Japan's Environmental Politics and Governance

Environmental issues stretch across scales of geographic space and require action at multiple levels of jurisdiction, including the individual level, community level, national level, and global level. Much of the scholarly work surrounding new approaches to environmental governance tends to overlook the role of sub-national governments, but this study examines the potential of sub-national participation to make policy choices which are congruent with global strategies and national mandates.

This book investigates the emerging actors and new channels of Japan's environmental governance, which has been taking shape within an increasingly globalized international system. By analyzing this important new phenomenon, it sheds light on the changing nature of Japan's environmental policy and politics, and shows how the links between global strategies, national mandates, and local action serve as an influential factor in Japan's changing structures of environmental governance. Further, it demonstrates that decision-making competencies are shared between actors operating at different levels and in new spheres of authority, resulting from collaboration between state and non-state actors. It highlights a number of the problems, challenges, and critiques of the actors in environmental governance, and raises new empirical and theoretical puzzles for the future study of governance over environmental and global issues. Finally, it concludes that changes in the tiers and new spheres of authority are leading the nation towards an environmentally stable future positioned within socio-economic and political constraints.

Demonstrating that bridging policy gaps between local action, national policy, and global strategies is potentially a way of reinventing environmental policy, this book will be of interest to students and scholars of Environmental Studies, Environmental Politics and Japanese Politics.

Yasuo Takao is Senior Lecturer of Political Science in the Department of Social Sciences and Security Studies of Curtin University, Western Australia.

Routledge Studies in Asia and the Environment

The role of Asia will be crucial in tackling the world's environmental problems. The primary aim of this series is to publish original, high quality, research-level work by scholars in both the East and the West on all aspects of Asia and the environment. The series aims to cover all aspects of environmental issues, including how these relate to economic development, sustainability, technology, society, and government policies; and to include all regions of Asia.

1 **Climate Change Governance in Chinese Cities**
   Qianqinq Mai and Maria Francesch-Huidobro

2 **Sustainability in Contemporary Rural Japan**
   Challenges and opportunities
   Stephanie Assmann

3 **Deliberating Environmental Policy in India**
   Participation and the role of advocacy
   Sunayana Ganguly

4 **Japan's Environmental Politics and Governance**
   From trading nation to EcoNation
   Yasuo Takao

5 **Climate Change Policy in Japan**
   From the 1980s to 2015
   Yasuko Kameyama

Japan's Environmental Politics and Governance

From trading nation to EcoNation

Yasuo Takao

LONDON AND NEW YORK

First published 2016
by Routledge
2 Park Square, Milton Park, Abingdon, Oxon OX14 4RN

and by Routledge
711 Third Avenue, New York, NY 10017

First issued in paperback 2018

Routledge is an imprint of the Taylor & Francis Group, an informa business

© 2016 Yasuo Takao

The right of Yasuo Takao to be identified as author of this work has been asserted by him in accordance with sections 77 and 78 of the Copyright, Designs and Patents Act 1988.

All rights reserved. No part of this book may be reprinted or reproduced or utilized in any form or by any electronic, mechanical, or other means, now known or hereafter invented, including photocopying and recording, or in any information storage or retrieval system, without permission in writing from the publishers.

Trademark notice: Product or corporate names may be trademarks or registered trademarks, and are used only for identification and explanation without intent to infringe.

British Library Cataloguing in Publication Data
A catalogue record for this book is available from the British Library

Library of Congress Cataloging in Publication Data
Names: Takao, Yasuo, author.
Title: Japan's environmental politics and governance : from trading nation to econation / Yasuo Takao.
Description: Abingdon, Oxon ; New York, NY : Routledge, 2016. | Series: Routledge studies in Asia and the environment ; 4 | Includes bibliographical references and index.
Identifiers: LCCN 2016022519| ISBN 9781138855908 (hardback) | ISBN 9781315720043 (ebook)
Subjects: LCSH: Environmental policy–Japan. | Decentralization in government–Japan. | Central-local government relations–Japan. | Environmental economics–Japan.
Classification: LCC GE190.J3 T35 2017 | DDC 333.70952–dc23
LC record available at https://lccn.loc.gov/2016022519

ISBN 13: 978-1-138-33955-2 (pbk)
ISBN 13: 978-1-138-85590-8 (hbk)

Typeset in Times New Roman
by Wearset Ltd, Boldon, Tyne and Wear

To my wife, Susan Takao

Contents

List of illustrations ix
Acknowledgments x
List of abbreviations xii

Introduction (theoretical frameworks) 1

1 The transformation of Japan's environmental policy 40

2 The rigidity of Japan's nuclear energy policy: state-centric gate-keeping 74

3 The state of local capacity-building: decentralized policy-making 110

4 Tokyo's metropolitan cap-and-trade: policy learning and diffusion 152

5 Shiga's cooperation with UNEP: transnational sectoral network 180

6 Kitakyushu's environmental business: utility-based transnationalism within norms 210

7 Yokohama's normative commitment: image and reputation 242

8 Expert citizens' role: civic science in environmental policy 271

Conclusion 300

Appendix I	318
Appendix II	319
Appendix III	320
Appendix IV	322
Index	324

Illustrations

Figures

I.1	Local government as a decentralized coordination agent	5
I.2	Multi-level/cross-scale interactions and local government	6
3.1	Expenditure on Japan's foreign aid and cooperation	131

Tables

2.1	Japan's nuclear power organizations	97
3.1	Local capacity for decentralized policy-making	114
3.2	ODA extended by local governments, 2002–2003 and 2008–2009	132
4.1	Tokyo's policy learning in the introduction of its cap-and-trade	171
5.1	Creating the International Lake Environment Committee through transnational support networks	181
6.1	Kitakyushu's transformation from previous experience to international environmental business	211
7.1	Yokohama's historical legacy and international orientation	243

Acknowledgments

People who live in the immediate environment experience the greatest environmental exposure risks and thus demand a greater role in prescribing solutions. Global strategies to environmental problem-solving cannot be contemplated without local demand and action. At the same time, local environmental problems require global solutions. The ideas for this book originated in a series of conversations with community leaders in Japan. The insight that sub-national governments may be able to bring together the plurality of stakeholders across scales of geographic space and at multiple levels of jurisdictions was gained from my direct observations at community level. Decentralized governance is normally understood as a process of the delegation of decision-making power to entities on the local level, but it is not necessarily about weakening national authority. The United Nations Development Programme (UNDP) defines decentralized governance as a coordinated relationship, which is developed by the balancing act of decision-making power and responsibility among national and sub-national governments, community, and market. In my project, these ideas were further developed through the close examination of decentralized international cooperation, not only to reconnect local action with national policy, but also to turn global strategies into local action, for environmental problem-solving.

For many observers of environmental governance, the challenges that environmental problems pose today are associated predominantly with what happens on the global level. However, it is equally true that one of the most obvious changes currently occurring is the change at the sub-national level, and it involves sub-national efforts to incorporate local action better into formal processes of national mandates and global strategies. The book presents a first attempt to better understand the potential role played by sub-national governments in overcoming the policy coordination difficulty that the cross-scale and multi-level approaches to environmental governance may create. It concludes that changes in the tiers of authority and in the new spheres of authority are leading the "EcoNation" of Japan towards an environmentally stable future. Ongoing changes at the sub-national level hold intriguing possibilities for reshaping the future landscape of policy-making and politics related to the environment. Further research on decentralized environmental governance holds great promise both for furthering the knowledge of environmental risk reduction, and for enhancing the involvement of sub-national actors in new forms of environmental governance.

In writing this book, I have accumulated debts of gratitude to many thoughtful individuals and organizations. These people, far more than I could possibly list, deserve thanks for the assistance and the useful suggestions they have extended me. Many are laypeople who have provided me with exceptional insights into my topic of research. I do thank each and every one. There are, however, a number of organizations and individuals to whom I would like to express my special appreciation; these are the ones who have made my research in Japan productive. First and foremost, I wish to thank Masaharu Hori, Thomas Schrock, and Stephen Weatherford, who have wholeheartedly provided me with advice and moral backing. I am also immensely grateful to my many mentors and sponsors who have selflessly supported my project over the past decade. These include: Kenrō Taura (Kiko Network), Toshiko Chiba, Yuko Nishida, and Naomi Okamoto (Tokyo Metropolitan Government's Bureau of the Environment), Hiroya Kotani (International Lake Environmental Committee), Azuma Kido and Akiko Teraishi (KITA Environmental Cooperation Center), Bernadia Irawati Tjandradewi and Akiko Murayama (CITYNET), Ryo Mori (ECO Communication Center), and Masanori Moori (EcoCity Shiki).

The production of this book would not have proceeded far without the editorial assistance of Freyja Bottrell. Her professional skills at putting complex pieces of my manuscript together contributed to the completion of this book. I am also grateful to anonymous reviewers for Routledge and editors for their constant encouragement. My special appreciation goes to the Australia-Asia-Pacific Institute at Curtin University for generously funding my various research trips to Japan.

A part of this book draws upon my earlier publications including "The transformation of Japan's environmental policy," *Environmental Politics*, Vol. 21, No. 5 (2012), © Taylor & Francis; "Making climate change policy work at the local level: capacity-building for decentralized policy making in Japan," *Pacific Affairs*, Vol. 85, No. 4 (2012), © University of British Columbia; "Sub-national level of participation in international environmental cooperation: the role of Shiga Prefecture for Lake Biwa environment in Japan," *Local Environment*, Vol. 18, No. 1 (2013), © Taylor & Francis; "Local levels of participation in Japan's foreign aid and cooperation: issues arising from decentralized international cooperation," *Asian Survey*, Vol. 54, No. 3 (2014), © The Regents of the University of California; "Policy learning and diffusion of Tokyo's metropolitan cap-and-trade: making a mandatory reduction of total CO_2 emissions work at local scales," *Policy Studies*, Vol. 34, No. 4 (2014), © Taylor & Francis.

Finally, my wife, Susan Takao, has played an important part in providing research assistance, critical commentary, and professional editing. For their patience and moral support, I also thank my daughter, Maia, and my son, Makoto, who will soon receive his Ph.D. in Ethnomusicology.

Abbreviations

ACF	Advocacy Coalition Framework
ASEAN	Association of Southeast Asian Nations
AWAREE	Awareness in Environmental Education
BAPPEKO	Surabaya's Developmental Planning Agency
BEMS	Building Energy Management System
BIWASO	Lake Biwa Comprehensive Development Project
BOE	Bureau of the Environment of the TMG
BWR	Boiling Water Reactor
C40	Climate Leadership Group
CASBEE	Comprehensive Assessment System for Built Environment
CBARAD	Community Based Adaptation and Resilience Against Disasters
CBO	Environmental Collateralized Bond Obligation
CCP	Cities for Climate Protection
CEMS	Community Energy Management System
CIA	Central Intelligence Agency
CITYNET	Regional Network of Local Authorities for the Management of Human Settlements
CLAIR	Council of Local Authorities for International Relations
COD	Chemical Oxygen Demand
COP-3	United Nations Framework Convention on Climate Change Conference
CPT	Cleaner Production Technology
CYO	CITYNET Yokohama Project Office
DAC	Development Assistance Committee
DPJ	Democratic Party of Japan
DRRM	Disaster Risk Management
DSP	Democratic Socialist Party
EA	Environment Agency
EANET	Acid Deposition Monitoring Network in East Asia
ECs	Expert Citizens
EIA	Environmental Impact Assessment
EMES	Environmental Management of Enclosed Coastal Seas

EMS	Environmental Management System
EPDC	Electric Power Development Co., Ltd
ERMS	Emissions Reduction Market System
ESCAP	United Nations—Economic and Social Commission for Asia and the Pacific
ESD	Education for Sustainable Development
EU	European Union
EU-ETS	European Union Emissions Trading System
EUCC	Electric Utility Coordination Council
FBR	Fast Breeder Reactor
GE	General Electric
GEF	Global Environmental Facility
GEMS	Global Environmental Monitoring System
GEN	Green Energy Law Network
GGRS	Greenhouse Gas Reduction Scheme
GHG	Greenhouse Gases
GIWA	Global International Waters Assessment
HABITAT	United Nations Human Settlements Programme
HEMS	Home Energy Management System
IAEA	International Atomic Energy Agency
IBRD	International Bank for Reconstruction and Development
ICAP	International Carbon Action Partnership
ICLEI	International Council for Local Environmental Initiatives
IGES	Kitakyushu Urban Center of the Institute for Global Environmental Strategies
ILEC	International Lake Environment Committee
ILEK	Integrated Local Environmental Knowledge
IMF	International Monetary Fund
ISO	International Organization for Standardization
ITTO	International Tropical Timber Organization
IULA-ASPAC	International Union of Local Authorities Asia-Pacific
JAEC	Japan Atomic Energy Commission
JAERI	Japan Atomic Energy Research Institute
JAIF	Japan Atomic Industry Forum
JAPCO	Japan Atomic Power Company
JBIC	Japan Bank for International Cooperation
JCM	Joint Crediting Mechanism
JCP	Japanese Communist Party
JICA	Japan International Cooperation Agency
JIS	Japan Industrial Standards
JSP	Japan Socialist Party
KITA	Kitakyushu International Techno-cooperation Association
KWAN	Kitakyushu for Asia Women Forum
LAS-E	Local Authority's Standards in the Environment
LBMI	Lake Basin Management Initiative

LDP	Liberal Democratic Party
MDGs	Millennium Development Goals
MEAs	Multilateral Environmental Agreements
METI	Ministry of Economy, Trade and Industry
MEXT	Ministry of Education, Culture, Sports, Science, and Technology
MHA	Ministry of Home Affairs
MHW	Ministry of Health and Welfare
MIAC	Ministry of Internal Affairs and Communications
MITI	Ministry of International Trade and Industry
MLG	Multi-level Governance
MM21	Minato Mirai 21
MMD-SNTV	Single-Non-Transferable-Vote, Multi-Member System
MOC	Memorandum of Cooperation
MOE	Ministry of the Environment
MOF	Ministry of Finance
MOFA	Ministry of Foreign Affairs
MOHA	Ministry of Home Affairs
NEPA	China's National Environmental Protection Agency
NGOs	Non-governmental Organizations
NHK	Japanese Broadcasting Corporation
NIMBY	Not-in-My-Backyard
NISA	Nuclear and Industry Safety Agency
NLCTP	National Level Cap-and-Trade Program
NRA	Nuclear Regulatory Authority
NRDC	National Resources Defense Council
NTT	Nippon Telegraph and Telephone
OCD	Office of Civil Defense
ODA	Official Development Assistance
OECD	Organisation for Economic Co-operation and Development
PCAs	Pollution Countermeasure Agreements
POS	Political Opportunity Structures
PPWSA	Phnom Penh Water Supply Authority
PR	Proportional Representation
RECLAIM	Regional Clean Air Initiatives Market
RGGI	Regional Greenhouse Gas Initiative
RLCTP	Regional Level Cap-and-Trade Program
SCAP	Occupation Supreme Commander of the Allied Powers
SDPJ	Social Democratic Party of Japan
SMD	Single-Member Districts
SO_x	Sulfur Oxide
STA	Science and Technology Agency
SWM	Solid Waste Management
TEPCO	Tokyo Electronic Power Company
THM	Takakura Home Method

TMA	Tokyo Metropolitan Assembly
TMG	Tokyo Metropolitan Government
TPLCS	Total Pollutant Load Control System
U-BCF	Upward Biological Contact Filtration
UCLG	United Cities and Local Governments
UK	United Kingdom
UN	United Nations
UNCRD	United Nations Centre for Regional Development
UNDESD	United Nations Initiative of the Decade of Education for Sustainable Development
UNEP	United Nations Environmental Programme
UNESCAP	United Nations Economic and Social Commission for Asia and the Pacific
UNESCO	United Nations Educational, Scientific and Cultural Organization
UNFCCC	United Nations Framework Convention on Climate Change
UNU	United Nations University
UNU-IAS	United Nations University Institute of Advanced Studies
US	United States of America
USIS	United States Information Service
VETS	Voluntary Emissions Trading Scheme
WATSAN	Water and Sanitation
WHO	World Health Organization
WLC	World Lake Conference
WLV	World Lake Vision
YSCP	Yokohama Smart City Project

Introduction (theoretical frameworks)

This book is about the future shape of globalized environmental policy and governance—which is much discussed but little understood. Environmental problems stretch across scales of geographic space and require action at multiple levels of jurisdictions, such as individual level, community level, national level, and global level. Multi-level governance and cross-scale coordination will open up opportunities for a variety of stakeholders to participate in decision-making. While potentially increasing the capacity of environmental governance, cross-scale and multi-level approaches may face difficulties in policy coordination created by the plurality of stakeholders and may also be attended with organizational complexity. Much of the scholarly work to date surrounding new approaches to environmental governance tends to overlook the role of subnational governments.[1] This book will examine an aspect of the potential of subnational participation to make policy choices, mediated by local governments, which are congruent with global strategies and national mandates in a consistent way. The findings from this book should be interpreted as a set of heuristic test cases to yield a good, but not necessarily conclusive, explanation for the possibility of generalization. Nonetheless, the global environmental challenges facing the international community suggest that a new approach to environmental risk reduction needs to be framed as a cross-scale and multi-level issue. I start from the perplexing fact that in the early 1970s Japan had one of the world's strongest environmental regulation regimes but today appears to have lost its innovative edge to other Organisation for Economic Co-operation and Development (OECD) countries. Environmental policy-making in Japan has developed as the nation has gone through different phases of environmental protection, namely from addressing domestic industrial pollution to global climate change. The dynamics of environmental policy-making have changed as environmental issues reveal multilayered and complex connections over the cross-border effects of environmental risks. In the process of global environmental challenges, Japan has lagged behind major European countries in environmental initiatives and innovations. Thus the question is how Japan should regain its reputation. Obviously, state-centric governance, which ensures that state sovereignty does not integrate at the supranational level more than it desires and thus does not impinge on its sovereignty, will not solve environmental problems. Multi-level and cross-scale governance, in which the state still can accept and reject international agreements yet pay the insurance premium in its sovereignty to reduce environmental threats, has a potential for environmental problem-solving.

A shared space of emerging relations among individuals and organizations in the policy area of environmental protection has expanded physically (e.g., geographic space) and non-physically (e.g., shared experiences, ideas, values) over the past two decades. It serves as a foundation for environmental policy-making. Policy ideas reside in a shared space, which exists at cross-scale/multi-level interactions. The experience of a Japanese environmental activist provides a useful story to illustrate this point. Kenrō Tarura graduated from the Graduate School of International Cooperation Studies, Kobe University in 1995. Two years later, the COP-3 (United Nations [UN] Framework Convention on Climate Change Conference) negotiations that Japan hosted in Kyoto had a profound effect on his career path. In 1998 he joined the Kiko Network, which was created as an umbrella organization of Japanese environmental citizens' groups to coordinate their activities before and after COP-3. After that, he worked as head of the Secretariat involving policy analysis, policy proposals, information dissemination, public awareness campaigns, and school education programs. Kenrō was destined to find it no longer easy to separate policy-addressees from policy-makers, or to distinguish between public and private actors in policy-making while actively promoting the diffusion of climate mitigation and adaptation measures. He helped less resourceful citizens bring their capacity onto an equal footing with policy-makers. He proposed that local knowledge would play a key role and would be necessary in judging the usefulness of professional expertise as policy predictions at higher levels of government could fail to equal the diversity of local experiences. He understood himself to be a player in a global game when feeding ideas, along with other NGOs (non-governmental organizations), into the international negotiation process. His career offers probably the best example of actors moving relatively freely across traditional levels and spheres of authority when pursuing public purposes.

Kenrō's story indicates that *ba* (field of sharing or interaction), where environmental concerns are made visible through sharing the feelings, thoughts and experiences of people, has transformed over time to transcend multiple spaces depending on the nature of the environmental issues and the actors involved.[2] In all likelihood, the earliest case of environmental problems that became salient in the history of modern Japan was a serious pollution problem which arose in the late nineteenth century due to mines and smelting factories, such as the Ashio Copper Mine, located in mountainous communities. The *ba* space took shape exclusively between the Meiji national leaders and the directly affected farmers. Due to Japan's drive to catch up with the West, little had been done to control the pollution, although some statutory regulations, such as the 1911 Factory Law, were implemented. In post-WWII Japan, industrial pollution problems spread throughout major industrial areas. Human tragedies such as the cases of Minamata disease (mercury poisoning) and of *itai-itai* disease (cadmium poisoning) increased public awareness. Anti-pollution residents' movements against big industries in Minamata and other areas had a dramatic effect on publicizing the issues. By the late 1960s, a majority of Japanese people had come to believe that industrial development must not be allowed at the expense of a healthy living environment.[3] Some local authorities were quick to initiate new environmental policies and the national government followed, particularly by enacting or amending 14 pollution control laws in what became known as the "Environmental Pollution Diet" of 1970.[4] The cost of environmental risk reduction was relatively concentrated on a limited number of polluters and victims in the affected areas, although the number of stakeholders in policy-making increased significantly. Therefore, the formation of environmental policy essentially took place within a domestic-level process.

Additionally, the oil crisis of 1973 served as an external shock to trigger the transformation of the interaction field. The business and government sectors showed great concern about energy efficiency rather than showing a genuine concern for environmental degradation. In the mid-1970s, the focus of environmental protection shifted from identifiable sources of industrial pollution to diffuse, no-point sources of non-industrial pollution. The disintegration of anti-industrial pollution movements marked a transformed field where Japanese environmental movements failed to establish powerful national interest groups while the government sector facilitated manufacturers' initiatives in energy conservation.[5] Despite the dominance of this industrial coalition, however, pioneering local authorities were exploring an alternative interaction field in the absence of national environmental initiatives while most localities acted in a piecemeal fashion according to national-level guidance. These frontrunners clearly demonstrated their willingness and capability to contribute to environmental risk reduction. There were several cases, such as those in Toyonaka and Hino Cities, which were reported as being faithfully citizen-led policy-making for municipal environmental plans. The local initiatives were meant to enhance an individual sense that they could make a difference—that is, their sense of political efficacy—in policy-making. The frontrunners sought to ensure the informed participation of all stakeholders through information disclosure and environmental impact assessment—specific modes of participatory accountability mechanisms—at the local level. They also structured incentive mechanisms to gain local officials' responsiveness through environmental performance disclosure and environmental policy coordination.[6]

The two international oil crises in 1973 and 1979 acted as a catalyst for adaptation to changes in the international environment. Yet the interaction *ba* remained domestic in the sense that the oil crises caused unilaterally systemic effects on policy formation in terms of international causes and domestic effects, while providing little room for the interaction of domestic and international factors. This policy environment, however, appears to have significantly changed over the last three decades. As environmental risks spill over to other domains in a non-territorial way, the interaction *ba* has rapidly expanded beyond national boundaries. It has transformed from a predominantly contentious interaction among domestic players to a far more complex process in which sub-national

4 *Introduction*

actors, for example, involve both local coordination with national policy and local adaptations to global environmental strategies. To reduce environmental risks at the regional and international levels, Japanese local governments have been working with counter-partners, such as overseas local authorities, domestic/ international NGOs and international organizations, building transnational coalitions and exchanging information to work internationally on global environmental strategies. Most local environmental officials have experience in international environmental cooperation, such as bilateral cooperation (e.g., Kitakyushu-Dalian), sectoral networks (e.g., Shiga-United Nations Environmental Programme [UNEP] partnership over environmental lake management), and international networks (e.g., Yokohama's CITYNET to support South–South cooperation).[7]

With the enactment of the Basic Environmental Law in 1993, which defined environmental policy principles and directions, Japan's environmental policy was facing another turning point. A series of new legislation, such as the Container and Packaging Recycling Law of 1995, the Environmental Impact Assessment Law of 1997, and the Basic Law for Establishing the Recycling-based Society of 2000, reflected an adaptation to a new policy-making environment at the international level. Probably, external pressure, which was globalized in the sense that environmental problems largely required global strategies and global solutions demanded national pledges, was the most important factor determining the course of events regarding this new development. In the years following the Rio Earth Summit in 1992, Japan, like any other country, was under pressure to implement concrete measures to achieve sustainable development, something agreed on at the UN conference. In December 1993, Japan's National Action Plan for Agenda 21 (national plan of action to achieve sustainable development) was submitted to the UN. One year later, the Basic Environment Plan was adopted under the direction of the Basic Environment Law. The action plan identified the measures to be undertaken by the national and local governments, as well as the roles of citizens, social groups and businesses involved in effectively pursuing environmental policies. In 1997 the Japanese government hosted the Kyoto Protocol Climate Conference (COP-3) and it pledged "internationally acceptable CO_2 reductions" as its reputation was at stake in the success or failure of the conference.[8] Since the conference was reported and discussed almost every day somewhere in Japanese national newspapers, the course of COP-3 events certainly raised public awareness on the impact of climate change in Japan.

Local action, national policy, and global strategies

Bridging policy gaps among local action, national policy, and global strategies is potentially a way of reinventing Japan's environmental policy. Today, the ultimate addressees of international regulation have largely shifted from state actors to societal actors, especially in the global environmental agenda. Consumers and businesses are expected to alter their behavior in the locally place-specific environment. Over the past three decades, as presented in the following chapters, some pioneering balancing acts between the global and local have been initiated by local governments. The institutionalization of sub-national participation for policy coordination will be beneficial to further development of environmental governance. As Figures I.1 and I.2 illustrate, my claim is that sub-national actors occupy a strategic position because they act as an intermediate agent in reconnecting local action with national policy and turning global strategies into local actions for problem-solving. On the one hand, local government, as part of the state apparatus, has varying degrees of political access to the national authority while, as a potential partner of civil society groups, assuring individuals' safety and health in local communities. On the other hand, beyond being an active part of national policy at the international level, local government deliberately decides whether or not to engage in the area of international environmental and development cooperation. This is because it wishes to implement a cohesive policy that would meet specific local needs, either due to a lack of support from the national government or due to the absence of national regulation. To examine this claim, the unit of analysis in this book is the agents of sub-national participation for policy integration between different levels and spheres of authority. The territorial state is hardly capable of providing a complex set of governance functions to solve the spillover effects of environmental problems and there is a need to allocate those functions to different governance levels and spheres.

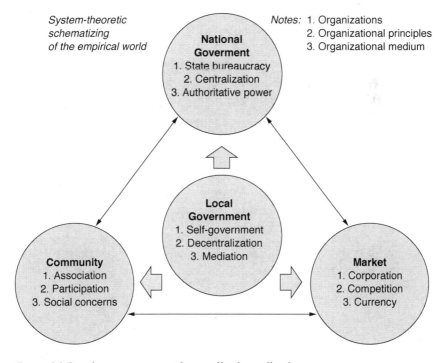

Figure I.1 Local government as a decentralized coordination agent.

6 Introduction

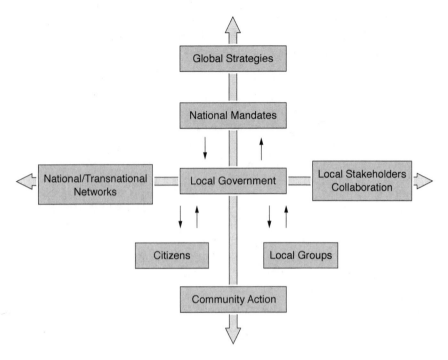

Figure I.2 Multi-level/cross-scale interactions and local government.

While the conventional focus of governance is on the processes and structures for rule-making and enforcement, I use a decentralized analysis whereby the link between individual agents and structural transformation is of crucial importance. This book takes an actor-specific approach, with special reference to local governments. The ultimate objective is to pave the way for a new form of environmental governance.

The framework of policy coordination among local actions, national mandates, and global agendas is grounded in foundational propositions: (1) state actors no longer have exclusive power to unilaterally design policies or regulations; (2) societal actors may perform a state function while state actors may provide a private good function, thus reflecting a blurring of the state–society divide; (3) in the area of policies formerly left to national state actors, sub-national state actors are capable of contributing to the policy-making process without national supervision; (4) ongoing decentralization of state spatial organization will weaken the national regulatory level and lead to a rediscovery of sub-national forms of governance, thus expecting greater interaction among actors within the center-periphery divide; (5) state actors are no longer the exclusive addressees of international rules and regulations, indeed societal actors are increasingly the ultimate addressees of the rules and regulations; (6) as the territorial division of the sovereign nation-state system has become increasingly unaccountable to basic human needs, societal and sub-national actors decide to engage in foreign policy, thus bypassing or even challenging the exclusive jurisdiction of state actors in the domestic-foreign divide.

Environmental governance also needs to consider structural conditions for joint problem-solving among actors involved in decision-making, while the rigid separation of local, national, and international affairs is problematic for environmental risk reduction: (1) global environmental problems, such as climate change, require local action; (2) local environmental problems, such as air pollution, require globally-overarching cooperation; and (3) although the role of governance without government has expanded over the last three decades, national governments still occupy the crucial position to accept or reject international agreements. Inescapably, environmental problem-solving involves multiple agencies and levels of government and is sought in the coalition-building of diverse stakeholders. It is driven by competitive or dominant coalitions while redefining the institutional structures of state-society, center-periphery, and domestic-foreign relations. The possible source of cohesion amid all the blurring and fragmentation of state-society, center-periphery, and domestic-foreign relations lies in the peculiar role of sub-national actors, especially local government.

Environmental protection and risk reduction, once provided, become public goods as none is excluded from the consumption opportunities of the benefits. But the policy area of environmental protection can be seen as "soft politics" in the sense that national governments are very reluctant to invest in this policy area as they tend to address themselves to economic efficiency and priority at the national level. The nature of environmental politics points to an environmental risk-reduction theory of cost-sharing/burden-sharing (politics) and incentive mechanisms/coordinating devices (governance). At the domestic level, taxation or regulation (backed by penalties) is a device that facilitates the provision of public goods yet "a corporate bias" reflects the desire of the national government to insulate itself from popular pressures. At the international level, there is no compulsory device and the provision of environmental risk reduction thus requires the aggregate effort of stakeholders but their participation is voluntary. These deficiencies are further compounded by institutional fragmentation. Not surprisingly, at the domestic level, environmental initiatives cut across the boundaries of departmental jurisdiction and cause "turf wars" among them. At the international level, there are more than 500 multilateral environmental agreements (MEAs) whose autonomous secretariats have been operating to achieve implementation, assessment, and enforcement. MEAs have been developed primarily as a way of problem-solving issue-by-issue, which may result in the duplication of activities and resources and inconsistencies among the decisions of different agreements.

Due to a fluid patchwork of overlapping jurisdictions, there is a growing need to provide a venue for policy coordination for problem-solving. The merit of including local governments to take up a decentralized coordination role in global environmental governance can be presumed based on a number of grounds: (1) local government has a permanent physical infrastructure and multi-tasking jurisdictions; (2) local government provides political access, leverage, and opportunities to civil society groups; (3) local government is open to a range of popular interests which are less represented within the corporatist sector at the national level; (4) local government can be pragmatically competent to deal with policy problems in national elite networks but also motivated by its concerns for local experience; (5) local government is potentially willing and capable of contributing to the national policy-making process; (6) local government takes part in transnational coalitions, externally to influence multilateral rule-making or internally to promote cooperation with other subnational and societal actors; (7) local government has been targeted by the UN for promoting the decentralized functions of global environmental governance. Local government is thus located in a strategic position to straddle the division between state and society, that between the center and the periphery, and that between the domestic and the foreign.

Of course, the traditional view is to be skeptical about what role local governments play, whether individually or collectively. This view is prominent particularly because only national state actors control material resources based on the monopoly of the legitimate use of physical force. Realists may argue that only a superior availability of material resources ensures the possibility of compliance with policy coordination. Yet simple coercion is only one potential tool for coordination. To explore the potential for local governments to coordinate the different fields of regulation, this book takes into account an alternative to the notion of power deriving from the potential use of economic and military force. Local government derives its authority from six principal sources of influence: (1) *expertise* is a key factor in the influence of local governments as they are not only skilled in the physical side of regulatory and technical knowledge but also motivated by their concerns for the local relevance of expertise; (2) local governments rely on *moral authority* to maintain their influence as they address themselves to the importance of meeting societal needs rather than economic efficiency and profitability; (3) *political legitimacy* deriving from popular explicit and implicit consent to their action is another factor in a sphere of influence; (4) *continuity* of representing public preferences is an important power source for local governments, with the support of their permanent physical infrastructure; (5) local governments act on *institutional authority* that derives from the public holding office while following the rules and aims of their institution; and (6) local governments are able to delegate many of their decisions to respond more effectively to others and at the same time they may have *delegated authority* whose rights and privileges are given by the delegator. In other words, compliance with policy coordination is not explicitly backed by force. The ability to influence others is socially recognized by the general public. The coordination agent uses these sources of influence to convince, encourage, induce, persuade, and promote deference in others.

Multi-level governance and cross-scale coordination

The term "governance" is defined to describe and explain the different ways in which actors organize themselves to solve their shared problems. In the discipline of political science, primary interests in governance are concerned with the changing patterns of relationships between the public sector and other actors[9] and the necessity to address the simultaneity and interaction of domestic and foreign affairs.[10] In the conventional usage of political theory, the term "government" refers to formal state institutions and the processes in which they operate to maintain social order and provide public goods. News media often treat the term government as a synonym for governance, both referring to the state steering of public affairs. Since the early 1990s, there has been a significant switch in the academic literature favoring the term governance rather than government.[11] This transition from government to governance recognizes the fact that governments are not the only decision-making authority in problem-solving. The focal point of governance has evolved around the search for an alternative to conventional top-down government control while pointing out a declining capacity on the part of governments, managing alone, to solve problems. The policy-making environment reflects increasingly blurred boundaries between levels of government, between state and civil society, and between domestic and foreign affairs. The field of effective political power thus needs to be "shared, bartered and struggled over by diverse forces and agencies at national, regional and global levels."[12] In most perspectives on governance, however, the ways of problem-solving still clearly embrace governmental institutions while including non-governmental institutions operating within the public space.[13] There is a marked dichotomy between a governmental top-down approach and a cross-scale approach—sharing responsibilities among levels of government, civil society groups, and firms.

Environmental governance cannot function well at a fixed scale; it needs to be neither small-scale nor large-scale, but cross-scale.[14] The framing of the cross-scale and multi-level provides a variety of stakeholders with access to decision-making. Better ways of matching the level of policy coordination to the scale of environmental risks and social processes are presumed to increase the capacity of environmental governance to adapt to change and uncertainty,[15] while cross-scale and multi-level arrangements may impose constraints on policy integration and be attended with organizational complexity.[16] In this context, this book will explore the ability of local-level, bottom-up, participatory approaches to make a choice, mediated by local governments, to be congruent with global strategies and national top-down regulatory mandates in a consistent way. From the viewpoint of policy coordination by local governments, accountability and legitimacy are primary challenges since roles and responsibilities are dispersed among a wide variety of stakeholders. Local governments are in a position either to act as an agent whose power is delegated by the national authority in a hierarchical, principal-agent chain-of-command where the agent is accountable to the principal or relies on public engagement, namely a venue whereby the general public participates in exacting accountability through a horizontal form of social responsibility. They also understand themselves as being agents in global strategies[17] and thus ensure mutual accountability for maintaining their congruent actions with international institutions, functionally independent of their national governments. They may even not act on behalf of their national governments or state-centric international institutions while participating in transnational networks of non-state actors to enhance social accountability beyond national boundaries. However, the strategic position of local governments lies in the fact that, as seen in this book, local governments normally do not explicitly challenge the hierarchy of territorial jurisdictions to assemble policy ideas and legitimacy to meet policy objectives. But rather they serve to establish a connection between *hierarchized* tiers (i.e., distribution of national decision-making competencies to sub-national and supra-national levels) of, and *de-hierarchized* new spheres (i.e., decision-making competencies shared between state and non-state actors, and between domestic and foreign affairs) of[18] authority through the very process of policy learning and knowing.

As the unit of analysis is an agent of sub-national participation, the actor-specific approach will focus on how different types of actors are linked with, and move across, traditional governmental levels and different spheres of authority. Local governments are presumed to be intersecting actors in multiple autonomous spheres of authority spanning many jurisdictions for coordinated action. Local governments are expected to act to build stronger horizontal and vertical linkages. Liesbet Hooghe and Gary Marks, while drawing on the literature on multi-level governance, identify two ideal types of multi-level governance: Type I governance—that "conceives of dispersion of authority to multi-task, territorially mutually exclusive jurisdictions in a relatively stable system with limited jurisdictional levels and a limited number of units"—and Type II governance—that "pictures specialized, territorially overlapping jurisdictions in a relatively flexible, non-tiered system with a large number of jurisdictions".[19] Type I is state-centric governance, which is based on a nationally led framework embedded within institutional boundaries for extending decision-making authority above and below the national state while national governments remain central actors. Type II is cross-scale governance, which is concerned with new-shared spheres (*ba*) of authority resulting from interactions between state and non-state actors in the frontiers of the center-periphery, public-private, and domestic-foreign. These spheres are confined neither to a fixed scale nor to a rigid hierarchy of scales, but they are the cross-scale result of adaptive processes between state and non-state actors for problem-solving. As Hooghe and Marks acknowledge that both types co-exist, or are not necessarily mutually exclusive, this book seeks to provide a better understanding of the relationships and the dynamics underlying transitions between these two types of multi-level governance. In particular, it will locate and illustrate the processes of transitions between the different types and show the importance of resource mobilization for problem-solving. The transitional process facilitates the dual responses of sub-national participation to both globalizing and localizing trends and thus acknowledges the fact that, while being globalized, environmental policy agenda requires local action.

Different institutional approaches to multi-level governance provide sub-national actors with distinctive channels for resource mobilization for environmental risk reduction.[20] Type I, for example, through sub-national participation in diplomatic representation, is institutionalized to clarify sub-national roles in achieving national goals within the context of international obligations or to establish a division of labor among levels of government with a state-centric gate-keeping capacity (its capacity to influence policy decisions).[21] This is the most common approach (based on the established institutional boundaries of polity) that arises out of the traditional state-centric framework. In essence, national policy either regulates or enables the sub-national level of participation in global environmental governance. In this process, the sub-national level of participation beyond national borders tends to be legitimized by domestic benefits rather than sharing the costs of environmental risk reduction beyond national borders.[22] As national governments extend incentive schemes as well as top-down policies towards sub-national actors, sub-national actors have primarily an implementation role to play if national environmental targets are to be met. The key issue of state-centric policy coordination for national government is to effectively monitor progress at the sub-national level for an understanding of aggregate progress at the national scale and further within the context of international obligation.[23] Type II is the most integrated approach (involving the restructuring of state polity), where sub-national authorities are given the right to represent themselves legitimately at the international level and are capable of contributing to the policy-making process without national supervision. In other words, sub-national authorities are institutionally empowered in an autonomous way. The channels, for example, through sub-national participation in the Committee of the Regions and sub-national collaboration with the European Commission without the supervision of national government, are institutionalized to allow sub-national governments to move independently across different spheres of authority to influence decision-making at the international level.[24] This institutional structure for environmental cooperation is organized around decentralized, dense networks between a variety of governments and other actors active in a joint domain.[25] The density of the networks is likely to absorb the underperformance or failure of one organization and continue to jointly generate governance capacity.[26] Yet the problems of accountability require agencies to specialize in a specific method of accountability with shared professional expertise.[27]

As compared to some federal systems, such as those of Austria, Belgium, Germany, and Switzerland, where sub-national authorities can conduct foreign policies in matters of their competence, Japan's unitary system does not formally recognize the legal right of sub-national authorities to represent themselves at the international level. One would expect that Japan is more approximate to Type I with the gate-keeping capacity of the national government. But once attention is directed towards the bottom-up political mobilization of sub-national authorities, static notions of governance cannot easily account for the dynamics of real-life experience in Japan. This is primarily due to the connections between *hierarchized* tiers and *de-hierarchized* new spheres of authority. In Japan's unitary system, as case studies in this book suggest, local governments, while mobilized across institutional boundaries of polity, independently participate in environmental governance at the international level, either due to a lack of support from the national government or in the absence of national regulation. Without the familiar ground of institutionalized rules or the right to represent themselves legitimately at the international level, local governments find a way through non-institutionalized or informal channels to move across levels of government and deal directly with a transnational network of local governments, non-state actors and supranational actors in a rather ad hoc fashion. Informal extra-national channels, such as the establishment of independent overseas offices for lobbying and representing their interests, are sought to push for the increased involvement of sub-national actors in decision-making at the international level, while engaging in direct exchanges with host nations and international organizations.[28]

As the detailed implementation of global environmental strategies is specified, the necessity of sub-national participation at the local scale will become more salient. Internationally agreed environmental goals need to be implemented in coordination with local realities and conditions. International environmental bodies, such as UNEP, need to be strengthened to assist multi-level integration for the management of international environmental goods, and they must work closely with a variety of stakeholders and governments right down to the sub-national level. In other words, one party needs the assistance and cooperation of the other in order to achieve policy outcomes. But the fundamental question is whether local governments are willing and capable enough to contribute to multi-level integration without national supervision. Sub-national mobilization, which takes place in the midst of unfamiliar rules or little institutionalization across national boundaries, requires sufficient resources and the strong commitment of sub-national leadership, knowledge, experience, and political will to act upon environmental policy. Equally important, although sub-national participation can be conceived as horizontally ordered at new-shared spheres of authority, local governments do not normally challenge the hierarchized tiers of territorial jurisdictions in an explicit way while bypassing the state-centric gate-keeping. This is mainly because the multi-task jurisdictions (not only concerning environmental issues) of local governments continually have to deal with the hierarchical territorial tiers of authority on a daily basis while simultaneously moving across different spheres of authority. In particular, the financial need of such sub-national participation in de-hierarchized new spheres brings back the local government to deal with the hierarchical territorial tiers in order to access national financial resources.

Normative or ethical dimensions for governance

Governance is widely assumed to be utility-driven for problem-solving. Indeed, functionalists tend to assume that governance will shape its form in response to collective needs yet neglect the dynamic process of governance in which agents purposively steer a polity.[29] Instrumentalists regard governance as a strategic choice of means-ends rational calculations, which is based on decision-making environments.[30] Likewise, neoliberal institutionalists see the form of governance as fixed with pre-determined material interests. As a result, these approaches may overlook the activities of individual agents involved in shaping governance systems. From the viewpoint of multi-level and cross-scale consultations and negotiations among agents, economic efficiency and local values cannot be easily conciliated and a potential for conciliation is unlikely to be found at a single territorial level. Developmental and environmental issues reveal a dimension of cultural values and social norms, which affect locals with a locally specific profile. While agents may try to be strategically rational and structural constraints may be unavoidable, governance functions need to rely on reconciliation between environmental/structural demands and locally adaptive agents. Local norms at the time they are established may be stable and resistant to change.[31] Over time, however, multi-level and cross-scale consultations and negotiations among agents may change their values, identities, and preferences. This book claims that local governments or sub-national actors[32] can indeed contribute ideas and solutions to finding a common ground as not only are they equipped with expert knowledge but they are also motivated by their concern for local experience and knowledge.

In governance practice, norms and moral values play an important role. This is a matter of "governance of governance" about how a normative or moral dimension pertains to a governance system in itself.[33] International governing actors, such as the World Bank, the International Monetary Fund (IMF) and the OECD, for example, have come under public scrutiny as they commit themselves to benchmarks of "good" governance, that is, the norms of accountability, transparency, responsiveness, equity, and participatory decision-making, as well as administrative and economic efficiency. A theme shared among many governance theorists is the notion that governance is strategically goal-oriented for problem-solving. However, this focus can easily lead to a neglect of norms and principles and thus to the problems of governance failure. Actors may misrepresent a plurality of values for a particular goal, for example, for that of a cost-benefit calculation. In a dispersed and relational setting of the governance system, there is a plurality of actors and no formal control system that facilitates the ways of interaction among these actors, except for mutual self-regulations. A governmental top-down approach may be less relevant in an increasingly complex social order and state authority has significantly been *de-hierarchized*. Nonetheless, governments can clearly act as a coordinator and contribute their own distinctive resources to solving complex coordination problems that involve a wide range of actors.[34] In this context, this book emphasizes the expected coordination role to be played by local governments or sub-national actors in remoralizing the collective action of governance. Each organization draws on its particular power resources in pursuit of its particular objectives. The suitability of local governments or sub-national actors lies in their relative openness to a range of social needs and consumers' interests whose voices are less likely to be heard at the national level of predominantly business-interest mediation. Local governments' coordination is one of decentralized mechanisms through which it is possible to deal with the problems of governance failure.

Participation is the essence of multi-level and cross-scale approaches by which all of the stakeholders' interests contribute to their inputs in an inclusive way, while not responding to any particular interest but still making a better decision or providing a public good for all. Perhaps this most difficult task could be compensated for by holding each other accountable for the actions undertaken. This simultaneous involvement of governmental and non-governmental actors who must give account could result in organizational complexity or in imposing constraints on actual accountability. In the issue area of environmental problems, since no single territorial level alone can tackle the challenges of environmental risk reduction, solutions must be flexibly sought by linking the cross-scale of the environmental problem with the jurisdictional and practical reach of governmental and non-governmental actors. Socially mobilized citizen groups and economic actors have no particular barriers for environmental regulations to be approved and implemented at both the national and international levels. But territorial national governments normally wish to act as the sole legitimate representatives of domestic interests and prevent supra-national organizations from bypassing them without their permission and implementing regulations at the local level. The compatibility between territorial interests and policy-specific functional interests thus corresponds to accountability coordination between governmental and non-governmental actors. Accountability also draws attention to the problems of compatibility between economic efficiency and social values. This primarily involves accountability coordination between business and social actors. The key reason that socially mobilized citizens' groups find it difficult to be accountable to stakeholders is more fundamental, and concerns their self-defining orientation. There are no uniform criteria that are externally accepted for evaluating the performance of their social and political activities. There is no simple uniform quantity like those of income or profit which evaluate the performance of business firms. Without their self-defining missions, activities, and achievements, socially mobilized citizens' groups' accountability cannot exist in the absence of externally accepted criteria. They, for example, may find many kinds of economic inefficiency quite valuable—e.g., those that involve environmental cost-sharing, charity, and voluntarism in their activities. Nonetheless, once defining themselves, they must render their criteria acceptable to the public. Otherwise, they will not gain trust and confidence among the public. A possible source of cohesion for accountability coordination lies in the peculiar role of local governments. Local authorities are more likely to assert values based on social needs or collectivist values as a counter to both values based on profit maximization, or the interests of the business sector, and values based on fragmented or individualistic modes of private consumption. As described in this book, local governments also do not simply ignore hierarchical constraints to attain their desired goals but negotiate with national authorities to steer policy-making. Without directly challenging the governmental tiers or acting without the national government's permission, local governments may be capable of deliberately crossing the domestic-foreign divide and entering cross-border cooperation agreements to implement an environmental cohesion policy.

While they may mobilize their own locally specific resources beyond national boundaries to understand themselves as part of global strategies, they are normally willing to keep redefining their relations with the governmental tiers through coordination and negotiation. It may be an overestimation to designate local governments as the only possible venue of accountability coordination, but it would equally be a mistake to underestimate the potential for local governments' strategic position to bring all the stakeholders together.

The normative dimension of environmental governance is often seen from the viewpoint of sustainability.[35] Negotiation and interaction between numerous stakeholders spreading across the hierarchical territorial tiers and newly shared spheres of authority can be institutionalized through the normative concept of sustainability.[36] Nonetheless, while sustainable development is defined by the Brundtland Report as "development that meets the needs of the present without compromising the ability of future generations to meet their own needs,"[37] the normative concept has been defined in many different ways. In order to tap the diverse meanings of sustainability, the two positions, "weak sustainability" and "strong sustainability," can be placed at the far ends of the typology as extremes.[38] The idea of weak sustainability states that human-made capital can take the place of natural capital and that any developmental and environmental problems will thus be solved through technological progress. As a counter to weak sustainability, strong sustainability is the idea that the existing stock of natural capital cannot be duplicated by human-made capital and that a more decentralized and self-reliant way of life will create a human society less destructive towards nature. In practice, however, the two rigid ways of sustainability thinking lead to a convergence on a theory-modest approach to sustainable development. Again, local governments occupy a strategic position since they straddle both the division between state and community and that between market and community. In one respect, their interests do relate to the interests of manufactured capital, for their concern to defend locally available jobs is broadly consistent with the concern of economic priorities and production. Yet demands for higher wages by local employees may conflict with well-being in reducing environmental risks. This dilemma is mitigated or even transcended through the adoption of a reflective equilibrium. Local authorities move their communities towards a more plausible middle ground marking the intersection of weak and strong sustainability. Thus the economic and environmental capital is complimentary, so to speak. Indeed, in Japan, while calling for a change in consumers' behavior, local governments have innovated better technologies for reducing pollution and have been creating locally specific renewable resources as substitutes for non-renewables. As illustrated in this book, some local authorities demonstrate an ability to use local experience and knowledge to promote international environmental business.

Learning and knowing about governance

Social reality is never made by only pre-determined objective facts but agents constitute it through purposive acts of learning. In particular, normative aspects of environmental problems are to be constructed and learned.[39] Agents use instruments, which are available in governance-related regulations and programs, to achieve their desirable goals. One such instrument is learning, which assumes agents do not know what can possibly be done in regard to problem-solving. Another related instrument is capacity-building, which assumes agents lack the information, knowledge, and resources to achieve socially desirable goals. These ways of learning and knowing bring together the actor-specific dimensions of effective governance with the concept of decision-making participation. Equally important, collective learning is one of the most important mechanisms of adaptive governance to deal with the transformative changes and uncertainties that characterize social-ecological systems.[40] These systems can be seen as relationships between people and nature where the environment is not external to the community.[41] Participation by a variety of stakeholders at multi-levels and spheres of authority is essential to knowledge-sharing and effective learning about those relationships. Social interaction in the process of participation helps stakeholders come to better understand alternative knowledge production and accept commonly shared norms. It may thus result in a more coherent transfer of ideas and practices. *De-hierarchized* and horizontal governance is then expected to facilitate the exchange of new knowledge and the process of reflexive learning, which is essential in the face of environmental uncertainty. Yet it should be noted that collective learning is not necessarily a voluntary act but it can be constrained by *hierarchized* tiers of authority. Agents can even be forced to learn.

Learning in the policy literature can be analytically differentiated from mere copying or mimicking.[42] Probably the most commonly assumed form of learning is "lesson-drawing" in reference to lessons gleaned from previous experience.[43] Policy failure can thus lead to a reconsideration of existing policy reasoning, subsequent to policy learning.[44] The experience is taken into account as it provides useful lessons on the likely consequences of policy options. Rational or Bayesian learning assumes a linear relationship from information to decision-making such that agents use new information to update their prior beliefs and adopt policy ideas with the highest expected utility.[45] Trial-and-error[46] or bounded rationality[47] provide alternative bases of explanation for policy learning, while some argue that the two theories of bounded learning and rational learning are not necessarily incompatible or converging in their predictions of policy diffusion.[48] Others address an unwarranted tacit assumption that lesson-drawing is a voluntary act by rational actors.[49] Such a voluntary act is more relevant to the *de-hierarchized* and horizontal dimension of governance where agents are free to move easily across numerous levels and spheres of authority. Lesson-drawing may encompass possible occurrences of both voluntary and coercive processes. Coercive forms do not always have to be non-rational. Lesson-drawing may take place with negotiated or obligatory forms of "indirect coercion" laying in the middle of the voluntary-coercive continuum.[50] Such forms can be observed in the *hierarchized* and vertical dimension of governance, which is characterized by command and control. It is likely that lesson-drawing cannot be entirely voluntary since it is also influenced by cultural values and local norms. In other words, the role of learning is directed by the normative values of alternative choices embedded in the locally specific structure within which the agent operates.[51]

The view of learning as a foundation for improving policy-making was subsequently embraced and expanded by many others with the conceptualization of various forms of policy learning. The policy literature provides the foundation for different modalities of learning: (1) the broad level of learning about policy elites' beliefs, key policy objectives, or general policy direction, (2) the operational level of learning of regulatory/promotional instruments or implementation designs, and (3) the strategic level of learning to understand the political feasibility and its policy process. Peter Hall defines what he calls "social learning" as a conscious attempt to adjust both the macro objectives/beliefs and the micro instruments of policy in light of policy experience and new information.[52] Social learning is not merely determined by drawing on past experience but also heavily influenced by new ideas and broader societal conflicts and debates. Paul Sabatier's "policy-oriented learning," however, is primarily concerned with the attainment or revision of a coalition's belief system.[53] In his view, learning can alter part of such a belief system but changes in policy elites' beliefs are often the result of non-conscious factors external to the make-up of a polity.[54] In contrast, at the operational level of policy learning, cognitive/conscious factors that are internal to learning agents can be one of the key determinants of how policy is implemented. In a conventional sense, the study of policy learning assumes that agents are utility maximizers who are able to choose the optimal option to achieve their policy objectives while drawing on fully rational learning. Purposive acts at the operational level, however, give special importance to bounded rationality and cognitive factors in learning. Another important level of learning is about strategies for advocating policy ideas to increase the political feasibility of policy proposals. Lesson-drawing is a political learning in which agents manipulate the policy process.[55] Learning agents can advance problems and ideas by learning how to enhance the political feasibility from lesson-drawing. As an analytical tool, the strategic level of learning is not concerned with a change in internalized policy beliefs, but rather strategic behavior to achieve policy goals.

The acceptance of new knowledge and ideas, external to agents, is complex and considered in the political context of collective and mutual learning. New knowledge can adversely affect the existing understanding of policy problems and thus potentially undermine the core beliefs of the decision-makers. In the scientific-technical area of environmental policy, policy and scientific experts dominate decision-making while the public shies away from holding policy debate. As scientific uncertainty in large-scale environmental problems increases, there are calls for the subjection of scientific expertise to social scrutiny. Social representation and local knowledge would be necessary to judge the usefulness of expert knowledge as scientific predictions could fail to meet the diversity of local conditions.[56] Experts tend to consider local knowledge "unscientific" and claim that the public needs to be educated (the deficit model).[57] The public has limited resources to participate in environmental decisions so that they may choose minimal contributions to export the cost to others (free-riding problem). There is a wide gap between scientific/expert knowledge and local daily-life knowledge impacting on two-way symmetrical communication to facilitate effective and collaborative learning. In this context, the intermediary role of local governments or sub-national actors,[58] which are not only equipped with expert knowledge but are also socially competent at the local level, is expected to bridge the gap between expert knowledge and local knowledge to allow for adaptive governance. To this end, local government can interpret and reevaluate scientific/expert knowledge to fit to the locally specific conditions of environmental problems while applying local knowledge accumulated in local communities to scientific reasoning. The normative significance of the intermediary role is to help less resourceful citizens place their capacity on an equal footing with the experts and thus offer democratic benefits through the deliberative process by which citizens who bear the consequences of policy-making should be able to be a part of the decisions. In essence, public participation does not automatically make expert knowledge democratically accountable. The key rationale for the intermediary role of local governments lies in the importance of extending the principles of democracy to the production of expert and scientific knowledge. The intermediary role of local governments can be developed as a new form of participation, yet little guidance is provided in the literature on how technically competent sub-national actors can contribute to the mitigation of the growing public disenchantment with expert knowledge.

Political choice and governance

The complexity of governance can be captured at three different levels of analysis: politics, polity, and policy. In the past, in order to describe a particular type of polity-structuring and policy-making arrangement, the term governance was often used apolitically as a set of institutional principles and rules for collective action in the pursuit of shared goals. However, as the addressees of global strategies for environmental protection have significantly swung from state actors to non-state actors, the political feasibility of problem-solving has become a key issue of governance to meet societal demands from stakeholders with divergent opinions and different interests. The process of decision-making is likely to be formed in a more contentious way. Political mobilization by stakeholders to influence the process of environmental rule-making takes place as much within institutional boundaries of the polity as across these boundaries. In essence, the theory of governance cannot explain change without introducing the strategic level of analysis to understand political feasibility and policy process.

Lesson-drawing is a political learning in which agents manipulate the policy process and which also involves adaptation, in the sense of responding to external constraints and opportunities. The advocacy coalition framework (ACF) is a good fit for explaining the collective actions of human agents and policy outcomes in political conflicts over a long period of time.[59] Political opportunity structures (POS) are the most frequently used approaches to explain how structures determine the variations of agent behavior.[60] Political learning is a venue for understanding the actual process of policy-making and thus learning about strategies for advocating policy ideas. Agents need to be aware of the relationships between political strategy and political feasibility within a given advocacy coalition. They also need to be aware of the prospects and external opportunity structures that may affect them. From the viewpoint of multi-level and cross-scale approaches, they need to know the political feasibility beyond their causal role explicated in policy-making within institutional boundaries and then understand how political mobilization occurs across institutional boundaries and outside of conventional procedures.

Environmental problems involve multiple interacting policy cycles over a long period of time among agents at multiple levels and spheres of authority. The ACF is ideally suited for the analysis of such policy processes. (1) Because of the cross-sectoral impacts of cost sharing, environmental problem-solving involves multiple actors and levels of government and spheres of authority. The framework allows us to explain the process of policy change through the interactions of those actors who seek to influence decisions in environmental policy. (2) Environmental policy is also guided by scientific knowledge and technology.[61] The transmission of policy ideas from networks of experts can be very intensive, and it may reveal how scientific knowledge guides policy-makers' learning. (3) The politicization of science and policy objectivity is inevitable since the policy core beliefs of environmental issues are deeply divided and perhaps even irreconcilable.[62] How expert knowledge is biased or compromised by the policy core beliefs of clashing coalitions is well worth finding out, as is examining how the policy core beliefs are constrained by the political feasibility to achieve their objectives. How and why coalitions alter their policy core beliefs if there is any such potential to be found also deserves further examination.

It would appear that POS provide the most useful approaches to cross-national comparisons of environmental policy.[63] The assumption is that domestic structures determine the variations in how political systems meet social demands. These traditional approaches deal primarily with the structural nature of state institutions. If Japan has less fragmented political institutions than other nations, then the political institutions are more capable of imposing government policy on society. Stable or simply pre-fixed institutions are presumed to make a comparative analysis. However, the parsimonious distinction of "open"/"closed" and "strong"/"weak"—the former referring to the input processes of policy cycle as open and closed access to the political system and the latter referring to the output phases of policy cycle as polity's strong and weak capacity to impose policy[64]—is too simplistic to explain the specific outcomes of policy-making. Herbert Kitschelt's concept of POS has thus been embraced and expanded further by other scholars to include more dynamic and more informal aspects of polity, such as "shifts in ruling alignments and the availability of potential allies"[65] and "cultural models" (cultural impact on the elite's and the public's reaction to challengers).[66] Unfortunately, the different versions of POS are designed to examine their impact on different dependent variables: mobilization strategies, movement development, and policy implementation. These variables are chosen to primarily explain movement features. The POS approaches tend to focus on movement activism and neglect the explanation of policy change. While some formal institutional structures may be stable over time, others are contingent or constantly in a process of transformation.[67] Although ascribing a significant part of policy change to social movements, POS do not systematically explain how changes in political opportunity translate into policy change.

A less fragmented Japan might not always be able to conduct more effective policy than other fragmented nations. It is necessary to identify "issue-specific" as well as general openings in the Japanese polity, since there is a possibility of factors that might vary across issues and constituencies.[68] Within the structure-agency debate, agents' action can be understood only when observed in the structural context of political opportunities, but political opportunity structures can be prone to change over time. In this respect, rather than focusing attention on the structural nature of state institutions, one may capture a dynamic ongoing process of policy-making that stretches over a long time period and involves various interests and participants. Indeed, a better understanding of Japan's environmental policy requires the encompassing of over six decades of policy transformation in post-WWII Japan involving multiple interacting cycles among agents and levels and spheres of authority. The ACF is most widely used for the analysis of such policy processes.[69] However, this framework was initially proposed by Paul Sabatier and Hank Jenkins-Smith in the federal and pluralistic context of American political institutions where various advocacy coalitions have relatively equal power.[70] The key question is whether the ACF can consistently explain policy-making in the Japanese political system, which is generally known as a centralized unitary system and a single-party-dominated system post-WWII. In the ACF, the policy subsystem, which is composed of advocacy coalitions in a given policy area, is the unit of analysis for explaining policy changes. The ACF is particularly suited to policy change in a policy subsystem marked by societal and political confrontation. In this sense, the ACF may not be fully fit for Japanese policy-making, since Japanese society is far less fragmented than other major industrialized nations in terms of class cleavages and consensus building is of greater importance. In post-WWII Japan, political affiliation was not based on strong societal cleavages, but rather social networks, which would weaken the emergence of a cleavage-based political process.[71] Just like political opportunity shapes political behavior, so too does the cultural environment where community activity is located.

Like POS, the ACF presents a broader political environment or "stable system parameters" (stable external factors) within which policy subsystems operate.[72] However, the ACF does not clearly specify what parameters actually shape the broader political environment and how they create it. The ACF tends to neglect the process by which policy change takes place in established institutional arrangements linking political systems and social demands.[73] The POS are more suited to identifying which institutional factors determine the size and strength of coalitions and constrain or open the strategic options of coalition-building and cross-coalition interaction. The wealth of institutional detail that the literature on Japan's environmental policy provides gives a basis for examining the process of how political systems respond to societal demands. Yet the political opportunity structures are not always stable. Changing political environments, such as unstable political alignments and divided elites, provides a greater potential to alter the levels and patterns of institutional access to policy-makers in the policy subsystem, while the interaction of actors and structures may recreate access levels and patterns. The predominance of economic over environmental concerns in Japan's national policy reflects the distribution of power within the government. The power of the Japanese economic bureaucracy extends into environmental policy, yet a long-term process of political realignment since the early 1990s would seem to have changed the nature of resources and constraints external to the policy subsystem of environmental policy.

If, first, the ACF-suggested causal mechanism cannot solely account for cross-national differences in policy-making and, second, the POS or macro-state structures do not explain well the causal mechanisms of specific policy outcomes either, then the explanatory utility that links the ACF argument with the POS-structuralist approach will merit greater research attention. State structures do not determine the specific content and course of decision-making, yet coalition-building and cross-coalition interaction take place in the framework of state and societal institutions. These structures shape the type and size of advocacy coalitions and the level of activity and commitment needed to build a support basis for specific policy. As such, an integrated approach encompassing both institutional structures and advocacy coalitions may be considered to work in tandem.[74]

Given the constitutional structure of Japan's political system, this book assumes that advocacy coalitions do not all have equal power and the power relations between these coalitions could lead to the presence of a dominant coalition.[75] The patterns of coalition stability reveal in the post-WWII process of Japan's industrialization that the elite consensus trickles down to public preference. In this sense, policy change can be observed when stability and incremental policy-making over long periods are interrupted by a rising coalition or pressures external to the subsystem (or even "internal subsystem events"[76]). In a comparative perspective, domestic structures (i.e., state institutions and institutional links between state and society) seem to account for variation in policy subsystem activity. POS's explanation of how domestic structures shape political mobilization could complement the ACF.

The case of Japan's environmental policy provides a conceptual rationale for the potential complementarity of the POS and the ACF, since the relative closedness of Japan's political opportunity structure largely determines the adoption of specific coalition strategies and the outcomes of coalition-building. (1) The greater the degree of territorial centralization, the smaller the formal access of any one part of the system to act (POS assumption). The territorial centralization of unitary states is prone to confrontational strategies for conflict resolution with respect to the challenger (POS assumption). Yet country-specific cultural models need to be combined with the political structure to assess the exact nature and scope of political mobilization. Japan seems to be a highly homogenous society and less fragmented in terms of class cleavage.[77] Despite the territorial centralization, socially mobilized citizens are less likely to adopt direct, confrontational strategies. The general direction of policy is less likely to be revised as long as the dominant advocacy coalition that created the program stays in power (ACF assumption). (2) The smaller the level of party fragmentation, the less the political access available to challenging groups (POS assumption). If political fragmentation is measured by the number of parties within a coalition, then one-party dominance makes the matter of political fragmentation less relevant regarding policy outcome. Equally important, electoral institutions structurally shape the degree of party fragmentation. Japan's now-defunct single-non-transferable-vote, multi-member system (MMD-SNTV) largely accounted for the long-time Liberal Democratic Party (LDP) dominance, although the system was not the optimal system for the LDP.[78] Nonetheless, personalized politics, inherent to the MMD-SNTV,[79] created intra-party opposition within the LDP itself. In this sense, the LDP was regarded as a coalition of factions.[80] Fragmentation in intra-party factional politics often prevented the LDP from effectively achieving policy outcomes. Unstable policy outcomes are more likely to persist if the benefits that a coalition seeks to produce are not given but negotiated in factional politics (ACF assumption). (3) The greater the degree of bureaucratic compartmentalization, the greater the political pressure different domestic groups could exert on policy-making (POS assumption). Bureaucratic pluralism has significant effects on policy-making in Japan.[81] In Japan, coalition-building takes place between a particular national ministry and private institutions, especially business associations and other interest groups, who share a set of policy goals and beliefs. The politics of coalition bargaining are handled within the sectionalism-driven national bureaucracy over the allocation of budgets, accompanied by politicians' intervention.[82] Coalition bargaining often involves political compromise rather than policy coordination among national ministries. Yet the impact of bureaucratic compartmentalization might vary across issues and constituencies. In a given issue area, actors within a dominant advocacy coalition may show substantial consensus on the policy belief of the issue and thus demonstrate their capacity to impose a consistent policy on constituencies (ACF assumption). Such an issue area in Japan was nuclear energy that the pro-nuclear coalition promoted in post-WWII. In the issue area of climate change, by contrast, Japan's bureaucracy-led coalition-building of sectoral interests was deeply divided and thus failed to initiate climate change policy. (4) Government control over market forces determines the capacity of political systems to effectively implement policies (POS assumption). The strategies and actions of a minority coalition are most effectively organized at the sub-national level, as the national government tends to insulate itself from the diverse pressures of different interests and addresses itself to production-oriented state provision.[83] The differing policy priorities of national and sub-national authorities provide the latter with relative openness to popular pressures and minority coalition's local solutions (POS assumption). Japanese state elite's commitment to a "developmental state" saw environmental improvements as a by-product of energy conservation measures.[84] Energy conservation was aimed at maintaining private sector profitability while limiting institutional access in channeling social demands into the political system. Nonetheless, perturbations to the subsystem, such as public opinion and political realignments, may cause fundamental changes in national policy (ACF assumption). Changes in public opinion might prompt instability in the policy subsystem and create the potential for rapid policy change. In Japan, by 1970 a high degree of societal mobilization against industrial pollution created a new support base for environmental policies and led to devastating losses at local elections for the governing Liberal Democratic Party (LDP). The clear changes in public opinion created a basis for rapid policy change at the national level, although the conservative industrial coalition would seem not to have altered its deep core beliefs.

In regard to further exploring the possibilities for cross-fertilization between the POS and the ACF, however, there is little attention paid by both POS and ACF scholars to the political mobilization that occurs across institutional boundaries.[85] Environmental policy is increasingly made in both a domestic and an international arena. The POS at the international level do matter, especially in environmental policy, in the sense that international pressures influence domestic opportunity structures.[86] International structures can alter the nature and patterns of institutional access at the domestic level to actors who seek to promote their policy beliefs and mobilize their skills and resources in forming coalitions with allies.[87] Equally important, the application of the ACF at the international level is also necessary to account for trans-boundary and global problems. According to the ACF, policy shifts are the result of catastrophic events at the international level as well as domestic changes external to the policy subsystem.[88] As environmental problem-solving involves different levels and spheres of authority and is sought by coalitions of diverse stakeholders, the ACF is suited to the examination of environmental problems that are influenced by factors outside national boundaries and to that of sub-national actors' participation whose salience the trans-boundary problems enhance for policy integration.

To what extent can the POS be applied to structural factors at the international level? The assumption is that international structures determine variations in how domestic political systems meet social demands. This potential approach deals with the structural nature of the international system. The United States (US) has long shouldered more security responsibilities for Japan and the US has often pressured Japan to subordinate its interest to US wishes, especially on the trade front. If Japan is unable to invent a serious alternative to the "unequal alliance" and continues to accept dependence on the US, then Japan's autonomy will be constrained by close patron-dependent relationships. Japan's industrial advocacy coalition, which remains in power, is likely to adopt wait-and-see environmental policies with an eye to this trading partner and to be quite sensitive to US wishes. Nonetheless, it is important to note that, in the absence of a

24 *Introduction*

centralized political authority at the international level, self-help serves as a guardian to protect the interests of national governments and foreign pressure may have a limited capacity to impose its wishes on national and sub-national actors. In the issue area of Japan's nuclear energy, for example, despite the opposition of the US government, the dominant coalition that instituted Japan's nuclear energy programs adopted a Calder Hall reactor from Britain as the first commercial nuclear power station, which started operation in 1965. It was reported that the pro-nuclear coalition of business leaders and their allied conservative politicians pursued a nuclear program free of the restrictions imposed by the United States on their use of by-product plutonium.[89]

The above approach of explaining the impact of the security environment simply highlights the interplay between separated levels of politics. The external environment is claimed to affect domestic politics ("second image reversed").[90] A more recent approach, the "two-level-games" theory, does suggest a shift from strictly delineated domestic-foreign dichotomies to an interactive levels approach while viewing international negotiations as influenced simultaneously by both domestic and international constraints.[91] This approach is subject to criticism on the grounds that it places the sub-national level of participation on the second level of the game and thus still presumes the domestic-foreign divide. Equally important, it is inadequate to consider the effect of international norm diffusion (e.g., causal beliefs based on global scientific understandings and planetary responsibility) on sub-national agents and specific domestic settings.[92] Local and provincial actors have increasingly considered themselves players in a global game to cope with the local impacts of climate change.[93] The dynamics of the sub-national level of participation would seem to reveal a convergence, rather than a simple interplay of domestic and international politics. This can be seen as a rapidly expanding sphere of action in which the boundaries of domestic and foreign affairs are eroding.[94] The boundary-eroding dynamics have become highly salient in the field of international environmental cooperation precisely because the causes of environmental risk are locally specific in character yet local action can simultaneously be a part of global strategies.

The ACF should be understood as being shaped simultaneously by domestic and foreign issues. Global forces and strategies increasingly influence the policy beliefs and interests of advocacy coalitions. Such an understanding requires an examination of the globally based account of strategies and motives of domestic actors in advocacy coalitions and an investigation of foreign actors' participation in advocacy coalitions. An advocacy coalition can be an integral part of a transnational advocacy network to help foreign actors further their policy goals in other localities. This process also enhances the salience of sub-national government actors. In an early debate on transnational politics, Robert Keohane and Joseph Nye confined the concept of transnationalism to the activities of non-governmental actors, differentiating their activities from those of "transgovernmental actors" or "sub-units of governments on those occasions when they act relatively autonomously from higher authority in international politics."[95] According to Thomas Risse-Kappen, however, the interactive relations of government actors across national boundaries can be considered transnational "when at least one actor pursues her own agenda independent of national decisions."[96] The necessity of this redefinition suggests that the distinction between state-based actors and non-governmental actors has become blurred as sub-national government actors look to transnational networks to gain support in the absence of action by national governments.[97] Transnational networks steer members towards two primary public goals: influencing and changing the behavior of nation-states within the international arena and governing transnational issues outside normal national jurisdiction. Epistemic communities[98] and transnational advocacy networks,[99] in which non-state actors operate in alliances with other non-state actors and state actors, see the sovereign state as the object of their advocacy activities. Their focus remains on the first public goal to hold the target state to account for international commitments. In contrast, public transnational networks, which sub-units of government (sub-national governments, legislators, and judges) establish, often in cooperation with international organizations, authoritatively enable governing to take place towards the second public goal. In this context, the individual and organizational "constituents" of the networks recognize the network authorities as authoritative based on their legal-formal ability to exercise control and coordination.[100] One of the largest public transnational networks, Cities for Climate Protection, was initiated by the International Council for Local Environmental Initiatives (ICLEI) in 1993 and involves more than 1,000 local governments worldwide. These sub-national actors, often from countries with limited national commitments, are integrating climate change mitigation into a form of inter-municipal governance beyond national boundaries.

Finally, one of the most important concepts in the ACF literature concerns "policy brokers" who seek a "political compromise" and reduce conflicts between the competing advocacy coalitions.[101] This is particularly important as I claim that sub-national actors can strategically act as an intermediate agent in reconnecting local action with national policy and turning global strategies into local action for problem-solving. The term intermediate agent was previously used in this chapter to describe "policy coordinators" who neutralize the policy inefficiencies caused by political frictions, and reduce the transaction costs of reaching an agreement to shape institutions and their interactions. In contentious policy subsystems, however, policy disagreements often result in political conflicts between the advocacy coalitions. A political compromise may become necessary for reaching an agreement but it puts a brake on current gains in policy efficiency and appropriate conduct. Potential policy brokers who may not consider the policy concerned as a fundamental issue become seriously concerned about the maintenance of the policy subsystem and thus act as brokers.[102] However, it is important to note that they may instead promote a particular coalition that matches their policy belief and thus act as policy participants rather than policy brokers. In contentious policy subsystems where conflicts are driven more by differences in policy core beliefs/values than by technical differences in secondary beliefs (related to policy instruments and specific policy proposals), the perception of actors to see their opponents as more powerful than they actually are, known as the "devil shift,"[103] becomes an impediment to arriving at a compromise between the competing advocacy coalitions. Policy brokers may thus choose one coalition over others to see a desirable policy outcome. It is likely that the policy area of environmental issues is a case in point. This policy area shows the low level of inter-coalition belief compatibility as environmental policy contests are often deeply divided over fundamental values.

Why then does anyone decide to act as a policy broker? The potential policy brokers are conceived from elected officials, political parties, and bureaucrats, each with neutral competence. However, bureaucrats may become policy advocates rather than brokers if their agencies' mission is clearly defined.[104] They strive to maximize their budget, as well as to extend their operating autonomy and thus protect their own agency's special interests. Elected officials at the national level tend to provide business interest groups with closer access than public interest groups and simultaneously act strategically to seek voters' maximization (material self-interest). Political parties may be internally divided on the issue concerned yet work together to maintain their internal party cohesion (institutional self-interest). Those actors who may not have strong policy core beliefs in dispute pursue their material self-interests in the capacity of policy brokers to guide a political compromise between the competing advocacy coalitions.[105] In other words, they are not expected to be purely neutral actors. In this context, the experience of Japanese local governments indicates the potential of another type of policy brokers. Local governments structurally hold a strategic position between the state and civil society and between domestic and foreign affairs in terms of their ability to influence others. Such structural positions create informational advantage while getting familiar with both sides and can increase their potential to influence others. In this sense, local governments can potentially act to find feasible policy compromises. Yet Japanese local governments did not always seek the stability or status quo of the policy environment and they were often revisionist policy brokers.[106] They were innovative in the policy area of environmental issues and pushed their innovative ideas while creating demand for the proposed solution.[107] Local governments in general are associated with the quality of life in the immediate environment (need) rather than economic efficiency (production) and tend to develop their policy core beliefs based on the association. Local governments, which are not only equipped with expert knowledge but are also socially competent at the local level, provide information that might not otherwise be heard by either local communities or other stakeholders. They could help local capacity-building to effectively engage resourceful stakeholders in reaching policy compromises. To this extent, policy comprises can be largely achieved by policy efficiency and appropriate policy conduct rather than driven by a strategic interest-base. It is safe to say that the distinction between advocate and broker is a continuum rather than a dichotomy.

Organization of this book

This book is divided into two parts. The first part (Introduction and Chapters 1 and 3) sets the context for my discussion of a series of case studies, which are presented in the second part of Chapters 2 and 4–8. This introductory chapter provides a conceptual and theoretical framework that informs the transformation of Japan's environmental policy and politics. Chapter 1 conducts a historical survey of environmental policy and politics by examining how environmental policy-making has developed as Japan has progressed through different phases of environmental protection from addressing domestic to global issues. Chapter 2 introduces the first test case to examine the traditional state-centric coordination of Japan's nuclear energy policy. Japan's nuclear energy has been a strong top-down national undertaking and it establishes a division of labor among levels of government with a state-centric gate-keeping capacity. The case studies, which are conducted in Chapters 4–8, represent a sharp contrast to the state-centric, hierarchical and centralized form of policy coordination. These case studies reveal that the dynamics of environmental problem-solving are much more de-hierarchized and open up opportunities for a variety of actors to participate in decision-making. Chapter 3 provides the state of local capacity in Japan for climate change countermeasures and involvement in international environmental cooperation, in order to locate the specific case studies within the overall picture of Japan's sub-national governing capacity. Chapter 4 casts light on the exceptional case of Tokyo's metropolitan cap-and-trade for a mandatory reduction of total CO_2 emissions as the Tokyo Metropolitan Government has exceptionally strong independent sources of revenue as well as administrative ability. Chapters 5–7 illustrate and explain the three localities (Shiga prefecture, Kitakyushu city, and Yokohama city) that have been the most engaged in international environmental cooperation, showing a higher level of commitment compared to other localities. The three studies of those localities demonstrate that locally specific needs and adaptive capacity continue to ensure difference and diversity among the more self-motivated local governments, in contrast with weaker municipalities that remain over-dependent on national supervision. Chapter 8 examines the importance of public participation in the production and use of environmental expertise and science, with special reference to "expert citizens" in Japan who can facilitate and mediate between expert knowledge and lay people. As uncertainty, inherent in the complexity of environmental science, increases, there are calls for refashioning expert knowledge into a more citizen-expert interactive governance.

Notes

1 In this book, sub-national governments in Japan are referred to as local governments. The local government system consists of two tiers: prefectures and municipalities (Article 1-3 of the Local Autonomy Law).
2 The concept of "*ba*" was initially developed by philosopher Kitarō Nishida. *Ba* can be defined as a shared space for emerging human relationships. In my view, *ba* serves as a foundation for new policy creation. The shared *ba* can be physical as well as non-physical. Policy ideas are embedded in both the physical space (e.g., cross-scale/multi-level interactions) and the non-physical space (e.g., shared experience and ideas). All these *ba* may be linked with one another for knowledge creation. See Kitarō Nishida, *An Inquiry into the Good*, trans. Masao Abe and Christopher Ives (New Haven, CT: Yale University Press, 1990).

3 Ellis S. Krauss and Bradford L. Simcock, "Citizens' movements: the growth and impact of environmental protest in Japan," in Kurt Steiner, Ellis S. Krauss, and Scott C. Flanagan, eds., *Political Opposition and Local Politics in Japan* (Princeton, NJ: Princeton University Press, 1980), pp. 187–227; Margret A. McKean, "Political socialization through citizens' movements," in K. Steiner, E. Krauss, and S. Flanagan, eds., *Political Opposition and Local Politics in Japan* (Princeton, NJ: Princeton University Press, 1981), pp. 228–73; Steven R. Reed, "Environmental politics: some reflections based on the Japanese case," *Comparative Politics*, Vol. 13, No. 3 (1981), pp. 253–69.

4 Michio Muramatsu, "The impact of economic growth policies on local politics in Japan," *Asian Survey*, Vol. 15, No. 9 (1975), pp. 799–816; Jeffrey Broadbent, *Environmental Politics in Japan: Networks of Power and Protest* (Cambridge, UK: Cambridge University Press, 1998).

5 Miranda A. Schreurs, *Environmental Politics in Japan, Germany and the United States* (Cambridge, UK: Cambridge University Press, 2002); David Vogel, "Environmental policy in Japan and West Germany," Paper presented at the annual meeting of the Western Political Science Association, Newport Beach, CA, March 1990.

6 Yasuo Takao, "Making climate change policy work at the local level: capacity-building for decentralized policymaking in Japan," *Pacific Affairs*, Vol. 85, No. 4 (2012), pp. 767–88.

7 Yasuo Takao, "Local levels of participation in Japan's foreign aid and cooperation: issues arising from decentralized international cooperation," *Asian Survey*, Vol. 54, No. 3 (2014), pp. 540–64.

8 Schreurs, *Environmental Politics in Japan, Germany, and the United States*, pp. 186–7.

9 Bob Jessop, "The rise of governance and the risks of failure: the case of economic development," *International Social Science Journal*, Vol. 50, No. 155 (1998), pp. 29–45; Garry Stoker, "Governance as theory: five propositions," *International Social Science Journal*, Vol. 50, No. 155 (1998), pp. 17–28.

10 James N. Rosenau, "Toward an ontology for global governance," in Martin Hewson and Timothy J. Sinclair, eds., *Approaches to Global Governance Theory* (Albany, NY: State University of New York Press, 1999), chp 13.

11 Jan Kooiman, ed., *Modern Governance: New Government-Society Interactions* (London: Sage, 1993); R.A.W. Rhodes, *Understanding Governance: Policy Networks, Governance, Reflexivity and Accountability* (Buckingham, UK: Open University Press, 1997).

12 David Held, Anthony McGrew, David Goldblatt, and Jonathan Perraton, *Global Transformations; Politics, Economics, Culture* (Cambridge, UK: Polity, 1999), p. 447.

13 Thomas G. Weiss, "Governance, good governance, global governance: actual challenges governance conceptual and actual challenges," *Third World Quarterly*, Vol. 21 (2000), pp. 795–814.

14 W. Neil Adger, Katrina Brown, Jenny Fairbrass, Andrew Jordan, Jouni Paavola, Sergio Rosendo, and Gill Seyfang, "Governance for sustainability: towards a 'thick' analysis of environmental decision-making," *Environment and Planning*, Vol. 35 (2003), pp. 1095–110.

15 Brian Walker, Nick Abel, John Anderies, and Paul Ryan, "Resilience, adaptability, and transformability in the Goulburn-Broken Catchment, Australia," *Ecology and Society*, Vol. 14, No. 1 (2009), on-line journal, available from: www.ecologyandsociety.org/vol14/iss1/art12/ [accessed December 26, 2009].

16 Claudia Pahl-Wostl, Joyeeta Gupta, and Daniel Petry, "Governance and the global water system: a theoretical exploration," *Global Governance*, Vol. 14, No. 4 (2008), pp. 419–35.

17 Karen T. Litfin, "Advocacy coalitions along the domestic-foreign frontier: globalization and Canadian climate change policy," *Policy Studies Journal*, Vol. 28, No. 1 (2000), pp. 236–52.

18 James Rosenau, *Along the Domestic-Foreign Frontier: Exploring Governance in a Turbulent World* (Cambridge, UK: Cambridge University Press, 1997).
19 Liesbet Hooghe and Gary Marks, "Types of multi-level governance," *European Integration Online Papers*, Vol. 5 (2001), on-line journal, available from: http://eiop.or.at/eiop/texte/2001011.htm [accessed 20 March 2015].
20 Gary Marks, "An actor-centred approach to multi-level governance," *Regional and Federal Studies*, Vol. 6, No. 2 (1996), pp. 20–40; Elizabeth Bomberg and John Peterson, "European Union decision making: the role of sub-national authorities," *Political Studies*, Vol. 46, No. 2 (1998), pp. 219–35.
21 Marks, "An actor-centred approach to multi-level governance," pp. 31–2; Bomberg and Peterson, "European Union decision making," pp. 227–8; Chris Skelcher, "Jurisdictional integrity, polycentrism, and the design of democratic governance," *Governance*, Vol. 18, No. 1 (January 2005), p. 94.
22 Stanley Hoffmann, "Obstinate or obsolete? The fate of the nation-state and the case of Western Europe," *Daedalus*, Vol. 95, No. 3 (1966), pp. 862–915; Paul Taylor, *The Limits of European Integration* (New York: Columbia University Press, 1983); Andrew Moravcsik, "Preferences and power in the European Community: a liberal intergovernmentalist approach," *Journal of Common Market Studies*, Vol. 31, No. 4 (1993), pp. 473–524.
23 Carlo Aall, Kyrre Groven, and Gard Lindseth, "The scope of action for local climate policy: the case of Norway," *Global Environmental Politics*, Vol. 7, No. 2 (2007), pp. 83–101.
24 Liesbet Hooghe and Gary Marks, "Europe with the regions: channels of regional representation in the European Union," *The Journal of Federalism*, Vol. 26, No. 1 (1996), pp. 73–82; Marks, "An actor-centred approach to multi-level governance," pp. 31–2; Bomberg and Peterson, "European Union decision making," pp. 223–7.
25 Kristine Kern and Harriet Bulkeley, "Cities, Europeanization and multi-level governance: governing climate change through transnational municipal networks," *Journal of Common Market Studies*, Vol. 47, No. 2 (2009), pp. 309–32; Eva Gustavsson, Ingemar Elander, and Mats Lundmark, "Multilevel governance, networking cities, and the geography of climate-change mitigation: two Swedish examples," *Environment and Planning C: Government and Policy*, Vol. 27 (2009), pp. 59–74.
26 Peter Haas, "Addressing the global governance deficit," *Global Environmental Politics*, Vol. 4, No. 4 (2004), p. 7.
27 Eva Sørensen and Jacob Torfing, "The democratic anchorage of governance networks," *Scandinavian Political Studies*, Vol. 28, No. 3 (2005), pp. 195–218; Carol Harlow and Richard Rawlings, "Accountability in multilevel governance: a network approach," *European Law Journal*, Vol. 13, No. 4 (2007), pp. 542–62.
28 For the European experience of such extra-national channels, see Hooghe and Marks, "Europe with the regions," pp. 82–90; Bomberg and Peterson, "European Union decision making," pp. 228–31; Charlie Jeffery, "Sub-national mobilization and European integration: does it make any difference?" *Journal of Common Market Studies*, Vol. 38, No. 1 (2000), pp. 1–23; Jenny Fairbrass and Andrew Jordan, "Multi-level governance and environmental policy," in Ian Bache and Matthew Flinders, eds., *Multi-level Governance* (Oxford: Oxford University Press, 2005), pp. 147–64.
29 Robert O. Keohane, "The demand for international regimes," in Stephen D. Krasner, ed., *International Regimes* (Ithaca, NY: Cornell University Press, 1983), pp. 141–71.
30 David Lake and Robert Powell, *Strategic Choice and International Relations* (Princeton, NJ: Princeton University Press, 1999).
31 Amitav Acharya, "How ideas spread: whose norms matter? Norm localization and institutional change in Asian regionalism," *International Organization*, Vol. 58, No. 2 (Spring, 2004), pp. 239–75.

32 For the details of sub-national actors, see the intermediary role of "expert citizens" in Chapter 8.
33 Jan Kooiman and Svein Jentoft, "Meta-governance: values, norms and principles, and the making of hard choices," *Public Administration*, Vol. 87, No. 4 (2009), pp. 818–36.
34 Bob Jessop, *The Future of the Capitalist State* (Cambridge, UK: Polity Press, 2002).
35 Lamont C. Hempel, *Environmental Governance: The Global Challenge* (Washington, DC: Island Press, 1996); W. Neil Adger, Saleemul Huq, Katrina Brown, Declan Conway, and Mike Hulme, "Adaptation to climate change in the developing world," *Progress in Development Studies*, Vol. 3, No. 3 (2003), pp. 179–95; Carl Folke, Thomas Hahn, Per Olsson, and Jon Norberg, "Adaptive governance of social-ecological systems," *Annual Review of Environment and Resources*, Vol. 30 (2005), pp. 441–73.
36 Folke, Hahn, Olsson, and Norberg, "Adaptive governance of social-ecological systems," pp. 441–73.
37 World Commission on Environment and Development (WCED), *Our Common Future* (Oxford: Oxford University Press, 1987), p. 43.
38 John Robinson, "Squaring the circle? Some thoughts on the idea of sustainable development," *Ecological Economics*, Vol. 48, No. 4 (2004), pp. 369–84; Colin C. William and Andrew C. Millington, "The diverse and contested meanings of sustainable development," *The Geographical Journal*, Vol. 170 (2004), pp. 99–104.
39 Karen T. Litfin, *Ozone Discourse: Science and Politics in Global Environmental Cooperation* (New York: Columbia University Press, 1994); Rodger A. Payne, "Persuasion, frames and norm construction," *European Journal of International Relations*, Vol. 7, No. 1 (2001), pp. 37–61.
40 William C. Clark, "Social learning," in Andrew S. Goudie and David J. Cuff, eds., *Encyclopaedia of Global Change: Environmental Change and Human Society* (Oxford: Oxford University Press, 2001), pp. 382–4; Folke, Hahn, Olsson, and Norberg, "Adaptive governance of social-ecological systems," pp. 441–73; Derek R. Armitage, Melissa Marschke, and Ryan Plummer, "Adaptive co-management and the paradox of learning," *Global Environmental Change*, Vol. 18, No. 1 (2008), pp. 86–98.
41 Fikret Berkes, Johan Colding, and Carl Folke, "Introduction," in Fikret Berkes, Johan Colding, and Carl Folke, eds., *Navigating Social-Ecological Systems: Building Resilience for Complexity and Change* (Cambridge, UK: Cambridge University Press, 2003), pp. 1–30.
42 Paul DiMaggio and Wlater Powell, ed., *The New Institutionalism in Organizational Analysis* (Chicago, IL: University of Chicago Press, 1991).
43 Richard Rose, "What is lesson-drawing?" *Journal of Public Policy*, Vol. 11, No. 1 (1991), pp. 3–30.
44 Peter May, "Policy learning and failure," *Journal of Public Policy*, Vol. 12, No. 4 (1992), pp. 331–54; Chang Lee and David Strang, "The international diffusion of public sector downsizing: network emulation and theory-driven learning," *International Organization*, Vol. 60, No. 4 (2006), pp. 883–909.
45 Covadonga Meseguer, "Learning about policies: a Bayesian approach," European Forum Working Paper Series 5, Florence, European University Institute, 2003.
46 Charles E. Lindblom, "The science of 'muddling through'," *Public Administration Review*, Vol. 29 (1959), pp. 79–88.
47 David Strang and John Meyer, "Institutional conditions for diffusion," *Theory and Society*, Vol. 22, No. 4 (1993), pp. 487–511; Kurt Weyland, "Theories of policy diffusion: lessons from Latin American pension reform," *World Politics*, Vol. 57, No. 2 (2005), pp. 262–95.
48 Meseguer, "Learning about policies."
49 Simon Bulmer, David Dolowitz, Peter Humphreys, and Stephen Padgett, *Policy Transfer in the European Union Governance* (London: Routledge, 2007), p. 13.

50 David P. Dolowitz and David Marsh "Who learns what from whom: a review of the policy transfer literature," *Political Studies*, Vol. 44, No. 2 (1996), pp. 347–9.
51 Martha Finnemore, "Norms, culture, and world politics: insights from sociology's institutionalism," *International Organization*, Vol. 50, No. 2 (1996), pp. 325–47.
52 Peter Hall, "Policy paradigms, social learning and the state: the case of economic policy making in Britain," *Comparative Politics*, Vol. 25, No. 3 (1993), pp. 275–96.
53 Paul A. Sabatier, "Knowledge, policy-oriented learning, and policy change: an advocacy coalition framework," *Knowledge*, Vol. 8 (1987), pp. 649–92.
54 Paul A. Sabatier and Hank Jenkins-Smith, "An advocacy coalition framework of policy change and the role of policy-oriented learning therein," *Policy Sciences*, Vol. 21, No. 2–3 (1988), p. 134.
55 David Robertson, "Political conflict and lesson-drawing," *Journal of Public Policy*, Vol. 11, No. 1 (1991), pp. 55–78.
56 Alan Irwin and Brian Wynne, *Misunderstanding Science? The Public Reconstruction of Science and Technology* (Cambridge, UK: Cambridge University Press, 1996); Harry H. Collins and Robert J. Evans, "The third wave of science studies: studies of expertise and experience," *Social Studies of Science*, Vol. 32, No. 2 (2002), pp. 235–96; Sheila Jasanoff, "Transparency in public science: purposes, reasons, limits," *Law and Contemporary Problem*, Vol. 69, No. 21 (2006), pp. 21–45.
57 Steven Yearley, "Making systematic sense of public discontents with expert knowledge: two analytical approaches and a case study," *Public Understanding of Science*, Vol. 9 (2000), pp. 105–22.
58 For the details of sub-national actors, see the intermediary role of "expert citizens" in Chapter 8.
59 Sabatier and Jenkins-Smith, "An advocacy coalition framework of policy change and the role of policy-oriented learning therein," pp. 129–68; Paul A. Sabatier and Hank C. Jenkins-Smith, eds., *Policy Change and Learning: An Advocacy Coalition Approach* (Boulder, CO: Westview Press, 1993).
60 Herbert P. Kitschelt, "Political opportunities structures and political protest: anti-nuclear movements in four democracies," *British Journal of Political Science*, Vol. 16 (1986), pp. 57–85; Sidney Tarrow, *Struggle, Politics, and Reform: Collective Action, Social Movements, and Cycles of Protest* (Ithaca, NY: Cornell University Press, 1989).
61 The ACF considers scientific knowledge as a "stable system parameter," which affects the constraints and opportunities of actors within the policy subsystem of environmental policy. As scientific uncertainty in environmental protection increases, however, it is unrealistic to consider this external factor as stable. It is necessary to examine the ways by which scientific knowledge and technology shape the channels and political opportunities offered to coalition-building and cross-coalition interaction.
62 Christopher M. Weible, Paul A. Sabatier, and Kelly McQueen, "Themes and variations: taking stock of the advocacy coalition framework," *The Policy Studies Journal*, Vol. 37, No. 1 (2009), pp. 121–40.
63 Kitschelt, "Political opportunities structures and political protest"; Tarrow, *Struggle, Politics, and Reform*.
64 Kitschelt, "Political opportunities structures and political protest," pp. 61–82.
65 Sidney Tarrow, *Power in Movement: Social Movements, Collective Action and Mass Politics* (New York and London: Cambridge University Press, 1994), p. 18.
66 Hanspeter Kriesi, Ruud Koopmans, Jan Willem Duyvendak, and Marco G. Giugni, *New Social Movements in Western Europe: A Comparative Analysis* (Minneapolis, MN: University of Minnesota Press, 1995), p. 33.
67 Kriesi, Koopmans, Duyvendak and Giugni, *New Social Movements in Western Europe*.

68 David S. Meyer and Debra C. Minkoff, "Conceptualizing political opportunity," *Social Forces*, Vol. 82, No. 4 (2004), pp. 1457–92.
69 Sabatier and Jenkins-Smith, *Policy Change and Learning: An Advocacy Coalition Approach*; Paul A. Sabatier and Hank Jenkins-Smith, "The advocacy coalition framework: an assessment," in Paul A. Sabatier, ed., *Theories of the Policy Process* (Boulder, CO: Westview Press, 1999), pp. 117–66; Paul A. Sabatier and Christopher M. Weible, "The advocacy coalition framework: innovations and clarifications," in Paul A. Sabatier, ed., *Theories of the Policy Process*, 2nd ed. (Boulder, CO: Westview Press, 2007), pp. 189–220.
70 Sabatier and Jenkins-Smith, "An advocacy coalition framework of policy change and the role of policy-oriented learning therein," pp. 129–68.
71 Scott C. Flanagan and Bradley M. Richardson, *Japanese Electoral Behavior: Social Cleavages, Social Networks and Partisanship* (London: Sage, 1977).
72 Sabatier and Jenkins-Smith, "The advocacy coalition framework," p. 149.
73 Michael Mintrom and Sandra Vergari, "Advocacy coalitions, policy entrepreneurs, and policy change," *Policy Studies Journal*, Vol. 24, No. 3 (1996), pp. 420–34.
74 The macro-environment of "stable system parameters" constraining coalition strategies is parallel to the concept of the POS; however, the ACF does not specify how these parameters shape venues to influence public policy.
75 Hanspeter Kriesi and Maya Jegen, "The Swiss energy policy elite: the actor constellation of a policy domain in transition," *European Journal of Political Research*, Vol. 39 (2001), p. 252.
76 Sabatier and Weible, "The advocacy coalition framework: innovations and clarifications," pp. 204–5.
77 Flanagan and Richardson, *Japanese Electoral Behavior*.
78 In 1994, the electoral system replaced it with a SMD (single-member district)/SNTV/PR (proportional representation) system. Voters were allocated two votes to cast: one for an SMD candidate and another for a party in the PR system.
79 Multi-member districts tend to provide incentives for candidates to represent narrow interests of their constituencies by reducing the vote-share threshold that they need to secure an electoral success. See, for example, Gary W. Cox, "Centripetal and centrifugal incentives in electoral systems," *American Journal of Political Science*, Vol. 34, No. 4 (1990), pp. 903–35.
80 See, for example, Gary W. Cox and Frances Rosenbluth, "The electoral fortunes of legislative factions in Japan," *American Political Science Review*, Vol. 87, No. 3 (1993), pp. 577–89.
81 Michio Muramatsu and Ellis S. Krauss, "The conservative policy line and the development of patterned pluralism," in Kozo Yamamura and Yasukichi Yasuba, eds., *The Political Economy of Japan, Vol. 1: The Domestic Transformation* (Stanford, CA: Stanford University Press, 1987), pp. 516–54; Seizaburō Satō and Tetsuhisa Matsuzaki, *Jimintō Seiken* [Liberal Democratic Party government] (Tokyo: Chuōkōron-sha, 1986).
82 In recent years, the rational choice theories of politician dominance and electoral determinism have become one of the influential approaches to a better understanding of state-society relations in Japan. Mark Ramseyer and Frances Rosenbluth, *Japan's Political Marketplace* (Cambridge, MA: Harvard University Press, 1993); Ellis S. Krauss and Robert J. Pekkanen, *The Rise and Fall of Japan's LDP: Political Party Organizations as Historical Institutions* (Ithaca, NY: Cornell University Press, 2010).
83 Peter Saunders, "Rethinking local politics," in Martin Boddy and Colin Fudge, eds., *Local Socialism?* (London: Macmillan, 1984), pp. 22–48.
84 Jeffrey Broadbent, "Japan's environmental politics: recognition and response processes," in Hidefumi Imura and Miranda Schreurs, eds., *Environmental Management in Japan* (Bangkok: The World Bank and Elsevier Press, 2005), p. 119.

Introduction   33

85 For those who apply the ACF to global subsystems, see Litfin, "Advocacy coalitions along the domestic-foreign frontiers," pp. 236–52.
86 Bert Klandermans, *The Social Psychology of Protest* (Oxford: Blackwell, 1997); Sidney Tarrow, "Transnational politics: contention and institutions in international politics," *Annual Review of Political Science*, Vol. 4 (2001), pp. 1–20.
87 David S. Meyer, "Political opportunity and nested institutions," *Social Movement Studies*, Vol. 2, No. 1 (2003), pp. 17–35.
88 Paul A. Sabatier, "Policy change over a decade or more," in Paul A. Sabatier and Hank C. Jenkins-Smith, eds., *Policy Change and Learning: An Advocacy Coalition Framework* (Boulder, CO: Westview Press, 1993), pp. 22–3.
89 Tetsuo Arima, *Genpatsu, Shōriki, CIA* [Nuclear power generation, Shōriki and CIA] (Tokyo: Shinchō Shinsho, 2008).
90 Peter Katzenstein, "International relations and domestic structures: foreign economic policies of the advanced industrial states," *International Organization*, Vol. 30, No. 1 (1976), pp. 1–45; Peter Gourevitch, "The second image reversed: the international sources of domestic politics," *International Organization*, Vol. 32, No. 4 (1978), pp. 881–912.
91 Robert D. Putnam, "Diplomacy and domestic politics: the logic of two-level games," *International Organization*, Vol. 42, No. 3 (1988), pp. 427–60.
92 Thomas Risse-Kappen, ed., *Bringing Transnational Relations Back In: Non-State Actors, Domestic Structures, and International Institutions* (New York: Cambridge University Press, 1995); Jeffrey T. Checkel, "International norms and domestic politics: bridging the rationalist-constructivist divide," *European Journal of International Relations*, Vol. 3, No. 4 (1997), pp. 473–95.
93 Zdravko Mlinar, "Local responses to global change," *Annals of the American Academy of Political and Social Science*, Vol. 540 (1995), pp. 145–56; Litfin, "Advocacy coalitions along the domestic-foreign frontier," pp. 236–52.
94 Rosenau, *Along the Domestic-Foreign Frontier: Exploring Governance in a Turbulent World*.
95 Robert Keohane and Joseph Nye, Jr., "Transgovernmental relations and international organizations," *World Politics*, Vol. 27, No. 1 (1974), p. 41.
96 Thomas Risse-Kappen, "Introduction," in Thomas Risse-Kappen, ed., *Bringing Transnational Relations Back In: Nonstate Actors, Domestic Structures and International Institutions* (New York: Cambridge University Press, 1995), p. 9.
97 Harriet Bulkeley, "Down to earth: local government and greenhouse policy in Australia," *Australian Geographer*, Vol. 31, No. 3 (2000), pp. 289–308; Michele Betstill and Harriet Bulkeley, "Transnational networks and global environmental governance: the cities for climate protection program," *International Studies Quarterly*, Vol. 48, No. 2 (2004), pp. 471–93.
98 Peter Haas, "Do regimes matter? Epistemic communities and Mediterranean pollution control," *International Organization*, Vol. 43, No. 3 (1989), pp. 377–403.
99 Margaret Keck and Kathryn Sikkink, *Activists beyond Borders: Advocacy Networks in International Politics* (Ithaca, NY: Cornell University Press, 1998).
100 Liliana Andonova, Michele Betsill, and Harriet Bulkeley, "Transnational climate governance," *Global Environmental Politics*, Vol. 9, No. 2 (2009), p. 56.
101 Sabatier, "Policy change over a decade or more," pp. 18–19; Sabatier and Jenkins-Smith, "The advocacy coalition framework: an assessment," pp. 117–66.
102 Sabatier, "Policy change over a decade or more," p. 27.
103 Sabatier and Jenkins-Smith, *Policy Change and Learning*; Sabatier and Jenkins-Smith, "The advocacy coalition framework: an assessment," pp. 117–66.
104 Sabatier and Jenkins-Smith, *Policy Change and Learning*, p. 27.
105 Karin Ingold and Frédéric Varone, "Treating policy brokers seriously: evidence from the climate policy," *Journal of Public Administration Research and Theory*, Vol. 22, No. 2 (2012), pp. 319–46.

106 In Japan, local government as a broker has a broad jurisdiction over a wide range of policy areas. Local governments are better able to negotiate because they have directly elected chief executives on the presidential rather than the parliamentary system, and their personnel system controls an entire government rather than just one department. Chief executives hold greater powers over personnel and organization. See Reed, "Environmental politics," pp. 253–70.

107 Muramatsu, "The impact of economic growth policies on local politics in Japan," pp. 799–816.

References

Aall, Carlo, Kyrre Groven, and Gard Lindseth (2007). "The scope of action for local climate policy: the case of Norway." *Global Environmental Politics*, Vol. 7, No. 2, pp. 83–101.

Acharya, Amitav (2004). "How ideas spread: whose norms matter? Norm localization and institutional change in Asian regionalism." *International Organization*, Vol. 58, No. 2, pp. 239–75.

Adger, W. Neil, Katrina Brown, Jenny Fairbrass, Andrew Jordan, Jouni Paavola, Sergio Rosendo, and Gill Seyfang (2003). "Governance for sustainability: towards a thick, analysis of environmental decision-making." *Environment and Planning*, Vol. 35, pp. 1095–110.

Adger, W. Neil, Saleemul Huq, Katrina Brown, Declan Conway, and Mike Hulme (2003). "Adaptation to climate change in the developing world." *Progress in Development Studies*, Vol. 3, No. 3, pp. 179–95.

Andonova, Liliana, Michele Betsill, and Harriet Bulkeley (2009). "Transnational climate governance." *Global Environmental Politics*, Vol. 9, No. 2, pp. 52–73.

Arima, Tetsuo (2008). *Genpatsu, Shōriki, CIA* [Nuclear power generation, Shōriki and CIA]. Tokyo: Shinchō Shinsho.

Armitage, Derek, Melissa Marschke, and Ryan Plummer (2008). "Adaptive co-management and the paradox of learning." *Global Environmental Change*, Vol. 18, No. 1, pp. 86–98.

Berkes, Fikret, Johan Colding, and Carl Folke (2003). "Introduction." In Fikret Berkes, Johan Colding, and Carl Folke, eds., *Navigating Social-Ecological Systems: Building Resilience for Complexity and Change*. Cambridge, UK: Cambridge University Press, pp. 1–30.

Betstill, Michele and Harriet Bulkeley (2004). "Transnational networks and global environmental governance: the cities for climate protection program." *International Studies Quarterly*, Vol. 48, No. 2, pp. 471–493.

Bomberg, Elizabeth and John Peterson (1998). "European Union decision making: the role of sub-national authorities." *Political Studies*, Vol. 46, No. 2, pp. 219–35.

Broadbent, Jeffrey (1998). *Environmental Politics in Japan: Networks of Power and Protest*. Cambridge, UK: Cambridge University Press.

Broadbent, Jeffrey (2005). "Japan's environmental politics: recognition and response processes." In Hidefumi Imura and Miranda Schreurs, eds., *Environmental Management in Japan*. Cheltenham, UK: The World Bank and Elsevier Press, pp. 102–34.

Bulkeley, Harriet (2000). "Down to earth: local government and greenhouse policy in Australia." *Australian Geographer*, Vol. 31, No. 3, pp. 289–308.

Bulmer, Simon, David Dolowitz, Peter Humphreys, and Stephen Padgett (2007). *Policy Transfer in the European Union Governance*. London: Routledge.

Checkel, Jeffrey T. (1997). "International norms and domestic politics: bridging the rationalist-constructivist divide." *European Journal of International Relations*, Vol. 3, No. 4, pp. 473–95.

Clark, William C. (2001). "Social learning." In Andrew S. Goudie and David J. Cuff, eds., *Encyclopaedia of Global Change: Environmental Change and Human Society*. Oxford: Oxford University Press, pp. 382–4.

Collins, Harry H. and Robert J. Evans (2002). "The third wave of science studies: studies of expertise and experience." *Social Studies of Science*, Vol. 32, No. 2, pp. 235–96.

Cox, Gary W. (1990). "Centripetal and centrifugal incentives in electoral systems." *American Journal of Political Science*, Vol. 34, No. 4, pp. 903–35.

Cox, Gary W. and Frances Rosenbluth (1993). "The electoral fortunes of legislative factions in Japan." *American Political Science Review*, Vol. 87, No. 3, pp. 577–89.

DiMaggio, Paul and Walter Powell, ed. (1991). *The New Institutionalism in Organizational Analysis*. Chicago, IL: University Chicago Press.

Dolowitz, David P. and David Marsh (1996). "Who learns what from whom: a review of the policy transfer literature." *Political Studies*, Vol. 44, No. 2, pp. 347–9.

Fairbrass, Jenny and Andrew Jordan (2005). "Multi-level governance and environmental policy." In Ian Bache and Matthew Flinders, eds., *Multi-level Governance*. Oxford: Oxford University Press, pp. 147–64.

Finnemore, Martha (1996). "Norms, culture, and world politics: insights from sociology's institutionalism." *International Organization*, Vol. 50, No. 2, pp. 325–47.

Flanagan, Scott C. and Bradley M. Richardson (1977). *Japanese Electoral Behavior: Social Cleavages, Social Networks, and Partisanship*. London: Sage.

Folke, Carl, Thomas Hahn, Per Olsson, and Jon Norberg (2005). "Adaptive governance of social-ecological systems." *Annual Review of Environment and Resources*, Vol. 30, pp. 441–73.

Gourevitch, Peter (1978). "The second image reversed: the international sources of domestic politics." *International Organization*, Vol. 32, No. 4, pp. 881–912.

Gustavsson, Eva, Ingemar Elander, and Mats Lundmark (2009). "Multilevel governance, networking cities, and the geography of climate-change mitigation: two Swedish examples." *Environment and Planning C: Government and Policy*, Vol. 27, pp. 59–74.

Haas, Peter (1989). "Do regimes matter? Epistemic communities and Mediterranean pollution control." *International Organization*, Vol. 43, No. 3, pp. 377–403.

Haas, Peter (2004). "Addressing the global governance deficit." *Global Environmental Politics*, Vol. 4, No. 4, pp. 1–15.

Hall, Peter (1993). "Policy paradigms, social learning and the state: the case of economic policy making in Britain." *Comparative Politics*, Vol. 25, No. 3, pp. 275–96.

Harlow, Carol and Richard Rawlings (2007). "Accountability in multilevel governance: a network approach." *European Law Journal*, Vol. 13, No. 4, pp. 542–62.

Held, David, Anthony McGrew, David Goldblatt, and Jonathan Perraton (1999). *Global Transformations: Politics, Economics, Culture*. Cambridge, UK: Polity.

Hempel, Lamont C. (1996). *Environmental Governance: The Global Challenge*. Washington, DC: Island Press.

Hoffmann, Stanley (1966). "Obstinate or obsolete? The fate of the nation-state and the case of Western Europe." *Daedalus*, Vol. 95, No. 3, pp. 862–915.

Hooghe, Liesbet and Gary Marks (1996). "Europe with the regions: channels of regional representation in the European Union." *The Journal of Federalism*, Vol. 26, No. 1, pp. 73–82.

Hooghe, Liesbet and Gary Marks (2001). "Types of multi-level governance." *European Integration Online Papers*, Vol. 5, on-line journal. Available from: http://eiop.or.at/eiop/texte/2001011.htm [accessed March 20, 2015].

Ingold, Karin and Frédéric Varone (2012). "Treating policy brokers seriously: evidence from the climate policy." *Journal of Public Administration Research and Theory*, Vol. 22, No. 2, pp. 319–46.

Irwin, Alan and Brian Wynne (1996). *Misunderstanding Science? The Public Reconstruction of Science and Technology*. Cambridge, UK: Cambridge University Press.

Jasanoff, Sheila (2006). "Transparency in public science: purposes, reasons, limits." *Law and Contemporary Problem*, Vol. 69, No. 21, pp. 21–45.

Jeffery, Charlie (2000). "Sub-national mobilization and European integration: does it make any difference?" *Journal of Common Market Studies*, Vol. 38, No. 1, pp. 1–23.

Jessop, Bob (1998). "The rise of governance and the risks of failure: the case of economic development." *International Social Science Journal*, Vol. 50, No. 155, pp. 29–45.

Jessop, Bob (2002). *The Future of the Capitalist State*. Cambridge, UK: Polity Press.

Katzenstein, Peter (1976). "International relations and domestic structures: foreign economic policies of the advanced industrial states." *International Organization*, Vol. 30, No. 1, pp. 1–45.

Keck, Margaret and Kathryn Sikkink (1998). *Activists beyond Borders: Advocacy Networks in International Politics*. Ithaca, NY: Cornell University Press.

Keohane, Robert O. (1983). "The demand for international regimes." In Stephen D. Krasner, ed., *International Regimes*. Ithaca, NY: Cornell University Press, pp. 141–71.

Keohane, Robert and Joseph Nye, Jr. (1974). "Transgovernmental relations and international organizations." *World Politics*, Vol. 27, No. 1, pp. 39–62.

Kern, Kristine and Harriet Bulkeley (2009). "Cities, Europeanization and multi-level governance: governing climate change through transnational municipal networks." *Journal of Common Market Studies*, Vol. 47, No. 2, pp. 309–32.

Kitschelt, Herbert P. (1986). "Political opportunities structures and political protest: antinuclear movements in four democracies." *British Journal of Political Science*, Vol. 16, pp. 57–85.

Klandermans, Bert (1997). *The Social Psychology of Protest*. Oxford: Blackwell, 1997.

Kooiman, Jan, ed. (1997). *Modern Governance: New Government-Society Interactions*. London: Sage.

Kooiman, Jan and Svein Jentoft (2009). "Meta-governance: values, norms and principles, and the making of hard choices." *Public Administration*, Vol. 87, No. 4, pp. 818–36.

Krauss, Ellis S. and Robert J. Pekkanen (2010). *The Rise and Fall of Japan's LDP: Political Party Organizations as Historical Institutions*. Ithaca, NY: Cornell University Press.

Krauss, Ellis S. and Bradford L. Simcock (1980). "Citizens' movements: the growth and impact of environmental protest in Japan." In Kurt Steiner, Ellis S. Krauss, and Scott C. Flanagan, eds., *Political Opposition and Local Politics in Japan*. Princeton, NJ: Princeton University Press, pp. 187–227.

Kriesi, Hanspeter and Maya Jegen (2001). "The Swiss energy policy elite: the actor constellation of a policy domain in transition." *European Journal of Political Research*, Vol. 39, No. 2, pp. 251–87.

Kriesi, Hanspeter, Ruud Koopmans, Jan Willem Duyvendak, and Marco G. Giugni (1995). *New Social Movements in Western Europe: A Comparative Analysis*. Minneapolis, MN: University of Minnesota Press.

Lake, David and Robert Powell (1999). *Strategic Choice and International Relations*. Princeton, NJ: Princeton University Press.
Lee, Chang and David Strang (2006). "The international diffusion of public sector downsizing: network emulation and theory-driven learning." *International Organization*, Vol. 60, No. 4, pp. 883–909.
Lindblom, Charles E. (1959). "The science of 'muddling through'." *Public Administration Review*, Vol. 29, pp. 79–88.
Litfin, Karen T. (1994). *Ozone Discourse: Science and Politics in Global Environmental Cooperation*. New York: Columbia University Press.
Litfin, Karen T. (2000). "Advocacy coalitions along the domestic-foreign frontier: globalization and Canadian climate change policy." *Policy Studies Journal*, Vol. 28, No. 1, pp. 236–52.
McKean, Margret A. (1980). "Political socialization through citizens' movements." In K. Steiner, E. Krauss, and S. Flanagan, eds., *Political Opposition and Local Politics in Japan*. Princeton, NJ: Princeton University Press, pp. 228–73.
Marks, Gary (1996). "An actor-centred approach to multi-level governance." *Regional and Federal Studies*, Vol. 6, No. 2, pp. 20–40.
May, Peter (1992). "Policy learning and failure." *Journal of Public Policy*, Vol. 12, No. 4, pp. 331–54.
Meseguer, Covadonga (2003). "Learning about policies: a Bayesian approach." European Forum Working Paper Series 5, Florence, European University Institute.
Meyer, David S. (2003). "Political opportunity and nested institutions." *Social Movement Studies*, Vol. 2, No. 1, pp. 17–35.
Meyer, David S. and Debra C. Minkoff (2004). "Conceptualizing political opportunity." *Social Forces*, Vol. 82, No. 4, pp. 1457–92.
Mintrom, Michael and Sandra Vergari (1996). "Advocacy coalitions, policy entrepreneurs, and policy change." *Policy Studies Journal*, Vol. 24, No. 3, pp. 420–34.
Mlinar, Zdravko (1995). "Local responses to global change." *Annals of the American Academy of Political and Social Science*, Vol. 540, pp. 145–56.
Moravcsik, Andrew (1993). "Preferences and power in the European Community: a liberal intergovernmentalist approach." *Journal of Common Market Studies*, Vol. 31, No. 4, pp. 473–524.
Muramatsu, Michio (1975). "The impact of economic growth policies on local politics in Japan." *Asian Survey*, Vol. 15, No. 9, pp. 799–816.
Muramatsu, Michio and Ellis S. Krauss (1987). "The conservative policy line and the development of patterned pluralism." In Kozo Yamamura and Yasukichi Yasuba, eds., *The Political Economy of Japan, Vol. 1: The Domestic Transformation*. Stanford, CA: Stanford University Press, pp. 516–54.
Nishida, Kitarō (1990). *An Inquiry into the Good*, trans. Masao Abe and Christopher Ives. New Haven, CT: Yale University Press.
Pahl-Wostl, Claudia, Joyeeta Gupta, and Daniel Petry (2008). "Governance and the global water system: a theoretical exploration." *Global Governance*, Vol. 14, No. 4, pp. 419–35.
Payne, Rodger A. (2001). "Persuasion, frames and norm construction." *European Journal of International Relations*, Vol. 7, No. 1, pp. 37–61.
Putnam, Robert D. (1988). "Diplomacy and domestic politics: the logic of two-level games." *International Organization*, Vol. 42, No. 3, pp. 427–60.
Ramseyer, Mark and Frances Rosenbluth (1993). *Japan's Political Marketplace*. Cambridge, MA: Harvard University Press.

Reed, Steven (1981). "Environmental politics: some reflections based on the Japanese case." *Comparative Politics*, Vol. 13, No. 3, pp. 253–70.

Rhodes, R.A.W. (1997). *Understanding Governance: Policy Networks, Governance, Reflexivity and Accountability.* Buckingham, UK: Open University Press.

Risse-Kappen, Thomas, ed. (1995). *Bringing Transnational Relations Back In: Non-State Actors, Domestic Structures, and International Institutions.* New York: Cambridge University Press.

Risse-Kappen, Thomas (1995). "Introduction." In Thomas Risse-Kappen, ed., *Bringing Transnational Relations Back In: Nonstate Actors, Domestic Structures and International Institutions.* Cambridge, UK: Cambridge University Press, pp. 3–33.

Robertson, David (1991). "Political conflict and lesson-drawing." *Journal of Public Policy*, Vol. 11, No. 1, pp. 55–78.

Robinson, John (2004). "Squaring the circle? Some thoughts on the idea of sustainable development." *Ecological Economics*, Vol. 48, No. 4, pp. 369–84.

Rose, Richard (1991). "What is lesson-drawing?" *Journal of Public Policy*, Vol. 11, No. 1, pp. 3–30.

Rosenau, James (1997). *Along the Domestic-Foreign Frontier: Exploring Governance in a Turbulent World.* Cambridge, UK: Cambridge University Press.

Rosenau, James N. (1999). "Toward an ontology for global governance." In Martin Hewson and Timothy J. Sinclair, eds., *Approaches to Global Governance Theory.* Albany, NY: State University of New York Press, chp 13.

Sabatier, Paul A. (1987). "Knowledge, policy-oriented learning, and policy change." *Knowledge*, Vol. 8, pp. 649–92.

Sabatier, Paul A. (1993). "Policy change over a decade or more." In Paul A. Sabatier and Hank C. Jenkins-Smith, eds., *Policy Change and Learning: An Advocacy Coalition Approach.* Boulder, CO: Westview Press, pp. 13–39.

Sabatier, Paul A. and Hank C. Jenkins-Smith (1988). "An advocacy coalition framework of policy change and the role of policy-oriented learning therein." *Policy Sciences*, Vol. 21, No. 2–3, pp. 129–68.

Sabatier, Paul A. and Hank C. Jenkins-Smith, eds. (1993). *Policy Change and Learning: An Advocacy Coalition Approach.* Boulder, CO: Westview Press.

Sabatier, Paul A. and Hank Jenkins-Smith (1999). "The advocacy coalition framework: an assessment." In Paul A. Sabatier, ed., *Theories of the Policy Process*, 2nd ed. Boulder, CO: Westview Press, pp. 117–66.

Sabatier, Paul A. and Christopher M. Weible (2007). "The advocacy coalition framework: innovations and clarifications." In Paul A. Sabatier, ed., *Theories of the Policy Process*, 2nd ed. Boulder, CO: Westview Press, pp. 189–220.

Satō, Seizaburō and Tetsuhisa Matsuzaki (1986). *Jimintō Seiken* [Liberal Democratic Party government]. Tokyo: Chuōkōron-sha.

Saunders, Peter (1984). "Rethinking local politics." In Martin Boddy and Colin Fudge, eds., *Local Socialism?* London: Macmillan, pp. 22–48.

Schreurs, Miranda A. (2002). *Environmental Politics in Japan, Germany and the United States.* Cambridge, UK: Cambridge University Press.

Skelcher, Chris (2005). "Jurisdictional integrity, polycentrism, and the design of democratic governance." *Governance*, Vol. 18, No. 1, pp. 89–110.

Sørensen, Eva and Jacob Torfing (2005). "The democratic anchorage of governance networks." *Scandinavian Political Studies*, Vol. 28, No. 3, pp. 195–218.

Stoker, Garry (1998). "Governance as theory: five propositions." *International Social Science Journal*, Vol. 50, No. 155, pp. 17–28.

Strang, David and John Meyer (1993). "Institutional conditions for diffusion." *Theory and Society*, Vol. 22, No. 4, pp. 487–511.

Takao, Yasuo (2012). "Making climate change policy work at the local level: capacity-building for decentralized policymaking in Japan." *Pacific Affairs*, Vol. 85, No. 4, pp. 767–88.

Takao, Yasuo (2014). "Local levels of participation in Japan's foreign aid and cooperation: issues arising from decentralized international cooperation." *Asian Survey*, Vol. 54, No. 3, pp. 540–64.

Tarrow, Sidney (1989). *Struggle, Politics, and Reform: Collective Action, Social Movements, and Cycles of Protest*. Ithaca, NY: Cornell University Press.

Tarrow, Sidney (1994). *Power in Movement: Social Movements, Collective Action and Mass Politics*. New York and London: Cambridge University Press.

Tarrow, Sidney (2001). "Transnational politics: contention and institutions in international politics." *Annual Review of Political Science*, Vol. 4, pp. 1–20.

Taylor, Paul (1983). *The Limits of European Integration*. New York, Columbia University Press.

Vogel, David (1990). "Environmental policy in Japan and West Germany." Paper presented at the annual meeting of the Western Political Science Association, Newport Beach, CA, March 1990.

Walker, Brian, Nick Abel, John Anderies, and Paul Ryan (2009). "Resilience, adaptability, and transformability in the Goulburn-Broken Catchment, Australia." *Ecology and Society*, Vol. 14, No. 1, on-line journal. Available from: www.ecologyandsociety.org/vol. 14/iss1/art12/ [accessed March 20, 2015].

Weible, Christopher M., Paul A. Sabatier, and Kelly McQueen (2009). "Themes and variations: taking stock of the advocacy coalition framework." *The Policy Studies Journal*, Vol. 37, No. 1, pp. 121–40.

Weiss, Thomas G. (2000). "Governance, good governance, global governance: actual challenges governance conceptual and actual challenges." *Third World Quarterly*, Vol. 21, pp. 795–814.

Weyland, Kurt (2005). "Theories of policy diffusion: lessons from Latin American pension reform." *World Politics*, Vol. 57, No. 2, pp. 262–95.

William, Colin C. and Andrew C. Millington (2004). "The diverse and contested meanings of sustainable development." *The Geographical Journal*, Vol. 170, pp. 99–104.

World Commission on Environment and Development (WCED) (1987). *Our Common Future*. Oxford: Oxford University Press.

Yearley, Steven (2000). "Making systematic sense of public discontents with expert knowledge: two analytical approaches and a case study." *Public Understanding of Science*, Vol. 9, pp. 105–22.

1 The transformation of Japan's environmental policy

In the 1970s, Japan was known as the leading innovator in environmental policy and other OECD countries found much to emulate. Two decades later, Japan appears to be falling behind on policy innovation; the Fukushima nuclear disaster has revealed the failures of Japan's environmental safety; and Japan is falling behind when it comes to climate change action. This chapter will conduct a historical survey of post-WWII Japan by examining the possible causes of the rise and fall of Japanese environmental policy. To this end, this chapter will explore its domestic policy subsystem, the international arena, and the arena where domestic and foreign issues converge, the emerging space in which traditionally national regulations cross-nationally become more alike in the processes and performances of environmental policy. Agents act simultaneously across the different tiers of authority and new spheres of authority, which evolved from interactions between state and non-state actors, are emerging.[1] Sub-national authorities have indeed increasingly become recognized as direct contributors to global environmental strategies. In this book, I do not use the term convergence as purely structural in the sense that similarity in environmental regulations is deterministically reduced to a set of globalization forces, but rather as actor-specific in the form of negotiated convergence/coordination where actors constantly reason about interest-driven utility and environmental norms.[2] Although not all actors implement identical regulations, policy coordination will primarily determine the nature and scope of policy convergence beyond the simple interplay of domestic and foreign affairs. Each of three approaches—the domestic/foreign divide, interaction, and convergence—offers a partial answer to the rise and fall of Japanese environmental policy.

What accounts for changes in environmental policy over time? I will examine how environmental policy-making has developed as Japan has gone through different phases of environmental protection, from addressing domestic to global issues. To this end, I will demonstrate that compelling analyses of the empirical puzzle of the loss of Japan's leadership role in environmental policy innovation can be conducted by combining the traditionally separated but increasingly interactive levels, and the emerging convergence, of domestic and foreign politics. I will argue that changes in both decision-making arrangements and political coalition-building that are shaped by differences in domestic-foreign linkages, represent different features of environmental policy-making.

In the 1960s, advanced economies in major countries, such as the United States, West Germany, and Japan, ushered in the era of national environmental policy-making. By the early 1970s, Japan had some of the world's strongest environmental regulations, yet was also known for its strong commitment to economic development and business interests. However, by 1990, Japan was no longer a clear leader.[3] According to the ENVIPOLCON (Environmental governance in Europe: the impact of international institutions and trade on policy convergence) database, including 40 environmental policy issues (air, water, waste, noise, energy and climate, nature protection, and others) in 21 European countries, the United States (US), Mexico, and Japan from 1970,[4] Japan was ahead of most countries in the early years (fifth place in 1970) in terms of the presence-of-policy of each environmental issue area but failed to retain this high position (sixteenth place in 1990). The strictness of Japan's environmental polices also toppled from a high ranking in 1970 to a very low position in 1990, while all the other countries became stricter from 1970 to 1990 regarding almost all environmental policies.[5]

Why was Japan able to get environmental issues on the agenda and take legislative action only for a short period of time in the early years? Many scholars argue that the severity of industrial pollution made it impossible to ignore and thus concerns regarding this prevailed over pro-development policies in electoral processes.[6] Additionally, some focus on actors, emphasizing Japan's anti-industrial pollution movements as an ultimate factor.[7] The policy shift was ascribed to political pressures that these movements generated as both the electoral threat to the ruling party and the productivity threat to big business grew rapidly.[8] Opposition-controlled localities are also considered to be a continuing source of pressure on the national government.[9] Opposition parties in control of local governments were quick to adopt stricter pollution prevention measures than those imposed at the national level. But their labor constituency was reluctant to endorse high pollution-related expenses[10] and, once the national ruling party incorporated some of the opposition's more popular measures into its platform, the momentum from local activism waned in the mid-1970s.

At a general level, policy expansion is explained as the government's response to increased needs. In any democratic nation, one normally expects that the weight of popular pressure and opinion, to some extent, influences the process of decision-making towards policy expansion. The literature identifies domestic problem pressure and demand as political motivations for environmental policy expansion.[11] To explain the rise of Japan's environmental regulations, a range of country-specific factors, such as the strength of the environmental advocacy coalition, the political opportunity structure and external events,[12] might be relevant. Although no single factor explains the scope of any policy change, in my view, local governments' "will and skill" for environmental policy innovations were a primary necessary condition for rapid legislative action at the national level in the early 1970s. There are two fundamental preconditions for this. First, local government occupies a strategic position straddling the division between the state and citizens. Local government is in a position to develop a safeguard to meet pressing needs beyond the reach of the national state. Second, local government acts as an immediate rescue center to assure individuals' security, a place to which local residents resort directly. This is primarily because the state's inability to manage leaves it up to local communities to deal with the increasing presence of problem pressures and residents' demands. Local communities are thus at the forefront of coping with this issue. In the 1960s and early 1970s, Japanese local governments pioneered and developed a compensation scheme for industrial pollution victims, set stricter emissions regulations than those required by national law, and began to extensively use pollution control agreements or Pollution Countermeasure Agreements (PCAs), which were not required by national law but concluded between polluter(s) and host local government(s) to enforce stringent measures to combat pollution.[13] In the 1970s, local governments even initiated the implementation of total pollutant load controls. The national government eventually accepted the necessity of these local actions and adopted some of the local innovations, such as the compensation scheme and the Total Pollutant Load Control System (TPLCS), at the national level.[14]

To explain why Japan began in the 1980s to lag behind major European countries such as Germany in environmental initiative and innovation, some focus on the circumstances under which environmental policy was initiated and argue that the policy environment had fundamentally changed due to improved air quality.[15] Others point out the failure of Japanese environmental movements to establish powerful national interest groups[16] as Japan subsequently had a very small and weakly organized community of environmental groups.[17] The disintegration of anti-industrial pollution movements was seen as a reflection of shifts in public opinion.[18] Such studies view policy formation as an essentially domestic-level process taking place within states. My objective, however, is to examine how the dynamics of environmental policy-making changed over time as environmental issues became internationalized.[19]

Traditional approaches of explaining this emerging phenomenon simply highlight the mutual interplay between separated levels of politics. Domestic factors are considered to be a determinant of foreign policy ("second image")[20] or the external environment is claimed to affect domestic politics ("second image reversed").[21] The "two-level-games" theory further suggests a shift from the domestic-foreign divide to an interactive levels approach while seeing the national representative in international negotiations as the key actor who takes into account the demands of actors at two levels: the domestic level and the international level.[22] Yet this approach is still state-centric, although emphasizing the important influence of non-state and sub-national actors. It views these actors as interest groups who simply demand that the national representative protect their interests in international negotiations and restrict the scope of acceptable negotiation outcomes. In other words, non-state and sub-national actors impose constraints on the negotiations but do not directly operate in international institutional contexts. The use of "multi-level governance" helps us avoid these pitfalls of the two-level game. The assumption of multi-level governance is that beyond the two-level theorization there are other levels which matter as well.[23] Gary Marks and others draw attention to multi-level policy networks that may involve sub-national actors, such as socially mobilized groups and sub-national governments, interacting directly with international organizations.[24] Some multi-level theories acknowledge that the legitimacy of multi-level governance depends on the legitimacy of democratic norms embedded within multi-level policy networks.[25] Sub-national actors have increasingly considered themselves direct players in a global game to cope with the local impact of climate change.[26] The dynamics of the sub-national level of participation reveal convergence, rather than a simple interplay of domestic and international politics. This can be seen as a rapidly expanding sphere of action in which the boundaries of domestic and foreign affairs are eroding. Boundary-eroding dynamics have become highly salient in the field of international environmental cooperation precisely because the causes of environmental risk are locally specific in character yet local action can simultaneously be part of global strategies. The necessity of integrating local actions to ensure the optimal reduction of environmental risks has been provided for in multilateral environmental agreements (MEAs).[27]

In my view, the different dynamics of actors, interests, institutions, and political coalitions reflect the differences between division, interaction, and convergence in domestic-foreign linkages. The first analytical framework—division—views environmental policy-making as a fundamentally domestic-level process. Actors in the process of political coalition-building treat the reduction of environmental risk as a local or national public good whose benefits accrue to the public of a nation and correspond to national boundaries. The question of who bears the cost of providing the public good at the local or national level lies at the heart of environmental politics. In this insulated national game, domestic groups pressure the government to adopt favorable environmental policies, and politicians seek to maximize votes by constructing coalitions among domestic groups. Changes in the external environment are seen as exogenous in the sense that international affairs can influence domestic actors but only through one-way causation of the international-to-domestic connection.

The second analytical framework—interaction—refers to environmental policy-making based on the simultaneous interplay between domestic interests and international bargaining or the two-way causation of domestic and international factors while presuming the different levels of domestic/foreign affairs. Environmental degradation may well spread beyond national borders and could have a regional/global range. Public intervention is thus required to provide both local/national and regional/international public goods for environmental risk-reduction. Policy-makers deal with two sets of constraints: domestic constraints on cost-sharing for environmental risk-reduction and foreign pressures on collective action over resources to contribute regional/international environmental benefits. Environmental politics is a locus where policy-makers must choose how to reconcile international and domestic concerns. This decision-making arrangement creates new actors, especially national foreign policy actors—the export sector and the foreign policy elite—and as domestic factors, including the distribution of domestic coalitions, impinge, the statesman seeks to maintain policy cohesion between the international and (intra-)national levels. It is inevitable then that the complexity of environmental policy-making entails much less coherence of the policy sector than that experienced in the insulated domestic-level process.

The third analytical framework—convergence—is defined as a penetration phenomenon where environmental policy-making at one level of government serves as decision-making in the political process of another. The reduction of industrial pollution by a municipal authority will improve air quality in the locality and, at the same time, the locally specific action may directly contribute to global governance for greenhouse gas emissions reduction. Environmental politics tends to revolve around coordinating the provision of intermeshed public goods. Beyond the state-centric presumption adopted by the second analytical framework, political actors interact across those levels and participate in multi-level coalition-building. The converged spheres of authority are linked by multiple actors moving across different governmental levels. This decision-making arrangement may involve sub-national actors dealing directly with foreign actors—overseas sub-national actors and international organizations. These emerging spheres provide potentials for policy integration among local action, national policy, and global strategies.

The next section explores the expansion of environmental regulations over industrial pollution and voluntary agreements between business and government in the 1970s and the use of pro-business, market-oriented approaches to environmental protection in the 1980s. These two decades saw policy formation as an essentially domestic-level process. The following section presents the case study of Japan's international bargaining over climate change in the 1990s. Environmental policy formation in the 1990s was quite compatible with much in the interactive two-level-games of constraints and opportunities on both the domestic and international levels. The penultimate section gives a view of, relatively unexplored, sub-national participation in international environmental regimes. It illustrates the emerging phenomenon of convergence from the perspective of the cross-border and cross-level harmonization of politics and policy. The final section analyses the transformation of these environmental affairs in terms of an eclectic interpretation of environmental politics operating along the lines of domestic/foreign division, interaction, and convergence.

The 1970s and 1980s: national environmental policy

After World War II, Japan's state-led corporatist policy networks with big business were set up to provide public opinion with less of an opportunity to affect policy outcomes. The passage of the 1967 Basic Law for Environmental Pollution Control was a result of coalition-building in which a Ministry of Health and Welfare (MHW) draft (recommending strict industrial liability) had been emasculated by the economic ministries and the peak business organizations to give priority to development over the environment.[28] Meanwhile, the "big four" shocks internal to the policy subsystem in the 1960s, which might have been considered to be a potential path for policy change, acted as a catalyst for the collapse of the national consensus towards industrialization in post-WWII Japan and for an increase in public awareness of environmental costs.[29] These four incidents, that is, Minamata disease (Methylmercury), Niigata Minamata disease (Methylmercury), *Itai-itai* disease (Cadmium poisoning), and Yokkaichi asthma (Sulfur dioxide), achieved sufficient exposure through legal challenges in the court of Japan and the extensive media coverage.[30]

As the advocacy coalition framework (ACF) suggests, changes in public opinion might prompt instability in the policy subsystem and create the potential for rapid policy change. By 1970 a high degree of societal mobilization against industrial pollution created a new support base for environmental policies and led to devastating losses at local elections for the governing Liberal Democratic Party (LDP). Local authorities, the layer of government closest to the people, were quick to respond to popular demands[31] and disgruntled voters elected a wave of candidates from the opposition coalitions to local chief executive positions in highly urbanized areas where the quality of life was deteriorating. LDP politics subsequently entailed a crisis effort to advance environmental policies into an electorally attractive proposition.[32] Its leadership rushed to radically revise the 1967 Basic Law, without first coordinating with peak business organizations.[33] In 1970 the National Diet of Japan, the so-called "Environmental Pollution Diet," passed radical improvements to the 1967 Basic law, including comprehensive government countermeasures against a wide range of types of environmental pollution, pledging the steepest reduction of environmental pollutants in the world.[34] The conservative industrial coalition of the bureaucracy, LDP, and business, responded to environmentalists' demand with an emphasis on strict regulations rather than market-based solutions. However, the policy's core belief in pro-development had never been in dispute within the conservative coalition, who instituted the environmental protection program and remained in power. The opportunity structure in the 1960s and 1970s was relatively closed to the demands of anti-industrial pollution movements due to the dominant conservative coalition.

The minority anti-industrial pollution coalition was neither easily identifiable in terms of its policy beliefs nor formally networked at the national level. The anti-pollution activities of residents' movements (*jūmin undō*) were not led by those external to the community, but rather internally initiated and organized by community leaders.[35] The movements were concerned with environmental threats to their livelihood and largely treated industrial pollution as a local problem confined to the host community of polluters. Anti-pollution struggles became a community-wide initiative at most. Redistribution policy co-opted the individual victims of industrial pollution in the form of compensation.[36] The benefits of the redistributive policy prevented potential anti-pollution actors from becoming united for anti-pollution coalition-building. Besides, opposition parties closely represented labor unions, whose interests were in ensuring the job security of their companies and those parties were thus reluctant to endorse environmental activism.[37] In this context, while the policy-relevant coalition-building was largely restricted to the business and political elites and more or less excluded societal actors and opposition parties, the intermediary role accorded to local governments was important. Local governments did not act as neutral intermediaries but rather as environmental-advocate intermediaries between the national government and citizens' movements and between industry and citizens' movements.

In 1964 the City of Yokohama pioneered such a role by concluding its PCAs with two electronic power companies. In 1959 the original citizens' movement, relevant to the PCAs, was launched in Isogo Ward as a support group for fishermen who were forced to leave their jobs due to land reclamation projects. Initially they were not really concerned about industrial pollution per se, but concerned about their livelihoods. In the following year, the Isogo Medical Association took part in the movement and petitioned the municipal government to take specific pollution countermeasures over the enterprises that were invited to the landfill site. As Ichio Asukata was elected as a socialist mayor of the city in April 1964, the Isogo citizens' association requested the national ministries to conduct an environmental preparatory investigation on the construction of the power plants. Since the Ministry of International Trade and Industry (MITI) directly regulated the electronic power companies, the mayor, who was a progressive mayor yet had direct connections with the national government, first negotiated with the MITI. In the negotiation process, MITI officials experienced a political crisis when Mishima's environmental protection movement successfully cancelled the plans to build Shizuoka prefecture's industrial complexes, which the MITI had proposed. To avoid further deterioration of its relations with citizens' movements, the MITI had to accept Asukata's demand that the city should stipulate its own pollution control standards. Once the MITI approved, the city began to negotiate with the companies. As a scientific report on Isogo's coal-fired power, which a group of academics produced, served as a source of persuasion, Asukata forced the companies to sign the PCAs as part of the land sale contracts.[38]

Recognition or encouragement from national ministries facilitated the rapid diffusion of PCAs among local governments. In 1970 the Ministry of Home Affairs (MHA), which had been in charge of local affairs, announced that it would guide local governments for the conclusion of PCAs.[39] In the 1970s local governments did not have to deal with the gate-keeping capacity of national ministries to conclude PCAs; they found familiar ground rules through formal national channels in order to create extra-legal pollution control agreements with industries. Since the conclusion of the Tokyo Metropolitan Government (TMG)—Tokyo Electronic Power Company (TEPCO) PCA in 1968, this highly publicized story became known as a better way of obtaining voter approval for development plans. The diffusion of PCAs tended largely to be mimicked by other localities as a catch up policy diffusion mechanism. PCAs also provided Japan's environmental politics with another factor which kept citizens' movements at the local level.

In the mid-1970s, the focus of environmental protection shifted from identifiable sources of industrial pollution to diffuse, no-point sources of non-industrial pollution. Environmental citizens' movements began to acknowledge that pollution did not necessarily come from a single identifiable source, such as electronic power manufacturers and oil refineries. The protection of people's health and the environment required the inclusion of diffuse pollutant sources, such as cars and household appliances. At the same time, the conventional NIMBY (not-in-my-backyard) problem became more salient as was seen in the often-cited "Tokyo garbage war" between Kōtō and Suginami Wards in the early 1970s.[40] Every resident needed household waste collection services, but no one wished to live near a waste disposal site.[41] Local communities thus had difficulties in building larger coalitions of environmental groups and gaining wider public support. They were unable to display the same level of community solidarity as that which had been a key characteristic of the earlier movements. Japan's environmental policy community was too fragmented and weak to have a concerted, direct voice in national policy-making. A potential key actor, the Environment Agency (EA), purposed with coordinating an anti-pollution advocacy coalition at the national level, was only established in 1971, and it was at the sub-cabinet level and remained a weak body, secondary to larger economic ministries. Over 3,000 citizens' environmental groups were mobilized yet never grew into a nationally coordinated movement or a national political party like Germany's Greens.

By the mid-1970s, the LDP began to regain electoral momentum, incorporating some local policy innovations into its own platform. The national government had caught up with local governments; the national standard was no less stringent than locally-imposed measures for air quality.[42] After 1974 there were no more reported cases of prefectures passing stricter air quality rules than the national standards.[43] In the late 1970s, when public responsiveness to environmental pollution significantly declined, progressive local chief executives in major metropolitan areas departed from the political arena.[44] Nationwide surveys indicated a significant drop—from over 20 percent in 1973 to 9 percent in 1981—in the percentage of the public who felt adversely affected by air pollution.[45] Conservative coalition-building thus prevailed in the absence of an attentive public and highly mobilized societal actors. In the early 1980s, the salience of environmental regulations decreased rather abruptly even while improving energy efficiency.

Following the industrial pollution crisis in the late 1960s, the most important factor for policy expansion was a perturbation external to the policy subsystem as the 1973 oil crisis triggered a greater concern with energy efficiency. Japanese leaders viewed the nation as the potential victim of uncontrollable external forces as Japan relied on imports to meet 85 percent of its energy needs.[46] In 1978 the government created tax incentives for investment in energy conservation facilities and, just after the second oil crisis in 1979, began to apply the Energy Conservation Law to energy conservation measures.[47] In the 1980s, the government played a regulatory role in two fundamental ways: creating financial incentives to boost energy-saving initiatives and investment, and energy efficiency standardization for manufacturing facilities, transportation, buildings, houses, and consumer products. On average, in the 1980s, Japan spent 1.0 energy unit per unit of GDP, against the OECD average of 1.5, Britain 1.3, West Germany 1.5, the US 1.9, and China 3.8.[48] The government's regulations to improve the energy efficiency of production were not part of its environmental policy, but rather conceived of as industrial policy to manage Japan's energy demand/supply. Nonetheless, efforts to maximize energy efficiency consequently contributed to emission reductions, so that "most of Japan's new environmental improvements during this period came as a by-product of energy conservation measures."[49] This was an example of policy subsystem-spanning problems or the interdependence among policy subsystems in which policy-making occurs beyond traditional subsystem boundaries or within several different policy domains. The spanning problems became particularly salient in environmental issues, as they were tangled with economic policy, energy security, nuclear power generation, industrial policy, agriculture policy, and education. Additionally, overlapping coalitions in the context of subsystem-spanning allowed multiple memberships. A set of overlapping coalitions can be defined as coalitions that share at least one agent in common. In Japan, for example, a member of the conservative industrial coalition might also be a member of the pro-nuclear energy coalition to ensure energy supplies and increase production. That the subsystem of environmental policy spanned across multiple policy domains indicated the complexity of environmental issues as a policy subsystem.

In the 1980s, the LDP's vote share rebounded nationally and locally. Its electoral success brought back the old coalition-building to Japan's environmental politics. Coordinating with LDP's business clients, industrial pollution control became integrated as part of traditional industrial policy.[50] The oil crises overshadowed genuine concerns for environmental degradation. The Keidanren (Japanese association of business organizations) worked with the MITI, which tended to see technology as the solution to environmental problems, to strengthen energy efficiency to free manufacturers from their dependence on imported energy.[51] In order to facilitate manufacturers' initiatives regarding energy conservation, the government offered support through low-interest loans and tax relief as well as opportunities to learn from collaborative government-industry-university research.[52] The output of Japan's pollution-intensive sector as a percentage of non-pollution-intensive sector production halved from nearly 70 percent in 1975 to 35 percent in 1989, while its import/export ratios of polluting products rapidly increased from as low as 20 percent in 1976 to a high of 95 percent in 1990.[53] In short, the conservative industrial coalition effectively facilitated the decline of pollution-intensive industries in Japan. It seems that alternating inter-related coalitional beliefs between environmental policy and energy policy effectively helped to hold the conservative forces together to achieve their goals over time.

The 1990s: environmental foreign policy

Without environmental degradation, there would be no need for environmental protection. However, the export sector's need for environmental protection did not derive from anticipated environmental degradation, but rather from changing international market conditions to which it needed to adjust quickly. By the time business, led by Europe, was fully engaged in the process of establishing environmental standards leading up to the 1992 Earth Summit, the Japanese export sector acknowledged that not complying with international environmental management standards (ISO14000) would disadvantage Japanese products sold in overseas markets.[54] In 1996 the business coalition of the Keidanren and the Japan Industrial Standards (JIS) Committee adopted International Organization for Standardization (ISO) international standards as part of JIS, virtually in their original form.[55]

By the mid-1980s, at the government level, Japan was under increasing pressure from major OECD countries to play an international role appropriate to its economic power. In particular, Japan was strongly criticized for exporting polluting industries to Southeast Asia. Prime Minister Yasuhiro Nakasone pledged to actively participate in preserving the global environment. In 1984 the United Nations (UN) General Assembly established the World Commission on Environment and Development (or Brundtland Commission) in response to a Japanese proposal. In the wake of the 1987 Brundtland Report, there was wide recognition among major OECD countries that global strategies would be needed to address inter-related social, environmental, and development issues. In 1988 atmospheric scientists at the Toronto Conference sought to get climate change on the international policy agenda, calling for a target of a 20 percent reduction in greenhouse gases (GHG) to below 1988 levels in 15 years. The Japanese government could not afford to risk damaging its international reputation by failing to respond to its international commitments and so established the Cabinet Meeting concerning Global Environmental Conservation in 1989 to coordinate policy among key ministries.[56] In short, foreign pressure hit the Japanese policy agenda even though, in the absence of a strongly mobilized body of domestic environmental non-governmental organizations (NGOs), there was no serious criticism from within.

The Japanese government's contributions to the issue of climate change fitted well with its effort to ease foreign pressure about doing more to contribute to international "public goods." In general, regardless of their contribution to sharing the costs of CO_2 emissions reduction, individual countries may receive the benefits of global strategies to mitigate climate change and there is an aspect of public goods theory in this context.[57] The benefits of climatic risk reduction are non-excludable so that any one country has a strong incentive to take a free ride on the efforts of others. Thus, even if uninvolved in the cost-sharing, Japan could be seen to benefit from it. However, if others found Japan's contributions to be less than expected, Japan might suffer damage to its reputation, which might entail other material losses, such as carbon tariffs paid to other countries.

Environmental foreign policy affects material interests in a way quite different from that of domestic environmental policy. Differences in developmental paths among countries have revealed specific geographical orientations. Climate change has been seen as a site for dialogue to tackle the North–South divide.

Japan has provided technical training to people from developing countries to diffuse environment-friendly technologies, and official development assistance (ODA) loans in fields related to climate change. In 1992, with an eye to the Rio Summit, the Cabinet adopted the ODA-guiding principle that "environmental conservation and development should be pursued in tandem," which was incorporated into Japan's first ODA Charter.[58] At the summit, Japan pledged a substantial increase in its environmental ODA—an increment of about US$7.0–7.7 billion in a five-year period.[59] Other parties taking part in the climate negotiations expected Japan's greater economic capability to incur more international responsibility for environmental protection by extending environmental aid to developing countries.

Despite its cost-sharing in the form of foreign aid, Japan's necessary but costly policies were perceived by business as likely to affect profits or market share. In the 1970s and 1980s, Japan set the benchmark in energy efficiency that other major OECD countries aspired to emulate. Yet, in the 1990s, Japan and certain environmentally advanced countries switched positions in terms of government and industry initiatives in environmental risk reduction. Climate change/carbon taxes were adopted in the early 1990s in Scandinavia and the Netherlands, and later in Britain and Germany, while Japan's business community was largely left to voluntary self-regulation to reduce CO_2 emissions. European countries have caught up to Japan in the field of industrial energy efficiency and even overtaken Japan in certain industrial sectors.[60] As the government claims,[61] Japan's CO_2 emissions per GDP are the lowest among OECD countries.[62] However, Japan's GDP is overvalued in currency conversions because of the high cost of living and thus Japan appears to be much more environmentally-efficient than it actually is. By using purchasing power currency values rather than simple currency conversions, Japan's CO_2 emissions per GDP are only equivalent to the EU-15 average.[63] Japan is relatively efficient but it is largely because the energy-efficient residential and transportation sectors make up for the high level of commercial and industrial CO_2 emissions per unit of GDP. Japanese housing consumes far less energy than housing in major OECD countries, although significant growth in the residential sector's proportional share of total CO_2 emissions has continued. The commercial and industrial sectors are expected to play a critical role in reducing CO_2 emissions, yet any reductions have been driven by Keidanren-led voluntary action.[64] The business community has successfully avoided mandatory requirements, such as tax or cap-and-trade schemes at the national level.[65]

International pressure alone does not suffice in accounting for Japan's climate change diplomacy. Japanese domestic politics became entangled via international negotiations, which can be conceived as a two-level game. In this game, the "win-set" is the range of possible options that are likely to be accepted by the domestic constituencies and international negotiations arrive at an agreement when there is an overlap between the win-sets of the states involved in the negotiations.[66] The negotiator uses a simultaneous calculation of constraints and opportunities on both the domestic and international levels; the state of domestic affairs could be used to affect the processes and outcomes of international bargaining, and foreign pressures might be used to persuade the domestic constituencies. "The larger each win-set, the more likely they are to overlap. Conversely, the smaller the win-sets, the greater the risk that the negotiations will break down."[67]

Domestically, regarding interests and actors, the coalition-building around climate change differed significantly from that around industrial pollution. Since the costs and benefits of industrial pollution in the 1970s were relatively concentrated on a narrow range of industrial interests and affected residents in industrial cities, these groups intensified their political conflict in a direct way. A dichotomy of polluters-versus-victims interest representation effectively influenced the course of events regarding pollution control and compensation. In contrast, a proposed agreement over climate change tends to impose both diffused and uncertain adaptation/mitigation costs on a sectoral basis while offering diffused benefits to a wide range of social groups. So the question becomes who needs to adapt to the adverse impact of climate change or mitigate the magnitude of climate change. Adaptation and mitigation are inter-related in the sense that the former activities have consequences for the latter or vice versa in both positive and negative ways. Synergies, trade-offs, and conflicts between adaptation and mitigation may exist in managing the environmental risks. The nature of these inter-relationships is locally specific at the sector level since GHG emissions are the consequences of human action or organizational processes that take place in a given space.[68]

Due to the scientific technicality of climate change, EA technocrats, who were well informed at international conferences, began to assume a major role in the policy debate while drawing on help from scientists in the fields of energy, economics, and atmospheric science. The EA, established in 1971 with the aim of coordinating the administration of environmental policies, still had to rely in practice on the exclusive exercise of other ministries' jurisdiction over environment-related matters. In this respect, climate change was an ideal area where the agency could expand its jurisdiction for policy coordination. Yet this environmental coalition faced tenacious resistance from an industrial coalition. Not surprisingly, the MITI took on the issue of climate change as a matter of industrial policy. The ministry, together with a strong business lobby, opposed a carbon tax as well as an emissions trading system.[69] Climate change also presented a challenge for energy demand/supply policy to take GHG emissions constraints into consideration. MITI's Agency of Natural Resources and Energy, in collaboration with coal, electricity, gas, nuclear and petroleum industries, had been instrumental in managing energy demand/supply after the two oil crises of 1973 and 1979.[70] On the other hand, as negotiations took place in the international arena, climate change put the Ministry of Foreign Affairs (MOFA) in a position to be at the forefront of coalition-building. As Japanese diplomats and conservative politicians had been obsessed with international reputation, Japan's leadership in the negotiations was conceived of as its international contribution. In 1995 the government officially announced its willingness to host the UN

Framework Convention on Climate Change Conference (COP-3) and staked its reputation on the success of the conference. The objective of the ministry in hosting COP-3 was to adopt a successful multilateral protocol and thus enhance its reputation as a leader in the Asia-Pacific. To this end, the host nation needed to be assured of US participation in the protocol and had no choice but to persuade other countries to bend to the wishes of the US.[71]

In 1990 Japan's Cabinet adopted an Action Program to Arrest Global Warming, which stated that the stabilization targets of CO_2 emissions at 1990 levels by 2000 would be achieved in two ways: reductions on a per capita basis, and the stabilization of the absolute total amount of CO_2 emissions.[72] As COP-3 approached, these apparently unattainable targets remained intact without any careful re-examination. Japan was criticized by some countries and environmental groups for not accepting legally binding targets at COP-2 but faced hardly any domestic pressure. In Japan it was rare for environmental NGOs to meet government officials to exchange their views on the matter of climate change. On May 30, 1997 the Kiko Forum (succeeded by the Kiko Network in April 1998), for example, had direct talks with MITI officials about the ministry's position, yet the MITI simply ignored a request to change the ministry's stance over climate change.[73] The wait-and-see attitude of most local authorities towards the outcome of negotiations at the Kyoto Climate conference also seemed to indicate that they simply monitored the negotiations without getting directly involved and only discovered Japan's climate change pledge, which might affect local governments for achieving the national mandate, at the end of the negotiations. Japan eventually failed to present its host nation's domestic plan at the opening of COP-3. As negotiations at COP-3 progressed, Japan had to submit a proposal for reducing GHG emissions. The relevant agencies and ministries thus began to represent their own beliefs and interests for Japan's proposal. Prime Minister Ryūtarō Hashimoto was expected to act as an intermediary agent in neutralizing the policy inefficiencies, caused by political frictions, or to seek a political compromise. In August 1997 Hashimoto instructed the EA, the MITI and the MOFA to come up with a mutually agreeable proposal so that Japan, as the host nation, would enhance its reputation.

The environmental coalition, led by the EA and the National Institute for Environmental Studies, argued, using a model based on the introduction of a carbon tax, that a 7.6 percent CO_2 reduction from 1990 levels by 2010 could be achieved without undermining economic growth.[74] The EA pointed out that the lessons drawn from the oil crises of 1973 and 1979 helped to increase energy conservation and efficiency and subsequently added a comparative advantage to Japanese products.[75] The industrial coalition, however, argued that Japan had produced the lowest per capita CO_2 emissions among OECD countries and thus would find it much more difficult than others to reduce GHG emissions. In its view, it was unfair for Japan's industries to reduce GHG emissions at the same rate as their counterparts in other countries. As Keidanren announced its voluntary action plan in June 1997, the MITI decided to propose reduction targets without imposing mandatory requirements on business. The ministry emphasized that reducing CO_2 emissions to 1990 levels by 2010 would be the best Japan could do to combat climate change.[76] The coalition of diplomatic interests insisted on a 6.5 percent reduction in GHG emissions, using pressure from the European Union (EU) (who proposed a 15 percent reduction) as one of its primary arguments against the 0 percent reduction proposed by the coalition of business interests.[77] By the end of September 1997, these ministries and the agency were unable to reach an agreement.

MOFA officials who had direct contact with the US and the EU delegations sought a specific percentage reduction as being minimally acceptable to the EU and possibly supported by the US, with some kind of allowance.[78] Internationally, Japan's delegation was quite sensitive to US wishes, due to its close relations with the US. To ensure US participation in the protocol, the Prime Minister's Office intervened as a policy broker in the domestic political game, and settled Japan's proposal on being a 5 percent reduction. This rate was a political compromise on policy being just enough to be a solution to domestic pressures rather than a policy efficiency consideration. However, this proposed reduction had specific conditions attached which were domestically acceptable; namely, alternative reduction rates would be applied to good performers on emissions reduction in terms of emissions per GDP, emissions per capita, and population growth.[79] After these conditions were taken into account, Japan's reduction target was expected to come down to 2.5 percent. Japan attempted to act as a mediator between the US and the EU but Japanese negotiators found themselves caught between the two major players. Japan's limited success in playing the role of mediator could be largely explained by domestic differences in policy beliefs and interests between the industrial coalition and the environmental coalition—the smaller the autonomy of Japanese negotiators from domestic pressure, the smaller the win-set. In the end, Japan's 6 percent reduction was both internationally accepted by delegations from other countries and ratified and implemented by the domestic constituencies.[80] Despite its publicized 15 percent reduction proposal, the EU achieved far lighter obligations easily at Kyoto. The US, however, was pushed to agree to a target that went far beyond its stabilization target.

In response to the Kyoto Protocol, Japan's Act on Promotion of Global Warming Countermeasures—Act No. 117 of 1998 (Climate Change Law) stipulated a local government's statutory obligation to promote policy measures for emissions reduction. Article 4 states: "Local governments shall promote policies to limit greenhouse gas emissions in accordance with the natural and social conditions of their areas." In 2002, as Japan ratified the Kyoto Protocol, the National Diet passed the revised Climate Change Law to introduce the new CO_2 emissions reduction programs targeted at all sectors to achieve the 6 percent CO_2 emissions reduction commitment under the Protocol. Article 20 of the revised law states:

> In view of the Kyoto Protocol Target Achievement Plan, prefectural and municipal governments shall endeavor to formulate and to implement comprehensive, plan-based programs for the control of greenhouse gases, in accordance with the natural and social conditions of their local areas.

The responsibility of local governments in formulating and implementing their climate change action plans is clearly specified in the revision. A share of the internationally pledged 6 percent target, however, is not allocated to individual prefectures but local governments are instead expected to set up their own mitigation target. The institutional issue boils down to local authorities' capability of contributing to problem-solving. The revised Climate Change Law neither clearly grants legal/formal authority nor provides decentralized financial power to local governments to reduce GHG emissions at the local level. Local governments lack sufficient jurisdiction over the adaptation/mitigation-related policy areas, such as energy supply (e.g., construction permits for power plants), transport infrastructure (e.g., railway, highway, shipping and vehicle regulations), and commercial activities (e.g., market regulations). These key jurisdictions belong to national ministries and agencies. The law has yet to allow an adequate delegation of power to lower levels of government. Local action cannot be effective in isolation from components of the institutional frameworks at the national scale. Ideal state-centric governance, through sub-national participation, is institutionalized to clarify sub-national roles in achieving national goals within the context of international obligations or to establish a division of labor among levels of government with a state-centric gate-keeping capacity (its capacity to influence policy decisions). If bridging policy gaps among local action, national policy, and global strategy is potentially a way of reinventing Japan's environmental policy, then the state of national top-down promotion of adaptation and mitigation in Japan is failing to provide much in the way of substantial participation in environmental governance.

The 1990s and the 2000s: sub-national participation

In the process of the Kyoto Protocol negotiations, Japan's negotiators needed to represent the national interest, which could not be defined by one unitary actor in the nation. Domestic stakeholders, who did not have identical preferences, wished the international negotiation outcome to reflect their preferences. In this context, domestic agents were seen simply as constraints on the negotiators; these agents had different preferences, only over the domestic concerns with international agreements. While being constrained simultaneously by domestic and international factors, the negotiators still acted on the delineated divide between the domestic level (politics within a territorially bounded entity) and the foreign level (politics between territorially bounded entities). In this sense, sub-national actors were unable to enter the international game as direct players in their own right. However, there was a rapidly expanding sphere of action in which domestic affairs and foreign affairs were eroding. Local and provincial actors increasingly recognized themselves as direct players in a global game to cope with the local impact of global issues. By the late 1970s, Chadwick Alger, a farsighted scholar, pointed out the importance of the sub-national level of participation in the resolution of global social issues.[81] He discussed the macro–micro relations of individual actions in pursuit of global solutions yet noted that the state-centric constraints of the mind-set and the territorial constraints of state authority had prevented people from participating in international cooperation and decision-making.[82] In the 1990s, as Alger witnessed, a marked upsurge was under way around the world to develop movements through which people and sub-national authorities could respond to global change and network with overseas counterparts to solve problems poorly attended by the state.[83]

The 1992 Earth Summit recognized the importance of sub-national participation in the resolution of global social issues. Agenda 21, which was adopted at the summit, also stressed the vital importance of international cooperation at the local level.[84] Sub-national participation is desirable for two basic reasons: the need for locally specific responses to global strategies (as the causes and effects of climate change are local in character) and the need for a decentralized form of international environmental cooperation (especially as partnerships between local authorities in the North and South can help the developing world to build the capacity of local governments).[85] As global strategies for environmental risk reduction reach the implementation stage, they demand local action. The linkages between international environmental regimes (based on multilateral agreements) and the local environment converge to follow the details of locally specific needs for global strategies. The implementation of international agreements links people in small-scale social structures to a global environmental regime and then increases the visibility of sub-national action in a global game.

Ever since the acknowledgment of a vital community role in the implementation of global strategies for sustainable development within the Agenda 21 framework, the position of local communities has been further promoted and strengthened by a series of decision-making processes at both the national and international levels. A new confidence in local governments has also developed as the participating countries at the 1996 UN Human Settlements Programme (HABITAT II) have been working hard towards the adoption of a World Charter for Local Self-government by UN member states to make a commitment to decentralization.[86] Nearly two-thirds of the 2,509 actions designated in Agenda 21 require the involvement of local governments, and more than 6,400 local governments in 113 countries are working on their own Local Agenda 21, based on action plans identified by people in their communities.[87] At the 2005 UN Word Summit on the Millennium Development Goals (MDGs), community networks and local governments were recognized as key partners.[88] A striking upsurge is under way around the globe regarding the number of sub-national government partnerships and networks. It was reported in 2004 that over 70 percent of the world's cities participate in city-to-city international cooperation programs, networks, and partnerships.[89]

In the EU, sub-national participation which is mandated in EU treaties allows direct contact between sub-national authorities and supranational institutions (e.g., participating in the Committee of the Regions, connecting with the EU commissioners, and influencing Members of the European Parliament). Increased freedom of sub-national participation may also derive from changes in the formal powers of sub-national authorities within national boundaries: in 1992 the French government passed national legislation allowing its local authorities to sign agreements with overseas counterparts (Art 131, Loi d'orientation No. 92-125). Sub-national actors (local governments, socially mobilized groups, and businesses) thus try to influence environmental policy-making through institutionalized channels in both the national and supranational arenas. To this end, they move across traditional levels of authority for coalition-building with different types of actors who share the same policy goals. Such institutional rules are yet to be seen in Japan. Article 34 of Japan's Basic Environment Law, enacted in 1993, acknowledges the role of local governments as the subjects of international environmental cooperation.[90] In 1993 the International Council for Local Environmental Initiatives (ICLEI) established its Tokyo office with the aim of promoting local initiatives (or Local Agenda 21) in Japan and other Asian countries.[91] Yet the Japanese government has neither clearly regulated nor enabled sub-national participation in international environmental cooperation. However, in the absence of national policy, a few front-runner local authorities are both willing and capable of contributing to bridging policy gaps between local action and global strategies. Without the familiar ground of institutionalized rules or the right to legitimately represent themselves at the international level, sub-national actors find through political mobilization a way to move across levels of government and deal directly with overseas counterparts and supranational actors in a rather ad hoc fashion.

To reduce environmental risks at the regional and international levels, Japanese local governments have been working with counter-partners, such as overseas local authorities, domestic/international NGOs, and international organizations, building transnational coalitions and exchanging information to work internationally on global environmental strategies. As of August 2013, in Japan all 47 prefectures, all 20 "designated cities" (i.e., with a population of over 500,000), and all 42 "core cities" (i.e., with a population of over 300,000) have engaged at least once in some form of international environmental cooperation; 43 out of 47 prefectures and 23 out of around 800 cities (i.e., with a population of over 50,000) have been engaging in some form of international environmental cooperation activities.[92] According to a 2002 Ministry of the Environment survey (of 47 prefectures and 40 major cities), 68 percent of sub-national government environmental officials "have experience in international environmental cooperation,"[93] which can be categorized into four patterns that are not necessarily mutually exclusive: bilateral cooperation/partnerships, and sectoral, regional, and international networks/coalitions.

One of the early pioneering efforts was the Kitakyushu-Dalian bilateral cooperation. The City of Kitakyushu was once a polluted steel town and is now renowned for having successfully overcome some of Japan's worst environmental problems. As the city accumulated environmental management expertise, a neighboring city across the Yellow Sea, Dalian, was about to experience every imaginable environmental problem, much like those experienced in Kitakyushu. Trans-boundary spillover effects from Dalian's pollution became a serious concern for Kitakyushu. As early as 1981, Kitakyushu began to transfer the know-how of environmental management to Dalian. While unilateral flows of resources and environmental knowledge and information emerged from Kitakyushu to Dalian, the city-to-city cooperation was more committed to mutual gains from environmental risk reduction.[94] This persuaded Japan's MOFA to acknowledge the importance of locally initiated approaches as an alternative to nationally defined ODA projects. The Japanese government thus pledged ODA funds to China to implement a proposed Dalian-Kitakyushu pollution control plan. The national government financed the project, but it depended on the Dalian-Kitakyushu partnership for successful planning and implementation. Thus self-governing inter-sub-national networks demonstrated the capacity to secure environmental risk reduction which did not rest on the power of national governments. The process of negotiations was enmeshed in territorially overarching spheres of authority, and the reallocation of decision-making brought the previous functions of the state down to the inter-sub-national arena.

The oldest sectoral network initiated by a Japanese local government is the International Lake Environment Committee Foundation (ILEC). Created in 1986 by Shiga prefecture to support environmentally sound management of lakes and their environments, something the UN Environmental Programme (UNEP) promotes in developing countries,[95] its activities, such as creating information databases and reporting and monitoring trends, aim to enhance environmental knowledge in the provision of national and international benefits for reducing the degradation of lakes.[96] Although the health of Lake Biwa in Shiga as a public good exclusively accrues to the residents, the benefits of knowledge about lake-environmental risk reduction are non-exclusive at the international level. UNEP gave requested assistance directly to the sub-national actor for its strategies to build a sectoral network of decentralized governance, and the sub-national actor responded by initiating an ILEC policy network, acknowledging the necessity of information sharing for solutions of fresh water eutrophication.[97] In this network, like-minded civil society organizations, scientists, and government officials from many parts of the world operated rather freely across traditional levels of authority in policy innovation and coordination by diffusing ideas and influencing policy measures while not completely superseding the jurisdictional level of the national state. Other major sectoral networks followed in the 1990s: the International Environmental Management of Enclosed Coastal Seas (EMES) Center (established by Hyogo prefecture in 1994), the Acid Deposition Monitoring Network in East Asia (EANET) (established in 1998 with the UNEP Regional Resource Centre of Asia and the Pacific as the Secretariat and managed by Niigata prefecture), and the Kushiro International Wetland Centre (established in 1995 to implement the Ramsar Convention on Wetlands of International Importance and operated by the City of Kushiro).

Regional environmental networks exist where the benefits of environmental risk reduction accrue to the public of nations with contiguous borders or of neighboring nations across the sea. In 2000, for example, Kitakyushu city established the Kitakyushu Initiative Network, comprising 62 cities from 18 member countries of the UN Economic and Social Commission for Asia and the Pacific (UNESCAP) to coordinate the reduction of urban environmental risks.[98] Other major regional networks are: the Asian Network of Major Cities (ANMC-21) (created in 2001 as a metropolitan multi-issue-oriented network with the Tokyo Metropolitan Government as the Secretariat), the Environmental Cooperation Network of Asian Cities (established in 1997 by the City of Kitakyushu with seven cities in Southeast Asia), and the Northern Forum (proposed by the government of Hokkaido in 1974 and set up in 1991 with 15 regional governments from eight northern countries).

The Regional Network of Local Authorities for the Management of Human Settlements (CITYNET) is an international environmental network among local authorities with an Asia-Pacific origin (including those authorities outside of the region), which has Category II Status within the UN Economic and Social Council. In 1987 it was established with the support of UNESCAP, the UN Development Programme (UNDP), and UN-HABITAT. The City of Yokohama has hosted the Secretariat of CITYNET to promote environmentally sustainable cities through consultation services, training and workshops, joint research projects, information dissemination, and by convening forums for members.[99] As of 2009, the membership comprised 139 organizations (local authorities, municipal associations, NGOs, research institutions, and private companies). The main objective of the network is to promote South–South cooperation among sub-national actors through reciprocity.[100] This networking organization operates as an external support agency, matching supply with demand for expertise and experience and sharing lessons learned among the members. The dynamics of CITYNET are driven by actors such as the City of Yokohama and UNDP's agencies that find the blurring of traditional levels of authority not only useful in transferring effective practices but also normatively desirable.[101]

The above practices of Japanese local governments reveal the underlying dynamics and tendencies that have been shaping the sub-national level of participation in the resolution of transnational issues. First, geographical proximity is becoming less relevant to international environmental cooperation, although directing the necessity of network establishment. In the European border regions, the local population, companies, universities, and others engage in cross-border contacts on a daily basis, and this turns local authorities on the border towards cross-border cooperation to promote their interests and solve cross-border problems. Geographical proximity is the natural and conventional criteria of partner selection. Some coastal cities and provinces in Northeast Asia border the Yellow Sea without a land border, yet they still share some geographical space with one another concerned with solving shared problems. A case in point is the inter-municipal cooperation between Dalian (China) and Kitakyushu (Japan) over pollution control. Geographical proximity is one of the most important factors driving local governments' activities across geographical borders but other factors allow the activities to transcend the constraints of the geographical fragmentation. Perhaps the most influential factor is the dual dynamics of internationalization and globalization. Internationalization can be seen as a phenomenon in which the external environment influences domestic policy-making and implementation ("second image reversed") while globalization can be narrowly defined as a process of policy convergence, especially in the policy area of environmental standards. While globalization cannot be accounted for by a set of driving forces in a deterministic way, this book directs attention to agent-specific and ideational factors as well as structural and economic factors. This increased dual dynamics facilitates the development of sub-national participation through greater spatial interaction. Kitakyushu and cities in Southeast Asia are geographically far apart but internationalization and globalization have made the physical distance less relevant to their partner selection. Equally important, as sub-national participation has been increasingly incorporated into global strategies,[102] the linkages of international environmental cooperation have revealed and emphasized different geographical orientations, that is, North–North, North–South, and South–South focuses. Yokohama's CITYNET offers a dialogue place to tackle the North–South divide and South–South cooperation.

Second, in the light of decentralized cooperation contributing to a range of major worldwide objectives, local governments face institutional and resource-related challenges. National governments, international associations, such as the United Cities and Local Governments (UCLG), and international organizations, such as the World Bank, have significantly facilitated sub-national governments to act as credible agents in international development work and environmental cooperation.[103] In particular, national government policy and commitment critically affect the level of financial resourcing and feasibility for decentralized cooperation. The task of sub-national governments is to find a way to work with national governments that provides sufficient legal and financial support while preserving a meaningful degree of independence and autonomy for their activities. Kitakyushu–Dalian bilateral cooperation over pollution control is a successful example of this kind. Local learning and knowledge persuaded Japan's MOFA to pledge ODA funds to China for implementing the Dalian–Kitakyushu-proposed decentralized cooperation. In this case, the sub-national government thus occupied a strategic position to change the policies and practices of the national government. Kitakyushu's commitment to global strategies for environmental protection required more institutionalized national aid to related projects. In response to this kind of need, the MOFA established a Grassroots Grant Aid Program in 1989, which was designed to provide overseas local authorities and community organizations with grants for international development work.

Third, it is self-evident that internal structuring and capacity-building is critical to the success of local government's participation in international environmental cooperation. A supportive internal infrastructure with an autonomous capacity will provide a necessary foundation for sound environmental management. Organizational strengthening is a sustained effort to improve management structures and change the organizational culture of the administration, while capacity-building is primarily directed towards human resource developments such as staff training and performance management. One important dimension of organizational strengthening is citizens' direct participation. The notion of organizational responsiveness and accountability derives from the viewpoint of citizens as service recipients; citizens are seen as mere beneficiaries of decision-making. To enhance participatory governance, management structures are to encourage citizens not only to be passive users but also to act as makers of service delivery.[104] The benefits of participatory mechanisms become marked for the promotion of decentralized cooperation. In light of the ongoing decentralization of government, sub-national government is often assumed to be a better fit to make a decision as close to people as possible and organizational strengthening is thus closely linked to the needs of people.[105] Community support through the participatory process is a key condition for gaining democratic legitimacy for the performance of sub-national governments.

Finally, in relation to capacity-building, community awareness is a fundamental precondition for the success of local governments' multi-level and cross-scale activities. A higher level of community awareness of the non-central-government-level linkages with foreign partners would seem to be present in successful and sustainable international cooperation.[106] Both a consultative, participatory process (within communities) and a mutual learning process (with foreign partners) in international environmental cooperation are expected to raise community awareness. This success factor can be seen as a "soft infrastructure" that facilitates the formation of norms and values of social networks for creating bridges between diverse individuals and groups and thus creates public trust in the necessity and capabilities of international environmental cooperation. Nonetheless, these norms and values are produced between individuals through social and mutual learning (or exists in their relationships) but cannot be directly used by individuals. The stock of such norms and values accumulated in non-material forms needs to be maintained, invested, and converted into physical outcomes such as sub-national participation in a decentralized form of international cooperation. This process can be described as the conversion of tacit expectation to explicit policy outcomes.[107] In other words, it requires an institutional medium for the physical materialization of public trust. In terms of decentralized cooperation, the institutionalized participation of individuals and groups is expected to act as a better-suited medium. Sub-national government officials and practitioners are yet to pay much attention to the formation of public trust and the conversion mechanisms and processes from public trust to the success of international environmental cooperation.

Conclusion

In the 1970s and 1980s, the formation of environmental policy was essentially a domestic-level process occurring within the Japanese state. The outputs from the two international oil crises were used as inputs to the domestic political game in adaptation to changes in the international environment. As an exogenous variable explaining the expansion of environmental policy, the oil crises are apolitical in the sense that they caused unilaterally systemic effects on policy formation in terms of international causes and domestic effects, while providing little room for the interaction of domestic and international factors. The expansion of environmental policy was a direct product of decisions made in the process of electoral politics. The government party advanced environmental policies into an electorally attractive proposition. The industrial coalition saw the costs of pollution reduction as relatively concentrated on a limited body of polluters and victims in the affected industrial areas. Some of the world's strongest environmental regulations were thus imposed on the business sector, yet the environmental improvements were seen by the industrial coalition as a by-product of energy efficiency measures. The cost-sharing worked within the limits of the state and thus corresponded to national boundaries.

The shift in Japan's environmental responses from industrial pollution to climate change created far more complex and uncertain constraints on decision-making. Japan's diplomacy over climate change was shaped both by what other countries would accept and by what domestic constituencies would ratify and implement. In the process of the Kyoto Protocol negotiations, domestic constituencies' demands were not exogenous in the sense that Japan's delegation had to manipulate domestic politics to explore a possibility of bargaining advantage over other countries. In the domestic political game of climate change, foreign pressures were not exogenous either in that the Japanese negotiators simultaneously employed foreign pressures to alter the scope of domestic constraints on the negotiations. Environmental politics was an arena where decision-makers had to choose how to reconcile domestic constraints and foreign pressures. At the domestic level, the environmental risk reduction of global issues such as climate change tended to impose diffused and uncertain costs on a sectoral basis while bringing diffused benefits to a wide range of social groups. Primarily due to the scientific technicality of climate change, and the uncertain costs of adapting to it, the domestic political game took place in the national bureaucracy. The bureaucracy-led coalition-building of sectoral interests was unable to respond to foreign pressures in a concerted way and thus failed to initiate climate change policy.

International environmental cooperation can progress successfully when there is agreement on how to realistically reduce environmental risks. Environmental impacts are manifested locally and vulnerability and adaptive capacity are determined by local conditions. Local action provides a vehicle to identify how incentives and interests interact at different levels of governance. This better enables the national authority to address environmental challenges as local environmental problems demand global strategies. In Japan, a number of front-runner local authorities have come to see their actions as part of a global game. Bridging policy gaps among local action, national policy, and global strategy is potentially a way of reinventing Japan's environmental policies, but the institutionalization of sub-national participation for policy integration is yet to develop.

Notes

1 James Rosenau, *Along the Domestic-Foreign Frontier: Exploring Governance in a Turbulent World* (Cambridge, UK: Cambridge University Press, 1997).
2 See Daniel W. Drezner, "Globalization and policy convergence," *International Studies Review*, Vol. 3, No. 1 (2001), pp. 53–78.
3 Duncan Liefferink, Bas Arts, Jelmer Kamstra, and Jeroen Ooijevaar, "Leaders and laggards in environmental policy: a quantitative analysis of domestic policy

outputs," *Journal of European Public Policy*, Vol. 16, No. 5 (2009), pp. 677–700; Katharina Holzinger, Christoph Knill, and Thomas Sommerer, "Is there convergence of national environmental policies? An analysis of policy outputs in 24 OECD countries," *Environmental Politics*, Vol. 20, No. 1 (2011), pp. 20–41.

4 Katharina Holzinger, Christoph Knill, and Bas Arts, eds., *Environmental Governance in Europe: The Impact of International Institutions and Trade* (Cambridge, UK: Cambridge University Press, 2008).

5 Liefferink, Arts, Kamstra and Ooijevaar, "Leaders and laggards in environmental policy," pp. 685–8.

6 Ellis S. Krauss and Bradford L. Simcock, "Citizens' movements: the growth and impact of environmental protest in Japan," in Kurt Steiner, Ellis Krauss, and Scott Flanagan, eds., *Political Opposition and Local Politics in Japan* (Princeton, NJ: Princeton University Press, 1980), pp. 187–227; Margaret A. McKean, *Environmental Protest and Citizen Politics in Japan* (Berkeley, CA: University of California Press, 1981); Steven Reed, "Environmental politics: some reflections based on the Japanese case," *Comparative Politics*, Vol. 13, No. 3 (1981), pp. 253–69.

7 McKean, *Environmental Protest and Citizen Politics in Japan*; Michael R. Reich, "Mobilizing for environmental policy in Italy and Japan," *Comparative Politics*, Vol. 16, No. 4 (1984), pp. 379–402.

8 Jeffrey Broadbent, *Environmental Politics in Japan: Networks of Power and Protest* (Cambridge, UK: Cambridge University Press, 1998), pp. 114–19.

9 Michio Muramatsu, "The impact of economic growth policies on local politics in Japan," *Asian Survey*, Vol. 15, No. 9 (1975), pp. 799–816; Krauss and Simcock, "Citizens' movements," pp. 187–227; Terry E. MacDougall, "Political opposition and big cities elections in Japan, 1947–1975," in Kurt Steiner, Ellis Krauss, and Scott Flanagan, eds., *Political Opposition and Local Politics in Japan* (Princeton, NJ: Princeton University Press, 1980), pp. 55–94; Reed, "Environmental politics," pp. 253–69; Gesine Foljanty-Jost, *Ökonomie und ökologie in Japan: politik zwischen wachstum und umweltschutz* (Opladen: Leske & Budrich, 1995).

10 McKean, *Environmental Protest and Citizen Politics in Japan*, p. 183.

11 Tanja A. Börzel, "Pace-setting, foot-dragging, and fence-sitting: member state response to Europeanization," *Journal of Common Market Studies*, Vol. 40, No. 2 (2002), pp. 193–214.

12 See, for example, Martin Jänicke, "Trend-setters in environmental policy: the character and role of pioneer countries," *European Environment*, Vol. 15 (2005), pp. 129–42.

13 The number of the Pollution Countermeasure Agreements (PCAs) increased rapidly from 30 in 1967 through 854 in 1970 to over 17,841 in 1980. See Geoffrey W.G. Learne, "Environmental contracts: a lesson in democracy from the Japanese," *U.B.C. Law Review*, Vol. 25 (1991), pp. 361–85.

14 The Total Pollutant Load Control System (TPLCS) seeks to reduce and control the total amount of pollutant load which flows into water areas. In 1973 this method was first implemented in Japan under the newly enacted Interim Law for Conservation of the Environment of the Seto Inland Sea.

15 See, for example, Gesine Foljanty-Jost, "Kankyō seisaku no seikō no jōken" [Conditions for the success of environmental policy], *Leviathan*, Vol. 27 (2000), pp. 35–48.

16 See, for example, Broadbent, *Environmental Politics in Japan*.

17 Miranda A. Schreurs, *Environmental Politics in Japan, Germany and the United States* (Cambridge, UK: Cambridge University Press, 2002).

18 David Vogel, "Environmental policy in Japan and West Germany," paper presented at the annual meeting of the Western Political Science Association, Newport Beach, CA, March 1990.

19 One major stimulus to Japan's attention to international environmental norms was the first UN Conference on the Human Environment, Stockholm 1972.

20 Kenneth N. Waltz, *Man, the State, and War: A Theoretical Analysis* (New York: Columbia University Press, 1959).
21 Peter Katzenstein, "International relations and domestic structures: foreign economic policies of the advanced industrial states," *International Organization*, Vol. 30, No. 1 (1976), pp. 1–45; Peter Gourevitch, "The second image reversed: the international sources of domestic politics," *International Organization*, Vol. 32, No. 4 (1978), pp. 881–912.
22 Robert D. Putnam, "Diplomacy and domestic politics: the logic of two-level games," *International Organization*, Vol. 42, No. 3 (1988), pp. 427–60; Peter B. Evans, Harold K. Jacobson, and Robert D. Putnam, *Double-edged Diplomacy: International Bargaining and Domestic Politics* (Berkeley, CA: University of California Press, 1993).
23 Gary Marks, "Structural policy and multi-level governance in the EC," in Alan Cafruny and Glenda Rosenthal, eds., *The State of the European Community, Vol. 2: The Maastricht Debates and Beyond* (Boulder, CO: Lynne Reinner, 1993), pp. 391–410; Liesbet Hooghe, "Sub-national mobilization in the European Union," *West European Politics*, Vol. 18, No. 3 (1995), pp. 175–98.
24 Gary Marks, François Nielsen, Leonard Ray, and Jane Salk, "Competencies, cracks and conflicts: regional mobilization in the European Union," *Comparative Political Studies*, Vol. 29, No. 2 (1996), pp. 164–92.
25 Simona Piattoni, "Multi-level governance: sfide analitiche, empiriche, normative," *Rivista Italiana di Scienza Politica*, Vol. 35, No. 3 (2005), pp. 417–45.
26 Zdravko Mlinar, "Local responses to global change," *Annals of the American Academy of Political and Social Science*, Vol. 540 (1995), pp. 145–56; Karen T. Litfin, "Advocacy coalitions along the domestic-foreign frontier: globalization and Canadian climate change policy," *Policy Studies Journal*, Vol. 28, No. 1 (2000), pp. 236–52.
27 A large number of MEAs, while imposing direct legal obligations on member states, prescribed the necessary planning and operational actions at the sub-national level, for example, Article 3 of the 1971 Convention on Wetlands of International Importance, Article 5 of the 1972 Convention concerning the Protection of the World Cultural and Natural Heritage, Article 4-2-c of the 1989 Basel Convention on the Control of Transboundary Movements of Hazardous Wastes and Article 4 of the 1997 Kyoto Protocol.
28 McKean, *Environmental Protest and Citizen Politics in Japan*, p. 19; Broadbent, *Environmental Politics in Japan*, p. 118.
29 Krauss and Simcock, "Citizens' movements," pp. 193–5.
30 See Norie Huddle and Michael Reich, *Island of Dreams: Environmental Crisis in Japan* (New York: Autumn Press, 1975); Frank Upham, "Litigation and moral consciousness in Japan: an interpretative analysis of four Japanese pollution suits," *Law and Society Review*, Vol. 10, No. 4 (1976), pp. 579–619.
31 Krauss and Simcock, "Citizens' movements," pp. 221–2.
32 Muramatsu, "The impact of economic growth policies on local politics in Japan," pp. 799–816; Broadbent, *Environmental Politics in Japan*, pp. 112–33.
33 Broadbent, *Environmental Politics in Japan*, pp. 120–1.
34 In this session of the Diet, 14 pollution control bills were passed; nationwide regulations were to be applied to air and water pollution, traffic pollution and noise, hazardous material transport, waste disposal and sewage, toxic waste, and Natural Parks. Equally important, the new laws held polluters financially responsible to their victims under civil law, and clarified the division of regulatory powers between national and sub-national governments. All regulatory power over business operators was delegated to municipal governments. This regulatory mechanism did not, however, specify any nationally-defined mandatory emission standards but left regulation and enforcement to sub-national authorities. In the following year, the Environmental Agency, a successor to the Pollution Control Office, was established

64 *Japan's environmental policy*

to coordinate the implementation of these new laws. See Broadbent, *Environmental Politics in Japan*, pp. 123–24; Jeffrey Broadbent, "Japan's environmental regime: the political dynamics of change," in Uday Desai, ed., *Environmental Politics and Policy in Industrialized Countries* (Cambridge, MA: The MIT Press, 2002), pp. 312–14.
35 McKean, *Environmental Protest and Citizen Politics in Japan*, p. 8.
36 Kent E. Calder, *Crisis and Compensation: Public Policy and Political Stability in Japan, 1949–1986* (Princeton, NJ: Princeton University Press, 1988).
37 McKean, *Environmental Protest and Citizen Politics in Japan*, p. 183.
38 The description of the Yokohama PCA case in this section is based on Masayasu Narumi, "Gigyō to bōshi keiyaku teiketsu" [Industry and pollution control agreements], in Atsushi Satō and Michio Nishihara, eds., *Kōgai taisaku* [Pollution countermeasures], Vol. 1 (Tokyo: Yūhikaku, 1969), pp. 335–48; Yu Matsuno, "Local government, industry and pollution control agreements," in Hidefumi Imura and Miranda A. Schreurs, eds., *Environmental Policy in Japan* (Cheltenham, UK: Edward Elgar, 2005), pp. 215–48.
39 Matsuno, "Local government, industry and pollution control agreements," p. 224.
40 McKean, *Environmental Protest and Citizen Politics in Japan*, pp. 102–8.
41 See Daniel P. Aldrich, *Site Fights: Divisive Facilities and Civil Society in Japan and the West* (Ithaca, NY: Cornell University Press, 2008).
42 Japan, Environmental Agency (JEA), *Zenkoku kankyō gyōsei binran* [National list of environmental administration], 1979 ed. (Tokyo: JEA, 1979).
43 Japan, Environmental Agency (JEA), *Zenkoku kankyō gyōsei binran* [National list of environmental administration], 1998 ed. (Tokyo: JEA, 1998).
44 Kyoto Governor Ninagawa Torazō (1950–1978) and Tokyo Governor Minobe Ryōkichi (1967–1979) retired in 1978 and 1979 respectively and Osaka Governor Kuroda Ryōichi (1971–1979) was voted out of office in 1979.
45 These surveys were conducted by the Public Relations Office in the Prime Minister's Office in 1971, 1973, 1975, 1979, and 1981. Respondents were asked about the pollution problems they had personally experienced in the last five years. The number of environmental protest incidents dramatically dropped in 1974 and local protests remained sporadic throughout the 1980s. See Japan, Environmental Agency (JEA), *White Paper on the Environment* (Tokyo: Printing Office of the Ministry of Finance, 1982), chps 2-1-3; Broadbent, *Environmental Politics in Japan*, p. 288.
46 Japan's energy self-sufficiency ratio dropped from 14 percent in 1970 to 4 percent in 2000 (the lowest ratio among industrialized countries). See Japan, Ministry of the Environment (JMOE), *Japanese Official Assistance in the Environmental Field* (2006), available from: www.env.go.jp/earth/coop/coop/images/pdf [accessed December 14, 2009].
47 In accordance with the law, a wide range of conservation measures was adopted. The most extensive was the "Top Runner Program," which: set energy efficiency standards for vehicles and household appliances; required energy-intensive plants, transportation businesses, and large office buildings to submit energy-conservation plans and reports; and provided incentives for integrated management of energy use at plants and offices.
48 Calculated from Organisation for Economic Co-operation and Development (OECD), *OECD Factbook 2009: Economic, Environmental and Social Statistics* (Paris: OECD, 2009), p. 117. Primary energy supply per unit of GDP is based on tonnes of oil equivalent (toe) per thousand 2000 US dollars of GDP calculated using PPPs.
49 Jeffrey Broadbent, "Japan's environmental politics: recognition and response processes," in Hidefumi Imura and Miranda Schreurs, eds., *Environmental Policy in Japan* (Washington, DC: Edward Elgar and the World Bank, 2005), p. 119.
50 Institute of Developing Economies (IDE), Japan External Trade Organization, *Development of Environmental Policy in Japan and Asian Countries* (New York: Palgrave Macmillan, 2007).

51 IDE, *Development of Environmental Policy in Japan and Asian Countries*.
52 Yong Ren, "Japan's environmental management experiences," in Hidefumi Imura and Miranda Schreurs, eds., *Environmental Policy in Japan* (Washington, DC: Edward Elgar and the World Bank, 2005), pp. 307–10.
53 Muthukumara Mani and David Wheeler, while drawing on emissions per unit of output, designated as pollution-intensive industries five sectors: iron and steel, nonferrous metals, industrial chemicals, pulp and paper, and metallic mineral products. Using the same pollution-intensity measure, they identified five non-pollution-intensive sectors: textiles, non-electrical machinery, electrical machinery, transport equipment, and instruments. See Muthukumara Mani and David Wheeler, "In search of pollution havens? Dirty industry in the world economy, 1960–1995," *Journal of Environment and Development*, Vol. 7, No. 3 (1998), pp. 215–47.
54 The International Organization for Standardization (ISO) was established in 1946 with the aim of creating international standards to promote international exchange in manufactured products and services.
55 Japan, Environmental Agency (JEA), *Kankyō ni yasashii kigyō kōdō chōsa* [Survey on environment-friendly business practices], 1996 ed. (Tokyo: JEA, 1997).
56 Japan, Environmental Agency (JEA), *White Paper on the Environment* (Tokyo: Printing Office of the Ministry of Finance, 1990), chp 9.
57 Mancur Olson, *The Logic of Collective Action: Public Goods and the Theory of Groups* (Cambridge, MA: Harvard University Press, 1965); Mancur Olson and Richard Zeckhauser, "An economic theory of alliances," *Review of Economics and Statistics*, Vol. 48, No. 3 (1966), pp. 266–79.
58 Japan, Ministry of Foreign Affairs (JMOFA), *Japan's Official Development Assistance* (2001), available from: www.mofa.go.jp/policy/oda/white/2001/contents.pdf [accessed December 23, 2009].
59 Although the volume of environmental ODA increased, Japan's accountability for the implementation of this new policy initiative was limited by bureaucratic politics, yen-loan-denominated aid, and commercial strings attached to aid ("tied aid"). See David Potter, "Assessing Japan's environmental aid policy," *Pacific Affairs*, Vol. 67, No. 2 (1994), pp. 200–15.
60 International Energy Agency (IEA), *Energy Statistics of OECD Countries 2004–2005* (Paris: OECD/IEA, 2007).
61 Japan, Ministry of Economy, Trade and Industry (JMETI), *Kikōhendō o meguru kokusai dōkō ni tsuite* [International trends in climate change] (Tokyo: METI, 2007).
62 If CO_2/unit of GDP is kg CO_2/1,000 US$ at 2000 prices, then Japan was the smallest polluter per unit of economic output in 2004. The ratio of Japan's figure to other major developed countries' emissions per unit of GDP were, as a multiple of Japan's: Britain 1.4 times, Germany 1.6, France 1.8, EU 27 1.9, US 2.0, Canada 3.2. See JMETI, *Kikōhendō o meguru kokusai dōkō ni tsuite*, p. 4.
63 IEA, *Energy Statistics of OECD Countries 2004–2005*.
64 Keidanren was to resolve problems of the business community and make proposals to government officials. In May 2002, Keidanren merged with Nikkeiren (Japan Federation of Employers' Associations) to form Nippon Keidanren (Japan Business Federation or JBF). The JBF membership of 1,609 comprises 1,295 companies, 129 industrial associations, and 47 regional economic organizations (May 28, 2009).
65 The Tokyo Metropolitan Government's cap-and-trade program, which started in April 2010, was the world's first urban model of mandatory reduction of total emissions.
66 Putnam, "Diplomacy and domestic politics," pp. 439–40.
67 Putnam, "Diplomacy and domestic politics," p. 438.
68 See, for example, Martin L. Parry, Osvaldo F. Canziani, Jean P. Palutikof, Paul J. van der Linden, and Clair E. Hanson, eds., *Contribution of Working Group II to the*

Fourth Assessment Report of the Intergovernmental Panel on Climate Change (Cambridge, UK: Cambridge University Press, 2007), chp 18.
69 See, for example, Shizuka Oshitani, *Global Warming Policy in Japan and Britain: Interactions between Institutions and Issue Characteristics* (Manchester, UK: Manchester University Press, 2006).
70 Katsuto Uchihashi, *Kyōsei no daichi atarashii keizai ga hajimaru* [The great land of cohabitation] (Tokyo: Iwanami Shoten, 1995), pp. 163–70.
71 The Japanese government had always accommodated its plan to the interests of the US in climate change treaty negotiations. When the US stood alone in public opposition, Japan proposed a "pledge and review" system in which parties would unilaterally pledge specific actions subject to performance review by an international body. See Yasuko Kameyama, "Climate change and Japan," *Asia-Pacific Review*, Vol. 9, No. 1 (2002), pp. 33–44; Yasuko Kameyama, "Evaluation and future of the Kyoto Protocol: Japan's perspective," *International Review for Environmental Strategies*, Vol. 5, No. 1 (2004), pp. 71–82.
72 Japan, Ministry of the Environment (JMOE), *Basic Environment Plan* (reference) (2009), available from: www.env.go.jp/en/policy/plan/basic/referenc.html [accessed December 26, 2009].
73 Yasuko Kawashima, "Japan's decision-making about climate change problems: comparative study of decisions in 1990 and 1997," *Environmental Economics and Policy Studies*, Vol. 3 (2000), p. 44.
74 Keiji Takeuchi, *Chikyū ondanka no seijigaku* [Politics of global warming] (Tokyo: Asahi shinbunsha, 1998), p. 156.
75 Japan, Ministry of the Environment (JMOE), *Quality of the Environment in Japan 1994* (1994), chp 2, available from: www.env.go.jp/en/wpaper/1994/index.html [accessed December 26, 2009].
76 Toshiaki Tanabe, *Chikyū ondanka to kankyō gaikō* [Global warming and environmental diplomacy] (Tokyo: Jijitsūshin sha, 1999), pp. 122–3.
77 For the position of the foreign policy coalition and the process of Japan's negotiations, see Tanabe, Japan's chief negotiator and Ambassador for Global Environmental Affairs at COP-3, *Chikyū ondanka to kankyō gaikō*.
78 Tanabe, *Chikyū ondanka to kankyō gaikō*.
79 UN Framework Convention on Climate Change (UNFCCC), FCCC/AGBM/1997/Misc.1/Add.6, 23 October 1997, available from: http://unfccc.int/cop4/resource/docs/1997/agbm/misc01a06.htm [accessed August 23, 2011].
80 Schreurs, *Environmental Politics in Japan, Germany and the United States*, pp. 176–209.
81 Chadwick F. Alger, "Foreign policies of US publics," *International Studies Quarterly*, Vol. 21, No. 2 (1977), pp. 277–318.
82 Chadwick F. Alger, "Creating local institutions for sustained participation in peace building," paper presented at the 26th annual convention of the International Studies Association, Washington, DC, March 4–6, 1985; Chadwick F. Alger, "Perceiving, analysing and coping with the local–global nexus," *International Social Science Journal*, Vol. 40, No. 3 (1988), pp. 321–40; Chadwick F. Alger and Saul Mendlovitz, "Approaches to global issues by local activists in the United States," paper presented at the 26th annual convention of the International Studies Association, Washington, DC, March 4–6, 1985.
83 Chadwick F. Alger, "The world relations of cities: closing the gap between social science paradigms and every human experience," *International Studies Quarterly*, Vol. 34, No. 4 (1990), pp. 493–518.
84 UN Conference on Environment and Development (UNCED), *Agenda 21*, Rio de Janeiro: UNCED, June 3–14, 1992, available from: www.un.org/esa/sustdev/documents/agenda21/english/adenda21toc.htm [accessed June 5, 2009].
85 Michael Shuman, *Toward a Global Village: International Community Development*

Initiatives (London: Pluto, 1994); Lara Green, Chris Game, and Simon Delay, *Why Should My Local Authority Be Involved in an Overseas Project?* (Birmingham, UK: Birmingham University, School of Public Policy, 2005).
86 Economic and Social Commission for Asia and the Pacific (ESCAP), *Local Government in Asia and the Pacific: A Comparative Analysis of Fifteen Countries* (Bangkok: ESCAP, 1999).
87 International Council for Local Environmental Initiatives (ICLEI), *Local Governments for Sustainability* (2008), available from: www.iclei.org [accessed June 1, 2009]. Chapter 28 of Agenda 21 states, "By 1996, most local authorities in each country should have undertaken a consultative process with their populations and achieved a consensus on a Local Agenda 21 for the community."
88 United Nations (UN), *UN General Assembly 2005 World Summit Outcome* (New York: United Nations, 2005).
89 United Cities and Local Governments (UCLG), "Press Kit," 2004 World Urban Forum Barcelona, September 13–17, 2004.
90 Japan, Ministry of the Environment (JMOE), The Basic Environmental Law, Act No. 91 of 1993 (2007), available from: www.env.go.jp/en/laws/policy/basic/ch2-3.html#section6 [accessed December 22, 2009].
91 The ICLEI refers to Local Agenda 21 as a participatory, multi-sectoral process in which local participants voluntarily create long-term, strategic action plans and implement them, integrating environmental, social and economic priorities, to achieve sustainability. See International Council for Local Environmental Initiatives (ICLEI), *The Local Agenda 21 Initiative: ICLEI Guidelines for Local Agenda 21* (Freiburg: ICLEI, 1993).
92 Citizens' International Plaza, CLAIR, Database of International Cooperation Activities by Japanese Local Governments, available from: www.plaza-clair.jp/jichitai/jichitai1-1.html [accessed August 27, 2013].
93 Japan, Overseas Environmental Cooperation Center (JOECC), *Chihō kōkyōdantai ni yoru kokusai kankyō kyōryoku shiryōshū* [A database of international environmental cooperation by local governments] (Tokyo: JOECC, 2003).
94 City of Kitakyushu, Bureau of the Environment, *Kitakyūshū kōgai taisakushi* [Kitakyushu's history of pollution control measures] (Kitakyushu: City of Kitakyushu, 1998), pp. 215–18; Kitakyushu International Techno-cooperative Association (KITA), *KITA nijyū-nen shi* [Twenty-year history of KITA] (Kitakyushu: KITA, 2001), pp. 230–52.
95 Hiroya Kotani, *Jidenteki kokusai koshō kankyō iinkai ron* [Autobiographical account of the International Lake Environment Committee], unpublished, 2006.
96 International Lake Environment Committee Foundation (ILEC), *International Lake Environment Committee* (2009), available from: www.ilec.or.jp/eg/index.html [accessed December 20, 2009].
97 *Kyoto Shinbun*, "Sekai no Biwako e" [Lake Biwa for a globalized world], May 11, 2010.
98 Kitakyushu Initiative Network, Secretariat (KINS), *Kitakyushu Initiative for a Clean Environment* (2008), available from: http://kitakyushu.iges.or.jp/cities/index.html [accessed December 21, 2009].
99 CITYNET relocated from Yokohama, Japan to Seoul, South Korea in March 2013.
100 Bernadia Tjandradewi and Peter J. Marcotullio, "City-to-city networks: Asian perspectives on key elements and areas for success," *Habitat International*, Vol. 33 (2009), pp. 165–72.
101 Akiko Murayama and Bernadia Tjandradewi, Interview by the author, May 24, 2010, CITYNET, Yokohama.
102 Marike Bontenbal, "Understanding North–South municipal partnership conditions for capacity development: a Dutch–Peruvian example," *Habitat International*, Vol. 33, No. 1 (2009), pp. 100–5.

103 Bontenbal, "Understanding North–South municipal partnership conditions for capacity development," pp. 100–5.
104 Andrea Cornwall and John Gaventa, "From users and choosers to makers and shapers: re-positioning participation in social policy," *IDS Bulletin*, Vol. 31, No. 4 (2000), pp. 50–62.
105 See, for example, Harry Blair, "Participation and accountability at the periphery: democratic local governance in six countries," *World Development*, Vol. 28, No. 1 (2000), pp. 21–39; John Gaventa, *Toward Participatory Local Governance: Six Propositions for Discussion* (Brighton, UK: Institute of Development Studies, 2001).
106 Jacobus Christian De Villiers, "Strategic alliances between communities, with special emphasis on the twinning of South African cities and towns with international partners," Ph.D. thesis, Graduate School of Business, University of Stellenbosch, 2005.
107 Paul Alder and Seok-Woo Kwon, "Social capital: prospects for a new concept," *Academy of Management*, Vol. 27, No. 1 (2002), pp. 17–40; Jon Gant, Casey Ichniowski, and Kathryn Shaw, "Social capital and organizational change in high-involvement and traditional work organizations," *Journal of Economics and Management Strategy*, Vol. 11, No. 2 (2002), pp. 289–328.

References

Alder, Paul and Seok-Woo Kwon (2002). "Social capital: prospects for a new concept." *Academy of Management*, Vol. 27, No. 1, pp. 17–40.
Aldrich, Daniel P. (2008). *Site Fights: Divisive Facilities and Civil Society in Japan and the West*. Ithaca, NY: Cornell University Press.
Alger, Chadwick F. (1977). "Foreign policies of US publics." *International Studies Quarterly*, Vol. 21, No. 2, pp. 277–318.
Alger, Chadwick F. (1985). "Creating local institutions for sustained participation in peace building." Paper presented at the 26th annual convention of the International Studies Association, Washington, DC, March 4–6, 1985.
Alger, Chadwick F. (1988). "Perceiving, analysing and coping with the local–global nexus." *International Social Science Journal*, Vol. 40, No. 3, pp. 321–40.
Alger, Chadwick F. (1990). "The world relations of cities: closing the gap between social science paradigms and every human experience." *International Studies Quarterly*, Vol. 34, No. 4, pp. 493–518.
Alger, Chadwick F. and Saul Mendlovitz (1985). "Approaches to global issues by local activists in the United States." Paper presented at the 26th annual convention of the International Studies Association, Washington, DC, March 4–6, 1985.
Blair, Harry (2000). "Participation and accountability at the periphery: democratic local governance in six countries." *World Development*, Vol. 28, No. 1, pp. 21–39.
Bontenbal, Marike (2009). "Understanding North–South municipal partnership conditions for capacity development: a Dutch–Peruvian example." *Habitat International*, Vol. 33, No. 1, pp. 100–5.
Börzel, Tanja A. (2002). "Pace-setting, foot-dragging, and fence-sitting: member state response to Europeanization." *Journal of Common Market Studies*, Vol. 40, No. 2, pp. 193–214.
Broadbent, Jeffrey (1998). *Environmental Politics in Japan: Networks of Power and Protest*. Cambridge, UK: Cambridge University Press.
Broadbent, Jeffrey (2002). "Japan's environmental regime: the political dynamics of

change." In U. Desai, ed., *Environmental Politics and Policy in Industrialized Countries*. Cambridge, MA: The MIT Press, pp. 295–355.

Broadbent, Jeffrey (2005). "Japan's environmental politics: recognition and response Processes." In H. Imura and M. Schreurs, eds., *Environmental Policy in Japan*. Washington, DC: Edward Elgar and the World Bank, pp. 102–34.

Calder, Kent E. (1988). *Crisis and Compensation: Public Policy and Political Stability in Japan, 1949–1986*. Princeton, NJ: Princeton University Press.

Citizens' International Plaza, CLAIR (2013). Database of International Cooperation Activities by Japanese Local Governments. Available from: www.plaza-clair.jp/jichitai/jichitai1-1.html [accessed August 27, 2013].

City of Kitakyushu, Bureau of the Environment (1998). *Kitakyūshū kōgai taisakushi* [Kitakyushu's history of pollution control measures]. Kitakyushu: City of Kitakyushu.

Cornwall, Andrea and John Gaventa (2000). "From users and choosers to makers and shapers: re-positioning participation in social policy." *IDS Bulletin*, Vol. 31, No. 4, pp. 50–62.

De Villiers, Jacobus Christian (2005). "Strategic alliances between communities, with special emphasis on the twinning of South African cities and towns with international partners." Ph.D. thesis, Graduate School of Business, University of Stellenbosch, 2005.

Drezner, Daniel W. (2001). "Globalization and policy convergence." *International Studies Review*, Vol. 3, No. 1, pp. 53–78.

Economic and Social Commission for Asia and the Pacific (ESCAP) (1999). *Local Government in Asia and the Pacific: A Comparative Analysis of Fifteen Countries*. Bangkok: ESCAP.

Evans, Peter B., Harold K. Jacobson, and Robert D. Putnam (1993). *Double-edged Diplomacy: International Bargaining and Domestic Politics*. Berkeley, CA: University of California Press.

Foljanty-Jost, Gesine (1995). *Ökonomie und ökologie in Japan: politik zwischen wachstum und umweltschutz*. Opladen: Leske & Budrich.

Foljanty-Jost, Gesine (2000). "Kankyō seisaku no seikō no jōken" [Conditions for the success of environmental policy]. *Leviathan*, Vol. 27, pp. 35–48.

Gant, Jon, Casey Ichniowski, and Kathryn Shaw (2002). "Social capital and organizational change in high-involvement and traditional work organizations." *Journal of Economics and Management Strategy*, Vol. 11, No. 2, pp. 289–328.

Gaventa, John (2001). *Toward Participatory Local Governance: Six Propositions for Discussion*. Brighton, UK: Institute of Development Studies.

Gourevitch, Peter (1978). "The second image reversed: the international sources of domestic politics." *International Organization*, Vol. 32, No. 4, pp. 881–912.

Green, Lara, Chris Game, and Simon Delay (2005). *Why Should My Local Authority Be Involved in an Overseas Project?* Birmingham, UK: Birmingham University, School of Public Policy.

Holzinger, Katharina, Christoph Knill, and Bas Arts, eds. (2008). *Environmental Governance in Europe: The Impact of International Institutions and Trade*. Cambridge, UK: Cambridge University Press, 2008.

Holzinger, Katharina, Christoph Knill, and Thomas Sommerer (2011). "Is there convergence of national environmental policies? An analysis of policy outputs in 24 OECD countries." *Environmental Politics*, Vol. 20, No. 1, pp. 20–41.

Hooghe, Liesbet (1995). "Sub-national mobilization in the European Union." *West European Politics*, Vol. 18, No. 3, pp. 175–98.

Huddle, Norie and Michael Reich (1975). *Island of Dreams: Environmental Crisis in Japan*. New York: Autumn Press.

Institute of Developing Economies (IDE), Japan External Trade Organization (2007). *Development of Environmental Policy in Japan and Asian Countries.* New York: Palgrave Macmillan.

International Council for Local Environmental Initiatives (ICLEI) (1993). *The Local Agenda 21 Initiative: ICLEI Guidelines for Local Agenda 21.* Freiburg: ICLEI.

International Council for Local Environmental Initiatives (ICLEI) (2008). *Local Governments for Sustainability.* Available from: www.iclei.org [accessed June 1, 2009].

International Energy Agency (IEA) (2007). *Energy Statistics of OECD Countries 2004–2005.* Paris: OECD/IEA.

International Lake Environment Committee Foundation (ILEC) (2009). *International Lake Environment Committee.* Available from: www.ilec.or.jp/eg/index.html [accessed December 20, 2009].

Jänicke, Martin (2005). "Trend-setters in environmental policy: the character and role of pioneer countries." *European Environment,* Vol. 15, pp. 129–42.

Japan, Environmental Agency (JEA) (1979). *Zenkoku kankyō gyōsei binran* [National list of environmental administration]. 1979 ed. Tokyo: JEA.

Japan, Environmental Agency (JEA) (1982). *White Paper on the Environment.* Tokyo: Printing Office of the Ministry of Finance.

Japan, Environmental Agency (JEA) (1990). *White Paper on the Environment.* Tokyo: Printing Office of the Ministry of Finance.

Japan, Environmental Agency (JEA) (1994). *Quality of the Environment in Japan 1994.* Available from: www.env.go.jp/en/wpaper/1994/index.html [accessed December 26, 2009].

Japan, Environmental Agency (JEA) (1997). *Kankyō ni yasashii kigyō kōdō chōsa* [Survey on environment-friendly business practices]. 1996 ed. Tokyo: JEA.

Japan, Environmental Agency (JEA) (1998). *Zenkoku kankyō gyōsei binran* [National list of environmental administration]. 1998 ed. Tokyo: JEA.

Japan, Ministry of Economy, Trade and Industry (JMETI) (2007). *Kikōhendō o meguru kokusai dōkō ni tsuite* [International trends in climate change]. Tokyo: METI.

Japan, Ministry of the Environment (JMOE) (1994). *Quality of the Environment in Japan 1994.* Available from: www.env.go.jp/en/wpaper/1994/index.html [accessed December 26, 2009].

Japan, Ministry of the Environment (JMOE) (2006). *Japanese Official Assistance in the Environmental Field.* Available from: www.env.go.jp/earth/coop/coop/images/pdf [accessed December 14, 2009].

Japan, Ministry of the Environment (JMOE) (2007). The Basic Environmental Law, Act No. 91 of 1993. Available from: www.env.go.jp/en/laws/policy/basic/ch2-3.html#section6 [accessed December 22, 2009].

Japan, Ministry of the Environment (JMOE) (2009). *Basic Environment Plan* (reference). Available from: www.env.go.jp/en/policy/plan/basic/referenc.html [accessed December 26, 2009].

Japan, Ministry of Foreign Affairs (JMOFA) (2001). *Japan's Official Development Assistance.* Available from: www.mofa.go.jp/policy/oda/white/2001/contents.pdf [accessed December 23, 2009].

Japan, Overseas Environmental Cooperation Center (JOECC) (2003). *Chihō kōkyōdantai ni yoru kokusai kankyō kyōryoku shiryōshū* [A database of international environmental cooperation by local governments]. Tokyo: JOECC.

Kameyama, Yasuko (2002). "Climate change and Japan." *Asia-Pacific Review,* Vol. 9, No. 1, pp. 33–44.

Kameyama, Yasuko (2004). "Evaluation and future of the Kyoto Protocol: Japan's perspective." *International Review for Environmental Strategies*, Vol. 5, No. 1, pp. 71–82.

Katzenstein, Peter (1976). "International relations and domestic structures: foreign economic policies of the advanced industrial states." *International Organization*, Vol. 30, No. 1, pp. 1–45.

Kawashima, Yasuko (2000). "Japan's decision-making about climate change problems: comparative study of decisions in 1990 and 1997." *Environmental Economics and Policy Studies*, Vol. 3, pp. 29–57.

Kitakyushu Initiative Network, Secretariat (KINS) (2008). *Kitakyushu Initiative for a Clean Environment*. Available from: http://kitakyushu.iges.or.jp/cities/index.html [accessed December 21, 2009].

Kitakyushu International Techno-cooperative Association (KITA) (2001). *KITA nijyū-nen shi* [Twenty-year history of KITA]. Kitakyushu: KITA.

Kotani, Hiroya (2006). *Jidenteki kokusai kosho kankyo iinkai ron* [Autobiographical account of the International Lake Environment Committee]. Unpublished, 2006.

Krauss, Ellis S. and Bradford L. Simcock (1980). "Citizens' movements: the growth and impact of environmental protest in Japan." In Kurt Steiner, Ellis Krauss, and Scott Flanagan, eds., *Political Opposition and Local Politics in Japan*. Princeton, NJ: Princeton University Press, pp. 187–227.

Kyoto Shinbun (2010). "Sekai no Biwako e" [Lake Biwa for a globalized world]. May 11, 2010.

Learne, Geoffrey W.G. (1991). "Environmental contracts: a lesson in democracy from the Japanese." *U.B.C. Law Review*, Vol. 25, pp. 361–85.

Lieffernik, Duncan, Bas Arts, Jelmer Kamstra, and Jeroen Ooijevaar (2009). "Leaders and laggards in environmental policy: a quantitative analysis of domestic policy outputs." *Journal of European Public Policy*, Vol. 16, No. 5, pp. 677–700.

Litfin, Karen T. (2000). "Advocacy coalitions along the domestic-foreign frontier: globalization and Canadian climate change policy." *Policy Studies Journal*, Vol. 28, No. 1, pp. 236–52.

MacDougall, Terry E. (1980). "Political opposition and big cities elections in Japan, 1947–1975." In Kurt Steiner, Ellis Krauss, and Scott Flanagan, eds., *Political Opposition and Local Politics in Japan*. Princeton, NJ: Princeton University Press, 1980, pp. 55–94.

McKean, Margaret A. (1981). *Environmental Protest and Citizen Politics in Japan*. Berkeley, CA: University of California Press.

Mani, Muthukumara and David Wheeler (1998). "In search of pollution havens? Dirty industry in the world economy, 1960–1995." *Journal of Environment and Development*, Vol. 7, No. 3, pp. 215–47.

Marks, Gary (1993). "Structural policy and multi-level governance in the EC." In A. Cafruny and G. Rosenthal, eds., *The State of the European Community, Vol. 2: The Maastricht Debates and Beyond*. Boulder, CO: Lynne Reinner, pp. 391–410.

Marks, Gary, François Nielsen, Leonard Ray, and Jane Salk (1996). "Competencies, cracks and conflicts: regional mobilization in the European Union." *Comparative Political Studies*, Vol. 29, No. 2, pp. 164–92.

Matsuno, Yu (2005). "Local government, industry and pollution control agreements." In H. Imura and M.A. Schreurs, eds., *Environmental Policy in Japan*. Cheltenham, UK: Edward Elgar, pp. 215–48.

Mlinar, Zdravko (1995). "Local responses to global change." *Annals of the American Academy of Political and Social Science*, Vol. 540, pp. 145–56.

Muramatsu, Michio (1975). "The impact of economic growth policies on local politics in Japan." *Asian Survey*, Vol. 15, No. 9, pp. 799–816.
Narumi, Masayasu (1969). "Gigyō to bōshi keiyaku teiketsu" [Industry and pollution control agreements]. In Atsushi Satō and Michio Nishihara, eds., *Kōgai Taisaku* [Pollution countermeasures], Vol. 1. Tokyo: Yūhikaku, pp. 335–48.
Olson, Mancur (1965). *The Logic of Collective Action: Public Goods and the Theory of Groups*. Cambridge, MA: Harvard University Press.
Olson, Mancur and Richard Zeckhauser (1966). "An economic theory of alliances." *Review of Economics and Statistics*, Vol. 48, No. 3, pp. 266–79.
Organisation for Economic Co-operation and Development (OECD) (2009). *OECD Factbook 2009: Economic, Environmental and Social Statistics*. Paris: OECD.
Oshitani, Shizuka (2006). *Global Warming Policy in Japan and Britain: Interactions between Institutions and Issue Characteristics*. Manchester, UK: Manchester University Press.
Parry, Martin L., Osvaldo F. Canziani, Jean P. Palutikof, Paul J. van der Linden, and Clair E. Hanson, eds. (2007). *Contribution of Working Group II to the Fourth Assessment Report of the Intergovernmental Panel on Climate Change*. Cambridge, UK: Cambridge University Press.
Piattoni, Simona (2005). "Multi-level governance: sfide analitiche, empiriche, normative." *Rivista Italiana di Scienza Politica*, Vol. 35, No. 3, pp. 417–45.
Potter, David (1994). "Assessing Japan's environmental aid policy." *Pacific Affairs*, Vol. 67, No. 2, pp. 200–15.
Putnam, Robert D. (1988). "Diplomacy and domestic politics: the logic of two-level games." *International Organization*, Vol. 42, No. 3, pp. 427–60.
Reed, Steven (1981). "Environmental politics: some reflections based on the Japanese case." *Comparative Politics*, Vol. 13, No. 3, pp. 253–69.
Reich, Michael R. (1984). "Mobilizing for environmental policy in Italy and Japan." *Comparative Politics*, Vol. 16, No. 4, pp. 379–402.
Ren, Yong (2005). "Japan's environmental management experiences." In H. Imura and M. Schreurs, eds., *Environmental Policy in Japan*. Washington, DC: Edward Elgar and the World Bank, pp. 287–314.
Rosenau, James (1997). *Along the Domestic-Foreign Frontier: Exploring Governance in a Turbulent World*. Cambridge, UK: Cambridge University Press.
Schreurs, Miranda A. (2002). *Environmental Politics in Japan, Germany and the United States*. Cambridge, UK: Cambridge University Press.
Shuman, Michael (1994). *Toward a Global Village: International Community Development Initiatives*. London: Pluto.
Takeuchi, Keiji (1998). *Chikyū ondanka no seijigaku* [Politics of global warming]. Tokyo: Asahi shinbunsha.
Tanabe, Toshiaki (1999). *Chikyū ondanka to kankyō gaikō* [Global warming and environmental diplomacy]. Tokyo: Jijitsūshin sha.
Tjandradewi, Bernadia and Peter J. Marcotullio (2009). "City-to-city networks: Asian perspectives on key elements and areas for success." *Habitat International*, Vol. 33, pp. 165–72.
Uchihashi, Katsuto (1995). *Kyōsei no daichi atarashii keizai ga hajimaru* [The great land of cohabitation]. Tokyo: Iwanami Shoten.
UN Conference on Environment and Development (UNCED) (1992). *Agenda 21*, Rio de Janeiro: UNCED, June 3–14, 1992. Available from: www.un.org/esa/sustdev/documents/agenda21/english/adenda21toc.htm [accessed June 5, 2009].
UN Framework Convention on Climate Change (UNFCCC) (1997). FCCC/AGBM/1997/

Misc.1/Add.6, 23 October 1997. Available from: http://unfccc.int/cop4/resource/docs/1997/agbm/misc01a06.htm [accessed August 23, 2011].

United Cities and Local Governments (UCLG) (2004). "Press Kit," 2004 World Urban Forum Barcelona, September 13–17, 2004.

United Nations (UN) (2005). *UN General Assembly 2005 World Summit Outcome*. New York: United Nations.

Upham, Frank (1976). "Litigation and moral consciousness in Japan: an interpretative analysis of four Japanese pollution suits." *Law and Society Review*, Vol. 10, No. 4, pp. 579–619.

Vogel, David (1990). "Environmental policy in Japan and West Germany." Paper presented at the annual meeting of the Western Political Science Association, Newport Beach, CA, March 1990.

Waltz, Kenneth N. (1959). *Man, the State, and War: A Theoretical Analysis*. New York: Columbia University Press.

2 The rigidity of Japan's nuclear energy policy
State-centric gate-keeping

This chapter presents the first test case that will examine the traditional state-centric coordination of government policy. Nuclear energy in Japan has been a strong top-down national undertaking, establishing a division of labor among levels of government with a state-centric gate-keeping capacity (a state's capacity to influence policy decisions at sub-national levels of government). The key aim of state-centric policy coordination is to effectively control progress at sub-national levels and ensure aggregate progress at the national scale and further within the context of international obligations. Central-local relations are institutionalized to clarify sub-national roles in achieving national goals and extend incentives as well as giving tutelage towards sub-national governments. Sub-national actors are expected primarily to play an implementation role in achieving national targets. The issue area of nuclear energy, however, is the most complex of all; state-centric coordination occurs both within and across policy subsystems.[1] As far as issues of nuclear energy are concerned, the foreign policy, industrial policy, energy and environmental protection subsystems are closely related to each other. The actions of actors from these subsystems are causally linked to each other. The nuclear energy policy subsystem in Japan has largely been nested within another subsystem, namely, industrial policy, and partially overlapped with other subsystems, especially environmental protection and foreign policy. Overlapping subsystem boundaries are thus presumed to affect policy coordination while the success of policy coordination requires the policy beliefs of political actors to be congruent with each other.[2] The situation of nuclear energy generation is further complicated when dealing with nuclear security, which automatically brings international-level attention to domestic issues. According to the advocacy coalition framework (ACF), policy change can be the result of shocking events, both internal and external to the policy subsystem.[3] It appears that neither the Fukushima meltdowns (an internal subsystem event or failures in subsystem practices) nor the consequent change in public opinion (an external subsystem event or public preference in favor of a nuclear phase-out) changed the policy beliefs of the dominant pro-nuclear coalition. Consequently, Shinzo Abe declared a nuclear phase-out would be irresponsible for the resource-poor nation.

The catastrophic Fukushima accident in March 2011 led to a review of the safety of nuclear power plants worldwide. In the aftermath, Germany permanently shut down eight of its reactors and pledged to close all of the country's 17 reactors by 2022. Switzerland also announced plans to phase out its reactors operation by 2034. In June 2011 Italians voted against a return to nuclear energy in a national referendum, cancelling a law that would allow for the construction of new reactors. In the United States (US), on the other hand, the Energy Policy Act of 2005 created incentives such as loan guarantees and tax credits to promote reactor construction and the United Kingdom (UK) government also decided in 2008 to support the building of new nuclear power stations. In these pro-nuclear energy countries, however, little progress has been made towards building new nuclear power stations and the building of new reactors in the world's most nuclear-dependent country, France, is being delayed due to rising costs in a post-Fukushima safety climate. While there is continued growth in nuclear energy production and use in non-OECD Asia, following the Fukushima catastrophe, even China suspended the approval of all new reactors until the completion of a nuclear-safety review. In Japan, however, Shinzo Abe's Liberal Democratic Party (LDP) government has stubbornly shown its eagerness for idle reactors to be restarted against a public opinion that has remained largely opposed to it due to nuclear safety fears following the Fukushima disaster.

The opposition Democratic Party of Japan (DPJ), which was in power during the time of the Fukushima disaster, had pledged to phase out nuclear power generation. By September 2013, all 54 of the country's commercial reactors were offline. On April 11, 2014, Abe's Cabinet officially reversed the DPJ's decision by adopting a new Basic Energy Plan that would push for restarting the idled reactors.[4] This new plan declared nuclear energy as "an important source of base-load electricity supply." Currently 24 reactors are in the process of restart approvals, which are required to meet the upgraded safety standards of the Nuclear Regulatory Authority (NRA). In August 2015, Japan put its first nuclear reactor, the Sendai 1 reactor, back into operation under new safety rules. Japan's government plans to raise the share of nuclear power generation back to 20–22 percent by 2030 while also "working to reduce nuclear dependence as much as possible."

Before the Fukushima Daiichi meltdowns, the Japanese government had promoted nuclear energy as "safe, cheap and able to reduce CO_2 emissions in the fight against climate change." By then there was an established knowledge of the costs and the safety of nuclear energy that was credible in both policy-makers' and scientists' eyes in Japan. Researchers had initiated a series of pioneering research projects on this topic and consolidated the literature into a body of empirically solid findings indicating that nuclear power generation is more costly than coal, hydro and gas.[5] The cost items of nuclear energy generation, as found in the literature, are extremely complex, accounting for generation costs, decommissioning/waste disposal costs, capital costs (research and development and site preparation), and external costs to society (insurance and compensation for nuclear accidents). Following the Fukushima accident, the Cost Review Committee of the government's Energy and Environment Council estimated generation costs for 2010 to be ¥8.9 per kWh (11.4 US cents), which was one and a half times higher than the Ministry of International Trade and Industry (MITI)'s estimate for 1999.[6] This newest estimate included additional costs for post-Fukushima safety measures, government policy expenses, and future nuclear risk reduction. In 2012 the Japanese government virtually nationalized Tokyo Electronic Power Co. (TEPCO) with a one trillion yen ($9.59 billion) injection of public funds and subsequently added more taxpayer money for the compensation, decontamination, and decommissioning of the Fukushima Daiichi plant. It thus became clear that nuclear power was not viable without government subsidies. In December 2012 the LDP won a landslide victory in a House of Representatives election, ejecting the DPJ from power after three years. On April 11, 2014, Abe's Cabinet decided to break away from the energy strategy, initiated in 2012 by the DPJ government, to phase out nuclear power and push for the restart of reactors. Why does the conservative government take an unyielding pro-nuclear stance against public concerns? This chapter identifies the causal mechanisms of policy transformation to answer this question.

What accounts for the patterns and nature of Japan's nuclear energy policy? Traditionally, the literature described energy policy in Japan as dominated by what Jeffrey Broadbent calls the "ruling triad" or three main actors of the pro-growth coalition.[7] Japanese leaders were reluctant to equate environmental risk with a potential failure in nuclear energy policy and most scholars also did not focus on the environmental risks of nuclear energy, but rather on the industrial contributions of nuclear energy. Richard Samuels explained the transformation of Japan's nuclear energy policy as a continual process of negotiation and coordination between the bureaucracy and private industry.[8] In this process, a bureaucratic turf war was highlighted for control over jurisdiction and budgets[9] and a single veto player, the dominant LDP, allowed utilities to charge consumers and subsidized loans for nuclear energy development,[10] while anti-nuclear energy activism activities hardly moved outside the host communities where nuclear power plants were to be located.[11] In the early 1990s, due to growing opposition in Japan to nuclear energy, some began to argue that the influence of "outside forces" must not be underestimated.[12] The debate following the aftermath of the Fukushima disaster has revolved around the future role of nuclear power in Japan's energy policy and many argue that a transformation of energy systems is required to overcome domestic obstacles.[13] Studies of Japan's nuclear energy policy generated a wealth of institutional detail, yet individually they were not suited to the task of either identifying the factors that determine differences and similarities across countries in the patterns and nature of nuclear energy policy or examining the factors that cause policy change, as there is an increasing gap between public preference and government responsiveness in nuclear energy policy.

This chapter will combine the dimensions of collective action (ACF) with the more static forms of institutional access (political opportunity structures—POS) to help identify the causal variables and mechanisms that explain nuclear energy policy in different domestic structures. Political opportunity structures are not always stable, changing political environments, such as unstable political alignments and divided elites, provide a greater potential to alter the levels and patterns of institutional access to policy-makers in the policy subsystem, while the interaction of actors and structures may recreate the access levels and patterns. The predominance of economic over environmental concerns in Japan's nuclear energy policy reflects the distribution of power within the government. The power of the Japanese economic bureaucracy extends into nuclear energy policy yet a long-term process of political realignment since the early 1990s would seem to have changed the nature of the resources and constraints external to the policy subsystem of nuclear energy.

External subsystem events or shocks also define a broader political environment and they are necessary but not sufficient for policy change.[14] Types of external events, such as "socio-economic conditions" and "public opinion," which are identified by the ACF, are fluid, unstable, and always changing. It is not clear under what conditions they are sufficient to account for policy change. Crises and disasters, whether external or internal to the policy subsystem, may abruptly bring about changes in economic conditions or turn public opinion against current policy. The electoral process may further link the changing tide of public preference to policy changes. The specific causal link between external/internal events and policy change can vary from one case to another.

Finally, factors, internal to coalitions, such as different self-interests of individual groups within a coalition, deserve closer examination. The ACF assumes that core beliefs hold advocacy coalitions together and do not change easily. However, such policy core beliefs can be unstable within an advocacy coalition as material groups, such as utility companies in nuclear energy policy, seek their own material gains.[15] In other words, there is a potential for policy change due to internal subsystem factors. We need to examine the ways in which the self-interests of groups, rather than their normative commitment, come first in explaining the intra-decision-making and maintenance of an advocacy coalition.

International structural factors

Public policy is made increasingly in both a domestic and an international environment. "Dynamic system events" at the international level do matter,[16] especially in nuclear energy policy, in the sense that foreign pressures influence domestic opportunity structures (that affect the resources and constraints of the subsystem actors) or affect variations in how domestic political systems meet social demands.[17] Foreign pressures can alter the nature and patterns of institutional access at the domestic level regarding actors who seek their policy beliefs and mobilize their skills and resources in forming coalitions with allies.[18] However, it is important to note that, in the absence of centralized authority at the international level, foreign pressure may have a limited capacity to impose its wishes on national and sub-national actors. The subsystem coalition that remains in power may seek to manipulate the anarchic nature of international structures in order to achieve their domestic objectives over time. Japan has pretty much behaved as submissive to US foreign policy wishes, requests, and demands, but has sometimes broken ranks with the US.

Japan's nuclear energy policy became linked with US foreign policy in order to contain the Soviet Union in the context of the emerging Cold War. In 1949 as US President Harry S. Truman announced that the Soviets now also possessed an atomic bomb, a bilateral nuclear arms race began. In the same year, the US Senate was able to add an amendment to the 1946 Atomic Energy Law to the agenda, in order to permit the commercialization of nuclear technology with a foreign partner yet keep nuclear technology under control in the US power bloc.[19] At the end of 1952, a new US President, Dwight D. Eisenhower, was elected to power and, in December 1953, he gave a speech, "Atoms for Peace," at the General Assembly of the United Nations (UN). The US government officially changed its policy about the control of nuclear science and technology in order to spread the benefits of its peaceful application at home and abroad. Eisenhower's intent was to distribute nuclear technology know-how with strict US supervision. Once the Korean War broke out in 1950, the Japanese government faced US officials' push for a large-scale Japanese rearmament (based on conventional military capabilities) to ease the military burden of the US in East Asia; however, it was clear that there had been no consideration by US officials about supplying its former wartime enemy Japan with nuclear weapons technology. But Japan had become an important ally, supplying a staging point for American military operations into Northeast Asia and the Russian Far East. It became necessary for the US military to sustain US nuclear force capabilities wherever required, even on Japanese soil.[20]

The structural factor at the international level was a necessary condition but not a sufficient one for determining the course of Japan's nuclear energy policy, while imposing and opening opportunities for domestic actors. Before the end of the Allied Occupation in 1952, conservative Diet members, such as Yasuhiro Nakasone, who already considered nuclear power as a viable option for the nation to ensure energy supplies, had petitioned the US government to allow Japan to develop a nuclear industry.[21] Nakasone believed that the self-sustaining fuel cycle of nuclear energy was necessary for the resource-poor nation.[22] In 1951 it was reported that Nakasone requested that John Foster Dulles, US Secretary of State, not ban Japan's nuclear research in the peace treaty negotiations.[23] In the early 1950s, the Yoshida administration repeatedly asked the US government for electric-power loans to reduce electricity shortages to aid Japan's reconstruction and eventually applied directly to the US Export-Import Bank and the International Bank for Reconstruction and Development (later known as the World Bank).[24] Extended loans to Japanese utilities were primarily used to import thermal-power generation equipment from the Westinghouse and General Electric (GE) companies and thus encourage US exports. After the loans, Japanese utilities were able to directly deal with these US suppliers who were destined to manufacture nuclear reactors.

Eisenhower's "Atoms for Peace" speech at the UN generated expectations among Japanese conservative politicians and utilities about what would follow to help Japan secure a stable source of energy. At the end of 1953, the US government launched an "Atoms for Peace" program that supplied nuclear equipment and technology to its allied nations. In March 1954, three conservative parties led by Yasuhiro Nakasone jointly submitted a 1954 budget to the House of Representatives, in order to revise the initial budget to add a new item for nuclear development that passed without any viable deliberation. The budget item was initially allocated to build an indigenous experimental reactor.[25] On November 14, 1955, however, the Japanese government signed the US–Japan nuclear cooperation agreement on the peaceful use of nuclear fuel for experimental US reactors. Under the agreement, the US government supplied Japan with two research reactors, subject to the condition under which used enriched uranium had to be returned to the US to prevent Japan from fuel reprocessing. This development set a clear direction that favored the use of established foreign equipment and technology.

Probably, the most noteworthy factor at the behavioral level was Matsutarō Shōriki's capacity to introduce Japan's first commercial nuclear power plant imported from the UK against US wishes, although Japan eventually switched to US-made light water reactors. Shōriki was well known as a staunch anti-communist media magnate who ran the *Yomiuri Shinbun* newspaper and the Nippon Television Network Service. Both the Central Intelligence Agency (CIA) and the US Defense Department needed to exploit Shōriki's media network as part of an anti-communism campaign in Japan. The Cold War structure allowed him to first negotiate with CIA agents and the US Information Service (USIS), in order to promote nuclear power in Japan. On March 1, 1954, a Japanese tuna fishing boat, the Daigo Fukuryū Maru (No. 5 Lucky Dragon) was exposed to radioactive fallout from a US hydrogen-bomb test on Bikini Atoll, soon after the US government began to supply nuclear technology to its allied nations. This incident evoked anti-nuclear sentiment among Japanese people. In order to create a favorable image in the public towards nuclear energy, the CIA and the USIS turned to the Shōriki's networks.[26]

By the mid-1950s, Japan's initial institutional setting over nuclear energy began to take a centralized shape under the eye of the prime minister. In December 1955, the Japanese government passed the Atomic Energy Basic Law, creating the Japan Atomic Energy Commission (JAEC) attached to the Prime Minister's Office to oversee the introduction of nuclear energy to Japan. Shōriki was elected as a Diet member of the House of Representatives in February 1955. He then became the first head of the JAEC who was responsible for the introduction of the first commercial reactor, and he was also appointed director of the newly established Science and Technology Agency (STA), which operated under the aegis of the JAEC. Despite the US–Japan nuclear cooperation agreement of 1955, the US government required an additional agreement between the two nations to impose further conditions on the future use of enriched uranium on which US-made power reactors would run in Japan. By contrast, the British option became more favorable regarding the earlier introduction of commercial nuclear reactors in Japan, as the UK-built Calder Hall type reactors ran on natural uranium yet were initially designed for the production of plutonium for nuclear weapons. Pro-nuclear Shōriki pushed forward his proposal to install a Calder Hall nuclear plant, although the Ministry of Foreign Affairs persuaded him to reconsider this option, given Japan's dependence on the militarized US for defence.[27] In October 1957, the UK experienced the worst nuclear accident in its history, known as the Windscale reactor fire. It appeared that the Calder Hall type reactors were clearly unsafe in earthquake-prone countries such as Japan. However, immediate utility and benefits of nuclear energy outweighed nuclear safety considerations; the UK–Japan nuclear agreement was thus concluded in June 1958. Meanwhile, the Soviet Union launched the world's first nuclear power plant in 1954; by September 1956, it was reported by the CIA that there was a high probability the Soviet Union would propose a nuclear energy program to Japan in international nuclear commerce as it had done to Egypt, India, Indonesia, and Iran.[28] Later that same month, US EAC Chair Lewis Strauss informed Japan's nuclear energy investigation representation that the US government would remove the confidentiality clauses attached to the delivery of power reactors for non-military use in Japan. By 1957 the Japanese government had a contract to purchase 20 US-made light water reactors.[29]

In the late 1950s, as discussed below in detail, a private sector-led pro-nuclear coalition took shape in Japan, utilizing government funding yet avoiding government control. Despite the state-centric institution of nuclear programs, Shōriki, who was determined to promote private companies seeking market entry into nuclear commerce against state-dominated operations, acted as an intermediary for requests from Keidanren (Japan Business Federation), a peak body for business lobbying, and the Japanese utilities pursuing the immediate commercialization of foreign reactor technology. As Japanese private industry was eager to get ready-for-use nuclear power plants, the major US manufacturers of electrical machines, unlike the CIA and the Pentagon, consistently sought the opening of a large market in Japan and strongly supported the entry of private businesses into the public sector-proposed market in Japan. US–Japan relations consequently saw the emergence of a transnational inter-corporate coalition for technology transfer between each of Japan's nuclear power industrial groups and a foreign supplier of nuclear technology.[30] As explained in another section of this chapter, Shōriki and the private utilities successfully made a deal with the Finance Ministry, while Japan's nuclear power plants would be operated privately. The ministry accepted the financial responsibility of the state for any indemnifications in excess of the fixed sum for accidents.[31] This event marked a private business-initiated pro-nuclear coalition, in cooperation with foreign partners.

The revised US–Japan nuclear cooperation agreement of 1968 ensured that the uranium and plutonium would be supplied with the safeguards carried out by the International Atomic Energy Agency (IAEA). In 1976 Democrat Jimmy Carter won the US presidency and brought his personal ideology to US foreign policy. He instituted a strict policy to control the spread of fissile materials. He was determined to deny even the US's closest non-nuclear allies, including Japan, access to these materials. All of that changed immediately after Republican Ronald Reagan's presidential election in 1980. Ronald Reagan reversed the Carter doctrine, which had banned the US from using plutonium for civilian use with its allies. Accordingly, the US–Japan nuclear cooperation of 1987 allowed

Japan to introduce a program for reprocessing and transporting plutonium while reserving the US's right to halt the Japanese plutonium program due to national security concerns. Nuclear technology, which has dual-use potential for military and civilian uses, thus poses structural constraints on nuclear energy policy.

Scientific and technical constraints

Nuclear energy policy is guided by the basic attributes of nuclear energy. These basic attributes are known in the ACF as "relatively stable parameters," which are claimed to be very difficult to change and thus impose constant constraints on, yet hardly become the subject of coalition strategies.[32] Nuclear power generation is non-dispatchable in the sense that sources of nuclear-generated electricity cannot be turned on or off at the request of power grid operators. As nuclear power plants do not power up quickly, their power output cannot be adjusted to a fluctuating demand. In theory, nuclear-generated electricity needs to provide the base-load up to night-time demand; otherwise it wastes a great deal of energy. This technological limit can be circumvented by exporting nuclear-generated electricity as France does with about 15 percent of its nuclear-generated electricity being exported to neighboring countries. Yet there is no such option for the island nation of Japan. Although Japan is dependent on imports of fossil fuels from overseas, the technical limits suggest that nuclear energy does not automatically become the only viable option for the resource-poor nation to ensure energy supplies. There are thus specific structural limits on the expansion of Japan's nuclear power generation (accounting for about 30 percent of the country's electricity before Fukushima).

Nevertheless, the basic attributes of nuclear energy could become the focus of coalition strategies in attaining or revising policy objectives, while nuclear technology is in a process of invention and ongoing re-invention in the longer term. The new specificity and uncertainty of scientific information may affect configurations of resources for coalition-building. Especially, since the policy core beliefs of nuclear issues are deeply divided and even irreconcilable, the politicization of science and technology is inevitable.[33] As uncertainty, inherent in the complexity of advanced nuclear technology, increases, it is unrealistic to consider the attributes of nuclear energy as a "stable system parameter" as the ACF may suggest. We need to examine the ways by which scientific knowledge and technology shape the channels and political opportunities offered to coalition-building and cross-coalition interaction.

Japan is a resource-poor country lacking necessary domestic reserves of natural resources, and it must import most of its energy resources, including uranium, to meet its energy needs. There were concerns about the long-term supply and potential shortage of uranium and a plutonium-fueled breeder appeared to be a way to resolve these concerns. During World War II, the idea of fast-breeder technology was raised by scientists in the US atomic bomb program. If reactors produce more plutonium than they consume, then they are regarded as fast breeder reactors (FBR). For the past seven decades, several countries, including Japan, have had development programs, aiming to pursue the FBR to solve issues with long-term energy supply. But advanced nuclear technology is increasingly uncertain as many already designed reactors remain net consumers of plutonium. To build its nuclear infrastructure quickly, Japan's government aimed to achieve a fully independent, closed fuel cycle, which the resource-poor nation adopted in the 1960s.[34] FBRs, which were expected to be net producers of plutonium, were considered to be the key technology in nuclear fuel recycling in Japan. The fast breeder reactor Monju was the experimental facility of the fuel cycle project along with the fuel reprocessing plant in Rokkasho. Yet in the aftermath of the sodium leak and cover-ups of the Monju incident in 1995, the fast breeder reactor commercialization had been postponed far into the future while the Rokkasho plant was unable to reprocess spent reactor waste as its full operation had been postponed due to a series of problems. As a result, the Rokkasho plant had functioned as a "temporary" nuclear waste storage facility. The nuclear fuel cycle required the chain progression of differing stages so that a single stage failure would have a domino effect on others. The Japanese government was unable to easily give up any fuel cycle project. In the view of utility companies, fuel reprocessing was clearly a loss-making business but Rokkasho was a de facto nuclear storage for those companies. The utility industry was not in a position to stop the fuel reprocessing project and unavoidably shared the expenses with the government. While allowing the utility industry less costly offshore fuel reprocessing, the government chose to press ahead with plutonium utilization in existing light water reactor designs. These actions continue to demonstrate the rigidity of Japan's nuclear policy and partially accounts for Shinzo Abe's stubborn eagerness for idled reactors to be restarted against the odds of public opinion after Fukushima.

The dominant pro-nuclear coalition at early formative stages

Why did Japan build nuclear plants in earthquake and tsunami prone areas in the first place? The initial answer lies in the formation of the pro-nuclear advocacy coalition in Japan. Economic growth in modern Japan was portrayed as a case of "techno-nationalism."[35] In post-WWII Japan, both conservative politicians and national bureaucrats often emphasized the importance of technological autonomy for national security, while initially depending on science and technology developed in other countries. Techno-nationalists believed that Japan's autonomous technological capacity would lay the foundations for its prosperity and security. The pro-nuclear coalition actors' bottom-line value was energy security based on Japan's autonomous technological capacity. The bottom-line value held pro-nuclear coalition actors together and represented something worthy of pursuit not only to policy elites in nuclear energy policy but also to those in other policy areas as well. According to the ACF, the paradigmatic belief legitimizing the actors' pursuit of these values can be seen as "deep core beliefs" at the broadest level and is thus very difficult to change.[36] Towards the end of the Allied Occupation in Japan, Nakasone already claimed that technologically driven nationalism would be a way to achieve Japan's restoration to the world stage.[37] In contrast, "policy core beliefs" are policy-specific or subsystem-wide in scope and involve fundamental policy choices.[38] The Japanese government had indeed promoted nuclear energy as a "safe and cheap" form of energy. In the early 1990s, it began to claim that clean nuclear energy would be able to address the problem of climate change while contributing to the Japanese economy. These beliefs were expected to represent normative commitments, bind the pro-nuclear coalition together in the policy subsystem and seek to materialize beliefs into nuclear energy policy. If it occurs, policy change is likely when dealing with policy core beliefs at the policy subsystem level as well as "secondary beliefs" at the narrower operational level of regulatory/promotional instruments or implementation designs.[39]

The key ally status that the United States had bestowed on Japan provided an opportunity to undertake nuclear policy formation while conservative politicians sought to ensure energy and private utilities were dealing with power shortages to catch up with Japan's postwar reconstruction. The initial stage of the pro-nuclear coalition revolved around the developmental value of nuclear energy, leaving behind its environmental risks. The Science Council of Japan, a peak body of the academic community, strongly opposed the 1954 budget approval and expressed its concern by emphasizing the importance of the basic research.[40] However, Japanese business leaders, with assistance from allied conservative politicians, responded to the Atoms for Peace speech in December 1953 as a business opportunity to regroup the old *zaibatsu* whose banking system was not affected by the Allied Occupation policy of *zaibatsu* dismemberment and remained intact.[41] To overcome their dependence on US special procurements from the Korean War, they pursued the rapid expansion of private investment in capital-intensive industries, one of which was the nuclear energy industry.[42] In the late 1950s, there subsequently emerged five major nuclear business groups in the equipment and engineering industry. Each group aligned with a foreign source of nuclear technology: Mitsubishi Atomic Power Industries–Westinghouse, Sumitomo Atomic Energy Industries–United Nuclear, Japan Atomic Energy Enterprise Co. (Toshiba/Mitsui)–General Electric (GE), Tokyo Atomic Industry Research Institute (Hitachi/Nissan)–GE, and First Atomic Power Industry Group (FAPIG-Daiichi)–Nuclear Power Group. While the Keidanren actively lobbied for the Japanese government to develop Japan's nuclear energy industry under the leadership of the business community, in March 1956 the Japan Atomic Industry Forum (JAIF), an association of suppliers and industrial buyers of nuclear energy, was established to take the direction of nuclear power development into their own hands.[43]

The Japanese electric utility industry was a pro-nuclear advocate from the beginning. In the mid-1950s, power utility companies had to have a strategy to overcome power shortages for Japan's postwar reconstruction and thus nuclear energy was becoming an attractive option as an alternative source.[44] The Japan Atomic Energy Research Institute (JAERI), which was established in 1956 under the jurisdiction of the STA to receive the two research reactors from the US, further decided to purchase a prototype Boiling Water Reactor (BWR) from GE. In October 1963 this GE demonstration reactor was the first to produce electricity in Japan while also providing information about commercializing foreign reactor technology. Private industry, led by the JIAF, accordingly sought access to the technology. It also requested state funding for commercialization and thus tried to minimize capital investment. As the utility industry was moving fast to commercialize it, the JAEC decided to import the British Calder Hall reactor, a large-scale commercialized magnox-type reactor. The MITI attempted to gain control over the Calder Hall importation through its state agency Electric Power Development Co., Ltd (EPDC).[45] To receive this reactor, however, the Japan Atomic Power Company (JAPCO) was created in 1957 in favor of the private utilities, with the investment ratio of 20 percent and 80 percent, government (EPDC) and private sector.[46] It is important to note here that the Keidanren and its allied politicians successfully prevented the MITI from establishing its formal jurisdiction over nuclear power R&D while private industry also deflected MITI's ambitions for the control of reactor importation. At the same time, according to the 1961 Atomic Power Indemnification Law, private industry successfully avoided full financial responsibility for accidents, as any indemnification over five billion yen would become the government's responsibility.[47] Early coalition-building was thus taking place in the pro-nuclear mechanism of interest representation by conservative politicians and industry groups that linked the economic environment to the political system. In the policy subsystem of nuclear energy, the autonomy of big business largely dictated the terms of agreement between sectors at the early stage of pro-nuclear coalition-building.

When the JAPCO finally got Calder Hall on line in 1966, the academic community condemned a range of issues from budget blowouts through major design problems to construction delays. Understandably, in 1963 the JAPCO had already decided to choose a US-designed light water reactor as Japan's second commercial reactor.[48] Since the disastrous fiscal experience of Calder Hall, only light water reactors have been constructed in Japan; three such commercialized reactors came, for the first time, on line in 1970. The utility companies purchased reactor designs from US suppliers and built them with the co-operation of Japanese engineering companies, which needed to ensure the environmental risks and public safety to buyers' local needs. In essence, the technology transfer was based on a "turn-key" contract in which the reactor design was supplied by foreign suppliers, but not made to buyers' locally specific needs. GE-designed Fukushima Daiichi No. 1 reactor was built on this turn-key basis in the late 1960s. This dependence on foreign technology and equipment helped to minimize the industry's capital investments.

The intra-coalition adjustment of beliefs to interests and power

In general, Japan's quasi-corporatist policy-network—that is, close ties between the national bureaucracy, the LDP, and big business—tends to be much less open, as decision-making that reflects the predominance of economic over other issues is much more centralized. Unlike the pluralist environment in which the ACF was initially proposed in the research area of US environmental policy-making, Japan's coalition-building tends to produce the dominant coalition that remains in power and have fewer influential actors in the policy subsystem. Nonetheless, coalition-building in nuclear energy policy does not support the conventional view of the bureaucracy-dominant models.[49] The national bureaucracy served as guarantor to private suppliers and industrial buyers of nuclear energy whose commitments were to overcome power shortages. The MITI negotiated with business groups and sought the approval of the LDP rather than leading the peak players. In this context, the primary focus of nuclear energy politics resided in intra-coalition adjustments rather than inter-coalition competition. In essence, power utility companies were "material groups" who sought to maximize their self-interests of profits and market shares, not those who were to pursue public purposes.[50] There was thus a political-tactical side to coalition-building that required the dominant coalition to ensure the maintenance of material groups' viability. In this sense, policy core beliefs were subordinated to interests.

In the mid-1950s, the MITI appeared to have lost the initiative over nuclear energy programs as Nakasone and his allies legislatively created the STA.[51] The maintenance of the pro-nuclear coalition in which the utility industry had gained an advantage over the MITI in the 1950s began to change in the early 1960s. In the mid-1960s, the "dual structure" of reactor development was established as the MITI-utilities group promoted the commercial nuclear enterprise and the independently staffed STA group specialized in research and test reactors.[52] The regulatory authorities had been compartmentalized to the extent that different state agencies, primarily the MITI and the STA, held jurisdiction over both the promotion side and the regulation side. The MITI then began to emerge with more formal negotiators. The MITI's strategy was to establish an economic incentive mechanism of electricity rate calculation in which the more utilities invest the more they earn.[53] MITI-initiated electricity rate systems served as a key mechanism in ensuring continuous large-scale investments in nuclear power plants by the utility industry. Cost and earning return methods were revised by the 1960 ministerial ordinance to calculate the cost base with fixed assets including construction in progress and working capital, to figure out the proper level of the electricity rate and thus decide the level of corporate earnings. Half of the amount of construction in progress was entitled to be included in the cost base. This incentive was widely used to promote investments in nuclear power plants as any government-approved construction plans would increase their corporate earnings. Nuclear fuel was also treated as part of their fixed assets and even spent nuclear fuel was treated as such in anticipation of its recycling. In other words, such radioactive waste continued to be a source of corporate earnings. In 1980 the government introduced a new item, "specified capital investment," which was adopted as part of the cost base. The specified capital investment, which was done by the utility industry on unviable enterprises, such as Japan

Nuclear Fuel Limited (established to build a nuclear fuel cycle infrastructure), was now included for cost accounting. The institutionalization of corporate earnings based on the electricity rate provided a foundation for building increasingly closer relationships between the MITI and the private utilities.

Conservative politicians were more committed to the policy core belief that nuclear power would be the only viable option for the resource-poor nation to ensure energy and increase production. However, the Keidanren and the utility companies were material interest groups. In general, these groups are presumed to be preoccupied with maximizing profits and more sensitive to changing "bottom-line" self-interest positions. To this extent, the stated policy core belief of the Keidanren and the utility companies could be fluid. To make these organizations more consistent with the normative commitments of the pro-nuclear advocacy coalition, the MITI indeed manipulated the rules and budgets of governmental institutions to ensure constant corporate profits. The pro-nuclear commitments involved a huge range of both investment and operation risks. The MITI thus established the corporate earnings-guaranteed system with the aim of protecting the utility investors from such risks by transferring the risks to the public, setting a limit on liability for nuclear accidents, and reducing the cost of disposing of radioactive waste. Within the dominant pro-nuclear coalition, the continued promotion of nuclear power generation involved mutual adjustments among those public and private actors' interests. This process can be seen as "policy-oriented learning,"[54] which resulted from experience at the operational level of learning of regulatory/promotional instruments or implementation designs. Such learning was highly unlikely to change the policy core attributes of nuclear energy policy.

Institutional top-down incentives to neutralize local demands

Apart from elite-centered coalition-building, the stability of the dominant coalition required an effort to co-opt potential minority coalition members into the pro-nuclear camp. Acting under pressure from the power utility companies, the LDP leadership had party-tactical motives to extend subsidies to the depopulated areas of proposed nuclear plants, in order to silence residents' voices. Fukushima Prefecture, where the Daiichi Nuclear Power Plant is located, received a cumulative 269 billion yen (US$2.8 billion) in subsidies by fiscal year 2009.[55] The power utility companies also donated large sums to local governments near the nuclear power plants, even though they were already paying large sums in taxes to local governments. It is reported that over the past 20 years the TEPCO spent more than 40 billion yen (US$0.4 billion) on payments known internally as "funds to deal with local communities."[56]

The oil crisis of 1973 served as a catalyst to accelerate the introduction of nuclear power generation. But the JAIF acknowledged that the utility industry had struggled to manage the problems of plant siting and in 1973 requested that the national government establish a location subsidy scheme, which would extend material benefits in the form of national subsidies to local governments for inviting nuclear power generating facilities into their areas.[57] In the early 1970s, the Japanese government indeed began to redirect national funds more decisively to rural areas as put forward in the Plan to Remodel the Japanese Archipelago by then MITI Minister Kakuei Tanaka in 1969.[58] As a new direction for regional policy, the system of electric power location subsidies was created in 1974 by the promulgation of three electric power laws. Under these laws, national subsidies were provided to local governments that agreed to have power generation plants in their areas. The Electric Power Development Tax was accordingly introduced to yield a cost burden of utility companies to consumers. This indirect tax was embedded into electricity bills to fund the national subsidies. The tax on electricity was initially 0.085 yen per kWh and its revenue was placed in a special account to be allocated to the MITI and the STA.[59]

In the 1980s, however, the incentive mechanism of the location subsidies increasingly became less effective at securing new site selections for nuclear reactors. Although the number of reactors in operation constantly increased, the number of approved new sites rapidly dropped from 10 in the 1970s to five in the 1980s, and one in the 1990s.[60] This decline and delays with approval procedures were largely due to prefectural governors' "veto power."[61] By the decision of the MITI Departmental Council, it became customary in the mid-1970s to obtain a prefectural governor's consent to formally apply to the Electric Utility Coordination Council (EUCC) for setting nuclear power development plans in his/her community. In the 1980s, some prefectural governors began to use their veto power, although lacking legal authority, as a bargaining tool for their own political ends. The most well-known case occurred in 1985 when the governor of Hokkaido, Takahiro Yokomichi, refused permission for the Power Reactor & Nuclear Fuels Corporation to conduct a preliminary environmental survey at the proposed site. He was not convinced that available techniques for handling high-level radioactive waste by solidifying it were safe.[62] The LDP claimed that the governor had no legal right to stop it. In the 1990s, political trends favored decentralization reforms and further strengthened governors' political influence in site arrangements. Nonetheless, once site arrangements went beyond what the governor was able to delay, individual nuclear power development plans were approved by the EUCC and incorporated into a national plan of power demand and supply.

As far as the policy area of nuclear energy was concerned, my claim that local government occupies a strategic position straddling the division between the state and citizens and developing a safeguard to meet local needs was less relevant in explaining the actual processes and structures for rule-making and enforcement of nuclear energy generation. Although local communities were indeed at the forefront of coping with nuclear-related public safety and environmental risks, local authorities were largely co-opted by the national government. The national government that ultimately authorized the construction of nuclear power plants tenaciously pursued its long-term national energy strategies by insulating them from popular pressures and rendering them more responsive to a voice within the pro-nuclear coalition at the national level. In short, the policy area of nuclear energy was among the most nationally regulated in Japan and local governments could have little freedom to initiate balancing acts between national mandates and local concerns for policy coordination. The necessary preconditions for my claim to be valid are to meet the following requirements: local governments, while operating across institutional boundaries of polity, need to participate independently in a given policy area, either due to the national government's lack of interest or in the absence of national regulation, or they need to be institutionally empowered as autonomous actors. State-centric governance over nuclear energy is a nationally led framework embedded within institutional boundaries for extending channels that can serve to incentivize local action for effectively making progress at national scales.

The minority anti-nuclear coalition in the quasi-corporatist regime

From the viewpoint of the pro-nuclear coalition, nuclear energy development aimed to secure energy for the resource-poor nation as well as maintaining private sector profitability while limiting institutional access to channeling local concerns/social demands into the political system. At the national level, the dominant coalition members saw nuclear energy policy as instrumental in managing energy demand/supply for production, rather than as a matter of public safety and environmental risk. In contrast, the policy priority of local governments, with community welfare at the top of the list, provided social actors with relative openness to local solutions. In the subsystem of nuclear energy policy, however, the pro-nuclear coalition predominantly controlled the process of nuclear energy rule-making at the national level, with state-centric gate-keeping resources, such as legal powers, sources of finance, claiming legitimacy, and control over information and expertise. The presence of strong state control largely constrained local governments in initiating specific balancing acts between national mandates and local concerns over nuclear energy development. Opposition parties were systematically excluded from most of the policy-making process and the anti-nuclear energy movement largely consisted of the NIMBY (not-in-my-backyard) phenomenon.

The earliest case of anti-nuclear struggles was the 1966 Nagashima incident in which activist fishermen derailed a plan for the construction of the Ashihama nuclear power plant. From the mid-1960s to the mid-1970s, the policy-relevant coalition-building was largely restricted to the business and political elites and more or less excluded societal actors and opposition parties. It is important to note here that the host communities of nuclear facilities were excluded from nuclear policy-making in the absence of coordination among themselves yet dependent on compensation for the construction of nuclear reactors. During this period, fisheries' cooperative associations locally spearheaded a number of anti-nuclear power generation struggles, which rarely became community-wide initiatives. Fishermen were not so much concerned about the safety of the nuclear power plant per se, but about nuclear power generation's threat to their livelihoods. Redistribution policy co-opted the host communities of nuclear facilities and their fishermen and farmers in the form of subsidies and compensation. The benefits of the redistributive policy largely prevented potential anti-nuclear actors from becoming united for anti-nuclear coalition-building.

According to the ACF, some external factors provide or recreate an opportunity for policy change,[63] while affecting the behavior of resource mobilization for anti-nuclear advocacy. "External shocks" are considered to be a trigger for anti-nuclear coalition-building and gain political support from greater awareness by the public. Probably the earliest external shock was the Daigo Fukuryū Maru (No. 5 Lucky Dragon) March 1954 incident in which a Japanese tuna fishing boat encountered radioactive fallout from a US hydrogen-bomb test on Bikini Atoll. The food contamination, which was caused by radioactive fallout carried by the prevailing westerlies from the test site, was reported almost every day somewhere in the national newspapers,[64] but a storm of hostile public opinion against nuclear tests did not give rise to a socially mobilized force against the civilian use of nuclear power. The mid-1950s to the mid-1960s was a decade of high expectation for nuclear power as a new energy source. According to the Management and Coordination Agency's public opinion poll in March 1969, 65.3 percent of the respondents were in favor of the "positive promotion of nuclear power for peaceful uses" while in sharp contrast only 4.6 percent said they were against it.[65] Since the late 1950s, the Japan Socialist Party (JSP) voting share had continually declined, with the Japan Communist Party (JCP) not yet influential enough to cause the LDP concern. The conservative LDP government attempted to avoid the rise of political divisions among its conservative supporters by extending material benefits to the host communities. The redistribution of government resources for compensation was intended to increase the insulation of grassroots demands by excluding external support from anti-nuclear forces.[66] Up to the late 1960s, all opposition parties were also in favor of the civilian use of nuclear power. The process of nuclear energy was largely depoliticized at local levels.

The number of approvals for construction of new nuclear reactors between 1969 and 1972 rapidly increased to 17, in contrast to only four approved new reactors between 1965 and 1968.[67] In the early 1970s, the JCP still maintained its support for the civilian use of nuclear power although local JCP members at the designated sites of new nuclear reactors began to get involved in anti-nuclear resident movements. In January 1972 the JSP officially adopted a clear stance on abolishing the civilian use of nuclear energy and in the following year its support for those movements was well underway. In 1973 the JSP mobilized the party's largest supporter, the General Council of Trade Unions of Japan or Sōhyō, to prevent the JAEC from holding a public hearing about the Fukushima Daini reactor. In the following year, the Sōhyō established a united front with some local residents against the announced experiment to test the first Japanese nuclear powered ship, Mutsu, in the outer sea and successfully postponed it. On the other hand, the Dōmei private sector labor confederation, in which its 200,000-strong membership of the Federation of National Electric Power

Workers Unions financially supported the Democratic Socialist Party (DSP), continued to promote nuclear energy projects. Given their ambiguous and divided stances towards nuclear energy, the opposition parties and labor unions were yet to exploit the political opportunities, which were created by local protests against the increased license permits for new nuclear reactors, to present a challenge to the pro-nuclear coalition.

During the period of the pro-nuclear Nakasone administration (1982–1987), 16 license permits were issued for the construction of new nuclear reactors. On April 26, 1986, a catastrophic nuclear accident, exogenous to the policy subsystem, occurred at the Chernobyl Nuclear Power Plant in Ukraine. The *Asahi Shinbun* opinion poll of August 1986, for the first time, showed that the number of respondents against the "promotion" of nuclear power generation exceeded that for the promotion. In January 1988 about 1,500 people demonstrated outside the headquarters of the Shikoku Electric Power Co. protesting an output test at a nuclear reactor, and in the following month 5,000 protesters of 522 citizens' groups (mostly with no affiliations to any political party) from around Japan held a rally in front of the headquarters.[68] In urban areas, rather than the host rural communities of nuclear facilities, socially mobilized groups emerged; in April 1988, nearly 20,000 citizens who represented 243 groups met together in Tokyo for promotional activities of de-nuclear power generation through national legislation. The reported cases of collective protests against nuclear power generation increased rapidly from 12 in 1987 to 83 in 1988.[69] Newly elected chairperson of the JSP, Takako Doi, mobilized Japanese women while collaborating with the Life Club Cooperative Society (consumers' organization), scientists, and the All-Japan Local Government Workers' Union, and collected 3.5 million signatures for this cause. The representative groups petitioned for the passage of anti-nuclear energy legislation, on behalf of the signatories. It was expected that the approving law-makers would submit a bill sponsored by themselves. However, opposition parties remained divided over nuclear energy issues and they were unable to propose an energy bill alternative to the existing one. The signature campaign was not inclusive enough to mobilize the supporters of pro-nuclear parties (the LDP and the DSP). In essence, despite the catastrophic Chernobyl accident and the resultant changes in public opinion, the policy core of a nuclear energy program had not changed as the pro-nuclear LDP remained in power. In this context, anti-nuclear policy-relevant coalition-building became salient with its policy core beliefs in nuclear risks and that a future nuclear accident could be a real possibility in Japan.

Cross-coalition interactions in the institutional structure of policy monopoly

While the pro-nuclear coalition that instituted the nuclear energy program remained in power, its policy-makers established a coordination mechanism of interests internal to the coalition. The mechanism aimed to make them more consistent with its policy objectives while responding to both the necessity of the nuclear fuel cycle and the assurance of corporate earnings at the operational level of policy learning. At the same time, however, the pro-nuclear LDP government was required to coordinate some cross-coalition interactions, in order to favor the existence of the pro-nuclear dominance. At the strategic level of learning to understand the political feasibility, the government structured these interactions into a set of responses to the minor anti-nuclear coalition and potential anti-nuclear forces. The various forms of responses, such as material benefits, strategic project delays, state agencies' reorganization, and consultation procedures, were used to selectively neutralize or silence opposition voices. When the incentive mechanism of the location subsidies and compensation measures became less effective, the government strategically reduced the number of approved new sites and delayed controversial projects. To continue to provide support to these projects, it began the tactical process related to state agencies' reorganization and new consultation procedures. The government attempted to utilize the minimum amount of coordinated behavior needed to keep the dream of a fully independent fuel cycle alive. In essence, the dominant coalition was challenged by the minority coalition but the distribution of power was so concentrated that cross-coalition interactions were very limited. The nuclear policy subsystem was in the process of forming and minority coalition actors were not interacting with any regularity to influence policy formulation and implementation.

Take, for example, the introduction of consultation procedures in 1979. At an early stage before utility companies formally applied to the EUCC about setting up their nuclear power development plans, the site selection of nuclear power plants had been already settled in essence by the pro-nuclear coalition members.[70] It was the time of nuclear power development when compensation (through the procurement of land and providing compensation for fisheries) to individuals, i.e., farmers and fishermen, who would be directly affected by the facility, appeared to prove effective in making successful site arrangements. But some local residents often saw the compensation offer as a bribe rather than as a form of benefit-sharing between the host community and the beneficiaries of the facility. In the late 1970s, before the delivery of the EUCC, the MITI held the first public hearings at which local voices were supposed to be heard about the nuclear power development plan.[71] However, the hearings were not early enough for meaningful consultation to consider alternatives to the proposed plan. Accordingly, the MITI issued the reactor installation permit, which was subject to the consent of the prime minister, on the advice of the STA. Once the permit was issued, the MITI exclusively controlled the licensing process. Despite the limited points of oppositions' access, the dominant pro-nuclear coalition seem to have largely prevented oppositions from adopting "confrontational," sustained strategies coordinated outside established policy channels.[72]

The effects of unstable political alignments on the policy subsystem

One ACF hypothesis concerning policy change is that significant events external to the policy subsystem, such as an election loss for a governing party, "are a necessary, but not sufficient, cause of change in the policy core attributes of a government program."[73] In July 1993, intra-party fighting within the LDP led to the party losing its majority in the general election after 38 years of uninterrupted rule. A small group of dissidents who split from the LDP seized power as part of a non-LDP eight-party coalition. Nonetheless, major policy change did not occur as anti-nuclear citizens' groups failed to exploit this opportunity. Even the Socialists who had been acting as a pivot for anti-nuclear coalition-building were about to transform into pragmatic centrists by breaking with their anti-nuclear stance. The JSP decided to form a "grand coalition" government with the LDP. As the Socialists left the ruling coalition in 1994, the LDP managed to get back in via a majority coalition with its bitter Socialists rival. By the summer of 1996 the LDP was able to form a single party government again. Despite its return to power, the one-party predominance of the LDP appeared to have ended under the 1994 electoral reform, which was one reason for the 1993 split of the LDP.[74]

The old electoral system of multimember district (MMD) with single non-transferable vote (SNTV) from 1947 to 1993, in which the voter casts only one ballot for multiple seats, caused intraparty rivalry (i.e., factional politics) in the LDP as multiple LDP candidates often ran for election in the same district. The new electoral system adopted in 2004, which was a mixed system of 300 single-member districts (SMD) and 200 (later amended to 180) proportional representation (PR) seats, was expected to make election campaigns less personal and more party focused. Recent experiences in elections suggest that the new electoral system certainly increased party competition but the expected pathway to a stable two-party system of alternating governments remains uncertain.[75] Within the LDP, the personal voter mobilization organizations adapted well to the new SMD system with a broader constituency and thus undermined the possible emergence of party-centric politics. From the viewpoint of potential policy change in nuclear energy, however, it is important to acknowledge that the focus of intraparty conflict significantly shifted under the new electoral system. Ellis Krauss and Robert Pekkanen argue:

> The high level of conflict in the LDP in the first few years of the twenty-first century reflects a shift from vertical cleavages (i.e., along factional lines) to horizontal cleavages (i.e., vested interests' "forces of resistance" versus reformers over a policy issue).[76]

Four former Prime Ministers, including LDP's Jun'ichiro Koizumi, had criticized Abe's pro-nuclear policies and in November 2013 Koizumi publicly declared at the Japan National Press Club that Japan should immediately abandon nuclear energy. Some senior LDP members, such as Tarō Kōno and Sēichiō Murakami, spoke in opposition to the LDP's official line of nuclear energy policy. LDP Diet members from urban election districts participated in study groups to reassess Japan's nuclear energy policy. It is safe to say that a significant proportion of LDP members were prevented from expressing their anti-nuclear stances. LDP nuclear energy policy reformers were yet to represent an official force within the ruling party but the new election system structured incentives for LDP politicians to focus on policy issues rather than notorious factionalism. Within the pro-nuclear coalition, those LDP members put into question the effectiveness of their nuclear energy policy. In longer terms, the new electoral system provided conditions for substantial change from the status quo of Japan's nuclear energy policy.

The national bureaucracy flexibly adapted to the unstable political alignments. From 1988 to 1996, the EUCC had frozen the approval of new sites for nuclear plants.[77] In 1993 the newly formed non-LDP coalition announced "jōhō kōkai e no torikumi" (initiatives for active information release) over nuclear energy generation.[78] In March 1996, the STA and the MITI launched a national Round Table whose original vision was to bring diverse voices around the nuclear policy issue to gain public acceptance. The invited discussants, who primarily represented business and academics, though also included a few critics, were unable to offer viable policy recommendations.[79] By 1994, when its coalition with the LDP was inaugurated, the Social Democratic Party (SDP), formerly JSP, had changed its position to the acceptance of the nuclear reactors in operation and thus undermined the basis of mass mobilization. As the JSP had previously provided an organizational basis for those activists to mobilize interested citizens against nuclear power plants, the JSP's pragmatic approach to its changed policy stance institutionally weakened a pivot of the anti-nuclear coalition-building. In 1996 when the LDP reconstituted itself once again, the EUCC began to process the applications for construction of new nuclear reactors, with eight new reactors approved between 1996 and 2001. The party realignment external to the policy subsystem thus brought about the rather restricted scope of institutional access to the minority anti-nuclear coalition.

The changing tide of public opinion over nuclear safety

On December 8, 1995, a sodium leak and fire at the Monju fast-breeder reactor in Fukui prefecture nearly became a major catastrophe that could have spilled deadly plutonium into the environment. Following the incident, an attempted cover-up by the operator ignited the weight of popular pressure and opinion to reconsider Japan's nuclear power policy. In January 1996 the governors of Fukui, Fukushima, and Niigata, which hosted more than half of Japan's nuclear plants, called for national consensus building through public engagement over nuclear power policy. In September 1999 Japan's first critical accident, at the uranium conversion facility, JCO Co. Ltd (Japanese nuclear fuel cycle company), killed two workers and released radiation into the living area of nearby residents.

These events revealed a failure in nuclear safety regulation in Japan. With regard to environmental safety regulation, radioactive contamination was excluded from the Basic Environment Law of 1993. There were no detailed, comprehensive statutory regulations in preparation for large-scale radioactive contamination. Due to the 2001 reorganization of government ministries, the MITI was reorganized into the Ministry of Economy, Trade and Industry (METI). The STA was then abolished and some of its functions were transferred to the Ministry of Education, Culture, Sports, Science, and Technology (MEXT). The regulation of commercial reactors, non-commercial reactors, and nuclear fuel facilities came within the jurisdiction of the METI. The Nuclear and Industry Safety Agency (NISA) was then created in 2001 as a branch of the METI to ensure the safety of nuclear power production and the safety of energy-related industries. NISA's lack of independence from the METI, which pursued the promotion of nuclear power, was widely criticized.[80] The appointment of NISA's executives was internally made as part of the personnel reshuffling of the METI, which did not help in the development of nuclear safety specialists. The 2001 reorganization of national ministries thus failed to separate nuclear regulation from the promotion function for the most basic safety requirements and provided a breeding ground for collusive ties between the regulator and the industry.

A shift in public opinion (i.e., external events) after a catastrophe could impose constraints on subsystem actors and change the distribution of resources among policy coalitions. Emerging public support holding a specific policy stance provides policy participants with resources to exploit for policy change and for imposing constraints on subsystem actors.[81] According to nationwide opinion polls between 1980 and 2000, those supporting the idea of the "reduction" or "abolition" of nuclear power generation remained in the minority, representing between 20 and 30 percent;[82] however, fluctuations of around 30 percent in the 1990s reflected Japanese people's increasing turn away from its "promotion."[83] In the 1990s, an anti-nuclear energy sentiment in the Japanese public began to take root due to several nuclear-related accidents and cover-ups (i.e., internal subsystem events)[84] although the causal links between the accidents and changes in public opinion (i.e., the redistribution of public support as a critical resource) require further examination. Anti-nuclear policy-relevant coalition-building became salient with the belief that a future nuclear accident would be a real possibility in Japan. Recipients of nuclear policy compensation were transforming in part into a driving force for anti-nuclear policy-relevant coalition-building. By the late 1990s, anti-nuclear coalition groups began to mobilize public support for anti-nuclear policy and work on broad exchanges between urban (Tokyo and Osaka) and rural (host communities) movements. A nationwide network, the Green Energy Law Network (GEN), which was formed in May 1999, sought legislative change for renewable energy promotion. In 2000 another network, the National Parliamentarians' Association for Promoting Renewable Energy, which was established in November 1999 as a non-partisan alliance of 256 politicians, joined the GEN and together they drew up a bill for promoting renewable energies.[85] The activists' causal beliefs in nuclear risks were extended to those concerned about finding a viable option for Japan to ensure energy security and climate change.

Technical resources were also mobilized by the activists to engage in a public debate, drawn largely from findings supplied by environmental scientists that nuclear energy is not cheap if back-end and recovery costs are taken into account. The accumulation of new evidence helped to revise the policy beliefs of the minority coalition while linking nuclear energy policy to renewable energy and climate change policy. In this process, policy-oriented learning was taking place across pro- and anti-nuclear belief systems as contentious interaction between the two coalitions, informed by policy experts and scientists, prevailed.[86] In the late 1990s, the focus on the pre-defined subsystem of nuclear energy began to increasingly experience policy diffusion and spillover effects across policy subsystems. In Japan, climate change bargaining and decision-making were conducted in relation to nuclear energy plans. Policy-oriented learning from adjacent policy subsystems was expected to represent important elements of public policy-making. Yet cross-sector coalition-building and conflict has hardly been theorized in political science.[87]

Seeking revisions at the level of policy elites' beliefs

The Democratic Party of Japan (DPJ) came to power in 2009 and the LDP was no longer the largest party in the lower house. The DPJ already controlled the upper house, and the party now represented 64 percent of lower-house seats. The DPJ ran on a platform of political and policy reforms, promising a departure from the LDP ways of politics. However, the DPJ came to power with a pro-nuclear energy policy, mainly because labor unions, related to utility companies and electronic product manufacturers, provided an important support base for vote mobilization. Most DPJ members shared a belief in the benefits of nuclear power generation, without having regularly received donations from the utility companies. The DPJ was then destined to deal with the catastrophic disaster. The DPJ government was blamed for an erratic response to the Fukushima Daiichi accident. In the aftermath, the DPJ's stance towards nuclear power became volatile, changing from Prime Minister Naoto Kan's call to end Japan's dependence on nuclear power to his successor Yoshihiko Noda's move to restart existing reactors. However, in just over three years (to 2012), the DPJ fell from power in a landslide electoral loss to the LDP.

Three months after the Fukushima disaster, the DPJ government created the Energy and Environment Council, which consisted of cabinet members aiming to enact future energy and environmental policy. The METI previously had exclusive jurisdiction over domestic energy policy, but the Council was now chaired by the Minister of State for National Policy to evade bureaucratic policy-making. In June–August 2012, the Council suggested three scenarios presuming to reduce the ratio of nuclear power generation by 2030 to 0 percent, 15 percent, or 20–25 percent, and conducted national discussions including public hearings, debate-based polling, and collecting public comments. The review of the national debate by the Council resulted in a proposal, "N-power operation zero (the abandonment of nuclear power generation) in the 2030s."[88] As a result of the Fukushima disaster, it appeared that the DPJ government was changing its policy core beliefs. Concurrently with the DPJ initiatives, however, the METI demonstrated its tenacious ability to maintain its jurisdiction over energy policy-making, establishing a subcommittee of its Advisory Committee for Natural Resources and Energy in October 2011 to discuss a basic energy plan. The METI was sensitive enough to respond to public criticism by including anti-nuclear critics who represented a third of the subcommittee members. Once the N-power operation zero was formulated in October 2012, however, the subcommittee never convened due to a fierce backlash from the Keidanren.[89] The DPJ was unable to control business interests' opposition to "N-power operation zero." Soon thereafter, the national election of December 16, 2012 returned power to the old guard LDP, which immediately abolished the Energy and Environment Council.

The LDP government used the subcommittee of the Advisory Committee for Natural Resources and Energy as an upgraded platform to discuss the Basic Energy Plan while most anti-nuclear critics were removed from the subcommittee.[90] Momentum for a fundamental change in energy policy ceased abruptly. The Abe administration brought the old policy-making process back in as an energy policy driver. In June 2012, as Table 2.1 shows, the DPJ government deflected criticism over a collusive relationship between the NISA and the utility industry or between regulation and promotion, with the establishment of the Nuclear Regulation Authority (NRA) as an independent agency of the Ministry of the Environment. But the LDP government made use of the Working Group for New Safety Levels, created within the NRA, to resume nuclear power plant operations. Abe's policy speech at the 183rd ordinary session of the Diet (February 28, 2013) declared that nuclear power plant operations would resume.

In post-Fukushima Japan, however, there is an important exogenous change that may alter the political resources and opportunities of both pro-nuclear and anti-nuclear coalitions. The incident entailed profound changes in public opinion. According to opinion polls, conducted by Japanese Broadcasting Corporation (NHK), Fuji News Network (FNN), *Sankei Shinbun* and *Asahi Shinbun*, in April 2013 immediately after the Fukushima incident, 41–44 percent of the respondents were in favor of "reduction" or "abolition."[91] Four months after the incident, the percentage dramatically soared to around 70 percent and stabilized thereafter.[92] In short, majority opinion clearly shifted from "just about right" (status quo) to "reduction." This divided the majority of the policy elite from the majority of eligible voters. Of course, changes in public preferences about a single policy area would neither directly provide new opportunities nor create resources for anti-nuclear coalition-building. In general, Japanese voters have cared primarily about economic and social security policies in the past. Opinion polls conducted immediately before and after the December 2012 election reported that respondents were most interested in the economy and employment (32 percent on December 11 by *Mainichi Shinbun* and 35 percent on December 18 by *Asahi*

Shinbun), followed by social security and welfare (23 percent on December 11 by *Mainichi Shinbun* and 30 percent on December 18 by *Asahi Shinbun*). But 7 percent and 17 percent mentioned energy issues, including nuclear energy, as reported by *Mainichi Shinbun* and *Asahi Shinbun* respectively, in the same polls. In particular, opposition parties, which have been divided over the future of nuclear energy, were yet to exploit the public sentiment in electoral politics.

On December 14, 2014, Prime Minister Abe emerged as the big winner in the Lower House election as the LDP and Komeito, its junior partner in the ruling coalition, won 325 out of 475 seats. Not surprisingly, the economy was the biggest concern among voters while a state of disarray among opposition parties shifted attention away from the highly divisive issue of restarting the idled

Table 2.1 Japan's nuclear power organizations

2005	
Cabinet Office (former Prime Minister's Office)	
JAEC	Japanese Atomic Energy Commission
NSC	Nuclear Safety Commission
Ministry of Economy, Trade and Industry – METI (formerly Ministry of International Trade and Industry – MITI)	
ANRE	Agency of Natural Resources and Energy
NISA	Nuclear and Industrial Safety Agency
Ministry of Education, Culture, Sports, Science and Technology – MEXT (dissolved Science and Technology Agency – STA)	
JAERI	Japan Atomic Energy Research Institute
JNC	Japan Nuclear Cycle Development Institute
Private Sector	
Keidanren	Japan Business Federation
JAIF	Japan Atomic Industry Forum
FEPCO	Federation of Electric Power Companies
JAPCO	Japan Atomic Power Company
J-Power	Electric Power Development Company
JEMA	Japan Electrical Manufacturers' Association

2012 (post-Fukushima)	
Cabinet Office	
JAEC	Japanese Atomic Energy Commission
Ministry of the Environment – MOE	
NRA	Nuclear Regulatory Authority (merger of NSC and NISA)
JAEA	Japan Atomic Energy Agency (merger of JAERI and JNC)
Ministry of Economy, Trade and Industry – METI	
ANRE	Agency of Natural Resources and Energy
Ministry of Education, Culture, Sports, Science and Technology – MEXT	
STPB	Science and Technology Policy Bureau

reactors. Only the SDP and JCP clearly said no to a reboot of the reactors while the DPJ ambiguously supported restarts with evacuation plans for locals.[93] The Future Generation Party even unconditionally agreed to put the reactors back online. Prime Minister Abe was ready to keep pushing his policy agenda. Meanwhile, the dominant nuclear energy coalition would continue to use institutional veto points (e.g., the new electoral system, which tends to cause partisan swings for the re-election of candidates, made it very difficult for any party to achieve a fundamental policy change; and Japan's parliamentary system, in which prime ministers emerge out of the majority party in parliament, reduces competition) to prevent any policy change whenever necessary. In longer terms, Japan's single-member district rules may reduce the scope for policy differences among major parties and lead the country's party system to become consolidated around two major parties. In this context, Steven Reed argues that civil society and local assemblies hold the key to third-party survival.[94] The party organization needs to be embedded within civil society, with its capacity to produce a significant number of local assembly members. In my view, Japan's third parties, who are rooted in civil society, have the potential to exploit public sentiment in electoral politics for policy change. These parties are in a strategic position to increase the salience of nuclear energy issues in electoral processes. When the public is not indifferent, major parties do not drift away from the public sentiment. In April 2015 the Japanese government announced an optimal energy mix for 2030 that consists of 20–22 percent from nuclear power and up to 24 percent from renewable energy. Third parties can be conceived of policy brokers, although they do not act as neutral arbiters but have a strategic interest to seek power or to be re-elected. They may have some policy bent towards the anti-nuclear coalition, while understanding the realistic sphere of policy elites' decision-making. Given the divisive and polarized nature of nuclear energy policy, they may seek stability between the coalitions in a bid to reduce reliance on nuclear power as much as possible in a realistic fashion.

Conclusion

In Japan, nuclear energy has been a major national undertaking with significant implications for foreign policy, domestic politics, and environmental and social issues. Nuclear energy policy arises out of a state-centric framework to secure energy for the resource-poor nation. The policy area indicates the issue-specific "closed" structures which allow for limited access to the political system. As the dominant pro-nuclear coalition stayed in power from the early post-war period until 1993, the essence of nuclear energy policy remained unchanged over time. Although there were some instances of internal conflicts and material competition within the dominant coalition, the coalition's policy core beliefs were rigidly held by policy elites. Its fundamental value priorities, especially the relative importance of economic development over environmental protection, guided its more specific beliefs, such as nuclear promotion taking priority over nuclear safety. The national government extended incentive schemes as well as top-down policies towards sub-national actors. Until the late 1980s, anti-nuclear energy forces were essentially composed of local ad hoc activists often tied to the NIMBY movement with little concern for formal organization and nationwide networking. In the policy area of nuclear energy, the national government seeks to regulate or enable a sub-national level of participation in promoting nuclear energy. Due to a great degree of territorial centralization in Japan, national authorities closely attend this policy area. The strong commitment of the national leadership provides local governments with little chance to initiate balancing acts between national mandates and local actions. The key issue is state-centric policy coordination for the national government to effectively achieve aggregate progress at a national scale.

Coalitions do not all have equal power. If one coalition operates in a situation of dominance, the dominant coalition is likely to achieve its desired policy outcomes, with little consideration given to the preferences of minor coalitions. The power structure of dominance helps to ensure stability in policy-making over time. In a comparative perspective, institutional structures determine the overall distribution of power among coalitions in a given policy subsystem. Some of the important institutional structures that account for the existence of the dominant pro-nuclear coalition in Japanese nuclear energy include: (1) US–Japan security ties that structurally affect the nuclear policy-making process in such a way as to focus on national representatives in international negotiations; (2) Japan's policy-specific experience by which stakeholders have developed expectations regarding the benefits of national undertaking; (3) the Japanese electoral system of 1947–1993, that is, MMD with SNTV, which fostered one-party LDP dominance; (4) Japan's centralized fiscal structure that provides the government party with clientelistic tools, that is, subsidies and grants, to silence anti-nuclear voices; (5) Japan's unitarism in which the distribution of decision-making competences is concentrated on the national level; (6) Japan's closed pre-parliamentary phase in which social actors have fewer opportunities to express their views and influence the project.

The dominant coalition tends to create a longer period of stable policy equilibrium in a given policy subsystem. Under external pressure, such as public opinion, the policy monopoly of the dominant coalition may become less effective and may even be replaced by a rising coalition. The Fukushima Daiichi nuclear disaster has indeed had a dramatic impact on public opinion and nuclear policy far beyond Japan. This experience demonstrates that public opinion may alter the policy elites' perception of nuclear energy promotion but it is hardly sufficient to cause policy change. The Japanese government tenaciously shows its eagerness for idled reactors to be restarted against the odds of public opinion. The conservative government takes an unyielding pro-nuclear stance against public concerns. The basic distribution of power within the policy subsystem of nuclear energy generation in Japan is concentrated in the hands of pro-nuclear coalition forces and this dominance produces the asymmetric patterns of cross-coalition interactions. The interest coordination mechanism internal to the dominant pro-nuclear coalition makes nuclear projects more consistent with its policy core beliefs to secure Japan's energy. In theory, the dominant coalition can be challenged by minority anti-nuclear coalition forces that display their capabilities to translate anti-nuclear public sentiments into electoral shifts while exploiting the political opportunities and resources in electoral processes. Proponents of nuclear policy change failed to skillfully exploit such opportunities in the parliamentary election of December 2014.

This chapter has shown that the following casual mechanisms help in understanding the rigidity of Japanese nuclear energy policy.

1. Domestic opportunity structures, while being capable of constraining collective action in the policy subsystem, adhere to certain international structures. One such dominant international structure in Japan's nuclear energy policy is found in US–Japan security ties through which the United States provides a guarantee of pro-nuclear energy development to Japan.
2. In a macro-perspective, the political opportunity structure, i.e., high territorial centralization, one-party dominance, bureaucratic pluralism, and opposition fragmentation, has systemic impact on coalition strategies and frames the nature and patterns of completion among coalitions. Japan's nuclear energy indicates that coalition behavior was framed by the low degree of "openness" in the political opportunity structure, i.e., high territorial centralization and one-party dominance.
3. Both the specificity of scientific knowledge and the local application of scientific information may structurally influence policy choice and the likelihood for policy change. The Japanese dominant coalition does not easily give up any nuclear fuel cycle project due to a potential domino effect on the chain progression of the fuel cycle. The island nation of Japan is also subject to the place-based application of nuclear knowledge, which makes continual progress.
4. Whether external or internal to the policy subsystem, accidents and disasters are fluid and evolving and remain as an indeterminate factor for major policy change. But the effect of these events may institutionally redistribute resources and policy access within the policy subsystem. The likelihood of major policy change largely depends on deliberate attempts by proponents of change to skillfully exploit such opportunities. The failure of opposition parties in the December 2014 election is a case in point.
5. In an institutional structure where a dominant coalition strives for a policy monopoly, the policy process is likely to remain at an impasse as long as the dominant governing coalition is in power. The largely uninterrupted LDP rule has not fundamentally altered power relations within the policy subsystem.
6. The institutionally closed access of the policy subsystem does not necessarily invite confrontational strategies by proponents of policy change (cf. POS's assumption). As observed in this study, the political-tactical side of cross-coalition relations, such as material incentives, project delays, and consultation offered by the dominant coalition, may successfully prevent likely protest activities in favor of current policy.

7 Interests and political power can be critical for a coalition to make its organizations more consistent with normative commitments. The intra-coalition adjustment of beliefs to interests and power is found in the rise of MITI's power and the MITI's manipulation of governmental rules and budgets for the utility companies.

Whether the policy monopoly of the pro-nuclear coalition will continue business-as-usual is an open question given the uncertainty resulting from external factors such as growing public pressure to curb the use of nuclear energy.

Notes

1. Matthew Zafonte and Paul Sabatier, "Shared beliefs and imposed interdependencies as determinants of ally networks in overlapping subsystems," *Journal of Theoretical Politics*, Vol. 10, No. 4 (1998), pp. 473–505.
2. Zafonte and Sabatier, "Shared beliefs and imposed interdependencies as determinants of ally networks in overlapping subsystems," pp. 475–82.
3. Christopher M. Weible, Paul A. Sabatier, and Kelly McQueen, "Themes and variations: taking stock of the advocacy coalition framework," *Policy Studies Journal*, Vol. 37, No. 1 (2009), p. 124.
4. Japan, Ministry of Economy, Trade and Industry (METI), Agency for National Resources and Energy, *Enerugī kihon keikaku* [Strategic Energy Plan] (2014), available from: www.enecho.meti.go.jp/category/others/basic_plan/pdf/140411.pdf [accessed December 22, 2014].
5. Takeshi Murota, *Genshiryoku no keizaigaku* [The economics of nuclear power] (Tokyo: Nihon Hyoronsha, 1981); Takeshi Murota, *Genpatsu no keizaigaku* [The economics of nuclear power generation] (Tokyo: Asahi Bunko, 1993); Ken'ichi Ōshima, *Saiseikanō enerugī no seiji keizaigaku* [The political economy of renewable energies] (Tokyo: Tōyō Shinpōsha, 2010); Ken'ichi Ōshima, *Genpatsu no kosuto* [The cost of nuclear power generation] (Tokyo: Iwanami Shinsho, 2011).
6. Japan, Cost Review Committee, Environment and Energy Council, "Kosuto-tō kenshō iinkai hōkokusho" [Cost Review Committee Report], December 2011, available from: www.cas.go.jp/jp/seisaku/npu/policy09/archive02_hokoku.html [accessed May 22, 2014].
7. Jeffrey Broadbent, *Environmental Politics in Japan: Networks of Power and Protest* (Cambridge, UK: Cambridge University Press, 1998).
8. Richard J. Samuels, *The Business of the Japanese State: Energy Markets in Comparative and Historical Perspective* (Ithaca, NY: Cornell University Press, 1987), pp. 228–56.
9. Hitoshi Yoshioka, "Reorganization of the administration and regulation of nuclear development," in Shigeru Nakayama and Hitoshi Yoshioka, eds., *A Social History of Science and Technology in Contemporary Japan*, Vol. 4 (Melbourne: Trans Pacific Press, 2006), pp. 189–273.
10. Linda Cohen, Mathew D. McCubbins, and Frances Rosenbluth, "The politics of nuclear power in Japan and the United States," in Peter F. Cowhey and Mathew D. McCubbins, eds., *Structure and Policy in Japan the United States* (Cambridge, UK: Cambridge University Press, 1995), pp. 177–202.
11. Hayden Lesbirel, *NIMBY Politics in Japan: Energy Siting and the Management of Environmental Conflict* (Ithaca, NY: Cornell University Press, 1998).
12. Peter Dauvergne, "'Outside forces' and the politics of reciprocal consent," *Asian Survey*, Vol. 33, No. 6 (1993), pp. 576–91.

13 See, for example, Jeff Kingston, "Japan's nuclear village: power and resilience" in Jeff Kingston, ed., *Critical Issues in Contemporary Japan* (Abingdon, UK: Routledge, 2013), pp. 107–19; Llewelyn Hughes, "Japan's energy conundrum," in Robert Pekkanen, Steven R. Reed, and Ethan Scheiner, eds., *Japan Decides 2014: The Japanese General Election* (Basingstoke, UK: Palgrave Macmillan, 2016).
14 Paul A. Sabatier and Hank Jenkins-Smith, "The advocacy coalition framework: an assessment," in Paul A. Sabatier, ed., *Theories of the Policy Process* (Boulder, CO: Westview Press, 1999), pp. 117–66.
15 Paul A. Sabatier, "The advocacy coalition framework: revisions and relevance for Europe," *Journal of European Public Policy*, Vol. 5, No. 1 (1998), p. 116.
16 Paul A. Sabatier and Hank C. Jenkins-Smith, eds., *Policy Change and Learning: An Advocacy Coalition Approach* (Boulder, CO: Westview Press, 1993), pp. 22–3.
17 Bert Klandermans, *The Social Psychology of Protest* (Oxford, UK: Blackwell, 1997); Sidney Tarrow, "Transnational politics: contention and institutions in international politics," *Annual Review of Political Science*, Vol. 4 (2001), pp. 1–20.
18 David S. Meyer, "Political opportunity and nested institutions," *Social Movement Studies*, Vol. 2, No. 1 (2003), pp. 17–35.
19 Tetsuo Arima, *Genpatsu/Shōriki/CIA* [Nuclear power, Shōriki and the CIA] (Tokyo: Shinchō Shinsho, 2011), p. 37.
20 It was reported that two secret agreements over the introduction and basing of nuclear weapons in Japan were negotiated during the Cold War. The first one, which was negotiated in the 1960 revision process of the US–Japan Security Treaty, was to allow transit of US nuclear weapons through Japanese territory and waters without prior consultation. The second one, which was reported as a secret part of the 1969 agreement reverting Okinawa to Japan, was to re-introduce US nuclear weapons on Okinawa in case of emergency. See, for example, *Japan Times*, "Kishi 'understood' secret nuke pact, '63 letter indicates," June 26, 2010.
21 Samuels, *The Business of the Japanese State*, 234.
22 Morris Low, *Science and the Building of a New Japan* (New York: Palgrave Macmillan, 2005), pp. 66–67.
23 Arima, *Genpatsu/Shōriki/CIA*, p. 44.
24 Laura Elizabeth Hein, *Fueling Growth: the Energy Revolution and Economic Policy in Postwar Japan* (Cambridge, MA: Council on East Asian Studies, Harvard University, Distributed by Harvard University Press, 1990), p. 261.
25 Hiroshi Honda, "Nihon no genshiryoku seiji katei" [The political process of Japanese nuclear power], *Hokudai Hogaku Ronshu* [Hokkaido University Law Journal], Vol. 54, No. 1 (2003), p. 354.
26 For more details on the relationships between Shōriki and the CIA, see Arima, *Genpatsu/Shōriki/CIA*, which is based on de-classified documents stored in the National Archives and Records Administration in Washington, DC.
27 Arima, *Genpatsu/Shōriki/CIA*, pp. 146–92.
28 Arima, *Genpatsu/Shōriki/CIA*, pp. 184–5.
29 Peter Kuznick, "Japan's nuclear history in perspective: Eisenhower and Atoms for War and Peace," *Bulletin of the Atomic Scientists*, April 13, 2011, on-line journal, available from: http://thebulletin.org/japans-nuclear-history-perspective-eisenhower-and-atoms-war-and-peace [accessed December 22, 2014].
30 Morris Low, Shigeru Nakayama, and Hitoshi Yoshioka, *Science, Technology and Society in Contemporary Japan* (Cambridge, UK: Cambridge University Press, 1999), p. 78; Shigeru Nakayama, *Science, Technology and Society in Postwar Japan* (London: Kegan Paul International, 1991), pp. 150–1.
31 Samuels, *The Business of the Japanese State*, pp. 239–40.
32 Sabatier, "The advocacy coalition framework," p. 102.
33 Weible, Sabatier, and McQueen, "Themes and variations," pp. 121–40.
34 Susan E. Pickett, "Japan's nuclear energy policy: from firm commitment to difficult

dilemma addressing growing stocks of plutonium, program delays, domestic opposition, and international pressure," *Energy Policy*, Vol. 30, No. 15 (2002), p. 1338; International Atomic Energy Agency (IAEA), "IAEA mission to review NISA's approach to the 'comprehensive assessment for the safety of existing power reactor facilities' conducted in Japan," *IAEA Report*, Tokyo and Ohi, January 2012.

35 See, for example, Richard Samuels, *Rich Nation, Strong Army: National Security and the Technological Transformation of Japan* (Ithaca, NY: Cornell University Press, 1994).
36 Paul A. Sabatier and Christopher M. Weible, "The advocacy coalition framework: innovations and clarifications," in Paul A. Sabatier, ed., *Theories of the Policy Process* (Boulder, CO: Westview Press, 2007), p. 194.
37 Matthew Penney, "Nuclear nationalism and Fukushima," *The Asia-Pacific Journal: Japan Focus*, on-line journal, available from: http://japanfocus.org/-matthew-penney/3712/article.html [accessed May 22, 2014].
38 Sabatier and Weible, "The advocacy coalition framework," pp. 194–5.
39 Sabatier and Weible, "The advocacy coalition framework," p. 196 and p. 198.
40 Hitoshi Yoshioka, *Genshiryoku no shakaishi* [The social history of nuclear power] (Tokyo: Asahi Shinbunsha, 1999).
41 *Japan Times*, "U.S. banker honored here," September 20, 1975.
42 Hiroshi Okumura, *Nihon no rokudai kigyō shūdan* [Japan's six biggest business groups] (Tokyo: Asahi Shinbunsha, 1994).
43 Takeshi Kawai, *Fushigina kuni no genshiryoku* [A strange nation's nuclear power] (Tokyo: Kadokawa Shoten, 1961), pp. 76–7; Tokunosuke Nakajima and Ikurō Anzai, *Nihon no genshiryoku hatsuden* [Atomic power in Japan] (Tokyo: Shin Nihon Shuppansha, 1979).
44 Takuji Okamoto, "Denryoku kyōkyū taisei no kakuritsu" [The establishment of electricity supply systems], in Shigeru Nakayama, Kunio Gotō, and Hitoshi Yoshioka, eds., *Nihon no kagaku gijutsu dai nikan* [Japanese science and technology Vol. 2] (Tokyo: Gakuyō Shobō, 1995), pp. 295–317.
45 Samuels, *The Business of the Japanese State*, pp. 238–39.
46 Yoshioka, *Genshiryoku no shakaishi*, p. 83.
47 Nihon Genshiryoku Sangyō Kaigi, ed., *Nihon no genshiryoku: 15-nen no ayumi* [Japan's nuclear power: 15 years of progress], Vol. 1 (Tokyo: Nihon Genshiryoku Sangyō Kaigi, 1971), pp. 121–8.
48 Samuels, *The Business of the Japanese State*, p. 240.
49 For the bureaucracy-dominant models, see, for example, Chalmers Johnson, *MITI and the Japanese Miracle: The Growth of Industrial Policy, 1925–1975* (Stanford, CA: Stanford University Press, 1982).
50 Paul A. Sabatier, "The advocacy coalition framework: revisions and relevance for Europe," p. 116.
51 Samuels, *The Business of the Japanese State*, p. 236.
52 Low, Nakayama, and Yoshioka, *Science, Technology and Society in Contemporary Japan*, p. 77.
53 Takeshi Murota, "Denkijigyōhō to genshiryoku hatsuden" [Electricity Business Act and atomic power generation], *Jiyū to Seigi* [Freedom and Justice], Vol. 42, No. 9 (1991), pp. 11–22; Yu Tanaka, *Nihon no denki ryōkin wa naze takai: yosui hatsuden no iranai riyū* [Why are Japan's electricity fees so expensive? Reasons for no necessity of pumped storage power generation] (Tokyo: Hokuto Shuppan, 2000), pp. 133–5.
54 Sabatier and Weible, "The advocacy coalition framework," p. 198.
55 Fukushima Prefecture, *Fukushima ni okeru dengen ricchi chiiki taisaku kōfukin ni kansuru shiry ō* [Report on electric power development promotion subsidies] (Fukushima: Energy Department of Fukushima Prefecture, 2010).
56 *The Asahi Shinbun*, "TEPCO quietly paid 40 billion yen to areas near nuclear plants," September 15, 2011.

57 Japan Atomic Industry Forum (JAIF), *Infure fukyō no nakadeno genshiryoku sangyō* [Nuclear power industry in an inflationary recession] (Tokyo: JAIF, 1973).
58 Kent Calder, *Crisis and Compensation: Public Policy and Political Stability in Japan 1949–1986* (Princeton, NJ: Princeton University Press, 1988), chp 6.
59 Ken'ichi Ōshima, *Saiseikanō enerugī no seiji keizaigaku*, pp. 32–5.
60 Japanese Atomic Energy Commission (JAEC), "Shirō dai-ichi yon-gō" [Report No. 4-1], March 16, 2010.
61 Hideyasu Kodama, "Nihon ni okeru genshiryoku hatsudensho ricchi ukeire no seiji katei" [Political processes of the site selection of Japan's nuclear power plants], *Seisaku Kagaku* [Policy Science] Vol. 5, No. 2 (1998), p. 41.
62 *New Scientist*, "A country without 'nuclear toilet'," October 3, 1985.
63 Sabatier and Weible, "The advocacy coalition framework," pp. 191–3.
64 Masayuki Nagasaki, *Kakumondai nyūmon: rekishi kara honshitsu o saguru* [Introduction to nuclear problems: a historical inquiry into the essence] (Tokyo: Keisō Shobō, 1998), pp. 58–9.
65 Japan, Management and Coordination Agency, "Genshiryoku no heiwa riyō ni kansuru yoron" [Opinion polls on peaceful uses of nuclear power], March 1969, available from: www8.cao.go.jp/survey/s43/S44-03-43-21.html [accessed August 2, 2014].
66 Shigeru Tanaka, "Seijiteki sōten to shakaiteki seiryoku no tenkai" [Political issues and the development of social forces], in Juichi Aiba, ed., *Kōza Shakaigaku*, Vol. 9 [Lecturers on sociology, Vol. 9] (Tokyo: Tokyo University Press, 2000), pp. 127–61.
67 JAEC, "Shirō dai-ichi Yon-gō."
68 Akihiko Takada, "Genpatsu nyūweibu no kenkyū" [Investigation on "nuke new weave"], *Seikei Daigaku Bungakubu Kiyō* [Seikei University, Faculty of Letters, Research Report], Vol. 26 (1990), pp. 131–88.
69 Hiroshi Honda, "Nihon no genshiryoku seiji katei (4)" [Political processes of nuclear energy in Japan, no. 4], *Hokudai Hōgaku Ronshū* [Hokkaido University Law Review], Vol. 54, No. 4 (2003), p. 318.
70 Kunio Gotō and Hitoshi Yoshioka, eds., *Tsūshi nihon no kagakugijyutsu dai yonkan: tenkanki 1970–1979* [The overview of Japanese history of science and technology, Vol. 4: transitional period of 1970–1979] (Tokyo: Gakuyō Shobō, 1995), pp. 160–1.
71 The decision of the MITI Departmental Council in January 1979 stipulated the implementation of the public hearings.
72 Cf. Herbert P. Kitschelt, "Political opportunities structures and political protest: anti-nuclear movements in four democracies," *British Journal of Political Science*, Vol. 16 (1986), pp. 57–85.
73 Weible, Sabatier, and McQueen, "Themes and variations," p. 129.
74 Ellis S. Krauss and Robert J. Pekkanen, *The Rise and Fall of Japan's LDP* (Ithaca, NY: Cornell University Press, 2011).
75 Ethan Scheiner, Steven R. Reed, and Michael F. Thies, "The end of LDP dominance and the rise of party-oriented politics in Japan," *Journal of Japanese Studies*, Vol. 38, No. 2 (2012), pp. 357–80; Michael F. Thies, "Changing how the Japanese vote: the promise and pitfalls of the 1994 electoral reform," in John Fuh-sheng Hsieh and David Newman, eds., *How Asia Votes* (New York: Chatham House, 2002), pp. 92–117; Steven R. Reed and Michael F. Thies, "The consequences of electoral reform in Japan," in Matthew Soberg Shugart and Martin P. Wattenberg, eds., *Mixed-Member Electoral Systems* (New York: Oxford University Press), pp. 380–403; Gary W. Cox, Frances Rosenbluth, and Michael F. Thies, "Electoral reform and the fate of factions: the case of Japan's Liberal Democratic Party," *British Journal of Political Science*, Vol. 29 (1999), pp. 33–56.
76 Ellis S. Krauss and Robert Pekkanen, "Explaining party adaptation to electoral reform: the discreet charm of the LDP?" *Journal of Japanese Studies*, Vol. 30, No. 1 (2004), p. 32.

77 JAEC, "Shirō Dai-ichi Yon-go."
78 Japan Atomic Energy Commission (JAEC), *Genshiryoku hakusho* [Nuclear white paper], 1993 ed. (Tokyo: Ōkurasho Insatsukyoku, 1993), chps 2–10.
79 Baku Nishio, "Sekinin aru mirai sentaku o: Shakaitō 'genshiryoku seisaku' e no teigen" [Responsible future choice: JSP's proposal for "nuclear policy"] *Gekkan Shakaitō* [Monthly Socialist Party] No. 461 (1993), pp. 88–95.
80 Department of Nuclear Safety and Security and Department of Nuclear Energy, "IAEA mission to review NISA's approach to the 'comprehensive assessment for the safety of existing power reactor facilities' conducted in Japan," *IAEA Report*, Tokyo and Ohi, Japan, January 23–31, 2012.
81 Sabatier and Weible, "The advocacy coalition framework," p. 203.
82 Atsuko Kitada, "Public opinion on nuclear power generation measured in continuous polls over the past 30 years and changes after Fukushima Daiichi nuclear power plant accident," *Nihon Genshiryoku Gakkai Wabun Ronbunshi* [Atomic Energy of Japan Review] Vol. 12, No. 3 (2013), pp. 177–96.
83 It should be noted that the *Asahi Shinbun* opinion poll offered for a choice of two alternatives: approval or disapproval of "promotion" and the disapproval ratio remained between 40 and 50 percent between 1986 and 2000. The higher percentage implies that those who support the status quo were included in the disapproval.
84 Sabatier and Weible, "The advocacy coalition framework," pp. 204–5.
85 Miranda A. Schreurs, *Environmental Politics in Japan, Germany and the United States* (Cambridge, UK: Cambridge University Press, 2002), p. 221.
86 Ōshima, *Saiseikanō enerugī no seiji keizaigaku*; Ōshima, *Genpatsu no kosuto*.
87 Matthew Zafonte and Paul Sabatier, "Shared beliefs and imposed interdependencies as determinants of ally networks in overlapping subsystems," pp. 473–505; Michael D. Jones and Hank C. Jenkins-Smith, "Trans-subsystem dynamics: policy topography, mass opinion, and policy change," *The Policy Studies Journal*, Vol. 37, No. 1 (2009), pp. 37–58.
88 Japan, Energy and Environment Council, "Strategy for innovative energy and environment," September 14, 2012, available from: www.cas.go.jp/jp/seisaku/npu/policy09/pdf/20120914/20120914_1.pdf [accessed July 3, 2014].
89 Ken'ichi Ōshima, "Enerugi seisaku tenkan no totatsuten to kadai [The goals and problems of energy policy change], *Kankyo to Kogai* [Environment and Pollution], Vol. 43, No. 1 (2013), pp. 2–6.
90 Ōshima, "Enerugi seisaku tenkan no totatsuten to kadai," p. 4.
91 Kitada, "Public opinion on nuclear power generation measured in continuous polls over the past 30 years and changes after Fukushima Daiichi nuclear power plant accident," p. 179.
92 Kitada, "Public opinion on nuclear power generation measured in continuous polls over the past 30 years and changes after Fukushima Daiichi nuclear power plant accident," p. 179.
93 *Jiji Tsūshin*, "Genpatsu saikadō yotō maemuki, jisetai nozoki yatō hantai" [Governing party's forward-looking attitudes towards restart: opposition parties against it, except for Jisedai], December 3, 2014, available from: www.jiji.com/jc/zc?k=2014 12/2014120300796 [accessed March 3, 2015].
94 Steven R. Reed, "Survival of 'third parties' in Japan's mixed-member electoral system," in Kenji E. Kushida and Phillip Y. Lipscy, ed., *Japan under the DPJ: the Politics of Transition and Governance* (Stanford, CA: The Walter H. Shorenstein Asia-Pacific Research Center, 2013), chp 4.

References

Arima, Tetsuo (2011). *Genpatsu/Shōriki/CIA* [Nuclear power, Shōriki and the CIA]. Tokyo: Shinchō Shinsho.
Asahi Shinbun (2011). "TEPCO quietly paid 40 billion yen to areas near nuclear plants." September 15, 2011.
Broadbent, Jeffrey (1998). *Environmental Politics in Japan: Networks of Power and Protest*. Cambridge, UK: Cambridge University Press.
Calder, Kent (1988). *Crisis and Compensation: Public Policy and Political Stability in Japan 1949–1986*. Princeton, NJ: Princeton University Press.
Cohen, Linda, Mathew D. McCubbins, and Frances Rosenbluth (1995). "The politics of nuclear power in Japan and the United States." In Peter F. Cowhey and Mathew D. McCubbins, eds., *Structure and Policy in Japan the United States*. Cambridge, UK: Cambridge University Press, pp. 177–202.
Cox, Gary W., Frances Rosenbluth, and Michael F. Thies (1999). "Electoral reform and the fate of factions: the case of Japan's Liberal Democratic Party." *British Journal of Political Science*, Vol. 29, pp. 33–56.
Dauvergne, Peter (1993). "'Outside forces' and the politics of reciprocal consent." *Asian Survey*, Vol. 33, No. 6, pp. 576–91.
Department of Nuclear Safety and Security and Department of Nuclear Energy (2012). "IAEA mission to review NISA's approach to the 'comprehensive assessment for the safety of existing power reactor facilities' conducted in Japan." *IAEA Report*, Tokyo and Ohi, Japan, January 23–31, 2012.
Fukushima Prefecture (2010). *Fukushima ni okeru dengen ricchi chiiki taisaku kōfukin ni kansuru shiry ō* [Report on electric power development promotion subsidies]. Fukushima: Energy Department of Fukushima Prefecture.
Gotō, Kunio and Hitoshi Yoshioka, eds. (1995). *Tsūshi nihon no kagakugijyutsu dai yonkan: tenkanki 1970–1979* [The overview of Japanese history of science and technology, Vol. 4: transitional period of 1970–1979]. Tokyo: Gakuyō Shobō.
Hein, Laura Elizabeth (1990). *Fueling Growth: The Energy Revolution and Economic Policy in Postwar Japan*. Cambridge, MA: Council on East Asian Studies, Harvard University, Distributed by Harvard University Press.
Honda, Hiroshi (2003). "Nihon no genshiryoku seiji katei" [The political process of Japanese nuclear power]. *Hokudai Hogaku Ronshu* [Hokkaido University Law Journal], Vol. 54, No. 1, pp. 337–94.
Honda, Hiroshi (2003). "Nihon no genshiryoku seiji katei (4)" [Political processes of nuclear energy in Japan, no. 4]. *Hokudai Hōgaku Ronshū* [Hokkaido University Law Review], Vol. 54, No. 4, pp. 315–82.
Hughes, Llewelyn (2016). "Japan's energy conundrum." In Robert Pekkanen, Steven R. Reed, and Ethan Scheiner, eds., *Japan Decides 2014: The Japanese General Election*. Basingstoke, UK: Palgrave Macmillan.
International Atomic Energy Agency (IAEA) (2012). "IAEA mission to review NISA's approach to the 'comprehensive assessment for the safety of existing power reactor facilities' conducted in Japan." *IAEA Report*, Tokyo and Ohi, January 2012.
Japan Atomic Energy Commission (JAEC) (1993). *Genshiryoku hakusho* [Nuclear white paper], 1993 ed. Tokyo: Ōkurasho Insatsukyoku.
Japan Atomic Industry Forum (JAIF) (1973). *Infure fukyō no nakadeno genshiryoku sangyō* [Nuclear power industry in an inflationary recession]. Tokyo: JAIF.
Japan, Cost Review Committee, Environment and Energy Council (2011). "Kosuto-tō kenshō

iinkai hōkokusho" [Cost Review Committee Report]. December 2011. Available from: www.cas.go.jp/jp/seisaku/npu/policy09/archive02_hokoku.html [accessed May 22, 2014].
Japan, Energy and Environment Council (2012). "Strategy for innovative energy and environment." September 14, 2012. Available from: www.cas.go.jp/jp/seisaku/npu/policy09/pdf/20120914/20120914_1.pdf [accessed July 3, 2014].
Japan, Management Coordination Agency (1969). "Genshiryoku no heiwa riyō ni kansuru yoron" [Opinion polls on peaceful uses of nuclear power]. March 1969. Available from: www8.cao.go.jp/survey/s43/S44-03-43-21.html [accessed August 2, 2014].
Japan, Ministry of Economy, Trade and Industry (METI), Agency for National Resources and Energy (2014). *Enerugī kihon keikaku* [Strategic Energy Plan]. Available from: www.enecho.meti.go.jp/category/others/basic_plan/pdf/140411.pdf [accessed 22 December 22, 2014].
Japan Times (1975). "U.S. banker honored here." September 20, 1975.
Japan Times (2010). "Kishi 'understood' secret nuke pact, '63 letter indicates." June 26, 2010.
Japanese Atomic Energy Commission (JAEC) (2010). "Shirō dai-ichi yon-gō" [Report No. 4-1]. March 16, 2010.
Jiji Tsūshin (2014). "Genpatsu saikadō yotō maemuki, jisetai nozoki yatō hantai" [Governing party's forward-looking attitudes towards restart; opposition parties against it, except for Jisedai], December 3, 2014. Available from: www.jiji.com/jc/zc?k=201412/2014120300796 [accessed March 3, 2015].
Johnson, Chalmers (1982). *MITI and the Japanese Miracle: The Growth of Industrial Policy, 1925–1975*. Stanford, CA: Stanford University Press.
Jones, Michael D. and Hank C. Jenkins-Smith (2009). "Trans-subsystem dynamics: policy topography, mass opinion, and policy change." *The Policy Studies Journal*, Vol. 37, No. 1, pp. 37–58.
Kawai, Takeshi (1961). *Fushigina kuni no genshiryoku* [A strange nation's nuclear power]. Tokyo: Kadokawa Shoten.
Kingston, Jeff (2013). "Japan's nuclear village: power and resilience." In Jeff Kingston, ed., *Critical Issues in Contemporary Japan*. Abingdon, UK: Routledge, pp. 107–19.
Kitada, Atsuko (2013). "Public opinion on nuclear power generation measured in continuous polls over the past 30 years and changes after Fukushima Daiichi nuclear power plant accident." *Nihon Genshiryoku Gakkai Wabun Ronbunshi* [Atomic Energy of Japan Review], Vol. 12, No. 3, pp. 177–96.
Kitschelt, Herbert P. (1986). "Political opportunities structures and political protest: anti-nuclear movements in four democracies." *British Journal of Political Science*, Vol. 16, pp. 57–85.
Klandermans, Bert (1997). *The Social Psychology of Protest*. Oxford, UK: Blackwell.
Kodama, Hideyasu (1998). "Nihon ni okeru genshiryoku hatsudensho ricchi ukeire no seiji katei" [Political processes of the site selection of Japan's nuclear power plants]. *Seisaku Kagaku* [Policy Science], Vol. 5, No. 2 (1998), pp. 29–49.
Krauss, Ellis S. and Robert Pekkanen (2004). "Explaining party adaptation to electoral reform: the discreet charm of the LDP?" *Journal of Japanese Studies*, Vol. 30, No. 1, pp. 1–34.
Krauss, Ellis S. and Robert J. Pekkanen (2011). *The Rise and Fall of Japan's LDP*. Ithaca, NY: Cornell University Press.
Kuznick, Peter (2011). "Japan's nuclear history in perspective: Eisenhower and Atoms for War and Peace." *Bulletin of the Atomic Scientists*, April 13, 2011, on-line journal. Available from: http://thebulletin.org/japans-nuclear-history-perspective-eisenhower-and-atoms-war-and-peace [accessed December 22, 2014].
Lesbirel, Hayden (1998). *NIMBY Politics in Japan: Energy Siting and the Management of Environmental Conflict*. Ithaca, NY: Cornell University Press.

Low, Morris (2005). *Science and the Building of a New Japan*. New York: Palgrave Macmillan.
Low, Morris, Shigeru Nakayama, and Hitoshi Yoshioka (1999). *Science, Technology and Society in Contemporary Japan*. Cambridge, UK: Cambridge University Press.
Meyer, David S. (2003). "Political opportunity and nested institutions." *Social Movement Studies*, Vol. 2, No. 1, pp. 17–35.
Murota, Takeshi (1981). *Genshiryoku no keizaigaku* [The economics of nuclear power]. Tokyo: Nihon Hyoronsha.
Murota, Takeshi (1991). "Denkijigyōhō to genshiryoku hatsuden" [Electricity Business Act and atomic power generation]. *Jiyū to Seigi* [Freedom and Justice], Vol. 42, No. 9, pp. 11–22.
Murota, Takeshi (1993). *Genpatsu no keizaigaku* [The economics of nuclear power generation]. Tokyo: Asahi Bunko.
Nagasaki, Masayuki (1998). *Kakumondai nyūmon: rekishi kara honshitsu o saguru* [Introduction to nuclear problems: A historical inquiry into the essence]. Tokyo: Keisō Shobō.
Nakajima, Tokunosuke and Ikurō Anzai (1979). *Nihon no genshiryoku hatsuden* [Atomic power in Japan]. Tokyo: Shin Nihon Shuppansha.
Nakayama, Shigeru (1991). *Science, Technology and Society in Postwar Japan*. London: Kegan Paul International.
New Scientist (1985). "A country without 'nuclear toilet'," October 3, 1985.
Nihon Genshiryoku Sangyō Kaigi, ed. (1971). *Nihon no genshiryoku: 15-nen no ayumi* [Japan's nuclear power: 15 years of progress], Vol. 1. Tokyo: Nihon Genshiryoku Sangyō Kaigi.
Nishio, Baku (1993). "Sekinin aru mirai sentaku o: Shakaitō 'genshiryoku seisaku' e no teigen" [Responsible future choice: JSP's proposal for "nuclear policy"]. *Gekkan Shakaitō* [Monthly Socialist Party], No. 461, pp. 88–95.
Okamoto, Takuji (1995). "Denryoku kyōkyū taisei no kakuritsu" [The establishment of electricity supply systems]. In Shigeru Nakayama, Kunio Gotō, and Hitoshi Yoshiok, eds., *Nihon no kagaku gijutsu dai nikan* [Japanese science and technology, Vol. 2]. Tokyo: Gakuyō Shobō, pp. 295–317.
Okumura, Hiroshi (1994). *Nihon no rokudai kigyō shūdan* [Japan's six biggest business groups]. Tokyo: Asahi Shinbunsha.
Ōshima, Ken'ichi (2010). *Saiseikanō enerugī no seiji keizaigaku* [The political economy of renewable energies]. Tokyo: Tōyō Shinpōsha.
Ōshima, Ken'ichi (2011). *Genpatsu no kosuto* [The cost of nuclear power generation]. Tokyo: Iwanami Shinsho.
Ōshima, Ken'ichi (2013). "Enerugi seisaku tenkan no totatsuten to kadai" [The goals and problems of energy policy change]. *Kankyo to Kogai* [Environment and Pollution], Vol. 43, No. 1, pp. 2–6.
Penney, Matthew (2012). "Nuclear nationalism and Fukushima." *The Asia-Pacific Journal: Japan Focus*, on-line journal. Available from: http://japanfocus.org/-matthew-penney/3712/article.html [accessed May 22, 2014].
Pickett, Susan E. (2002). "Japan's nuclear energy policy: from firm commitment to difficult dilemma addressing growing stocks of plutonium, program delays, domestic opposition, and international pressure." *Energy Policy*, Vol. 30, No. 15, pp. 1337–55.
Reed, Steven R. (2013). "Survival of 'third parties' in Japan's mixed-member electoral system." In Kenji E. Kushida and Phillip Y. Lipscy, eds., *Japan under the DPJ: the Politics of Transition and Governance*. Stanford, CA: The Walter H. Shorenstein Asia-Pacific Research Center, chp 4.

Reed, Steven R. and Michael F. Thies (2003). "The consequences of electoral reform in Japan." In Matthew Soberg Shugart and Martin P. Wattenberg, eds., *Mixed-Member Electoral Systems*. New York: Oxford University Press, pp. 380–403.

Sabatier, Paul A. (1998). "The advocacy coalition framework: revisions and relevance for Europe." *Journal of European Public Policy*, Vol. 5, No. 1, pp. 98–130.

Sabatier, Paul A. and Hank C. Jenkins-Smith, eds. (1993). *Policy Change and Learning: An Advocacy Coalition Approach*. Boulder, CO: Westview Press.

Sabatier, Paul A. and Hank Jenkins-Smith (1999). "The advocacy coalition framework: an assessment." In Paul A. Sabatier, ed., *Theories of the Policy Process*. Boulder, CO: Westview Press, pp. 117–66.

Sabatier, Paul A. and Christopher M. Weible (2007). "The advocacy coalition framework: innovations and clarifications." In Paul A. Sabatier, ed., *Theories of the Policy Process*. Boulder, CO: Westview Press, 2007, pp. 189–220.

Samuels, Richard J. (1987). *The Business of the Japanese State: Energy Markets in Comparative and Historical Perspective*. Ithaca, NY: Cornell University Press.

Samuels, Richard (1994). *Rich Nation, Strong Army: National Security and the Technological Transformation of Japan*. Ithaca, NY: Cornell University Press.

Scheiner, Ethan, Steven R. Reed, and Michael F. Thies (2012). "The end of LDP dominance and the rise of party-oriented politics in Japan." *Journal of Japanese Studies*, Vol. 38, No. 2, pp. 357–80.

Schreurs, Miranda A. (2002). *Environmental Politics in Japan, Germany and the United States*. Cambridge, UK: Cambridge University Press.

Takada, Akihiko (1990). "Genpatsu nyūweibu no kenkyū" [Investigation on "nuke new weave"]. *Seikei Daigaku Bungakubu Kiyō* [Seikei University, Faculty of Letters, Research Report], Vol. 26, pp. 131–88.

Tanaka, Shigeru (2000). "Seijiteki sōten to shakaiteki seiryoku no tenkai" [Political issues and the development of social forces]. In Juichi Aiba, ed., *Kōza Shakaigaku* 9 [Lecturers on sociology, Vol. 9]. Tokyo: Tokyo University Press, pp. 127–61.

Tanaka, Yu (2000). *Nihon no denki ryōkin wa naze takai: yosui hatsuden no iranai riyū* [Why are Japan's electricity fees so expensive? Reasons for no necessity of pumped storage power generation]. Tokyo: Hokuto Shuppan.

Tarrow, Sidney (2001). "Transnational politics: contention and institutions in international politics." *Annual Review of Political Science*, Vol. 4, pp. 1–20.

Thies, Michael F. (2002). "Changing how the Japanese vote: the promise and pitfalls of the 1994 electoral reform." In John Fuh-sheng Hsieh and David Newman, eds., *How Asia Votes*. New York: Chatham House, pp. 92–117.

Weible, Christopher M., Paul A. Sabatier, and Kelly McQueen (2009). "Themes and variations: taking stock of the advocacy coalition framework." *Policy Studies Journal*, Vol. 37, No. 1, pp. 121–40.

Yoshioka, Hitoshi (1999). *Genshiryoku no shakaishi* [The social history of nuclear power]. Tokyo: Asahi Shinbunsha.

Yoshioka, Hitoshi (2006). "Reorganization of the administration and regulation of nuclear development." In Shigeru Nakayama and Hitoshi Yoshioka, eds., *A Social History of Science and Technology in Contemporary Japan*, Vol. 4. Melbourne: Trans Pacific Press, pp. 189–273.

Zafonte, Matthew and Paul Sabatier (1998). "Shared beliefs and imposed interdependencies as determinants of ally networks in overlapping subsystems." *Journal of Theoretical Politics*, Vol. 10, No. 4, pp. 473–505.

3 The state of local capacity-building

Decentralized policy-making

This chapter will examine the state of local capacity-building for climate change countermeasures in Japan and Japanese local government involvement in international environmental cooperation. The aim is to draw an overall picture of sub-national participation in climate change policy and international environmental cooperation by highlighting the governing capacity gaps between pioneering local governments and other local governments. Climate change policy needs to be led by both global strategies and national mandates in an integrated way; however, climate change impacts are manifested locally and their adaptive capacity is determined by local conditions. I claim that a possible source of cohesion for policy integration lies in the decentralized role of local governments, for they occupy a strategic position since they straddle both the division between global collective action and national self-interest and that between the international and the national. In one respect, local governments have a potential to reconnect local action with national policy and turn global strategies into local actions for problem-solving. This strategic position enables local governments to take up a key role in the decentralized functions of international cooperation. Yet the necessary precondition for local governments to efficiently and effectively participate in decentralized policy coordination lies in their governing capacities. The chapter first lays out the basic components of local capacity for decentralized policy-making and assesses current local capacity in view of Japan's climate policy. The second section examines the state of Japanese local governments' capacity in international environmental cooperation and assesses the issues arising from decentralized international cooperation. The bulk of the data employed in the study is derived from existing up-to-date government databases. The data suggests that only the largest municipalities, as well as prefectures, have the governing capacity to develop a comprehensive approach to climate adaptation and mitigation, while medium-sized municipalities have the potential to take a participatory approach to climate policy. It argues that some pioneering localities realize their potential to take initiatives under political leadership but most localities act in a piecemeal fashion according to clear national-level guidance. It also suggests that financial capacity is significantly related to international environmental cooperation, but factors internal to unexpectedly active localities require further examination.

In the 1970s, Japanese local government was known for its progressive policy on industrial pollution control, with other Organization for Economic Cooperation and Development (OECD) countries emulating Japan's local environmental innovations. In the late 1960s, when industrial pollution fueled local environmental activism in Japan, it became apparent that the centralized image of Japan would require closer examination. Some scholars suggested that Japan was less centralized than most academic Japan-specialists had initially thought and its local government system had much more discretion than they had expected.[1] In the absence of national legislation, Japanese local governments, pressured at the time by developing movements of residents in their pollution-affected localities, exercised their discretionary power for policy innovations.[2] They played a critical role in policy diffusion to the national level to tackle pollution problems.

However, the local policy environment appears to have significantly changed, particularly over the last two decades. Japan's local environmental responses have shifted from predominantly contentious activities in domestic politics to a far more complex process that involves both local coordination with national policy and local adaptations to global environmental strategies. On the global level, the importance of local policy-making can be traced back to ideas incorporated into Agenda 21 (an action plan for sustainable development adopted at the 1992 Earth Summit), with an emphasis on the local level of participation, the layer of government closest to the people.[3] Ever since the acknowledgment of the community's vital role in the implementation of global strategies for sustainable development within the Agenda 21 framework, the position of local communities has been further promoted and strengthened by a series of decision-making processes at both the national and international levels. In 1993 the International Council for Local Environmental Initiatives (ICLEI) launched the notion of Local Agenda 21, a participatory, multi-sectoral process in which local participants voluntarily create long-term, strategic action plans and implement them to achieve sustainability by integrating environmental, social, and economic priorities.[4] Article 34 of Japan's Basic Environmental Law, which was enacted in the same year, acknowledged the role of local governments as the subjects of international environmental cooperation.

A local level of participation in climate change policy is increasingly expected on two basic grounds: the need for locally specific responses to global strategies and the need for a decentralized form of redistributing global environmental functions.[5] Global strategies for environmental risk reduction require local action while local environmental problem-solving demands global coordination.[6] From the viewpoint of local policy-making, the central issue boils down to local authorities' willingness and capability to contribute to problem-solving to cater for both locally specific needs and global strategies. Yet the key problem for local capacity-building is an inadequate delegation of power to lower levels of government.[7] First, in many countries, local governments do not have the fiscal capacity to include funding requirements in their environmental programs. Second, they often lack sufficient jurisdiction over the implementation of environmental policies. Equally important, there exists two fundamental blockages within local administrations: lack of information and expertise and incapability in interdepartmental coordination.[8] From the viewpoint of multi-level governance, action at local scales cannot be effective in isolation from components of the institutional frameworks at national scales.[9] The reputation of Japanese local governments for being innovative in the 1970s is well worth inquiring into to inform an exploration of their adaptation to the new policy environment. The case of Japan's efforts in local capacity-building offers an opportunity to examine how to make climate change policy work at the local level.

Assessing local capacity-building

There exists a great deal in the literature examining the advantages of decentralized public policy. Earlier research on decentralized decision-making for service delivery found numerous benefits. First, as environmental problems are often location-specific, differences in geographical areas can be effectively dealt with in decentralized decision-making.[10] Second, decentralized units are positioned well to make the processing of interest articulation and aggregation easier since public preferences are available in the immediate environment[11] or as voters move from one community to another to satisfy their service preferences.[12] Third, the specific operations of decentralization provide chances for enhancing the visibility of service performance and the traceability of responsibility, and thus increase accountability to stakeholders.[13] Lastly, subject to inter-jurisdictional competition, decentralized control over the economy responds to citizens' needs and prevents the central government from interfering with markets.[14]

What government level of policy-making, then, is better suited to environmental issues? The impact of decentralized governance on environmental quality has been documented in the empirical literature but evidence reported in a number of studies shows mixed results. Some studies provide evidence that devolving authority did result in inefficient regulatory competition or "a race to the bottom" that would lower environmental quality to compete for capital.[15] They also report evidence of "free riding" by sub-national governments that chose lower environmental standards than the national government would choose, to export the environmental costs to their neighbors.[16] Others argue that there is no evidence of such destructive regulatory competition and many sub-national governments do not even exercise their discretion in favor of lower environmental standards.[17] These results appear to be mixed yet a list of preconditions necessary for decentralized environmental policies to be efficient would explain these apparently mixed results in a more consistent way. For decentralization to realize the potential benefits of efficiency and equitability, the literature suggests several capacity-based preconditions: intergovernmental cooperation at the sub-national level without centralized intervention;[18] fiscal autonomy and discretion;[19] administrative capacity;[20] democratic political institutions;[21] responsive local officials;[22] and civic engagement.[23] These preconditions are primarily a question of sufficient resources, that is, sufficient financial resources, jurisdiction, discretion, adequate staff and expertise, and accountability mechanisms.

In this chapter, while drawing on the above literature, as Table 3.1 shows, the local capacity necessary for policy decentralization to be effective is examined from two viewpoints: government performance evaluations and citizens' orientations. Government performance can be evaluated both procedurally and substantially. Evaluations of local government performance thus draw on two fundamental causal paths: *governmental procedures* (the quality of representational links between citizens and local government—accountability and attentiveness) and *governmental performance* (the evaluations of policy-making and implementation activities of local government—efficiency and fairness). Citizens' orientation can be observed both individually and collectively. The orientations of citizens are thus linked into two causal paths: the individual's subjective makeup of *political involvement* (personal orientations and expectations) and the interpersonal makeup of *social relations* relevant to collective action (collective orientations and expectations among citizens).

The quality of governmental procedures requires two basic conditions: *accountability mechanisms* (referring to mechanisms that allow wide, effective participation in light of the governmental ability to provide access and to hold officials accountable) and *officials' attentiveness* (officials' actual attentiveness to what the people think).[24] The equality of accountability can be observed by assessing the institutional mechanisms of a linkage process that relates the government to the citizenry. These include climate change-specific ones such as Local Agenda 21, action plans, and environmental impact assessments. Accountability mechanisms are crucial structures of legitimate government, but they are only effective to the extent that officials acknowledge the incentive structures designed to increase their attentiveness. Evidence of officials' attentiveness can be sought in the incentive structures of climate change such as environmental performance disclosure and personnel management.

The quality of governmental performance is tapped by two conditions: *officials' efficiency* (officials' capacity to accomplish their tasks without undue waste of time or resources) and *fairness of government outputs* (fairness of cost-sharing in local government's outputs). These two conditions address procedural efficiency and overall fairness respectively. Key indicators for such efficiency in climate policy, as discussed later, are chief executives' leadership, administrative ability, and fiscal capacity. In this policy area, fairness involves mitigation cost-sharing rather than the potential benefits of environmental risk reduction, since these benefits are both non-excludable and non-rival. As indicated in this study, environmental impact assessments at early stages and citizen involvement are a minimal condition for overall fairness.

The subjective makeup of political involvement is shaped by two prominent conditions: *political interest* (personal feelings of responsibility for citizen participation) and *political efficacy* (personal feelings about the prospect for successful citizen participation).[25] In addition to predispositions, social networks provide

Table 3.1 Local capacity for decentralized policy-making

Capacity	Dimension	Definition	Empirical indicators
Governmental procedures	Accountability mechanisms	Access to hold officials accountable	Institutions that press officials to take account of citizens' views
	Officials' attentiveness	Attentiveness to public preference	Facts if officials actually take proper account of citizens' view
Governmental performance	Officials' efficiency	Ability to perform tasks efficiently	Efficiency of leadership and administration
	Fairness of government outputs	Fairness of cost-sharing	Wide, effective participation
Citizens' orientations	Political interest	Responsibility for citizen participation	Interest in politics
	Political efficacy	Prospect for citizen participation	Perception of government institutions
	Interpersonal trust	Shared expectations among citizens	Trust in people

a potential for a higher level of political participation. The interpersonal makeup of social relations is accounted for by a primary condition: *interpersonal trust* (shared expectations situated in relationships between citizens).[26] The subjective and interpersonal makeup can be observed by citizens' perceptions.

The following section will assess the local capacity of Japan to meet locally specific conditions as well as national policy frameworks and international agreements while drawing on the analytical framework of those key components.

Citizens' orientation: political involvement and expectation

Political interest

Today Japanese public concerns about climate change are particularly high; a 2007 government survey found that 92.3 percent of the public expressed "very" or "modest" concern about the issue.[27] If major trends in public opinion are paralleled by coverage in the mass media, then the near explosion of climate change coverage that began in 1989 indicates a sudden upward trend in public awareness about climate change. Newspaper articles with key words, *chikyū kankyō* (global environment) and/or *chikyū ondanka* (global warming), increased rapidly in number from seven in 1986 through 1,430 in 1989 to 2,633 in 1992 when the Earth Summit took place.[28] Yet, a number of studies found that, despite this public awareness, societal actors were yet to be mobilized to influence the policy-making process.[29] In the 1960s and early 1970s, Japanese politics of industrial pollution involved the costs of industrial poisoning, namely the visible costs of human life itself. The immediate causes of industrial pollution, unlike non-industrial pollution, were easy to identify and confront. In contrast, in the 1990s the objectives of Japan's environmental policy moved away from one-dimensional pollution controls towards a sustainable society and environment. The general public had a limited capacity to confront diffused, "no-point sources" of pressure on the environment. The low visibility of long-term mitigation benefits that the general public is supposed to receive tend to prevent the general public from citizen participation.[30] In this context, the importance of environmental education has already been identified by local authorities and a range of climate change education in the curriculum of schools has been implemented across the nation.[31]

Political efficacy

According to the Nippon Telegraph and Telephone (NTT) Data survey, the lower the level of government, the higher the citizens' expectation of representation. The survey asked who "should decide on important issues of municipal governance." As high as 88 percent of respondents answered, "Residents should directly participate in decision-making," in sharp contrast to only 11 percent answering, "Publicly elected representatives should decide." Although a mere 8 percent had experienced direct participation in such decision-making at some level, 37 percent had not yet had a chance to participate but wished to do so when the opportunity arose.[32] This is a significant percentage of potentially proactive citizens. It is clear that there is plenty of room for the incorporation of local environmental policy-making in inclusive democracy-building.

As the same survey shows that 47 percent felt their views to be represented at the municipal level while only 8 percent at the national level, Japanese local governments are relatively trusted institutions. Indeed, positions as local civil servants are deemed to be one of the most desirable jobs among university graduates.[33] Communication processes between local administration and citizens are expected to enhance the transparency and social equity of cost-sharing for climate action and thus increase personal feelings about the prospect for successful citizen participation. Yet Japanese local governments are now facing the challenge of meeting the needs of multi-sectoral climate action.

Over the past decade, some form of direct citizen participation (*shimin sanka*) in local policy-making has become common among municipalities. The 1993 enactment of the national Basic Environmental Law encouraged local governments to prepare their own environmental basic bylaws and plans, and the national grant program paid 50 percent of actual costs for preparing such plans, in anticipation of compliance with the *senshinsei* (advancement) of the planning process (i.e., citizens' participatory role in the process).[34] This triggered abrupt increases in the nationally defined inclusion of citizens in preparing local environmental plans. As of 2013, Basic Environmental Bylaws had been enacted in 59.2 percent of 1,194 local governments (cf. 95.2 percent of local governments with population of over 0.5 million) and Basic Environmental Plans had been prepared by 57.7 percent of those local governments (cf. 100 percent local governments with population of over 0.5 million).[35] In preparing their basic environmental plans, these local governments normally created a sole participatory mechanism, advisory environmental councils (*shingikai*), whose membership composition was similar to the national councils representing business, interest groups, and academics rather than concerned ordinary citizens.[36] This national top-down promotion provided little provision for substantial citizen participation in local environmental policy-making. Nonetheless, it is important to note that there are two pioneering cases, Toyonaka City[37] and Hino City,[38] reported as the only, purely, faithfully citizen-led environmental policy-making; it is reported that a group of openly invited citizens in both cities collectively conducted data collection, site investigations, measurements, and assessments and local assemblies adopted their draft plans in March 1999 and September 1999 respectively. Otherwise, a dozen examples of substantial participation were reported as cases of collaboration between citizens and local administration. On balance, therefore, the local policy-making environment to increase personal feelings about the prospect for successful citizen participation is at an early embryonic stage.

Interpersonal trust

A series of nationwide surveys, although providing limited measurement indexes used to compare different localities in Japan, indicate that a positive relationship is present between social trust and participation.[39] The 2005 Cabinet Office survey asked questions concerning the degree of trust in people on a scale of 1 (not trusted) to 9 (most trusted): 25.6 percent of "designated cities"—populations of at least 0.5 million—indicated 6 or more, compared to cities/towns 27.8 percent and villages 28.3 percent, while the rate of regular participation in voluntary work was 8.7 percent in designated cities, 13.8 percent in cities/towns, and 18.2 percent in villages.[40] The levels of both social trust and participation were relatively low in major cities such as Tokyo and Osaka while higher in rural localities. All in all, the higher the level of social trust the greater the involvement in voluntary work. It is important to note here that since the introduction of the Non-profit Organization Law in 1998, the number of legally registered voluntary organizations rose rapidly to over 45,000 in March 2012. The rise of organized voluntary activity in major and medium-sized cities seems to be producing a new type of social capital, bridging capital, bringing different groups together for more inclusive social networks.[41] The role of these organizations as mobilization agencies is yet to be examined.

Governmental procedures: accountability and attentiveness

Accountability mechanisms

Making climate change policy work requires the informed participation of all stakeholders. Probably the most notable development of information disclosure in environmental policy is the introduction of evaluation and announcement programs regarding greenhouse gas (GHG) emissions reduction. In these programs, large GHG-emitting business facilities are required to submit a GHG emissions reduction plan. This plan is evaluated and the results are officially announced. As of April 2010, 36 percent (17) of 47 prefectures and 32 percent (6) of 19 designated cities were implementing such mandatory measures at some level.[42] In Kyoto City, since 2005, 148 designated facilities have been required to submit their CO_2 emissions reduction plans and outcome reports, documentation that has been released to the public.[43] In a similar way, the Tokyo Metropolitan Government designated 1,332 facilities in 2005 and officially announced the evaluation of their submitted five-year reduction plans. In 2008 the experience of information disclosure under this mandatory reporting system led the Tokyo Metropolitan Government to introduce mandatory targets for a reduction in overall emissions for large-scale emitters as part of an emissions trading program.[44] The world's first urban cap-and-trade program, which required mandatory CO_2 reductions from large commercial and industrial buildings, launched in Tokyo on April 1, 2010. One year later, Saitama became the second local government in Japan to implement a mandatory emissions trading scheme while agreeing to link their cap-and-trade programs with Tokyo. Its target-setting emissions trading program set reduction targets of around 600 designated facilities and allowed them to trade allowances.

To make informed citizens active, there are specific modes of participatory accountability mechanisms available at the local level of Japan's climate change policy: Local Agenda 21; local climate change action; and local environmental impact assessments (EIA).

Local Agenda 21

An integrated approach to Local Agenda 21 is expected to provide an opportunity for local governments to engage their local communities and other local governments to develop actions for climate adaptation and mitigation. In January 1993, for the first time in Japan, Kanagawa prefecture made a Local Agenda 21 program, and by March 2003, all remaining 46 prefectures and 330 municipalities had followed suit.[45] In Japan, the policy area of Local Agenda 21 came under the jurisdiction of Environmental Agency (reorganized as the Ministry of the Environment in 2001), which supervised local adoption through prefectural departments of the environment. This narrow, vertical tutelage was incapable of effective coordination among environmental and non-environmental policy areas. Most municipalities had already had "long-term comprehensive plans" (*sōgō keikaku*) at the highest level of local governmental plans, as defined in the Local Autonomy Law (Article 2-4). Local government officials tended to see Local Agenda 21 as one among various administration activities, not as a plan to integrate these activities. Unlike the ICLEI definition of Local Agenda 21,[46] Japan's Environmental Agency saw Local Agenda 21 as the final product of community plans rather than as an interactive process itself between stakeholders for increasing local accountability in making communities more sustainable.[47] Local Agenda 21 programs in Japan were consequently reported to indicate peculiar patterns: over 70 percent of these Local Agenda 21s were regarded as a mere administration plan rather than a societal, voluntary process of local community consultation[48] and almost all were aimed at a narrowly defined issue of the environment rather than at a broadly conceived inter-issue linkage of sustainability, except for a few localities such as Kyoto and Minamata Cities and Nirayama Town where the integration of planning and action across economic, social and environmental spheres was sought.[49]

It was reported that, as of March 2003, at the first phase of planning and policy-making, 40 percent of Local Agenda 21 programs at the prefectural level and 67 percent at the municipal level provided citizens with direct access to decision-making at some level.[50] Nonetheless, a very few cases, such as Hikone, Joetsu, Kasumigaura, Kyoto, and Toyonaka Cities, were recognized as a citizen-led partnership with the local administration that had determined the content or direction of Local Agenda 21 programs.[51] It was also found that only Osaka prefecture had reviewed and altered its Local Agenda 21 program every fiscal year while 72 percent of Local Agenda 21 programs at the prefectural level and 58 percent at the municipal level were equipped with a program review mechanism.[52] Overall, the state of Local Agenda 21 adoption in Japan is still far from achieving a participatory process of continual policy formation.

Climate change action

Article 4 of the 1998 Climate Change Law states: "Local governments shall promote policies to limit greenhouse gas emissions in accordance with the natural and social conditions of their areas." This gives statutory recognition to the advantages of decentralization and that the nature of environmental problems is often location-specific and can be managed in different geographical areas. A significant number of Japanese local governments have accordingly been implementing their action plans for emissions reductions in their geographical areas; as of December 2014, 100 percent (47) of 47 prefectures, 80 percent (16) of 20 designated cities, and 21.4 percent (383) of all 1,788 local governments, had drawn up such plans.[53] It was found that almost all of these plans had stated their emissions reduction targets and designated reduction measures but very few had clearly articulated their locally specific measures as credible or achievable for emissions reduction targets.[54]

In December 2004, Kyoto City enacted the Kyoto City Global Warming Countermeasures Ordinance to reduce GHG emissions to 10 percent below 1990 levels by 2010, becoming the first local government in Japan to put such a specialized ordinance into effect. Five prefectures (Kyoto and Osaka in 2005, Nagano in 2006, Wakayama and Shizuoka in 2007) and six municipalities (Kawagoe in 2007, Kashiwa in 2007, Chiyoda Ward in 2008, Kusatsu in 2008, Hiroshima in 2009, and Kawasaki in 2010) followed suit in enacting such ordinances. As of April 2015, 38 percent (18) of 47 prefectures have enacted and implement their climate change countermeasure-specific ordinances for climate mitigation.[55] The ordinance-based countermeasures have been taken partly due to a recognition that the energy consumption of Japanese households has grown much faster than the industrial sector[56] and changes in lifestyle and social beliefs are thus crucial to the success of effective GHG emissions reduction. The success of such changes requires a greater collaboration between local administrations and citizens for information sharing that ensures a better informed citizenry and publicly monitored administrative decisions. As of 2010, 42 percent of 1,358 local governments have been practicing some form of collaboration with citizens for emissions reduction countermeasures, yet only 10 percent of these collaborative schemes have been initiated or requested by their local residents.[57] In other words, a large majority of collaborations have been led by the local administration.

Stakeholder meetings for the introduction of Tokyo's cap-and-trade system are regarded as one such administration-led collaboration. At the 2007 meetings, the Tokyo Metropolitan Government successfully sought ex post facto approval of administrative initiatives from business establishments, environmental NGOs, and academics.[58] Since the administration-led system, targeted for mandatory emissions reductions among big emitters, was well-prepared and well-documented, the Tokyo Chamber of Commerce, along with the general public, came to fully support the cap-and-trade system in 2008.[59] Kyoto City is another active locality with a citizen-led, rather than administration-led, approach to collaboration. Its Miyako Agenda 21 Forum (as of 2008, consisting of 551 members drawn from citizens' groups, academics, and business associations), in partnership with local administration, has promoted action plans towards becoming a low carbon city and engaged in a range of educational promotions to raise public awareness.[60]

Environmental impact assessments (EIA)

The project level is critically important for assessing climate change risks and for developing suitable adaptation measures. Generally speaking, a government requires policy tools to screen projects for the risks posed by climate change. The aim of EIA is to assess the impact of a proposed project on the environment and develop measures to avoid or minimize those impacts. Local governments are naturally expected to incorporate climate impact and adaptation within the context of EIA procedures. Long before the 1997 enactment of the national EIA Law, some local governments had already implemented relatively comprehensive assessments over proposed projects under public pressure to take preventive measures rather than ex post countermeasures against industrial pollution.[61] Kawasaki City was the first local government in Japan to enact an EIA Ordinance in 1976 while both the Tokyo Metropolitan Government and Kanagawa prefecture followed suit in 1980. As of March 2012, all major localities (47 prefectures and 17 designated cities) enacted their EIA ordinances under the direction of the national EIA Law.[62] The objective of local EIA was to now carry it out "within the law" but also to apply it flexibly to cover smaller and more diverse projects for meeting local needs rather than just those the national law designated.

All local EIA procedures have independent review commissions (*shinsakai*), which act as advisory assessors to provide technical/expert opinions at various stages of EIA. Most local EIA ordinances also stipulate an administrative obligation for public hearings (*kōchōkai*) that local chief executives consider necessary to hold at any stage. Equally important, EIA brings citizen participation to a new dimension. In the area of industrial pollution, the third party (the general public) had not been specifically stipulated in Japan's legal system and thus normally could not act as a formal participant, yet EIA has provided a new way of opening up the scope of participation to the general public. In fact, most local EIA procedures define participants as "those who have opinions from the standpoint of protecting the environment" (no geographically defined limits).[63] Nonetheless, there is a major problem commonly found in these local EIA systems; consultation at an early stage of projects does not normally fall within the scope of EIA, and thus the public find it impossible to consider alternatives to the proposed projects. As of 2004, three prefectures (Tokyo, Hokkaido, and Hyogo) and one municipality (Zushi) had an institutionalized system of citizen participation explicitly prescribed in their EIA ordinances, and three prefectures (Tokyo, Saitama, and Mie) and two municipalities (Kyoto and Kawasaki) had an EIA mechanism for early draft plans, which was embedded in their EIA ordinances.[64] The only exception is the Tokyo Metropolitan Government, which provides public access to early draft plans involving the public and authorities with environmental, social, and economic responsibilities as part of the EIA process in an integrated way. However, it is very important to note that the practice of incorporating climate change adaptation measures within the existing systems of EIA remain at a very early stage. Only a few Japanese local governments, such as the Tokyo Metropolitan Government, have shown their intent to seriously use EIA procedures in this context.

Officials' attentiveness

In Japan, the heads of local governments and members of local assemblies are elected by direct public election (Article 93 of Japan's constitution). This is a "dual representation system" whereby both the assembly and the chief executive officer of local governments are directly elected as representative organs by residents. There are thus two channels through which the will of residents can be heard. Local assemblies are to function as deliberative organs to represent their residents. However, the capacity of local assemblies to keep their chief executives in check has been seriously constrained by the phenomenon of *ōru yotōka* (all parties ruling together without political opposition).[65] As a result, incentives for local officials' attentiveness are largely institutionalized in their executive branches, providing a way of reaching out to citizens in a direct way. The effectiveness of a local government's attentiveness to what the people think significantly derives from local administration. Japanese local governments have directly elected mayors or governors on the presidential system. These chief executives have greater control over an entire government personnel and organization than the prime minister at the national level. In general, local authorities, the layer of government closest to the people, are under constant pressure to respond to popular demands quickly. In the field of local environmental policy in Japan, there are two areas of development for incentive structures brought to officials' attention: environmental performance disclosure and environmental policy coordination.

Environmental performance disclosure

In general, sub-national government ensures better information disclosure than national government does. Local governments are not distracted by the secrecy needed in "high politics." The number of local government information disclosure ordinances rose rapidly from 56 in 1985 to 178 in 1990; as of October 2014, 100 percent (47) of 47 prefectures, 100 percent (20) of 20 designated cities, and 99.9 percent (1717) of 1719 municipalities in Japan had enacted information disclosure ordinances and were providing disclosure at some level.[66] The information release ratio by the Tokyo Metropolitan Government between 2000 and 2004, for example, was 97 percent of 13,402 disclosure requests.[67] Indeed, the information disclosure of government performance has become a common practice among prefectures and major cities; those authorities introducing a government performance appraisal system increased markedly from 18.1 percent of all local governments in 2004 to 59.3 percent in 2013 (47 of 47 prefectures and 19 of 20 designated cities).[68] It should be noted that there are no legal obligations for local authorities either to introduce such a system or to comply with a nationally defined way of evaluation when they decide to introduce one. Performance evaluation is generally carried out by their administrative organizations (self-evaluation) and primarily focuses on a post facto examination of project outcomes. As of October 2013, self-evaluation without external evaluation accounted for 54.4 percent of 1,060 local performance appraisal systems and a dual mechanism of internal and external evaluation represented 43.7 percent of those systems.[69] Yet there is some evidence that the number of local governments implementing their evaluation at the policy-level as well as at the program-level is on the increase: 39 percent of prefectures and 22 percent of designated cities.[70] In this context, the use of both the specific policy-level and ante facto evaluation for EIA, as described previously, is likely to provide a greater incentive to local officials' attentiveness.

Environmental policy coordination

In Japan, pollution countermeasure agreements (PCAs) with specific enterprises have been an effective measure of local environmental policy to regulate major "point source polluters." In 1993 there were 42,000 such agreements between local authorities and individual enterprises.[71] Yet there had been a lack of transparency in PCAs that were left at a great distance from well-planned policy implementation. As the scope of local environmental policies expanded beyond industrial grounds, local authorities would exercise their power over diffuse, "no-point sources" of pressures on the environment. In the early 1990s, as the objectives of Japan's environmental policy moved away from one-dimensional pollution control towards a sustainable society and environment, the scope of regulatory objects was to expand from business activities through city planning to consumer behavior. The expansion of policy scope necessitated policy coordination between environmental and other departments and required expertise for a diverse set of administrative tools.

When responsibilities overlap, conflict may result. Inter-departmental coordination is thus required. There have been more examples of institutionalization for "comprehensive environmental policy-making." One such example is the creation of a Global Warming Countermeasures Promotion Office, which is expected to draw up large-scale GHG emissions reduction plans, to be implemented on a top-down basis. This office is usually attached to the chief executives' office for policy coordination. As of 2009, eight prefectures and six designated cities operated such headquarters for climate change policy.[72] Some local governments recognize that *jinji-idō* (organization-wide job rotation practice), which is carried out every year before the new fiscal year starts in April, would disrupt policy continuity and prevent employees from developing their expertise. To overcome the adverse effect of a personnel reshuffle, in 2009 Kyoto City created a new job classification, *kankyō-shoku* (environmental specialists) for managing environmental issues.[73] Informally, the Tokyo Metropolitan Government has been giving priority to employees' preferences for personnel reshuffling. As a result, there has been a substantial increase in the number of experienced environmental specialists.[74]

Governmental performance: efficiency and fairness

Officials' efficiency

Local officials occupy a better position to respond to locally specific preferences than officials in higher levels of government. Their performance can be facilitated and constrained by locally specific characteristics, such as the type of service to be provided, the differences between fiscal need and fiscal capacity available to them, the size and location of their localities, the patterns of intergovernmental relations, their relationships with neighboring local governments, and other factors. In Japan, it appears that the chief executives of localities with a larger population (or larger tax base) tend to see themselves as administratively more competent in exercising their discretion in carrying out responsibilities. According to a survey of local chief executives' perceptions (allowing only yes or no responses), 49.6 percent of 1,905 respondents saw local government as not competent enough to carry out the responsibilities demanded by decentralization in terms of transferring responsibility to local bodies. The percentage of those of prefectures (100 percent) and cities (70.2 percent) claiming to be competent, as compared with towns and villages (39.1 percent), were large enough to call this finding into question.[75]

Political leadership

A large majority of Japanese local authorities have displayed a copycatting behavior (*yokonarabi*) regarding climate change policy by implementing nationally-subsidized policy measures or following nationally-defined policy measures that neighboring localities have adopted. Under these circumstances, a number of case studies have come to the conclusion that political leadership—usually mayoral or gubernatorial—is a key ingredient in a local government's ability to introduce progressive low carbon measures.[76] In order to exercise their leadership over stakeholders and residents, these chief executives would require necessary resources, such as sufficient fiscal capacity and staff resources, chief executives' jurisdiction over a given policy or program, sufficient staff support, public support, political parties' support, and a friendly mass media. It then largely depends on their ability and willingness to mobilize those resources to influence others. It was reported that, without some form of chief executives' commitment, progressive proposals may never get onto the policy agenda while being initially presented by an informal policy network of those (government officials, NGOs and academics) interested in low carbon issues.[77] At the stage of policy formation, however, the exercise of chief executives' power may not promote but rather undermine the policy rationale if it is politicized to the extent to which there exist tensions between the chief executives and local assemblies or influential local figures (Tokyo Governor Shintarō Ishihara created such tensions with big business over his intention to introduce Tokyo's cap-and-trade in 2002–2007).[78] From the viewpoint of local administration, the department concerned is less likely to commit itself to progressive policy-making if there are such tensions or there is a high likelihood of changing hands to a new chief executive (Nagano Governor Yasuo Tanaka failed to win the goodwill of his government officials for cooperation in 2002–2006).[79] To make these recalcitrant actors commit to or support progressive low carbon measures, the ideal chief executive would require sufficient financial resources and political opportunities to be exploited by political leadership (Tokyo Governor Ishihara's bid for the 2016 Olympic Games under the slogan, "Carbon Minus Olympics" legitimized stringent mitigation measures in 2006).[80]

Administrative ability

As of April 2014, the total number of local government employees in environmental administration stood at 14,148 (7,203 for pollution and 6,945 for environmental conservation). Within the context of administrative reforms, the overall size of local administration in terms of employment had decreased by nearly 16 percent between 1994 and 2014; in contrast, the number of local government employees in environmental conservation increased rapidly by 52 percent during the same period.[81] In every prefecture and designated city, along with a bureau for environmental administration (177 employees on the prefectural average and 198 employees on the designated-city average), multiple sections were established within this environmental bureau. As far as other municipalities were concerned, only 13 percent (233 municipalities) had an independent department of environmental administration. In nearly 90 percent of municipalities with populations of less than 10,000, and in about 66 percent of municipalities with populations of more than 10,000 but less than 30,000, there existed no specialist responsible for environmental administration.[82] As of October 2014, specialized staffs consisting of four to 20 people (who were in charge of climate change countermeasures) represented 68 percent (32) of 47 prefectures, and staffs of zero to four people accounted for 91 percent (1,586) of 1,741 municipalities.[83]

An environmental management system can support local governments' climate change adaptation and mitigation measures by providing procedures for managing the environmental impacts of their own organizational activities. Japanese local governments have applied recognized environmental management systems or developed their own environmental management systems. In 1998 Shiroi Town in Chiba prefecture was the first local government in Japan to acquire the ISO 14001 international environmental management standards certificate, in order to take on initiatives in promoting projects that would reduce the burden on the environment. The number of accredited local governments grew rapidly, peaking at 513 localities in 2004, though declining to 269 localities in 2009. This decline was due primarily to an amalgamation of localities but also to the introduction of new standards in environmental management systems (EMS), such as Local Authority's Standards in the Environment (LAS-E). As ISO 14001 had been initially used for manufacturing facilities, by 2008 32 percent of ISO 14001 accredited local governments declared that they would adapt ISO 14001 as their own.[84] As of January 2008, 37 percent of local governments were performing under some form of EMS and 22 percent of these local governments had developed their own EMS.[85]

In a broad sense, administrative review provides local policy-makers with a mechanism to improve the effectiveness and efficiency of initial decisions. Over time, the review process is likely to lead to a better decision as the evaluation outcome is reported back to the initial decision maker. A policy cycle or sequenced policy process is a guide for policy development. As described previously, nearly 60 percent (1,060) of all 1,789 local governments managed a system of administrative evaluation in 2013 yet only 35 percent (325) of 930 towns/villages had administrative evaluation at some level in the same year. A characteristic feature observed in the trends of administrative evaluation is that most of these local governments (95 percent) implemented at the project level, yet a limited number of them carried it out at the policy level (12 percent) and at the implementation level (49 percent).[86] While reviewing project management is very important to improve the quality of service delivery, policy and implementation review is essential to developing policies and strategies. In this sense, local administrative evaluation is yet to be improved to enhance administrative ability in order to develop local climate policy.

Financial capacity

To achieve local policy innovation, local governments must have fiscal flexibility in budgetary choices. They can enjoy little freedom in budgeting unless their revenue can expand beyond the rate of inflation. Yet Japanese local authorities' revenue is the most regulated in the world. The Local Tax Law imposes a common legal framework on all local governments, setting state-mandated local tax rates and assessment methods. In Japan, the Local Allocation Tax has also heavily influenced local governments, which have a low fiscal capacity. This tax (i.e., national transfer payments to local governments) serves the purpose of equalization between wealthier and poorer local governments. The transfer payment forces a nationally established spending level on the poorer local governments, although increasing the elasticity of their income by not specifying how to spend it. In practice, a small proportion of current expenditure is dispensable and much additional revenue is often used up by rising costs. The ratio of current expenditure to revenue is thus a useful index of fiscal elasticity measurements. This ratio for both prefectures and municipalities has increased significantly since the early 1990s when the bubble economy began to collapse. The ratio of prefectures rose from 70.7 percent in 1990 to 93.0 percent in 2013, while that for municipalities also increased from 69.7 percent in 1990 to 90.2 percent in 2013.[87] Massive budget deficits have remained in most Japanese local governments as their spending has far exceeded revenues. Since the early 1990s, their budget deficits and outstanding debt have increased significantly. Existing local borrowing as a percentage of GDP rose rapidly from 15 percent in 1991 (when the bubble economy burst) to 40 percent in 2003, and has fluctuated between 40 percent and 42 percent over the decade since 2003.[88] In fiscal year 2005, a high of 27.5 percent (514) of all local governments (1,874) showed a borrowing burden ratio of more than 18 percent (debt service/total value of ordinary financial resources). Only the Tokyo Metropolitan Government seemed to stand out in this fiscal crisis with US$2,450 of its per capita local tax revenue in fiscal year 2005, amounting to roughly twice the prefectural average.[89] In this respect, there is a potential for financially weak local authorities to move towards lax emissions control standards (or fiscal crisis as an incentive to be a free rider on the environmental protection effort of others) in order to increase their tax base.

Some areas of climate policy such as economic incentives require a significant degree of fiscal autonomy and capacity at the local government level. By December 2007, 238 municipal programs were reported to offer subsidies, funding, and/or tax incentives for the promotion of energy efficiency and new energy.[90] So far the Tokyo Metropolitan Government is the only local government in Japan that has been able to implement a package of measures as a comprehensive system of environmental policies. In 2009 it started its own tax system to promote energy saving for small-and-medium-sized companies.[91] Its fiscal elasticity significantly accounts for the scope of Tokyo Metropolitan initiatives. The Tokyo Metropolitan Government has much freedom for budgetary choice to meet the fiscal needs of a comprehensive system of economic incentives while being constrained by nationally defined revenue-raising regulations like any other local government.

Fairness of government outputs

To assure greater fairness, projects need to be assessed at the early stages of problem identification and throughout the planning and decision-making processes. In Japan, only a few local authorities, such as Kobe and Kawasaki Cities, have carried out a comprehensive process of evaluating the environmental impact of policies, plans, or individual projects and their alternatives at earlier stages. Probably the most advanced process is found in a new practice of the Tokyo Metropolitan EIA, which was revised in 2002. Under this EIA, the Tokyo Metropolitan Government has assessed environmental impact at earlier stages and responded to the accumulative, compound environmental impact in greater-area development plans.[92] But it is important to note that such progressive measures are confined to a small minority of front-runner localities in Japan.

The policy process is usually considered in a cyclic way through different stages: agenda setting, policy formulation, decision-making, implementation, monitoring, and evaluation. Citizen participation is a key determinant in fostering fairness in the policy process as it brings the government closer to the local residents. The key issue is how civil society actors are able to interact with the policy process and affect policy positions, approaches, and actions in each of these stages. A number of case studies on Japanese localities do point to two driving forces for promoting environmental equity: socially mobilized citizens and mayoral/gubernatorial leadership.[93] Using the frameworks of political opportunity structures,[94] it can be argued that the institutional environment for a greater degree of participatory access functions as a filter between mobilized citizens and a local government's capacity to enhance equity. Formal institutional access, which provides incentives for civil society participation to thrive in fair decision-making, ranges from the legal-administrative institution of central-local relations and electoral systems, to party systems and political alliances. However, those case studies illustrate that the opportunity structure for direct forms of citizen participation, which appears to be either empowered or constrained by demographics, seems to play a primary role in promoting environmental equity. Although a lack of case studies makes my observation only suggestive rather than definitive, there seems to be a threshold size, probably exceeded only in the multi-million population cities, at which a greater number of organizations and more complex decision-making processes come to outweigh the political efficacy of direct forms of citizen involvement. Equally important, no reports on the smaller size categories of fewer than 30,000 people (as of 2014, 937 out of 1,718 municipalities, excluding the 23 Special Wards of Tokyo) are found in those case studies. I would expect fewer political actors to be involved in small villages that are less complex and reveal less diversity. Within this limit, the smallness of local governments is likely to nurture political participation by the virtue of their accessibility and intimacy.

The direct forms of citizen involvement for promoting overall fairness can be categorized into three basic patterns: doing citizens' planning on their own with the help of relatively neutral municipal authorities (Hino City's Basic Environmental Plan in 1999 with a population of 170,000, Toyonaka City's Agenda 21 in 1999 with a population of 390,000); citizens' planning collaboration on equal terms with local administration (Hikone City's Basic Environmental, and Action Plans in 2001 with a population of 110,000 and Shiki City's Basic Environmental Plan and EcoCity in 1999 with a population of 65,000); citizens' agenda setting and local administration's planning (Date City's Basic Environmental Plan in 1999 with a population of 35,000 and Ichikawa City's Basic Environmental Plan in 2000 with a population of 450,000).[95]

Assessing the capacity of local engagement for international cooperation

Foreign policy has traditionally been the exclusive jurisdiction of the state. In the past 20 years, however, there has been an unprecedented expansion of decentralized international cooperation at the local level and of the multiple modes and mechanisms of cooperation created. Unlike national governments, local governments deliberately decide whether or not to engage in international cooperation at their discretion. Why do they get involved and go beyond what is mandated under national policy? The potential answer is not simply about the global agenda regarding environment and development, or national mandates, but also stems from local needs and the adaptive capacity to get involved. In the light of widespread, ongoing trans-local cooperation, one persistent challenge is to understand the factors which enable local actors to take up a key role in international cooperation. Fiscal capacity is expected to be a significant indicator of local government's engagement in international cooperation, yet plenty of wealthy local authorities eschew any role. Administrative ability is required, yet many competent local authorities and teams likewise decide not to get involved. Local authorities, with their similar physical and social environments in which people live, are not all equally responsive to national policies or global strategies. The problem concerns the assumption that local structural factors, national policy, and global strategies generate a uniform impact across different stages of decision-making by different local actors. What then might account for the different outcomes of the two most-similar localities? This section will thus make an initial assessment of factors internal to local governments. The following chapters of case studies will further examine how different motivations operate at successive stages of decision-making across local actors, rather than having a uniform impact.

The idea of decentralized international cooperation emerged in the field of international municipal relations. The United Nations Center for Human Settlements (UN-Habitat) broadly defined decentralized international cooperation as a locus "whereby cities (and indeed other institutions) work together on defining their problems and devising appropriate solutions on the basis of shared experience among peer groups."[96] Such a broad definition can be used to include all possible local entities other than governmental administrative structures in decision-making processes. There is no agreement in the literature on the definition of international cooperation in which local actors take up a major role. A number of relevant terms are often used interchangeably (trans-local cooperation, decentralized international cooperation, local official development assistance [ODA], city-to-city cooperation, and development assistance) which may make the definition more ambiguous. As the chapters of case studies in this book attempt to explain the motivations of Japanese local governments, the term "international cooperation" is used to refer to any formalized form of problem-solving cooperation that is delivered between a local government and any local entities in at least one state other than their own, or an international institution, or a multinational economic actor. The nature of such cooperation reveals different geographical linkages, that is, North–North, North–South, and South–South. In practice, since the 1992 Earth Summit, recognition of local governments as key players in global sustainability strategies and the areas of development assistance and environmental cooperation have become a focal point of decentralized international cooperation activities. The 2000 Millennium Development Goals, which identify local authorities as crucial actors in tackling poverty challenges, have created a further legitimate setting for sub-national involvement. Where necessary, the terminology of international cooperation is further clarified in the following chapters.

Post-World War II, Japan's foreign aid has evolved through different stages. The state-centric approach to Japan's aid policy naturally brings into focus bureaucratic politics, mercantilist interests, responses to the security environment, and foreign pressures of various kinds. Japan's international cooperation at the sub-national level has accordingly played a role that is largely seen as complementary to national aid policy. Local governments cooperate with state agencies to support national programs for training officials from developing countries and dispatch local experts to developing countries. Since the late 1980s, as described in the selected cases, some pioneering Japanese local authorities have initiated and managed their own North–South policies in the area of international environmental and development cooperation, both through the Local Allocation Tax (national general grants) and ODA funding from the national government. To explain the upsurge of local participation, the literature predominantly focuses on an analysis of the role of structural factors at the national and international levels. It connotes the spreading of decentralized international cooperation from a common source of internationally shared principles and rules (such as the international recognition of local authorities as key players in global strategies);[97] the decentralization policies implemented in many developing countries;[98] and the international agenda for localizing foreign aid,[99] which created a setting to promote the decentralized functions of international cooperation. At the national level, the Japan-specific literature identifies four structural changes in aid policy, which facilitated the patterns of cooperation dispersion that were based on mimicking, rather than trial-and-error learning behaviors among local authorities.[100] (1) Since the early 1990s when Japan introduced new aid guidelines (the 1992 ODA Charter),[101] the country has refocused its foreign aid towards environmental and "softer" types of aid such as poverty alleviation and social infrastructure such as educational and medical facilities. (2) The ongoing decentralization of government in developing countries is reflected in the request-based disbursement of Japan's ODA, which leaves it to the recipient to identify needs and formulate aid requests. (3) Since fiscal year 1998, the Japanese government has continued the trend of cutting its ODA budget. (4) In the late 1990s, Japan began to promote the "community participation model" (*kokumin-sanka gata*) that would involve local authorities in international cooperation programs.[102] All of these preconditions are claimed to provide a favorable basis for local authorities' involvement. But the question of

130 *Local capacity-building*

why they are getting involved cannot be answered without analysis of local decision-making. The implementation of their programs needs to be locally specific, addressing their own particular conditions and needs. The key issue thus boils down to local authorities' willingness and adaptive capacity to contribute to international cooperation.

National regulation and promotion

In 1997 and 1998 the (currently Cabinet Office) Committee on Economic Cooperation announced two policy directions towards the greater involvement of local governments in international cooperation projects; in 1999 the national government formally began to promote the community participation model. Decentralized international cooperation, in which local governments take up a key role, has also been recognized by Japanese aid agencies.[103] There are two main channels, the Ministry of Foreign Affairs (MOFA) and the Ministry of Internal Affairs and Communications (MIAC) (known as Home Affairs or MOHA, until 2001), through which national funds are provided to extend local know-how and experience to developing countries. Both ministries acknowledge the valuable contribution that local governments can make towards international cooperation. Their policy directions and funding have been a top-down catalyst for the local level of participation.

The MOFA created an ODA grant aid program for the promotion of Japanese local authorities' overseas technological cooperation in 1971 (it ceased to exist in 2003). The Ministry has extended financial support and provided information to aid local authorities in accepting specialists from developing countries for training as well as dispatching experts. In the late 1990s, the Ministry's Japan International Cooperation Agency (JICA), responsible primarily for the technical cooperation component of Japan's bilateral ODA, began to strengthen the involvement of local governments. The ODA reforms, initiated by the Ministry in 1998, facilitated JICA's efforts to incorporate local authorities through the "contracting-out method," by which JICA would assign some ODA projects to Japanese local governments.[104] Today, although local authorities need to decide if they wish to participate in ODA projects by contributing their own resources to meet JICA's request, JICA still provides them with resources such as facilities and past project experience.

In the late 1980s, the MOHA began to allocate transfer payments for *kokusaika suishin taisakuhi* (promotion expenditure for internationalization) through the Local Allocation Tax to local governments. These payments to local governments peaked at US$1.3 billion in 1997 and fluctuated at around US$1.2 billion per year thereafter, yet they were not reported as a budgetary sum for ODA in *Japan's Official Development Assistance White Paper.*[105] Given the national incentives, local governments initiated their own international cooperation projects, independently funded by their own financial resources (including national transfers through the block grant). As Figure 3.1 shows, the amount of spending on these projects reached about US$70 million in 1994 and has hovered around

Local capacity-building 131

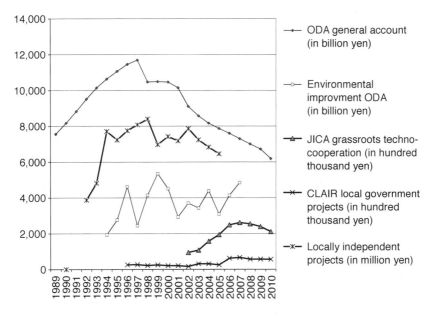

Figure 3.1 Expenditure on Japan's foreign aid and cooperation.

Sources: Ministry of Foreign Affairs, *Seifu kaihatsu enjo hakusho* [Government white paper on ODA], 2011 ed.; JICA, *Gyōmu jisseki hōkokusho* [Report on projects performance], various years, www.jica.go.jp/about/jica/jisseki/index.html [accessed August 1, 2013]. The figures for spending on international cooperation projects independently funded by local governments and the CLAIR figures are provided by the International Office, Ministry of Internal Affairs and Telecommunications and Japan Local Government Centre (CLAIR Sydney), respectively.

Note
"Locally independent projects" are international cooperation projects both conducted and funded by local authorities' independent sources. JICA is an independent governmental agency that coordinates ODA projects for the national government. "JICA grass-roots techno-cooperation," which was introduced in 2002, aims to contribute to developing countries at the grass-roots level in collaboration with partners in Japan, such as local governments. CLAIR is a joint organization of Japanese local governments to promote and support local-level internationalization. "CLAIR local government projects" have been designating innovative and exemplary international cooperation projects of local governments as "Model Projects" since 1996.

$50 million to $60 million per year since then. In 1988 the MOHA authorized the establishment of the Council of Local Authorities for International Relations (CLAIR), and the Ministry continues to provide administrative guidance through CLAIR to individual municipalities and prefectures regarding their engagement in international development and environmental cooperation.

Levels of local engagement for international cooperation

The involvement of local governments as a percentage of bilateral ODA can be a crude indicator of their activity level in international cooperation. The Development

132 Local capacity-building

Assistance Committee (DAC) statistics displayed in Table 3.2 show that among seven major OECD countries, Japan's figure is at the bottom with 0.1 percent in 2002–2003, while the 2008–2009 figure indicates a significantly increasing trend of 0.5 percent.[106] Although the data collection coverage and method differs slightly with each member state in reporting DAC statistics, the reported figures at the aggregate level place Japan in a comparative perspective. For Japan, which undertakes regular data collection, its local government contributions represent only a small share of total bilateral ODA. In other words, we are looking at a comparatively low activity level of Japanese local governments in the area of bilateral ODA.

However, it is important to note that Japan's figures in Table 3.2 may misrepresent the true nature and scope of decentralized international cooperation. International cooperation projects funded by local authorities' independent sources are not included in the technically specific ODA statistics that were reported by the Japanese government to the OECD Development Co-operation Directorate.[107] As Figure 3.1 indicates, those independent projects peaked at 8.4 billion yen (US$76 million) in 1998 and since 2002 have begun to decline, yet those seen as a percentage of the national ODA general account show a long-term upward trend. Indeed, independently funded projects as a percentage of total ODA continually increased from 0.4 percent in 1992 to 0.9 percent in 2005. This spending is equivalent to 10 percent of Australia's ODA and 50 percent of New Zealand's. The overall decline trend is not an across-the-board phenomenon among the projects involved in international cooperation. JICA and CLAIR, the two channels through which national funds are provided to extend local know-how and experience to developing countries, have remained steady in terms of spending levels against the backdrop of severe fiscal constraints at home.

Table 3.2 ODA extended by local governments, 2002–2003 and 2008–2009

Country	Total amount	As % of bilateral ODA	
	2003 (US$ million)	2002–2003	2008–2009
Spain	321.0	18.0	13.0
Germany	687.3	11.0	8.0
Belgium	59.8	5.0	4.0
Italy	27.3	2.0	0.7
Canada	17.5	0.9	N/A
France	39.5	0.4	N/A
Japan	9.9	0.1	0.5

Sources: adopted from DAC statistics (*DAC Journal*, Vol. 6, No. 4 [2005], p. 16; *DAC Peer Review*, various issues); and Ignacio Martinez and José Antonio Sanahuja, "Decentralized development aid in Spain and the effectiveness challenge," Instituto Complutense de Estudios Internacionales (ICEI), ICEI Paper, no. 18 (2010), p. 1.

Notes
There was no such category of aid reported in the United States and Britain. The term "local government" used in this report refers to various sub-national levels of government. Over 90 per cent of the German figures account for imputed students' costs.

Local capacity-building 133

According to the CLAIR database of international cooperation, forms of international cooperation include the acceptance of specialists and government officials for training from developing countries, dispatch of experts to developing countries, joint investigation with developing countries towards finding solutions to urban problems, holding seminars and conferences, partnering with international organizations, and hosting international inter-city network programs.[108] As of August 2013, in Japan all 47 prefectures, all 20 designated cities (i.e., with a population of over 500,000), and all 42 core cities (i.e., with a population of over 300,000) have engaged at least once in some form of international cooperation.[109] Over the past decade, however, the Japanese sub-national level of participation in international cooperation has reached a crossroads. In a 1997–1998 national survey,[110] nearly 80 percent of core cities had engaged in some form of international cooperation, yet the rate dropped to less than 40 percent in 2005 (11 out of 28 responding core cities), while participation rates in 100 percent of prefectures and designated cities remained intact during the same period.[111] Core cities have evolved a distinctive form of international cooperation, engaging primarily in the acceptance of technical trainees. A total 82 percent of prefectures and 92 percent of designated cities have conducted training under JICA-funded programs; they continue to receive national aid for international cooperation activities.[112] Unlike prefectures and designated cities, core cities have independently run more than 90 percent of their own technical training.[113] It is not surprising that as their financial capacity average index dropped from 0.90 in 1996 to 0.77 in 2011, core cities have favored cutting their independent training programs.[114] On the other hand, all prefectures and designated cities, likely driven by national incentives and guidelines, have continued to train specialists and officials from developing countries even though their own financial capacity indexes varied in 2011 from 1.16 to 0.24 and from 1.07 to 0.69, respectively. Nonetheless, their spending on international cooperation activities peaked in 1998 and has steadily declined since then. It is important to note here that the decline has taken place mainly in the acceptance of trainees and the dispatch of experts, and not in locally initiated areas of partnerships with international organizations and inter-city network programs.[115] Five prefectures and eight cities are involved in partnerships with international organizations and/ or inter-city network programs with activities that go beyond their national guideline mandate and financial incentives.[116] Projects with international organizations were reported in 2006 to account for about one-half of the national total of Japan's spending on international cooperation projects independently funded by local governments.[117] The question is, why do these local governments deliberately decide to engage in such extensive cooperation?

To answer this question, the local governments of Shiga (prefecture), Yokohama (designated city), and Kitakyushu (designated city) were chosen for the case studies in Chapters 5, 6, and 7 respectively. Landlocked Shiga (financial capacity index 0.54; government employees 13.0 per 1,000 people),[118] which has actively worked with an international organization, is a critical case to identify potential motives, because other landlocked prefectures with similar enabling indicators (Gifu—0.52 and 11.8 per 1,000; Gunma—0.56 and 12.5 per 1,000; and Tochigi—0.56 and 12.4 per 1,000) cooperate only minimally.

The two other governments have been the most active in international cooperation. Yokohama (0.98 and 5.8 per 1,000), with Japan's second largest port (international connection indicator: 81 million tons for foreign cargo-handling in 2011),[119] has partnerships with multiple international organizations and puts together international inter-city network programs. Another large city, Nagoya (1.01 and 8.9 per 1,000), which has Japan's largest port (international connection indicator: 130 million tons for foreign cargo-handling in 2011), has primarily delivered training sessions through JICA programs. This places Yokohama in a critical position to be examined to find potential determinants.

Kitakyushu (0.69 and 7.4 per 1,000) is by far the most active among Japan's localities. It has the longest experience, over 30 years, of partnership with international organizations, developing international inter-city networks and producing the largest number of trainees, more than 400 per year from 2005 to 2012.[120] Given that its financial capacity index is the second worst among designated cities, Kitakyushu, with a population of less than one million, deserves a close examination of its motives. At the aggregate level, financial capacity is both positively and significantly related to international cooperation,[121] but factors internal to unexpectedly active localities such as Shiga and Kitakyushu require further examination.

Preliminary assessment of factors internal to local governments

Following a case study of Tokyo's cap-and-trade program, which the exceptional performance and financial strength of the capital megacity have helped develop (Chapter 4), studies of these three localities will focus on the role of local governments in international cooperation dynamics that are integral to their political policy structure. The focus of their international cooperation has been on voluntary activity; they decided whether or not to engage in international cooperation by going beyond what was expected by the national government. There is a clear privileging of an actor-specific approach, a focus upon who is involved in decision-making, how, and why. The logic of deliberate choice in the selection of international cooperation activities, the interpretation of internationally shared norms and principles, the response to nationally defined guidelines, and the conceptual adaptation by decision-makers were all central to the analysis of these three cases. Structures, such as international norms in the North–South context and national policy mandates, provided the political context within which Shiga, Kitakyushu, and Yokohama acted. These structures constrained or facilitated local action, rather than being determinants. Nonetheless, it was the local actors who interpreted the role of these structures and adapted them to meet their own conditions and needs.

Local needs and adaptive capacity continue to ensure difference and diversity among the more self-motivated local governments, in contrast with weaker municipalities that remain over-dependent on national supervision. Japanese local government choice in selecting international cooperation activities appears to reflect four major analytically distinct mechanisms: tutelage (by the national government), mimicry (emulating neighbors), learning (revising after drawing lessons), and pioneering (innovation). The majority of local governments that engaged in international cooperation simply worked with state agencies to support national programs for training specialists from, and dispatching local experts to, developing countries. Tutelage, exercised via conditions attached to national subsidies or top-down administrative guidance, is most likely to be important in explaining similarities among local authorities' international cooperation. Mimicry also favors the diffusion of similar patterns of international cooperation; it explains how and why some cities copy neighboring localities' practices in order to catch up, rather than making their own policy choices. Learning is based on lessons drawn from experience, which gives guidance about the likely consequences of policy options. Pioneering is the initiative in which local actors use new information to update their prior beliefs and adopt new policy ideas. While both tutelage and mimicry tend to have a uniform impact on international cooperation activities among "bandwagoning" local actors, learning and pioneering can reveal different motivations within international cooperation decision-making, as illustrated in the three case studies.

Policy learning and innovation are not inevitable processes deriving from greater fiscal capacity or other enabling factors. It is true that earlier studies indicate a positive and significant correlation between fiscal capacity and international cooperation at the aggregate level. There appears to be a threshold enabling capacity at which limited resources come to outweigh the motivations of active engagement in international cooperation. Yet, among the largest local governments, their motivations and purposes continue to produce difference and diversity. Some are actively cooperative; others are simply cooperative within the nationally defined guidelines. Some actors are more willing to adopt policy ideas than others; not all policy-makers are equally sensitive to the same information. This may be a result of various factors. The voluntary activity of decentralized international cooperation may need to focus more on agency than on structural explanations. If local governments are required to decide whether or not to engage in international cooperation at their discretion, then factors internal to agency, such as past experience, prior beliefs, political leadership, and public support can be more influential determinants than external opportunity structures such as international recognition and national policy. Agency is influential to the extent that it individually or collectively interprets and adapts external opportunity structures to local needs. If there are any incongruities among equally capable agencies in regard to the interpreted external opportunity structures, then the sources of these incongruities are likely to derive from agencies' probable motivations and purposes.

In the ODA Charter of 1992, the Japanese Cabinet, for the first time, acknowledged the potential role of local governments in implementing foreign aid. As Japan continues to make tougher cuts in foreign aid budgets, policy coordination between local initiatives and national policy strategies has become critical for the efficient use of shrinking budgets. In environmental management where a wealth of local experience and expertise is available to others, especially developing countries, the national government needs to be actively involved in resourcing local governments. The challenge to any national enabling framework for local government participation is how to link the national level of policy-making with local strategies. Understanding local initiatives and motives will help the nation to focus on how the national government can better enable local governments to address foreign aid challenges. This will ultimately serve as a guide for bridging policy gaps between local action and national policy strategies. The implementation barriers to local governments for decentralized international cooperation reveal a lack of coordination among JICA, CLAIR, and Japanese ministries, causing a fragmentation of sub-national participation. Thus, a broad institutionalization of decentralized international cooperation and policy integration is yet to be developed in Japan.

Conclusion

Since the early 1990s, the focus of Japan's environmental policy has shifted from one-dimensional industrial pollution controls to a comprehensive environmental governance strategy. Boundary-eroding dynamics have become highly salient in the field of international environmental cooperation precisely because the causes of environmental risk are locally specific in character yet local action can simultaneously be a part of global strategies. To meet the need for a decentralized form of redistributing global environmental functions, the position of local governments has been promoted and strengthened by a series of decisions made at both the national and international levels. In Japan, a number of front-runner local authorities have come to see their actions as part of a global game. Nonetheless, local officials have a limited capacity to handle diffuse pressures on the environment, which requires their accountability mechanisms as well as their accumulated expertise and encouragement of citizens' political involvement. The international agreement made by Japan to reduce GHG emissions puts pressure on local authorities to take initiatives for climate adaptation. Most Japanese localities are yet to take such an opportunity to exercise their policy initiative. The institutionalization of sub-national participation for policy integration is yet to develop.

International environmental cooperation needs to be established not to primarily influence sovereign states but rather to enhance governance practices in a form of decentralized cooperation in which local actors take up a key role. Sub-national actors, often from countries with limited national commitments, are integrating environmental risk reductions into a form of inter-municipal coordination (e.g., Cities for Climate Protection) beyond national boundaries. They also establish public transnational networks in cooperation with international organizations, which authoritatively enable their networks to exercise policy coordination. Japan's unitary system does not formally recognize the legal rights of local governments to represent themselves at the international level. In the absence of national government action, however, the Japanese statist tradition does not prevent local governments from not operating on behalf of the Japanese national government. Either due to a lack of support from the national government or in the absence of national regulation, as discussed in the following chapters, Japanese local governments have transnationally reached out as alternative means of environmental management for problem-solving. They are often able to bypass the established central-local relations, yet not completely superseding them, so that the national government could have a chance to better understand local initiatives and motives. To meet locally specific needs, they or the sphere of government closest to the people, eventually needs to serve as the intermediary between local communities and the national government.[122]

This chapter concludes that in Japan, with regard to the government's competence/efficiency, only the largest municipalities and prefectures possess a substantial degree of expertise and resources which they can use to reduce urban energy intensity and CO_2 emissions and further engage in international environmental cooperation. Depending on the local capacity of political leadership, administrative ability and financial discretion, some forward-looking localities have been ushering in a new level of development for operating innovative environmental programs. Probably the most exceptional case is the Tokyo Metropolitan Government whose strong independent sources of revenue allow for a comprehensive system of climate policy including the 2010 introduction of its cap-and-trade system. As for international environmental cooperation, the voluntary nature of such local engagement may require the examination of agencies' probable motivations and purposes beyond their fiscal capacity and administrative ability, rather than that of structural explanations. Of course, limited resources may come to outweigh the motivations of active engagement in international cooperation. In this sense, resources, such as finance, personnel, and expertise, are the necessary preconditions for motivating local authorities.

Yet efficiency and equity is seen as a trade off against each other. In those localities, the size of the population appears to be too large and diverse to facilitate direct forms of participation for ensuring the fairness of government's outputs. Instead, the large localities tend to address the issue of policy process fairness, such as EIA at earlier stages. It is only in pioneering medium-sized municipalities that mobilized citizen groups demonstrate some success in holding governmental procedures accountable and responsive to their communities in a direct way. Direct participation itself becomes a process of spontaneous learning for citizens to gain much subjective political competence and to develop quasi-professional expertise regarding climate change and comprehensive environmental governance.

Notes

1 Richard Samuels, *The Politics of Regional Policy in Japan* (Princeton, NJ: Princeton University Press, 1983); Steven Reed, *Japanese Prefectures and Policy Making* (Pittsburgh, PA: University of Pittsburgh Press, 1986).

2 Michio Muramatsu, "The impact of economic growth policies on local politics in Japan," *Asian Survey*, Vol. 15, No. 9 (1975), pp. 799–816; Kurt Steiner, Ellis Krauss, and Scott Flanagan, eds., *Political Opposition and Local Politics in Japan* (Princeton, NJ: Princeton University Press, 1980); Steven Reed, "Environmental politics: some reflections based on the Japanese case," *Comparative Politics*, Vol. 13, No. 3 (1981), pp. 253–69.
3 United Nations Conference on Environment and Development, *Agenda 21*. Rio de Janeiro: UNCED, June 3–14, 1992, available from: www.un.org/esa/sustdev/documents/agenda21/english/adenda21toc.htm [accessed December 3, 2014].
4 International Council for Local Environmental Initiatives (ICLEI), *The Local Agenda 21 Initiative: ICLEI Guidelines for Local Agenda 21* (Freiburg: ICLEI, 1993).
5 Michael Shuman, *Toward a Global Village: International Community Development Initiatives* (London: Pluto, 1994); Lara Green, Chris Game, and Simon Delay, *Why Should My Local Authorities Be Involved in an Overseas Project?* (Birmingham, UK: Birmingham University, 2005).
6 Hugh Dyer, "Environmental ethics and international relations," *Paradigms*, Vol. 8, No. 1 (1994), pp. 58–77; Karen Litfin, "Advocacy coalitions along the domestic-foreign frontier: globalization and Canadian climate change policy," *Policy Studies Journal*, Vol. 28, No. 1 (2000), pp. 236–52.
7 Harriet Bulkeley and Heike Schroeder, "Governing climate change post-2012: the role of global cities case-study – Los Angeles," Working Paper 122, Wallingford, UK, Tyndall Center for Climate Change Research, 2008; Kristine Kern and Alber Gotelind, "Governing climate change in cities: modes of urban climate governance in multi-level systems," OECD Conference Proceedings, Paris, OECD, 2009.
8 Claudia Holgate, "Factors and actors in climate change mitigation: a tale of two South African cities," *Local Environment*, Vol. 12, No. 5 (2007), pp. 471–84; Barry Rabe, "Governing the climate from Sacramento," in Stephen Goldsmith and Donald Kettl, eds., *Unlocking the Power of Networks* (Washington, DC: Brookings Institution Press, 2009), pp. 34–61.
9 Thomas Dietz, Elinor Ostrom, and Paul Stern, "The struggle to govern the commons," *Science*, Vol. 302 (2003), pp. 1907–12; Liesbet Hooghe and Gary Marks, "Unravelling the central state, but how? Types of multi-level governance," *American Political Science Review*, Vol. 97, No. 2 (2003), pp. 233–43.
10 Thomas H. Tietenberg, "On the efficient spatial allocation of air pollution control responsibility," in Horst Siebert, Ingo Walker, and Klaus Zimmermann, eds., *Regional Environmental Policy: The Economic Issues* (New York: New York University Press, 1979), pp. 79–83; Horst Siebert, *Economics of the Environment: Theory and Policy* (Berlin and Heidelberg: Springer Verlag, 1992).
11 Wallace E. Oates, *Fiscal Federalism* (New York: Harcourt Brace and Jovanovich, 1972).
12 Charles Tiebout, "A pure theory of local expenditures," *The Journal of Political Economy*, Vol. 64, No. 5 (1956), pp. 416–24.
13 George Peterson, *Decentralization in Latin America: Learning through Experience* (Washington, DC: World Bank, 1997).
14 Barry R. Weingast, "The economic role of political institutions: market-preserving federalism and economic development," *Journal of Law, Economics and Organization*, Vol. 11, No. 1 (1995), pp. 1–31; Ronald McKinnon, "The logic of market-preserving federalism," *Virginia Law Review*, Vol. 83, No. 7 (1997), pp. 1573–80.
15 Per G. Fredriksson and Daniel Millimet, "Strategic interaction and the determination of environmental policy across U.S. states," *Journal of Urban Economics*, Vol. 51, No. 1 (2002), pp. 101–22; Arik Levinson, "Environmental regulatory competition: a status report and some new evidence," *National Tax Journal*, Vol. 56, No. 1 (2003), pp. 91–106.

Local capacity-building 139

16 Eric Helland and Andrew Whitford, "Pollution incidence and political jurisdiction: evidence from the TRI," *Journal of Environmental Economics and Management*, Vol. 46, No. 3 (2003), pp. 403–24; Hilary Sigman, "Transboundary spillovers and decentralization of environmental policies," *Journal of Environmental Economics and Management*, Vol. 50, No. 1 (2005), pp. 82–101.

17 John List and Shelby Gerking, "Regulatory federalism and environmental protection in the Unites States," *Journal of Regional Science*, Vol. 40, No. 3 (2000), pp. 453–71; Wallace E. Oates, "A reconsideration of environmental federalism," in John List and Aart de Zeeuw, eds., *Recent Advances in Environmental Economics* (Cheltenham, UK: Edward Elgar Publisher, 2002), pp. 1–32.

18 Paul Shapiro and Jeffrey Petchey, "The welfare economics of environmental regulatory: two parables on state vs. federal control," in John B. Braden and Stef Proost, eds., *The Economic Theory of Environmental Policy in a Federal System: New Horizons in Environmental Economics* (Cheltenham, UK: Edward Elgar Publisher, 1997), pp. 122–46.

19 Paul Seabright, "Accountability and decentralization in government: an incomplete contracts model," *European Economic Review*, Vol. 40, No. 1 (1996), pp. 61–89.

20 Ariel Fiszbien, "The emergence of local capacity: lessons from Colombia," *World Development*, Vol. 25, No. 7 (1997), pp. 1029–43; Anne M. Larson, "Natural resources and decentralization in Nicaragua: are local governments up to the job?" *World Development*, Vol. 30, No. 1 (2002), pp. 17–31; Asian Development Bank, *Capacity Building to Support Decentralization in Indonesia* (Manila: ADB, 2005).

21 Richard Crook and James Manor, *Democracy and Decentralization in Southeast Asia and West Africa: Participation, Accountability and Performance* (Cambridge, UK: Cambridge University Press, 1998); Krister Andersson and Frank van Laerhoven, "From local strongman to facilitator: institutional incentives for participatory municipal governance in Latin America," *Comparative Political Studies*, Vol. 40, No. 9 (2007), pp. 1085–111.

22 Jonathan Rodden, "Comparative federalism and decentralization: on meaning and measurement," *Comparative Politics*, Vol. 36, No. 4 (2004), pp. 481–500.

23 Robert D. Putnam, *Making Democracy Work: Civic Traditions in Modern Italy* (Princeton, NJ: Princeton University Press, 1993); Edward P. Weber, *Pluralism by the Rules: Conflict and Cooperation in Environmental Regulation* (Washington, DC: Georgetown University Press, 1998); Paul Selman, "Social capital, sustainability and environmental planning," *Planning Theory and Practice*, Vol. 2, No. 1 (2001), pp. 13–30.

24 The accountability mechanism for monitoring provides incentives for the attentiveness of officials to constituents. But it is procedurally operational only to the extent that officials recognize and act on the incentives.

25 The indices for citizens' orientations are adopted from the civic culture literature: Gabriel A. Almond and Sidney Verba, *The Civic Culture* (Princeton, NJ: Princeton University Press, 1963), chps 10, 11; and Sidney Verba and Norman Nie, *Participation in America: Political Democracy and Social Equality* (New York: Harper & Row, 1972), chps 9–13.

26 The index for interpersonal trust is adopted from the social capital literature: Putnam, *Making Democracy Work*, chp 6.

27 Japan, Cabinet Office, *Chikyū ondanka taisaku ni kansuru yoron chōsa* [Public opinion survey on global warming countermeasures], available from: www8.cao.go.jp/survey/h19/h19-globalwarming/index.html [accessed November 12, 2009]. The Japanese government has not conducted opinion polls on this subject since 2007.

28 The figures are calculated by the author from two major national newspapers (i.e., through on-line indexing services provided by digital news archives): *Asahi Shinbun* and *Yomiuri Shinbun*.

29 Taisuke Miyauchi, "Kankyō jichi no shikumizukuri" [Environmental self-governance

140 *Local capacity-building*

and its organization], *Kankyō Shakaigaku Kenkyū* [Journal of Environmental Sociology], Vol. 7 (2001), pp. 56–71; Takeshi Wada, "Nijūisseiki no chikyū kankyō to shakai hatten" [The Earth's environment for the twenty-first century and social development], *Yuibutsuron to Gendai* [Materialism and Today], Vol. 29 (2002), pp. 2–15; Kōichi Hasegawa, *Kankyō undō to atarashii kokyōken* [Environmental movements and new public space] (Tokyo: Yūhikaku, 2003).

30 Hasegawa, *Kankyō Undō to Atarashii Kokyōken*; Shun'ichi Hiraoka and Takeshi Wada, "Chihō jichitai ni okeru shiminsankagata no chikyū ondanka taisaku o suishinsuru shikumi to shakaiteki haikei" [Political system and social background for the promotion of climate mitigation through citizens' participation in local government], *Ritsumeikan Sangyōshakai Ronshū* [Ritsumeikan University Industrial Society Papers], Vol. 41, No. 2 (2005), p. 49.

31 Takeshi Wada and Kenrō Taura, *Shimin chiiki ga susumeru chikyū ondanka bōshi* [Climate change countermeasures by citizens and community] (Kyoto: Gakugei Shuppan, 2007), pp. 132–52; Hideki Kitagawa (ex-Kyoto Prefecture official of Bureau of the Environment), Interview by author, May 13, 2010, Kyoto; Kenrō Taura, Interview by author, May 13, 2010, Kyoto; Japan Center for Climate Change Actions, "Chiiki no dōkō" [Regional trends], available from: www.jccca.org/trend_region/ [accessed November 1, 2011].

32 In August 2001 NTT Data conducted this survey on 1,000 people aged 20 and over who resided in 10 cities in the capital region. See NTT Data, "Denshi seifu to minshushugi ni kansuru shutoken shimin chōsa" [Investigation report on citizens in the capital region for e-government and democracy], December 2001.

33 Nikkei Human Resources, *Nikkei Navi 2006*, available from: http://job.nikkei.co.jp [accessed June 15, 2006].

34 Hideyuki Takahashi, "Jichitai kankyō kihon keikaku no genjō to kadai" [The state and problems of local basic environmental plans], *Kikan Gyōsei Kanri Kenkyū* [Administrative Management Quarterly], Vol. 89 (2000), pp. 20–1.

35 In February–March 2013, the Ministry of the Environment conducted this survey on all 1,789 local governments. See Japan, Ministry of the Environment (MOE), "Kankyō kihon keikaku ni kakawaru chihō kōkyō dantai ankēto chōsa" [Survey on basic environmental plans by local government], September 2013.

36 Takahashi, "Jichitai kankyō kihon keikaku no genjō to kadai," pp. 21–2.

37 Kenji Kawasaki, "Aratana dankai o mukaeta shimin sanka" [An emerging new phase for citizen participation], *Chihō Zaimu* [Local Finance], No. 568 (2001), pp. 276–7.

38 Makoto Kayashima, "Hinoshi ni okeru kankyō kihon keikaku sakutei" [Formulation of Hino City's basic environmental plan], *Tokyo no Jichi* [Autonomy Tokyo], Vol. 18, No. 33 (1999), pp. 18–25.

39 See, for example, Japan, Cabinet Office, "Sōsharu kyapitaru" [Social capital], 2002 ed., survey report, June 2003; Japan, Cabinet Office, "Community regeneration and social capital," survey report, August 2005; NHK Broadcasting Culture Research Institute, "Zenkoku kenmin ishiki chōsa" [An attitude survey on prefectural inhabitants], 1978 and 1996.

40 Japan, Cabinet Office, "Community regeneration and social capital."

41 Japan, Cabinet Office, "Sōsharu kyapitaru," p. 5.

42 Material provided by the Bureau of the Environment, Tokyo Metropolitan Government (TMG).

43 Kunimitsu Imai (Kyoto City Department Chief of Countermeasure Planning for Global Warming), Interview by author, May 18, 2010, Kyoto, Japan.

44 Toshiko Chiba (Tokyo Metropolitan Department Chief of Global Warming Countermeasures), Interview by author, May 20, 2010, Tokyo, Japan; Teruyuki Ōno, "Tokyo wa mou hajimete imasu" [Tokyo has already started!] *Gaikō Fōramu* [Diplomacy Forum], No. 260 (2010), pp. 42–5.

45 Japan, Ministry of the Environment, Press Release, May 13, 2003.

46 ICLEI provides the working definition of Local Agenda 21: "Local Agenda 21 is a participatory, multi-sectoral process to achieve the goals of Agenda 21 at the local level through the preparation and implementation of a long-term, strategic action plan that addresses priority local sustainable development concerns." See ICLEI, "Second Local Agenda 21 survey," Background Paper No. 15 (DESA/DSD/PC2/BP15), January 2002, p. 6.
47 See Japan, Environmental Agency (EA), "Rōkaruajenda 21 sakutei gaido" [Guidelines for formulating Local Agenda 21], June 1995.
48 Japan, Ministry of the Environment (MOE), "Rōkaruagenda 21 no sakutei jōkyōtou chōsa kekka nit suite" [Results on the investigation of the state of Local Agenda 21 programing], March 2003, available from: www.env.go.jp/press/press.php?serial=4101 [accessed December 3, 2009]; Takahiro Nakaguchi, "Nihon no rōkaruagenda to rōkaruakushon no genjō to kadai" [The state and problem of Japan's Local Agenda 21 and local action], Architectural Institute of Japan Seminar, August 2002.
49 Kōji Kanagawa, "Jichitai keikaku to pātonashippu kankei ni okeru rōkaruagenda 21 no ichizuke" [Positioning Local Agenda 21s in the local planning structure and partnership relations], *Toshi Kenkyū* [Urban Studies], Vol. 4 (2004), pp. 43–50.
50 Japan, Ministry of the Environment, "Rōkaruagenda 21 no sakutei jōkyōtou chōsa kekka nit suite."
51 Kenji Kawasaki, "Shimin to gyōsei no pātonāshippu ni yoru jichitai kankyō manējimento" [Local environmental management by a partnership between citizens and administration], *Chiiki Kaihatsu* [Regional Development], No. 426 (2000), pp. 54–62; Japan ICLEI, "Nihon no jichitai no ajenda 21 jisshi jōkyō chōsa hōkoku" [Report on the state of practice of Japanese local government's Agenda 21], May 2001.
52 Japan, Ministry of the Environment (MOE), Press Release, May 13, 2003.
53 Japan, Ministry of the Environment (MOE), *Chihō kōkyō dantai ni okeru chikyū ondanka taisaku no suishin ni kansuru hōritsu shikō jōkyō chōsa kekka* [Report on the state of local governments' law implementation regarding the promotion of global warming countermeasures], March 2015, available from: www.env.go.jp/earth/dantai/h261001/mat02.pdf [accessed August 1, 2015]. Article 20-3 (2008 amendment to the Climate Change Law) obligates prefectures and designated cities, core cities (with population of over 300,000 but not large enough to be designated), and special cities (with a population of at least 200,000) to formulate measures to reduce CO_2 emissions from business activities and households in their areas.
54 Japan, Ministry of the Environment (MOE), *Chihō kōkyō dantai ni okeru chikyū ondanka taisaku no suishin ni kansuru hōritsu shikō jōkyō chōsa kekka*, pp. 80–96.
55 Material provided by the Bureau of the Environment, Tokyo Metropolitan Government (TMG).
56 Japan, Ministry of Economy, Trade and Industry (METI), *Energī hakusho* [White paper on energy], 2010 ed., chp 1-1-2, Available from: www.enecho.meti.go.jp/topics/hakusho/2010energyhtml/ [accessed November 3, 2011].
57 See Japan, Ministry of the Environment (MOE), "Kankyō kihon keikaku ni kakawaru chihō kōkyō dantai ankēto chōsa," pp. 62, 70.
58 Tokyo Metropolitan Government (TMG), "Sutēkihorudā mītingu" [Stakeholder meetings], available from: www2.kankyo.metro.tokyo.jp/kikaku/kikouhendouhousin/index.htm [accessed May 21, 2010].
59 Chiba, Interview by author, May 20, 2010, Tokyo; Naomi Okamoto (Tokyo Metropolitan Section Chief of Emissions Reduction Countermeasures), Interview by author, 23 June 2011.
60 Kitagawa, Interview by author, May 13, 2010, Kyoto; Imai, Interview by author, May 18, 2010, Kyoto.
61 Mitsuru Tanaka and Fumitoshi Okiyama, "Chihō kōkyō dantai ni okeru kankyō

asesumento sēdo no rekishi kara no kyōkun" [Lessons on the history of environmental impact assessment by Japanese local governments], *Asesumento Gakkaishi* [Journal of Environmental Impact Assessment], Vol. 8, No. 2 (2010), pp. 6–16.

62 Japan, Ministry of the Environment (MOE), *Environmental Impact Assessment Network*, available from: www.env.go.jp/policy/assess/2-3selfgov/2-3system/list1.html [accessed November 3, 2014].

63 Ken'ichirō Yanagi, "Chihō jichitai asesu jōrei no saikin no dōkō bunseki" [A recent trend analysis of local government assessment ordinances], *NIRA Policy Research*, Vol. 13, No. 12 (2000), pp. 36–9.

64 Japan, Ministry of the Environment (MOE), "Senryakuteki kankyō eikyō hyōka ni tsuite" [Strategic environmental assessment], available from: www.env.go.jp/council/02policy/y0210-04/mat06.pdf [accessed December 3, 2009].

65 In 2010 over 99 percent of mayoral proposals sailed through local assemblies almost intact. See National Association of Chairpersons of City Councils, "Shichō tēshutsu ni yoru gian" [Mayor-proposed agenda items], available from: www.si-gichokai.jp/official/research/jittai22/pdf/08_jittai22.pdf [accessed November 3, 2011].

66 Japan, Ministry of Internal Affairs and Communications (MIAC), "Chihō kōkyō dantai ni okeru jōhō kōkai jōrei no seitei jōkyō" [The enactment of local information disclosure ordinances], March 31, 2015, available from: www.soumu.go.jp/main_content/000350962.pdf [accessed November 3, 2011].

67 Release Ratio = (Release + Partial Release)/(Cases Claimed – No Existence of Information). Data provided by Policy Information Office, Tokyo Metropolitan Government (TMG).

68 Japan, Ministry of Internal Affairs and Communications (MIAC), Press Release, March 25, 2014.

69 Japan, Ministry of Internal Affairs and Communications (MIAC), Press Release, March 25, 2014.

70 Japan, Ministry of Internal Affairs and Communications (MIAC), Press Release, March 16, 2011.

71 Japan, Ministry of the Environment (MOE), *Chihō kōkyō dantai no kankyō hozen taisaku chōsa* [Investigation on the environmental conservation measures of local governments] (Tokyo: MOE, 2005).

72 Local Green Government Portal, *Local Green Government Portal*, available from: www.climate-lg.jp/policy/gw-city.html [accessed December 14, 2010].

73 In Japan, positions for local government employees are typically classified into two categories: *ippan-shoku* (generalsists) and *gijutsu-shoku* (technical employees). Kyoto City was the first municipality to create such a classification for policy continuity and expertise accumulation.

74 Chiba, Interview by author, May 20, 2010, Tokyo.

75 *Sankei Shinbun*, January 8, 1996, carried a report on the survey of 1,905 chief executives (57.7 percent of all local chief executives) in Japan. City-town-village (*shi-cho-son*) are basic municipalities. The population of different city-town-village municipalities varies from under 1,000 to more than 1 million. Although a *shi* (city) has a population of at least 30,000, the population of a *son* (village) has normally several thousand, while the size of a *cho* (town) is midway between the two types of municipalities.

76 See, for example, Toshimasa Itakura, "Shimin sanka ni yoru kankyō jōrei zukuri" [Making an environmental ordinance through citizen participation], *Keikaku Gyōsei* [Planning Administration], Vol. 24, No. 3 (2001), p. 78; Kenshi Baba, Kazumasu Aoki, and Osamu Kimura, "Analysis of environmental and energy policy processes in local governments in Japan," *Denryoku Chūō Kenkyūjo Hōkoku* [Central Research Institute of Electric Power Industry Report], Socio-economic Research Center, Rep. No. Y05025 (May 2006); Yasuhira Fujii, "Tokubetsuku ni okeru kankyō kihon jōrei no seitei katei bunseki" [Analysis of basic environmental ordinance-making

processes in Special Wards], *Sōkan Shakai Kagaku* [Relative Social Sciences], Vol. 17 (2007), p. 76.
77 Kazumasu Aoki, "Senkuteki na jichitai ondanka bōshi seisaku no seihi o meguru seisaku katei bunseki" [Policy analysis of progressive preventive-measures for climate change by local governments], *Tomidai Keizai Ronshu* [Economic Journal of Toyama University], Vol. 56, No. 2 (2010), pp. 136–9.
78 Chiba, Interview by author, May 20, 2010, Tokyo; Okamoto, Interview by author, June 23, 2011, Tokyo.
79 Aoki, "Senkuteki na jichitai ondanka bōshi seisaku no seihi o meguru seisaku katei bunseki," pp. 144–7.
80 Chiba, Interview by author, May 20, 2010.
81 Japan, Ministry of Internal Affairs and Communications (MIAC), "Chihō kōkyō dantai teiin kanri chōsa kekka" [Report on the number of personnel of local public entities], March 2015.
82 The figures are based on the report, "Chihō kōkyō dantai no jōkyō ni tsuite" [The situation of local governments], provided on March 17, 2005 at a General Policy Meeting of the Central Environment Council.
83 Japan, Ministry of the Environment (MOE), *Chihō kōkyō dantai ni okeru chikyū ondanka taisaku no suishin ni kansuru hōritsu shikō jōkyō chōsa kekka*, p. 23.
84 The figures of ISO 14001 are provided by Japan Accreditation Board.
85 The figures are based on a survey on environmental management, conducted in January 2008 over 685 responding local governments by Knowledge Management Research & Institute.
86 Japan, Ministry of Internal Affairs and Communications (MIAC), Press Release, March 25, 2014.
87 Japan, Ministry of Internal Affairs and Communications (MIAC), Press Release, November 28, 2014.
88 Japan, Ministry of Finance (MOF), "Waga kuni no zaisei jijo" [The country's state of public finance], January 2015, available from: www.mof.go.jp/budget/budger_workflow/budget/fy2015/seifuan27/04.pdf [accessed August 6, 2015].
89 Japan, Ministry of Internal Affairs and Communications (MIAC), *Local Public Finance in Japan*, available from: www.soumu.go.jp/english/pdf/lpfij.pdf [accessed December 14, 2010].
90 Japan, Ministry of the Environment (MOE), *Chihō kōkyō dantai ni okeru chikyū ondanka taisaku no suishin ni kansuru hōritsu shikkō jōkyō chōsa kekka*.
91 Tokyo Metropolitan Government (TMG), *Hōdō pappyō shiryō* [Press Release Material] March 31, 2009.
92 Tokyo Metropolitan Government (TMG), *Environmental Impact Assessment System of the Tokyo Metropolitan Government* (Tokyo: TMG, 2006).
93 See, for example, Itakura, "Shimin sanka ni yoru kankyō jōrei zukuri," pp. 73–78; Fujii, "Tokubetsuku ni okeru kankyō kihon jōrei no seitei katei bunsei," pp. 71–7 Hiraoka and Wada, "Chihō jichitai ni okeru shiminsankagata no chikyū ondanka taisaku o suishinsuru shikumi to shakaiteki haikei," pp. 47–53.
94 Sidney Tarrow, *Struggle, Politics, and Reform: Collective Action, Social Movements, and Cycles of Protest* (Ithaca, NY: Cornell University Centre for International Studies, 1991); Hanspeter Kriesi, "The political opportunity structure of new social movements: its impact on their mobilization," in J. Craig Jenkins and Bert Klandermans, eds., *The Politics of Social Protest* (Minneapolis, MN: University of Minnesota Press, 1995), pp. 167–98.
95 Kawasaki, "Shimin to gyōsei no pātonāshippu ni yoru jichitai kankyō manējimento," pp. 56–61; Takahashi, "Jichitai kankyō kihon keikaku no genjō to kadai," pp. 19–34.
96 UN Center for Human Settlements (Habitat), "City-to-city cooperation: issues arising from experience," Habitat Report, Nairobi, May 25, 2001, p. 4.
97 Especially after the 1992 Earth Summit recognition of sub-national authorities as

144 *Local capacity-building*

key players in global environmental strategies, European cities and local governments had increasingly engaged in international cooperation. Global strategies such as the Habitat Agenda in 1996 and the UN Millennium Summit in 2000 highlighted the critical role of cities and regions in development.

98 A.H.J. Helmsing, "Decentralization, enablement and local governance in low income countries," Working Paper Series No. 342 (2000), The Hague, Netherlands, Institute of Social Studies; UN Development Program (UNDP), *The Challenge of Linking* (New York: UNDP Management Development and Governance Division, 2000); Jon Pierre, *Debating Governance, Authority, Steering and Democracy* (Oxford: Oxford University Press, 2000).

99 The 2005 Paris Declaration on Aid Effectiveness, signed by all OECD countries, recommended an action for local ownership of development strategies. The Accra Agenda for Action (AAA), which was the result of the mid-term 3rd High Level Forum on Aid Effectiveness in Accra, Ghana (September 2–4, 2008), recognized the need to support capacity-building initiatives of local authorities and emphasized the importance of local resources in the provision of technical cooperation.

100 Hitoshi Yoshida, *Jichitai no kokusai kyōryoku* [International cooperation by local governments] (Tokyo: Nihon Hyoronsha, 2001); Japan International Cooperation Agency (JICA), *Chihō jichitai no kokusai kyōryoku jigoyō e no sanka daiichi fēzu* [Participation of local authorities in international cooperation projects: Phase I] (Tokyo: JICA Research Institute, 1998); JICA, *Chihō jichitai no kokusai kyōryoku jigyō e no sanka daini fēzu* [Participation of local authorities in international cooperation projects: Phase II] (Tokyo: JICA Research Institute 2000); JICA, *Chiiki okoshi no keiken o sekai e* [Extending the experience of local revitalization to the world] (Tokyo: JICA Research Institute, 2003).

101 In 1992 the Japanese government adopted the ODA principles of (1) concern for the environment, (2) avoidance of military use of ODA, (3) attention to ODA recipients' military expenditure and development of weapons of mass destruction, and (4) attention to the promotion of democracy, market economy, and basic human rights. This new ODA policy involved prioritizing the promotion of environmental conservation as well as the political and strategic use of ODA in the post-Cold War environment.

102 In 1997 the Committee on Economic Cooperation Policy proposed the greater involvement of local authorities in international cooperation and in 1999 the Cabinet adopted the Medium-Term Policy on ODA that subsequently affirmed the importance of local authorities' role in coordination between levels of government.

103 JICA, *Chihō jichitai no kokusai kyōryoku jigyō e no sanka daini fēzu*; Japan Bank for International Cooperation (JBIC), *Yen shakkan gyōmu ni okeru chihō jichitai to kokusai ginkō tono renkei kyōka ni mukete* [JBIC's collaboration with local authorities for yen loan business] (Tokyo: JBIC, 2003).

104 Hitoshi Yoshida and Purnendra Jain, "Japan's new channels of aid and cooperation: local government as an actor," Ad hoc Expert Group Meeting on Tracking the Reforms in Aid Delivery, Management and Accountability, Mexico City, November 6–7, 2003, pp. 17–21.

105 Yoshida, *Jichitai no kokusai kyōryoku*, pp. 100–6.

106 No figures for UK local governments are available from the DAC statistics. Yet the most highlighted activity is the 1999 establishment of the UK Local Government Alliance for International Development. See UK, Department for International Development (UKDFID), "Strategic Grant Agreement between DFID and UK Local Government Alliance for International Development," December 23, 2003.

107 The DAC defines official development assistance (ODA) as (1) flows of official financing, (2) with the promotion of the economic development and welfare of developing countries as the main objective, and (3) on occasional terms of at least 25 percent grant element.

108 In Japan, several local governments, such as Kitakyushu and Yokohama, have been

hosting inter-city network programs for sustainable urban management—with the goal of capacity-building for city planning and environmental management in Asian countries.
109 Citizens' International Plaza, Council of Local Authorities for International Relations (CLAIR), Database of international cooperation activities by Japanese local governments, available from: www.plaza-clair.jp/jichitai/jichitai1-1.html [accessed August 27, 2013].
110 JICA, *Chihō jichitai no kokusai kyōryoku jigyō e no sanka daiichi fēzu*.
111 Eiji Wakasugi, "Shichōson ni yoru kokusai kyōryoku ni kansuru ikkosatsu" [An observation on international cooperation by local governments], *Kokusai Kyōryoku Kenkyū* [Studies on International Cooperation], Vol. 23, No. 1 (2007), p. 57.
112 In 1989 the MOHA instructed both prefectures and designated cities alone to prepare a comprehensive policy for the promotion of international cooperation and began to offer financial support to their initiated activities. Between 1992 and 2003, the MOFA also provided only prefectures and designated cities with subsidies for training experts from aid-recipient countries.
113 Yoshida, *Jichitai no kokusai kyōryoku*, pp. 34–9.
114 Financial capability index is the average during three fiscal years including the fiscal year stated of the figures obtained by dividing the total value of basic financial revenue by basic financial demand value. The indexes provided in this chapter are adopted from Japan, Statistics Bureau, MIAC, *e-Stat*, available from: www.e-stat.go.jp/SGT/chiiki/CommunityProfileTopDispatchAction.do?code=1 [accessed August 27, 2013].
115 Kazuki Yamazaki, "Chiiki kokusaika ni okeru kokusai kyōryoku no genjo to kadai" [The state and problems of international cooperation in the area of local-level internationalization], *Jichitai Kokusaika Fōramu* [Local-Level Internationalization Forum], No. 199 (2006), p. 3.
116 CLAIR, Database of international cooperation activities.
117 Yamazaki, "Chiiki kokusaika ni okeru kokusai kyōryoku no genjo to kadai," p. 3.
118 The number of local government employees per 1,000 people (as of April 2012) is based on MIAC, *Chihō kokyōdantai teiin kanri kankeki* [Management of local government personnel numbers], available from: www.soumu.go.jp/main_sosiki/jichi_gyousei/c-gyousei/teiin/index.html [accessed August 30, 2013].
119 The figures of foreign cargo-handling for both Yokohama and Nagoya are adapted from Nagoya Port Authority, *Port of Nagoya*, available from: www.port-of-nagoya.jp/port_of_nagoya/ [accessed August 30, 2013].
120 Kitakyushu International Techno-cooperative Association (KITA), *KITA*, available from: www.kita.or.jp/index.html [accessed August 30, 2013].
121 Hidenori Nakamua, Mark Elder, and Hideyuki Mori, "The surprising role of local governments in international environmental cooperation: the case of Japanese collaboration with developing countries," *Journal of Environment and Development*, Vol. 20, No. 3 (2011), p. 238.
122 In legal and formal terms, municipalities' departments do not directly communicate with the corresponding ministries of the national bureaucracy, but only through their prefectures. In other words, prefectures facilitate communication between the national government and municipalities, or deliver nationally defined advice and guidance to municipalities. However, designated cities have most of the powers of a prefecture, including their direct communication with national ministries.

References

Almond, Gabriel A. and Sidney Verba (1963). *The Civic Culture*. Princeton, NJ: Princeton University Press.

146 Local capacity-building

Andersson, Krister and Frank van Laerhoven (2007). "From local strongman to facilitator: institutional incentives for participatory municipal governance in Latin America." *Comparative Political Studies*, Vol. 40, No. 9, pp. 1085–111.

Aoki, Kazumasu (2010). "Senkuteki na jichitai ondanka bōshi seisaku no seihi o meguru seisaku katei bunseki" [Policy analysis of progressive preventive-measures for climate change by local governments]. *Tomidai Keizai Ronshu* [Economic Journal of Toyama University], Vol. 56, No. 2, pp. 337–71.

Asian Development Bank (2005). *Capacity Building to Support Decentralization in Indonesia*. Manila: ADB.

Baba, Kenshi, Kazumasu Aoki, and Osamu Kimura (2006). "Analysis of environmental and energy policy processes in local governments in Japan." *Denryoku Chūo Kenkyūjo Hōkoku* [Central Research Institute of Electric Power Industry Report] Socio-economic Research Center, Rep. No. Y05025.

Bulkeley, Harriet and Heike Schroeder (2008). "Governing climate change post-2012: the role of global cities case-study – Los Angeles." Working Paper 122, Wallingford, UK, Tyndall Center for Climate Change Research.

Citizens' International Plaza, Council of Local Authorities for International Relations (CLAIR) (2013). Database of international cooperation activities by Japanese local government. Available from: www.plaza-clair.jp/jichitai/jichitai1-1.html [accessed August 27, 2013].

Crook, Richard and James Manor (1988). *Democracy and Decentralization in Southeast Asia and West Africa: Participation, Accountability and Performance*. Cambridge, UK: Cambridge University Press.

Dietz, Thomas, Elinor Ostrom, and Paul Stern (2003). "The struggle to govern the commons." *Science*, Vol. 302, pp. 1907–12.

Dyer, Hugh (1994). "Environmental ethics and international relations." *Paradigms*, Vol. 8, No. 1, pp. 58–77.

Fiszbien, Ariel (1997). "The emergence of local capacity: lessons from Colombia." *World Development*, Vol. 25, No. 7, pp. 1029–43.

Fredriksson, Per G. and Daniel Millimet (2002). "Strategic interaction and the determination of environmental policy across U.S. states." *Journal of Urban Economics*, Vol. 51, No. 1, pp. 101–22.

Fujii, Yasuhira (2007). "Tokubetsuku ni okeru kankyō kihon jōrei no seitei katei bunseki" [Analysis of basic environmental ordinance-making processes in Special Wards]. *Sōkan Shakai Kagaku* [Relative Social Sciences], Vol. 17 (2007), pp. 71–7.

Green, Lara, Chris Game, and Simon Delay (2005). *Why Should My Local Authorities Be Involved in an Overseas Project?* Birmingham, UK: Birmingham University.

Hasegawa, Kōichi (2003). *Kankyō undō to atarashii kokyōken* [Environmental movements and new public space]. Tokyo: Yūhikaku.

Helland, Eric and Andrew Whitford (2003). "Pollution incidence and political jurisdiction: evidence from the TRI." *Journal of Environmental Economics and Management*, Vol. 46, No. 3, pp. 403–24.

Helmsing, A.H.J. (2000). "Decentralization, enablement and local governance in low income countries." Working Paper Series, No. 342. The Hague, Netherlands, Institute of Social Studies.

Hiraoka, Shun'ichi and Takeshi Wada (2005). "Chihō jichitai ni okeru shiminsankagata no chikyū ondanka taisaku o suishinsuru shikumi to shakaiteki haikei" [Political system and social background for the promotion of climate mitigation through citizens' participation in local government]. *Ritsumeikan Sangyōshakai Ronshū* [Ritsumeikan University Industrial Society Papers], Vol. 41, No. 2, pp. 39–55.

Holgate, Claudia (2007). "Factors and actors in climate change mitigation: a tale of two South African cities." *Local Environment*, Vol. 12, No. 5, pp. 471–84.
Hooghe, Liesbet and Gary Marks (2003). "Unravelling the central state, but how? Types of multi-level governance." *American Political Science Review*, Vol. 97, No. 2, pp. 233–43.
International Council for Local Environmental Initiatives (ICLEI) (1993). *The Local Agenda 21 Initiative: ICLEI Guidelines for Local Agenda 21*. Freiburg: ICLEI.
International Council for Local Environmental Initiatives (ICLEI) (2002). "Second Local Agenda 21 survey." Background Paper No. 15 (DESA/DSD/PC2/BP15), January 2002.
Itakura, Toshimasa (2001). "Shimin sanka ni yoru kankyō jōrei zukuri" [Making an environmental ordinance through citizen participation]. *Keikaku Gyōsei* [Planning Administration], Vol. 24, No. 3, pp. 73–8.
Japan Bank for International Cooperation (JBIC) (2003). *Yen shakkan gyōmu ni okeru chihō jichitai to kokusai ginkō tono renkei kyōka ni mukete* [JBIC's collaboration with local authorities for yen loan business]. Tokyo: JBIC.
Japan, Cabinet Office (2002). "Sōsharu kyapitaru" [Social capital], 2002 ed., survey report, June 2003.
Japan, Cabinet Office (2005). "Community regeneration and social capital," survey report, August 2005.
Japan, Cabinet Office (2007). *Chikyū ondanka taisaku ni kansuru yoron chōsa* [Public opinion survey on global warming countermeasures]. Available from: www8.cao.go.jp/survey/h19/h19-globalwarming/index.html [accessed November 12, 2009].
Japan Center for Climate Change Actions (2011). "Chiiki no dōkō" [Regional trends]. Available from: www.jccca.org/trend_region/ [accessed November 1, 2011].
Japan, Environmental Agency (EA) (1995). "Rōkaruajenda 21 sakutei gaido" [Guidelines for formulating Local Agenda 21]. June 1995.
Japan ICLEI (2001). "Nihon no jichitai no ajenda 21 jisshi jōkyō chōsa hōkoku" [Report on the state of practice of Japanese local government's Agenda 21]. May 2001.
Japan International Cooperation Agency (JICA) (1998). *Chihō jichitai no kokusai kyōryoku jigoyō e no sanka daiichi fēzu* [Participation of local authorities in international cooperation projects: Phase I]. Tokyo: JICA Research Institute.
Japan International Cooperation Agency (JICA) (2000). *Chihō jichitai no kokusai kyōryoku jigyō e no sanka daini fēzu* [Participation of local authorities in international cooperation projects: Phase II]. Tokyo: JICA Research Institute.
Japan International Cooperation Agency (JICA) (2003). *Chiiki okoshi no keiken o sekai e* [Extending the experience of local revitalization to the world]. Tokyo: JICA Research Institute.
Japan, Ministry of Economy, Trade and Industry (METI) (2010). *Enerugī hakusho* [White paper on energy]. 2010 ed. Available from: www.enecho.meti.go.jp/topics/hakusho/2010energyhtml/ [accessed November 3, 2011].
Japan, Ministry of the Environment (MOE) (2003). "Rōkaruagenda 21 no sakutei jōkyōtou chōsa kekka nit suite" [Results on the investigation of the state of Local Agenda 21 programing]. March 2003. Available from: www.env.go.jp/press/press.php?serial=4101 [accessed December 3, 2009].
Japan, Ministry of the Environment (MOE) (2003). Press Release, May 13, 2003.
Japan, Ministry of the Environment (MOE) (2005). *Chihō kōkyō dantai no kankyō hozen taisaku chōsa* [Investigation on the environmental conservation measures of local governments]. Tokyo: MOE.
Japan, Ministry of the Environment (MOE) (2009). "Senryakuteki kankyō eikyō hyōka ni

148 Local capacity-building

tsuite" [Strategic environmental assessment]. Available from: www.env.go.jp/council/02policy/y0210-04/mat06.pdf [accessed December 3, 2009].

Japan, Ministry of the Environment (MOE) (2013). "Kankyō kihon keikaku ni kakawaru chihō kōkyō dantai ankēto chōsa" [Survey on basic environmental plans by local government]. September 2013.

Japan, Ministry of the Environment (MOE) (2014). *Environmental Impact Assessment Network*. Available from: www.env.go.jp/policy/assess/2-3selfgov/2-3system/list1.html [accessed November 3, 2014].

Japan, Ministry of the Environment (MOE) (2015). *Chihō kōkyō dantai ni okeru chikyū ondanka taisaku no suishin ni kansuru hōritsu shikō jōkyō chōsa kekka* [Report on the state of local governments' law implementation regarding the promotion of global warming countermeasures]. March 2015. Available from: www.env.go.jp/earth/dantai/h261001/mat02.pdf [accessed August 1, 2015].

Japan, Ministry of Finance (MOF) (2015). "Waga kuni no zaisei jijō" [The country's state of public finance]. January 2015. Available from: www.mof.go.jp/budget/budger_workflow/budget/fy2015/seifuan27/04.pdf [accessed August 6, 2015].

Japan, Ministry of Internal Affairs and Communications (MIAC) (2010). *Local Public Finance in Japan*. Available from: www.soumu.go.jp/english/pdf/lpfij.pdf [accessed December 14, 2010].

Japan, Ministry of Internal Affairs and Communications (MIAC) (2011 and 2014). Press Release. March 16, 2011, March 25, 2014, and November 28, 2014.

Japan, Ministry of Internal Affairs and Communications (MIAC) (2013). *Chihō kokyōdantai teiin kanri kankeki* [Management of local government personnel numbers]. Available from: www.soumu.go.jp/main_sosiki/jichi_gyousei/c-gyousei/teiin/index.html [accessed August 30, 2013].

Japan, Ministry of Internal Affairs and Communications (MIAC) (2013). *e-Stat*. Available from: www.e-stat.go.jp/SGT/chiiki/CommunityProfileTopDispatchAction.do?code=1 [accessed August 27, 2013].

Japan, Ministry of Internal Affairs and Communications (MIAC) (2015). "Chihō kōkyō dantai ni okeru jōhō kōkai jōrei no seitei jōkyō" [The enactment of local information disclosure ordinances]. March 31, 2015. Available from: www.soumu.go.jp/main_content/000350962.pdf [accessed November 3, 2015].

Japan, Ministry of Internal Affairs and Communications (MIAC) (2015). "Chihō kōkyō dantai teiin kanri chōsa kekka" [Report on the number of personnel of local public entities]. March 2015.

Kanagawa, Kōji (2004). "Jichitai keikaku to pātonashippu kankei ni okeru rōkaruagenda 21 no ichizuke" [Positioning Local Agenda 21s in the local planning structure and partnership relations]. *Toshi Kenkyū* [Urban Studies], Vol. 4, pp. 43–50.

Kawasaki, Kenji (2000). "Shimin to gyōsei no pātonāshippu ni yoru jichitai kankyō manējimento" [Local environmental management by a partnership between citizens and administration]. *Chiiki Kaihatsu* [Regional Development], No. 426, pp. 54–62.

Kawasaki, Kenji (2001). "Aratana dankai o mukaeta shimin sanka" [An emerging new phase for citizen participation]. *Chihō Zaimu* [Local Finance], No. 568, pp. 276–7.

Kayashima, Makoto (1999). "Hinoshi okeru kankyō kihon keiaku sakutei" [Formulation of Hino City's basic environmental plan]. *Tokyo no Jichi* [Autonomy Tokyo], Vol. 18, No. 33, pp. 18–25.

Kern, Kristine and Alber Gotelind (2009). "Governing climate change in cities: modes of urban climate governance in multi-level systems," OECD Conference Proceedings, Paris, OECD.

Kitakyushu International Techno-cooperative Association (KITA) (2013). *KITA*. Available from: www.kita.or.jp/index.html [accessed August 30, 2013].
Kriesi, Hanspeter (1995). "The political opportunity structure of new social movements: its impact on their mobilization." In J. Craig Jenkins and Bert Klandermans, eds., *The Politics of Social Protest*. Minneapolis, MN: University of Minnesota Press, pp. 167–98.
Larson, Anne M. (2002). "Natural resources and decentralization in Nicaragua: are local governments up to the job?" *World Development*, Vol. 30, No. 1, pp. 17–31.
Levinson, Arik (2003). "Environmental regulatory competition: a status report and some new evidence." *National Tax Journal*, Vol. 56, No. 1, pp. 91–106.
List, John and Shelby Gerking (2000). "Regulatory federalism and environmental protection in the Unites States." *Journal of Regional Science*, Vol. 40, No. 3, pp. 453–71.
Litfin, Karen (2000). "Advocacy coalitions along the domestic-foreign frontier: globalization and Canadian climate change policy." *Policy Studies Journal*, Vol. 28, No. 1, pp. 236–52.
Local Green Government Portal (2010). *Local Green Government Portal*. Available from: www.climate-lg.jp/policy/gw-city.html. [accessed December 14, 2010].
McKinnon, Ronald (1997). "The logic of market-preserving federalism." *Virginia Law Review*, Vol. 83, No. 7, pp. 1573–80.
Miyauchi, Taisuke (2001). "Kankyō jichi no shikumizukuri" [Environmental self-governance and its organization]. *Kankyō Shakaigaku Kenkyū* [Journal of Environmental Sociology], Vol. 7, pp. 56–71.
Muramatsu, Michio (1975). "The impact of economic growth policies on local politics in Japan." *Asian Survey*, Vol. 15, No. 9, pp. 799–816.
Nagoya Port Authority (2013). *Port of Nagoya*. Available from: www.port-of-nagoya.jp/port_of_nagoya/ [accessed August 30, 2013].
Nakaguchi, Takahiro (2002). "Nihon no rōkaruagenda to rōkaruakushon no genjō to kadai" [The state and problem of Japan's Local Agenda 21 and local action]. Architectural Institute of Japan Seminar, August 2002.
Nakamua, Hidenori, Mark Elder, and Hideyuki Mori (2011). "The surprising role of local governments in international environmental cooperation: the case of Japanese collaboration with developing countries." *Journal of Environment and Development*, Vol. 20, No. 3, pp. 219–50.
National Association of Chairpersons of City Councils (2011). "Shichō tēshutsu ni yoru gian" [Mayor-proposed agenda items]. Available from: www.si-gichokai.jp/official/research/jittai22/pdf/08_jittai22.pdf [accessed November 3, 2011].
Nikkei Human Resources (2006). *Nikkei Navi 2006*. Available from: http://job.nikkei.co.jp [accessed June 15, 2006].
NTT Data (2001). "Denshi seifu to minshushugi ni kansuru shutoken shimin chōsa" [Investigation report on citizens in the capital region for e-government and democracy]. December 2001.
Oates, Wallace E. (1972). *Fiscal Federalism*. New York: Harcourt Brace and Jovanovich.
Oates, Wallace E. (2002). "A reconsideration of environmental federalism." In John List and Aart de Zeeuw, eds., *Recent Advances in Environmental Economics*. Cheltenham, UK: Edward Elgar Publisher, pp. 1–32.
Ōno, Teruyuki (2010). "Tokyo wa mou Hajimete Imasu" [Tokyo has already started!]. *Gaikō Fōramu* [Diplomacy Forum], No. 260, pp. 42–5.
Peterson, George (1997). *Decentralization in Latin America: Learning through Experience*. Washington, DC: World Bank, 1997.

Pierre, Jon (2000). *Debating Governance, Authority, Steering and Democracy*. Oxford: Oxford University Press.
Putnam, Robert D. (1993). *Making Democracy Work: Civic Traditions in Modern Italy*. Princeton, NJ: Princeton University Press.
Rabe, Barry (2009). "Governing the climate from Sacramento." In Stephen Goldsmith and Donald Kettl, eds., *Unlocking the Power of Networks*. Washington, DC: Brookings Institution Press, pp. 34–61.
Reed, Steven (1981). "Environmental politics: some reflections based on the Japanese case." *Comparative Politics*, Vol. 13, No. 3, pp. 253–69.
Reed, Steven (1986). *Japanese Prefectures and Policy Making*. Pittsburgh, PA: University of Pittsburgh Press.
Rodden, Jonathan (2004). "Comparative federalism and decentralization: on meaning and measurement." *Comparative Politics*, Vol. 36, No. 4, pp. 481–500.
Samuels, Richard (1983). *The Politics of Regional Policy in Japan*. Princeton, NJ: Princeton University Press.
Seabright, Paul (1996). "Accountability and decentralization in government: an incomplete contracts model." *European Economic Review*, Vol. 40, No. 1, pp. 61–89.
Selman, Paul (2001). "Social capital, sustainability and environmental planning." *Planning Theory and Practice*, Vol. 2, No. 1, pp. 13–30.
Shapiro, Paul and Jeffrey Petchey (1997). "The welfare economics of environmental regulatory: two parables on state vs. federal control." In John B. Braden and Stef Proost, eds., *The Economic Theory of Environmental Policy in a Federal System: New Horizons in Environmental Economics*. Cheltenham, UK: Edward Elgar Publisher, pp. 122–46.
Shuman, Michael (1994). *Toward a Global Village: International Community Development Initiatives*. London: Pluto.
Siebert, Horst (1992). *Economics of the Environment: Theory and Policy*. Berlin and Heidelberg: Springer Verlag.
Sigman, Hilary (2005). "Transboundary spillovers and decentralization of environmental policies." *Journal of Environmental Economics and Management*, Vol. 50, No. 1, pp. 82–101.
Steiner, Kurt, Ellis Krauss, and Scott Flanagan, eds. (1980). *Political Opposition and Local Politics in Japan*. Princeton, NJ: Princeton University Press.
Takahashi, Hideyuki (2000). "Jichitai kankyō kihon keikaku no genjō to kadai" [The state and problems of local basic environmental plans]. *Kikan Gyōsei Kanri Kenkyū* [Administrative Management Quarterly], Vol. 89, pp. 20–1.
Tanaka, Mitsuru and Fumitoshi Okiyama (2010). "Chihō kōkyō dantai ni okeru kankyō asesumento sēdo no rekishi kara no kyōkun" [Lessons on the history of environmental impact assessment by Japanese local governments]. *Asesumento Gakkaishi* [Journal of Environmental Impact Assessment], Vol. 8, No. 2, pp. 6–16.
Tarrow, Sidney (1991). *Struggle, Politics, and Reform: Collective Action, Social Movements, and Cycles of Protest*. Ithaca, NY: Cornell University Centre for International Studies.
Tiebout, Charles (1956). "A pure theory of local expenditures." *The Journal of Political Economy*, Vol. 64, No. 5, pp. 416–24.
Tietenberg, Thomas H. (1979). "On the efficient spatial allocation of air pollution control responsibility." In Horst Siebert, Ingo Walker, and Klaus Zimmermann, eds., *Regional Environmental Policy: The Economic Issues*. New York: New York University Press, pp. 79–83.

Tokyo Metropolitan Government (TMG) (2006). *Environmental Impact Assessment System of the Tokyo Metropolitan Government*. Tokyo: TMG.
Tokyo Metropolitan Government (TMG) (2009). *Hōdō pappyō shiryō* [Press Release Material]. March 31, 2009.
Tokyo Metropolitan Government (TMG) (2010). "Sutēkihorudā mītingu" [Stakeholder meetings]. Available from: www2.kankyo.metro.tokyo.jp/kikaku/kikouhendouhousin/index.htm [accessed May 21, 2010].
United Kingdom, Department for International Development (UKDFID) (2003). "Strategic Grant Agreement between DFID and UK Local Government Alliance for International Development." December 23, 2003.
United Nations Center for Human Settlements (Habitat) (2001). "City-to-city cooperation: issues arising from experience." Habitat Report, Nairobi, May 25, 2001.
United Nations Conference on Environment and Development (1992). *Agenda 21*. Rio de Janeiro: UNCED, June 3–14, 1992, Available from: www.un.org/esa/sustdev/documents/agenda21/english/adenda21toc.htm [accessed December 3, 2014].
United Nations Development Program (UNDP) (2000). *The Challenge of Linking*. New York: UNDP Management Development and Governance Division.
Verba, Sidney and Norman Nie (1972). *Participation in America: Political Democracy and Social Equality*. New York: Harper & Row.
Wada, Takeshi (2002). "Nijūisseiki no chikyū kankyō to shakai hatten" [The Earth's environment for the twenty-first century and social development]. *Yuibutsuron to Gendai* [Materialism and Today], Vol. 29, pp. 2–15.
Wada, Takeshi and Kenrō Taura (2007). *Shimin chiiki ga susumeru chikyū ondanka bōshi* [Climate change countermeasures by citizens and community]. Kyoto: Gakugei Shuppan.
Wakasugi, Eiji (2007). "Shichōson ni yoru kokusai kyōryoku ni kansuru ikkosatsu" [An observation on international cooperation by local governments]. *Kokusai Kyōryoku Kenkyū* [Studies on International Cooperation], Vol. 23, No. 1, pp. 55–66.
Weber, Edward P. (1988). *Pluralism by the Rules: Conflict and Cooperation in Environmental Regulation*. Washington, DC: Georgetown University Press.
Weingast, Barry R. (1995). "The economic role of political institutions: market-preserving federalism and economic development." *Journal of Law, Economics and Organization*, Vol. 11, No. 1, pp. 1–31.
Yamazaki, Kazuki (2006). "Chiiki kokusaika ni okeru kokusai kyōryoku no genjo to kadai" [The state and problems of international cooperation in the area of local-level internationalization]. *Jichitai Kokusaika Fōramu* [Local-Level Internationalization Forum], No. 199, pp. 2–4.
Yanagi, Ken'ichirō (2000). "Chihō jichitai asesu jōrei no saikin no dōkō bunseki" [A recent trend analysis of local government assessment ordinances]. *NIRA Policy Research*, Vol. 13, No. 12, pp. 36–9.
Yoshida, Hitoshi (2001). *Jichitai no kokusai kyōryoku* [International cooperation by local governments]. Tokyo: Nihon Hyoronsha.
Yoshida, Hitoshi and Purnendra Jain (2003). "Japan's new channels of aid and cooperation: local government as an actor." Ad hoc Expert Group Meeting on Tracking the Reforms in Aid Delivery, Management and Accountability, Mexico City, November 6–7, 2003.

4 Tokyo's metropolitan cap-and-trade

Policy learning and diffusion

The purpose of this chapter is to cast light on the exceptional: the Tokyo Metropolitan Government (TMG), which has never received any Local Allocation Tax money, not since the 1953 establishment of this equalization grant system. Wealthy Tokyo has been able to utilize a much greater degree of financial flexibility and autonomy than any other local government. The mega metropolis has initiated many policy innovations ahead of the national government. One of these innovations was Japan's first mandatory emissions trading scheme, launched in April 2010 by the TMG. The process of adopting such a policy idea is extremely complex and requires a close examination of the political context in which the idea is learned, articulated, contested, adapted, and accepted by agents, both individual and collective. Why and how was the world's first urban scheme for a mandatory reduction of total emissions adopted in Tokyo and not elsewhere? What might cause the diffusion of this idea in other urban areas? One key explanation behind idea adoption is a policy evolution of trial-and-error lessons about effective policy design, desirable policy goals, and politically feasible judgments. This study finds that both agency effects and structural opportunities of policy adoption in the case of Tokyo's cap-and-trade are too specific to result in a more coherent diffusion of ideas, policies, and practices in other urban areas. Although there are signs of a diffusion of Tokyo's cap-and-trade throughout Japan, this is more likely to derive from mimicking behaviors than from learning. The policy transfer of Tokyo's cap-and-trade requires continuous learning about adaptive capacity to make it a better fit for locally specific conditions.

Metropolitan regions generate the bulk of greenhouse gas (GHG) emissions as they are responsible for the consumption of the majority of the world's energy. Sub-national governments in these population centers are increasingly initiating action on climate change. In this chapter, the Tokyo Metropolitan cap-and-trade system will be used as a single case study. Launched in April 2010 by the TMG, it is the world's first urban model of a mandatory reduction of total CO_2 emissions. Experimentation at local scales presents a unique testing opportunity for both sub-national and national governments to achieve their climate policy goals.

Climate change mitigation, once provided, becomes a global public good. No country can be excluded from the consumption opportunities of mitigation benefits. But the effectiveness of mitigation depends on the aggregate effort of all countries, and equally important, it will inevitably need to adapt to local conditions for the implementation of mitigation measures. Specific policy tools can enhance the effectiveness of mitigation at the local scale. Policy learning is one such tool used to overcome impediments to policy-relevant decision-making. Learning, which may lead to policy diffusion, may be a key candidate for disentangling the mechanisms of local policy innovation. The process of adopting policy ideas raises questions regarding why a specific policy idea is adopted in one place and not elsewhere and why some agents can be more responsive to the same idea than others.

This chapter will present a map of causal pathways and factors accounting for policy diffusion effects. It is a detailed case study that looks beneath the aggregate relationships of policy learning and diffusion to more qualitative evidence of governing bodies interacting at different phases of policy adoption within the urban scheme of a mandatory reduction of total emissions. The causal mechanism of policy adoption will be described as sequences of events regarding the adoption of Tokyo's cap-and-trade. The focus is on the whole causal process leading to a better process-oriented understanding of adopting policy ideas. Yet, to pinpoint complex diffusion patterns, it attempts to observe the process in a highly specific way by conceptualizing a diffusion mechanism of learning. It is the objective of this study to disentangle the process of policy adoption by an agent, the TMG, which constitutes the unit of analysis. The chapter is structured to examine how the adoption of Tokyo's cap-and trade can be explained in terms of the lessons learned from their own past or from other places elsewhere. I ultimately argue that Tokyo's policy learning is not easily adopted elsewhere due to the unique characteristics of the capital megacity.

Policy learning and diffusion

Karl Deutsch pioneered and emphasized the role of learning as resulting from the flow of communications and feedback about policy impacts.[1] The view of learning as a foundation for improving policy-making was subsequently embraced and expanded on by many others with the conceptualization of various forms of policy learning. Policy diffusion, which is facilitated by learning as a leading diffusion mechanism,[2] can be divided into two types: policy diffusion in a narrow sense and policy transfer. Policy transfer focuses on a limited, specific form of policy diffusion, which refers only to those cases caused by cognitive/conscious factors of learning agents. If it is the case that prior knowledge and its utilization are not independently responsible for policy adoption, then it cannot be said that policy transfer occurs.[3] Policy diffusion in a narrow sense includes cases where policy adoption is more the consequence of structural factors, such as similar modernizing and globalizing forces, without agents,[4] while the involvement of agents increases the likelihood of diffusion.[5] In a broader perspective, this subcategory of diffusion without agents, who are aware of prior knowledge, is seen as a way of explaining "policy convergence,"[6] alongside the structural forces of globalization.[7] All in all, from the viewpoint of structure-agency relationships, the diffusion literature emphasizes the importance of a structural account for adopting policy ideas, while the transfer literature identifies the significance of an agency-centered account for policy adaptation.[8]

The diffusion literature identifies a number of agent-involved patterns of adopting policy ideas. (1) One of the key diffusion determinants is communication between policy elites who interact with each other in their networks.[9] They tend to adopt a policy idea when they interact with their counterparts who have already adopted the policy idea.[10] (2) Geographical proximity of neighboring polities is likely to encourage the diffusion of policy ideas. Policy diffusion tends to be clustered geographically as policy elites emulate their neighbors when faced with similar problems.[11] (3) Policy innovation "frontrunners' serve as a point of reference for other policy elites, who do not wish to be among the latecomers, to catch up, favoring the diffusion of policy ideas.[12] David Dolowitz and David Marsh call it "perceptual transfer" as agents have feelings of being left behind.[13] (4) Similarity between systems sharing much of the same cultural, economic, and institutional features is another potential contribution to policy diffusion. Policy elites are likely to direct more attention to policy ideas that are adopted under cultural, economic, and institutional conditions similar to their own.

Policy diffusion also takes place across countries. According to a state-centric understanding, state officials communicate with each other, neighboring states influence each other, and "laggard" states follow leader states.[14] However, cross-national policy diffusion does not always occur between sovereign states; rather it can be transnationally carried out among social actors, sub-national governments, business actors and/or international organizations. Policy learning can thus stretch across scales for geographic space at multiple levels of jurisdiction. Cross-scale and multi-level learning provides a multiplicity of lessons for policymakers to make policy development better fit locally specific conditions in an adaptive way. But learning differs across learning agents. Some are more capable of using new information to update their prior beliefs and adopt innovative policy ideas while others are less so. In this sense, factors internal to an agent are most important for a better understanding of policy diffusion and learning. At the same time, such learning helps the process of collective learning develop "consensual knowledge" by knowledge sharing.[15]

When involved in policy diffusion, agents have different objects to be transferred. The primary focus of research interests in this area was initially on material, utility-based objectives, such as policy goals, structure, and instruments between governments.[16] Mark Evans and Jonathan Davies then distinguish between the "soft" transfer of ideas, principles, symbols, and attitudes and the "hard" transfer of those material objectives.[17] One might expect soft transfer to come before hard transfer as the latter requires an investigation of the founding role played by the soft transfer of discourse. In this context, Diane Stone seeks to address the role of ideational-based policy diffusion played by non-governmental actors in transnational networks—as a complement to the government-centric hard transfer.[18] Networks of experts (epistemic communities) are seen as knowledge-transfer agents who have control over knowledge production and thus guide policy learning.[19]

Yet, given such opportunities for policy ideas to spread, not all policy-makers are equally sensitive to the same information.[20] Some are more capable or willing to adopt policy ideas than others. Policy diffusion is thus not an inevitable process. Factors that are internal to agency, such as fiscal capacity, resourcing, prior beliefs, attentiveness to policy ideas, public demand, political leadership, and electoral/party politics, can be more influential determinants of adopting policy ideas than the external opportunity structures.[21] The public policy literature produces a better understanding of how domestic factors affect the process of policy adoption from abroad while the diffusion literature in structuralists' international relations tends to ignore domestic circumstances.[22] Global strategies and national mandates, which are internationally agreed by the states concerned, need to lead climate mitigation. However, climate change impacts are manifested locally and the capacity for policy operation is largely determined by local conditions. It is therefore expected that the relationship between structural factors and agency effects is strongly interactive in the sense that global strategies and national mandates promote or constrain Tokyo's actions, yet Tokyo interprets these structures and adapts them to local conditions.

The learning and diffusion of Tokyo's metropolitan cap-and-trade deserves a closer examination. Because of the cross-sectoral impacts of cost sharing, environmental problem-solving normally involves multiple agencies and multi-level policy networks or the multiplicity of learning and diffusion processes associated with policy adoption.[23] This allows us to map the spread of policy ideas that agents wish to promote or prevent through interactions in policy networks, conferences, and negotiations. Equally important, climate mitigation policy is influenced more by scientific knowledge and technology than any other policy area. Scientific knowledge needs to be translated in political terms for local action. The operational level of learning may reveal how experts' control over scientific knowledge guides policy-makers' learning. The politicization of science and policy objectivity is inevitable since the core beliefs of environmental issues are deeply divided and even irreconcilable. It is well worth finding out how scientific knowledge is biased or compromised by the core beliefs of clashing coalitions, as well as examining how core beliefs are constrained by the political feasibility.

Lesson-drawing from within and outside of the nation

Learning could be a key source of policy innovation. Policy learning can take place in transnational networks as well as in the hierarchies of the state. The involvement of social actors and sub-national actors in climate change policy can lead to the "transnationalization of policy."[24] National governments and international organizations work with them to incorporate their interests into a policy network for policy development. Transnational policy communities of

156 *Tokyo's metropolitan cap-and-trade*

policy experts and scientists share their knowledge and ideas and form a transnational network through regular interaction.[25] These interactions can involve a process of mutual learning about problem-solving and the development of a collective understanding. In regard to climate change mitigation, attention also needs to be drawn to the "soft" forms of learning, such as the diffusion of norms, which provides a justification for the "hard" learning of policy tools. Climate change norms are related to sustainable development and the equitable distribution of responsibilities. These international norms serve to direct the demands of specific policy tools. As illustrated in this book, some local authorities demonstrate an ability to utilize local experience and knowledge so a policy tool can promote international norms while straddling both the division between state and community and that between market and community.

Learning in the hierarchies of the state

The Agency for Natural Resources and Energy, which is a branch of Japan's Ministry of Economy, Trade and Industry (METI, formerly Ministry of International Trade and Industry), has been instrumental in managing energy demand/supply. Not surprisingly, the METI takes on the issue of climate change as a matter of industrial policy. Climate change presents a challenge for energy demand/supply policy to take GHG emissions constraints into consideration. The national Energy Efficiency Law, which is the basis of energy policy implementation for the national agency, was revised in 1998 to require business operators with overall annual energy consumption of 3,000 kl in crude oil equivalent or more to periodically report their energy unit consumption, energy conservation measures, and three-to-five year conservation plans.[26] According to this revision, when energy conservation activities were inadequate, measures, such as public disclosures and fines, would be applied to the underperforming business operator. Energy policy had thus been the exclusive jurisdiction of the national level. Yet the Bureau of the Environment of the TMG (BOE) directed attention to the mandatory national reporting scheme as its own policy tool lesson, which triggered the 2000 introduction of the Enterprise Planning System for Mitigation Measures (a voluntary emissions reduction scheme with a mandatory reporting system) by the TMG.[27] This program targeted business facilities with emissions of 1,500 kl in crude oil equivalent or more, who were required to report a target, based on the average from the past three consecutive years' emissions, and plan to implement the required basic reduction measures set by the TMG. Under this scheme, it was also required for the targeted facilities to make their reports on reduction plans and the results available to the public. The TMG publicly named the facilities that had failed to comply with disclosure obligations. In the operational process of this program, the targeted facilities were identified by utilizing existing surveys for the implementation of the national Energy Efficiency Law and conducting the TMG's independent surveys.[28]

In essence, the process of adopting the TMG's mandatory reporting scheme is a redesign of the national policy instrument and constitutes evidence of instrumental learning in the hierarchies of the state. This is a case of a spillover of instrumental ideas from one policy domain, energy policy, to another, environmental policy. At the operation level of learning, conscious factors that are internal to the TMG appear to be the key determinants of adopting the instrumental idea. The BOE used learning tools, such as independent surveys and formal evaluations, to draw lessons from the national instrumental design. However, such lesson-drawing can be inadequate as instrumental ideas may be adopted without acknowledging the initial policy-making environment of a specific policy domain at a different level of government.[29] The process of the TMG's lesson-drawing over the mandatory reporting system will be examined further in the following sections.

Learning in transnational networks

The latest addition to Tokyo's climate policy package is a cap-and-trade scheme. The idea of a market-based cap-and-trade originated in the 1980s in the United States (US) to address acid rain caused by sulfur dioxide emissions. As this policy idea diffused from the US clean air scheme to global climate policy, the multi-national European Union Emissions Trading System (EU-ETS) was launched in 2005. In Tokyo, from 2001 and 2002, think tanks and academics acted as transfer agents, shuttling knowledge about cap-and trade, and were invited to work with BOE officials.[30] The BOE accepted the fundamental ideas of cap-and-trade, but as the transferred policy instruments had to be adapted to the urban scale there was little practical experience from around the world for BOE officials to draw on. As described below, the "hard" transfer of policy instruments from overseas was limited, and domestic processes were soon shaping the detailed programs of Tokyo's cap-and-trade. In the following sections, I will trace the different phases of adopting policy ideas within the urban scheme of Tokyo's cap-and-trade, including an analysis of whether the BOE was able to establish an improved understanding of the instrumental redesign.

Horizontal diffusion among localities at the domestic level

This section will explore the spread of Tokyo's mandatory reporting system to others and inquire into why and how instances of learning or copying occurred. Besides Tokyo's mandatory reporting system, which was introduced in 2000, there are two other potential lessons regarding conveying learning to others: the 2005 revision of Tokyo's mandatory reporting system[31] and the 2005 national mandatory GHG Accounting and Reporting system (which was part of the 2005 Act on the Promotion of Global Warming Countermeasures).[32] As described later, the TMG failed to introduce a mandatory reduction of total CO_2 emissions in 2004. Instead, in March 2005, the TMG strengthened the enforcement mechanism of Tokyo's mandatory reporting system; in the revised reporting system, the targeted business facilities were now advised by the TMG guidelines, required to submit and announce a five-year GHG reduction plan, and this plan was evaluated, rated by the TMG and announced on the TMG website. The instrumental role of Tokyo's mandatory reporting system shifted from information management to regulatory measures. This experience provided the basis for the introduction of a mandatory reduction of total CO_2 emissions in Tokyo. In contrast to this, in June 2005, the national government finally adopted a national mandatory reporting system for emissions reduction; however, in this system, the individual reports on business operators were disclosed only upon request, and enforcement mechanisms, such as government advice, ratings, evaluations, and public announcements, were not put in place. While it is worth examining if the adoption of this national mandatory reporting scheme was the outcome of policy convergence (since a number of OECD countries, including Australia, Britain, Canada, France, Israel, New Zealand, and the United States, had already put such reporting schemes in place or were considering introducing them), it is observed that the TMG led the adoption of a mandatory reporting of emissions reduction and the national government eventually followed suit. But the policy instrument was not directly transferable to a national level of governance since national strategies occurred in the learning process of wider socio-political landscapes and technical practices.

As of October 2012, 30 out of 47 prefectures and seven out of 20 designated municipalities (with populations of greater than half a million) were implementing some form of mandatory systems for emissions reporting. What was transferred? Learning implies an improved understanding, as reflected by a decision to produce more efficient and effective policy outcomes than the previous ones.[33] Along this line, I have used the existence of convincing enforcement mechanisms as an indicator for learning outcomes regarding Tokyo's mandatory reporting system at the same level of government. Aggregate patterns of diffusion over time (2000–2012) showed that a majority of those local governments copied rather than learned from the experience of Tokyo's 2000 mandatory reporting system while introducing their mandatory reporting systems without adequate mechanisms to enforce them. There were only three localities (the cities of Sapporo and Nagoya, and Kagawa prefecture) that imposed obligations on targeted facilities to disclose both their emissions reduction plans and the results. In 2005, as the national mandatory GHG Accounting and Reporting system introduced the national government's duty of information disclosure upon request, several local governments, such as Saitama, Hyogo, Kyoto, Osaka, Nagano, and Shizuoka prefectures, rather than business operators themselves, also began to disclose the plans and results of individual business facilities. However, no local governments adopted the instrumental ideas of formal evaluation, rating, and announcement as prescribed in Tokyo's 2005 mandatory reporting system. It is safe to say that most local authorities essentially wished to implement voluntary emissions reduction schemes together with the mimicking behavior of mandatory reporting.[34]

The way taken by learning agents involved in adopting mitigation policy instruments seems to be heavily influenced by industrial structures and previous growth patterns on emissions in each locality. In 2006 the industrial sector in Tokyo was responsible for only 9 percent of all CO_2 emissions (cf. Japan's average of 36 percent), but large-scale office buildings in the commercial sector, which represented only 1 percent of all businesses in Tokyo, accounted for about 40 percent of all CO_2 emissions.[35] These office buildings were targeted for Tokyo's mandatory reporting. In the same year, Chiba prefecture, whose industrial sector represented 65 percent of all CO_2 emissions, had failed to introduce a mandatory reporting system, and Aichi prefecture, whose industrial sector accounted for 53 percent of all CO_2 emissions, in 2003 adopted a mandatory reporting system but with no mechanism to force the targeted facilities to submit their reports.[36] In contrast, a few localities (the cities of Kyoto and Sapporo and the prefectures of Kyoto, Osaka and Saitama) that approximated the institutionalization of Tokyo's mandatory reporting enforcement tended to show a much lower share of industrial CO_2 emissions by sector.[37] In 2006, 6 percent of Sapporo city's CO_2 emissions and 18 percent of Kyoto city's came from the industrial sector. The reasoning thus hypothesizes that the higher the share of the industrial sector of all CO_2 emissions, the less likely it is that learning agents adopt effective mitigation policy tools. Previous growth patterns on emissions also seem to be associated with the effectiveness of policy instruments. The front-runners of effective mandatory reporting can be found in the low growth environment of GHG emissions.[38] GHG emissions in Tokyo increased by approximately 3 percent from 1990 to 2006, those in Osaka prefecture showed negative 4 percent and those in Saitama prefecture indicated positive 1.5 percent during the same period. On the other hand, Fukushima prefecture, whose GHG emissions increased by 28 percent from 1990 to 2006, had been unable to adopt a mandatory reporting system. Akita prefecture, which had equally fast emissions growth with a 13 percent increase during the same period, eventually introduced a mandatory reporting system in 2011 but with only the right to counsel the targeted facilities who failed to submit their reports.[39] It is similarly hypothesized that the faster the GHG emissions increase in previous years, the less likely it is that learning agents will adopt effective mitigation policy tools.

Altering policy elites' beliefs

As the seventh session of the Conference of the Parties (COP7) – Marrakesh Climate ended in November 2001 with an agreement regarding the implementation details of the Kyoto accord, a policy network of communication among BOE officials, local NGOs, and academic researchers emerged through informal debates and study sessions. To take part in the new commitment which Japan internationally agreed to in Marrakesh, the 2002 Tokyo Metropolitan Environmental Master Plan made a clear target of Tokyo achieving a 6 percent GHG reduction by 2010 from the 1990 level, although the national reduction goals did not specify the statutory responsibility of local governments.[40] There was a consensus amongst policy network experts recognizing that Tokyo's voluntary emissions reduction scheme with the mandatory reporting system alone could not achieve the emissions reduction goal. In February 2002, Governor Shintarō Ishihara launched "Tokyo's Climate Change Strategy" at the opening speech of the first plenary session of the Tokyo Metropolitan Assembly (TMA), prioritizing a mandatory reduction of CO_2 emissions from large-scale buildings in the industrial and commercial sectors and beginning deliberations on the possible establishment of Tokyo's ETS.[41] Tokyo's policy success in introducing a mandatory reduction scheme for diesel vehicle emissions in 1999 provided a convincing basis for learning by allowing BOE officials to trace the course of the events leading to success. BOE officials saw this specific lesson as a reference point. In this scheme, the BOE worked with the metropolitan department of small-to-medium enterprises to create demand for particulate-matter removal devices (DPF) and promote a market-driven reduction mechanism with the TMG's subsidies for the purchase of those devices.[42]

Learning, as part of the process of adopting the idea of a mandatory reduction policy, entailed new understandings of general policy direction, involving a rethinking among the policy elites on the dominant view of voluntary reduction and fundamental aspects of mitigation policy. The change in their policy beliefs from voluntary to mandatory reduction appeared to be the direct result of non-conscious factors, especially those regarding internationally agreed commitments and national policies, external to the make-up of the Tokyo metropolitan polity. But these structural factors are not sufficient to account for the alteration of the general policy direction. Cognitive/conscious factors that were internal to the learning agents are necessary in considerations of the result. The policy networks of BOE officials and other like-minded experts were characterized by consensual knowledge. Members of these networks used the formal evaluation of Tokyo's mitigation policy as a learning tool, and the necessity of mandatory reduction was communicated through the channels of informal debates and study sessions.[43] Equally important, Tokyo's initiative to control diesel vehicle emissions can be identified as the most influential lesson learned by BOE officials. This innovation convinced them to pursue a policy model of mandatory reduction.[44]

Political feasibility and gubernatorial leadership

Combating climate change is a political problem. In Japan, there is little evidence that the divide between the environmental and industrial advocacy coalitions at the national level will be resolved over climate change policy. In contrast, it appears that Tokyo's cap-and-trade program has successfully gained goodwill and cooperation from both citizens' groups and business establishments. Tokyo's success in implementing the cap-and-trade program can be attributed largely to political learning about maneuvering and manipulating policy processes in order to advance the policy idea of mandatory reduction. In February 2002, as mentioned above, Governor Ishihara entered mandatory emissions reduction on the policy-making agenda. A handful of BOE officials informally worked with an environmental non-profit organization and came up with the idea of the mandatory reduction of "total" CO_2 emissions.[45] To this end, they proposed an absolute, aggregate cap on large-scale facilities that would be induced to trade excess reductions among themselves to achieve the overall reduction target (cap-and-trade). In November 2002, the TMG officially announced its policy shift towards a mandatory reduction of total CO_2 emissions.[46]

In May 2003, the policy idea of cap-and-trade was referred to a sub-committee of the Tokyo Metropolitan Environmental Council, which consisted of 15 members—including four members from the business sector (Tokyo Electric Power, Tokyo Gas, Toyota Motor, and the Association of Building Engineering and Equipment).[47] These members of the industrial advocacy coalition at the national level attempted to affect local policy-making. Not surprisingly, BOE officials could not avoid a bitter split between the locally coordinated environmental coalition (academics, scientists, and citizens' groups) and the industrial advocacy coalition. The core beliefs of the environmental coalition, which was calling for mandatory emissions reduction, were based on Japan's moral responsibility as a big emitter, while those of the industrial advocacy coalition, which emphasized the economic rationale of voluntary measures, were concerned about economic welfare over environmental objectives. Both Toyota and Tokyo Electric Power strongly opposed the proposals of mandatory reduction of total CO_2 emissions and the necessary provision of penalties.[48] As the TMG anticipated, neither of the coalitions was led to alter their policy beliefs. Yet the Council Secretariat had initially maneuvered the sub-committee membership so that pro-cap-and-trade members occupied the majority of the seats at the sub-committee. It appeared that the expected sub-committee's report would be in favor of BOE's proposals for cap-and-trade. By the sixth session of the sub-committee in November 2003, this momentum abruptly changed as business operators intensively lobbied the Headquarters of the Governor to ensure they could retain their voluntary measures.[49] In May 2004, the Council Secretariat submitted the final report, from which the phrases "mandatory reduction" and "penalties" were uniformly missing, to Governor Ishihara. The TMG subsequently dropped the institutionalization of cap-and-trade from its policy-making agenda list. Instead, as describe previously, it moved towards regulatory measures by strengthening its mandatory reporting system in 2005.

In 2006 Tokyo's bid to become the host city for the summer Olympic Games in 2016 returned the idea of cap-and-trade to the policy-making agenda.[50] To win the right to host the games, Governor Ishihara made the environment a top priority, formulating a "Carbon-minus Olympics" strategy.[51] Tokyo's bid for the games brought different TMG departments together and led to the formation of an interdepartmental consensus regarding stringent mitigation measures. In the following year, Governor Ishihara demonstrated his political commitment to addressing climate change issues, allocating US$600 million to a "Global Warming Countermeasures Fund" over the next 10 years. Unlike other local authorities, the TMG had a great deal of freedom in budgetary choice, which allowed it to create such a fund. The governor had sufficient financial resources and political opportunities, allowing Tokyo's bid for the games to be exploited by the political leadership. The metropolitan administration was ready to commit itself to progressive policy-making since there was no likelihood of there being a new governor in the near future.

In June 2007, the TMG officially created a cap-and-trade policy agenda again.[52] By this time, BOE officials had attempted to advance the idea of adopting a cap-and-trade scheme by learning the political feasibility from lesson-drawing. They were less concerned with a change in the policy beliefs of business operators, but rather were concerned with promoting strategic behavior to achieve the policy goal of a mandatory reduction of total CO_2 emissions. From 2007 to 2008, the MTG held three administration-led "stakeholder" meetings and 28 public meetings with business establishments. The TMG and the Keidanren (Japan Business Federation) failed to reach a mutually satisfying resolution but the Tokyo Chamber of Commerce came to fully support a cap-and-trade scheme by the end of the consultation process.[53] In June 2008, members of the Metropolitan Assembly who relied heavily on support from small-to-medium businesses (representing over 99 percent of business enterprises in Tokyo) for their electoral success unanimously passed a cap-and-trade program by revising the existing Environmental Conservation Ordinance.

BOE officials judged the probability of a successful cap-and-trade enactment and assessed the opportunity costs associated with advancing this proposal. The cap did not apply to small and medium-sized business facilities, yet through their offset-credit approach these facilities were allowed to create credits, known as offsets, through energy-saving measures. Then the large-scale facilities under the cap were allowed to purchase such credits to meet their obligations. Governor Ishihara introduced the Environmental Collateralized Bond Obligation (CBO) Program in order to provide smaller businesses with a means of raising funds to achieve CO_2 reductions.[54] The TMG was thus able to convince the Tokyo Chamber of Commerce of the viability of the implementation designs. In other words, political learning led to instrumental learning.

The characteristics of the mega capital also increased the political feasibility of cap-and-trade proposals. No steel or petroleum facilities, which fell under the category of the targeted facilities under the cap, happened to be located in Tokyo. Equally important, electric power plants, while being required to submit their plans and results of emissions reduction and renewable energy development (energy supply-side regulations), were exempted from the cap-and-trade system. The TMG was thus able to limit instances of direct confrontation with the most powerful lobbying groups. Although their policy rationale was well documented and prepared with convincing data, BOE officials were obviously unwilling to challenge the core beliefs of the industrial coalition. These policy elites were aware of the relationship between their past failed strategy and its impact on the prospects of cap-and-trade.[55]

The evidence indicates that resource and leadership similarities might facilitate the political learning of similar cap-and-trade at local scales elsewhere but they were not sufficient preconditions to facilitate political learning. The structural factors—especially those relating to geographic location and the centralization of political and business activities—seemed to have provided the TMG with another political opportunity to push its mandatory reduction of total CO_2 emissions through the policy processes. The unique location of Tokyo persuaded many big business operators to reluctantly concede to the mandatory reduction.[56] Tokyo is the city with the highest concentration of corporate headquarters (more 50 percent of enterprises having more than 3,000 employees) and hosts the national government's functions. This does not necessarily make the city significantly different from its counterparts in other countries, but the structure of the national bureaucracy does make a significant difference. Japan's regulatory agencies distinctively practice informal/administrative regulations rather than market-based regulations, although there has been a push towards a market-driven regulatory system since the early 1990s. Therefore, proximity to the national bureaucracy becomes crucial in running their business operations. The business value of information obtained through face-to-face contact with the national bureaucracy encourages the concentration of headquarters in Tokyo to overcome bureaucratic hurdles. The comparative advantages of business operation in Tokyo are likely to outweigh the costs associated with mandatory emissions reduction. It is thus less likely that the introduction of Tokyo's cap-and-trade system would induce large-scale business operators to move out of Tokyo to situate their headquarters elsewhere within the nation. The concentration of corporate headquarters then allows Tokyo's cap-and-trade system to prioritize CO_2 emissions reduction from large-scale buildings that account for 40 percent of all CO_2 emissions in Tokyo.

Horizontal and vertical coordination in governing Tokyo's cap-and-trade

BOE officials clearly recognized that GHG emissions reduction (i.e., provision of the public good) would require the aggregate efforts of all actors and all countries for problem-solving, before launching Tokyo's cap-and-trade system in April 2010.[57] In 2008 the TMG began to urge other local authorities to adopt mandatory cap-and-trade programs and promote an integrated cap-and-trade system that would cover the entire nation. The national government's compulsion in the hierarchies of the state is far more effective than local government's cooperation to introduce a cap-and-trade program at the local level. Lacking an authority capable of compelling other localities to adopt the policy idea of a cap-and-trade program, the TMG had to win the goodwill of other local authorities through a sort of coordinated cooperation. The TMG took initiatives to expand its local system, which targeted the end-use of energy in office buildings, to the neighboring prefectures of Saitama, Kanagawa, and Chiba, while holding a seminar on Tokyo's mitigation measures for all other prefectures and designated cities in August 2008 and July 2009. In September 2010 the TMG and Saitama prefecture agreed to establish a linked system in which credits from excess emissions reductions and small and medium-sized facility credits (offsets) would become tradable between the two jurisdictions.[58] In the April of the following year, Saitama's mandatory emissions trading scheme, which set an absolute cap at the facility level (i.e., 581 facilities as of 2013), started by being bilaterally linked to Tokyo.

Governor Ishihara used to insist, "Once we start our emissions trading system, our neighbors, such as Kanagawa, Chiba and Saitama, in the national capital region will follow suit."[59] However, his anticipation and enthusiasm seemed to be too optimistic for Kanagawa and Chiba to show any willingness to do so. These two prefectures had a much higher share of industrial CO_2 emissions by sector or large-scale energy-intensive factories (namely, steel and petro-chemical industries) than Tokyo and Saitama. In 2011, about 45 percent of Kanagawa's CO_2 emissions and around 65 percent of Chiba's CO_2 emissions came from the industrial sector, as compared with only 6 percent of Tokyo's and 29 percent of Saitama's (primarily from cement plants).[60] The limits of Kanagawa's and Chiba's effort to introduce a mandatory emissions trading scheme became visible due to the financial necessity of those local governments to invite and persuade large-scale factories to locate there. There were serious concerns about the possibility that mandatory cap-and-trade programs, backed up by an enforcement mechanism, would force the factories to exercise choice by moving to another locality where environmental regulations would be low enough to meet their business needs. Kanagawa's Governor Shigefumi Matsuzawa was quoted as saying, "The industrial heartland of Japan, such as Kanagawa, Aichi and Osaka, has great difficulty in adopting it [a mandatory cap-and-trade scheme]."[61]

In November 2009, in response to Prime Minister Yukio Hatoyama's declaration for the target reduction in Japan's GHG emissions to be 25 percent below 1990 levels by 2020, the TMG proposed a nationwide cap-and-trade system by outlining a two-tier system: National Level Cap-and-Trade Program (NLCTP) and Regional Level Cap-and Trade Program (RLCTP). The former would impose an absolute cap on around 500 super large-scale energy and resource suppliers (i.e., power plants and steel plants) while the latter would be managed by prefectures and large cities by targeting large facilities (i.e., factories, office buildings, and public facilities).[62] The TMG has contributed to a useful debate on national government-level programs, on which the METI will have a great impact. So far, in 2005 the Ministry of the Environment (MOE) introduced Japan's Voluntary Emissions Trading Scheme (JVETS) for a preliminary investigation into this scheme, in which 31 companies voluntarily participated in the initial experimentation. Further, in 2008 a MOE investigation committee introduced the Experimental Emissions Trading Scheme (a voluntary scheme) by experimenting with a combination of an absolute cap and an intensity-based one.[63] The TMG continues to state that any national cap-and-trade system should be mandatory and have an absolute cap as reducing GHG emissions depends on the aggregate effort of all actors concerned.

Transnational networks in sharing Tokyo's experience

BOE officials obviously borrowed the idea of EU-ETS but they had to adapt their policy instruments to the specific urban scale. Tokyo's cap-and-trade system has five-year compliance periods, which are much longer than the one-year period under EU-ETS. The compliance mechanism is designed to allow large-scale buildings to gradually reduce CO_2 emissions through long-term strategic investments in energy efficiency, while the EU-ETS's short compliance periods enabled the designated facilities to easily use its emissions trading scheme, in a bid to achieve their reduction obligations.[64] Tokyo's cap-and-trade is also intended to avoid too much dependence on emissions trading, as the designed facilities could not engage in emissions trading unless they achieved the required reduction target. Emission reductions exceeding the yearly obligation may be traded from the second year of each compliance period. In other words, Tokyo's cap-and-trade can be regarded as an urban-scale system prioritizing mandatory emissions reductions over market-driven emissions trading.

At the early stage of Tokyo's mitigation measures, it was recognized by Governor Ishihara that Tokyo should make an international contribution to building a mutual learning network to combat climate change by sharing Tokyo's local experience and local human capital with counterpart organizations. Following the TMG's announcement in 2007 to join the International Carbon Action Partnership (ICAP), whose members are major cities and state governments, in March 2008 the TMG agreed with the State of California to link up its emissions credit trading with California's trading scheme. Tokyo and other major cities in the world have worked together through a network Climate Leadership Group (C40) to share and strengthen their efforts to become low-carbon cities. As big cities in developing countries become interested in Tokyo's mitigation measures, the TMG has also been conveying Tokyo's experience to those energy-intensive cities. Tokyo's efforts to link with other carbon markets, however, are expected to face a serious difficulty in linking one system with another, due to different operational methods used for different targets and different market rules. While emissions trading markets in the EU and US revolve around the targeted industries, i.e., utilities and energy-intensive industries, Tokyo's scheme has a focus on the end-use of energy, i.e., office buildings. Even if systems are compatibly linked with one another, BOE officials express their concern about an influx of low priced allowances, which may delay domestic emission reductions.[65] In other words, "soft" forms of transfer—such as the idea of low-carbon links among mega cities—are appealing, but the "hard" transfer of policy tools and implementation is a difficult sell.

Assessing the determinants of policy learning and diffusion

GHG emissions are the consequence of human actions or organizational processes that take place in a given space. Climate mitigation may be led by national mandates, but the causes of this global issue are locally specific in character and implementation needs to be locally specific to meet local conditions. In the absence of national policy, for example, this necessity has led to the creation of some pioneering sub-national ETS programs, such as the Regional Greenhouse Gas Initiative (RGGI) in the Northeastern United States, the Greenhouse Gas

Reduction Scheme (GGRS) in Australia's New South Wales, the Regional Clean Air Initiatives Market (RECLAIM) in Los Angeles, and the Emissions Reduction Market System (ERMS) in Chicago, all of which were designed at the sub-national level. These cases have increased the potential ability of local authorities to learn lessons drawn from previous experiences in mitigation at sub-national scales.[66] Metropolitan areas are responsible not only for the bulk of national economic output but also for the costs of high carbon-intensities. They are particularly vulnerable to the urban-specific impacts of climate change and thus need to take these impacts into consideration for climate change mitigation.[67] Such consideration is yet to be given to mitigation experiments at city scales, such as with Tokyo's cap-and-trade program.

Vertical linkages

It took many years to establish Tokyo's cap-and-trade program. The TMG began to curtail Tokyo's CO_2 emissions in 2000 by seeking innovations in its own voluntary emissions reduction scheme with a mandatory reporting system. Once Governor Ishihara got the issue of mandatory reduction on the TMG policy-making agenda in 2002, the "soft" transfer of a market-based cap-and-trade solution became the initial driver of Tokyo's climate policy in the early stages. The adoption of this basic idea from overseas bypassed the exclusive jurisdiction of the national government without, however, directly challenging the existing inter-governmental relations. The detailed instruments of Tokyo's climate policy package involved multiple policy cycles in interactive domestic-level processes while diffusing upwards or downwards between national and sub-national governments.

The institutional approach to national-local coordination on climate change policy that is commonly used in most countries is a top-down model (or a hierarchically ordered system of direct/indirect coercion) where national governments require sub-national authorities to work within nationally defined frameworks as well as assist sub-national authorities to develop their capacity to take action on their own. But not all national governments have made such a strong commitment to climate action. In the absence of strong national policy, as seen in the case of Tokyo's cap-and-trade initiative, some sub-national authorities are capable enough to independently act to address climate change by lesson-drawing. If local action one-sidedly enhances policy diffusion to higher levels of government, this can be seen as a bottom-up model (a decentralized form of learning or copying). The case in point is that Japanese local governments initially led the adoption of policy innovations against industrial pollution and the policy laggard, the national government, followed suit. The case study of Tokyo's cap-and-trade, however, has found that a third model, that of interactive/mutual learning processes among levels of government, is revealed in the process of adopting policy ideas. It is safe to say that the analytical importance of organizational learning through interactions between levels of government can tap into the abundant information of policy diffusion.[68] In general, mitigation policy instruments are less likely to be directly transferable to a different level of government while there is a growing need for coordinated decision-making processes between different levels of government. Learning agents are faced with a different structural context at each level of government. They interpret the structural context and make a conscious effort to gain an improved understanding of what factors constrain a direct policy transfer. In this study, the learning of mandatory reporting in national energy policy triggered the introduction of mandatory reporting in a different policy domain at the local level, that is, local environmental policy, to meet local conditions. The national government eventually made policy development fit better in the national structural context of the same environmental policy domain and then introduced a national mandatory reporting scheme in a less stringent way to reduce GHG emissions.

Horizontal linkages

Policy diffusion can also occur through national networks of communication among local governments to keep up with policy innovation "front-runners" or to emulate neighbors. This is based on interactions among governmental units that legally or socio-economically have the same status at the same level. The expected competition among local governments diffuses the horizontal dimension of policy innovation among localities. The horizontal competition at the sub-national level assumes that the policy process need not follow the administrative chart of the centralized structure. Instead it reveals the actual learning behavior of local policy elites rather than the formal rules in the hierarchical structure. In the area of environmental policy, some studies provide evidence that the sub-national authorities' communication networks did result in inefficient regulatory competition or "a race to the bottom" that would lower environmental quality in order to compete for capital.[69] Others report evidence of "free riding" by sub-national authorities that chose lower environmental standards in order to export the environmental costs to their neighbors.[70] These two behavioral tendencies have been considered to be key constraints on the diffusion of progressive environmental policy; they are driven by structural factors, such as fiscal or capital demand for a common low base.

In this study, there is no clear evidence that a mandatory reporting system supports the claim of horizontal competition to catch up with front-runners. This can be partly explained by the nature of the cost-benefit of mitigation measures. In Japan, the focus of environmental protection has shifted from identifiable sources of industrial pollution to diffuse, no-point sources of climate change. Since the costs and benefits of industrial pollution are relatively concentrated on a narrow range of industrial interests and affected residents in industrial cities, these groups intensified their political conflict in a direct way. A dichotomy of polluters-versus-victims interest representation effectively influenced the adoption of policy ideas regarding pollution control and compensation. In contrast, climate change policy tends to impose both diffused and uncertain adaptation costs on a sectoral basis while offering diffused benefits to a wide range of social groups. Laggard government agencies are thus less willing to learn about mitigation instruments and emulate their neighbors. This study has found that the process of horizontal diffusion of mandatory reporting is characterized by copying in terms of symbolic terms, rather than a rational concern with an improved understanding of policy ideas. A majority of local governments that had engaged in policy instrument transfer emulated Tokyo's mandatory reporting system without adequate mechanisms to enforce their own systems.

There is also no clear evidence of an association between mitigation tools and "a race to the bottom." The previous findings of this constraint on progressive or costly policy diffusion are based primarily on the American experience in a federal system. In theory, elected local officials in Japan's unitary system do not have to be accountable to their voters to the extent that national regulations set limits on the financial discretion of local governments and extend fiscal equalization to reduce the inequality of fiscal capacity among localities. Japanese local governments tend to compete less with each other than those in federal systems, such as the United States, in the pursuit of revenue policy. According to a perceived "race to the bottom," local governments are expected to choose economic advantages over potentially costly environmental tools. The findings suggest that national networks of communication among local governments do not necessarily operate under a "lowest common denominator" mechanism in which local governments, while adhering to sub-optimal choices, failed to achieve more efficient and effective policy outcomes than previous outcomes. The assumption of "a race to bottom" does not fully account for why 37 (55 percent) of 67 large local authorities have adopted the idea of mandatory reporting and the rest have not, and why at least seven (15 percent) of those authorities are implementing mandatory reporting with convincing enforcement mechanisms.[71] It is also important to note that local governments, which adopted this policy idea after the introduction of the 2005 national mandatory GHG Accounting and Reporting system, tended to emulate this national practice rather than Tokyo's system in a horizontally competitive way.

Learning agents as diffusion determinants

In this study, opportunity structures that influenced policy-making choices and helped to bring about the adoption of Tokyo's cap-and-trade are unique in the sense that others are unlikely to have such structures. First, Tokyo has the largest concentration of corporate headquarters in the world, which flock there seeking national government offices in the Kasumigaseki section of Tokyo to conduct informal communication and lobbying. The business value of this office location probably outweighs that of any other location in Japan. This allowed the TMG to adopt a specific yet efficient coverage for a mandatory reduction of total CO_2 emissions, which targeted only large-scale buildings but accounted for nearly a half of Tokyo's CO_2 emissions. The total CO_2 emissions in Tokyo were characterized by a high rate in the commercial sector but a low rate in the industrial sector. So far there is no evidence of a cap-and-trade-induced pattern of business migration moving out of the business and political center of Tokyo's metropolitan area. Second, the TMG has a great deal of freedom of budgetary choice, which allows it to offer a more comprehensive incentive program for mitigation measures. The concentration of business activities in Tokyo ensures the revenue-raising capacity to implement a package of mitigation measures, with its per capita local tax revenue amounting to roughly twice the level of the prefectural average. The TMG was able to offer subsidies, funding, and tax incentives as a mechanism to spur the demand of emissions credits and started its own tax system to promote energy saving in small and medium-sized companies. This study also suggests that there are two structural conditions to which almost all of the 47 prefectures and the 20 designated cities seem to have adapted for mitigation policy instruments: industrial structures and previous growth patterns on emissions in each locality. The higher the share of the industrial sector in all CO_2 emissions, the less likely it is that learning agents adopt effective mitigation policy tools. The faster GHG emissions increased in previous years, the less likely it is that learning agents adopt effective mitigation policy tools.

However, even if such hypotheses were generally applied to localities, not all learning agents would be equally sensitive to the same information. The key issue boils down to learning agents' willingness and capability to contribute to the locally specific policy-making process.[72] There were two exceptions where, despite being one of the lowest growth environments for emissions, the localities had not adopted any form of mandatory reporting.[73] Why were the cities of Fukuoka, with a low growth rate in the industrial sector, and Shizuoka, with a low growth rate in GHG emissions, still unable to adopt the policy idea of mandatory reporting? These exceptional cases are yet to be examined to answer this question. Nonetheless, this study demonstrates that the TMG's practice of continuous learning successfully drove the implementation of a mandatory reduction of all CO_2 emissions. A full explanation required the examination of factors that were internal to the TMG or agency effects. The linear stages of policy process (i.e., agenda setting, policy formulation, and implementation) did not reflect the TMG's actual practice, and the policy evolution involved multiple interacting cycles (a voluntary reduction policy with mandatory reporting, regulatory measures, a mandatory reduction policy, an incentive mechanism, and a tax policy) rather than a single policy cycle. The process of BOE's learning did not necessarily show a linear relationship from information to decision-making or systematic policy evaluation, but rather an evolutionary process of trial-and-error in pursuit of the political feasibility of policy adoption.

The process tracing of the TMG's multiple interacting policy cycles has found a set of individual and collective agent effects on the adoption of Tokyo's cap-and-trade scheme. (1) Without Governor Ishihara's commitment, progressive proposals may have never got onto the policy agenda despite being initially presented by an informal policy network of those interested in low carbon issues. (2) The TMG's mandatory emissions reporting scheme was a result of instrumental learning or a redesign of the national policy instrument of energy conservation reporting. (3) A key departure from prior policy ideas towards Tokyo's cap-and-trade was the change in the shared policy beliefs of the environmental coalition from voluntary reduction to mandatory reduction, which policy network members had learned from the policy experience of a voluntary emissions reduction plan with mandatory reporting. (4) Tokyo's regulatory measures to control diesel vehicle emissions, whose reductions had previously created a market-driven reduction mechanism, convinced BOE officials to pursue a policy model of mandatory reduction. (5) The TMG's failure to adopt a mandatory reduction of all CO_2 emissions in 2004 entailed policy advocates learning about political strategies for increasing the feasibility of policy adoption. (6) BOE officials became more sophisticated in ensuring the successful cap-and-trade policy enactment, while learning about creating incentives to meet the TMG's reduction goals. (7) The mandatory emissions reporting provided the TMG with the accumulated data necessary for implementing the cap-and-trade scheme.

Conclusion

The development of Tokyo's cap-and-trade system presents a case study on policy learning and diffusion from multiple sources, by a variety of agents, and over an extended period of time. The preliminary analysis in this chapter suggests that there is evidence of both endogenous and exogenous sources of learning regarding Tokyo's climate change policy. All in all, domestic processes in conjunction with policy ideas from overseas are reflected in its policy package. The key finding is that the opportunity for transferring overseas ideas into Tokyo arose from its adaptive capacity, which is determined by local conditions.

The international recognition of the Marrakech Accords and Japan's commitment to these agreements certainly created a legitimate setting for Tokyo's involvement in mandatory reduction. However, there was little evidence that the change in the TMG officials' policy beliefs from voluntary to mandatory reduction was the direct result of non-conscious factors, especially those of internationally agreed commitments and national policies, external to the make-up of the Tokyo metropolitan polity. These structural factors are not sufficient to account for the alteration of the general policy direction. Cognitive/conscious factors that were internal to the learning agency are necessary to consider the result. Think tanks and academics were the key agents of the soft transfer of overseas cap-and-trade concepts; these experts facilitated the emergence of BOE officials' policy learning. As the modes of mandatory reduction had been widely discussed, Governor Ishihara became a necessary agent in the sense that he used his official capacity to create a cap-and-trade policy agenda, enhancing the political feasibility. It was not surprising that neither the environmental coalition nor the industry advocacy coalition were led to change their core beliefs. But the TMG was able to convince small and medium-sized businesses (representing over 99 percent of business enterprise in Tokyo) of the viability of the implementation designs by providing financial incentives for GHG emissions reduction. In other words, the strategic level of learning advanced the policy adoption

Table 4.1 Tokyo's policy learning in the introduction of its cap-and-trade

1998	National mandatory reporting system of energy conservation (introduced)
2000	Tokyo's mandatory emissions reporting system (introduced)
2004	Tokyo's mandatory reduction of total CO_2 emissions (failed to introduce)
2005	Tokyo's mandatory emissions reporting system (revised)
2005	National mandatory GHG Accounting and Reporting (introduced)
2005	European Union Emissions Trading System (EU-ETS) (launched)
2007	International Carbon Action Partnership (joined by Tokyo)
2007	Tokyo's cap-and-trade scheme (back on policy agenda)
2010	Tokyo's cap-and-trade scheme (launched)

by manipulating the policy process while not being concerned with a change in their internalized policy beliefs.

As Table 4.1 indicates, the evolution of Tokyo's climate change policy involved multiple interacting policy cycles, based on its practice of continuous learning over time. The policy development was largely a function of agency effects, rather than events outside the subsystem of the TMG while reconstructing the policy ideas, exogenous to the Tokyo metropolitan polity, to ensure a better fit with prior local experience. It was based on the sequence of policy learning, rather than concentrating upon what lessons were drawn from a single policy blueprint. The process tracing in this case study described how multiple ideas and lessons were chosen and integrated into a climate policy package. The TMG's trial-and-error process, both in the policy and political processes, lies at the heart of the evolutionary learning of policy adoption, while complementing rationality as optimization. Tokyo's policy learning is not easily adopted elsewhere due to the interaction of structure and agency peculiar to the capital megacity. Other local authorities require a capacity of lesson-drawing to understand the applicability of Tokyo's experience in their context. Otherwise, if there is to be any diffusion, it is more likely to be mimicking by other localities to catch up as a diffusion mechanism or prompted by the national government in a semi-coercive fashion.

Notes

1 Karl W. Deutsch, *The Nerves of Government* (New York: Free Press of Glencoe, 1963).
2 This study is concerned primarily with learning, but the literature identifies other diffusion mechanisms, such as competition, coercion, and social emulation (Dietmar Braun and Fabrizio Gilardi, "Taking 'Galton's Problem' seriously: toward a theory of policy diffusion," *Journal of Theoretical Politics*, Vol. 18, No. 3 (2006), pp. 298–322; Beth Simmons, Frank Dobbin, and Geoffrey Garrett, "Introduction: the international diffusion of liberalism," *International Organization*, Vol. 60, No. 4 (2006), pp. 781–810).
3 Colin J. Bennett, "Understanding ripple effects: the cross-national adoption of policy instruments for bureaucratic accountability," *Governance*, Vol. 10, No. 3 (1997), p. 215.

4 David P. Dolowitz and David Marsh, "Who learns what from whom: a review of the policy transfer literature," *Political Studies*, Vol. 44, No. 2 (1996), pp. 343–57.
5 See, for example, Michael Mintrom and Sandra Vergari, "Policy networks and innovation diffusion: the case of state education reform," *Journal of Politics*, Vol. 60, No. 1 (1998), pp. 126–48; Chang K. Lee and David Strang, "The international diffusion of public sector downsizing: network emulation and theory-driven learning," *International Organization*, Vol. 60, No. 4 (2006), pp. 883–909.
6 Colin J. Bennett, "What is policy convergence and what causes it?" *British Journal of Political Science*, Vol. 21 (1991), pp. 215–33; Katharina Holzinger and Christoph Knill, "Causes and conditions of cross-national policy convergence," *Journal of European Public Policy*, Vol. 12, No. 5 (October 2005), pp. 775–96.
7 Mark Evans, "Policy transfer in critical perspective," *Policy Studies*, Vol. 30, No. 3 (2009), pp. 243–68; Diane Stone, "Transfer agents and global networks in the 'transnationalization' of policy," *Journal of European Public Policy*, Vol. 11, No. 3 (2004), pp. 545–66; Diane Stone, "Private philanthropy or policy transfer? The transnational norms of the open society institute," *Policy and Politics*, Vol. 38, No. 2 (2010), pp. 269–87.
8 David Marsh and J.C. Sharman, "Policy diffusion and policy transfer," *Policy Studies*, Vol. 30, No. 3 (2009), pp. 269–88.
9 Robert Savage, "Diffusion research traditions and the spread of policy innovations in a federal system," *Publius*, Vol. 15, No. 4 (1985), pp. 1–27; Everett M. Rogers, *Diffusion of Innovations* (New York: The Free Press, 1995).
10 Mintrom and Vergari, "Policy networks and innovation diffusion," pp. 126–48.
11 Jack L. Walker, "The diffusion of innovations among American states," *American Political Science Review*, Vol. 63 (1969), pp. 880–99; Francis S. Berry and William D. Berry, "Innovation and diffusion models in policy research," in P.A. Sabatier, ed., *Theories of the Policy Process* (Boulder, CO: Westview Press, 1999), pp. 172–78.
12 Berry and Berry, "Innovation and diffusion models in policy research," pp. 172–78; Kristine Kern, Helge Jörgens, and Martin Jänicke, "The diffusion of environmental innovations: a contribution to the globalization of environmental policy," WZB Working Paper, 2001, No. FS II 01 – 302.
13 David P. Dolowitz and David Marsh, "Who learns what from whom," p. 349.
14 Berry and Berry, "Innovation and diffusion models in policy research," pp. 172–8.
15 Stone, "Transfer agents and global networks in the 'transnationalization' of policy," p. 548.
16 David P. Dolowitz, "A policy-maker's guide to policy transfer," *Political Quarterly*, Vol. 74, No. 1 (2003), pp. 101–08.
17 Mark Evans and Jonathan Davies, "Understanding policy transfer: a multi-level, multi-disciplinary perspective," *Public Administration*, Vol. 77, No. 2 (1999), pp. 361–85.
18 Stone, "Transfer agents and global networks in the 'transnationalization' of policy," pp. 545–66; Stone, "Private philanthropy or policy transfer?" pp. 269–87; Diane Stone, "Transfer and translation of policy," *Policy Studies*, Vol. 33, No. 6 (2012), pp. 483–99.
19 Claire Dunlop, "Policy transfer as learning: capturing variation in what decision-makers learn from epistemic communities," *Policy Studies*, Vol. 30, No. 2 (2009), pp. 289–311; Stone, "Transfer and translation of policy," p. 488.
20 Berry and Berry, "Innovation and diffusion models in policy research," pp. 172–8; Fabrizio Gilardi, "Who learns from what in policy diffusion processes?" *American Journal of Political Science*, Vol. 54 (2010), pp. 650–66.
21 Walker, "The diffusion of innovations among American states," pp. 880–99; Virginia Gray, "Innovations in the States: a diffusion study," *American Political Science Review*, Vol. 67 (1973), pp. 1174–91; Savage "Diffusion research traditions and the spread of policy innovations in a federal system," pp. 1–27.

Tokyo's metropolitan cap-and-trade 173

22 Marsh and Sharman, "Policy diffusion and policy transfer," p. 279.
23 Evans and Davies, "Understanding policy transfer," pp. 361–85; Richard Common, *Public Management and Policy Transfer in Southeast Asia* (Aldershot: Ashgate, 2001); Mark Evans, ed., *Policy Transfer in Global Perspective* (Aldershot: Ashgate, 2004).
24 Stone, "Transfer agents and global networks in the 'transnationalization' of policy," pp. 545–66.
25 Bennett, "What is policy convergence and what causes it?" pp. 224–5.
26 Ministry of Economy, Trade and Industry (METI), "Enerugi shiyō no gōrika ni kansuru hōritsu [Energy efficiency law], 2012, available from: www.meti.go.jp/press/2011/03/20120313001/20120313001-7.pdf [accessed December 10, 2012].
27 Tokyo Metropolitan Government (TMG), "Tomin no kenkō to anzen o kakuhosuru kankyō ni kansuru jōrei" [Local ordinance for the environment to protect public health and safety], 2000, available from: www.reiki.metro.tokyo.jp/reiki_honbun/g1011328001.html [accessed December 8, 2012].
28 Toshiko Chiba, Section Chief of Climate Change Countermeasures, TMG's Bureau of the Environment, Interview with author May 20, 2010.
29 Peter May, "Policy learning and failure," *Journal of Public Policy*, Vol. 12, No. 4 (1992), p. 333.
30 Yuko Nishida, Department of Urban/Global Environment, TMG's Bureau of the Environment, Interview with author June 23, 2011.
31 Tokyo Metropolitan Government (TMG), "Chikyū ondanka taisaku keikakusho seido" [Enterprise planning system for mitigation measures], 2006, available from: www.kankyo.metro.tokyo.jp/climate/attachement/h18riifuretto.pdf [accessed December 10, 2012].
32 Japan e-Gov, "Chikyū ondanka taisaku no suishin ni kansru hōritsu" [Act on the promotion of global warming countermeasures], 2011, available from: law.e-gov.jp [accessed December 10, 2012].
33 Richard Rose, "What is lesson-drawing?" *Journal of Public Policy*, Vol. 11, No. 1 (1991), pp. 3–30.
34 Information for the mandatory reporting systems at the local level was adopted from the Ministry of the Environment's database. See Japan, Ministry of the Environment (MOE), "Sonota jichitai no hōkoku seido" [Reporting systems of other local governments], 2012, available from: http://ghg-santeikohyo.env.go.jp/document/lg_system2 [accessed December 8, 2012]; Japan, Ministry of the Environment (MOE), "Todōfuken no hōkoku seido" [Prefectural reporting systems], 2012, available from: http://ghg-santeikohyo.env.go.jp/document/lg_system#L8 [accessed December 8, 2012].
35 Tokyo Metropolitan Government (TMG), *Tokyo Cap-and-Trade Program: Japan's First Mandatory Emissions Scheme* (Tokyo: Bureau of the Environment, TMG, 2010), p. 8.
36 MOE, "Sonota jichitai no hōkoku seido."
37 MOE, "Sonota jichitai no hōkoku seido"; MOE, "Todōfuken no hōkoku seido."
38 MOE, "Sonota jichitai no hōkoku seido."
39 MOE, "Sonota jichitai no hōkoku seido."
40 Noriko Sugiyama and Tsuneo Takeuchi, "Local policies for climate change in Japan," *The Journal of Environment and Development*, Vol. 17, No. 4 (2008), pp. 425–41.
41 Tokyo Metropolitan Assembly (TMA), Minutes of the first plenary session of the Tokyo Metropolitan Assembly, February 20, 2002.
42 TMA, Minutes of the first plenary session, February 20, 2002.
43 Naomi Okamoto, Section Chief of Total Emission Reduction, TMG's Bureau of the Environment, Interview with author June 23, 2011.
44 Keiji Endo, General Manager, Environmental Issues, Tokyo Trucking Association, Interview with author June 29, 2011.

45 Yuko Nishida, Interview with author June 23, 2011.
46 Tokyo Metropolitan Government (TMG), *Toshi to chikyū no ondanka soshi ni kansuru kihon hōshin* [Policy direction for the city and its mitigation measures] (Tokyo: Bureau of the Environment, 2002).
47 Tokyo Metropolitan Government (TMG), "Tokyoto kankyō shingikai iin meibo" [List of members of the Tokyo Metropolitan Environmental Council], 2003, available from: www.kankyo.metro.tokyo.jp/attachement/list_040223.pdf [accessed December 10, 2012].
48 Tokyo Metropolitan Government (TMG), "Dai sankai kikaku seisaku bukai gijiroku" [Minutes of the 3rd session of the policy planning committee], 2003, available from: www.kankyo.metro.tokyo.jp/attachement/030526.pdf [accessed December 10, 2012].
49 Yoshihiro Kageyama, Executive Officer, Environment Department, Tokyo Electric Power Company, Interview with author June 23, 2011; Masami Hasegawa, Environmental Policy Bureau, Japan Business Federation, Interview with author June 27, 2011.
50 Kazumasu Aoki and Yuko Motoki, "Tokyo ni okeru chikyū ondanka taisaku o meguru seisaku katei ni kansuru yobiron-teki kōsatsu" [Some consideration on the policy processes of climate change countermeasures in Tokyo], *Tomidai Keizai Ronshū* [Toyama University Journal of Economics], Vol. 53 (2007), pp. 131–81.
51 Tokyo Metropolitan Government (TMG), "Orinpikku pararinpikku gyōgitaikai shōchi katsudo hōkoku" [Report on bids activities for the 2016 Olympic Games and Paralympics] (Tokyo: TMG Bids Committee, 2010), pp. 389–90.
52 Tokyo Metropolitan Government (TMG), "Tokyo ni okeru kikō hendō taisaku no seika to tenkai" [Achievements and developments of climate change countermeasures in Tokyo]. Press Release, March 31, 2007.
53 Tokyo Metropolitan Government (TMG), "Sutēkihorudā mītingu" [Stakeholder meetings], 2012, available from: www.kankyo.metro.tokyo.jp/climate/plan/climate_change/stakeholder_meetings.html [accessed December 5, 2012].
54 Tokyo Metropolitan Government (TMG), *Tokyo Climate Change Strategy* (Tokyo: Tokyo Metropolitan Government, 2007), p. 8.
55 Toshiko Chiba, Interview with author May 20, 2010.
56 Keiji Okamoto, Managing Director, Japan Building Owners and Managers Association, Interview with author June 17, 2011; Takeshi Imada, Principal Senior Manager, Real Estate Companies Association of Japan, Interview with author July 4, 2011.
57 Yuko Nishida, Interview with author June 23, 2011.
58 Tokyo Metropolitan Government (TMG), Press Release, September 17, 2010.
59 Naomi Okamoto, Interview with author June 17, 2011.
60 Naomi Okamoto, Interview with author June 17, 2011.
61 *Nikkei Ekorojī* [Nikkei Ecology], September 25, 2008, p. 14.
62 TMG, *Tokyo Cap-and-Trade Program*, pp. 28–29.
63 GHG missions can be reduced by imposing an absolute cap on the quantity of the emissions or by allowing some maximum intensity relative to some mitigation measure of output or input, such as the number of vehicles purchased by consumers at the level of an economic sector and the amount of energy usage mandated by some production process at the firm level.
64 Kōji Miyazawa, Section Chief of Emission Trading, TMG's Bureau of the Environment, Interview with James Tulloch May 5, 2015, published in *Allianz Lab*, Allianz Life Insurance Japan, available from: http://life.allianz.co.jp/about_us/az/lab/012.html [accessed June 5, 2015].
65 Yuko Nishida, Interview with author June 23, 2011; Sven Rudolph and Takeshi Kawakastu, "Tokyo's greenhouse gas emissions trading scheme: a model for sustainable megacity carbon markets?" Joint Discussion Paper Series in Economics, MAGKS, No. 25, 2012.
66 David Cash and Susanne Moser, "Linking global and local scales: designing dynamic

assessment and management process," *Global Environmental Change*, Vol. 10, No. 2 (2000), pp. 109–20.
67 Stephane Hallegatte, Fanny Henriet, and Jan Corfee-Morlot, "The economics of climate change impacts and policy benefits at city scale: a conceptual framework," OECD Environment Working Paper 4, 2008, Paris, OECD; Jason Corburn, "Cities, climate change and urban heat island mitigation: localizing global environmental science," *Urban Studies*, Vol. 47, No. 2 (2009), pp. 413–27.
68 Harriet Bulkeley and Susanne Moser, "Responding to climate change: governance and social action beyond Kyoto," *Global Environmental Politics*, Vol. 7, No. 2 (2007), pp. 1–10.
69 Per G. Fredriksson and Daniel Millimet, "Strategic interaction and the determination of environmental policy across US states," *Journal of Urban Economics*, Vol. 51, No. 1 (2002), pp. 101–22; Arik Levinson, "Environmental regulatory competition: a status report and some new evidence," *National Tax Journal*, Vol. 56, No. 1 (2003), pp. 91–106.
70 Eric Helland and Andrew Whiford, "Pollution incidence and political jurisdiction: evidence from the TRI," *Journal of Environmental Economics and Management*, Vol. 46, No. 3 (2003), pp. 403–24; Hilary Sigman, "Transboundary spillovers and decentralization of environmental policies," *Journal of Environmental Economics and Management*, Vol. 50, No. 1 (2005), pp. 82–101.
71 MOE, "Sonota jichitai no hōkoku seido"; MOE, "Todōfuken no hōkoku seido."
72 In cross-nationally comparative perspective, the problem lies at an inadequate delegation of power to lower levels of government. In many countries, sub-national governments often lack sufficient jurisdiction over the implementation of climate change policies. See, for example, Kristine Kern and Alber Gotelind, "Governing climate change in cities: modes of urban climate governance in multi-level systems," OECD Conference Proceedings, 2009, Paris, OECD.
73 MOE, "Sonota jichitai no hōkoku seido."

Bibliography

Allianz Life Insurance Japan (2015). *Allianz Lab*, May 5, 2015. Available from: http://life.allianz.co.jp/about_us/az/lab/012.html [accessed June 5, 2015].
Aoki, Kazumasu and Yuko Motoki (2007). "Tokyo ni okeru chikyū ondanka taisaku o meguru seisaku katei ni kansuru yobiron-teki kōsatsu" [Some consideration on the policy processes of climate change countermeasures in Tokyo]. *Tomidai Keizai Ronshū* [Toyama University Journal of Economics], Vol. 53, pp. 131–81.
Bennett, Colin J. (1991). "What is policy convergence and what causes it?" *British Journal of Political Science*, Vol. 21, pp. 215–33.
Bennett, Colin J. (1997). "Understanding ripple effects: the cross-national adoption of policy instruments for bureaucratic accountability." *Governance*, Vol. 10, No. 3, pp. 213–33.
Berry, Francis S. and William D. Berry (1999). "Innovation and diffusion models in policy research." In Paul Sabatier, ed., *Theories of the Policy Process*. Boulder, CO: Westview Press, pp. 169–200.
Braun, Dietmar and Fabrizio Gilardi (2006). "Taking 'Galton's Problem' seriously: toward a theory of policy diffusion." *Journal of Theoretical Politics*, Vol. 18, No. 3, pp. 298–322.
Bulkeley, Harriet and Susanne Moser (2007). "Responding to climate change: governance and social action beyond Kyoto." *Global Environmental Politics*, Vol. 7, No. 2, pp. 1–10.

Bulmer, Simon, David Dolowitz, Peter Humphreys, and Stephen Padgett (2007). *Policy Transfer in the European Union Governance*. London: Routledge.
Cash, David and Susanne Moser (2000). "Linking global and local scales: designing dynamic assessment and management process." *Global Environmental Change*, Vol. 10, No. 2, pp. 109–20.
Common, Richard (2001). *Public Management and Policy Transfer in Southeast Asia*. Aldershot, UK: Ashgate.
Corburn, Jason (2009). "Cities, climate change and urban heat island mitigation: localizing global environmental science." *Urban Studies*, Vol. 47, No. 2, pp. 413–27.
Deutsch, Karl W. (1963). *The Nerves of Government*. New York: Free Press of Glencoe.
DiMaggio, Paul and Walter Powell, eds. (1991). *The New Institutionalism in Organizational Analysis*. Chicago, IL: University of Chicago Press.
Dolowitz, David P. (2003). "A policy-maker's guide to policy transfer." *Political Quarterly*, Vol. 74, No. 1, pp. 101–8.
Dolowitz, David P. and David Marsh (1996). "Who learns what from whom: a review of the policy transfer literature." *Political Studies*, Vol. 44, No. 2, pp. 343–57.
Dolowitz, David P. and David Marsh (2000). "Learning from abroad: the role of policy transfer in contemporary policy making." *Governance*, Vol. 13, No. 1, pp. 5–24.
Dunlop, Claire (2009). "Policy transfer as learning: capturing variation in what decision-makers learn from epistemic communities." *Policy Studies*, Vol. 30, No. 2, pp. 289–311.
Evans, Mark, ed. (2004). *Policy Transfer in Global Perspective*. Aldershot, UK: Ashgate.
Evans, Mark (2009). "Policy transfer in critical perspective." *Policy Studies*, Vol. 30, No. 3, pp. 243–68.
Evans, Mark and Jonathan Davies (1999). "Understanding policy transfer: a multi-level, multi-disciplinary perspective." *Public Administration*, Vol. 77, No. 2, pp. 361–85.
Finnemore, Martha (1996). "Norms, culture, and world politics: insights from sociology's institutionalism." *International organization*, Vol. 50, No. 2, pp. 325–47.
Fredriksson, Per G. and Daniel Millimet (2002). "Strategic interaction and the determination of environmental policy across US states." *Journal of Urban Economics*, Vol. 51, No. 1, pp. 101–22.
Gilardi, Fabrizio (2010). "Who learns from what in policy diffusion processes?" *American Journal of Political Science*, Vol. 54, pp. 650–66.
Gray, Virginia (1973). "Innovations in the States: a diffusion study." *American Political Science Review*, Vol. 67, pp. 1174–91.
Hall, Peter (1993). "Policy paradigms, social learning and the state: the case of economic policy making in Britain." *Comparative Politics*, Vol. 25, No. 3, pp. 275–96.
Hallegatte, Stephane, Fanny Henriet, and Jan Corfee-Morlot (2008). "The economics of climate change impacts and policy benefits at city scale: a conceptual framework." OECD Environment Working Paper 4, Paris, OECD.
Helland, Eric and Andrew Whiford (2003). "Pollution incidence and political jurisdiction: evidence from the TRI." *Journal of Environmental Economics and Management*, Vol. 46, No. 3, pp. 403–24.
Holzinger, Katharina and Christoph Knill (2005). "Causes and conditions of cross-national policy convergence." *Journal of European Public Policy*, Vol. 12, No. 5, pp. 775–96.
Japan e-Gov (2011). "Chikyū ondanka taisaku no suishin ni kansru hōritsu" [Act on the promotion of global warming countermeasures]. Available from: law.e-gov.jp [accessed December 10, 2012].

Japan, Ministry of Economy, Trade and Industry (METI) (2012). "Enerugi shiyō no gōrika ni kansuru hōritsu" [Energy efficiency law]. Available from: www.meti.go.jp/press/2011/03/20120313001/20120313001-7.pdf [accessed December 10, 2012].
Japan, Ministry of the Environment (MOE) (2012). "Sonota jichitai no hōkoku seido" [Reporting systems of other local governments]. Available from: http://ghg-santeikohyo.env.go.jp/document/lg_system2 [accessed December 8, 2012].
Japan, Ministry of the Environment (MOE) (2012). "Todōfuken no hōkoku seido" [Prefectural reporting systems]. Available from: http://ghg-santeikohyo.env.go.jp/document/lg_system#L8 [accessed December 8, 2012].
Kern, Kristine and Alber Gotelind (2009). "Governing climate change in cities: modes of urban climate governance in multi-level systems." OECD Conference Proceedings, Paris, OECD.
Kern, Kristine, Helge Jörgens, and Martin Jänicke (2001). "The diffusion of environmental innovations: a contribution to the globalization of environmental policy." WZB Working Paper, No. FS II 01 – 302.
Lee, Chang K. and David Strang (2006). "The international diffusion of public sector downsizing: network emulation and theory-driven learning." *International Organization*, Vol. 60, No. 4, pp. 883–909.
Levinson, Arik (2003). "Environmental regulatory competition: a status report and some new evidence." *National Tax Journal*, Vol. 56, No. 1, pp. 91–106.
Lindblom, Charles E. (1959). "The science of 'muddling through.'" *Public Administration Review*, Vol. 19, No. 2, pp. 79–88.
McCann, Eugene and Kevin Ward (2012). "Policy assemblages, mobilities and mutations: towards a multi-disciplinary conversation." *Policy Studies Review*, Vol. 10, No. 3, pp. 325–32.
Marsh, David and J.C. Sharman (2009). "Policy diffusion and policy transfer." *Policy Studies*, Vol. 30, No. 3, pp. 269–88.
May, Peter (1992). "Policy learning and failure." *Journal of Public Policy*, Vol. 12, No. 4, pp. 331–54.
Meseguer, Covadonga (2003). "Learning about policies: a Bayesian approach." European Forum Working Paper Series 5, European University Institute, Florence.
Meseguer, Covadonga (2006). "Rational learning and bounded learning in the diffusion of policy innovations." *Rationality and Society*, Vol. 18, No. 1, pp. 35–66.
Mintrom, Michael and Sandra Vergari (1998). "Policy networks and innovation diffusion: the case of state education reform." *Journal of Politics*, Vol. 60, No. 1, pp. 126–48.
Nikkei Ekorojī [Nikkei Ecology] (2008). September 25, 2008.
Rogers, Everett M. (1995). *Diffusion of Innovations*. New York: The Free Press.
Rose, Richard (1991). "What is lesson-drawing?" *Journal of Public Policy*, Vol. 11, No. 1, pp. 3–30.
Rudolph, Sven and Takeshi Kawakastu (2012). "Tokyo's greenhouse gas emissions trading scheme: a model for sustainable megacity carbon markets?" Joint Discussion Paper Series in Economics, MAGKS.
Sabatier, Paul A. (1987). "Knowledge, policy-oriented learning, and policy change." *Knowledge*, Vol. 8, No. 4, pp. 649–92.
Sabatier, Paul A. (1988). "An advocacy coalition framework of policy change and the role of policy-oriented learning therein." *Policy Sciences*, Vol. 21, No. 2, pp. 129–68.
Sabatier, Paul A. and Hank C. Jenkins-Smith, eds. (1993). *Policy Change and Learning: An Advocacy Coalition Approach*. Boulder, CO: Westview Press.

Savage, Robert (1985). "Diffusion research traditions and the spread of policy innovations in a federal system." *Publius*, Vol. 15, No. 4, pp. 1–27.

Schneider, Anne and Helen Ingram (1990). "Behavioral assumptions of policy tools." *Journal of Politics*, Vol. 52, No. 2, pp. 510–29.

Sharpe, Laurence James (1993). *The Rise of Meso-government in Europe*. London, Sage.

Sigman, Hilary (2005). "Transboundary spillovers and decentralization of environmental policies." *Journal of Environmental Economics and Management*, Vol. 50, No. 1, pp. 82–101.

Simmons, Beth, Frank Dobbin, and Geoffrey Garrett (2006). "Introduction: the international diffusion of liberalism." *International Organization*, Vol. 60, No. 4, pp. 781–810.

Stone, Diane (2004). "Transfer agents and global networks in the 'transnationalization' of policy." *Journal of European Public Policy*, Vol. 11, No. 3, pp. 545–66.

Stone, Diane (2010). "Private philanthropy or policy transfer? The transnational norms of the open society institute." *Policy and Politics*, Vol. 38, No. 2, pp. 269–87.

Stone, Diane (2012). "Transfer and translation of policy." *Policy Studies*, Vol. 33, No. 6, pp. 483–99.

Strang, David and John W. Meyer (1993). "Institutional conditions for diffusion." *Theory and Society*, Vol. 22, No. 4, pp. 487–511.

Sugiyama, Noriko and Tsuneo Takeuchi (2008). "Local policies for climate change in Japan." *The Journal of Environment and Development*, Vol. 17, No. 4, pp. 425–41.

Tokyo Metropolitan Assembly (TMA) (2002). Minutes of the first plenary session of the Tokyo Metropolitan Assembly, February 20, 2002.

Tokyo Metropolitan Government (TMG) (2000). "Tomin no kenkō to anzen o kakuhosuru kankyō ni kansuru jōrei" [Local ordinance for the environment to protect public health and safety]. Available from: www.reiki.metro.tokyo.jp/reiki_honbun/g1011328001.html [accessed December 8, 2012].

Tokyo Metropolitan Government (TMG) (2002). *Toshi to chikyū no ondanka soshi ni kansuru kihon hōshin* [Policy direction for the city and its mitigation measures]. Tokyo: Bureau of the Environment.

Tokyo Metropolitan Government (TMG) (2003). "Dai sankai kikaku seisaku bukai gijiroku" [Minutes of the 3rd session of the policy planning committee]. Available from: www.kankyo.metro.tokyo.jp/attachement/030526.pdf [accessed December 10, 2012].

Tokyo Metropolitan Government (TMG) (2003). "Tokyoto kankyō shingikai iin meibo" [List of members of the Tokyo Metropolitan Environmental Council]. Available from: www.kankyo.metro.tokyo.jp/attachement/list_040223.pdf [accessed December 10, 2012].

Tokyo Metropolitan Government (TMG) (2006). "Chikyū ondanka taisaku keikakusho seido" [Enterprise planning system for mitigation measures]. Available from: www.kankyo.metro.tokyo.jp/climate/attachement/h18riifuretto.pdf [accessed December 10, 2012].

Tokyo Metropolitan Government (TMG) (2007). *Tokyo Climate Change Strategy*. Tokyo: TMG.

Tokyo Metropolitan Government (TMG) (2007). "Tokyo ni okeru kikō hendō taisaku no seika to tenkai" [Achievements and developments of climate change countermeasures in Tokyo]. Press Release, March 31, 2007.

Tokyo Metropolitan Government (TMG) (2010). "Orinpikku pararinpikku gyōgitaikai shōchi katsudo hōkoku" [Report on bids activities for the 2016 Olympic Games and Paralympics]. Tokyo: TMG Bids Committee.

Tokyo Metropolitan Government (TMG) (2010). Press Release, September 17, 2010.
Tokyo Metropolitan Government (TMG) (2010). *Tokyo Cap-and-Trade Program: Japan's First Mandatory Emissions Scheme*. Tokyo: Bureau of the Environment, TMG.
Tokyo Metropolitan Government (TMG) (2012). "Sutēkihorudā mītingu" [Stakeholder meetings]. Available from: www.kankyo.metro.tokyo.jp/climate/plan/climate_change/stakeholder_meetings.html [accessed December 5, 2012].
Walker, Jack L. (1969). "The diffusion of innovations among American states." *American Political Science Review*, Vol. 63, pp. 880–99.
Weyland, Kurt G. (2005). "Theories of policy diffusion: lessons from Latin American pension reform." *World Politics*, Vol. 57, No. 2, pp. 262–95.
Wildavsky, Aaron (1979). *Speaking Truth to Power: The Art and Craft of Policy Analysis*. Boston, MA: Little Brown.

5 Shiga's cooperation with UNEP
Transnational sectoral network

The collaborative relationship between Shiga Prefecture and the United Nations Environmental Programme (UNEP) to create the International Lake Environment Committee (ILEC) was Japan's earliest experience of sub-national participation in international cooperation with counterparts from the developing world and international organizations. The ILEC is an international non-governmental standing committee, which has been hosted by Shiga's prefectural government since 1986. One of its key missions is to support environmentally sound lake management activities, which UNEP promotes in developing countries. The objective of this chapter is to examine the local government's autonomous capacity to mobilize resources across institutional boundaries of polity and independently participate in transnational environmental governance. From a state-centric view, a sub-national level of participation at the international level can only be feasible if it is an active part of national policy. In the case of the Shiga prefectural government's initiative for international lake-environmental cooperation, however, as Table 5.1 indicates, sub-national actors came to see themselves as direct players in the absence of national policy. The chapter examines under what conditions and in what ways such a sub-national level of participation takes place by conducting a case study of Shiga's collaboration with UNEP over lake-environment risk reduction. It reveals the formation process of transnational governance networks involving a sub-national government that is not operating on behalf of the national government. Shiga's cooperation with UNEP was primarily driven by the ad hoc, bottom-up political mobilization of sub-national actors. In general, without institutionalized channels for sub-national governments to participate in the international level, sub-national governments need to mobilize resources on such an ad hoc basis and pioneering sub-national actors need to be capable of effectively engaging in the formation process of transnational governance in unfamiliar territory.

This chapter is about the management story of Lake Biwa in Shiga prefecture. The lake is completely located within Shiga prefecture, situated across most municipalities in the prefecture, with its surface area of 674.4 square kilometers occupying one-sixth of the prefecture's total area. In the environmental policy area of Japanese history, as environmental impacts were manifested locally and adaptive capacity determined by local conditions, municipal governments

Table 5.1 Creating the International Lake Environment Committee through transnational support networks

Early 1970s	*Akashio* (freshwater "red tide") (detected)
1971	Chicago city's regulation over the use of phosphate (enacted)
1974	Masayoshi Takemura (reformist) as prefectural governor (1974–1986) (elected)
1978	Prefectural Movement Liaison Conference (established)
1979	Prefectural Ordinance Relating to the Prevention of Eutrophication in Lake Biwa (enacted)
Late 1970s	Learning about lake environment from Canada and New Zealand
Early 1980s	Learning about lake environment from Germany
1981	Takemura's proposal for an international conference on lake environment
1983	Shiga's first contact with the United National Environmental Programme (UNEP)
1984	Prefectural Ordinance Governing the Conservation of Natural Scenery (enacted)
1984	International Lake Environment Conference in Shiga (held)
1985	Shiga's partnership with the UNEP (established)
1986	International Lake Environmental Committee (ILEC) (launched)

became the first movers. Given the geographical setting of the lake, however, the initiatives for environmental policy were taking place at the prefectural level. The Shiga prefectural government reached out for international environmental cooperation on behalf of voters who found it impossible to ignore the severity of lake pollution and whose concern with it prevailed over pro-development policies in electoral processes. While the worsening eutrophication of the rivers and lakes became known as a worldwide problem, local knowledge and experience in Japan was not sufficient to cope with the Lake Biwa's environmental stresses. This led the prefectural Environmental Bureau to develop a lake environment policy network with overseas counterparts, which provided them with the process of learning about lake environments.[1] These actors transnationally engaged in policy innovation and coordination by diffusing ideas and influencing the policy measures adopted in other countries.[2] In the process of policy networking, the under-funded and overloaded UNEP[3] began to work with Shiga prefecture to meet the need to decentralize environmental governance functions, in order to pave the way for future environmental problem-solving.[4]

Transnationalism and sub-national government

Over the past two decades, sub-national levels of participation in transnational environmental governance have become noticeable within the European Union (EU). It is also increasingly being observed beyond the EU political process, yet little is known about the dynamics of sub-national participation in non-EU settings. While it is beyond the scope of this study to make comparisons of the behavior of sub-national units of European governments in this chapter, a case study of Shiga prefectural government's initiative for transnational lake-environmental governance provides a rare opportunity to open up the black box of that participation dynamic. Shiga prefecture in Japan was probably among one of the world's few sub-national governments to specifically acknowledge the unique properties of lakes, which make up 90 percent of the world's available surface fresh water, and then to address the lack of local awareness of the value of lakes for long-term preservation at the international level. To this end, Shiga also reached out to UNEP for support, without securing prior approval from the Japanese national government. An initial International Lake Environment Conference, held by the prefectural government in 1984, was attended by thousands of participants from around the world and became an unexpectedly huge success. In the wake of the conference's success, UNEP proposed the establishment of an international standing committee in Shiga to promote sustainable management of the world's lakes and reservoirs. This chapter will examine the potential for the participation of sub-national governments in transnational environmental governance by examining the origins, developments, and causes of Shiga's sub-national engagement in providing benefits on both the local and global scales for environmental risk reduction.

In the early debate on transnational politics, Robert Keohane and Joseph Nye confined the concept of transnationalism to the activities of non-governmental actors, differentiating from those of "transgovernmental actors" or "sub-units of governments on those occasions when they act relatively autonomously from higher authority in international politics."[5] According to Thomas Risse-Kappen, however, the interactive relations of government actors across national boundaries can be considered transnational "when at least one actor pursues her own agenda independent of national decisions."[6] The necessity of this redefinition suggests that the distinction between state-based actors and non-governmental actors has become blurred as sub-national government actors look to transnational networks to gain support in the absence of national government action.[7] In the revelatory case of Shiga, the Japanese statist tradition did not prevent the Shiga prefectural government from not operating on behalf of the Japanese national government. The result was a well-matched strategy of environmental governance that was both international and sub-national, in which the overloaded UNEP was requesting a division of labor for decentralized functions and in which Shiga prefectural government was seeking assistance in the absence of national policy.[8]

Transnational networks steer members towards two primary public goals: influencing and changing the behavior of nation-states within the international arena and governing transnational issues outside normal national jurisdiction. Epistemic communities[9] and transnational advocacy networks,[10] in which non-state actors operate in alliances with other non-state actors and state actors, see the sovereign state as the object of their advocacy activities. Their focus remains on their first public goal, to hold the target state accountable to their international commitments. In contrast, public transnational networks,[11] which sub-units of government (sub-national governments, legislators, and judges) establish, often in cooperation with international organizations, authoritatively enabled governing to take place towards the second public goal. In this context, the individual and organizational "constituents" of the networks recognize the network authorities as authoritative based on their legal-formal ability to exercise control and coordination.[12] One of the largest public transnational networks, Cities for Climate Protection (CCP), was initiated by the International Council for Local Environmental Initiatives (ICLEI) in 1993 and involves more than 1,000 local governments worldwide. These sub-national actors, often from countries with limited national commitments, are integrating climate change mitigation into a form of inter-municipal governance beyond national boundaries. Likewise, the collaborative relationship of Shiga-UNEP was not established to primarily influence sovereign states but rather to enhance governance practices in a form of decentralized cooperation, in which local actors take up a key role.

Yet the pattern of Shiga-UNEP ties is not easily accounted for by the concepts of transnational networks and governance. As discussed in the following section, this is primarily due to the connections between vertical territorial tiers of government and horizontally formed networks of governance. As compared to some federal systems, such as those of Austria, Belgium, Germany, and Switzerland, where sub-national authorities can conduct foreign affairs in matters of their competence, Japan's unitary system does not formally recognize the legal right of sub-national authorities to represent themselves at the international level. To establish the ILEC, without explicitly challenging the hierarchy of territorial jurisdictions, Shiga was nevertheless able to negotiate with UNEP directly. Political mobilization allowed the like-minded coalition of Shiga-UNEP to create the ILEC by bypassing the established relations of Japanese central-local relations, yet without completely superseding them. The formation of this collaboration can be seen to come from mutual dependence in a horizontal fashion. Once formed, however, Shiga had to continually provide support services for lake environmental management, both locally and transnationally. The necessity of collaboration maintenance brought back the prefectural government to deal with the hierarchical territorial tiers to access national financial resources. The ILEC, given a Japanese legal status in 1987, sought to exercise discretionary power over its allocated national funds by acting as an independent provider of policy innovation and expertise which the national government had been neither willing to manage nor capable of providing.[13]

The significance of sub-national participation in environmental governance

UNEP is the chief agency that is expected to promote the development, by various actors, of coherence among environmental institutions involved in multiple geographic scales. However, there are more than 500 multilateral environmental agreements (MEAs) whose autonomous secretariats have been operating to achieve implementation, assessment, and enforcement. MEAs have been developed primarily as a way of solving issue-by-issue or sectoral problems. The provision of environmental risk reduction has dealt with institutional fragmentation, which may result in the duplication of activities and resources, and the inconsistencies among decisions within different agreements.[14] To provide a blueprint for solving these problems, two basic categories of reform options are proposed: the establishment of a more authoritative and better-resourced international environmental organization[15] and functional integration either by "clustering" several MEAs[16] or via "policy networks" of cross-sectoral partnerships.[17] Support for the reform options is divided among scholars; however, the establishment of a strong international organization is not necessarily incompatible with the other reform options in the sense that clustering and policy networking are still necessary for more effective international environmental organization.

Clustering refers to the grouping of a number of international environmental agreements, in order to minimize institutional overlap and coordinate operations.[18] Thematic clusters, such as conservation and the global atmosphere, are seen as viable tools for making operations and funding more efficient. In contrast, cross-sectoral partnerships aim to build policy networks by bringing together different sectors, such as civil society, corporations, governments, and international organizations, to solve the environmental problems a single sector cannot govern.[19] Sub-national government can be a part of those policy networks. Both clustering and cross-sectoral reform options address concerns primarily in the horizontal dimension of environmental policy integration. Vertical policy integration across various territorial tiers of governance is also required to bring about a comprehensive integration of environmental strategies.[20] It is crucial to bridge policy gaps between local action, national policy, and global strategies. Much of the scholarly work to date surrounding transnational networks tends to overlook the role of sub-national governments while regarding the state as a single national entity. A review of these practices across a number of countries basically presents three institutional approaches to sub-national-national environmental policy linkages: state-centric governance, autonomous governance, and multi-level governance. Each approach provides sub-national actors with distinctive channels for political mobilization in a global environmental game.[21]

State-centric governance is a nationally led framework embedded within institutional boundaries for extending channels that can serve to incentivize sub-national action for international environmental cooperation. These channels, for example, through sub-national participation in diplomatic representation and in the parliamentary approval of treaties, are institutionalized to clarify sub-national roles in achieving national goals within the context of international obligations or to establish a division of labor among levels of government with a state-centric gate-keeping capacity.[22] This approach is based on the traditional state-centric framework, which is primarily driven by exclusive national benefits rather than sharing the cost of environmental risk reduction beyond sovereign territory. To this end, national policy either constrains or promotes a sub-national level of participation in transnational environmental governance. China most approximates this ideal-type as it extends incentive schemes as well as top-down policies towards sub-national actors.[23] Sub-national actors play an implementation role to meet national mandates or take part in making aggregate progress at a national scale and further within the context of internationally agreed goals. In an ideal type of state-centric governance, it is only the national governments that can entrust to an international environmental organization the power to set the limits of national sovereignty regarding environmental concerns. Sub-national authorities could operate only through the representatives of central state authorities in either the functional integration of clustering or cross-sectoral partnerships. In Risse-Kappen's view, sub-national activities that cross national boundaries are not considered transnational to the extent that they are operating on behalf of a national government. National governments thus pursue vertically non-overlapping jurisdictions of environmental policy integration between tiers of governance.

Perhaps, more relevant to non-EU settings is another ideal type, autonomous governance, which directs attention towards the bottom-up political mobilization of sub-national authorities. This ideal type assumes that, in a legal-formal sense, national governments are still the sole legitimate representatives of domestic interests at the international level. Yet sub-national authorities from countries with capacity limitations and environmental failures stemming from their national governments are more likely to reach out transnationally as an alternative means of problem-solving. These authorities seek to take part in transnational environmental networks, either due to a lack of support from the national government or in the absence of national regulation. Without the familiar ground of institutionalized rules or the right to represent themselves legitimately at the international level, the agency of sub-national actors finds a way through non-institutionalized or informal channels to move across levels of government and deal directly with counterparts in other countries and supranational actors in a rather ad hoc fashion. Informal extra-national channels, such as the establishment of independent overseas offices for lobbying and transnational associations representing sub-national governments, are sought to push for the increased involvement of sub-national authorities in decision-making at the international level.[24] Sub-national mobilization, which takes place on the basis of unfamiliar rules or little institutionalization across national boundaries, requires sufficient resources and the strong commitment of sub-national leadership, knowledge, experience, and political will to act upon environmental policy. As a result, not all sub-national authorities have enough potential to act as independent transnational actors. The creation of inter-sub-national networks and coalition-building with like-minded actors can characterize non-institutionalized channels for sub-national governments to participate in international environmental cooperation.

The third institutional approach (involving the restructuring of state polity) is an integral one or multi-level governance (MLG) that combines the two other institutional approaches into a synergistic dialogue of policy where national governments give sub-national authorities the right to represent themselves legitimately at the international level and contribute to the policy-making process without national supervision. In other words, national governments institutionally empower sub-national authorities as autonomous transnational actors. EU member states, for example, through sub-national participation in the Committee of the Regions and sub-national collaboration with the European Commission, institutionalize channels for their sub-national governments to move independently across different spheres of authority to influence decision-making at the international level.[25] If an ideal type of MLG is that of "a system of continuous negotiations among nested governments at several territorial tiers,"[26] then the formally independent but functionally interdependent sub-national level of participation can be seen as a dimension of MLG. This institutional structure for international environmental cooperation is organized around decentralized, dense networks between a variety of governments and other actors active in a joint domain.[27] These networks can be examined from a vertical and a horizontal dimension; they vertically involve the interdependence of government operations at different territorial levels and horizontally reveal the interdependence between governments and non-governmental actors across territorial levels.[28] The density of the networks is likely to absorb the underperformance or failure of one organization and continue to jointly generate governance capacity.[29] Yet the problems of accountability require agencies to specialize in a specific method of accountability with shared professional expertise.[30] The EU polity has been significantly restructured in such a way.[31]

Although these three institutional approaches are not necessarily mutually exclusive, the collaborative formation between Shiga and UNEP predominantly displays an instance of the second with its efforts to achieve a cross-sectoral solution. As the detailed implementation of global environmental strategies is specified, the necessity of sub-national participation at the local scale will become more salient. Internationally agreed environmental goals need to be implemented in coordination with local realities and conditions. UNEP and other environmental bodies need to be strengthened to assist multi-level integration for the management of international environmental goods, and they are expected to work closely with a variety of stakeholders and governments right down to the sub-national level.

The origins of Shiga's environmental coordination

As Shiga is a landlocked prefecture, the limits of local institutional capacity to cope with lake environment degradation, if left unattended by the national government, are seen as a key factor driving Shiga to reach out transnationally for policy learning and solutions. Today, prefectural officials in Shiga firmly believe that the participation of sub-national governments at the international level is a crucial part of environmental governance.[32] Shiga deliberately decided to engage in international environmental cooperation at its discretion, while other similarly landlocked prefectures remained within what was mandated under national policy. Factors internal to agency can be more influential determinants than external opportunity structures, which may have uniform impacts on other prefectures as well. This case study suggests that three key ingredients enabled the Shiga prefectural government to get involved in international environmental cooperation: the visibility of lake-environmental degradation and the traceability of responsibility, qualities of strong gubernatorial commitment and leadership, and the capacity-building capabilities of the prefectural administration.

In the early 1970s, the surface of Lake Biwa in the pristine north-western shore unexpectedly turned red due to a phenomenon known as *akashio* (freshwater "red tide").[33] The cause was traced to the phosphorous content of synthetic household detergents. Domestic waste water, contaminated by phosphate discharge, was not only a technical matter of eutrophication, but also could be harmful to human health. As it became a matter of concern for people's health, the local Women's Organization Liaison Committee (consisting of the Local Women's Association, labor union women's groups, and consumers' cooperatives) began to organize a movement campaigning for the reduction of synthetic detergent use. The administrative practice of reporting the environmental degradation of Lake Biwa did not attract much public attention but the "Three-Drop" citizens' movement (calling for the reduction of synthetic detergent use from five to three drops at a time), organized by the Committee in 1971, became a turning point to uncovering the problem by linking household practices with the technical eutrophication of the lake. In the mid-1970s, as eutrophication became toxic, the prefectural government joined this movement to campaign for the lake environment by framing it as a "causal story" that told who was to bear responsibility.[34] In 1978 the citizen-led synthetic detergent ban movement established a Prefectural Movement Liaison Conference, in cooperation with the prefectural government, to promote the use of "soap power" (*sekken undo* or soap campaign).[35] In the following year, this resulted in the passage of a prefectural Ordinance Relating to the Prevention of Eutrophication in Lake Biwa (*biwako jōrei*) for regulating synthetic detergent sales and use.

In 1974 this issue was raised in a gubernatorial election; as a challenger, Masayoshi Takemura, took a reformist stance with his support for the movement to ban synthetic detergents, and defeated the conservative incumbent, Governor Kin'ichirō Nozaki. The election had become polarized between Nozaki's pro-development conservatism and Takemura's environmental reformism; there was no other influential alternative but to let either a pro-business or a pro-life quality governor lead Shiga prefecture.[36] Once successfully elected, Takemura had more range to maneuver to seek resource commitments to international environmental cooperation that would have been unpopular in the political climate of pro-development. In 1978 once successfully re-elected for a second term without contestation (running on both government and opposition tickets), the governor instructed his staff members to "organize an international conference that will provide Shiga residents with an opportunity to learn precedents (on lake-environment risk reduction) abroad."[37] Obviously, it was also intended that prefectural officials would learn policies and practices from counterparts in other countries. At the stage of policy formation, the exercise of gubernatorial power effectively promoted this policy rationale as there was little politicized tension between the governor and prefectural assemblies or influential local figures. The prefectural department concerned committed itself to progressive policy-making since there was no likelihood of there being a change of hands to a new chief executive.[38]

As the city of Chicago began to regulate the use of phosphates in 1971, the worsening eutrophication of rivers and lakes became a worldwide environmental problem. Local knowledge and experience in Japan created a necessary body of knowledge on environmental problems, but it was not sufficient to cope with the environmental stresses of Lake Biwa. In the late 1970s, lack of experience and expertise led the prefectural Environmental Bureau to mobilize a variety of overseas partners in preparation for drafting a prefectural Ordinance on the Prevention of Eutrophication of Lake Biwa. Researchers in the Canada Centre for Inland Water were invited to share their internationally known expertise on eutrophication.[39] The activities and lessons of Lake Taupo in New Zealand, which had displayed a lake environment and water quality similar to Lake Biwa, provided prefectural officials with the process of learning about lake environments.[40] In the early 1980s, a delegation of the prefectural government went on a few fact-finding tours to Germany on the shore of Lake Constance (also similar to Lake Biwa) in order to gain input into the formulation of a 1984 prefectural Ordinance Governing the Conservation of Natural Scenery (*fukei jōrei*).[41] With growing momentum to develop relationships with overseas counterparts, prefectural officials planned to hold an unprecedented international conference to bring together interested citizens, scientists, and government officials whose ideas were laid down by Governor Takemura in 1981. This plan unintentionally became a stepping-stone towards the development of a lake environment policy network in which these actors transnationally engaged in incorporating diverse resources and perspectives, including local knowledge, and diffusing policy innovations to affected communities in the problem-solving process.[42]

Unlike one-dimensional industrial pollution controls over concentrated polluters, diffused pressures on the lake environment were difficult to confront. Targeting household detergents, however, made one diffuse source of pollution very clear: any consumer buying dangerous detergents was contributing to the problem. The citizen-led framing of public opinion about Lake Biwa pollution made the idea of holding an international conference into an attractive potential source of legitimacy and accountability for prefectural policy. Equally important, gubernatorial leadership was a key ingredient in Shiga's ability to get involved in international environmental cooperation. Without the governor's commitment, the unique idea of the international conference would never have made it onto the policy agenda. Such progressive moves might be facilitated only when progressives hold political power by a very comfortable electoral margin, or when the governor is in a strong enough position to remain undamaged by the scrutiny of voters. To realize his commitment, the long-serving governor won the goodwill of his government officials and their cooperation. Due to the technicality of lake management, the prefectural technocrats, who had become well informed through information sharing with overseas counterparts, began to assume a major role in the policy debate while drawing on help from scientists in the fields of lake-environmental conservation.

Shiga's initiatives in the absence of national support

Japan's Basic Environmental Law states (in Article 34) that the state shall take measures to promote activities by sub-national governments for international environmental cooperation. Nonetheless, international cooperation has not been stipulated as grounds for permissible functions in the Local Autonomy Law, which defines the scope of sub-national operation by an enumeration of specific responsibilities. The national government has neither regulated extra-national channels for a sub-national level of participation in international environmental cooperation nor institutionalized such channels for empowering sub-national governments. Without waiting for national regulations or getting national enabling support, a few front-runner municipalities have developed some form of partnership with international organizations: Osaka with UNEP since 1992, Fukuoka with the UN Human Settlements Programme (HABITAT) Regional Office since 1997, Kitakyushu with the UN Economic and Social Commission for Asia and the Pacific (UNESCAP) since 2000, Kawasaki with UNEP since 2005, and Nagoya with the UN Centre for Regional Development (UNCRD) since 1971. Yokohama has also hosted multi-lateral city-to-city network programs, the Regional Network of Local Authorities for the Management of Human Settlements (CITINET), which the Second Congress of Local Authorities for the Development of Human Settlements created in 1987 through an initiative of the UN Economic and Social Commission for Asia and the Pacific (ESCAP) and local authorities in Asia and the Pacific.[43]

The cases of the first four municipalities indicate that international environmental cooperation is likely to take place with the support of the national government when the city or prefecture has experienced and successfully overcome severe environmental problems in the past and wishes to transfer local experience and expertise to developing countries (the North–South dimension).[44] In contrast, Shiga's motives behind its collaboration with UNEP were to foster policy learning and find solutions in the absence of national support. In the case of Nagoya, the UNCRD was established in the city in 1971 by an agreement between the UN and the Japanese national government. Nagoya City has hosted the UNCRD since then and this is a special case of nationally initiated arrangements. Yokohama is a case where the city, pursuing its own commitment independent of national policy, hosts CITYNET for South–South cooperation not only in the field of the environment but in the general area of urban management.

The partnership between Shiga-UNEP to create the ILEC was the earliest experience in Japan of this kind regarding the national authorities. In April 1983, Shiga's preparatory office for the proposed conference was established at the prefectural Environmental Bureau. Governor Takemura requested sponsorship support from the national Ministry of Construction that had national jurisdiction over water resource development; its expected endorsement would have provided him with a major boost in his effort to hold the conference. However, the Land and Water Bureau of the ministry utterly renounced the conference proposal by saying, "it is not a consultation with us but an already fixed plan," and rejected the request.[45] Even the national Environment Agency technocrats, who were supposed to coordinate the administration of environmental policies, were quoted as saying, "Why on earth does a rural prefecture wish to hold an international conference?"[46] The prefectural officials construed these reactions as an indication of the Japanese statist tradition that could have welcomed the involvement of Shiga in joint problem-solving and policy learning but only insofar as the prefectural initiative is chartered by the national ministries.[47] Shiga's relations with the Ministry of Construction had already been sour, especially since 1972 when both parties reached a political agreement for the redevelopment of the Lake Biwa area, a plan referred to as a national project with the title Lake Biwa Comprehensive Development Project or "BIWASO." As BIWASO was concerned with water-resources development for the neighboring prefectures, the Shiga prefectural government accepted the national plan in exchange for material benefits to its local communities. The River Bureau in the national ministry regarded the sponsorship request as Shiga's pretext for another political gain over water-resource management.[48] The unsupportive responses by the ministries may also be associated with the legal system of environmental policy in Japan. Pollution prevention and control was mostly of local origin, reflecting local environmental conditions; the legal system had provided more local discretion than in any other policy areas. Air and Water Pollution Control Laws were cases in point whereby the national government left local governments to legally impose even stricter controls than national ones in accordance with the natural and social conditions of their areas, so much so that the national government had little understanding of the international environmental cooperation necessary for lake-environmental governance at the sub-national level.[49]

Nationally-led enabling frameworks to incentivize sub-national authorities also faced implementation barriers. The state administration revealed a lack of coordination among relevant ministries, causing the fragmentation of national policy-making for the promotion of the sub-national level of participation in international environmental cooperation. It was also subject to ministerial rivalries, namely, the Ministry of Home Affairs (MOHA) had initially gained primary control over the budget and administration of international environmental cooperation through its agency called the Council of Local Authorities for International Relations (CLAIR). The CLAIR, consisting mainly of temporary transferees from local governments, suffered from a lack of expertise whose accumulation was prevented by its frequent personnel reshuffle.[50] Meanwhile, in the ODA Charter of 1992, the Cabinet acknowledged the potential role of Japanese local governments to implement foreign aid.[51] The Ministry of Foreign Affairs (MOFA) accordingly began to support local governments' environmental ODA initiatives through the International Cooperation Agency (JICA) while seeing the local ODA as an alternative way of financing MEA implementation in the South. There was little program coordination between the MOHA and the MOFA.[52] The Environmental Agency, which had been established in 1971 with the aim of coordinating the administration of environmental policies, still had to rely in practice on the exclusive exercise of other ministries' jurisdiction over environment-related matters.

Probably, the real challenge to a national enabling framework for the sub-national level of participation was how to translate and implement norms, regulations, rules, and commitments, which had been internationally agreed by the Japanese national government, into operational actions. In fact, the necessity of integrating sub-national actions to ensure the optimal reduction of environmental risks had been provided for in the MEAs themselves. A large number of MEAs, while imposing direct legal obligations on member states, prescribed the necessary planning and operational actions at the sub-national level, for example, Article 3 of the 1971 Convention on Wetlands of International Importance, Article 5 of the 1972 Convention concerning the Protection of the World Cultural and Natural Heritage, Article 4.2(c) of the 1989 Basel Convention on the Control of Transboundary Movements of Hazardous Wastes and Article 4 of the 1997 Kyoto Protocol. The state-centric mindset of Japanese national authority tended to devote itself to its direct state obligations under MEAs but failed to develop policy frameworks to enable sub-national action for MEA implementation.[53] In legal-formal terms, sub-national authorities had to wait until the domestic application of individual treaties to sub-national operations was statutorily specified.

Shiga's mobilization along the domestic-foreign frontier

Acting out of its own interest or utility, Shiga had begun to recognize that sub-national action would not suffice in producing a desirable solution without international cooperation and policy learning. But this functional necessity did not automatically drive the prefectural government to engage in international environmental cooperation. Political mobilization was necessary. There was no constellation of existing rules by which the prefectural government may decide what to do and evaluate the behavior of others beyond the national boundary. Without any familiar ground for institutionalized rules or the right to legitimately represent itself at the international level, Governor Takemura found a way through political mobilization to move across spheres of authority and deal directly with the supranational actor, UNEP, in a rather ad hoc fashion.

In the absence of institutionalized channels through which the prefectural government was to be attached as a participant to the permanent representation of the Japanese state, Governor Takemura bypassed the national government by dealing directly with UNEP. A series of actions had their origins in bottom-up, self-directed mobilization with loose and opportunistic features. In April 1983 the informal channel opened up to Shiga when a prefectural official had an opportunity to meet visiting UNEP officials at the International Division of the national Environmental Agency in Tokyo. When the prefectural Environmental

Bureau sought sponsorship for the international conference, UNEP responded enthusiastically, providing a stark contrast to the cold response of the national Environment Agency. Director for Support Measures, UNEP Programme Bureau, Hisao Sakimura, who was clearly aware of the necessity of decentralized cooperation, reported back to Nairobi on the proposed conference; Executive Director Mostafa Tolba of UNEP immediately and strongly endorsed the idea.[54] The proposed conference subsequently attracted strong sponsorship not only from UNEP, but also from the United Nations University (UNU), the International Bank for Reconstruction and Development (IBRD) and the Organization for Economic Co-operation and Development (OECD).[55] Shiga prefecture had thus entered the first phase of enhanced cooperative relationships with UNEP. Due to the role it played in creating the ILEC, Shiga had received more substantial recognition, including warm appreciation and enthusiasm, at the international level than from its own national government.

The influence of individuals, especially the role played by Governor Takemura, should not be overstated, for systematic factors, such as the severity of lake pollution, the national government's inaction, and the over-loaded UNEP, provided specific structural circumstances under which the governor was able to be instrumental in taking the initiative for international environmental cooperation. It is safe to say that gubernatorial entrepreneurship was a necessary condition for establishing the ILEC in the sense that, without Takemura's commitment, the progressive initiative would never have made it onto the policy agenda.

Shiga's upward coordination with UNEP

Political mobilization took place as much outside domestic procedures as within conventional boundaries. Both UNEP and Shiga tried to find, in the blurring of the foreign-domestic divide, a way to improve or strengthen their positions and to pursue their goals. UNEP demonstrated its capacity to cross the foreign-domestic gate, without formal permission from the Japanese national government, to promote the decentralized functions of global environmental governance. Shiga was both willing to and capable of exploiting the informal channel across national boundaries without completely superseding the existing inter-governmental relations.

As a pre-conference session was scheduled in September 1983, Shiga's preparatory office began to recruit participants through media outlets. The preparatory office received a rather cold response from the major national newspapers. The then head of *Yomiuri Shinbun*'s branch office was quoted as saying, "If there is any interest in the lake conference at all, it would most likely be from Shiga's concerned residents."[56] The preparatory office remained committed to "framing" the lake environment as being better for public understanding or giving a quality of communication that would make the issues attractive to and persuasive for targeted audiences.[57] Much to their surprise, these newspapers learned that a press release successfully attracted much larger crowds than expected, with more than the admission capacity of 900 attendees registered across the nation within just one week.[58] In the spring of 1984 the international conference, scheduled to be held in August, was reported and discussed almost every day somewhere in the national newspapers. On the last day of the International Lake Environment Conference, the importance of the lake environment issue was highlighted even in one of *Asahi Shinbun*'s comic strips, known as *Fuji Santaro* (similar to *Doonesbury*). During the August 27–31 dates of the international conference, about 2,400 participants, including those from 28 other countries, were involved in the official proceedings, and an astonishing 10,000 citizens' representatives staged a variety of forums as an alternative to the official meetings.[59] It is important to note that Shiga's initiatives accordingly gained political legitimacy through mobilizing a large number of concerned citizens as well as government officials and scientists for the international conference. Yet the Takemura administration was strongly condemned by some members of the prefectural assembly for "spending millions of yen on a one-off conference."[60]

The real news from the international conference was made during UNEP Executive Director Mostafa Tolba's final speech in which he proposed the establishment of an international standing committee that was to co-organize a biennial World Lake Conference with the local host country taking over tasks and outcomes from the initial Shiga conference.[61] Immediately after the international conference, he visited the national Environment Agency in an attempt to redistribute some functions of international environmental governance to Japan, and requested that Director General Ueda Minoru of the agency create an "international Shiga committee" that would serve as a Secretariat for lake environmental monitoring and conference organization.[62] In contrast to the Environment Agency's dispassionate attitude, Governor Takemura enthusiastically responded to Tolba's call, declaring at a press conference, "We (Shiga prefectural government) will take the plunge to realize the proposal."[63] Noticeably absent from the initial supporters of the process towards establishing the ILEC was Japan's national bureaucracy. The driving force behind the process was an emerging like-minded coalition of the prefectural government and UNEP.

In September 1984 Shiga's preparatory office, while working on a final report of the International Lake Environment Conference, started to prepare for the creation of an international Shiga committee. Without challenging its existing relationships with the national government, it called for help to legitimize the process of Shiga's involvement from the two key national representatives of domestic interests: the International Division (of the national Environmental Agency) that had dealt with UNEP for over a decade, and the United Nations Policy Division (of the Ministry of Foreign Affairs). Two aides from each division planned to meet on a monthly basis with Shiga's preparatory office with a divisional expectation that the creation might gradually occur over years. Meanwhile, when the Japanese delegation (of the national Environmental Agency) was scheduled to attend a UNEP management board meeting in May 1985, Governor Takemura was also invited directly by Executive Director Tolba to report the outcomes of the International Lake Environment Conference. Shiga's preparatory office requested that the Ministry of Foreign Affairs issue the governor an official passport for being part of the Japanese delegation. At first, the ministry declined saying that there was no precedent for issuing official passports to sub-national government officials. Governor Takemura eventually managed to carry an official passport on condition that he be treated as an "advisor" to the Japanese delegation. Yet, much to the Japanese national government's displeasure, the UNEP Nairobi office treated Governor Takemura as the de facto chief of the Japanese delegation. As soon as he arrived in Nairobi, Executive Director Tolba had a lengthy meeting, attended by a Japan Broadcasting Corporation (NHK) reporter. At the meeting, Governor Takemura expressed his determination to push through the establishment of an international Shiga committee "within a year." Executive Director Tolba then promised to extend support through an UNEP management team. This story was immediately reported as the latest top breaking news in Japan. Once it became public knowledge, the national Environmental Agency was unable to back down from it.[64]

In December 1985 Governor Takemura and UNEP Planning Bureau Chief G.N. Golubev agreed to officially launch an International Lake Environmental Committee, or ILEC for short, on February 26, 1986. They made the prospectus for the establishment of the ILEC public, stating:

> We deem it necessary to convene an international conference on a regular basis for information sharing over lake environmental management and water use, create a permanent organization for providing accurate lake environmental information upon request, and for this organization to function as a consultative body for UNEP.[65]

The prefectural government pursued tackling the lake-environmental issue beyond the national boundary and found itself in an unfamiliar sphere of authority where it took initiatives in the absence of ground rules. Accessing informal channels did not automatically lead to sources of influence in the bottom-up political mobilization of the sub-national government. Informal, ad hoc channels provided Governor Takemura with points of access to his political entrepreneurship. The governor demonstrated that he was capable of avoiding the hierarchical constraints of the central state and of manipulating them to his advantage. In this context, the prefectural capability of acting independently was well matched by UNEP's necessity of having policy frameworks to support sub-nation level action. The overloaded UNEP was determined to meet the need for decentralizing environmental governance functions, in order to pave the way for future environmental problem-solving.[66]

Shiga's effort to bridge gaps between local action, national mandates, and global strategies

Financing decentralized governance

Since there were no domestic statutory provisions or procedures to allow for sub-national governments to engage in international environmental governance functions, in February 1986 the ILEC was initially started as a private organization neither regulated nor protected by domestic law (*nin'i dantai*). Its first task was environmental monitoring that would involve collecting data about the environmental quality of lakes around the globe. Although promising to offer initial set-up funds to this project, UNEP found itself unable to sign a contract with the unregistered ILEC.[67] In 1987 Governor Minoru Inaba, successor to Takemura, accordingly decided to re-establish it as a legally recognized foundational organization for public benefits (*zaidan hōjin*). This arrangement allowed the prefectural government to legally supply the ILEC with both its own funds and human resources. To gain legal status, however, the ILEC came under the supervisory jurisdiction of both the national Environmental Agency and the Ministry of Foreign Affairs. In fact, an ex-national Environmental Agency official was invited to take up the post of director of the board of the ILEC.[68] This situation was a double-edged sword, with the beneficial effects of improved access to national funds being offset by the potentially adverse effects of national supervision. ILEC's ties to the national agencies provided ILEC's big projects (such as the Lake Basin Management Initiative or LBMI, 2003–2005—setting up a decentralized basin governance system with the Global Environmental Facility or GEF, the world largest independent funder of projects to improve the global environment) with access to national funds, but the ILEC was accordingly held accountable to a nationally defined criteria.[69]

Fund-raising was critically important not only for building Shiga's coalition but also for maintaining its involvement in international environmental cooperation. The question of how to achieve sustainable ILEC financing remained unanswered. The ILEC was constantly faced with the limitations of its capacity to gain access to adequate resources. While financial responsibility for the World Lake Conference (WLC) rested with the local hosts, primary ILEC income was derived from fund-raising on an individual project basis. Take, for example, the GEF-funded LBMI for which the ILEC was the executing agency. It was also co-financed by the Japanese national government (supplied from Japan Trust Funds at the World Bank). The LBMI was thus dependent on funding not only from international organizations but also heavily from the national government. Yet it was a locally initiated project and was dependent for its legitimacy and successful implementation upon ILEC's reputation as an independent provider of objective expertise on lake-basin management. In a similar way, the ILEC continued to provide consultancy based on its initiatives and ideas to potential funders who consigned their implementation back to the ILEC. Such projects included: group training courses on lake water quality management in cooperation with the JICA, 1991–2005; modelling of water quality processes in Lake Biwa in 1999 for the Ministry of Construction; and monitoring the effects of stock farm wastes and effluent on lake water quality since 1997 for the Japan Livestock Technology Association. As its financial support did not keep pace with its functional needs, the ILEC sought external funds in such a way that its organizational autonomy would not be undermined. The ILEC accordingly attempted to act as an independent provider of expertise on lake-basin management for successful implementation.[70] In this sense, the subnational level of participation involved some degree of mutual and reciprocal relationships with other spheres of authority, although it was neither formally independent nor functionally interdependent on equal terms.[71]

Managing decentralized functions

Not surprisingly, another challenge the ILEC had to face was avoiding the duplication and overlap of its programs and resources (horizontal policy integration). Such potential duplication and overlap existed, for example, when it sought to monitor and provide early warning information on environmental threats and to facilitate communication among stakeholders. At UNEP, the Global Environmental Monitoring System (GEMS), which was inaugurated in 1972 as a result of the UN Stockholm Conference on the Environment, was already running a global monitoring program. For the water quality of lakes and reservoirs, the GEMS Water Programme was dedicated to providing data in cooperation with the World Health Organization (WHO). To its surprise, the ILEC found that the program database comprised only 34 lakes/reservoirs around the world, one of which was Lake Biwa.[72] Even more surprising, Lake Biwa was reported as having a maximum depth of 4 meters (as compared with 104.1 meters measured by the Geospatial Information Authority of Japan). This discrepancy was eventually explained by the acquisition of inaccurate or incomplete information, derived from government departments of water and wastewater management in WHO-designated countries. In 1986 the ILEC began to collect environmental and socio-economic data about major lakes and reservoirs in cooperation with universities, research institutes, and government departments around the world, and provided users with a "World Lakes Database" accessible at www.ilec.or.jp/database/database_old.html. Over time, however, the GEMS Water Programme also developed its own global database, GEMStat, accessible at www.gemsat.org, which contained data for 425 lake and reservoir stations. Since 1999, the Global International Waters Assessment (GEF-funded GIWA) had also been monitoring and assessing problems related to lakes. While each of these database projects sought to meet its own information needs, part of their requirements could overlap with each other. In this sense, information management requires avoidance of duplication and a more integrated process between local knowledge and international governance strategies.

Perhaps the most important initiative for integrating local action into international lake-environmental governance was the 2003 official launch of the World Lake Vision (WLV) (vertical policy integration). The drafting of this vision was initiated in 2001 by the Shiga prefectural government, the ILEC, and UNEP. A set of principles in the vision was intended to guide lake stakeholders in developing and implementing local lake visions and action plans as part of the environmental public goods of world order. In other words, local lake visions should be accountable not only for the local causes and effects of lake degradation, but also those that can be regional or international in nature, such as flood and drought due to the impacts of climate change.[73] To this end, local lake visions, while precise action would be determined by the local conditions, were encouraged to use existing international conventions and protocols (such as the Ramsar Convention on Wetlands of International Importance, the Convention on Biological Diversity, the Convention to Combat Desertification, and others) to implement the principles of the WLV.[74] At the eleventh WLC meeting, held in Nairobi in 2005, the vision expanded to include support functions, such as the LBMI, which acted as a clearing house for better practices and helpful lessons learned from lakes and reservoirs around the world.[75] As stakeholders participated in the management cycle of developing, implementing, and refining local lake visions, the WLV facilitated policy learning in which they looked beyond their national boundaries to study each other's policy initiatives and experiences. There was a potential for the development of common norms of expected lake management to facilitate the process of sub-national participation in providing the environmental public goods of world order.

The WLV resulted from a number of drafts that had been produced between 2001 and 2003 by a Drafting Committee, while going through a series of its meetings and consultations with scientists, policy-makers, politicians, and social groups. The need for the sustainable use of fresh water had been previously addressed in the international arena, such as stated in the Dublin Principles, Chapter 18 of Agenda 21, and the World Water Vision. However, the unique properties of lakes had never been specifically addressed in these previous efforts. In 2003 the WLV was introduced at the Third World Water Forum to attract the attention of citizens' groups, lake managers, scientists, and policy-makers, as it identified socioeconomic factors contributing to unsustainable lake use and threats arising from within lake drainage basins and beyond, defined seven management principles for the sustainable use of lakes, and proposed immediate actions and long-term strategies for addressing these threats. To integrate the WLV into a practical action program that could be adapted to locally specific needs, in 2005 the World Lake Vision Action Project was proposed at the Fourth World Water Forum. In the following year, a call for action reports from around the world started, and by February 2007, 27 reports were submitted to the project. The World Lake Vision Action Report Committee (WLVARC), comprising 30 lake management experts, has continued to synthesize the lessons learned from locally specific experiences into a comprehensive assessment of the application of the WLV principles and then facilitate further application of these principles to local lake visions around the world.[76]

Building decentralized capacity

The ILEC seeks to promote capacity-building in two ways: developing the abilities of individual lake managers and policy-makers and continuously improving lake basin governance. Lack of capacity in local lake governance, especially in the developing world, has been recognized by a series of WLCs, and one of ILEC's missions is to support "activities on environmentally sound management of lakes, which UNEP promotes for developing countries."[77] This is where Japan's ODA can utilize its international reputation as a responsible country in the North–South divide. Since 1991, the JICA (which coordinates Japan's ODA projects for the national government) has sponsored a range of ILEC training courses for government officials and lake managers who are responsible for the management of lake basins in developing countries. With lake resource development, where local societal measures have lost much of their management functions, government officials and lake managers have internationally acknowledged the utility of ILEC's way of thinking, the Integrated Lake Basin Management (ILBM), that is "a compilation of the lessons learned from lake basin management experiences globally, synthesized to address complex planning issues using a basin governance framework."[78]

Apart from the above-mentioned management capacity, the ILEC promotes the involvement of the public in identifying lake problems and in developing sustainable and publicly supportable solutions to these problems.[79] When the sources of lake environmental problems go beyond the local scale, the possibilities for direct public participation may become fewer. The ILEC attempted to develop an awareness-raising concept for identifying significant lake problems and developing practical solutions with the general public. It approached the Education Sector of the United Nations Educational, Scientific and Cultural Organization (UNESCO) in Paris for co-sponsorship to provide broad access to lake environmental learning. UNESCO declined to cooperate with the ILEC, although expressing its mission to raise public awareness worldwide. UNESCO appeared to be aware that most national leaders were politically sensitive to what would be taught about environmental issues at school.[80] One of ILEC's own pilot schemes, the "Five-Country Project," was instead launched by its scientific committee members in their home countries (Japan and Denmark in 1989, Brazil in 1990, and Argentina, Ghana, and Thailand in 1991). The project produced a number of useful outcomes but was still not on track for delivering on the promise of quality environmental awareness. In recent years, the ILEC targeted teachers for lake environmental education by providing a series of teacher training courses, 2000–2010, in cooperation with the JICA.

The determinants of Shiga's involvement in decentralized international cooperation

Shiga prefectural government played an indispensable role in providing an environmental public good for world order. Shiga's cooperation with UNEP approximates an autonomist institutional framework. This framework can be identified where national government has neither regulated nor enabled the sub-national level of participation but a few front-runner sub-national authorities are willing and capable of contributing to policy-making in the absence of national policy. Although sub-national actors cannot legitimately represent themselves at the international level, some actors are willing and capable enough to find a way, through informal channels, to access different spheres of authority. The case of

Shiga's experience has demonstrated a set of individual and collective agent effects under locally specific conditions.

1. Localized motives for international environmental cooperation appear central. Why did Shiga get involved and go beyond what is required under national mandates? We need to look beneath the aggregate relationships. Shiga's distinctive motivations are the ultimate independent variable in explaining its international environmental cooperation. Its initial motives were to foster policy learning and find solutions for the worsening eutrophication of Lake Biwa, in the absence of national support. The Shiga prefectural government sought to find solutions beyond the reach of the national government.
2. A sub-national level of participation in international environmental cooperation may be facilitated when there is significant electoral discretion, especially when an electoral success allows for a wide range of maneuvers creating a significant commitment of sub-national resources. In the case of Shiga, one explanation for the successful scope of Takeruma's gubernatorial leadership is derived from the polarized election between Nozaki's pro-development conservatism and Takemura's environmental reformism. Within the electoral process, there were no other influential alternatives besides letting either pro-business or life quality lead Shiga prefecture. Once successfully elected, Takemura may have had more range to maneuver in seeking resource commitments that would have been unpopular in an uncertain electoral position.[81]
3. The physical proximity of local communities to ecological effects may provide a potential for sub-national participation in decentralized environmental cooperation. An experience of environmental incidents may thus create or increase the need for sub-national participation and thus open up opportunities for environmental reformism. The worsening eutrophication of Lake Biwa, which had become a serious health hazard, triggered serious concerns about existing policy priorities in Shiga prefecture. These concerns allowed the prefectural government to reorient its policy towards quality of life and avoid the scrutiny of voters regarding the costs of policy shift.[82]
4. Sustainable sub-national participation may require credibility levels that vary with the patterns of coordination and negotiation among actors moving across traditional levels of authority over the existence of overlapping competencies. Sub-national authorities represent their constituencies; therefore, what is acknowledged by those interactions needs to be in the interest of the local territories (representation). The authorization of sub-national involvement in those negotiations does not necessarily take place just at the national level, but is also done at the international level while there is often neither permissive legislation nor specific provision in domestic law to regulate its involvement (authorization). The credibility of sub-national participation will also be enhanced through inclusive participation by the sub-national constituencies in agenda setting and policy-making (participation). In this

study, the Shiga prefectural government began to protect its constituencies for environmental risk reduction, subsequently multi-level negotiation and coordination occurred. The collective views of international environmental cooperation, cultivated by UNEP, then rendered legitimacy and acceptability to Shiga's sub-national participation.

5   The success of sub-national participation depends on sub-national authorities' capacity to represent themselves in multi-level negotiation and coordination as participants with persuasively distinct interests. To be successful, sub-national participation requires a capacity to move across and connect the national-local hierarchy, the public-private gap, and the foreign-domestic divide (political mobilization). It must demonstrate its capacity for governance functions: sustainable financing, scientific information monitoring and assessment, integration of local actions in international cooperation, and support for the capacity-building that is particularly needed in developing countries (policy-making and implementation). Without directly challenging the national government, Shiga prefectural government was able to cross the foreign-domestic divide. Without getting permission from either the Ministry of Foreign Affairs or the Environmental Agency, Shiga's sub-national utility was effectively mobilized to attract UNEP's need for redistributing environmental governance functions. The ILEC was driven to take a more integrated approach to coordination between local knowledge and international governance strategies. But it was less capable of ensuring its sustainable financing. The increased capacity of governance functions required a greater availability of financial resources yet the national government's funds were the primary source of financing for the major projects of environmental risk reduction. The ILEC sought to exercise discretionary power over national funds by acting as an independent provider of policy innovation and expertise, something which the national government had been less capable in providing environmental public goods.

Sub-national authorities are closest to environmental effects and they are closest to those who can best tackle environmental problems. They demonstrate the greatest potential for contributing to international policy integration. The ways in which sub-national levels of participation are institutionalized will vary from one country to another, reflecting political and administrative systems and historical traditions. Perhaps the ultimate precondition for an effective sub-national level of participation in international environmental governance is the internalization of norms and social understanding. The generation and diffusion of sub-national participatory values need to be reduced to the interest of stakeholders. The same norms need to be internalized by both sub-national and national agents so that they believe such norms exist and thus act accordingly. In the case of world lake management, policy networks are the norm for entrepreneurs who make purposive efforts to diffuse a common set of norms and worldview.

Conclusion

The findings in the case of Shiga's experience suggest a number of potential causal links for decentralized international cooperation that focus more on agency than on structural explanations. If local governments are required to decide whether or not to engage in international environmental cooperation at their discretion, then factors internal to agency—such as fiscal capacity, resourcing, past experience, prior beliefs, political leadership, and public support—can be more influential determinants than external opportunity structures such as international recognition and national policy. Agency is influential to the extent that it individually or collectively interprets and adapts the external opportunity structures to local needs. If there are any incongruities among equally capable agencies in regard to the interpreted external opportunity structures, then the sources of these incongruities are likely to derive from agencies' probable motivations and purposes.

There are two fundamental priorities or commitments that motivate local governments in relation to cooperative and non-cooperative behaviors: material motivations (the extent to which local authorities are committed to maximizing their local economic or material utility) and normative motivations (how committed local authorities are to obeying the norms of international cooperation for its own sake). In practice, while holding a mix of these motivations, local authorities are expected to show significant differences in the weighting of material and normative motivations. The case of Shiga's experience demonstrates how its motivations are causally linked with other independent variables that explain international environmental cooperation. These independent variables include immediate environmental risks, citizen-led issue framing, strong gubernatorial leadership, and the prefectural Environmental Bureau's adaptive capacity, factors that tend to be scarce in other local governments. Shiga's material motive of learning to allow for problem-solving was resourced by the facilitating effects of those variables in a sequential way. Therefore, the initial motives behind the formation of its partnership with UNEP were to foster policy learning and find solutions for environmental risk reduction. Today, prefectural officials in Shiga firmly hold normative beliefs that the participation of sub-national governments at the international level is a crucial part of environmental governance. In the past 30 years, the ILEC has established itself as a service provider for decentralized environmental cooperation from which all partners in a North–South context are to learn and benefit for lake environmental governance. As lake managers and policy-makers participate in the management cycle of developing, implementing, and refining local lake visions, the ILEC has facilitated policy learning in which they look beyond their practices to study each other's policy initiatives and experiences.

The emergence of the collaborative relationship between Shiga and UNEP can be seen to stem from mutual dependence among the two parties in the sense that one party needs the assistance and cooperation of the other in order to achieve policy outcomes. Although not involved in material resource exchange on equal terms, the formation of this relationship can be conceived as rather horizontally ordered and bypassing the exclusive jurisdiction of the national government without, however, directly challenging existing inter-governmental relations. Without sufficient institutional powers and legal competences, Shiga was eventually pressured to operate on behalf of the national government while trying to financially maintain the ILEC. The vertically ordered, traditional state-centric framework crept into the maintenance of the ILEC's transnational networks. In short, the sub-national level of participation involved some degree of mutual and reciprocal relationships with other spheres of authority, although it was neither formally independent nor functionally interdependent on equal terms.

In a governmental system of hierarchized tiers, the institutional capacity limitations of a national government are considered a precondition for sub-national governments to transnationally reach out for policy learning when they pursue their own agenda independent of national policy. The Shiga prefectural government experienced the institutional capacity limitations of the national government, which facilitated its policy learning beyond national borders and recognized the greater governance gap that the inability of the national bureaucracy created, to sense the need for a sub-national level of participation in international environmental governance. The prefectural government accordingly looked for overseas partners as a compensation mechanism. It called for help from UNEP to see how its counterparts in other countries are coping with lake environmental management.

Shiga was able to get involved only because the prefectural government successfully tapped into the legitimating power that was derived from its constituencies. In advanced democracies, sub-national authorities represent their constituencies; therefore, sub-national activities need to be in the interests of these sub-national territories. By mobilizing transnationally, sub-national authorities might simply promote their narrowly defined sub-national interests as if they were just lobbying for particular interests. In the case of Shiga, however, the prefectural government and its constituencies ended up sharing broad public interests in the sub-national level of participation at the international level. The legitimacy of its sub-national participation initially derived from the community values reflected in citizen-led issue framing. The experience of the international conference, which was then facilitated by electoral slack, raised public awareness and promoted the production and diffusion of information regarding the need for linking the framed sub-national issue to international environmental cooperation. This was instrumental in getting the establishment of the ILEC onto the policy agenda.

Notes

1 Hiroya Kotani, *Jidenteki kokusai koshō kankyō iinkai ron* [Autobiographical account of the International Lake Environment Committee], unpublished manuscript (Kusatsu, Shiga: ILEC, 2006), p. 3.

2 Shiga Prefecture, *Kankyō hakusho* [White paper on the environment] (Otsu, Shiga: Environmental Office, Shiga Prefecture, 1988), pp. 329–33; Tatsuo Kira, *Chikyū kankyō no naka no Biwako* [Lake Biwa in the global environment] (Kyoto: Jinbunshoin, 1990), pp. 223–5, 240–7.
3 Peter M. Haas, "Addressing the global governance deficit," *Global Environmental Politics*, Vol. 4, No. 4 (2004) pp. 1–15.
4 Kira, *Chikyū kankyō no naka no Biwako*, p. 242; Satoru Matsumoto, Associate Director of the International Lake Environment Committee Foundation, Interview with author, May 12, 2010.
5 Robert Keohane and Joseph Nye, Jr., "Transgovernmental relations and international organizations," *World Politics*, Vol. 27, No. 1 (1974), p. 41.
6 Thomas Risse-Kappen, "Introduction," in Thomas Risse-Kappen, ed., *Bringing Transnational Relations Back In: Nonstate Actors, Domestic Structures and International Institutions* (Cambridge, UK: Cambridge University Press, 1995), p. 9.
7 Harriet Bulkeley, "Down to earth: local government and greenhouse policy in Australia," *Australian Geographer*, Vol. 31, No. 3 (2000), pp. 289–308; Michele M. Betsill and Harriet Bulkeley, "Transnational networks and global environmental governance: the Cities for Climate Protection Program," *International Studies Quarterly*, Vol. 48, No. 2 (2004), pp. 471–93.
8 Kotani, *Jidenteki kokusai koshō kankyō iinkai ron*; *Kyoto Shinbun* [Kyoto Newspaper], "Anohi anotoki; jidai no shōgen" [On that day, at that time; historical witness], May 10 to May 17, 2010.
9 Peter M. Haas, "Do regimes matter? Epistemic communities and Mediterranean pollution control," *International Organization*, Vol. 43, No. 3 (1989), pp. 377–403.
10 Margaret E. Keck and Kathryn Sikkink, *Activists beyond Borders: Advocacy Networks in International Politics* (Ithaca, NY: Cornell University Press, 1998).
11 Liliana B. Andonova, Michele M. Betsill, and Harriet Bulkeley, "Transnational climate governance," *Global Environmental Politics*, Vol. 9, No. 2 (2009), pp. 59–61.
12 Andonova, Betsill, and Bulkeley, "Transnational climate governance," p. 56.
13 Hiroya Kotani, Interview by author, International Lake Environmental Committee (ILEC), May 12, 2010; Kira, *Chikyū kankyō no naka no Biwako*; *Kyoto Shinbun*, "Anohi anotoki; jidai no shōgen," May 11, 2010, p. 3; Shiga Prefecture, *Kankyō hakusho* (Otsu, Shiga: Environmental Office, Shiga Prefecture, 1988), pp. 329–32.
14 Joy Hyvarinen and Duncan Brack, *Global Environmental Institutions: Analysis and Options for Change* (London: Royal Institute of International Affairs, 2000); Ronald B. Mitchell, *International Environmental Agreements Database Project* (Version 2010.2), available from: http://iea.uoregon.edu/ [accessed July 25, 2010].
15 See, for example, Daniel C. Esty, "International governance at the global level: the value of creating a global environmental organization," *Environment Matters*, Annual Review 1999–2000 (2000), pp. 12–15; Ford Runge, "A global environmental organization (GEO) and the world trading system," *Journal of World Trade*, Vol. 35, No. 4 (2001), pp. 399–426.
16 See, for example, Konrad von Moltke, *On Clustering International Environmental Agreements* (Winnipeg, Canada: International Institute for Sustainable Development, 2001).
17 Michael Howlett, "Managing the 'Hollow State': procedural policy instruments and modern governance," *Canadian Public Administration*, Vol. 43, No. 4 (2000), pp. 312–31; Charlotte Streck, "Global public policy networks as coalitions for change," in Daniel C. Esty and Maria H. Ivanova, eds., *Global Environmental Governance: Options and Opportunities* (New Haven, CT: Yale School of Forestry and Environmental Studies, 2002), pp. 121–40.
18 Von Moltke, *On Clustering International Environmental Agreements*, p. 3.
19 Streck, "Global public policy networks as coalitions for change," pp. 121–40.
20 Ian Bache and Matthew Flinders, "Themes and issues in multi-level governance," in

Ian Bach and Matthew Flinders, eds., *Multi-Level Governance* (Oxford: Oxford University Press, 2004), p. 3.
21. Gary Marks, "An actor-centred approach to multi-level governance," *Regional and Federal Studies*, Vol. 6, No. 2 (1996), pp. 20–40; Elizabety Bomberg and John Peterson, "European Union decision making: the role of sub-national authorities," *Political Studies*, Vol. 46, No. 2 (1998), pp. 219–35; Liesbet Hooghe and Gary Marks, *Multi-Level Governance and European Integration* (Lanham, MD: Rowman & Littlefield, 2001).
22. Marks, "An actor-centred approach to multi-level governance," pp. 31–2; Bomberg and Peterson, "European Union decision making," pp. 227–8; Hooghe and Marks, *Multi-Level Governance and European Integration*, p. 78; Chris Skelcher, "Jurisdictional integrity, polycentrism, and the design of democratic governance," *Governance*, Vol. 18, No. 1 (2005), p. 94.
23. Yuan Hu, "Implementation of voluntary agreements for energy efficiency in China," *Energy Policy*, Vol. 35, No. 11 (2007), pp. 5541–8.
24. Liesbet Hooghe and Gary Marks, "Europe with the regions: channels of regional representation in the European Union," *The Journal of Federalism*, Vol. 26, No. 1 (1996), pp. 82–90; Bomberg and Peterson, "European Union decision making," pp. 228–31; Charlie Jeffery, "Sub-national mobilization and European integration: does it make any difference?" *Journal of Common Market Studies*, Vol. 38, No. 1 (2000), pp. 1–23; Jenny Fairbrass and Andrew Jordan, "Multi-level governance and environmental policy," in Ian Bache and Matthew Flinders, eds., *Multi-Level Governance* (Oxford: Oxford University Press, 2004), pp. 147–64; Guy Peters and Jon Pierre, "Multi-level governance and democracy: a Faustain bargain?" in Ian Bache and Matthew Flinders, eds., *Multi-Level Governance* (Oxford: Oxford University Press, 2004), pp. 75–89.
25. Hooghe and Marks, "Europe with the regions," pp. 73–82; Marks, "An actor-centred approach to multi-level governance," pp. 31–2; Bomberg and Peterson, "European Union decision making," pp. 223–7; Hooghe and Marks, *Multi-Level Governance and European Integration*, pp. 81–6.
26. Gary Marks, "Structural policy and multi-level governance in the EC," in Alan W. Cafruny and Glenda G. Rosenthal, eds., *The State of the European Community* (Boulder, CO: Lynne Rienner, 1993), p. 392.
27. Kristine Kern and Harriet Bulkeley, "Cities, Europeanization and multi-level governance: governing climate change through transnational municipal networks," *Journal of Common Market Studies*, Vol. 47, No. 2 (2009), pp. 309–32; Eva Gustavsson, Ingemar Elander, and Mats Lundmark, "Multilevel governance, networking cities, and the geography of climate-change mitigation: two Swedish examples," *Environment and Planning C: Government and Policy*, Vol. 27, No. 1 (2009), pp. 59–74.
28. Bache and Flinders, "Themes and issues in multi-level governance," p. 3.
29. Haas, "Addressing the global governance deficit," p. 4.
30. Eva Sorensen and Jacob Torfing, "The democratic anchorage of governance networks," *Scandinavian Political Studies*, Vol. 28, No. 3 (2005), pp. 195–218; Carol Harlow and Richard Rawlings, "Accountability in multilevel governance: a network approach," *European Law Journal*, Vol. 13, No. 4 (2007), pp. 542–62.
31. Hooghe and Marks, *Multi-Level Governance and European Integration*.
32. Shiga Prefecture, *Kankyō hakusho* [White paper on the environment] (Otsu, Shiga: Environmental Office, Shiga Prefecture, 1985), pp. 50–9; Shiga Prefecture, *Kankyō hakusho* (Otsu, Shiga: Environmental Office, Shiga Prefecture, 1988), pp. 329–33; Shiga Prefecture, *Kankyō hakusho* (Otsu, Shiga: Environmental Office, Shiga Prefecture, 1996), pp. 8–9; Hiroya Kotani, Interview by author, May 12, 2010.
33. Manabu Kondō, "Water resource management and inclusive democracy: a case study of the environmental NGO movement and its role in Shiga prefecture," *The Asian Journal of Biology Education*, Vol. 1 (2002), pp. 50–1.

34 Hiroya Kotani, Interview by author, May 12, 2010; Tatsuya Nakamura, Department of Environmental Policy, Shiga Prefecture, Interview by author, September 11, 2011. For the politics of telling compelling "causal stories" for agenda setting, see Deborah Stone, "Causal stories and the formation of policy agenda," *Political Science Quarterly*, Vol. 104, No. 2 (1989), pp. 281–300.
35 Biwako Kaigi, *Sukitōru biwako o mirai e* [The future of pristine Lake Biwa] (Otsu, Shiga: Lake Biwa Environmental Department, 1999), pp. 2–6.
36 Masayoshi Takemura, *Kusanone seiji watshi no hōhō* [Grassroots politics—my way] (Tokyo: Kodansha, 1986).
37 Kotani, *Jidenteki kokusai koshō kankyō iinkai ron*, p. 2.
38 Toshiaki Kagatsume, ILEC Managing Secretary General, Interview by author, May 12, 2010.
39 Kotani, *Jidenteki kokusai koshō kankyō iinkai ron*, p. 2.
40 Kotani, *Jidenteki kokusai koshō kankyō iinkai ron*, p. 3.
41 Kira, *Chikyū kankyō no naka no Biwako*, pp. 27–54.
42 Shiga Prefecture, *Kankyō hakusho* (Otsu, Shiga: Environmental Office, Shiga Prefecture, 1988), pp. 329–33; Kira, *Chikyū kankyō no naka no Biwako*, pp. 223–5, 240–7; Toshiaki Kagatsume, Interview by author, May 12, 2010.
43 The CITYNET Secretariat relocated from Yokohama, Japan to Seoul, South Korea in early 2013.
44 Hidenori Nakamura, Mark Elder, and Hideyuki Mori, "The surprising role of local governments in international environmental cooperation: the case of Japanese collaboration with developing countries," *Journal of Environment and Development*, Vol. 20, No. 3 (2011), pp. 219–50.
45 *Kyoto Shinbun*, "Anohi anotoki; jidai no shōgen," May 11, 2010, p. 3.
46 Kotani, *Jidenteki kokusai koshō kankyō iinkai ron*, p. 4; *Kyoto Shinbun*, "Anohi anotoki; jidai no shōgen," May 11, 2010, p. 3.
47 Hiroya Kotani, Interview by author, May 12, 2010; Kira, *Chikyū kankyō no naka no Biwako*; *Kyoto Shinbun*, "Anohi anotoki; jidai no shōgen," May 11, 2010, p. 3.
48 Hiroya Kotani, Interview by author, May 12, 2010.
49 Hiroya Kotani, Interview by author, May 12, 2010; *Kyoto Shinbun*, "Anohi anotoki; jidai no shōgen," May 11, 2010, p. 3.
50 Takuo Iwata, "The role of local government in international cooperation: a comparative study of Japan and France," *Miyazaki Daigaku Kyoiku Bunka Gakubu Kiyo* [Bulletin of Educational Culture Department, Miyazaki University], Vol. 20 (2009), p. 4.
51 Ministry of Foreign Affairs (MOFA), 2001, *Japan's Official Development Assistance*, available at: www.mofa.go.jp/policy/oda/white/2001/contents.pdf [accessed December 23, 2009].
52 David L. McConnell, "Education for global integration in Japan: a case study of the JET program," *Human Organization*, Vol. 55, No. 4 (1996), pp. 446–57; Iwata, "The role of local government in international cooperation," pp. 4–5.
53 Hiroshi Isozaki, "Kankyō jōyaku to chihō jichitai" [MEAs and local governments], *Kankyō to Kōgai* [The Environment and Pollution], Vol. 26, No. 3 (1997), pp. 2–6; Manabu Haneishi, "Kokusai jōyaku to chihō kōkyō dantai" [Treaties and local governments], *Toshi to Gabananasu* [Municipal Governance], Vol. 5 (2004), pp. 66–7.
54 Kotani, *Jidenteki kokusai koshō kankyō iinkai ron*, p. 4; *Kyoto Shinbun*, "Anohi anotoki; jidai no shōgen," May 11, 2010, p. 3; Satoru Matsumoto, Interview with author, May 12, 2010.
55 Shiga Prefecture, *Kankyō hakusho* (Otsu, Shiga: Environmental Office, Shiga Prefecture, 1985), pp. 50–1; *Kyoto Shinbun*, "Anohi anotoki; jidai no shōgen," May 11, 2010, p. 3.
56 Kotani, *Jidenteki kokusai koshō kankyō iinkai ron*, p. 5.
57 Hiroya Kotani, Interview by author, May 12, 2010; Tatsuya Nakamura, Interview by

author, September 11, 2011. For the notion of "framing," see David A. Snow, E. Burke Rochford, Steven K. Worden, and Robert Benford, "Frame alignment processes, micro-mobilization and movement participation," *American Sociological Review*, Vol. 51, No. 4 (1986), pp. 464–81; Keck and Sikkink, *Activists beyond Borders*, pp. 2–3.
58 *Kyoto Shinbun*, "Anohi anotoki; jidai no shōgen," May 11, 2010, p. 3.
59 Shiga Prefecture, *Kankyō hakusho* (Otsu, Shiga: Environmental Office, Shiga Prefecture, 1985), pp. 50–1; *Kyoto Shinbun*, "Anohi anotoki; jidai no shōgen," May 12, 2010, p. 3.
60 Kotani, *Jidenteki Kokusai Koshō Kankyō Iinkai ron*, p. 7.
61 Kira, *Chikyū kankyō no naka no Biwako*, pp. 240–1; Kotani, *Jidenteki kokusai koshō kankyō iinkai ron*, p. 7; *Kyoto Shinbun*, "Anohi anotoki; jidai no shōgen," May 15, 2010, p. 3.
62 Kotani, *Jidenteki kokusai koshō kankyō iinkai ron*, p. 7.
63 *Kyoto Shinbun*, "Anohi anotoki; jidai no shōgen," May 15, 2010, p. 3.
64 This section is based on Hiroya Kotani, Interview by author, May 12, 2010 and Toshiaki Kagatsume, Interview by author, May 12, 2010.
65 Kotani, *Jidenteki kokusai koshō kankyō iinkai ron*, p. 14.
66 Kira, *Chikyū kankyō no naka no Biwako*, p. 242; Satoru Matsumoto, Interview with author May 12, 2010.
67 Kotani, *Jidenteki kokusai koshō kankyō iinkai ron*, p. 19.
68 Kotani, *Jidenteki kokusai koshō kankyō iinkai ron*, p. 20.
69 Kotani, *Jidenteki kokusai koshō kankyō iinkai ron*, pp. 34–5; Hiroya Kotani, Interview by author, May 12, 2010.
70 International Lake Environmental Committee (ILEC), *How Can We Stop Degradation of the World's Lake Environment?* (Kusatsu, Shiga: ILEC, 2007).
71 Toshiaki Kagatsume, Interview by author, May 12, 2010; Satoru Matsumoto, Interview by author May 12, 2010.
72 Kotani, *Jidenteki kokusai koshō kankyō iinkai ron*, p. 18.
73 World Lake Vision Committee (WLVC), *World Lake Vision: A Call to Action* (Kusatsu, Shiga: World Lake Vision Project Secretariat, 2003), pp. 17–30.
74 WLVC, *World Lake Vision: A Call to Action*, p. 29.
75 Toshiaki Kagatsume, Interview by author, May 12, 2010; Satoru Matsumoto, Interview by author May 12, 2010.
76 World Lake Vision Action Report Committee (WLVARC), *World Lake Vision Action Report: Implementing the World Lake Vision for the Sustainable Use of Lakes and Reservoirs* (Kusatsu, Shiga: ILEC, 2007).
77 International Lake Environmental Committee (ILEC), *ILEC's Vision*, 2010, available at: www.ilec.or.jp/eg/about_ilec/vision.html [accessed December 23, 2013].
78 ILEC, *How Can We Stop Degradation of the World's Lake Environment?*; Hiroya Kotani, Interview by author, May 12, 2010.
79 WLVC, *World Lake Vision: A Call to Action*, p. 8.
80 Kotani, *Jidenteki kokusai koshō kankyō iinkai ron*, pp. 28–9.
81 However, for this to be possible, a precondition must hold: sufficient devolution to sub-national authorities, especially the adequacy of revenue resources devolved to them.
82 Making the need of sub-national participation credible, however, required the collaboration of overlapping competencies among different spheres of authority.

Bibliography

Aall, Carlo, Kyrre Groven, and Gard Lindseth (2007). "The scope of action for local climate policy: the case of Norway." *Global Environmental Politics*, Vol. 7, No. 2, pp. 83–101.

Andonova, Liliana B.L., Michele M. Betsill, and Harriet Bulkeley (2009). "Transnational climate governance." *Global Environmental Politics*, Vol. 9, No. 2, pp. 59–61.
Bache, Ian and Matthew Flinders (2004). "Themes and issues in multi-level governance." In Ian Bach and Matthew Flinders, eds., *Multi-Level Governance*. Oxford: Oxford University Press, pp. 1–11.
Betsill, Michele M. and Harriet Bulkeley (2004). "Transnational networks and global environmental governance: the Cities for Climate Protection Program." *International Studies Quarterly*, Vol. 48, No. 2, pp. 471–93.
Biwako Kaigi (1999). *Sukitōru biwako o mirai e* [The future of pristine Lake Biwa]. Otsu, Shiga: Lake Biwa Environmental Department.
Bomberg, Elizabety and John Peterson (1998). "European Union decision making: the role of sub-national authorities." *Political Studies*, Vol. 46, No. 2, pp. 219–35.
Bulkeley, Harriet (2000). "Down to earth: local government and greenhouse policy in Australia." *Australian Geographer*, Vol. 31, No. 3, pp. 289–308.
Esty, Daniel C. (2000). "International governance at the global level: the value of creating a global environmental organization." *Environment Matters*, Annual Review 1999–2000, pp. 12–15.
Fairbrass, Jenny and Andrew Jordan (2004). "Multi-level governance and environmental policy." In Ian Bache and Matthew Flinders, eds., *Multi-Level Governance*. Oxford: Oxford University Press, pp. 147–64.
Gustavsson, Eva, Ingemar Elander, and Mats Lundmark (2009). "Multilevel governance, networking cities, and the geography of climate-change mitigation: two Swedish examples." *Environment and Planning C: Government and Policy*, Vol. 27, No. 1, pp. 59–74.
Haas, Peter M. (1989). "Do regimes matter? Epistemic communities and Mediterranean pollution control." *International Organization*, Vol. 43, No. 3, pp. 377–403.
Haas, Peter M. (2004). "Addressing the global governance deficit." *Global Environmental Politics*, Vol. 4, No. 4, pp. 1–15.
Haneishi, Manabu (2004). "Kokusai joyaku to chiho kokyo dantai" [Treaties and local governments]. *Toshi to Gabanansu* [Municipal Governance], Vol. 5, pp. 66–7.
Harlow, Carol and Richard Rawlings (2007). "Accountability in multilevel governance: a network approach." *European Law Journal*, Vol. 13, No. 4, pp. 542–62.
Hoffmann, Stanley (1966). "Obstinate or obsolete? The fate of the nation-state and the case of Western Europe." *Daedalus*, Vol. 95, No. 3, pp. 862–915.
Hooghe, Liesbet and Gary Marks (1996). "Europe with the regions: channels of regional representation in the European Union." *The Journal of Federalism*, Vol. 26, No. 1, pp. 82–90.
Hooghe, Liesbet and Gary Marks (2001). *Multi-Level Governance and European Integration*. Lanham, MD: Rowman & Littlefield.
Howlett, Michael (2000). "Managing the 'Hollow State': procedural policy instruments and modern governance." *Canadian Public Administration*, Vol. 43, No. 4, pp. 312–31.
Hu, Yuan (2007). "Implementation of voluntary agreements for energy efficiency in China." *Energy Policy*, Vol. 35, No. 11, pp. 5541–8.
Hyvarinen, Joy and Duncan Brack (2000). *Global Environmental Institutions: Analysis and Options for Change*. London: Royal Institute of International Affairs.
International Lake Environmental Committee (ILEC) (2007). *How Can We Stop Degradation of the World's Lake Environment?* Kusatsu, Shiga: ILEC.
International Lake Environmental Committee (ILEC) (2010). *ILEC's Vision*. Available from: www.ilec.or.jp/eg/about_ilec/vision.html [accessed December 23, 2013].

Isozaki, Hiroshi (1997). "Kankyō jōyaku to chihō jichitai" [MEAs and local governments]. *Kankyō to Kōgai* [The Environment and Pollution], Vol. 26, No. 3, pp. 2–6.

Iwata, Takuo (2009). "The role of local government in international cooperation: a comparative study of Japan and France." *Miyazaki Daigaku Kyoiku Bunka Gakubu Kiyo* [Bulletin of Educational Culture Department, Miyazaki University], Vol. 20, pp. 1–15.

Japan, Ministry of Foreign Affairs (MOFA) (2001). *Japan's Official Development Assistance*. Available from: www.mofa.go.jp/policy/oda/white/2001/contents.pdf [accessed December 23, 2009].

Jeffery, Charlie (2000). "Sub-national mobilization and European integration: does it make any difference?" *Journal of Common Market Studies*, Vol. 38, No. 1, pp. 1–23.

Keck, Margaret E. and Kathryn Sikkink (1998). *Activists beyond Borders: Advocacy Networks in International Politics*. Ithaca, NY: Cornell University Press.

Keohane, Robert and Joseph Nye, Jr. (1974). "Transgovernmental relations and international organizations." *World Politics*, Vol. 27, No. 1, pp. 39–62.

Kern, Kristine and Harriet Bulkeley (2009). "Cities, Europeanization and multi-level governance: governing climate change through transnational municipal networks." *Journal of Common Market Studies*, Vol. 47, No. 2, pp. 309–32.

Kira, Tatsuo (1990). *Chikyū kankyō no naka no Biwako* [Lake Biwa in the global environment]. Kyoto: Jinbunshoin.

Kondo, Manabu (2002). "Water resource management and inclusive democracy: a case study of the environmental NGO movement and its role in Shiga prefecture." *The Asian Journal of Biology Education*, Vol. 1, pp. 45–58.

Kotani, Hiroya (2006). *Jidenteki kokusai koshō kankyō iinkai ron* [Autobiographical account of the International Lake Environment Committee]. Unpublished manuscript. Kusatsu, Shiga: ILEC.

Kyoto Shinbun [Kyoto Newspaper] (2010). "Anohi anotoki; jidai no shōgen" [On that day, at that time: historical witness]. May 10 to 17, 2010.

McConnell, David L. (1996). "Education for global integration in Japan: a case study of the JET program." *Human Organization*, Vol. 55, No. 4, pp. 446–57.

Marks, Gary (1993). "Structural policy and multi-level governance in the EC." In Alan W. Cafruny and Glenda G. Rosenthal, eds., *The State of the European Community*. Boulder, CO: Lynne Rienner, pp. 391–410.

Marks, Gary (1996). "An actor-centred approach to multi-level governance." *Regional and Federal Studies*, Vol. 6, No. 2, pp. 20–40.

Mitchell, Ronald B. (2010). *International Environmental Agreements Database Project* (Version 2010.2). Available from: http://iea.uoregon.edu/ [accessed July 25, 2010].

Nakamura, Hidenori, Mark Elder, and Hideyuki Mori (2011). "The surprising role of local governments in international environmental cooperation: the case of Japanese collaboration with developing countries." *Journal of Environment and Development*, Vol. 20, No. 3, pp. 219–50.

Peters, Guy and Jon Pierre (2004). "Multi-level governance and democracy: a Faustain bargain?" In Ian Bache and Matthew Flinders, eds., *Multi-Level Governance*. Oxford: Oxford University Press, pp. 75–89.

Risse-Kappen, Thomas (1995). "Introduction." In Thomas Risse-Kappen, ed., *Bringing Transnational Relations Back In: Nonstate Actors, Domestic Structures and International Institutions*. Cambridge, UK: Cambridge University Press, pp. 3–33.

Runge, Ford (2001). "A global environmental organization (GEO) and the world trading system." *Journal of World Trade*, Vol. 35, No. 4, pp. 399–426.

Shiga Prefecture (1985). *Kankyō hakusho* [White paper on the environment]. Otsu, Shiga: Environmental Office, Shiga Prefecture.

Shiga Prefecture (1988). *Kankyō hakusho* [White paper on the environment]. Otsu, Shiga: Environmental Office, Shiga Prefecture.

Shiga Prefecture (1996). *Kankyō hakusho* [White paper on the environment]. Otsu, Shiga: Environmental Office, Shiga Prefecture.

Skelcher, Chris (2005). "Jurisdictional integrity, polycentrism, and the design of democratic governance." *Governance*, Vol. 18, No. 1, pp. 89–110.

Snow, David A., E. Burke Rochford, Steven K. Worden, and Robert Benford (1986). "Frame alignment processes, micro-mobilization and movement participation." *American Sociological Review*, Vol. 51, No. 4, pp. 464–81.

Sorensen, Eva and Jacob Torfing (2005). "The democratic anchorage of governance networks." *Scandinavian Political Studies*, Vol. 28, No. 3, pp. 195–218.

Stone, Deborah (1989). "Causal stories and the formation of policy agenda." *Political Science Quarterly*, Vol. 104, No. 2, pp. 281–300.

Streck, Charlotte (2002). "Global public policy networks as coalitions for change." In Daniel C. Esty and Maria H. Ivanova, eds., *Global Environmental Governance: Options and Opportunities*. New Haven, CT: Yale School of Forestry and Environmental Studies, pp. 121–40.

Takemura, Masayoshi (1986). *Kusanone seiji watshi no hōhō* [Grassroots politics—my way]. Tokyo: Kodansha.

von Moltke, Konrad (2001). *On Clustering International Environmental Agreements*. Winnipeg, Canada: International Institute for Sustainable Development.

World Lake Vision Action Report Committee (WLVARC) (2007). *World Lake Vision Action Report: Implementing the World Lake Vision for the Sustainable Use of Lakes and Reservoirs*. Kusatsu, Shiga: ILEC.

World Lake Vision Committee (WLVC) (2003). *World Lake Vision: A Call to Action*. Kusatsu, Shiga: World Lake Vision Project Secretariat.

6 Kitakyushu's environmental business

Utility-based transnationalism within norms

In general, unless they are an active part of national policy, local governments' involvement in international environmental cooperation is driven by voluntary action as it is very difficult to justify voluntary activities to taxpayers. Despite this potential difficulty, Kitakyushu municipal government is by far the most active among Japan's local governments. As Table 6.1 shows, the city, with more than 30 years' experience in international environmental cooperation, appears to have an exceptionally strong commitment to decentralized international cooperation. Although Kitakyushu's financial capacity is the second worst among the 20 designated cities, it is an unexpectedly active locality. Why does the city get involved in international environmental cooperation? This chapter will look beneath the aggregate relationships to more qualitative evidence of the different motivations that operated at successive stages of decision-making across local, national, and foreign actors, while examining the expansion of the multiple modes and mechanisms of cooperation Kitakyushu created. I argue that Kitakyushu used lessons drawn from its historical experience to update its stakeholders' prior beliefs and adopt new policy ideas. The municipal government, especially the mayors of Kitakyushu City, has routinely utilized reasons of utility (i.e., local business interests) and norms (i.e., sustainability), with both these considerations affecting Kitakyushu's policy ideas and choices. City officials, local business and citizens' groups have even developed a complex way of balancing norms and utility. To this end, the municipal government has skillfully established a connection between hierarchical tiers of authority (i.e., the distribution of national decision-making competencies to Kitakyushu) and new de-hierarchical spheres of authority (i.e., its decision-making competencies shared with societal actors and local business and with overseas counterpart organizations). The process of policy learning and knowing has then facilitated the development of new policy ideas through this cross-scale and multi-level connection.

Historical learning into Kitakyushu models

In the past the iron and steel industry was a symbol of industrialization, supplying a wide range of industrial sectors with materials. By the beginning of the twentieth century Yawata, on the north coast of the present Kitakyushu area,

Table 6.1 Kitakyushu's transformation from previous experience to international environmental business

1960s	Kitakyushu located in one of the four largest industrial zones
1963	Fact-finding surveys on industrial pollution (started by Kitakyushu residents)
1970	The chronic lung diseases of residents (reported)
1971	Kitakyushu pollution prevention ordinance (enacted)
Mid-1970s	Dredging Dokai Bay (completed)
1980	Sludge dredging at the river (completed)
1981	Kitakyushu's environmental experts to Dalian (dispatched)
1987	Kōichi Sueyoshi (1987–2007) – Kitakyushu mayor (elected)
Early 1990s	Dramatic SO_x emissions reduction
1990	United Nations Global 500 Award (received)
1992	United Nations Local Government Honors (received)
1993	Dalian Environmental Model Zone (proposed by Kitakyushu)
1995	China's ODA request to Japan regarding the proposed Model Zone
1996	Japan's decision to fund the Model Zone project
1996	Hibikinada Development Plan (environmental business) (publicized by the city)
1997	Kitakyushu Eco-Town Project (approved by the national government)
2000	Kitakyushu Initiative for a Clean Environment (in partnership with the United Nations Economic and Social Commission for Asia and the Pacific to improve environmental management in the region)
2000s	Kitakyushu Initiative Network with 62 cities in 18 Asian countries
2009	Action Plan of the Kitakyushu Eco-Model City (offsetting emissions made in developing countries)
2010	Kitakyushu Asian Center for Low Carbon Society (established)

became the center of iron and steel production in Japan. Japan's victory in the Sino-Japanese War of 1895 had forced China to pay a financial indemnity equivalent to about 15 percent of Japan's gross national product (GNP) at that time. The indemnity was channeled into running Yawata's government-owned iron and steel industry and providing privileged access to quality iron ore from China.[1] The Yawata Iron and Steel Works (today's Nippon Steel Corporation) began production in 1901 and remained government-owned until 1934.[2] During the 1904–1905 Russo-Japanese War, when an Asian nation defeated a European nation for the first time in modern history, Japan became a world military power. The Yawata Iron and Steel Works supported Japan's military build-up, producing more than half of domestic steel output up to the late 1930s.[3] On August 9, 1945, an US B-29 bomber was going to drop an atomic bomb on Kokura (part of the present Kitakyushu City), Japan's large arsenal town, but found the site covered in clouds and turned west to the alternative target of Nagasaki. The hands of fate saved the lives of people there. At the end of World War II, however, the steel town of Yawata (part of the present Kitakyushu City) saw the widespread destruction of industrial infrastructure and suffering and chronic malnutrition among local residents. By 1947, a rising American fear of "communist expansionism" totally killed the spirit of the anti-fascist common cause shared between the Soviet Union and the Western democracies during World

War II. Ironically, the beginning of the Cold War provided the foundation for Yawata's revitalization. Once the Korean War broke in 1950, Japanese manufacturers received fresh orders for all the necessities of war. Yawata, which was the closest to Korea, put its steel plant into full operation to fill massive orders for steel building materials.[4]

Yawata Steel was the primary beneficiary of Japan's postwar alliance with the United States (US). Its prosperity was a foreign policy success for the American administrators who helped rebuild Japan's internal stability against a background of communist threats. Japan's strategic importance to the US created greater room for its government's maneuvers regarding neomercantilist practices. The steel industry in Japan became a main target for the implementation of industrial policy by the Japanese government. The Ministry of International Trade and Industry (MITI) implemented a wide range of policies designed to strategically allocate funds to the steel industry.[5] Japan's raw steel output rose rapidly from 9.4 million tons in 1955 to 102 million tons in 1975. Its export ratio of total steel production also increased from 15 percent in 1950 to a high of 39.4 percent in 1976.[6] During the first two decades of the US–Japan alliance, the US enjoyed a healthy balance of trade surplus with Japan. But by the late 1960s, Japan's balance of payments began to turn positive, mostly with the US. In 1967 the US Congress introduced a bill to set import quotas for steel. To avoid the establishment of such a system, the Japanese steel industry set up a voluntary export restraint system.[7] By the time the US returned from its failed Vietnam War, US–Japan trade conflicts had intensified, reflecting changes at the systemic level, namely that the American economic hegemony was declining. In 1971 the US ran a disastrous balance of payments, with a deficit of US$10.6 billion.[8] Ironically, the Japanese miracle economy that postwar US policy had promoted now appeared to thwart the aspirations of thousands of American steel workers.

Japan's economic success had to bear the burden of pressure and criticism not only from outside Japan but also from within. Rapid development came at a heavy environmental cost. The industrial smoke was rich in dust and sulfur dioxide. During the high economic period of 1955–1965, air and water pollution worsened rapidly. In 1963 Kitakyushu was born in the midst of industrial pollution by the amalgamation of five cities: Moji, Kokura, Wakamatsu, Yahata, and Tobata. In the 1960s, Kitakyushu developed into one of the four largest industrial zones in Japan, accounting for over 5 percent of Japan's industrial production. In those districts, many residents were surrounded by large factories involved in chemical, iron, and steel production. As early as 1950 it was a women's association in the Nakabaru district (Nakabaru Women's Association) of Tobata City (part of the present Kitakyushu City) that began to take environmental matters into its own hands. With the support of the Tobata City Council and administration, its spontaneous study groups successfully persuaded the Nihon Denso Power Plant to install a dust collector for the protection of local residents' health and safety.[9] In 1963 citizens' groups began to conduct a series of fact-finding surveys on dust fall, smoke, and offensive odors and followed this through by continually demanding environmental risk reductions from the factories and petitioning the city administration for improvements. In 1965, when women's associations in the Tobata Ward of Kitakyushu produced a documentary film, "We Want Our Blue Sky Back," the Shiroyama district of Kitakyushu indicated the worst air pollution on record in Japan, i.e., 80 tons of falling dust per month/km^2 on average being produced by its industrial complex.[10] In 1966 the Bay of Dokai in Kitakyushu recorded a chemical oxygen demand (COD) high of 36 mg/l, and was called the "dead sea."[11] The bay was highly contaminated by industrial and domestic wastewater and this environmental pollution progressed to such an extent that even coliform bacteria could not survive.

Yet the MITI encouraged large-scale mergers for greater international competitiveness, resulting in the merger of Yawata and Fuji in 1970.[12] By then, the chronic lung diseases local residents had developed were aggravated by air pollution. The merged Nippon Steel was by far the biggest local employer (employing nearly 50,000 people), but its advantageous position was about to dissolve due to popular public pressures, which the legendary women's associations had nurtured with other grassroots groups. In 1971, as a Kitakyushu pollution prevention ordinance was enacted, the city created the Environmental Pollution Control Bureau to implement a range of environmental regulations. In 1972, as a full-scale waste incineration facility was completed, a pollution prevention agreement was reached between the municipal government and 54 industrial plants in the city. In the mid-1970s, Dokai Bay was dredged; a total of 350,000 cubic meters of polluted sludge, containing more than 30 parts per million (ppm) of mercury, was removed. The total operation cost 2 billion yen (US$18 million), of which 71 percent was borne by the Kitakyushu business sector and 29 percent by the municipal government.[13] In addition to the industrial pollution, many houses had been illegally built along the city's main river, further contributing to river water pollution. The sludge dredging and removal project at the river was completed in 1980. Following the municipal regulations, each corporate firm developed its own environmental risk reduction plan to implement various countermeasures. Sulfur oxide (SO_x) emissions from steel works in Kitakyushu, for example, dropped from 27,575 tons/year in 1970 to 600 tons/year in 1990.[14] In collaboration with these groups and local business, a system, known as the "Kitakyushu Method" of overcoming the environmental problems, was adopted by the municipal government. Since 1973, the municipal government has spent US$4.6 billion on pollution control and prevention, with the corporate sector spending a further US$2.1 billion.[15] Kitakyushu developed, through lesson-drawing, its own local human capital for decentralized environmental cooperation. From the viewpoint of its involvement in international environmental cooperation, the city was well equipped, with both environmental risk-management skills and pollution prevention technologies or cleaner production technology (CPT), to share their accumulated assets with others.

Kitakyushu's trans-local cooperation with Dalian

From 1929 to 1944, regular passenger boats had been operating between Dalian in China and the Moji Ports (in the present area of Kitakyushu) in Japan.[16] Since the late nineteenth century, Moji had functioned as an international trading port and Japan's gateway to Northeast Asia. Japan's unconditional surrender to the Allies at the end of World War II broke off this connection. In 1972 Japan moved to open diplomatic relations with China, as the US rapprochement with China began against Soviet expansionism. Local residents in Kitakyushu accordingly resumed a goodwill relationship with those in Dalian. As China participated in the UN Conference on Human Environment at Stockholm in 1972, the national government began to express its environmental concerns at the policy level. In the following year, it established its own environmental protection agencies at both the national and local levels. In the early 1970s, the Chinese government took a rigid ideological approach to environmental problems as China was less industrialized and less environmentally damaged. Chinese official pronouncements blamed capitalists' profit maximization as the root cause of environmental degradation.[17] At the conference in Stockholm, the Chinese delegation identified the industrialized countries as the primary polluters, proposing that any victim country would be entitled to claim compensation from those countries.[18] At the same time, a Chinese spokesman stated that "Nature" had to be subject to the superiority of human needs.[19] However, by 1979 when Deng Xiaoping overthrew the Maoist model of politics and economics rapid changes were about to start in China's landscape.[20] Deng's policy completely reversed collectivism to individualistic rewards for profit maximization, and encouraged the emergence of new enterprises in Dalian. The local consequences for the environment were soon being felt. By the early 1980s, Dalian started experiencing serious environmental problems caused by enormous development aspirations, much like those experienced in Kitakyushu. In 1981, for the first time by request, Kitakyushu City dispatched three environmental experts to its sister city Dalian, who offered a seminar on pollution management. Residents in Dalian were faced with their limited capacity to deal with air pollution from the massive combustion of raw coal and extensive water contamination from thousands of new small enterprises.[21] China's National Environmental Protection Agency (NEPA) became an independent state organization in 1984. It recognized the financial losses caused by pollution but found difficulties in handling localized development with little capital for environmental management.[22]

In the early 1990s, Kitakyushu received worldwide praise for its collaborative achievements in restoring the environment and its preventive environmental efforts, winning the Global 500 Award (presented by the United Nations Environment Programme in 1990) and the UN Local Government Honors (at the 1992 Earth Summit in Rio de Janeiro). By 1990, however, acid rain began to affect all parts of Japan.[23] The Japanese government, researchers, and newspapers reported that China's coal-burning power plants had caused the acid rain affecting Japan, although the Chinese government did not accept this accusation.[24] In 1991, as local residents in Kitakyushu recognized that acid rain was the most pressing transnational air pollution problem, the city held the International Conference on Acid Rain in East Asia. In 1992 the Environmental Cooperation Center was created as part of a non-profit organization, the Kitakyushu International Techno-cooperation

Association (KITA), in response to the recognition that the domestic "Kitakyushu Method" alone could not cope with the spillover effect of environmental degradation.[25] Kitakyushu dispatched 49 pollution control experts to Dalian in 1993 and then a further 36 in 1995 in a bid to develop a trans-local network through their joint seminars on environmental control.[26]

By the early 1990s, Dalian was a state-designated city as well as one of the 14 Coastal Open Cities where local residents experienced every imaginable environmental problem. At the China-Kyushu symposium on environmental technology, held in November 1993, Mizuno Isao, director-general of KITA, proposed establishing a "Dalian Environmental Model Zone" through the joint efforts of Kitakyushu and Dalian. This notion received support from Song Jian, a member of China's State Council, who after the symposium visited Kitakyushu with Jie Zhenhua, Director General of China's NEPA. In January 1994 China's NEPA accordingly adopted this proposed idea as a priority project, which was expected to have nationwide influence. During his visit to China in September 1994, the mayor of Kitakyushu received official confirmation of support for the Model Zone project from both Vice-Premier Zhu Rongji and NEPA Director General Jie Zhenhua.[27]

Although the Kitakyushu side was ready to provide the project with its experience and expertise on pollution control and prevention, the inter-municipal coalition of Kitakyushu and Dalian had limited financial resources and staffing to implement the master plan of the Dalian Environmental Model Zone. In August 1994 both cities thus further agreed that they would target their national governments for fund-raising. In September 1995, the Chinese government subsequently made an Official Development Assistance (ODA) request for its Dalian Environmental Model Zone projects to be funded by the Japanese government. In February 1996, the Japanese government thus pledged ODA funds to China for the Dalian Environmental Model Zone project. Never before had such trans-local initiatives been adopted as ODA projects at the national level.[28] This turned out to be the first successful case in which city-to-city environmental cooperation aligned with Japan's large-scale ODA. This city-to-city effort grew into a project worth over US$300 million.

With assistance from the Japan International Cooperation Agency (JICA—a state agency), KITA conducted a site diagnosis on key polluting enterprises, helped them identify the origins of the pollution, put forward corrective countermeasures, and stipulated clean production plans. In December 1996, an Investigation for the Consolidation Plan of the Dalian Environmental Model Zone was set up by a joint team of a Dalian guidance group, a JICA group, and a Kitakyushu group of 20 experts who were recruited from KITA, local universities, and businesses.[29] The team, while working on a set of environmental targets to last beyond 2010, had already produced a wide range of practical environmental management and expertise to the Model Zone project. From 1996 to 2000, the Kitakyushu group conducted energy efficiency improvement projects. These projects were designed to develop an energy efficient boiler suitable for the coal used in Dalian, especially in winter when the air was heavily polluted by small-scale residential boilers.[30] The KITA Environmental Cooperation Center carried out an application study of preventive environmental strategies for the steel, cement, chemical, and dye industries in Dalian. In 1998 it presented a set of 18 proposals including pickling/heat treatment process improvement in steel works, the production conversion of sulfuric acid in a chemical plant, and a nitration process improvement of chlorobenzene in a dye factory.[31] In the same year, it co-organized with the UN Centre for Regional Development a training seminar in Dalian to inform and disseminate the outcomes of the Model Zone project, with special focus on "cleaner production" technologies and financial mechanisms.[32] In 2000 experts from Japan and China released a "Dalian Environmental Model Area—development investigation report," which drew a blueprint for Dalian's environmental protection work for the future. In recent years, Dalian's efforts in environmental protection have provided a market for environmental protection enterprises and technology exports for Kitakyushu. New Japan Chemical Environmental Consultancy Co., Ltd., and Aqua Tech Co., Ltd., both from Kitakyushu, established their representative offices in 2005 and 2006, respectively, signaling that decentralized environmental cooperation has entered into the substantial stage of international environmental business.[33]

The trans-local network of Kitakyushu-Dalian emerged as Dalian was inexperienced in coping with industrial pollution and Kitakyushu thus began to engage in diffusing its policy measures to the coastal city located across the Yellow Sea, in order to solve the cross-border problems of acid rain. They shared the common goal of environmental risk reduction and frequently exchanged information. Their network functioned as a trans-local advocacy coalition towards seeking out financial resources from both the Japanese and Chinese governments. Trans-local contacts amplified the demand for financial support for the Dalian Environmental Model Zone and echoed their demands back into the domestic arena. Neither of the cities could have done this alone. Their network allowed each city to reach beyond its own capability to advocate and instigate changes in a synergized way. The coalition of Kitakyushu city officials, KITA members, local businesses, universities, residents' groups, and Dalian city officials was not simply complementary to the national governments by engaging in assistance activities that were centrally defined, but rather it took the initiative on a trans-local basis in response to some sense of common local problems, crossing borders. Direct participation by the coalition in ODA encouraged the extensive participation of local communities in the development process of the Model Zone project. It provided local business, banks, residents with opportunities, not only to participate in ODA activities, but also to collaborate with overseas counterparts. In this respect, the considerable scope of their participation could develop accountability between the Model Zone project and local communities in the both cities. Some argue that the emphasis on local participation in ODA also offers the possibility of improving Japan's notorious reputation for ODA implementation, such as aid tied to orders for goods and services from Japanese big business and corrupt practices by government officials in recipient countries.[34] The Vice-Director of the KITA Environmental Cooperation Center, Hiroshi Mizoguchi, argues further in support of the Kitakyushu experience. He points out that grassroots ODA initiatives tend to be truly hands-on, providing follow-up support, creating self-reliance, and maintaining a long-term commitment rather than seeking a skimming strategy to produce short-term project outcomes that the national government requires from implementation agencies every fiscal year.[35]

Kitakyushu's promotion of international environmental businesses

In 1985, an Organisation for Economic Co-operation and Development (OECD) environmental report introduced Kitakyushu as "a city that was transformed from gray city to green city."[36] With its history of severe industrial pollution and its experience in using environmental management and technology to overcome it, Kitakyushu leaders found a natural business niche: using local environmental expertise to benefit from international cooperation. In 1980 the city established KITA, designed to use its local human resources and expertise in technology transfers to developing countries. In the late 1980s, Mayor Kōichi Sueyoshi (1987–2007) of Kitakyushu, a former national bureaucrat in the Construction Ministry, identified locally accumulated environmental technologies with a great business potential for municipal revitalization. He proposed a strategy to couple environmental policy with business opportunities.[37] Since the establishment of KITA, mayors and community leaders of Kitakyushu have nurtured the development of environmental business undertakings aimed at greatly benefiting both Kitakyushu and its partners in developing countries.[38] At the 2002 Johannesburg Summit, Mayor Sueyoshi received the "Earth Summit 2002 Sustainable Development Award." The city's environmental innovations have received international recognition through his mayoral leadership.

In 1987, when he was elected mayor on a platform of economic renewal for Kitakyushu, Sueyoshi had little idea of how the city could transform major heavy industry districts into those of "zero emissions environmental industries."[39] In 1989 the mayor asked a study group of academics to make recommendations for future uses of the 2,000 hectare Hibiki landfill area in Kitakyushu. He was impressed by the policy idea of "venous" industry (resource recycling industry) that Professor Toshifumi Yada, an economic geographer at Kyushu University, had introduced to him.[40] Yada suggested that communities were now far more open to the idea of encouraging and nurturing venous industries. In 1992 the mayor, with support from the study group, decided to use venous industries as a key concept for Kitakyushu's revitalization. In terms of the process of material flow, "arterial" industry operates in the industrial process of consumption while venous industry is one that, for environmental protection, uses advanced technologies to transform household and industrial waste created in the process of consumption and production into renewed resources and products. The city accordingly started to make a niche for itself in environmental business. At this stage, the Hibikinada Development Plan was neither widely understood nor broadly accepted by local residents.[41] In 1994 private enterprises launched a committee to study the feasibility of developing the environmental sector in Kitakyushu, while Nippon Steel played a key role in commercializing the business by creating Nishi-Nippon PET-Bottle Recycling Co. Ltd., in cooperation with some other companies. The energy intensive industries were in transition in the sense that they were losing competitiveness and thus sought to transform their business direction of heavy industry towards a more complex industrial structure. To be specific, major firms in Kitakyushu explored a new way of managing their excessive production capacity to utilize the unused landfill for new investment. The committee held a series of sessions for environmental business pilot and feasibility studies with the first part in March–August 1995 and the second part in February–May 1996. For the second part of the studies, the municipal departments and bureau chiefs participated to provide inputs from the administrative side. In 1996 Mayor Sueyoshi formally publicized the Hibikinada Development Plan via press releases.

After reviewing the findings of the pilot and feasibility studies, the mayor tenaciously negotiated with MITI to receive a cost-sharing national subsidy for developing "environmental industry."[42] He successfully persuaded MITI officials to adopt the Eco-Town policy, implemented since 1997, for supporting the innovation and entrepreneurship of Kitakyushu's and other localities' local recycling and zero emissions strategies. The national government promised the city to cover 50 percent of the project costs for developing material assets and equipment ("hardware" grants) and networking, information and promotional organizations ("software" grants). In August 1997 the mayor started chairing the Kitakyushu Council for the Promotion of Environmental Industry, which consisted of private companies, KITA, the prefectural administration, and academics.[43] The first meeting was at the beginning of the implementation phase of Kitakyushu's Eco-Town Project. The role of municipal support was to provide hard infrastructure, such as industrial roads and sewage, assist the software side, such as through public awareness campaigns and information disclosure, and coordinate stakeholders' needs and issues, including stakeholders' meetings and briefings for residents.[44] The Kitakyushu Eco-Town Project, initially developed in the eastern part of the Hibiki landfill area, consisted of the Practical Research Area (the clustering of research institutions for developing environmental technologies), the Hibiki Recycling Area (small and medium-sized recycling companies), and the Comprehensive Environmental Industrial Complex (environmental companies, established by investment from large companies, to treat industrial waste). The city also established the Eco-Town Center in the area so that the center would be used to hold the operation of all their facilities accountable to the citizens concerned and encourage citizens' involvement in the Eco-Town Plan. The Kitakyushu Eco-Town became the largest project in Japan, with 29 business facilities, 16 research institutions, 1,300 employees, and an investment amount of over US$0.6 billion in 2012.[45] In October 2014 the city announced an expansion of the area of the Eco-Town beyond the Hibikinada landfill area into the entire area of Kitakyushu.

In the 1990s, as environmental issues increasingly required global strategies to find solutions, Kitakyushu began to see itself as a direct contributor to the global solution, while seeking simultaneous improvements in its economy and environment. In 1997 as the Eco-Town Project in Japan was introduced by MITI, Kitakyushu Eco-Town became the first Eco-Town in Japan approved by the government. The Kitakyushu project aimed to be designated "Asia's International Resource-Recycling and Environmental Industry Base City."[46] The national government's subsidies for this project provided Kitakyushu with the financial support to attract companies that could develop high-tech model recycling facilities. With the Eco-Town project attracting much foreign attention, the municipal government held seminars and conducted feasibility field surveys on the creation of recycling Eco-Towns in the Chinese cities of Tianjin (2008–2009), Qingdao (2007–2008), and Suzhou (2005). Its Eco-Town cooperation with China's cities is now underway, using Kitakyushu as a reference.[47] In 2009 Kitakyushu started to provide Dalian with support for actions to create resource recycling facilities. Xi Jinping (then Vice-President of PRC) formally visited Kitakyushu on December 16, 2009. *The People's Daily* (December 17, 2009) even reported that China could draw from Kitakyushu's rich lessons in environmental protection and the development of advanced technologies as a model for application to Chinese cities. According to the Action Plan of the Kitakyushu Eco-Model City (April 2009), by 2050 the city would aim to achieve a 50 percent reduction in CO_2 emissions, compared to 2005 levels (15.6 million tons), and to offset 23.4 million tons of carbon emissions generated by environmental technology transfer from Kitakyushu to developing countries.[48] In other words, the latter will be achieved to offset emissions made in developing countries by environmental technology transfer, which is expected to help reduce the cost of carbon emissions reduction in those countries. This initiative is taking place through the Kitakyushu Initiative Network with 62 cities in 18 Asian countries. In June 2010 the Kitakyushu Asian Center for Low Carbon Society was established and began joint operations between the city, KITA and the Kitakyushu Urban Center of the Institute for Global Environmental Strategies (IGES) to spread low-carbon societies to other parts of Asia through the creation of environmental businesses.

Kitakyushu's environmental business in the North–South context

As discussed in Chapter 5, geographical proximity is the natural criterion for partner selection. A case in point is inter-municipal cooperation between Dalian and Kitakyushu over pollution control. Geographical proximity is strongly related to the development of international environmental cooperation, providing both opportunities and incentives; it is one of the most important factors driving trans-local activities. As international environmental cooperation has become a part of the global strategies for environmental risk reduction, the linkages of trans-local relations have revealed different geographical orientations, with a special focus on North–South issues. International environmental cooperation has been seen as a site for dialogue to tackle the North–South divide. In this respect, geographical proximity could undermine the normative commitment to solve the North–South divide, since Northern counterparts are partly driven by their immediate concerns about the transboundary spillover effects across geographically adjacent areas. Given the inequalities in terms of material, financial, and human resources between Northern and Southern counterparts, the smaller material benefits for Northern partners also appear to compromise the criteria of partner selection. However, Kitakyushu's environmental business is instead expected to form the basis of dialogue for mutual benefits and learning between Northern and Southern partners. The operation of the Kitakyushu Asian Center for Low Carbon Society has the potential to develop a compatible way of balancing the normative commitment to North–South solutions and commercial self-interest.

In practice, Kitakyushu already has more than 15 years' experience in international environmental cooperation that reaches beyond cross-border problems and transcends the constraints of geographical fragmentation. By 1998, the Kitakyushu municipal government often stated that exchange activities in international environmental cooperation are a locus for "mutual learning" which is a pillar of social trust, understanding, and cultural sensitivity in the context of the North–South divide. In November 1998, Kitakyushu and Semarang (the capital city of Central Java province) in Indonesia became "Environmental Partner Cities" at an international conference in Semarang. Kitakyushu was cited as saying: "The City of Kitakyushu also would like to learn sustainable development for the experience of cities in Indonesia."[49] To take root in the local community, both cities chose the tofu industry, tofu being is an important part of the diet of local residents in both places. As waste water from tofu shops was identified as a major source of river pollution in Semarang, Mitsuhiro Kihara, owner of a 100-year-old tofu shop in Kitakyushu, explained the importance of manufacturing technologies which can reduce waste water from tofu plants yet create local employment opportunities.[50] Between 2001 and 2004, KITA, with support from JICA, delivered catchment management mechanisms to the designated Bajak river basin, including those for river water monitoring, collection of wastewater, wastewater treatment, Japanese tofu production technology, hygiene management, and cultural exchange programmes.[51] To ensure public consultation at an early stage, community groups, tofu producers, academics, and government agencies concerned were invited to discuss the proposed project, including alternatives to it, and how to adapt the proposed ideas to locally specific conditions. It was reported that the implementation of the project helped to increase public awareness about the importance of improving water quality, sanitation, and hygiene to reduce water-borne diseases.[52]

In the general area of water management, Kitakyushu has been sharing waterworks technology with Asian cities as part of its initiative to improve water standards and human health. Hideo Ishii, a field officer at Kitakyushu's Water and Sewer Bureau, emphasizes the importance of a reliable water system, which is a prerequisite not only for human health and sanitation but also for the sustainable development of local regions.[53] This bureau has been involved in waterworks projects in Indonesia, Vietnam, and China and the case of Cambodia's capital of Phnom Penh has been a success story. In 1991 the Paris Peace Agreement ended Cambodia's civil war, yet the nation was not completely at peace. In 1993 the Phnom Penh Water Supply Authority (PPWSA) was able to supply water through the city's waterworks to only 25 percent of the city's population. In 1999 Kitakyushu agreed through the Japanese government to share its waterworks expertise with and dispatch skilled experts to Phnom Penh. In the same year, the city began to provide the expertise and specialists for the instalment of a block system of gridded and separated distribution pipes to detect water leakages. Water and Sewer Bureau official Kazuya Kubota recalled his experience:

> there was no data or records, since it was just after the civil war.... we had to quickly gather current data to begin the instalment process. One of the hardest jobs was to see if the pipes have been tampered with. I felt a fear for my life.[54]

In the midst of political instability, Phnom Penh was still fraught with danger. By 2006, the international water cooperation, as compared to 1993, stood out as crucial to achieving the outstanding results: the percentage of households in Phnom Penh served by the PPWSA increased from 25 percent to 90 percent; the period of time per day for water availability rose from 10 hours to 24 hours; and the non-revenue water rate (i.e., due to leakage and theft) dropped from 72 percent to less than 8 percent.[55] This success has attracted much attention from other Association of Southeast Asian Nations (ASEAN) nations.

Following its experience in Phnom Penh, Kitakyushu continued to supply safe water to other ASEAN nations. In 2009 Hai Phong (Vietnam) and Kitakyushu signed a five-year friendship cooperation agreement (MOU), in which both cities developed a five-year plan for 2009–2013 regarding environmental cooperation and other issues. In particular, Kitakyushu helped Hai Phong improve its water supply system through the transfer of water purification technology. In 2013 Hai Phong decided to introduce Kitakyushu's Upward Biological Contact Filtration (U-BCF) processing techniques in a small-scale treatment plant (5,000 m^3/day). This advanced treatment method, which was jointly developed in 1997 by Kitakyushu's Water and Sewer Bureau and a private company, Kobelco Eco-Solutions Company, aimed to lower operation costs as biological decomposition happens without any electric power or any chemicals.[56] Kitakyushu holds a national patent for this technology. The pilot water filtering project using U-BCF processing techniques was successfully installed and operated in Hai Phong. The Japanese government accordingly decided to grant ODA of US$15 million (no repayment required) to Hai Phong City to introduce U-BCF technology to main treatment plants.[57] A preparatory study through ODA cooperation began in July 2014. Hai Phong's project has become a means of spreading U-BCF from one city to another in Vietnam. The targeted localities in

Vietnam are Hanoi City, Hai Duong Province, Nam Dinh Province, Quang Ninh Province, Hai Phong City, Khanh Hoa Province, Binh Duong Province, and Tien Giang Province. In 2015 the City of Kitakyushu was ready to act as an advisor for the contracted project while Kobelco had won a US$225,000 contract to plan the system of a large water treatment facility in Hai Phong. The construction of this plant was scheduled to start in May 2015 and, once completed, is expected to treat 5,000 tonnes of water per day to serve nearly two million people in Hai Phong.[58] Currently, Kitakyushu is working on and devoting its energy to "Water Business," in which the city is investing in and consulting for water-related projects in developing countries.

Kitakyushu's shift from technology transfer to socio-technical export

The process of adopting environmental policy ideas is extremely complex and requires a close examination of different situations among developing countries in which the idea is learned, contested, adapted, and accepted by locals, both individual and collective. The manner in which environmental technology is applied has critical consequences on the contested interface between environment and development processes. Probably the most pressing issue facing the activities of international development is accessing advanced technological hardware and applied knowledge while addressing climate change. The implementation of the United Nations Framework Convention on Climate Change (UNFCCC) highlights the importance of low-carbon technology transfer, which implies high expectations of technological solutions to the development-environment dilemma. In this context, Kitakyushu's policy elites are drawing lessons from their experiences with Asian cities. In their view, that high expectation can be met so long as the process of technology transfer to the counterparts is an integral part of solving the interdependent problems of health, environment, wealth, and social relations rather than merely a physical transfer of technology.[59] Technical know-how itself is neutral but technological artefacts need to be embedded within the social and cultural fabric of communities in developing countries, implying that the hardware can be used and adapted to local conditions. In the past, Kitakyushu's international environmental cooperation has established a trans-local network through the transfer of environmental technologies the city has developed through creating solutions to pollution problems and manufacturing processes. Now the Kitakyushu Asian Center for Low Carbon Society, in cooperation with private firms, universities, and citizens' groups, is moving towards not only transferring technologies, but giving support for building green cities in Asia. The municipal government has adjusted itself in light of new information, experiences, or changing strategic considerations to address climate change. Kitakyushu's feasibility studies towards environmentally sustainable cities in Asia involve the public and local authorities with environmental, social, and economic responsibilities as part of the trans-local process in an integrated way.[60] Such policy-oriented learning is a crucial factor for Kitakyushu's policy change towards Asian cities. At the strategic level of learning, Kitakyushu seeks mutual benefits in trans-local relations: the city will revitalize Kitakyushu communities through overseas environmental business development, primarily by its local companies, while Asian cities will be able to control pollution and improve quality of life while reducing CO_2 emissions.[61]

Surabaya is the second largest city in Eastern Java, Indonesia. In the mid-1990s, fast-growing amounts of solid waste were posing a complex challenge for Surabaya's environmental policy. The city was able to collect less than half of the solid waste produced in the city. Since then, Kitakyushu, in cooperation with the JICA, the KITA, the IGES, JPec Co., Ltd. (a thermal power company), and other private firms, has been assisting Surabaya City through technology transfer to transform its waste management into an economically affordable yet environmentally sustainable system. The first large project, in 2004–2006, in close cooperation with the City of Kitakyushu and the KITA in the area of household composting, achieved a significant reduction of waste in the Surabaya waste disposal system. In 2004, the KITA, under the funding scheme of the Japan Fund for Global Environment (provided through an initial endowment from the Japanese government together with contributions from the private sector), began to cooperate with a local non-governmental organization (NGO), Pusdakota, in introducing a new system for solid waste management in a low-income neighbourhood.[62] The local residents were encouraged to separate organic and non-organic household waste at the source. Pusdakota collected the organic waste twice a week. JPec. Co., Ltd., provided the NGO with the Takakura Method, which was based on a simple method utilizing fermentative microorganisms. Pusdakota's composting center, through many months of collaborative work with JPec, was eventually able to produce a marketable compost of high quality within one or two weeks, rather than the three months needed for traditional open window composting methods. Over time, the Takakura Method was adapted and modified further to meet local needs at the household level.[63] This modified system was known as the Takakura Home Method (THM) and Pusdakota acquired a patent for it from the Indonesian government. Surabaya City was impressed by the achievement and benefits that the pioneering composting project brought to the community and decided to spread the waste management system to other communities in the city, in cooperation with other local NGOs. Neighborhood groups and the NGOs organized a range of events and awareness campaigns across the entire area of the city. The city was initially allocated a budget for building six composting centers that could compost a total of 60 m³ of waste per day, and as of 2012 there were 16 composting centers in the city that produced 7,000 tons of composting annually.[64]

Surabaya achieved considerable reductions in the amount of solid waste that was to be disposed of at the final landfill site; every day, 1,241 tons of waste was disposed in 2010 as compared with 1,819 tons of waste in 2005.[65] In other words, the spread of compost activities significantly contributed to a 30 percent reduction in the amount of waste. In 2011 there were 17,000 residences in the city that were using the composting bins at the household level.[66] Local residents learned that waste could be transformed into resources through waste separation at the household level and even produce a profit that provided low-income families with income earning opportunities. Community participation raised residents' awareness of the environmental importance and material benefits of waste separation. This lesson-drawing encouraged them further to separate and collect other valuable items, such as paper, cans, PET bottles, and metals from waste at the community level and implemented "Waste Bank" activities or bank *sampah* to which local residents brought valuable non-organic waste as a "deposit."[67] These activities facilitated household income through sales to businesses. Equally important, Surabaya city officials recognized that the waste management project was not only effective in reducing the amount of waste and improving the hygienic environment, but also in reducing levels of greenhouse gases (GHG), i.e., methane gas, which final disposal sites would produce.[68]

Surabaya's solid waste management strategies were thus quite successful but from the viewpoint of GHG emissions reduction at the up-scaling level, the city's action remained at an experimental stage of climate change countermeasures. In response to the urgent issue of climate change, in 2009 the Indonesian government pledged to cut its GHG emissions by 26 percent or up to 41 percent with international support by 2020 compared to 2009 levels. In 2010, when both the Office for International Environmental Strategies (City of Kitakyushu) and the Kitakyushu Asian Center for Low Carbon Society began to consider the provision of a comprehensive "package" of knowledge, planning, operation, and funding to help transform Asian cities into a low carbon society,[69] a new type of trans-local relations between Kitakyushu and Surabaya emerged under the banner of the so-called "Green Sister City." In November 2012 both cities agreed to become Green Sister Cities, while pledging to work on ongoing joint projects to develop low-carbon and environmentally sustainable societies. The Japanese government launched a Joint Crediting Mechanism (JCM),[70] which would "facilitate diffusion of leading low carbon technologies, products, systems, services, and infrastructure as well as implementation of mitigation actions, and contributing to sustainable development of developing countries,"[71] in August 2013 Japan and Indonesia agreed to develop a range of JCM projects on a large scale. The implementation of the JCM-related mitigation projects is expected to provide crediting opportunities through the JCM for Japan and its partners towards GHG reduction. GHG reduction on a local scale occurs in the areas of local government services, such as energy supply, waste management, water resource, and transport, along with global climate change strategies. As part of the JCM-related project on low-carbon and environmentally sustainable city planning in Surabaya, the City of Kitakyushu and the IGES organized a feasibility study to reduce GHG emissions in major sectors of energy consumption in Surabaya. During a feasibility study conducted in 2013–2014, two domestic stakeholders meetings were held in Kitakyushu and three information-sharing meetings were held in Surabaya between stakeholders in both cities. They produced a final report on low carbon plans for Surabaya in March 2014.[72] Kitakyushu is currently promoting the export of an integrated environmental system through stakeholders' participation from both cities at an earlier stage of master-planning.

This new project is intended to support Surabaya in its endeavor to build a low-carbon city by targeting four designated sectors: energy, solid waste, transportation, and water resources. The IGES and Asian Center for Low Carbon Society have been managing the project in cooperation with Surabaya's Developmental Planning Agency (BAPPEKO). The first task of the project team was expected to identify specific programs or measures which could reduce CO_2 emissions yet to bring about social, economic and environmental benefits in an integrated way.[73] To this end, the project was initially designed to develop a data management system to measure CO_2 emissions reduction in each sector and support the further development of plans with the available data to implement adaptation and mitigation projects. Contracted Japanese companies in charge of each sector conducted project feasibility studies in cooperation with their counterparts in Surabaya. The NTT Data Institute of Management Consultant, Inc., in collaboration with local firms and facilities, assessed energy savings in buildings and the supply of energy to industries. With assistance from the Transportation Section of Surabaya, Almec VPI Corporation examined the potential to improve the operation of public transportation and taxis. In the solid waste sector, three Japanese companies worked with counterparts in Surabaya for the feasibility study: Nishihara Corporation for the separation, recycling, and composting of household waste, Hitachi Zosen for the generation of power from incineration, and Amita for the manufacturing of raw materials for cement from waste from business establishments. Matsuo Sekkei Co. and Kitakyushu's Water and Sewer Bureau investigated energy savings at water and sewage plants. The investigators accordingly presented specific proposals for promoting the JCM to develop concrete measures. The final report states that, if implemented simultaneously, concrete measures in all four sectors could potentially reduce CO_2 emissions by approximately 150,000 t-CO_2/year.[74] Most of the proposed programs and measures will be implemented after the fiscal year of 2015. For those proposals, with a scale of several millions of US dollars, applications will be submitted to the Ministry of the Environment for equipment aid, and to JICA overseas investment and financing with a scale of 100 million US dollars.[75]

Public support for international environmental cooperation

Perhaps the most fundamental condition for the effective implementation of local governments' international environmental cooperation is public support or taxpayers/voters support. Some local authorities, such as Kitakyushu, have become involved in international environmental cooperation and have gone beyond what is mandated under national policy. It is safe to assume that part of this ability to get involved stems from public support. At the local level, community engagement as a part of a broader stakeholder engagement process provides a basis for increasing government accountability. Engaging the wider community in dialogue at an early stage can help local governments communicate the motivations for their international environmental cooperation, including any expected societal benefits and normative commitments, ease concerns about these being no direct benefits to the average taxpayers, and secure public acceptance. Yet civic disengagement from political processes has certainly attracted considerable attention in recent decades. To reverse the trend of civic disengagement, governments are required to strengthen their relations with citizens. These relations cover a wide range of interactions at different stages of agenda setting, policy formation, implementation, and evaluation. The level of interactions can be seen as a one-way relationship of information providers to recipients, through a two-way relationship of consultation, to a two-way partnership between government and citizens. Active participation at the third level is the highest order of public engagement. Surprisingly enough, a survey on climate change and developmental cooperation, conducted by the IGES in 2010, shows that over 50 percent of adults (685 respondents) in Kitakyushu supported the cooperation to help developing countries address environmental problems, "even without direct benefits to the citizens' own city."[76] To account for the surprising level of public support, we need to explore Kitakyushu's historical experience of severe environmental pollution and local residents' initiatives to overcome it, and examine the process of local multi-stakeholders' engagement in Kitakyushu's policy innovation. All in all, efforts to engage the general public in international environmental cooperation take many forms, yet in the policy area of Kitakyushu's international environmental cooperation, "engagement" is a means towards acceptance rather than true participation.

In around 1950, local residents in Tobata City (the present Tobata Ward of Kitakyushu) began to say, "the laundry gets dirty by dust fall." As described previously, the Nakabaru Women's Association in the city did its own field research and prepared credible documentation by conducting a fact-finding series on dust fall, smoke, and offensive odors. In 1951 they submitted a petition to the Tobata City Council. The city administration then served as a crucial mediator between this citizen group and the Nihon Denso Power Plant for the implementation of pollution prevention measures. In 1961 the Sanroku Women's Association in Tobata City began to carry out its own investigation into damages caused by soot from a carbon black manufacturer, Nippon Steel Chemical Co., Ltd. With the findings of their hand-made studies, the women's group turned to the municipal government for help. The mayor, accompanied by the group members, visited the headquarters of the manufacturer in Tokyo and mediated a settlement. During the 1960s, pollution from factories in Kitakyushu was so serious that the sky looked "colored with all seven colors of the rainbow." In 1963 the Kitakyushu municipal government successfully facilitated the conclusion of agreements between the local residents and polluters for the implantation of pollution controls, while creating an advisory body on environmental pollution in 1964 to advise the mayor about pollution countermeasures. This council consisted of city councilors, representatives from the women's associations and other residents' groups, academics, and corporations. In 1963 and 1964 the women's associations invited university professors and scientists to review their methods and activities, and organized factory tours and other field trips, in order to gain first-hand knowledge of the pollution problem. The women's associations launched *Aozora ga hoshii* [We want blue skies] as an in-house magazine that was distributed widely among Kitakyushu households. In 1965 the coordinating committee of the Tobata's women's associations and the Board of Education of Kitakyushu City jointly published a study report on the smoke and soot, also entitled "We want blue skies," which persuasively assessed the association between air pollution and school absenteeism among elementary students. The associations' activities in the 1960s expanded on a large scale, with over 6,000 members in 13 women's associations.[77] These activities conducted by the women's associations played a key role in the environmental movement raising public awareness of environmental pollution among the general public. Probably the single most important outcome of Kitakyushu's early initiatives in industrial pollution is that the socially mobilized citizens' groups did not engage in sustained contentious interactions with the targeted factories as the local government played a key role in neutralizing the pollution prevention inefficiencies, caused by the self-interested parties, and in reducing the transaction costs (i.e., costs of making an acceptable agreement with the other party) of reaching an agreement between the local residents and polluters. The local government relied on moral authority to maintain its influence by imposing social responsibilities on the corporations for pollution yet still sought a way for integrated improvement of the environment and economy.[78] This policy brief provided a basis for Kitakyushu's involvement in international environmental cooperation today.

Policy-oriented learning was instrumental in modifying the policy belief for adapting to the notion of sustainable development, e.g., the Johannesburg Declaration on Sustainable Development in 2002. To change production and consumption patterns, the municipal government determined to create a more sustainable city and the key target towards realizing the challenging determination was now to "take social responsibility by all stakeholders, including not only corporate firms but also citizens."[79] Considering this modified policy belief, citizens in Kitakyushu from various fields submitted over 1,000 ideas to launch a new environmental plan. A discussion forum of local multi-stakeholders led the city to declare the creation of the "World Capital of Sustainable Development" in October 2004, whose activities were designed to build a hub of human resource development in Asia.[80] From April to December 2003, the city called for ideas and opinions from citizens from different fields and sectors to create a new environmental plan for both local coordination with national policy and local adaptations to global environmental strategies. In October and December 2003, hundreds of stakeholders gathered, with representatives of different groups (citizens, government, industry, and academia), and exchanged ideas and opinions at the Multi-stakeholders Forum on the World Capital of Sustainable Development. A drafting committee, the Kitakyushu Committee on the World Capital of Sustainable Development, composed of 34 members from various sectors, was established and the committee, from March to October 2004, held four plenary meetings, 10 workshops, and four drafting meetings.[81] In the final version of this grand plan, three basic objectives were formulated on the basis of building sustainable cities to pass on to the next generation. These objectives are the creation of sharing "symbiosis" among all stakeholders, the pursuance of "green growth" through compatibility of the environment and economy, and the enhancement of the city's sustainability. In response to the grand plan, 250 concrete projects have been established by integrating the city's different policy areas, ranging from those that cover the environment and economy, through the promotion of employment, to international environmental cooperation.[82]

The first normative principle that has priority over other principles in the statement of the World Capital of Sustainable Development lies in the importance of "the power of its residents" for sustainable development in Kitakyushu and beyond.[83] In this context, the Regional Centre of Expertise (RCE) Kitakyushu was established in 2006 while acting under the United Nations (UN) initiative of the Decade of Education for Sustainable Development (UNDESD) 2005–2014. In response to the Johannesburg Plan of Implementation, in 2003 the United Nations University Institute for the Advanced Study of Sustainability (UNU-IAS) launched the RCEs, which were sub-national and trans-sub-national networks of multi-stakeholders on the Education for Sustainable Development (ESD). Japan's Ministry of the Environment funded the ESD projects and the UNU acknowledged RCE Kitakyushu in 2006. The missions of RCE Kitakyushu are to raise public awareness on sustainable development and serve, to this end, as a locus to integrate ESD-related activities in the fields of the environment, the economy, social issues, and international cooperation.[84] The ESD-related activities have put the objectives of the World Capital of Sustainable Development into concrete action by developing networks among societal groups. The Kitakyushu Citizens' Association of Global Warming and the "RISE Kitakyushu" have collaborated to embed the recycling society mentality—not only avoiding waste but re-using it as a resource—through a range of community-based recycling activities. The Kitakyushu for Asia Women Forum (KWAN), which introduced a system of "environmental household budgets" for keeping the record of environmental impact at the household level, has played a critical role as a core member of many ESD-related activities. Since 2010, 10 universities in Kitakyushu, with some financial support from the Ministry of Education, Culture, Sports, Science and Technology, operated the "Kitakyushu Manabito ESD Station" project, in order to strengthen the cooperation between the universities and local communities by providing a hub of ESD-related activities in Kitakyushu. Since the same year, the Kitakyushu ESD Council, consisting of representatives of 51 organizations including universities, community groups, industries, and governmental bodies, has been promoting ESD activities at the community level by using 130 public community centers across the city area.[85]

The 2010 IGES survey indicates that nearly 90 percent of 685 respondents in Kitakyushu "agreed" or "somewhat agreed" when they were asked if the city "should continue international environmental cooperation."[86] The public engagement activities in Kitakyushu seem to help the local residents have a clear understanding of international environmental cooperation. The results of the survey demonstrate a significant correlation between awareness and support: "the more the citizens were aware of, or had knowledge of, the city's international environmental cooperation projects, the more clearly they supported the city's continuous cooperation."[87] Another noteworthy finding is that 40 percent of the respondents would like to see the city's international environmental cooperation being used for the promotion of overseas business operations and employment opportunities in the city.[88] These results carry specific implications for Kitakyushu's further involvement in a new policy-making environment for trans-local relations. Given Kitakyushu's shift from technology transfer to socio-technical export to promote a low-carbon society in developing countries, the municipal government is expected to play a greater coordination role among multi-stakeholders. Given the correlation between public awareness and public support for international environmental cooperation, it is also important for the city to provide a place for continuing ESD activities to raise awareness of the concept of sustainable development. Equally important, both the survey results and Kitakyushu's historical experiences of international cooperation strongly suggest that linking the city's international environmental cooperation with the promotion of local business is a way of gaining the goodwill of the taxpayers/voters. Finally, as done in the past, the municipal government needs to continue acting as an intermediary to connect domestic private firms with local governments in developing countries to secure credible business opportunities.

Determinants of Kitakyushu's involvement in decentralized international cooperation

Despite the fact that its financial capacity index is the second worst among the designated cities and its population is less than one million, Kitakyushu's commitment to international environmental cooperation has been exceptionally strong. Kitakyushu's municipal government has played an indispensable role in providing environmental public goods for global strategies in the area of environmental issues. The case of Kitakyushu approximates neither exclusively state-centric nor exclusively autonomist in its institutional approach to international environmental cooperation. The city has been capable of effectively engaging in international environmental cooperation by using a number of avenues for the cross-fertilization, so to speak, of both institutional frameworks. From a state-centric point of view, Kitakyushu's participation at the international level has largely been an active part of national policy. Kitakyushu has developed its cooperative relationship with the national government to provide environmental management experience at the local level, which was formerly unattended by national ministries. The city has been quite successful in receiving national funds, that is, grants and subsidies, to build its environmental business capacity and carry out various public works projects, including creating a hub of human resource development in Asia. Yet the city's activities have not been simply complementary to already existing national policies by engaging in assistance activities that were nationally defined, but rather it has taken its own initiatives in response to locally specific issues and problems. The national government has often recognized the benefits and importance of Kitakyushu's policy innovations, such as the "Dalian Environmental Model Zone," and adopted them as part of national policy implementation. Over the years, the city has developed a capacity to act as an independent provider of expertise and human capital on environmental management for the successful implementation of national policy. The case of Kitakyushu shows the effect of certain explanatory factors on the development of its international environmental cooperation.

1. Process-tracing observation of Kitakyushu's experience reveals the ultimate independent variable, that is, a desire to promote environmental business, in explaining its international environmental cooperation. The municipal government has taken initiatives to create business opportunities from international environmental cooperation. To this end, Kitakyushu has used its accumulated technologies and human capital to achieve environmental improvement in developing countries. Kitakyushu's distinctive motivation for international environmental business stands out from other localities, although others are more or less materially motivated as well. The municipal government has been making efforts to deliberately utilize its environmental assets and local experience to bring economic benefits to the city, while promoting the norms of international cooperation for its own sake. In other words, Kitakyushu has continuously sought to make the competing goals of material utility and environmental protection compatible. The important point of this balancing act is that when motivated by self-interest to supply a public good, an agent needs to act within the framework of norms for environmental protection.

2. Economic utility-based considerations can embrace ethical ones. City departments' officials in Kitakyushu clearly wish to contribute for reasons other than merely self and utility-based objectives. They wish to show that they take part in environmental initiatives to settle the normative commitment to the North–South division. They feel a responsibility to utilize their accumulated human capital and local experience, especially when they would benefit as much materially as local communities in developing countries were reducing environmental risks. The key challenge of sub-national participation in international environmental cooperation is to ensure incentives for norm compliance so that sub-national participants will be better off participating than not participating.

3. The structural context of opportunities to supply a public good must be translated, by agents' actions, into policy outcomes. In the case of Kitakyushu's international environmental cooperation, mayoral leadership/political entrepreneurship is another crucial ingredient in the city's ability to initiate and promote international environmental business. In general, mayors in Japan have little formal authority and limited resources that are adequate to engage in the sub-national level of participation in international environmental cooperation. This obstacle was skillfully overcome by Mayor Sueyoshi, a

former national bureaucrat of the Construction Ministry, who had a "direct pipeline to the center." He was able to acquire a high degree of bargaining leverage with national ministries and thus derive significant financial resources from Kitakyushu's cooperative relationship with the national government. In the cooperative pattern of relationships between central and local authorities, national ministries were responsive to Kitakyushu's demands for the successful implementation of national policy and tolerated a measure of local flexibility in promoting international environmental business to meet locally specific needs. As the general public supported the mayor's initiatives, the depoliticization of municipal decision-making was epitomized in the course of events regarding the activities of environmental business development.

4   The structural opportunities for Kitakyushu to take initiatives for international environmental cooperation existed at the national and international levels. In the 1990s, local authorities were internationally recognized as key players in global strategies at the 1992 Earth Summit, the 1996 Habitat Agenda, and the 2000 Millennium Summit. The international agenda for localizing foreign aid was set to spread decentralized international cooperation activities at the 2005 Paris Declaration on Aid Effectiveness and the 2008 Accra Forum on Aid Effectiveness. In response to this global trend, the Japanese government introduced a new aid policy (the 1992 ODA Charter), which clearly shifted its focus to environmental and humanitarian aid. In the late 1990s, the government began to promote grassroots-level aid that would involve local authorities in international cooperation programs. In 2013, the MOE started "JCM model projects" that would facilitate the implementation of projects, which were managed by private companies under the JCM carbon crediting mechanism. The first bilateral document on the JCM was signed between Japan and Indonesia in August 2013. Kitakyushu's companies have got involved in JCM model projects from the beginning. Given a range of the opportunity structures, Kitakyushu effectively interpreted and adapted it to local needs. Not all equally capable local governments did transform the opportunities into fruitful policy innovations. Any incongruities among equally capable actors are likely to come from their motivations and purposes.

5   The focus of local government participation in international environmental cooperation has been on a voluntary basis. The biggest challenge local governments face in maintaining and strengthening their involvement in these activities is to ensure accountability to taxpayers/voters. Public acceptance is a necessary condition. Over the past three decades, Kitakyushu has worked hard to rebrand itself as a center for environmental technology transfer to Asia. Linking international environmental cooperation with overseas business development has been a way of rendering Kitakyushu's participation more accountable to local residents. The potential economic benefits enable the municipal government to take part in the credibility of the entire plan of international environmental cooperation activities. Equally

important, there is a significant correlation between awareness and public acceptance. Indeed, the majority of Kitakyushu's taxpayers/voters seem to support activities in developing countries, even without direct benefits to them. The surprising level of public support is closely associated with public engagement activities in Kitakyushu, which helped the local residents gain a clear understanding of international environmental cooperation. From the viewpoint of GHG emissions reduction, the city needs to consider the fact that a significant portion of socially mobilized citizens believe the city should make additional efforts to reduce GHG emissions in developing countries without expecting economic benefits or without doing so for carbon offsetting.

Conclusion

The answer to the question of why Kitakyushu is by far the most active among Japan's local governments boils down to the city's willingness and capability to contribute to the policy-making process of international environmental cooperation without the supervision of the national government. However, mayoral leadership never explicitly challenged or bypassed the hierarchy of territorial jurisdictions, but produced policy innovations in the area of environmental business that would become an active part of national policy. Kitakyushu's environmental policy and programs shaped their form not only in response to collective needs, but also through the dynamic process of mayoral leadership in which agents purposively steered the municipal polity. The real life experience of Kitakyushu was based on the connections between hierarchized tiers and de-hierarchized new spheres of authority. The municipal government, as part of the state apparatus, had close access to national ministries and then national aid provided the tools Kitakyushu's policy initiatives for international environmental cooperation needed to become financially secure. While the territorial state of Japan had difficulty in providing an integrated set of solutions for the spillover effects of environmental programs through unbundling the functions of environmental protection to different governance levels and spheres, Kitakyushu experienced new spheres where its activities were confined neither to a fixed scale nor to a rigid hierarchy of scales. Kitakyushu's environmental collaboration with developing countries was the result of an adaptive process between state and non-state actors and its function was cross-scale. The translocal process facilitated the two-way response of Kitakyushu's activities to both globalizing and localizing needs. Kitakyushu was an intersecting actor in multiple spheres of authority spanning many jurisdictions for coordinated action.

The advocacy coalition framework (ACF) can be applied as a useful analytical framework to understand the incorporation of sub-national actors into nationwide networks and examine the influence of those groups in a larger interinstitutional setting. The ACF assumes a policy-making environment that includes multiple actors and multiple levels of government. However, as compared with policy areas that are a dominantly national undertaking, such as nuclear energy policy in Japan, the policy areas of local autonomy, such as pollution control, can be organized by particular local governments. In Japan, policy innovations for pollution control and management initially occurred at the local level and then were emulated by the national government. The Kitakyushu Method is a case in point. The municipal government skillfully coordinated its collaborative achievements in restoring the environment and its preventive environmental efforts between citizens' groups and the business sector. The policy-making environment of Kitakyushu, which was encouraged by local experience and constrained largely by locally specific conditions, did not become contentious in meeting demands from stakeholders with different interests. The city successfully avoided a hard political choice between development and environment by simultaneously seeking both goals in a rather conciliatory way.

From the early 1950s to the mid-1980s in Japan, actors in the process of political coalition-building treated environmental protection as a local or national public good whose benefits extended to all the members of a community situated within the nation or all the citizens of the nation. Those benefits of environmental protection corresponded to national borders rendering the nature of local and national public goods territorial. As stakeholders in environmental protection had different priorities and preferences, the question of how to share the burden of financing them became highly politicized. The municipal government played a strategic role in bringing social cohesion to both the division between economy and environment and that between the business sector and social groups at the local level. In the 1990s, Kitakyushu policy elites clearly recognized that environmental degradation was spreading beyond national borders and could have a regional/global range. At the national level, policy-makers had to face two primary sources of constraints on environmental policy-making: domestic constituencies' demand and division over the cost-sharing for environmental risk reduction and international pressures to contribute regional/international environmental benefits (global public goods). Environmental politics became a locus where national policy-makers had to choose how to reconcile international and domestic concerns. The interplay between these two concerns can be viewed as mutually constitutive and thus less cohesive in managing the state of environmental problems. This decision-making arrangement provided an opportunity for mayoral leadership in Kitakyushu to demonstrate how to realistically reduce environmental risks by reconnecting local action with national mandates and turning global strategies into local action. Furthermore, an Asian intercity platform for low carbon society encompasses the possibility that Kitakyushu at the local level will take actions that shape climate change governance at other levels (convergence).

One of the most interesting findings of Kitakyushu's experience is that a one-sided mechanism of policy diffusion, which had initially operated through technology transfer to developing countries, was transformed into a locus for mutual learning for both Southern and Northern partners. Policy learning can be conceptualized as a horizontal mechanism of diffusion (voluntary act) while being constrained by hierarchical tiers of authority (coercion). Kitakyushu's participation and coordination at multi-levels and spheres of authority helped a variety of stakeholders on both the South and North sides come to better understand alternative knowledge production and thus produce a more coherent transfer of ideas and practice. Within both the distribution of national decision-making competencies to sub-national levels and the scope of national decision-making authorities to accept or reject international agreements, stakeholders in the trans-local relations between Kitakyushu and its partners in developing countries established a specific communication network that shaped the diffusion patterns of policy ideas and led to the adaptation and coordination of policy approaches. Kitakyushu's experience indicated learning through problem-solving or through trial and error while sharing information and expertise. Policy ideas and instrumental tools were transferred through regular meetings, the dispatch of experts, and site visits for investigation. The successful implementation of Kitakyushu's international environmental cooperation largely depended on joint problem-solving between practitioners from both sides at ground level or street level. It provided an opportunity for Kitakyushu to learn the addition of knowledge, the improvement of instrumental skills, and the acknowledgment of cultural values through adaptation processes in the Southern partners. New experiences and new ways of dealing with environmental problems formed the source of transformative learning that led local communities in developing countries to reconsider their existing way of living and change their policy beliefs.

The coalition of Dalian and Kitakyushu Cities also provided local residents with a participatory locus. As a non-profit organization, the KITA proposed the initial idea of a Dalian Environmental Model Zone project; the inter-municipal coalition effectively identified Japan's ODA funds as a means of achieving the project. The locally initiated ODA project, while implemented through inter-municipal networks, encouraged broad-based community participation. The successful fundraising gained popular support through processes of participation, although a wider range of people's association began at the implementation stage of the project. With a view to systematically transfer the environmental management and technology accumulated in Kitakyushu to Dalian, the team of citizens, professionals, researchers, and government officials worked on a set of environmental targets to last beyond the year 2010. It had not only transferred the basic expertise and technology, but also produced a wide range of locally specific and practical environmental measures to the Model Zone project. The Dalian-Kitakyushu inter-municipal network was a place where such a team was able to maintain a long-term commitment rather than seek a skimming strategy to produce short-term project outcomes that the national government would require every fiscal year.

Notes

1 John H. Boyle, *Modern Japan: The American Nexus* (Fort Worth, TX: Harcourt Brace & Company, 1993), p. 132; Akira Irie, "Japan's drive to great-power status," in Jansen Marius, ed., *The Cambridge History of Japan*, Vol. 5 (Cambridge, UK: Cambridge University Press, 1989), p. 767.
2 Chalmers Johnson, *MITI and the Japanese Miracle* (Stanford, CA: Stanford University Press, 1982), p. 111; William W. Lockwood, *The Economic Development of Japan*

(Princeton, NJ: Princeton University Press, 1968), p. 24. For the detailed development, see Yawata Seitetsusho, ed., *Yawata Seitetsusho 50-nen Shi* [Fifty-years history of the Yawata Iron and Steel Works] (Tokyo: Yawata Seitetsusho, 1950).
3 Sydney Crawcour, "Industrialization and technological change, 1885–1920," in Peter Duus, ed., *The Cambridge History of Japan*, Vol. 6 (Cambridge, UK: Cambridge University Press, 1988), p. 430; Johnson, *MITI and the Japanese Miracle*, pp. 86–87; Lockwood, *The Economic Development of Japan*, pp. 109, 508.
4 William Horsley and Roger Buckley, *Nippon: New Superpower* (London: BBC Books, 1990), pp. 51–2; Johnson, *MITI and the Japanese Miracle*, p. 200; Haruhiro Fukui, "Economic planning in postwar Japan: a case study in policy making," *Asian Survey*, Vol. 12, No. 4 (1972), pp. 333–6.
5 Johnson, *MITI and the Japanese Miracle*, pp. 207, 268–71; Hideki Yamawaki, "The steel industry," in Ryūtarō Komiya, Masahiro Okuno, and Kōtarō Suzumura, eds., *Industrial Policy of Japan* (Tokyo: Academic Press, 1988), pp. 281–305.
6 Figures from Japan Iron and Steel Federation, *Monthly Report of the Iron and Steel Statistics*, various issues.
7 Ryūtarō Komiya and Motoshige Itoh, "Japan's international trade and trade policy, 1955–1984," in Takashi Inoguchi and Daniel Okimoto, eds., *The Political Economy of Japan*, Vol. 2 (Stanford, CA: Stanford University Press, 1988), p. 197.
8 *International Economic Report of the President* (Washington, DC: GPO, March 1975), p. 137.
9 See City of Kitakyushu, Kitakyushu Kōgai Taisakushi Bukai [Kitakyushu Pollution Countermeasure Section], ed., *Kitakyushu kōgai taisakushi* [Kitakyushu history of pollution control measures] (Kitakyushu: City of Kitakyushu, 1998).
10 City of Kitakyushu, Bureau of the Environment, *Kitakyushushi no kankyō kokusai kyōryoku* [International Environmental Cooperation by Kitakyushu City] (Kitakyushu: Kitakyushu City, 1997), p. 3.
11 City of Kitakyushu, Bureau of the Environment, *Kitakyushushi no kankyō kokusai kyōryoku*, p. 3.
12 Johnson, *MITI and the Japanese Miracle*, pp. 76, 277–83; Yamawaki, "The steel industry," pp. 299–302.
13 Metropolitan Environmental Improvement Program (MEIP), "Japan's experience in urban environmental management: Kitakyushu," April 1996, Washington, DC: MEIP, World Bank, p. 62.
14 Figures provided by Environmental Cooperation Center, Kitakyushu International Techno-cooperation Association (KITA/ECC).
15 City of Kitakyushu, Bureau of the Environment, *Kitakyushushi no kankyō kokusai kyōryoku*, p. 5.
16 City of Kitakyushu, Kitakyushu Kōgai Taisakushi Bukai, ed., *Kitakyushu kōgai taisakushi*, pp. 177, 217.
17 See, for example, *People's Daily*, September 7, 1971.
18 *Beijing Review*, June 27, 1972 (Statement of Chinese spokesperson at the Conference in Stockholm).
19 *Beijing Review*, June 27, 1972 (Statement of Chinese spokesperson at the Conference in Stockholm).
20 Terry Cannon, "Introduction: the economic reforms, demographic processes and environmental problems," in Terry Cannon, ed., *China's Economic Growth* (London: Macmillan, 2000), pp. 4–11.
21 City of Kitakyushu, Kitakyushu Kōgai Taisakushi Bukai, ed., *Kitakyushu kōgai taisakushi*, p. 177.
22 Vaclav Smil, "Environmental problems in China: estimates of economic costs," *East-West Center Special Reports* No. 5 (1996), pp. 1–62; Eduard B. Vermeer, "Industrial pollution in China and remedial policies," *China Quarterly*, No. 156 (December 1998), pp. 986–1016.

23 *Asahi Shinbun*, March 3, 1991. Between December 1990 and January 1991, at 1,000 sites across Japan, the Citizen Bank and Eco Research Office in Tokyo led a campaign to measure quantities of acid rain. Hundreds of citizens' and consumers' groups and schools participated. They found that three-quarters of the sites were affected by acid rain.
24 See, for example, Japan, Environment Agency (Acid Rain Countermeasure Committee), *Final Report of the Third Acid Rain Investigation, 1993–1997*, cited in *Sankei Shinbun*, March 20, 1999; Hiroyuki Ishi, *Sanseiu* [Acid rain] (Tokyo: Iwanami Shoten, 1992), pp. 204–6; O. Nagafuchi, R. Suda, H. Mukai, M. Koga, and Y. Kodama, "Analysis of long-range transported acid aerosol in rime found at Kyūshū mountainous regions, Japan," *Water, Air, and Soil Science*, Vol. 85, No. 4 (1995), pp. 2351–6.
25 The KITA was established in 1980 as a non-profit organization under the joint auspices of the Kitakyushu Junior Camber, the Kitakyushu Chamber of Commerce and Industry, and the Western Japan Industry Club, in collaboration with Kitakyushu municipal government and Fukuoka prefectural government. Its mission was to contribute to the promotion of international cooperation at the grassroots level by providing training opportunities for technology transfer, research and development, and the updating of training materials.
26 City of Kitakyushu, Kitakyushu Kōgai Taisakushi Bukai, ed., *Kitakyushu kōgai taisakushi*, p. 177.
27 This section is based on Kitakyushu Kōgai Taisakushi Bukai, ed., *Kitakyushu kōgai taisakushi*, pp. 177–81 and 217–18; Kitakyushu International Techno-cooperation Association (KITA), *KITA nijyū-nen shi* [Twenty-year history of KITA] (Kitakyushu: KITA, 2001), pp. 230–7.
28 Azuma Kido, International Information Section Chief of KITA Environmental Cooperation Center, Interview by author, June 27, 2000 and Akiko Teraishi, International Information Section Manager of KITA Environmental Cooperation Center, Interview by author, June 28, 2000.
29 City of Kitakyushu, Kitakyushu Kōgai Taisakushi Bukai, ed., *Kitakyushu kōgai taisakushi*, pp. 178–80; 217–18.
30 Materials adopted from a KITA's internal report, KITA, "KITA's performed projects and financial report in FY 1998."
31 KITA, "KITA's performed projects and financial report in FY 1998."
32 KITA, "KITA's performed projects and financial report in FY 1998."
33 Interview by author with Mitsuyo Nakatsu, KITA, Kitakyushu, March 16, 2011.
34 See, for example, Zhaowen Tu, "Kan-nihonkai-ken e no teigen" [Proposals for the Japan sea rim sphere] *Sekai* [World] No. 549 (1991), pp. 164–5.
35 Hiroshi Mizoguchi, "Jyūkōgyō toshi to kankyō" [Industrial city and the environment], in NEAR Intellectual Infrastructure Committee, ed., *Bodaresu jidai no chiikikan kōryu* [Regional cooperation in a borderless age] (Tokyo: Aruku, 1999), pp. 146–7.
36 Organisation for Economic Co-operation and Development (OECD), *The State of the Environment, 1985* (Washington, DC: OECD Publications and Information Center, 1985), p. 29.
37 Kōichi Sueyoshi, *Kitakyushu ekotaun: zero emisshon no chōsen* [Kitakyushu eco-town: challenges to zero emission] (Tokyo: Kaizōsha, 2002).
38 Azuma Kido, Interview by author, June 27, 2000; Nozomi Hakozaki, Department of International Environmental Strategies, Kitakyushu, Interview by author, March 16, 2011.
39 Sueyoshi, *Kitakyushu ekotaun: zero emisshon no chosen*.
40 Sueyoshi, *Kitakyushu ekotaun: zero emisshon no chosen*.
41 Shingo Takasugi, *Kitakyushu Ekotaun o mi ni yuku* [Investigating the Eco-Town project] (Tokyo: Daiyamondo sha, 1999), p. 141.
42 Takasugi, *Kitakyushu Ekotaun o mi ni yuku*, pp. 142–3; Jun'ichi Kawasaki, "Kitakyushu

Ekotaun jigyō no tanjō made no ayumi" [Processes for the birth of Kitakyushu's Eco-Town], *Kyushu Kokusai Daigaku Keiei Keizai Ronshū* [Kyushu International University Business and Economics Review], Vol. 18, No. 3 (2012), p. 44.
43 Takasugi, *Kitakyushu Ekotaun o mi ni yuku*, p. 143.
44 Global Environment Centre (GEC), "Eco-Towns in Japan: implications and lessons for developing countries and cities," June 2005, p. 37.
45 Japan, Ministry of the Environment, "Kitakyushu-shi moderu jigyō" [Kitakyushu city model project], 2012, available at: www.env.go.jp/recycle/ecotown/ [accessed June 2, 2015].
46 For the details of Kitakyushu Eco-Town, see, GEC, "Eco-Towns in Japan," pp. 29–41.
47 City of Kitakyushu, "Technical cooperation through distance learning system," 2009, available at: www.hilife.or.jp/kankyoushuto_zenkokuforum/pdf/kitakyuushuu.pdf [accessed August 30, 2012].
48 City of Kitakyushu, "Action plan of Kitakyushu Eco-Model City," 2009, available at: www.city.kitakyushu.lg.jp/files/000025616.pdf [accessed August 30, 2012].
49 City of Kitakyushu, Environmental Management Division, Environment Bureau, *Semarang Conference on Sustainable Development: Urban Environmental Management in Times of Crisis and the Advancement of the Cooperation Network among Cities in the Asian Region* (Kitakyushu: City of Kitakyushu, 1998), p. 2.
50 City of Kitakyushu, Environmental Management Division, Environment Bureau, *Semarang Conference on Sustainable Development*, p. 8.
51 Mushtaq Ahmed Memon, "Public participation for urban environmental management: overview and analysis," The 5th Thematic Seminar: Kitakyushu Initiative Seminar on Public Participation for Urban Environmental Management, Institute for Global Environmental Strategies (IGES), 2004, pp. 10–11.
52 Memon, "Public participation for urban environmental management," p. 11.
53 Cited in Isao Naruse, "Hooked on water: City of Kitakyushu offers technical support for waterworks in Asia," *Highlighting Japan* (February 2014), p. 8.
54 City of Kitakyushu, International Policy Division, "International water cooperation," *Kitakyushu Bridges*, No. 38 (2012), p. 3.
55 City of Kitakyushu, International Policy Division, "International water cooperation," p. 2; Naruse, "Hooked on water," p. 9.
56 Masashi Yayama, "Upward biological contact filtration (U-BCF) in Vietnam," in Nobutaka Nakamoto, Nigel Graham, Robin Collins, and Rolf Gimbel, eds., *Slow Sand and Alternative Biofiltration Process: Further Developments and Applications* (London: IWA Publishing, 2014), pp. 508–14.
57 Material provided by Consulate General of Vietnam in Fukuoka, Japan on October 9, 2015.
58 *The Voice of Vietnam* (online newspaper) "Vietnam applies clean water technology from Japan," May 17, 2013, available at: http://english.vov.vn/Society/Vietnam-applies-clean-water-technology-from-Japan/260415.vov [accessed March 1, 2015].
59 See, for example, Kitakyushu Asian Center for Low Carbon Society, "Kitakyushu model initiative to export the 'Concept of Green Cities'," 2015, available at: http://asiangreencamp.net/eng/active3.html [accessed March 1, 2015] and Reiji Hitsumoto, Executive Director for International Environmental Strategies Office, "A green urban economy in Kitakyushu: the integral role of the private sector," City of Kitakyushu, 2012, pp. 17–24.
60 The "Kitakyushu Model," which the Kitakyushu Asian Center for Low Carbon Society announced in September 2013, is designed for green city development by organizing development know-how based on its experience in such an integrated way.
61 The Memorandum of Understanding for Green Sister Cities that the cities of Kitakyushu and Surabaya (Indonesia) signed in November 2012 is based on the principle of such mutuality.
62 Kitakyushu International Techno-cooperation Association (KITA), "Separation at

238 *Kitakyushu's environmental business*

source, collection and composting of waste in Surabaya, Indonesia: promoting the reduction and recycling of waste," FY 2007 Environmental Restoration and Conservation Agency Report, March 2007, p. 1.

63 KITA, "Separation at source, collection and composting of waste in Surabaya, Indonesia," p. 2.
64 D.G.J. Premakumara, "Kitakyushu City's international cooperation for organic waste management in Surabaya, Indonesia and its replication in Asia cities," Kitakyushu Urban Centre, IGES, March 2012, p. 5.
65 Premakumara, "Kitakyushu City's international cooperation for organic waste management in Surabaya, Indonesia and its replication in Asia cities," p. 5.
66 Premakumara, "Kitakyushu City's international cooperation for organic waste management in Surabaya, Indonesia and its replication in Asia cities," p. 5.
67 KITA, "Separation at source, collection and composting of waste in Surabaya, Indonesia," p. 38.
68 KITA, "Separation at source, collection and composting of waste in Surabaya, Indonesia," p. 4.
69 Hitsumoto, "A green urban economy in Kitakyushu," p. 22.
70 The JCM is a carbon crediting mechanism through which Japanese companies can earn carbon credits by investing in technology to cut greenhouse gas emissions in developing countries.
71 Ministry Economy, Trade and Industry (METI), "Recent development of the Joint Crediting Mechanism (JCM)," August 2014, available at: www.meti.go.jp/policy/energy_environment/global_warming/pdf/201409_JCM_ENG.pdf [accessed June 30, 2015].
72 Institute for Global Environmental Strategies (IGES), "FY2013 feasibility studies on Joint Crediting Mechanism projects towards environmentally sustainable cities in Asia: final report on technical assistance for designing a Low Carbon City plan in Surabaya, Indonesia," IGES, March 2014.
73 IGES, "FY2013 feasibility studies on Joint Crediting Mechanism projects towards environmentally sustainable cities in Asia."
74 IGES, "FY2013 feasibility studies on Joint Crediting Mechanism projects towards environmentally sustainable cities in Asia," p. ii.
75 IGES, "FY2013 feasibility studies on Joint Crediting Mechanism projects towards environmentally sustainable cities in Asia," p. iii.
76 Hidenori Nakamura and Mark Elder, "Practical measures to promote Japanese local governments' environmental collaboration with developing countries with citizens' support," *IGES Policy Brief*, No. 18 (2012), p. 18.
77 In this section, the description of the women's associations is based on City of Kitakyushu, Kitakyushu Kōgai Taisakushi Bukai, *Kitakyushu kōgai taisakushi*.
78 Azuma Kido, Interview by author, June 27, 2000 and Akiko Teraishi, Interview by author, June 28, 2000.
79 Hiroshi Mizoguchi, "Towards 'The World Capital of Sustainable Development' with a miracle of Kitakyushu's experience," Roundtable Paper, Asia Europe Environment Forum, Shenzhen, China, November 28–30, 2007, p. 83.
80 Mizoguchi, "Towards 'The World Capital of Sustainable Development' with a miracle of Kitakyushu's experience," pp. 83–4.
81 Hitsumoto, "A green urban economy in Kitakyushu," p. 8.
82 Mizoguchi, "Towards 'The World Capital of Sustainable Development' with a miracle of Kitakyushu's experience," p. 84.
83 City of Kitakyushu "Commitment of the residents of Kitakyushu to all people, the earth and future generations: towards the creation of a 'World Capital of Sustainable Development'," City of Kitakyushu, 2014, p. 4.
84 Kitakyushu ESD Council, "Regional Centres of Expertise on education for sustainable development," available at: http://archive.ias.unu.edu/resource_centre/RCE Kitakyushu.pdf [accessed June 30, 2015].

85 The description of RCE Kitakyushu is based on Masashi Suga, "RCE Kitakyushu: variety of ESD programs by local communities," available at: http://archive.ias.unu.edu/resource_centre/RCE%20Kitakyushu_full_paper.pdf [accessed June 30, 2015].
86 Nakamura and Elder, "Practical measures to promote Japanese local governments' environmental collaboration with developing countries with citizens' support," p. 5.
87 Nakamura and Elder, "Practical measures to promote Japanese local governments' environmental collaboration with developing countries with citizens' support," p. 5.
88 Nakamura and Elder, "Practical measures to promote Japanese local governments' environmental collaboration with developing countries with citizens' support," p. 5.

Bibliography

Beijing Review (1972). June 27, 1972 (Statement of Chinese spokesperson at the Conference in Stockholm).
Boyle, John H. (1993). *Modern Japan: The American Nexus*. Fort Worth, TX: Harcourt Brace & Company.
Cannon, Terry (2000). "Introduction: the economic reforms, demographic processes and environmental problems." In Terry Cannon, ed., *China's Economic Growth*. London: Macmillan, pp. 1–29.
City of Kitakyushu (2009). "Action plan of Kitakyushu Eco-Model City." Available from: www.city.kitakyushu.lg.jp/files/000025616.pdf [accessed August 30, 2012].
City of Kitakyushu (2009). "Technical cooperation through distance learning system." Available from: www.hilife.or.jp/kankyoushuto_zenkokuforum/pdf/kitakyuushuu.pdf [accessed August 30, 2012].
City of Kitakyushu (2014). "Commitment of the residents of Kitakyushu to all people, the earth and future generations: towards the creation of a 'World Capital of Sustainable Development'." Kitakyushu: City of Kitakyushu.
City of Kitakyushu, Bureau of the Environment (1997). *Kitakyushushi no kankyō kokusai kyōryoku* [International Environmental Cooperation by Kitakyushu City]. Kitakyushu: City of Kitakyushu.
City of Kitakyushu, Bureau of the Environment (Environmental Management Division) (1998). *Semarang Conference on Sustainable Development: Urban Environmental Management in Times of Crisis and the Advancement of the Cooperation Network among Cities in the Asian Region*. Kitakyushu: City of Kitakyushu.
City of Kitakyushu, International Policy Division (2012). "International water cooperation." *Kitakyushu Bridges*, No. 38, pp. 2–3.
City of Kitakyushu, Kitakyushu Kōgai Taisakushi Bukai [Kitakyushu Pollution Countermeasure Section], ed. (1998). *Kitakyushu kōgai taisakushi* [Kitakyushu history of pollution control measures]. Kitakyushu: City of Kitakyushu.
Crawcour, Sydney (1988). "Industrialization and technological change, 1885–1920." In Peter Duus, ed., *The Cambridge History of Japan*, Vol. 6. Cambridge: Cambridge University Press, pp. 385–450.
Fukui, Haruhiro (1972). "Economic planning in postwar Japan: a case study in policy making." *Asian Survey*, Vol. 12, No. 4, pp. 333–6.
Global Environment Centre (GEC) (2005). "Eco-Towns in Japan: implications and lessons for developing countries and cities." June 2005.
Hitsumoto, Reiji, Executive Director for International Environmental Strategies Office (2012). "A Green Urban Economy in Kitakyushu: the integral role of the private sector." City of Kitakyushu.

Horsley, William and Roger Buckley (1990). *Nippon: New Superpower*. London: BBC Books.
Institute for Global Environmental Strategies (IGES) (2014). "FY2013 feasibility studies on Joint Crediting Mechanism projects towards environmentally sustainable cities in Asia: final report on technical assistance for designing a Low Carbon City plan in Surabaya, Indonesia." IGES, March 2014.
International Economic Report of the President (1975). Washington, DC: GPO, March 1975.
Irie, Akira (1989). "Japan's drive to great-power status." In Jansen Marius, ed., *The Cambridge History of Japan*, Vol. 5. Cambridge, UK: Cambridge University Press.
Ishi, Hiroyuki (1992). *Sanseiu* [Acid rain]. Tokyo: Iwanami Shoten.
Japan, Environment Agency (Acid Rain Countermeasure Committee-ARCC) (1999). *Final Report of the Third Acid Rain Investigation, 1993–1997*. Tokyo: ARCC.
Japan, Ministry of Economy, Trade and Industry (METI) (2014). "Recent development of the Joint Crediting Mechanism (JCM)." August 2014. Available from: www.meti.go.jp/policy/energy_environment/global_warming/pdf/201409_JCM_ENG.pdf [accessed June 30, 2015].
Japan, Ministry of Foreign Affairs (1999). *Waga kuni no seifu kaihatsu enjo—ODA hakusho* [Japanese overseas development assistance—ODA white paper], Vol. 1. Tokyo: Kokusaikyōryoku Suishinkyōkai.
Japan, Ministry of the Environment (MOE) (2012). "Kitakyushu-shi moderu jigyō" [Kitakyushu city model project]. Available from: www.env.go.jp/recycle/ecotown/ [accessed June 2, 2015].
Johnson, Chalmers (1982). *MITI and the Japanese Miracle*. Stanford, CA: Stanford University Press.
Kawasaki, Jun'ichi (2012). "Kitakyushu Ekotaun jigyō no tanjō made no ayumi" [Processes for the birth of Kitakyushu's Eco-Town]. *Kyushu Kokusai Daigaku Keiei Keizai Ronshū* [Kyushu International University Business and Economics Review], Vol. 18, No. 3, pp. 39–48.
Kitakyushu Asian Center for Low Carbon Society (2015). "Kitakyushu model initiative to export the 'Concept of Green Cities'." Available from: http://asiangreencamp.net/eng/active3.html [accessed March 1, 2015].
Kitakyushu ESD Council (2015). "Regional Centres of Expertise on education for sustainable development." Available from: http://archive.ias.unu.edu/resource_centre/RCE Kitakyushu.pdf [accessed June 30, 2015].
Kitakyushu International Techno-cooperation Association (KITA) (1999). *KITA kankyō kyōryoku sentā jigō gaiyō* [KITA's performed projects and financial report in FY 1998]. Kitakyushu: KITA, 1999.
Kitakyushu International Techno-cooperation Association (KITA) (2001). *KITA nijyūnen shi* [Twenty-year history of KITA]. Kitakyushu: KITA, 2001.
Kitakyushu International Techno-cooperation Association (KITA) (2007). "Separation at source, collection and composting of waste in Surabaya, Indonesia: promoting the reduction and recycling of waste." FY 2007 Environmental Restoration and Conservation Agency Report, March 2007.
Komiya, Ryūtarō and Motoshige Itoh (1988). "Japan's international trade and trade policy, 1955–1984." In Takashi Inoguchi and Daniel Okimoto, eds., *The Political Economy of Japan*, Vol. 2. Stanford, CA: Stanford University Press, pp. 173–224.
Lockwood, William W. (1968). *The Economic Development of Japan*. Princeton, NJ: Princeton University Press.
Memon, Mushtaq Ahmed (2004). "Public participation for urban environmental

management: overview and analysis." The 5th Thematic Seminar: Kitakyushu Initiative Seminar on Public Participation for Urban Environmental Management, Institute for Global Environmental Strategies (IGES).
Metropolitan Environmental Improvement Program (MEIP) (1996). "Japan's experience in urban environmental management: Kitakyushu." April 1996. Washington, DC: MEIP, World Bank.
Mizoguchi, Hiroshi (1999). "Jyūkōgyō toshi to kankyō" [Industrial city and the environment] in NEAR Intellectual Infrastructure Committee, ed., *Bodaresu jidai no chiikikan kōryu* [Regional cooperation in a borderless age]. Tokyo: Aruku, pp. 140–51.
Mizoguchi, Hiroshi (2007). "Towards 'The World Capital of Sustainable Development' with a miracle of Kitakyushu's experience." Roundtable Paper, Asia Europe Environment Forum, Shenzhen, China, November 28–30, 2007.
Nagafuchi, O., R. Suda, H. Mukai, M. Koga, and Y. Kodama (1995). "Analysis of long-range transported acid aerosol in rime found at Kyūshū mountainous regions, Japan." *Water, Air, and Soil Science*, Vol. 85, No. 4, pp. 2351–6.
Nakamura, Hidenori and Mark Elder (2012). "Practical measures to promote Japanese local governments' environmental collaboration with developing countries with citizens' support." *IGES Policy Brief*, No. 18, pp. 1–12.
Naruse, Isao (2014). "Hooked on water: City of Kitakyushu offers technical support for waterworks in Asia," *Highlighting Japan*, February, pp. 8–9.
Organisation for Economic Co-operation and Development (OECD) (1985). *The State of the Environment, 1985*. Washington, DC: OECD Publications and Information Center.
Premakumara, D.G.J. (2012). "Kitakyushu City's international cooperation for organic waste management in Surabaya, Indonesia and its replication in Asia cities." Kitakyushu Urban Centre, IGES, March 2012.
Smil, Vaclav (1996). "Environmental problems in China: estimates of economic costs." *East-West Center Special Reports*, No. 5, pp. 1–62.
Sueyoshi, Kōichi (2002). *Kitakyushu ekotaun: zero emisshon no chōsen* [Kitakyushu eco-town: challenges to zero emission]. Tokyo: Kaizōsha.
Suga, Masashi (2015). "RCE Kitakyushu: variety of ESD programs by local communities." Available from: http://archive.ias.unu.edu/resource_centre/RCE%20Kitakyushu_full_paper.pdf [accessed June 30, 2015].
Takasugi, Shingo (1999). *Kitakyushu Ekotaun o mi ni yuku* [Investigating the Eco-Town project]. Tokyo: Daiyamondo sha.
The Voice of Vietnam (online newspaper) (2013). "Vietnam applies clean water technology from Japan." May 17, 2013. Available from: http://english.vov.vn/Society/Vietnam-applies-clean-water-technology-from-Japan/260415.vov [accessed March 1, 2015].
Tu, Zhaowen (1991). "Kan-nihonkai-ken e no teigen" [Proposals for the Japan sea rim sphere]. *Sekai* [World], No. 549, pp. 154–68.
Vermeer, Eduard B. (1998). "Industrial pollution in China and remedial policies." *China Quarterly*, No. 156, pp. 986–1016.
Yamawaki, Hideki (1988). "The steel industry." In Ryūtarō Komiya, Masahiro Okuno, and Kōtarō Suzumura, eds., *Industrial Policy of Japan*. Tokyo: Academic Press, pp. 281–305.
Yawata, Seitetsusho, ed. (1950). *Yawata seitetsusho 50-nen shi* [Fifty-year history of the Yawata Iron and Steel Works]. Tokyo: Yawata Seitetsusho.
Yayama, Masashi (2014). "Upward biological contact filtration (U-BCF) in Vietnam." In Nobutaka Nakamoto, Nigel Graham, Robin Collins, and Rolf Gimbel, eds., *Progress in Slow Sand and Alternative Biofiltration Process: Further Developments and Applications*. London: IWA Publishing, pp. 508–14.

7 Yokohama's normative commitment
Image and reputation

The city of Yokohama has been renowned as the hub of *kaikoku* (open-door policy) since 1858, when Tokugawa Japan opened the port of Yokohama to foreign trade and permitted foreigners to live there. As Table 7.1 demonstrates, Yokohama's commitment to *kokusai kōken* (contribution to the international community), which had been translated into policies and practices, has manifested itself in a variety of texts and speeches. This chapter will examine the ways in which norms may outweigh immediate utility, more specifically those ways in which Yokohama's reputation as an international city provided a foundation for shaping a collective self-understanding of normative commitment to international environmental cooperation. Among the largest Japanese ports (in terms of the value of foreign trade), both Yokohama and Nagoya are well known for their high fiscal capacity and staff resources, on the part of the city governments, yet the latter has conducted a minimal level of international environmental cooperation. The localized motives for Yokohama to take up an active role in decentralized international cooperation deserve a closer examination. This study finds that no matter who occupied the mayor's office, Yokohama's historical legacy and international orientation motivated it to respond to needs for development assistance and environmental cooperation. According to a nationwide survey, conducted in 2012 by the Brand Research Institute, Yokohama is ranked first in the nation as the most "internationalized" city. Yet, as local conditions and needs change, the patterns and nature of decentralized international cooperation will also be transformed, accordingly, to meet them. This can be seen in Yokohama's new strategy to promote international cooperation for the benefit of local business.

Local governments in Japan, like those in other OECD countries, remain small contributors to international environmental cooperation but they can be a significant part of environmental strategies at the global level by sharing their know-how and local experience with partner countries. Previous studies indicate, "Only the largest municipalities extend any significant amounts of aid."[1] More specifically, the scale of international environmental cooperation and their fiscal capacity have significant positive correlations with each other.[2] Indeed, Yokohama is one of the wealthiest municipalities in Japan. In 2008 and 2009, the city did not receive the Local Allocation Tax (national transfer payments to local

Table 7.1 Yokohama's historical legacy and international orientation

1858	US–Japan Treaty of Amity and Commerce
1858	Yokohama's port for foreign trade and its area for foreigners' residence (established)
1868	Meiji Restoration
1870s	Yokohama as the first landing site of Western influence
1923	Great Kantō Earthquake
1920s	Reconstruction of Yokohama as "an international trading city"
1945	Great Yokohama Air Raid (at the end of World War II)
1945	Yokohama as a supply base for US Occupation in Japan (until 1952)
1950s	Rapid recovery of foreign trade along with the expansion of the Port of Yokohama
1960s	Port of Yokohama as a supply base of imported natural resources for the Keihin Industrial Zone
1963	Ichio Asukata as Yokohama's mayor (1963–1978) (elected)
1964	Pollution Control Agreement between the city and a thermal power plant (concluded for the first time in Japan)
1983	Official launch of the Minato Mirai 21 (Port city of the future 21)
1986	Yokohama as the host city of the International Tropical Timber Organization headquarters (until the present)
1992	Yokohama as Secretariat of CITYNET (until 2013)
1996	Yokohama as the host city of the Food and Agriculture Organization (until the present)
2015	Minato Mirai 2050 Project Action Plan ("smartest future environmental city in the world, the centerpiece of global attention")

governments), whereby revenues are set aside as a shared resource among local authorities to be reallocated to each authority. The more affluent a city becomes, the less the municipal government receives the national transfer payments. The Local Allocation Tax is designed to ensure a similar level of government services and investment across the nation. In the fiscal years of 2008 and 2009, only 3 percent of the total number of local governments did not receive this tax. According to Yokohama City's 2013 budget, Local Allocation Tax as a percentage of total revenues was 1.4 percent and its financial strength index (total value of basic financial revenue/basic financial demand value) was 0.96, which was the fourth highest among all the 20 designated cities.[3] Given the average financial strength index of 0.49 for municipalities and that of 0.85 for designated cities, Yokohama financially occupies a preferable position to engage in international cooperation at its discretion, as fiscal capacity is one of the necessary conditions for decentralized international cooperation. As discussed previously, both Yokohama and Nagoya are well known as being two of the big three ports in terms of value of foreign trade and also as among the wealthiest governments among designated cities, yet Nagoya, with physical and socio-economic environments similar to Yokohama, has been weakly responsive to national policy and global strategies and cooperated only minimally. The following section will look beneath the structural factors to find more qualitative evidence of localized motives for Yokohama's involvement in decentralized international cooperation.

Foreign pressure on the future of a small fishing village

Yokohama was a sleepy fishing village of 101 households in 1853 when a fleet of four American warships ("black ships") under the command of Commodore Matthew Perry arrived at Uraga, which lay to the immediate south of Yokohama. The use of gunboat diplomacy threatened the Tokugawa Shogunate into ending Japan's 200-year-old policy of isolation (*sakoku*) and opening Japanese ports to United States (US) trade. Fear and fascination was the Tokugawa leaders' reaction on encountering Western technology. While looking to the US for advanced technology, the 1854 conclusion of the US–Japan Peace and Amity Treaty or the Kanagawa Treaty, named after the location where it was concluded, between the two sides ended Japan's policy of national seclusion. This treaty opened the ports of Hakodate and Shimoda to American ships to supply food, water, and coal, and for trade. The Kanagawa Treaty was followed by the 1858 US–Japan Treaty of Amity and Commerce, which formally established trade and diplomatic relationships between the two nations. This agreement initially designated Kanagawa, just north of Yokohama, as Japan's first treaty port for foreign trade (Article 3). However, Kanagawa was strategically an important traffic point of the Tōkaidō or one of the 53 stations of this road, connecting Edo to Kyoto and its location was too close to the de facto capital of Edo. Instead, the Tokugawa Shogunate ordered the establishment of the port at Yokohama. The Kanagawa River formed a natural barrier to foreigners in accessing the Tōkaidō. Probably none of the Shogunate advisors at that time would have imagined that, a century later, Yokohama would become the second largest city in Japan.[4]

Once opened, entry was also quickly sought by other Western powers, such as the Russians, the British and the French, with similar treaty demands. These treaties were unequal treaties, in which local officials gave extra-territorial rights to foreigners in Japan. A state of fear about the Tokugawa leaders' failure to deal with foreign pressure had spread across the nation and the issue of *jōi* (the principle of excluding foreigners) arose.[5] Yet Yokohama became renowned as the hub of the open-door policy (*kaikoku*) from 1858, when Tokugawa Japan permitted foreigners to live in a designated area. Westerners, while restricted from travelling outside of the settlement, began to reside in the designated foreigners' residence area (*kyoryūchi*), located in what is now Yamashita-cho (district). A moat surrounded this area, which was also called "inside the barrier" (*kannai*). The foreigners' settlement was a soft wet area of low-lying land, infested by mosquitoes and beset by foul smells.[6] As Western traders built their business buildings there, their residences moved to an inland section, the present Honcho area. The newly arrived Chinese merchants took over the less inhabitable areas for their housing and small businesses.[7] They provided daily necessities, such as Western clothing and hairdressing, for Westerners in Yokohama. Native villagers in Yokohama began to resettle in the present Motomachi, which was located between the low-lying commercial district and the inland residential district, and the Shogunate's compensation for their resettlement spurred entrepreneurs to do business with foreigners.

In 1866 the Shogun's advisors had to face the burden of growing pressure from within Japan and failed to deal with opposition from a military alliance of two clans, Chōshū (present Yamaguchi prefecture) and Satsuma (present Kagoshima prefecture). After the declaration of the imperial alliance to revive the emperor's authority, the Tokugawa regime ended in 1868. In 1867 mass movements with the slogan of *ējanaika* ("who cares?") abruptly started spreading across various regions in Japan, although they were not coordinated with any clear political platform. Common folk joined in these dancing festivals to express their millennial fears.[8] This phenomenon coincided with the end of Japanese feudalism. The Meiji government of modern Japan started in 1868 abolishing the divided feudal domains and becoming the sole national center by establishing a uniform state administration. The Meiji Restoration of 1868 (when the Meiji emperor was restored as the head of Japan) brought rapid change to the port of Yokohama. Western merchants, who had businesses already established in Shanghai and Hong Kong, were drawn to new business opportunities in Japan's first treaty port for foreign trade. Mitsui and other large Japanese trading houses also opened shop at the port of Yokohama. The port was initially developed for trading silk with foreign trading partners. As its infrastructure was built, Yokohama grew rapidly, becoming the first landing site of Western influences and a place for communication between the Japanese and foreigners.[9] The growth of the Yokohama boomtown was marked by the arrival of Western technology, including Japan's first telegraph lines between Yokohama and Tokyo (1869), Japan's first beer breweries (1869), Japan's first daily newspaper, the *Yokohama Mainichi Shinbun* (1870), Japan's first gas-powered street lamps (1872), and Japan's first railway, between Yokohama and Shimbashi in Tokyo (1872). In 1889 the city of Yokohama was established through the amalgamation of Kanagawa and Yokohama, which together accounted for 25,849 households. Rich Western merchants built exotic mansions and family-owned business combines (*zaibatsu*), such as Mitsubishi and Mitsui, prospered in cooperation with the Meiji government. Yokohama also became known for its international flair.

The foreign settlements ceased to exist in 1899 as a result of new treaties between Japan and the Western powers. Yet, an influx of foreigners and foreign culture and goods and an outflow of Japanese ones continued through the port of Yokohama. The early twentieth century brought a rapid growth in heavy industries to the port of Yokohama. Around 1915 Asano Sōichirō (the founder of the Asano *zaibatsu*) and other entrepreneurs built new factories on reclaimed land between Kawasaki and Kanagawa. This area grew to be the Keihin Industrial Zone, one of the four largest industrial districts in Japan. On September 1, 1923 the Great Kantō Earthquake destroyed about 80 percent of the total area of housing and 21,384 people died and 1,951 others went missing within the city boundaries.[10] In the aftermath of the disaster, the city officials tenaciously called for help from the national government by emphasizing the necessary reconstruction of Yokohama as a pivot to Japan's international connections and the necessity of foreign residents' protection on which Japan's international reputation would rest.[11] In the midst of emergency relief efforts, Mayor Katsusaburō

Watanabe of Yokohama (1922–1925) stated his firm commitment to the reconstruction of Yokohama as "an international trading city" and as "the gate way to the nation's capital (*teito no genkan*)."[12] Such a statement implied not only the city's physical reconstruction, but also the reconstruction of the city's pride. In the absence of sufficient financial support from the national government, the city officials chose to invest in the repair and expansion of the Port of Yokohama as a priority infrastructure project. The issuance of municipal bonds became an important mechanism for financing the reconstruction of the port.[13] As Yokohama's taxpayers continued to cover a significant part of the project financing into the 1930s, Chūichi Ariyoshi (1925–1931), who succeeded Watanabe as mayor of Yokohama in May 1925, praised local residents' efforts to restore the city's pride and normal functionality in the post-disaster reconstruction.[14]

Yokohama's strategic location for the Allied Occupation of Japan

The reconstructed infrastructure would be destroyed again but this time by a man-made disaster. Nearly a half of the city area was reduced to ashes by US air raids during World War II. The Great Yokohama Air Raid, occurring in a single morning, May 29, 1945, started the wave of firebombing that killed 3,650 people (and wounded an estimated 10,000 people) and reduced 34 percent of the city area to rubble.[15] On August 30, 1945, General Douglas MacArthur landed at Atsugi Air Base near Yokohama to head the Allied Occupation in Japan and drove himself to Yokohama. He provisionally set up his headquarters for the Occupation Supreme Commander of the Allied Powers (SCAP) in Yokohama (at the New Grand Hotel – Yokohama and the Yokohama Customs House), although the official headquarters later moved to the Dai-Ichi Insurance Building in the Marunouchi district of Tokyo. Yokohama served as the host to a large US military presence. It was from Yokohama that the SCAP confiscated 70 percent of the requisitioned land area (1,600 hectares) and 61 percent of the requisitioned buildings in Japan (outside of Okinawa). In particular, 90 percent of port facilities were laid under requisition and the Port of Yokohama functioned as a supply base which supported the US military operation during the Allied Occupation of 1945–1952. The outbreak of the Korean War of 1950–1953 set Yokohama's role as a key transshipment base for America's strategic needs.[16] Yokohama suddenly found itself in the international spotlight of the emerging Cold War.

When the Allied Occupation ended in 1952, US Navy facilities moved to an American base in Yokosuka, 25 km south of Yokohama. The Harbor Law, which was enacted in 1950, transferred the authority of port management from the national government to local authorities. In 1951 Yokohama city became the port management authority. In the same year, the Yokohama International Port City Construction Law was passed in the Nation Diet and, under the implementation of this law, Yokohama was designated to improve the port infrastructure and develop a waterfront area rapid transit system under a national aid program. The San Francisco Peace Treaty took effect in April 1952 and Japan became independent again. By 1952 Ōsanbashi Pier was released from requisition and returned to Yokohama and the port was reopened. Yokohama's recovery got underway during the period of the Korean War special procurement boom. The rapid recovery of foreign trade brought along with it the expansion of the Port of Yokohama. Heavy industries were re-established along the Keihin Industrial Zone. As the reclamation work of Daikoku-chō (80 hectares) was completed in 1961, Tokyo Electric Power, Nittō Chemical Industry, Asia Oil, Taiyō Fishery, and others moved onto this land to set up their facilities. The reclamation of the first section of Negishi Bay (364 hectares) was also completed in 1963 and Nippon Oil, Tokyo Gas, Toshiba, Ishikawajima-Harima Heavy Industries, and 155 other companies located their facilities in the new land.[17] With advanced shipping and railway facilities, the Port of Yokohama, which handled imports of natural resources for the Keihin Industrial Zone and exporting goods, again became a major point of international trade for Japan. During the 1960s, Yokohama's population grew rapidly and by 1980 the city had become the second largest in Japan.

Yokohama as the leading innovator in environmental policy

In the spring of 1947, the head of the State Department's Policy Planning, George Kennan urged that the US Occupation policy for Japan follow American communist containment policy. This was the point where the US government began to promote Japan's foreign trade, and provided loans and credits for recovery aid. In August 1951 the Yokohama Reconstruction Council was created to launch a derequisitioning movement demanding the early return of the requisitioned land. At the council, Mayor Ryōzō Hiranuma of Yokohama (1951–1959) brought together the worlds of politics, bureaucracy, and business at the local level through a common bond to revive Yokohama as an international port city. In February 1952 the council presented a Petition for the Problem Processing of the Requisitioned Land in Post-Peace Treaty to the Cabinet, the lower house and each political party. They requested that the national government pay 80 percent of the actual costs (*futankin*), which was a kind of specific national grant, for reconstruction activities performing as the execution of land readjustment projects. Eight months later, the national government responded that 100 percent of the expenses for *kannani* (83 hectares) would be borne in full by the national government and 50 percent of those for other areas (156 hectares) would be borne by the national government.[18] As Ōsanbashi Pier, located in the center of old Yokohama's waterfront, was released from US requisition and the Korean War affected shipping recovery by Japanese shipping companies, such as Nippon Yusen (NYK Line), Yokohama's recovery gained momentum.

The 1963 election of socialist leader Ichio Asukata as mayor of Yokohama (1963–1978) was probably the most important event for Yokohama's policy innovations for environmental protection. He launched the slogan of "direct democracy" (*chokusetsu minshushugi*) by implementing the practice of "Ten

Thousand Citizens' Meeting" (*ichiman ni'n shūkai*) to seek direct exchanges of views between the mayor and local residents.[19] Asukata's progressive innovations encompassed the policy areas of urban planning and environmental protection. In February 1965 Asukata announced a grand conception, "Yokohama's City Planning—Yokohama's Future Made by Its Citizens," and the city's urban planning entered a new phase when policy innovations were achieved to meet local geographical and social conditions. The Pollution Countermeasure Agreement (PCA), signed by the Yokohama city government and a thermal power plant in 1964, was the first in Japan and later became the most important precedent for environmental protection at the local level. The city further drafted an agreement with several firms that planned to set up their facilities on Yokohama's reclaimed land. The city required stricter pollution prevention measures beyond the nationally defined level as well as compensation for damage that might be caused in the future. According to the Tiebout migration, taxpayers may exercise choice by moving to a locality where service levels are closer to their needs.[20] In other words, firms might choose a less regulated locality rather than Yokohama. However, the business utility of the reclaimed land's location appeared to outweigh the appeal of any other location in Japan and thus did not prevent the incoming firms from concluding the agreement. The Port of Yokohama provided direct access to a full range of imported raw materials across the reclaimed land and it was linked to a transport system for the efficient movement of goods. The location was very close to Tokyo's consumption market as well as to national government offices in the Kasumigaseki section of Tokyo for informal communication and lobbying.

In May 1964, the Economic Planning Agency (a national agency) issued a permit to the state-owned Electric Power Development Co., Ltd (EPDC), established and controlled by the Ministry of International Trade and Industry (MITI), to construct a 265-megawatt coal-fired thermal power plant in Yokohama area. Local residents in Naka and Isogo Wards of Yokohama learned about the Tokyo Electric Power Company's (TEPCO's) plan to sell a part of its reclaimed land to EPDC in order to construct the power plant and thus established in June 1964 the Environmental Health and Preservation Committee calling for the environmental impact to be properly assessed before construction. In response to this demand by citizens, Yokohama City formally requested an advisory opinion addressed to the mayor by a group of four academics. On July 15, this group suggested the necessity of "a review of the city's siting plan of energy intensive industries" and "making changes in the siting of the coal-fired thermal power plant." In addition, a Pollution Section with seven full-time professional staff was established within the city's Department of Public Health in April 1964 and conducted a smoke diffusion test and simulation, in order to assess the environmental impact of the coal-fired thermal power plant.[21] As a result, Mayor Asukata was able to scientifically predict that the siting would cause serious air pollution.[22] The mayor firmly believed that the city must prevent the EPDC from buying the land from the TEPCO if the EPDC did not guarantee that sound pollution control measures would always be met.

Under these circumstances, the mayor structurally held a strategic position between the national government and local residents in terms of his ability to initiate the first PAC in Japan. As he was getting familiar with both the MITI through the operation of big business in Yokohama and the local citizens' groups through the implementation of direct exchanges of views with them, he was ready to find feasible policy compromises. Asukata did not seek the status quo of the policy environment but he was a revisionist policy broker. He pushed his innovative ideas while creating demand for the proposed solution. In this sense, Mayor Asukata became a policy advocate rather than a broker. The reclaimed land that the TEPCO tried to transfer to the EPDC was originally built and owned by the City of Yokohama. When the city sold it to the TEPCO, the reclaimed land was transferred subject to the condition that the TEPCO would not sell the land to third parties without the city's consent. While not having sufficient legal authority to force the firms to take effective pollution control measures, Mayor Asukata innovatively made use of the contractual obligation to persuade the EPDC to sign the PCA.[23] As the MITI was the ultimate decision-maker for the fate of the EPDC, the mayor approached the MITI, to request help in budgeting funds for the EPDC to take the pollution control measures proposed in the PAC. The process of Yokohama's negotiations with the MITI coincided with a landmark event in Mishima-Numazu (Shizuoka prefecture). The national plan for a petrochemical complex in this area, drawn up by the MITI, was forced to cancel due to the opposition of local residents.[24] MITI officials were shocked and found themselves confronted by the difficulty of building a plant against the opposition of the host community. The request of Yokohama municipal government was taken very seriously by the national government and the mayor was able to negotiate the agreement on an equal footing with the state-owned EPDC. The process of PAC negotiations took form in a more contentious way. In this sense, the theory of apolitical governance cannot fully account for the conclusion of the PAC without introducing the political feasibility of problem-solving to meet local residents' demands. This story can be seen as a political learning in which the socialist mayor manipulated the policy process and also involved adaptation, while engaging in sustained contentious interactions with the EPDC, which was under the control of the MITI.

Minato Mirai 21 (Port city of the future 21)—from ideas to implementation

The core of the Minato Mirai 21 (MM21) project is to reinvent Yokohama's waterfront area as an "international cultural center" and provide a "human environment surrounded by water, greenery and history."[25] MM21 occupies 188 hectares of waterfront land, 77 hectares of which are built on landfill. An area of 88 hectares is used for private-built investments and the remaining 100 hectares is designated for public facilities. In 1963, when Asukata was elected as mayor of Yokohama, "five insurmountable challenges" (*gojyūku*) on a grand scale (i.e., the Great Kantō Earthquake, the Japanese part of the Great Depression, the Great

Yokohama Air Raid, postwar requisition by US forces, and urban sprawl) had brought accumulated local experience and human capital to the city's administration. By request of the mayor, who sought to stop disorderly development in Yokohama, Akira Tamura from a consulting firm proposed six major projects in 1964. The history of MM21 can be traced back to one of these major projects: this project, "Yokohama City Center Plan Concept Proposal," was designed to reinvent and strengthen the city center for Yokohama to regain its reputation as an international port city. At that time, large shipbuilding docks and port facilities were located in the central part of Yokohama and the project targeted the Mitsubishi Dockyards, the National Railways freight station, and the Takashima rail yard for relocation. A large part of the present MM21 land was originally owned by Mitsubishi Heavy Industries and the Yokohama shipyard of Mitsubishi Heavy Industries had been operated under high operating conditions. Tamura and his team felt uncertain about how successfully the city could negotiate with Mitsubishi Heavy Industries for their relocation but they considered it key to planning the future of Yokohama.[26]

In 1967 negotiations began between the city and Mitsubishi Heavy Industries. As the city's development was about to enter the post-industrial phase, Yokohama required the consolidation of its urban structure. To participate in redevelopment, the private sector suffered from the uncertainty of changing land use control while the city and the Mitsubishi Heavy Industries carried out the negotiations. In 1976 they reached a basic agreement on the relocation the Mitsubishi Heavy Industries. Once interested private parties had a clear prospect for land use conversion and the public burden of infrastructure, the relocation of heavy industries' port and railroad yards to deep-water port facilities began in the late 1970s. The relocation was completed in 1983. From 1967 to 1983, the MM21 planning converted a solution into a step-by-step process in which the municipal government acted as an intermediary agent in reconnecting consumption-oriented community needs with production-oriented business needs.[27] The public sector was to construct and readjust infrastructure for investment incentives and the private sector was to invest in business and housing developments. Shifting away from Fordism (an industrial, mass-production, mass-consumption economy), the MM21 area was imagined as a human habitat for information sharing and communication in which housing services, commercial activities, and cultural spaces were treated as primary. Local history and experience was carefully incorporated into the idea of MM21. The municipal government was pragmatically competent enough to deal with policy problems in big business networks but also motivated by the locally specific needs of redevelopment and sustainability. The Investigatory Committee for the Redevelopment Planning of Yokohama City Center and Waterfront Area, which was established in 1978, announced its basic vision for the redevelopment of the area.[28] This vision was intended to integrate the two areas of the old *kannai* city center and the growing transport hub at Yokohama Station into a new city center. The city established the Minato Mirai 21 Corporation in 1984 and delegated the coordination role to this third party.

In April 1978, Mayor Michikazu Saigō (1978–1990) of Yokohama, a former national bureaucrat in the Home Affairs Ministry, took over Asukata's major projects. Asukata had often engaged in contentious interactions with the national government, but the new mayor had access to national ministries and the party in power, which provided a useful venue for major projects to be materialized. Shortly after taking office, Mayor Saigō successfully obtained a national permit of reclamation work for the landfill of 77 hectares in MM21 and the groundbreaking ceremony took place in December 1983. The seeds sowed in the Asukata era began to sprout. As Asukata returned to national politics in 1978, Tamura, the team leader for Yokohama's city planning, who had developed an inter-departmental Planning Office with young technocrats for project design and implementation, also resigned. The new mayoral leadership initially kept a distance from the legacy of the planning office yet as residents' and commercial organizations in the old *kannai* rallied in support of the contributions, made by the planning office, the Asukata-Tamura ideas were largely inherited and reinvented in Yokohama's post-industrial era.[29] The political legitimacy that derived from popular implicit consent given to the municipal government was an important source for the local administration to keep a consistent orientation in city planning. Environmental clean-up was the primary motivation for the land use conversion of the inner harbor area in MM21. It was characteristic of the MM21 design that administrative coordination permitted a great emphasis on environmental norms and cultural values as well as economic-utility through market mechanisms.

The municipal government, the closest agency responsible for meeting the weight of popular pressure and opinion, had a multi-task jurisdiction that allowed for a complex way of balancing environmental protection and economic utility. The city departments (especially the Urban Development Bureau) not only learned the physical side of technical knowledge but also were motivated by their concerns for the relevance of local expertise and their desire for international recognition. The awareness of being an environmentally friendly city was clearly observed among the city officials who had worked to introduce environmental challenges into local agenda. The MM21 project relocated polluting and energy-intensive plants from the central part of Yokohama, and cleaned up the underutilized brownfield sites of the former railway yard and contaminated sites. The MM21 redevelopment introduced public green spaces for parks and trees on the new waterfront; a quarter of the project area was allocated to these green spaces.[30] Since the 1983 official launch of MM21, energy efficiency had been a key concern in the project. The primary measures in reducing the energy included improved new building designs as well as heating and cooling technologies, although city officials were hardly aware in the early 1980s of climate change challenges to mitigation and adaptation.[31] It is important to note that some researchers point out Yokohama's failure to balance environmental protection and economic utility.[32] In their view, MM21 depended too much on major investors to move forward with the project work and it was more common to have situations where environmental protection was not a primary option. In

1988 the Basic Agreement on Town Development was signed between the land owners, including the municipal government, in the MM21 area, in order to maximize returns on their investments. They argue that these stakeholders occupied a strategic position in controlling the process of decision-making over city planning and design. Therefore, the formation and implementation of the MM21 project tended to be biased towards immediate utility. Environmental and social concerns might easily be undermined by the utility-based objectives of the corporate sector.

In 1990 Hidenobu Takahide, a former national bureaucrat of the Construction Ministry, was first elected as mayor of Yokohama, serving three four-year terms (1990–2002). As he took office, the Japanese economic bubble burst. The economic downturn dramatically slowed the pace of planned land use in the MM21 project while forcing some provisional land use adjustments to cope with the project delay.[33] Many constructions remained unfinished and demand for office space continued to decline.[34] Since private investments became less available to the MM21 project, the resultant delay appeared to suggest a project failure in the economic utility sense. Ironically enough, the delay in competitive investments provided the municipal government with an opportunity to avoid a potential corporate bias and consider economic calculations within the context of environmental norms, especially in relation to climate change mitigation and adaptation.[35] The city's Urban Development Bureau began to introduce and implement new concepts to the MM21 project. These concepts and challenges to city planning included a "smart city," "sustainable building," and a "smart grid," to which the original MM21 was adapted and reinvented for the public benefit. As part of sustainable building initiatives, the buildings in the MM21 area had been certified by the comprehensive assessment system for built environment (CASBEE), which was an environmental performance rating tool developed in 2001 under the guidance of Japan's Ministry of Land, Infrastructure and Transport.[36] In April 2010, the Yokohama Smart City Project (YSCP) was designated as a Next Generation Energy Infrastructure and Social System Demonstration Area by the Ministry of Economy, Trade and Industry (METI). Its annual budget was approximately $3.7 billion for the five years between 2010 and 2014. The municipal government has worked with private firms, such as, Toshiba, Nissan Motor, Panasonic, Meidensha, TEPCO, Tokyo Gas, and others to collaboratively carry out the introduction of energy management systems: renewable energy, CEMS (community energy management system), HEMS (home energy management system), BEMS (building energy management system), and new transportation systems.[37] This large-scale operational experiment is being undertaken in the targeted areas, especially the MM21 area. The findings and lessons drawn from this experiment will be utilized for Yokohama's long-term goals: greenhouse gas (GHG) emissions reduction per person by 60 percent from the 2004 level by 2050 and 10 percent renewable energy in primary energy supply by 2020. Another ambitious goal is to export the know-how overseas as a city-scale infrastructure package. The Minato Mirai

2050 Project Action Plan was launched in March 2015 to transform the MM21 district into the "smartest future environmental city in the world, the centrepiece of global attention."[38]

CITYNET: a regional network of local authorities for South–South cooperation

The city of Yokohama not only provided financial incentives to persuade corporate firms in the Tokyo metropolitan area to set up their offices and facilities in the MM21 area, they also invited international organizations and their specialized agencies to locate their offices in the MM21. In 1982 the city hosted the First Regional Congress of Local Authorities for the Development of Human Settlements in Asia and the Pacific and promoted the creation of inter-city exchange network activities to meet the challenges of rapid urbanization. In 1983 when the MM21 project was officially launched, the municipal government planned to build international conference facilities in the MM21 district, aiming to increase Yokohama's visibility as a dynamic international city. In 1987 the Second Regional Congress of Local Authorities for the Development of Human Settlements in Asia and the Pacific created a Regional Network of Local Authorities for the Management of Human Settlements (CITYNET) to strengthen cities' capacity to solve major environmental and social problems through "networking" between cities in the Asia Pacific and "bring together local governments, civil society, and the private sector to collectively act for more sustainable cities."[39] From 1987 to 1992, the United Nations Economic and Social Commission for Asia and the Pacific (UNESCAP) served as the Executing Agency and functioned as a secretariat of the regional network. Being a primary promoter, Yokohama won the new Secretariat's position in 1992. Between 1992 and 2013, Yokohama was home to the Secretariat of CITYNET, replacing the Secretariat functions of the UNESCAP. At the beginning of network activities, Yokohama was the only member city from among developed countries, and played an intermediary role in facilitating South–South cooperation among local authorities and communities.[40]

In the same period of time, the International Tropical Timber Organization (ITTO) was created under the auspices of the United Nations amidst growing concern about the environmental degradation of tropical forests. City officials in Yokohama made a strong appeal to member states to locate the ITTO headquarters in Yokohama. The city pledged to bear some of the operation costs of the headquarters and cover the cost of hosting the sessions of the International Tropical Timber Council, which was composed of all the member states. In 1986 Yokohama successfully won the bid to host the ITTO. A city official recalled Yokohama's inspiration for the bid, "This was an ideal that was very much in line with the city's vision, which was to be not only a hub of business and economic activity but also a contributor to the global environment."[41] This was the direct motivation for Yokohama in hosting the ITTO headquarters. Despite the considerable burden on the city's finances, Mayor Takahide emphasized Yokohama's reputation with its environmental contribution. Indeed, he stated, "The more important the ITTO becomes, the higher evaluation of the city's contribution will be."[42] Hosting CITYNET and the ITTO enhanced Yokohama's reputation and attracted the offices of other international organizations in the 1990s, such as the World Food Program (WFP) since 1996, the Food and Agriculture Organization (FAO) since 1997, and the United Nations University Institute of Advanced Studies (UNU-IAS) since 2004. City officials have learned about the fruits of a commitment to *kokusai kōken*; more than 160,000 visitors have attended international conferences held in the MM21. One of the city officials accordingly assessed the impact by saying, "This showcases our city around the world and gives pride to our citizens."[43]

When Yokohama became the new Secretariat of CITYNET, there were already other inter-city networks in the Asia Pacific, such as the International Union of Local Authorities Asia-Pacific (IULA-ASPAC). Yet CITYNET members continue to express their support for operating the CITYNET network, as they believe that the network is adapting to regionally specific needs while focusing on providing South–South cooperation support to the diverse membership of CITYNET.[44] CITYNET has two main categories of membership: full member and associate member. Full members are local authorities in the Asia Pacific while associate members represent local authorities outside of the region, as well as non-governmental organizations (NGOs), universities and research institutes, corporate firms, and national associations of local authorities. At its inception in 1987, CITYNET had only 26 members. Today (as of November 2015), full members number 85 and associate members number 45 in the Asia-Pacific and Europe.[45] CITYNET is a member-driven network in which local authorities work together to strengthen their capacity for solving major urban problems, such as water supply, sewage, climate adaptation and mitigation, public health, disaster management, and others. The founding members of CITYNET were primarily from South Asia and over time local governments and organizations from Southeast Asia joined CITYNET. The CITYNET network is occupied largely by low-income urban communities, with an annual GDP per capita of under US$2,400.[46]

As part of the process of CITYNET networking, local authorities are expected to serve as facilitators in bringing together urban stakeholders for information sharing and expertise exchanges. Few resources were available for CITYNET to share for South–South cooperation; most of its cooperation funding derived from the budgets of the low-income member cities. The subsidy of the Yokohama city government (and the Seoul Metropolitan government since 2013) has covered more than half of the total revenue of CITYNET.[47] To meet project-based needs, CITYNET has also engaged in fundraising activities through cooperation with donors and partners. Japanese donors, such as Japan International Cooperation Agency (JICA) and Japan's Council of Local Authorities for International Relations (CLAIR), continue to support CITYNET activities through Yokohama project offices. Given the limited resources available to the Secretariat of CITYNET, decentralization has been a key strategy in its own organizational functioning. In 2003 the Secretariat adopted a "cluster" approach, grouping member cities with similar needs relating to the environment, infrastructure, Millennium Development Goals, disaster management, and information communication technology.[48] This cluster initiative gave momentum to the trend of decentralization strategies. The groupings of CITYNET members began to develop their own projects, and to fund and coordinate their own activities, in order to meet their cluster's needs. They undertook cluster activities to develop their action plans and find partners.

Along with the adoption of cluster methods, the Secretariat simultaneously launched a new city-to-city concept called, the Memorandum of Cooperation (MOC).[49] The office promoted among member cities a MOC to clarify the objectives, methods, and expected outcomes of city-to-city cooperation. The MOC was expected to be instrumental in implementing a cost-effective project and providing a reliable avenue for Overseas Development Assistance (ODA) from developed countries. In 2004 CITYNET began to explore opportunities for ODA funding from the Japanese national government, leveraging the accountability and cost effectiveness that the MOCs could increase.[50] Under the grassroots cooperation scheme funded by the JICA, CITYNET implemented the Awareness in Environmental Education (AWAREE) project in Hanoi and Phnom Penh (2004–2007). CITYNET later launched the Post-AWAREE Project as a follow-up to raise awareness among local government officials and citizens about climate change mitigation and adaptation in Colombo, Dhaka, Da Nang (Vietnam), and Makati (Philippines) from 2007 to 2010. In these projects, the involvement of JICA gave member cities a state-level avenue for cooperation with their own national governments. As these national governments tackled issues including those propelled by CITYNET, the International Policy Office of Yokohama city became convinced that the national-local links were successful and beneficial to CITYNET member cities.[51]

Since its establishment in 2003, the cluster system had been transformed to meet the challenges of preparing, on a local scale, for globalized environmental issues. In 2010 the environment cluster, including water and sanitation (WATSAN) and solid waste management (SWM), was consolidated into the climate change cluster. At the same time, the Yokohama's YSCP, which had been designated by the METI, was launched to reduce CO_2 emissions. In October 2012, as part of the YSCP projects, CITYNET invited representatives from its member cities to Yokohama, with the financial support of the CLAIR. The invited cities, such as Bangkok, Colombo, Danang, Dhaka South, and Jakarta, participated in workshops and site-visits and got hands-on experience with Yokohama's approaches to combating climate change. Some might consider this invitation as one-way learning on the part of the Southern partners, but the participants reported the importance of interaction with regard to mutual practitioner-to-practitioner learning in addressing similar challenges, such as energy shortages, solid waste management, and disaster resilience, to combat climate change.[52] Yokohama's officials at the Secretariat often found themselves in an intermediary role in sharing/exchanging knowledge and expertise among and between local authorities and communities on the part of the Southern partners.[53]

One of the recently completed projects is the first phase of the Community Based Adaptation and Resilience Against Disasters (CBARAD) project, which is conducted by the CITYNET Yokohama Project Office (CYO) and the city of Yokohama, and funded by the JICA.[54] The CBARAD project began in August 2012 and the first phase of the project reached completion in March 2015. This is a pilot project in which Iloilo City in the Philippines was selected as this area had continually suffered flood damage due to its geographical conditions. The ultimate objective of this project is for the achievements of community-based adaptation and resiliency activities against floods to be replicated in other cities in the Philippines as well as abroad. Five flood-prone *barangays* (districts), that is, Balabago, Buntatala, Calubihan, Dungon A, and San Isidro, in Iloilo City were targeted for the first phase of the project. The Japanese government provided the project funds through the JICA to construct river flood ways and broaden the rivers, in order to mitigate floods. During the course of the project, to build the capacity of the communities on disaster risk reduction, the City of Yokohama made a range of "soft-side" contributions—from technical training sessions and site visits/field activities in Japan, through workshops on participatory risk assessment (based on hazard maps, historical timelines, and others) in Iloilo City, to several Yokohama Technical Advisory Visits to Iloilo City. Local citizens' groups, such as Tsurumi River Networking—TRnet and Plus Arts, in Japan have also been primary drivers in introducing community-based activities for disaster risk reduction to Iloilo communities. On the part of the designated districts, the municipal government of Iloilo has held several stakeholders' meetings and workshops for information sharing regarding the project's activities and helped to form a multi-stakeholder partnership among the concerned groups, such as the City Disaster Risk Management (DRRM) Office, West Visayas State University, the Bureau of Fire Protection, the national Office of Civil Defense (OCD), Philippine National Police, United Architects of the Philippines, and others. The participants have drafted action plans outlining the core activities of the project, while sharing their experience on disaster prevention in Japan and adapting the prevention measures to locally specific conditions. There are a total of 45 volunteer groups in the five districts, which are coordinated by the Barangay Disaster Risk Reduction and Management Committees for disaster preparedness, prevention and mitigation, response, and rehabilitation and recovery. The five districts have developed evacuation maps based on the identified evacuation centers, prepared a list of evacuees, provided the residents with hazard and evacuation maps and an evacuation manual, and established protocols for communicating early warnings and evacuation information. It is reported that community leaders now fairly understand the basic concepts and framework on which risk reduction programs should be adopted.[55]

Determinants of Yokohama's involvement in decentralized international cooperation

In the case of Yokohama, norms seem to outweigh immediate utility; its reputation as an international city provided a foundation for shaping a collective self-understanding of normative commitment to international contribution. It is safe to say that successive mayoral leadership, supported by strong fiscal capacity, facilitated Yokohama's engagement in international cooperation. Yet, no matter who occupied the mayor's office, Yokohama's historical legacy and international orientation motivated it to respond to needs for development assistance and environmental cooperation. As local conditions and needs change or policy elites consciously attempt to adopt new ideas in the light of policy experience and new information, the patterns and nature of decentralized international cooperation will also be transformed, accordingly, to meet the new needs or adjust to the new ideas. The different patterns of international cooperation (e.g., policy learning-driven cooperation, international environmental business, and norm-based cooperation) are thus not mutually exclusive over time. This can be seen in Yokohama's new strategy to promote international cooperation for the benefit of local business. Mayor Fumiko Hayashi (2009-the present) of Yokohama, a former president of BMW Tokyo Corp. and former chairman of major supermarket chain Daiei Inc., has been making efforts since 2011 to promote overseas business development for environmental solutions. Under this initiative, however, the mayor emphasizes that business benefits must be considered within the normative realm of Yokohama's commitment to *kokusai kōken*. In an exclusive interview, she says:

> since the open port of 1859, Yokohama has achieved respectable results of international exchange and cooperation with overseas cities and built a strong network with international organizations. In April 2015 (the municipal government) will set up a new International Bureau to shape international policy in a fully integrated way.[56]

It is characteristic of the case of Yokohama to show the effect of certain normative factors on the development of its international environmental cooperation. Perhaps the most interesting finding is that the city has involved extending the meaning of international norms to link its policies and practices with the historical experience and reputation of Yokohama.[57] The new practices of its South–South cooperation support to the diverse membership of the CITYNET have emerged as a result of the merging of international norms with local culture.

1 Sub-national levels of participation in international environmental cooperation may be facilitated when international norms relevant to this issue area are congruent with pre-existing local norms and historical experience.[58] For example, tracing Yokohama's identity-building process back to the idea of its open-door policy being linked with its international image and

reputation as Japan's first treaty port for foreign trade. The experience of identity-building or the domestic normative environment would seem to facilitate the success of international norm diffusion. Local actors were expected to be receptive to the new norm. A shared understanding of Yokohama's commitment to international connection was constructed through social processes of communication and clarification. The collective understanding became expressed in a variety of texts and speeches as a form of Yokohama's role expectation.[59] Taken collectively, these expressions of international municipal commitment spawned expectations among stakeholders in Yokohama—mayors, city departments, and local constituents. Perhaps the most interesting finding is that not only were Yokohama's policy beliefs and practices congruent with the international norm of environmental cooperation, but also this foreign idea helped to enhance the profile and prestige of Yokohama's pre-existing beliefs. By 2006, the municipal government made its desire to position itself centrally within the realm of international development/environmental cooperation clear; this consensus was reflected in the Yokohama General Plan of 2006.[60] Yet, generally speaking, it is important to note that the use of the international norm of environmental cooperation, based on the principle of shared responsibility over problem-solving, does not necessarily mean that an agent has internalized the norm. In the case of Yokohama, some mayors may strategically use that norm to justify their mayoral leadership while not believing in the normative validity. International norms can be instrumental in legitimizing agents' political interests.

2   A better match between international and domestic norms does not automatically lead to sub-national levels of participation in international environmental cooperation. Sub-national variations in international environmental cooperation, indicated by the changes in policy-making and implementation, could be explained by the ability of local agents to reconstruct and apply foreign norms to ensure a better fit with pre-existing local experience and norms, and to localize and realize the potential of these foreign norms to enhance the acceptance and reputation of pre-existing local beliefs. Without successive mayors' commitment, progressive proposals for international environmental cooperation, such as hosting the international intercity network programs for the environment, may have never made it onto Yokohama's agenda. By hosting the offices of international organizations, the mayors have "grafted" or reinterpreted the international norm of international environmental cooperation to develop a new significance for the port city, which is congruent with local beliefs and history. The city's departments, such as the International Policy Office (under the Management Bureau) and the Human Resources Division (under the Waterworks Bureau), have been instrumental in implementing the represented norms of Yokohama's missions and activities for international cooperation. While lacking its own organization for international environmental cooperation, Yokohama has provided the intercity networks and international organizations

with more a permanent loci of communication to persuade domestic actors in Japan and beyond to be part of collective problem-solving and raise public awareness of their missions and activities. The city has thus continued to signal its intention to share a keen interest in the environment internationally as well as domestically. Not surprisingly, all the interviewees mentioned in this chapter highlighted Yokohama's idealistic motivation towards international environmental cooperation.

3   An understanding of public opinion, which can be seen as the embodiment of citizens' concerns and beliefs, provides us with a broad image of the engagement of the public with a specific policy area. Some studies suggest that Yokohama's residents have become more supportive of international environmental cooperation in recent years. According to a 2010 survey on climate change and developmental cooperation, 60 percent of Yokohama's residents support the city's continuous cooperation to reduce environmental risks in developing countries, even without direct benefits to their own community.[61] In general, international environmental cooperation is a low-salience policy area at the local level and the general public thus tends to have a weak opinion, allowing policy-makers to have significant leeway in making policy decisions as they see fit. The general public is easily manipulated by political leaders, since the issue area is of little importance to, and hard to comprehend by, the general public. Comparatively speaking, however, Yokohama's residents have a rather strong opinion on international contribution, due to the city's historical precedents and experience. This public sentiment seems to constrain any leeway for policy-making and has encouraged successive municipal leaders to support the city as a center of Japan's internationalization. The role and reputation of Yokohama, identified as a *kokusai toshi* (international city), has been shaped by its collective self-understanding and the expectations of actors outside of the city. Successive mayors of Yokohama have said that their city would develop its "right place in the world."[62]

4   National government policy and practice is an enabling environment that will greatly influence the extent and success of a local government's involvement in international environmental cooperation. Yokohama's participation in international environmental cooperation has been an active part of national policy, although CITYNET has been involved beyond what was mandated under national policy. The establishment of the UNU in Japan was part of national policy to enhance the international status of Japan while Yokohama's officials enthusiastically invited the UNU-IAS to set up its institute at PACIFICO Yokohama. In 1973 the establishment of the UNU, with its headquarters in Tokyo, was approved on the basis of Secretary-General U Thant's proposal at the UN General Assembly. The establishment project was headed by Yasushi Akashi (a senior Japanese diplomat and United Nations administrator) and the Japanese government not only covered all the capital costs required for setting up the UNU-Center in Tokyo, but also contributed US$100 million to UNU's Endowment Fund.

The relocation of UNU-IAS to Yokohama in 2004 was a deliberate decision by the city to invite, as well as be a part of, aggregate progress at the national policy scale and further their aims within the context of Japan's international obligation. In essence, national policy enabled the local level of participation in international environmental cooperation. Unlike international environmental cooperation in the case of Shiga where the prefectural government participated due to a lack of support from the national government or in the absence of national regulation, Yokohama's cooperation with several international organizations was an integral part of national mandates. Until the mid-1980s, the UNU was the only international organization that the Japanese government hosted in the country. Japan's Ministry of Foreign Affairs (Economic Affairs Bureau and Economic Cooperation Bureau) accordingly decided to entice the member states to locate ITTO headquarters in Japan, in order to "enhance the role and status (of Japan) in international society."[63] Yokohama's bid to host the ITTO in 1986 was to take part in the national initiative as well as meeting Yokohama's mission for international cooperation.

5   Local human capital (namely, accumulated experience in environmental management) and a sense of mission to protect the environment provide a foundation for sub-national level of participation in international environmental cooperation. Policy subsystems normally involve actors from different levels of government, largely because local officials have considerable leeway in decision-making in the absence of national legislation or regulations. In the policy area of industrial pollution, the municipal government, under Asukata's leadership, pioneered innovative policy measures to combat industrial pollution, as the dominant conservative coalition (i.e., the ruling party, the bureaucracy, and big business) at the national level was unable and unwilling to manage the problem. The division between the state and Yokohama's residents left Mayor Asukata in a strategic position as a leader to develop a safeguard to ensure public health and safety beyond the reach of the national government. Accordingly, the city was developing the local human capital on environmental management and a sense of mission for environmental protection that city officials were to utilize later for promotion as an environmentally friendly international city. As progressive local chief executives, such as Mayor Asukata, adopted stricter pollution prevention measures than those imposed at the national level, the national ruling party eventually incorporated some of those progressive measures into its platform to overcome the electoral threat to its politicians. Experience and new information, such as the pollution-related productivity threat to big business, also facilitated policy learning for this policy change, although it did not lead to changes in the policy core beliefs of "growth-first." As a result, the momentum of coalition-building organized around particular local governments' activism waned in the mid-1970s and Mayor Asukata decided to return to national politics to become Chair of the Japan Socialist Party (JSP). The two successive Yokohama mayors, who were formerly

national bureaucrats, while showing their ability to get more financial benefits from the national government, successfully utilized the Asukata's legacies of environmental activism for international environmental cooperation.

Finally, within the broad scope of democracy, citizens should be at the center of policy-makers' considerations, and community-wide participation is thus expected to one of the key determinants of Yokohama's involvement in decentralized international cooperation. In other words, Yokohama's residents should be seen not only as a target object, but also as an acting agent of policy-making. Except for the brief period of Asukata's leadership over the issue areas of the city's industrial pollution, Yokohama's policy-making has been inclined towards top-down rather than participatory bottom-up approaches. As mentioned above, some scholars are critical that the MM21 project was a top-down, landowner/developer-led undertaking at some point. The case of Yokohama's involvement in international environmental cooperation suggests that the opportunity structure for direct forms of citizen participation is constrained by the city's demographics. As seen in Chapter 3, a greater number of organizations and the more complex decision-making processes in a multi-million person city would seem to override the political efficacy of citizens' direct participation.

Conclusion

Yokohama is one of Japan's most urbanized megacities, well known for its high fiscal capacity and its overseas social ties, foreign residents and visitors, and local economic dependence on trade. So is Nagoya but the city has minimally engaged in international environmental cooperation. The port of Atsuta (the present Nagoya port), situated in shallow water, was not a part of the Tokugawa policy to open Japanese ports to foreign trade. In 1951 a government ordinance designated the port of Nagoya as the Designated Special Major Port for Japan's international distribution bases. Post World War II, the port of Nagoya grew rapidly and became Japan's largest port in terms of foreign cargo-handling, as the export sector of automobile-related enterprises (especially Toyota-affiliated business) flourished in this area. Local historical legacies, which might provide a foundation for constructing a collective self-understanding of normative commitment to international environmental cooperation, are missing from the shared similarities of the two cities. Nagoya lacks a long history of exposure to international connections and influence. In other words, the two cities are most similar on specified variables, such as current international connection indicators and financial capacity indices, but differ in the independent variable of interest, that is, local historical experience that might lead to the dynamics of norm formation for international environmental cooperation. Although exact matching is impossible, Yokohama's historical legacy and international orientation is more likely to account for the higher level of its engagement in international environmental cooperation.

In the case of Shiga's ILEC, the limits of indigenous institutional capacity to cope with lake-environment degradation can be seen as a key factor driving

Shiga to reach out transnationally for policy learning and solution. Nonetheless, the prefectural government was willing and capable of developing its partnership with UNEP to create the ILEC. Shiga was bypassing gaining prior approval of the national government in the absence of a gate-keeping capacity by the national bureaucracy to decide whether sub-national authorities could represent the domestic interests of lake environment. As described in Chapter 5, Governor Takemura of Shiga led the course of the events without, however, totally ignoring the established central-local relations. In contrast, Yokohama's relationships with international organizations did not cross the domestic gate without prior approval from the national government. The city was willing to bid for hosting international organizations' facilities and was selected by the national government to become the legitimate representative of domestic interests in those relationships. Once approved, however, the municipal government was capable of contributing to the policy-making process of decentralized international cooperation without the supervision of the national government. Yokohama's experience approximates to the Type I of Marks and Hooghe in which central–local government relations establish a stable division of labor between levels of government over roles and responsibilities (as discussed in the Introduction).

Indeed, Yokohama was able to get involved in international environmental cooperation by going far beyond what was expected under national policy to meet Japan's international obligations. The city took part in the creation of a multi-actor cooperation network, CITYNET, among local authorities and communities in the Asia Pacific region and beyond. The city officials I interviewed actively facilitated the development of city-to-city cooperation to strengthen the ability of urban local governments to better manage their communities under the auspices of South–South cooperation. The city of Yokohama occupied an opportune position to act as an intermediate agent in connecting local action and experience among urban communities in developing countries and turning the benefits of mutual learning into local action for problem-solving. Yokohama's desire to enhance its role in the region helped to provide a mechanism to put local-to-local dialogue into practice. The horizontal network of local urban actors constantly suffered from a lack of financial resources, which depended on the budgets of low-income member cities. The subsidy of the Yokohama city government accounted for more than half of the total revenue of CITYNET. As it was necessary for CITYNET to raise funds for individual project activities, through cooperation with donors and partners, Yokohama project offices acted strategically as a policy broker to manage access to those necessary funds from Japanese donors, such as the JICA and CLAIR.

Despite Yokohama's activities within the institutional framework of state-centric governance, the findings in this chapter suggest a number of hypothetical causal links for decentralized international cooperation that focus more on agency than on structural explanations. The chapter has drawn attention to the fact that the municipal government deliberately decided to engage in international cooperation at its discretion. It suggests that factors internal to agency, such as past experience, prior beliefs, public support, fiscal capacity, and resourcing can be more influential determinants than external opportunity structures such as international recognition and national policy. Agency is influential to the extent that it individually or collectively interprets and adapts the external opportunity structures to local needs. If there are any incongruities among equally capable agencies in regard to the interpreted external opportunity structures, then the sources of these incongruities are likely to derive from agencies' probable motivations and purposes.

Local governments' decisions are either empowered or constrained by their fiscal capacity and administrative ability. It is also apparent that city size, which is positively correlated with fiscal capacity and administrative ability, is a factor in the degree of international engagement. Only large municipalities, such as Yokohama, extend any significant amount of foreign aid, and there are no reports thus far identified to show that municipalities with a population of fewer than 25,000 people have gone beyond the scope of international engagement mandated by the national government. Although a lack of case studies makes my observation suggestive rather than definitive, there appears to be a threshold enabling capacity at which limited resources start to outweigh the motivations for active engagement in international cooperation. Yet, among the largest municipal governments, such as Nagoya and Yokohama, their motivations and purposes continue to produce difference and diversity. Some are actively cooperative; others are simply cooperative within the nationally defined guidelines.

Chapters 5, 6, and 7 have focused on the role of three outstanding local Japanese authorities in international cooperation dynamics that are integral to their political policy structure. The focus of their international cooperation has been on voluntary activity; they decided whether or not to engage in international cooperation. There is a clear privileging of an actor-specific approach, a focus upon who is involved in decision-making, how, and why. The logic of deliberate choice in the selection of international cooperation activities, the interpretation of internationally shared norms and principles, the response to nationally defined guidelines, and the conceptual adaptation by decision-makers were all central to the analysis of the three cases. Structures, such as international norms in the North–South context and national policy mandates, provided the political context within which Shiga, Kitakyushu, and Yokohama acted. These structures constrained or facilitated local action, rather than acted as determinants. Nonetheless, it was the local actors who interpreted the role of these structures and adapted them to meet their own conditions and needs.

Local needs and adaptive capacity continue to ensure difference and diversity among the more self-motivated local governments, in contrast with weaker municipalities that remain over-dependent on national supervision. Japanese local government choice in selecting international cooperation activities appears to reflect four major analytically distinct mechanisms: tutelage (by the national government), mimicry (emulating neighbors), learning (revising after drawing lessons), and pioneering (innovation). The majority of local governments that engaged in international cooperation simply worked with state agencies to support national programs for training specialists from and dispatching local experts to developing countries.

Tutelage, exercised via conditions attached to national subsidies or top-down administrative guidance, is most likely to be important in explaining the similarities among local authorities' international cooperation. Mimicry also favors the diffusion of similar patterns of international cooperation; it explains how and why some cities copy neighboring localities' practices in order to catch up, rather than making their own policy choices. The two other mechanisms are found to be at work in the three case studies. Learning is based on lessons drawn from experience, which gives guidance on the likely consequences of policy options. Pioneering, especially found in the case of Kitakyushu, is the initiative in which local actors use new information to update their prior policy beliefs and adopt new policy ideas. While both tutelage and mimicry tend to have a uniform impact on international cooperation activities among "bandwagoning" local actors, learning and pioneering can reveal different motivations within international cooperation decision-making, as illustrated in the three case studies.

Notes

1 DAC Secretariat (Statistics and Monitoring Division, Development Co-operation Directorate), "Aid extended by local and state governments," *DAC Journal*, Vol. 6, No. 4 (2005), p. 9.
2 Hidenori Nakamura, Mark Elder, and Hideyuki Mori, "The surprising role of local governments in international environmental cooperation: the case of Japanese collaboration with developing countries," *Journal of Environment and Development*, Vol. 20, No. 3 (2011), pp. 219–50.
3 Ministry of Internal Affairs and Communications, "Heisei nijyūgo-nen chihō kōkyō dantai shuyō zaisei shihyō ichiran" [2013 table of measurement indexes of local public finance], available from: www.soumu.go.jp/iken/zaisei/H25_chiho.html [accessed July 25, 2015].
4 The historical description of opening the port for foreign trade in this section is based on Yokohama City, *Yokohama-shi shikō* [History of Yokohama city], Vol. 5 (Yokohama: Yokohama City, 1931), chps 2 and 3.
5 Akira Tanaka, "Bakumatsu no kiki ishiki" [Crisis consciousness in the Bakumatsu period], *Nihon no kinsei* [Modern Japan], Vol. 18 (Tokyo: Chūōkōron, 1994), pp. 103–45.
6 Tien-shi Chen, "Reconstruction and localization of ethnic culture: the case of Yokohama Chinatown as a tourist spot," *Senri Ethnological Studies*, Vol. 76 (2010), p. 31.
7 Takeomi Nishikawa and Izumi Ito, *Kaikoku Nihon to Yokohama Chūkagai* [Japan's open-door policy and Yokohama Chinatown] (Tokyo: Taishūkan Shoten, 2002), pp. 81–3.
8 Even a Yokohama's foreign resident heard a lot of rumors of such events. See Fred G. Notehelfer, ed., *Japan through American Eyes: The Journal of Francis Hall of Kanagawa and Yokohama, 1859–1866* (Princeton, NJ: Princeton University Press, 1992), p. 436.
9 John W. Dower, *Yokohama Boomtown: Foreigners in Treaty-Port Japan 1859–1872* (Cambridge, MA: MIT Visualizing Cultures, 2008).
10 City of Yokohama, Editorial Section of Municipal History, ed., *Yokohama shi shinsai shi* [A record of Yokohama city earthquake disaster], Vol. 1 (Yokohama: City of Yokohama, 1926), p. 15.

11 City of Yokohama, Editorial Section of Municipal History, ed., *Yokohama shi shinsai shi*, Vol.1, p. 71.
12 City of Yokohama, Editorial Section of Municipal History, ed., *Yokohama shi shinsai shi*, Vol.1, p. 79.
13 City of Yokohama, Editorial Section of Municipal History, ed., *Yokohama shi shinsai shi*, Vol.1, p. 45.
14 City of Yokohama, *Yokohama fukkō shi* [A record of Yokohama reconstruction], Vol. 4 (Yokohama: City of Yokohama, 1932), p. 737. Yet it is important to note that some observers consider the port-focused reconstruction as a nationally defined project as the ordinary citizens' needs, such as water and sewage, were neglected by the municipal government. See Caroline Norma, "Reconstruction in service of the Japanese nation: Yokohama city and the Great Kanto Earthquake of 1923," *Eras*, Edition 10, November 2008, available from: www.arts.monash.edu/publicatins/eras [accessed June 7, 2015].
15 City of Yokohama, General Affairs Bureau, *Yokohama no kūshū to sensai kanren shiryō* [Documents on Yokohama air raid and war casualties], 2000–2010, available from: www.city.yokohama.lg.jp/somu/org/gyosei/sisi/web-air-raid/chapter11.html [accessed June 7, 2015].
16 The descriptions in this section are based on City of Yokohama, General Affairs Bureau, *Yokohama-shi shi II* [History of Yokohama city II] Vol. 2-1 and Vol. 2-2 (Yokohama: City of Yokohama, 1999 and 2000), chp 1 and chp 1 respectively.
17 City of Yokohama, General Affairs Bureau, *Yokohama-shi shi II* [History of Yokohama city II] Vol. 3-1 (Yokohama: City of Yokohama, 2002), pp. 20–4.
18 For the details of derequisitioning and Yokohama's recovery, see the City of Yokohama, General Affairs Bureau, *Yokohama-shi shi II* [History of Yokohama city II] Vol. 2-2 (Yokohama: City of Yokohama, 2000), pp. 145–86.
19 Ichio Asukata, *Kakushin shisei no tenbō: Yokohama shisei yone'n no kiroku* [Views of reformist municipal government: a four-year record of Yokohama municipal government] (Tokyo: Shakai Shinpō sha, 1967).
20 Charles M. Tiebout "A pure theory of local expenditures," *Journal of Political Economy*, Vol. 64 (1956), pp. 416–24.
21 City of Yokohama, Department of Public Health, *Yokohama shi ni okeru kōgai no jittai to yosoku: Negishi Honmoku kōgyō chiku o megru shomondai no kaimei no tame ni* [The state and prediction of industrial pollution in Yokohama: a solution for the problems of the industrial districts of Negishi and Honmoku] (Yokohama: Department of Public Health, 1964).
22 This section's tracing of the course of the events is based on Nobuhiko Sukegawa and Katsumi Saruta, "Negishi Honmoku kōgyō chiku ni okeru karyoku hatsudensho ricchi ni tomonau kōgai mondai no keika" [The process of the pollution problems regarding the siting of the coal-fired thermal power plant in the districts of Negeshi and Honmoku], *Chōsa Kihō* [Investigation Quarterly: City of Yokohama], Vol. 6 (1965), pp. 58–71.
23 City of Yokohama, General Affairs Bureau, *Yokohama-shi shi II* [History of Yokohama city II] Vol. 3-2 (Yokohama: City of Yokohama, 2003), pp. 610–22.
24 Jack G. Lewis, "Civic protest in Mishima: citizens' movements and the politics of the environment in contemporary Japan," in Kurt Steiner, Ellis S. Krauss, and Scott C. Flanagan, eds., *Political Opposition and Local Politics in Japan* (Princeton, NJ: Princeton University Press, 1980), pp. 274–313.
25 Yokohama Minato Mirai 21 Corporation, *Minato Mirai 21 Information*, Vol. 85 (2004), p. 4.
26 Hiroshi Kishida and Morio Uzuki, *Toshi zukuri senryaku to purojekuto manēgimento: Yokohama Minato Mirai no chōsen* [City planning strategies and project management: Minato Mirai's challenge] (Tokyo: Gakugei Shuppan, 2009).
27 Takayuki Kaneda, Takeko Kondo, Shin'ichi Sakurai, and Yasuhiro Uozaki, "Wankō

sai-kaihatsu ni okeru kōmin kyōdō ni kansuru jisshō-teki kenkyū" [An empirical research on PPP in promoting redevelopments of old piers and yards in Japanese ports], *Kaiyō Kaihatsu* [Ocean Development], Vol. 70, No. 2 (2014), p. 135.
28 Until October 1981, MM21 was known as the "City Waterfront Area."
29 Interview by author with Shigenobu Sato, CITYNET, Yokohama, May 24, 2011.
30 Osman Balaba, "The use of indicators to assess urban regeneration performance for climate-friendly urban development: the case of Yokohama Minato Mirai 21," in Mitsuhiko Kawakami and Zhen-jiang Shen, eds., *Spatial Planning and Sustainable Development: Approaches for Achieving Sustainable Urban Form in Asian Cities* (Heidelberg: Springer, 2013), p. 107.
31 Balaba, "The use of indicators to assess urban regeneration performance for climate-friendly urban development," pp. 91–113.
32 See, for example, Limin Hee and Low Boon Liang, "Water margins: the redevelopment of waterfronts and waterways in Asian cities," The International Conference of the International Forum on Urbanism, November 26–28, 2009, Amsterdam.
33 As of 2015, the rate of development progress is 66 percent, or 86 percent when provisional use is included.
34 Lin Zhong-Jie, "From megastructure to megalopolis: formation and transformation of mega-projects in Tokyo Bay," *Journal of Urban Design*, Vol. 12, No. 1 (2007), pp. 85–6.
35 Lin Zhong-Jie, "From megastructure to megalopolis," p. 86; Balaba, "The use of indicators to assess urban regeneration performance for climate-friendly urban development," p. 111.
36 See Japan GreenBuild Council/Japan Sustainable Building Consortium, "Comprehensive assessment system for built environment," September 2015, available from: www.ibec.or.jp/CASBEE/english/overviewE.htm [accessed June 7, 2015].
37 Japan Smart City, "The Yokohama Smart City Project 2014," available from: http://jscp.nepc.or.jp/en/yokohama/ [accessed June 7, 2015].
38 Fumiko Hayashi (mayor of Yokohama), "Minato Mirai 21: revitalising the city," *Urban Solutions*, No. 5 (2004), p. 55.
39 CITYNET, "About us," 2014, available from: http://citynet-ap.org/category/about/ [accessed June 7, 2015].
40 Interview by author with Bernadia Irawati Tjandradewi, CITYNET, Yokohama, May 24, 2011.
41 Interview with Makoto Sekiyama, Director General for Foreign Affairs, the City of Yokohama, cited in *ITTO Tropical Forest Update*, Vol. 23, No. 3 (2014), pp. 22–23.
42 Yokohama City Council, Yokohama City Council Minutes, fourth plenary session, No. 13, December 20, 1991.
43 Yokohama City Council, Yokohama City Council Minutes, fourth plenary session, No. 13, December 20, 1991.
44 Interview by author with Bernadia Irawati Tjandradewi, CITYNET, Yokohama, May 24, 2011.
45 CITYNET, "CITYNET members map," available from: http://citynet-ap.org/category/members-and-partners/ [accessed November 7, 2015].
46 Bernadia Irawati Tjandradewi and Peter J. Marcotullio, "City-to-city networks: Asian perspectives on key elements and areas for success," *Habitat International*, Vol. 33 (2009), p. 167.
47 See *CITYNET Annual Report, 2007–2014*, available from: http://citynet-ap.org/category/publications-all/annual-reports/ [accessed November 7, 2015].
48 Interview by author with Bernadia Irawati Tjandradewi, CITYNET, Yokohama, May 24, 2011; Interviews by author with Akiko Murayama, CITYNET, Yokohama, May 24, 2011 and January 17, 2013.
49 Tjandradewi and Marcotullio, "City-to-city networks," p. 167.
50 Interviews by author with Akiko Murayama, CITYNET, Yokohama, May 24, 2011, and January 17, 2013.

51 Interview by author with Shigenobu Satō, CITYNET, Yokohama, May 24, 2011.
52 *CITYNET Annual Report*, 2012, pp. 10–11, available from: http://citynet-ap.org/category/publications-all/annual-reports/ [accessed November 7, 2015].
53 Interview by author with Bernadia Irawati Tjandradewi, CITYNET, Yokohama, May 24, 2011.
54 CITYNET Yokohama Project Office, Community Based Adaptation and Resilience Against Disasters Project (CBARAD), "Iloilo City of the Republic of the Philippines: Completion Report, August 2012–March 2015," available from: http://citynet-yh.org/english/wp-content/uploads/2015/10/2015-CBARAD-Annual-Report-.pdf [accessed November 7, 2015].
55 CITYNET Yokohama Project Office, Community Based Adaptation and Resilience Against Disasters Project (CBARAD), "Iloilo City of the Republic of the Philippines: Completion Report, August 2012–March 2015," p. 21.
56 Interview with Fumiko Hayashi, Mayor of Yokohama, cited in "Shin kōmin renkei saizensen" [On the frontiers of Public Private Partnership], *Nikkei BPnet*, February 18, 2015.
57 Amitav Acharya suggests the theory of constitutive localization. According to Acharya, international norms are not simply either accepted or rejected but may develop along a third trajectory of constitutive localization. See Amitav Acharya, "How ideas spread: whose norms matter? Norm localization and institutional change in Asian regionalism," *International Organization*, Vol. 58 (2004), pp. 239–75.
58 Jeffrey Checkel argues that the successful diffusion of norms is determined by the degree of "cultural match," that is, the degree to which the external norm resonates with the domestic normative environment. See Jeffrey T. Checkel, "Norms, institutions, and national identity in contemporary Europe," *International Studies Quarterly*, Vol. 43, No. 1 (1999), pp. 84–114.
59 See, for example, Mayor Hidenobu Takahide's speech, Yokohama City Council Minutes, regular meeting of the City Council, March 2, 1993; Mayor Hiroshi Nakada's speech, Yokohama City Council Minutes, regular meeting of the City Council, June 10, 2005; Mayor Fumiko Hayashi's speech, Yokohama City Council Minutes, Special Committee on Audit, September 28, 2010.
60 Yokohama City, "Yokohama General Plan (Long Term Vision)," June 23, 2006, available from: www.city.yokohama.lg.jp/seisaku/seisaku/vision/honbuneng.pdf [accessed November 7, 2015].
61 Institute for Global Environmental Strategies (IGES), "Practical measures to promote Japanese local governments' environmental collaboration with developing countries with citizens' support," *Policy Brief*, Vol. 18 (2012), p. 5.
62 See, for example, a speech made by Mayor Hiroshi Nakada at the 2004 ceremony of the US–Japan 150th Anniversary Program, available from: www.ajstokyo.org/150/speach/speach8_j.htm [accessed November 7, 2015].
63 Japan, Diet, House of Representatives, Minutes of the Committee on Foreign Affairs, March 25, 1988, No. 4.

References

Acharya, Amitav (2004). "How ideas spread: whose norms matter? Norm localization and institutional change in Asian regionalism." *International Organization*, Vol. 58, No. 2, pp. 239–75.
Asukata, Ichio (1967). *Kakushin shisei no tenbō: Yokohama shisei yone'n no kiroku* [Views of reformist municipal government: a four-year record of Yokohama municipal government]. Tokyo: Shakai Shinpō sha.
Balaba, Osman (2013). "The use of indicators to assess urban regeneration performance for climate-friendly urban development: the case of Yokohama Minato Mirai 21." In

Mitsuhiko Kawakami and Zhen-jiang Shen, eds., *Spatial Planning and Sustainable Development: Approaches for Achieving Sustainable Urban Form in Asian Cities*. Heidelberg: Springer, pp. 91–113.

Checkel, Jeffrey T. (1999). "Norms, institutions, and national identity in contemporary Europe." *International Studies Quarterly*, Vol. 43, No. 1, pp. 84–114.

Chen, Tien-shi (2010). "Reconstruction and localization of ethnic culture: the case of Yokohama Chinatown as a tourist spot." *Senri Ethnological Studies*, Vol. 76, pp. 29–38.

CITYNET (2014). "About us." Available from: http://citynet-ap.org/category/about/ [accessed June 7, 2015].

CITYNET (2015). "CITYNET members map." Available from: http://citynet-ap.org/category/members-and-partners/ [accessed November 7, 2015].

CITYNET (2015). *CITYNET Annual Report, 2007–2014*. Available from: http://citynet-ap.org/category/publications-all/annual-reports/ [accessed November 7, 2015].

CITYNET Yokohama Project Office, Community Based Adaptation and Resilience Against Disasters Project (CBARAD) (2015). "Iloilo City of the Republic of the Philippines: Completion Report, August 2012–March 2015." Available from: http://citynet-yh.org/english/wp-content/uploads/2015/10/2015-CBARAD-Annual-Report-.pdf [accessed November 7, 2015].

City of Yokohama (1931). *Yokohama-shi shikō* [History of Yokohama city], Vol. 5. Yokohama: City of Yokohama.

City of Yokohama (1932). *Yokohama fukkō shi* [A record of Yokohama reconstruction], Vol. 4. Yokohama: City of Yokohama.

City of Yokohama (2006). "Yokohama General Plan (Long Term Vision)." June 23, 2006. Available from: www.city.yokohama.lg.jp/seisaku/seisaku/vision/honbuneng.pdf [accessed November 7, 2015].

City of Yokohama, Department of Public Health (1964). *Yokohama shi ni okeru kōgai no jittai to yosoku: Negishi Honmoku kōgyō chiku o megru shomondai no kaimei no tame ni* [The state and prediction of industrial pollution in Yokohama: a solution for the problems of the industrial districts of Negishi and Honmoku]. Yokohama: Department of Public Health.

City of Yokohama, Editorial Section of Municipal History, ed. (1926). *Yokohama shi shinsai shi* [A record of Yokohama city earthquake disaster], Vol. 1. Yokohama: City of Yokohama.

City of Yokohama, General Affairs Bureau (1999). *Yokohama-shi shi II* [History of Yokohama city II], Vol. 2-1. Yokohama: City of Yokohama.

City of Yokohama, General Affairs Bureau (2000). *Yokohama-shi shi II* [History of Yokohama city II], Vol. 2-2. Yokohama: City of Yokohama.

City of Yokohama, General Affairs Bureau (2002). *Yokohama-shi shi II* [History of Yokohama city II], Vol. 3-1. Yokohama: City of Yokohama.

City of Yokohama, General Affairs Bureau (2003). *Yokohama-shi shi II* [History of Yokohama city II], Vol. 3-2. Yokohama: City of Yokohama.

City of Yokohama, General Affairs Bureau (2000–2010). *Yokohama no kūshū to sensai kanren shiryō* [Documents on Yokohama air raid and war casualties]. Available from: www.city.yokohama.lg.jp/somu/org/gyosei/sisi/web-air-raid/chapter11.html [accessed June 7, 2015].

DAC Secretariat (Statistics and Monitoring Division, Development Co-operation Directorate) (2005). "Aid extended by local and state governments." *DAC Journal*, Vol. 6, No. 4, pp. 1–53.

Dower, John W. (2008). *Yokohama Boomtown: Foreigners in Treaty-Port Japan 1859–1872*. Cambridge, MA: MIT Visualizing Cultures.
Hayashi, Fumiko (2004). "Minato Mirai 21: revitalising the city." *Urban Solutions*, No. 5, pp. 42–8.
Hee, Limin and Low Boon Liang (2009). "Water margins: the redevelopment of waterfronts and waterways in Asian cities." The International Conference of the International Forum on Urbanism, November 26–28, 2009, Amsterdam.
Institute for Global Environmental Strategies (IGES) (2012). "Practical measures to promote Japanese local governments' environmental collaboration with developing countries with citizens' support." *Policy Brief*, Vol. 18 (2012), pp. 1–12.
ITTO Tropical Forest Update (2014), Vol. 23, No. 3, pp. 22–3.
Japan, Diet, House of Representatives (1988). Minutes of the Committee on Foreign Affairs, March 25, 1988, No. 4.
Japan GreenBuild Council/Japan Sustainable Building Consortium (2015). "Comprehensive assessment system for built environment." September 2015. Available from: www.ibec.or.jp/CASBEE/english/overviewE.htm [accessed June 7, 2015].
Japan, Ministry of Internal Affairs and Communications (MIAC) (2013). "Heisei nijyūgo-nen chihō kōkyō dantai shuyō zaisei shihyō ichiran" [2013 table of measurement indexes of local public finance]. Available from: www.soumu.go.jp/iken/zaisei/H25_chiho.html [accessed July 25, 2015].
Japan Smart City (2014). "The Yokohama Smart City Project 2014." Available from: http://jscp.nepc.or.jp/en/yokohama/ [accessed June 7, 2015].
Kaneda, Takayuki, Takeko Kondo, Shin'ichi Sakurai, and Yasuhiro Uozaki (2014). "Wankō sai-kaihatsu ni okeru kōmin kyōdō ni kansuru jisshō-teki kenkyū" [An empirical research on PPP in promoting redevelopments of old piers and yards in Japanese ports]. *Kaiyō Kaihatsu* [Ocean Development], Vol. 70, No. 2, pp. 133–8.
Kishida, Hiroshi and Morio Uzuki (2009). *Toshi zukuri senryaku to purojekuto manēgimento: Yokohama Minato Mirai no chōsen* [City planning strategies and project management: Minato Mirai's challenge]. Tokyo: Gakugei Shuppan.
Lewis, Jack G. (1980). "Civic protest in Mishima: citizens' movements and the politics of the environment in contemporary Japan." In Kurt Steiner, Ellis S. Krauss, and Scott C. Flanagan, eds., *Political Opposition and Local Politics in Japan*. Princeton NJ: Princeton University Press, pp. 274–313.
Nakada, Hiroshi (2004). Speech at the 2004 ceremony of the US–Japan 150th Anniversary Program. Available from: www.ajstokyo.org/150/speach/speach8_j.htm [accessed November 7, 2015].
Nakamura, Hidenori, Mark Elder, and Hideyuki Mori (2011). "The surprising role of local governments in international environmental cooperation: the case of Japanese collaboration with developing countries." *Journal of Environment and Development*, Vol. 20, No. 3, pp. 219–50.
Nikkei BPnet (2004). "Shin kōmin renkei saizensen" [On the frontiers of Public Private Partnership], February 18, 2015.
Nishikawa, Takeomi and Izumi Ito (2002). *Kaikoku Nihon to Yokohama chūkagai* [Japan's open-door policy and Yokohama Chinatown]. Tokyo: Taishūkan Shoten.
Norma, Caroline (2008). "Reconstruction in service of the Japanese nation: Yokohama city and the Great Kanto Earthquake of 1923." *Eras*, Edition 10, November 2008. Available from: www.arts.monash.edu/publicatins/eras [accessed June 7, 2015].
Notehelfer, Fred G. ed. (1992). *Japan through American Eyes: The Journal of Francis Hall of Kanagawa and Yokohama, 1859–1866*. Princeton, NJ: Princeton University Press.

Sukegawa, Nobuhiko and Katsumi Saruta (1965). "Negishi Honmoku kōgyō chiku ni okeru karyoku hatsudensho ricchi ni tomonau kōgai mondai no keika" [The process of the pollution problems regarding the siting of the coal-fired thermal power plant in the districts of Negeshi and Honmoku]. *Chōsa Kihō* [Investigation Quarterly: City of Yokohama], Vol. 6, pp. 58–71.

Tanaka, Akira (1994). "Bakumatsu no kiki ishiki" [Crisis consciousness in the Bakumatsu period]. *Nihon no kinsei* [Modern Japan], Vol. 18. Tokyo: Chūōkōron, pp. 103–45.

Tiebout, Charles M. (1956). "A pure theory of local expenditures." *Journal of Political Economy*, Vol. 64, pp. 416–24.

Tjandradewi, Bernadia Irawati and Peter J. Marcotullio (2009). "City-to-city networks: Asian perspectives on key elements and areas for success." *Habitat International*, Vol. 33, pp. 165–72.

Yokohama City Council (1991). Yokohama City Council Minutes. Fourth plenary session, No. 13, December 20, 1991.

Yokohama City Council (1993). Yokohama City Council Minutes. First plenary session, No. 2, March 2, 1993.

Yokohama City Council (2005). Yokohama City Council Minutes. Second plenary session, No. 8, June 10, 2005.

Yokohama City Council (2010). Yokohama City Council Minutes. Special Committee on Audit, September 28, 2010.

Yokohama Minato Mirai 21 Corporation (2014). *Minato Mirai 21 Information*, Vol. 85, pp. 1–22.

Zhong-Jie, Lin (2007). "From megastructure to megalopolis: formation and transformation of mega-projects in Tokyo Bay." *Journal of Urban Design*, Vol. 12, No. 1, pp. 73–92.

8 Expert citizens' role
Civic science in environment policy

The aim of this chapter is to examine the importance of public participation in the production and use of environmental science, with special reference to "expert citizens" who can facilitate and mediate between experts and laypeople. Local government occupies a strategic position between state and civil society and between domestic and foreign affairs in terms of its ability to influence others. Local authorities, who are not only equipped with expert knowledge but also motivated by their concerns for local experience and problems, are expected to help laypeople effectively engage with resourceful stakeholders to redress inequitable distributions of environmental burdens and promoting two-way symmetrical communication rather than the one-way asymmetrical communication associated with expert persuasion. Yet the key problem boils down to local authorities' willingness and capability to utilize this strategic position to be responsive to the needs of society and thus foster legitimacy in policy-making. Not all local authorities possess this willingness and capability to help less-resourceful laypeople build their capacity to make decisions on an equal footing with experts. As uncertainty, inherent in the complexity of environmental science, increases, there are calls to refashion expert knowledge into a more citizen-expert interactive governance. In the United States (US), the way that lay people can participate in scientific knowledge application and policy-making is organized through grassroots and national environmental organizations, such as the National Resources Defense Council (NRDC). In Japan, such professional associations that build networks of interaction with scientific experts, policy-makers, interest groups, and the media, have yet to emerge on a wider scale. The study of expert citizens is largely unexplored in Japan's environmental policy. Nonetheless, voluntary citizens individually or collectively have developed their expertise over many years and have begun to play an intermediary role at the local level. This chapter will analyze the potential roles of expert citizens by conducting case studies of two Japanese localities, Shiki and Jōyō cities.

In his influential article, "Bowling alone: America's declining social capital," Robert Putnam has drawn attention to the fact that Americans no longer actively participate in politics or trust their government's ability to have the answers to economic and social problems.[1] In 1995 when he published this chapter, Japan's voter turnouts were the lowest in its electoral history and participation in electoral politics was at near-crisis levels. Voter turnouts for local elections dropped to 55 percent in the mid-1990s, the lowest level seen in postwar Japan.[2] Representative democracy in post-WWII Japan is now at a crossroads: Japan's voter turnout has been continually low and floating voters, who drift from party to party or between turnout and abstention at actual elections, have continued to increase. Does this mean that Japanese people are "bowling alone"? This is not necessarily a sign of widespread political apathy but can be a warning against the old pork barrel politics, which has given favors to special interest groups in the past. In this respect, political alienation rather than apathy may appropriately explain the degree and nature of political participation in Japan. The country is now facing a time like no other in the history of modern Japan; there is an exceptionally high demand for an alternative way of politics. Reformists or new political groups are expected to turn this opportunity into democracy building. Forward-looking citizens' groups in Japan are proposing an alternative form of political renewal in the issue area of environmental protection.

Generally speaking, laypeople are increasingly excluded from partaking, even indirectly, in environmental policy-making. One of the major factors, which may contribute to political alienation, is the increasingly technical area of policy-making since the public remains outside the policy debates. As Henrik Bang suggests, the key problem of contemporary politics is political exclusion rather than free riding.[3] Such exclusion appears to lead to the professionalization of political participation that can be seen as a venue of governance networks with the intertwining of scientific experts, policy-makers, interest groups, and the media.[4] Bang thus proposes to assume:

> The more ECs (expert citizens), and the more willing ECs become to cooperate with each other and more established top elites, the greater the likelihood that ECs will exclude laypeople from the discursive construction of new publics and modes of democratic governance.[5]

However, as the two case studies illustrate in this chapter, the development of expert citizens does not necessarily reinforce the exclusion of laypeople from the governance network of expert systems, but rather facilitates capacity-building supports for laypeople who are not directly tied to the emerging arena of governance networks. It is true that today experts from the state, civil society, and the market are increasingly working together, across hierarchical tiers and de-hierarchical new spheres of authority, to solve shared issues and problems. In a normative sense, though, the heart of democracy in a modern world lies in the balancing act of utility-driven interests and social integrity between expert-led political authorities and laypeople through which polity structuring should be carried out over time.[6] This chapter seeks to explore the potential of citizens' voluntary associations to develop their expertise and act as facilitators of a public space where laypeople can collaborate with each other and educate themselves to take part in political processes.

In the technically based area of environmental policy, policy and scientific experts tend to dominate decision-making while the public remains outside the policy debates. Lay ideas are often discounted as "unscientific." Environmental education is thus viewed as important in order for lay people to improve their environmental literacy[7] as they are less capable of scientific reasoning.[8] In the mid-1980s, Ulrich Beck's *Risk Society* made an influential contribution to a new theory of reflective modernity in which technologically induced risks lead to calls for the subjection of scientific expertise to social scrutiny.[9] A number of scholars subsequently began to refer to public participation in science. First-hand experience in the immediate environment emphasized the key role of local knowledge that would be necessary for judging the usefulness of scientific expertise as scientific predictions could fail to meet the diversity of local experiences.[10]

This chapter argues that a possible source of a congruence-building process amid all the disagreements between expert and lay knowledge and universal and local knowledge lies in the particular role of "expert citizens," as they hold a strategic position straddling the gaps between laypeople and experts. Expert citizens who are scientifically competent but also motivated by their concerns for local experience, individually or collectively, facilitate the filling of gaps between scientific expertise and local knowledge within the existing policy networks. In science-driven policy, expert citizens have the potential to make a fundamental contribution to environmental justice. Some people live in pleasant environments; others exist in hazardous environments. Expert citizens are placed in a strategic position to allow the parties to redress inequitable distributions of environmental burdens. In the quest for environmental justice, expert knowledge must be connected to place-based knowledge. Expert citizens can play an intermediary role in making expert knowledge more responsive to the needs of society, thus fostering the legitimacy of policy-making.

People who live in an immediate environment experience the greatest environmental exposure risks and thus demand a greater role in prescribing solutions. Local communities are demanding the redistribution of expertise, drawing on their first-hand experience—often known as local knowledge—to reduce the environmental risks they face.[11] Whatmore *et al.* identify the importance of public engagement in science as a means of building confidence in the expert knowledge claims on which policy relies.[12] In a case study of flood risk management, they argue how science should bring the knowledge of local people to land management practices at the catchment scale. Given the limits of predictive science knowledge, the ideal of "public participation" argues that the application of scientific knowledge would require the knowledge and value of ordinary citizens.[13] Another ideal, that of "co-production," encourages ordinary citizens to participate in the production of scientific knowledge.[14]

Yet public engagement with science remains problematic. Laypeople have limited resources to get involved in the various issues of science governance so that they may choose minimal contributions to export the cost to others (the free-riding problem). In this context, analyses of practical applications of public engagement with science reveal a range of new developments that have an impact on environmental communications. A varied literature highlights the linkages between ordinary citizens and scientific experts, rather than simply the citizen-expert dichotomy that assumes the former emphasizes social values while the latter deals in scientific facts. The literature saw a different citizen identity emerging as the response of laypeople to the problem: "expert citizens," "citizen experts," or "counter-experts." Some refer to expert citizens as organized groups, possibly affiliated with political parties and trade unions, that actually represent citizens to policy-makers.[15] Others treat expert citizens as "counter-experts" who present a challenge to the ability of traditional science in a contentious fashion.[16]

As Henrik Bang suggests,[17] expert citizens are defined as independent, voluntary professionals who are able to build cooperative networks in their individual or collective capacity between citizens and experts and pragmatically deal with policy problems in elite policy networks. As discussed below, the focus of my attention is directed at the intermediary role of expert citizens to make connections between otherwise unconnected actors (i.e., policy and scientific experts and laypeople) in a way that co-produces environmental policy. The objective of the intermediary role is to bridge the gap between scientific/expert knowledge production and local daily-life knowledge production for the adaptive governance of local communities. To this end, expert citizens are expected to interpret and reevaluate scientific/expert knowledge to fit into the locally specific conditions of environmental problems while applying local knowledge accumulated in local communities to scientific reasoning. The normative significance of the intermediary role is to help less resourceful citizens have their capacity be on an equal footing with experts and thus offer democratic benefits through the deliberative process by which citizens who bear the consequences of policy-making should be able to be part of decisions.

In this context, I emphasize the importance of expert citizens as agents who cast new light on environmental governance. Functionalists may argue that expert citizens will emerge in response to collective needs. Likewise, structuralists may suggest that environmental constraints will be constitutive, producing expert citizens. Moving beyond these assumptions, the intermediary role of the agents is neither simply the result of functional needs nor that of structural constraints, but also determined by the action of the agents who facilitate a negotiated solution with some degree of legitimacy to blend expert and local knowledge productions. This chapter highlights the ways expert citizens creatively use their strategic position to coordinate, facilitate, and persuade stakeholders for environmental risk reduction.

Expert citizens as an intermediary in the democratization of science

Disengagement from political processes has certainly attracted considerable attention in recent decades. To reverse the trend of civic disengagement, governments are required to strengthen their relations with citizens. These relations cover a wide range of interactions at different stages of agenda setting, policy formation, implementation, and evaluation. The level of interactions can be seen from a one-way relationship of information providers to recipients, through a two-way relationship of consultation, to a two-way partnership between government and citizens. Active participation at the third level is the highest order of public engagement. Public participation (that is, including citizens more directly in decision-making) is rare and confined to a very few Organisation for Economic Co-operation and Development (OECD) countries, such as the US and the United Kingdom (UK), and takes place primarily at the sub-national level.[18] In the UK, the introduction of public participation on a pilot basis (i.e., Engage for Change, Champions of Participation) is well established at local and national levels. However, both local and national public officials tend to believe that the issues are too complex for citizens to get involved and these officials have a limited competence to facilitate public participation.[19] With the Act of Decentralization of 2003, French communes were equipped with two options to organize a local consultation or a binding referendum. France has a tradition of communes' micro-level direct democracy but public participation at the national level is very limited. In Italy, by contrast, even at the local level politicians who have a vested interest in decision-making (patronage politics), and thus weak democratic trust, present a major challenge to establishing citizen engagement.[20]

In policy-making, the high level of scientific knowledge necessary to understand the available information makes it difficult for laypeople to comprehend. Disincentives to lay engagement in science-driven policy are thus much greater than those found in other policy areas.[21] Since ordinary citizens generally receive most of their scientific information from the mass media, media coverage is central to public knowledge. Not surprisingly, that coverage is less directly part of the scientific reasoning debate.[22] The media may engage with socially shared understandings used in the process of making sense of unfamiliar scientific knowledge,[23] yet the learning of environmental science requires much more time and commitment for laypeople to engage in the first place than in many other policy areas. While previous work suggests that citizens' engagement with scientists will develop their perception of capacities to participate in political processes about scientific matters[24] and that they are indeed capable of scientific knowledge acquisition,[25] both the social status of scientific experts and the legitimacy of "objective" knowledge may intimidate laypeople from having a perceived capacity to communicate with scientific institutions in the first place.[26]

It is at this point that "expert citizens" enter the debate on citizen alienation from political processes in the area of environmental science. My claim is that expert citizens can go far in addressing the alienation problem. Expert citizens are independent professionals in the non-profit sector, skilled in the physical side of the relevant sciences, and motivated by their concerns for the local relevance of scientific knowledge. In this chapter, the term "expert citizen" is defined in the Japanese political context as one who does not wish to deal with the strong state and corporatist interests at the national level but rather prefers to be involved at the local level as it is closest to their communities. The merchant nature of post-WWII Japan reflected the desire of the national government to insulate itself from popular pressures, including environmental ones, and direct its economic policy to promote profitability in the private sector. Environmental interests experience difficulties in finding a voice within economic priorities at the national level. Tension between national and local authorities reflects the relative openness of local government to popular pressures and social priorities. Japan has a small and locally organized community of environmental groups.[27] In the US, where generic rules of policy-making add an incentive to formally incorporate laypeople into the public realm of wider consultation, if laypeople wish to influence environmental policy-making at the national level, they can join national environmental organizations, such as the NRDC. Public participation is organized in a professional way; those national associations build networks of interaction with scientific experts, policy-makers, interest groups and the media expressing the opinions of citizens.[28] In the UK, the inclusion of not-for-profit organizations and independent think tanks as third parties is well accepted to implement good practice in public participation. To support public participation, these organizations, such as Involve and DEMOS, have been offering expertise and channeling citizen participation. In the UK, public officials and politicians appear to be more open to third-party collaboration than any other European OECD countries.[29]

Public participation does not automatically make expert knowledge democratically accountable. The key rationale for the "intermediary role" of expert citizens lies in the importance of extending the principles of democracy to the production of expert and scientific knowledge. In this chapter, while drawing on the literature about the division between laypeople and experts, the quality of expert citizens' role is tapped by two basic components: helping local capacity-building to effectively engage resourceful stakeholders in shared policy and decision-making and promoting two-way symmetrical communication rather than the one-way asymmetrical communication associated with expert persuasion. Expert citizens, who are capable not only of understanding expert knowledge but also of socially engaging at the local level, provide information that might not otherwise be heard by either laypeople or experts. Awareness raising is a two-way flow of communication and information exchange in order to improve mutual understanding between the actors. Yet technical assistance is directed towards laypeople, particularly in the drafting and formulation of a policy development plan. This assistance also requires persistent effort to ensure public participation. More importantly, expert citizens, who are expected to act as facilitators, need to apply a lateral coordination process to developing plans, solving problems, and making decisions. They need to bring together laypeople and experts through persuasion and negotiation, instead of giving hierarchically authority-based guidance and rules. To this end, again, they help less resourceful laypeople build their capacity to co-produce on an equal footing with experts, yet they are expected to be a neutral third party when facilitating a negotiated solution between the parties. The intermediary role of expert citizens can be considered as a new form of participation, yet little guidance is provided in the literature on how technically competent expert citizens' practices contribute to the mitigation of the growing public disenchantment with expert knowledge.

Why do Jōyō and Shiki matter?

Over the past decade, some forms of direct citizen participation (*shimin sanka*) in local policy-making have become common among Japanese local governments. The 1993 enactment of the national Basic Environmental Law encouraged local authorities to prepare their own environmental basic bylaws and plans, and the national grant program paid 50 percent of actual costs for preparing such plans, in anticipation of compliance with the advancement (*senshinsei*) of planning processes (i.e., citizens' participatory role in the process). This triggered abrupt increases in the nationally defined inclusion of citizens in preparing local environmental plans. As of 2013, Basic Environmental Bylaws had been enacted in 97 percent of prefectures and 58 percent of municipalities. In preparing their basic environmental plans, these local governments normally created a sole participatory mechanism, advisory environmental councils (*shingikai*), whose membership composition was similar to that of the national councils representing businesses, interest groups, and academics rather than concerned ordinary citizens. In their plan-implementation processes, as of 2013, public involvement played a limited role: with the establishment of advisory councils accounting for 68 percent of local governments, opinion surveys as an instrument of accountability representing 51 percent of the local governments, and public comments being solicited by 47 percent of the local governments. In 2013, 42 percent of the 1,034 local governments had been practicing some form of collaboration with citizens for CO_2 emissions reduction countermeasures, yet only 10 percent of those collaborative schemes had been initiated or requested by local residents. A large majority of the collaborations had been led by the local administration as the 1998 Climate Change Law stipulated a local government's statutory obligation to promote policy measures for emissions reduction. The national top-down promotion had thus failed to provide much in the way of substantial citizen participation in local environmental governance.[30]

In Japan, "Local Agenda 21" has become a field for political experimentation with new ways to create legitimacy and participatory accountability mechanisms which are expected to require deliberation between experts and citizens to address a broadly conceived inter-issue linkage (namely, economic development, environmental protection and social justice) of sustainability.[31] Local Agenda 21 has the potential to enhance public understanding and mitigate public disenchantment with expert knowledge. Yet most municipalities have already had "long-term comprehensive plans" (*sōgō keikaku*) at the highest level of local governmental plans, as defined in Local Autonomy Law (Articles 2-4). Local government officials tend to see Local Agenda 21 as one of a variety of administration activities, not as a plan to integrate stakeholders' activities into a participatory, multi-sectoral process. Unlike the International Council for Local Environmental Initiative's (ICLEI) definition of Local Agenda 21, Japan's Environmental Agency saw Local Agenda 21 as the final product of community plans rather than as an interactive process itself, existing between stakeholders to increase local accountability in making communities more sustainable.[32] Local

Agenda 21 programs in Japan are consequently reported to indicate peculiar patterns: over 70 percent of these Local Agenda 21s (as of 2012, the number of reported cases of such programs at the municipal level was 330) are regarded as a mere administration plan rather than a societal, voluntary process of local community consultation.[33]

Nonetheless, it is important to note that substantial citizen participation was reported in a dozen pioneering cases of collaboration between citizens and the local administration for environmental governance. There are two front-runner cases, Toyonaka and Hino cities, reported as being purely citizen-led environmental planning whereby a group of openly invited citizens made their own drafts and local assemblies literally adopted them as basic environmental plans in March 1999 and September 1999, respectively.[34] There are two other basic patterns of citizens' collaboration with local administration: one on relatively equal terms between citizens and local administration (e.g., Jōyō and Shiki cities) and the other based on citizens' agenda setting and local administration's planning (e.g., Date and Ichikawa cities).[35]

The necessity of citizen participation to achieve successful environmental policy has been recognized for some years, especially since the 1992 Rio Declaration. In Japan, a series of local adaptations to environmental decision-making has attempted to strengthen the principle of public involvement. Yet concerned citizens are faced with the "scientization" and "expertization" of environmental problems; the complexity of scientific knowledge to discuss environmental rules and regulations appears to put any venture to collaborate with administrators and scientists out of the reach of private citizens. Perhaps, the most interesting development for bridging gaps between science and society is the Creation and Sustainable Governance of New Commons through Formation of Integrated Local Environmental Knowledge (ILEK) project in Japan. The ILEK project has developed the novel concept of "bilateral knowledge translators" who are residential researchers (living in local communities) and local stakeholders at the same time.[36] They translate local knowledge into general scientific languages and stimulate knowledge-sharing between science and society. Since 2012, the project has been conducting a series of social experiments in the case study sites by using the presence of recruited bilateral translators.[37] The ultimate objective is to build a knowledge-based adaptive governance mechanism for local communities.

The Kiko Network (a Japanese non-governmental organization for addressing climate change) is probably the first organization in Japan to lead the way in acting as a coordinator between citizens and experts in environmental policy-making while being keenly aware of the need to play such a role in the advancement of expert knowledge.[38] Since 2000, the Kiko Network has served as a contractor for stakeholder coordination for local environmental planning in municipal projects, such as those for Jōyō, Yawata, Takashima, Hirakata, Ooyamazaki, Tanba, and Yao cities. In 2011 the organization started to organize and coordinate "Strategic Forums for Low Carbon Regional Development" where citizens, businesses, and experts participate in studying and sharing road maps towards a low-carbon society. Those forums (five cases in 2011 and eight cases in 2012) have been in operation as the Kiko Network provides information regarding the structure of carbon emissions and available natural and social resources that are highly specific to each locality. It is important to note that the Kiko Network is not the umbrella organization that individual citizens or their groups join if they want to influence national environmental policy. The Kiko Network has limited access to national policy-making. The Kiko Network president's membership in a government committee is probably the only direct venue where its voice is heard and represented at the national level. The Kyoto office of the Kiko Network, which was involved in my case study, has held education and training activities and collaborative activities with local governments and other citizens' groups at the local level.

Some farsighted independents who are locally active for climate change adaptation and mitigation have attempted to fulfil such talent needs through modularized training systems. Kazuho Seko, executive producer of the non-profit Training and Resource Center, proposes "collaboration coordinators" (*kyōdō kōdinētā*) who are competent enough to plan conferences and workshops and facilitate collaborative processes between citizens and other stakeholders. The Center has also provided training programs and management skills to local communities since 1997.[39] Ryo Mori, executive director of the non-profit ECO Communication Center, has also conducted a series of training programs for citizens' capacity-building to develop a participatory learning process related to community environmental management and for their scientific and local knowledge to facilitate environmental decision-making processes.[40] The Center itself has designed and coordinated the process of local environmental collaboration in 13 municipalities since 1993.[41]

Jōyō city was the first municipality with which the Kiko Network entered into a contract (2000–2003) to facilitate the collaborative processes of developing Jōyō's basic environmental bylaw and plan. Shiki city was also the first municipality to which ECO Communication Center provided the design and facilitation of workshops—Shimin Kankyō Daigaku (citizens' environmental university for facilitators' training) from 1993 to 1995, which was part of municipal projects for the Model City for the Promotion of Environmental Education as designated by the Ministry of Education in 1993. Both municipalities are cities on a river where local knowledge of the environment and local identities have emerged over a long period of time. The ratio of the daytime population per 100 nighttime population is 78.3 (2010) in Shiki and 80.9 (2010) in Jōyō; both cities are known as commuter towns where there are more workers living in the city than working there.[42] Shiki and Jōyō, with populations of 72,813 (2013) and 78,347 (2013), respectively, are normally categorized as small cities but the population of both cities has more than doubled since 1970, putting a greater strain on the local environment. As described in the following sections, collaboration between citizens and experts in both cities was conducted through joint environmental planning on far more equal terms than was done in most other Japanese localities. These two cases are quite similar to each other, with the one exception being the ways citizens actually participate in environmental policy-making and implementation.

The case of EcoCity Shiki in Shiki city

In 1995 a socially mobilized citizens' group called EcoCity Shiki began a citizen-led process of environmental planning that resulted in the non-governmental Shiki Citizen's Environmental Plan in 1998. In the same year, the municipal government openly solicited 26 members for a Citizen's Environmental Conference that was to meet to draft a governmental Basic Environmental Plan. It found more than half of its seats occupied by EcoCity Shiki members. While it took three years for EcoCity Shiki to complete its own fieldwork-based Shiki Citizen's Environmental Plan, the EcoCity Shiki-led Conference achieved its governmental mission within a matter of 10 months. The city administration subsequently integrated much of the non-governmental plan, made by EcoCity Shiki, into the 1999 Basic Environmental Plan. The following case study will examine the intermediary roles played by a collective body of expert citizens, EcoCity Shiki, in organizing a voluntary citizens' group for initiating and supporting the community plan and in facilitating the exchange process between expert knowledge and residents' concerns.

Shiki's experience addresses a most intriguing question: Why did the bureaucracy-led city authority take laypeople's ideas so seriously and subsequently collaborate with concerned citizens? One of the original members of EcoCity Shiki, Masanori Moori, unhesitatingly answered, "Certain antecedent conditions more favorable to citizen participation already existed in the city."[43] In 1972 the oldest environmental group in the Saitama region, the Council for the Promotion of Clean River, was established in Shiki. Thereafter, the city witnessed the creation of other Shiki-based environmental groups, such as Shiki City Livelihood Club, Two Trees Club, Field Club, and Ecosystem Conservation Society (Shiki Branch), and the number of environmental groups in the city increased to around 70 organizations by the early 1990s.[44] A dominant feature characteristic of most Japanese environmental movements in the early 1970s was their routine engagement in contentious politics against power-holders in the issue area of industrial pollution. Yet conservationists who were willing to collaborate with the city administration and business began to lead Shiki's organizations and by the mid-1980s their activities to promote environmental conservation became more noticeable. In 1985 Kihachirō Hosoda, who took a progressive stance with his strong support for direct citizen participation, was successfully elected as Shiki's mayor. He established a private advisory council, known as Shiki Citizen's Conference, in the following year to follow through on his campaign promise. The council continued to propose citizens' ideas to the municipal government until 2001 when he stepped down as mayor.

In the upsurge of conservation concerns, Shimin Kankyō Daigaku served as a place to bring all the environmental groups together to develop networks among themselves. The city held a series of participatory workshops on environmental issues in 1993 and 1994. As requested by some participants, it further offered another series of workshops for facilitators' training in 1995. ECO Communication Center Director Mori acted as an organizer of all these workshops while introducing the learning methods of participatory workshop and fieldwork experience to the participants. A shared sense of solidarity subsequently emerged among those who had studied together for three years. Some participants in the workshops became members of Shiki's Promotion Committee for Environmental Education. They were entrusted with the task of providing the contact point for local residents and the city administration. A major outcome of the training sessions occurred in July 1995 when Mori proposed a voluntary workshop, Local Agenda Shiki Workshop, based on the necessity of a citizen-initiated environmental plan. As momentum grew at this self-managed two-day workshop, discussions among 32 participants (10 of whom were municipal government employees participating in the capacity of individual citizens) paved the way for the coalition establishment of EcoCity Shiki in October 1995.[45] Both the municipal project for the Model City and the intermediary non-profit ECO Communication Center provided a number of insulated, issue-oriented citizen groups with an opportunity to network with one another for multi-dimensional community planning.

EcoCity Shiki accordingly chose the formulation of its own environmental plan at the start of their activity and this became a formative experience for the organization to develop the patterns of their activity. In October 1995, EcoCity Shiki members agreed to set up four working groups: "Water and Green," "Rubbish and Energy," "Health, Medical Care and Welfare," and "Community Building and Environmental Education." Using the experience gained from Shimin Kankyō Daigaku, the members mobilized two key operational patterns, fieldwork and workshops, to draft their environmental plan.[46] The former was conducted to identify emerging issues (e.g., the urban heat island effect, water quality in the river, and information about birds, fish, and plants in the river basin) in the local environment and apply the findings to their draft plan. The fieldwork was based on the assumption that local conditions were so variable that universal scientific predictions may fail. The latter was designed for individual views to be heard and taken into account and for a number of invited experts to communicate to the public in the environmental debate (e.g., waste reduction, biomass, transportation systems). A workshop-driven planning process was aimed at ensuring social equity and developing communications that would take the local context and its demands seriously.[47]

In March 1998 EcoCity Shiki completed its Shiki Citizen's Environmental Plan. Chapter 1 of the plan set forth the specific roles to be played by EcoCity Shiki in the processes of community building, stating, "EcoCity Shiki is to act as coordinator between different localities, generations, and actors. The members are to work in close cooperation with municipal administration, local business and residents and to vigorously engage in practical activities and become a promoter."[48] The members thus clearly recognized the importance of their developed competence to facilitate the complementarities between experts and ordinary citizens within the existing networks. At the time of the release of the plan, the city administration had already indicated its willingness to collaborate with EcoCity Shiki. The Environmental Promotion Department of Shiki City was cited as saying, "We'd like to incorporate some of their ideas into a municipal plan where possible, after taking into account the impact on administration and business and financial backing."[49] Director Mori then praised the potential competence of EcoCity Shiki as "developed enough to actually propose a public policy."[50]

In fiscal year 1998 the mayor secured a budget for making the city's administrative environmental plan as EcoCity Shiki presented a copy of its environmental plan to him. In May 1998 all 26 members who were publicly recruited from the citizenry began to discuss and draft an official environmental plan at the Citizen's Environmental Conference. They held nine major meetings until the completion of the first draft and prior to each formal meeting the chair and deputy-chair persons had an executive briefing with environmental specialists or scientists and the city department concerned to exchange information and opinions. They were able to produce a draft-only comprehensive plan at the ninth meeting and submitted the compilation of all the works to the city administration to assess their feasibility and operationality. Take, for example, "a 75 per cent reduction in municipal waste within 10 years," which was initially proposed by the non-governmental Shiki Citizen's Environmental Plan. It was based on EcoCity Shiki's findings that food waste represented nearly half of the total weight of household rubbish. In its view, avoiding or composting food waste could achieve a large part of the goal. Yūji Nishikawa of the Environmental Promotion Department recalled the collaborative process by saying, "it was difficult for us to adopt it as it was, because we were dealing with a group of diverse citizens from a population of 65,000."[51] From the viewpoint of the city administration, budget matters, such as capital expenditure and operation costs, preoccupied waste reduction. At that time, dioxin pollution was in the spotlight since scientists had detected high dioxin concentrations in farm produce in the neighboring city Tokorozawa. Environmental specialists pointed out the necessity of limits in the concentration of dioxin-like compounds in the discharge gas of waste incineration. Nonetheless, the city administration assessed the early draft and agreed to much of EcoCity Shiki's detailed action plan. At the tenth meeting in March 1999, it became the final draft. The collaborative process helped to develop a communication and policy network, so to speak, among expert citizens, local government officials and environmental specialists.

It is important to point out that EcoCity Shiki has taken local history and life experience seriously to increase the credibility of their policy ideas in the collaborative process. In other words, its knowledge production is gained through life experience and it is mediated through local history and cultural tradition. Director Moori of EcoCity Shiki makes explicit his reliance on evidence from local historical legacies, pictures, oral storytelling, and eye-witnessed evidence from many years' experiences.[52] The rivers shaped the physical landscape and influenced the cultural landscape of Shiki. He argues, "Our natural and cultural heritage provided Shiki's predecessors with a foundation of living wisdom."[53] EcoCity Shiki has carried out a series of heritage investigations, conducted numerous studies of water and habitat quality, did fieldwork with openly recruited citizens on a regular basis, organized eco-tours to foster a greater appreciation of the local environment and implemented some conservation projects. One of the most recent projects was a field investigation of "Shiki Ecomuseum: Learning from Mizuka (remnants of locally specific flood control facilities)," 2009–2010. EcoCity Shiki organized and coordinated extensive field research on Mizuka, which had been built around old family housing in the seventeenth and eighteenth centuries and remained intact, with 19 laypeople volunteering to act as investigators for this project. They were able to produce a monograph and share local knowledge with local residents. To increase the value of its distinctiveness and place, the Shiki community as a whole is regarded as an "ecomuseum," which is an important public space where community members can learn from their heritage to conserve their place-based knowledge and make the most of it for community planning.[54]

Expert citizens play an intermediary role in the exchange process between expert knowledge and residents' concerns at the local level. Probably the most critical question in finding a proper role for expert citizens is to ask if they act as a neutral third party in the collaborative processes of stakeholders or if they actually represent individual citizens to policy-makers and other experts. ECO Communication Center initially intended to train its members to become "coordinators." In other words, the coordinators are supposed to remain committed to strict neutrality in the exchange processes of stakeholders.[55] However, all observed facts indicate that EcoCity Shiki clearly attempted to represent individual citizens to policy experts while talking through technical matters to individual citizens with concrete views of everyday reality and persuading the experts to incorporate local concerns often overlooked by them into their plan. It appears that EcoCity Shiki has used a series of open workshops/seminars and fieldwork as a main accountability mechanism towards individual citizens. The relationship between ordinary citizens and expert citizens requires further case studies to identify the emerging roles played by expert citizens.

The case of the Citizen Environmental Discussion Group in Jōyō city

Jōyō city enacted a Basic Environmental Ordinance in 2002 and approved its Basic Environmental Plan in 2003. Jōyō was probably the first Japanese city where citizen participants produced a formal proposal for a legally binding ordinance without any tentative basis, prepared by the municipal administration, for discussion, and drafted it, in collaboration with an Examination Committee (*kentō iinkai*) of the city administration, until the final stage of technical wording. Notable differences between Jōyō and Shiki lie in the ways citizens actually participated in environmental policy-making and implementation. To promote the citizens' participatory role in the formulation of the ordinance, Jōyō city established an advisory Citizen Environmental Discussion Group (*kankyō shimin kondankai*), which consisted of 10 openly recruited citizens, six business representatives and four other organization representatives. To facilitate the process of ordinance-drafting and to coordinate in a collaborative process between the group and the city administration, the role of "environmental coordinator" was outsourced to the Kiko Network. Kenrō Taura from this environmental non-profit organization directly coordinated between the citizen group and the Examination Committee, whereas in the case of Shiki, ECO Communication Center did not get involved in the process of policy-making and implementation but, prior to this process, provided a series of workshops and field experiences for capacity-building to become expert citizens. To examine the science-society interface, we need inquiries where the unit of analysis is the actors who play an intermediary role between laypeople and experts in policy-making. The target of analysis is thus both the Kiko Network and the Citizen Environmental Discussion Group.

As discussed below, the ways of Jōyō citizens' involvement appear to be closely associated with the capacity and scale of environmentally concerned residents. An abandoned gravel pit that occupied 13 percent of the Jōyō area created a unique environmental problem of water contamination. In 1967 a Townspeople Conference against Gravel Digging was established to engage in a contentious interaction with business interests and the then town administration. The flood legends of the Kizu River, which runs along the city, had a significant influence on cultural landscape and life experience. Yet it was only in the late 1990s that citizens' groups finally propelled their concerns into the visibility of a conservation movement. In collaboration with the city administration, the scale of conservation activities in Jōyō grew much slower and smaller than in Shiki, with the number of environmental groups reaching around 20 in the late 1990s.[56]

In the past, Japanese local governments have made increasing use of private consultants who provided more technical and complex planning services. It is reported that local authorities in no small number have totally subcontracted the preparation of draft plans and ordinances to consultants.[57] Consultants normally extend technical support for their clients. The relationships between local authorities and consultants can be explained from a vertical principal-agent viewpoint. In this sense, the Kiko Network was not a consultant as it was contracted to facilitate the progression of discussion at each meeting of the Citizen Environmental Discussion Group and, in its independent capacity, to coordinate the interactive process between the group and the Examination Committee. Why then was it necessary for Jōyō City to outsource the coordinator's role to the Kiko Network?

An original member of the Citizen Environmental Discussion Group, Noriko Okamura, recalls the state of the group at an early stage by saying, "At the beginning we didn't understand many technical terms necessary for environmental planning.... We groped our way to the door in the dark and didn't know where to begin."[58] In this regard, the Department of Environmental Planning of Jōyō pointed out, "Without any coordinator, what would have happened in the midst of producing the formal proposal...."[59] Most members did not have a comprehensive understanding of the fundamentals of environmental conservation, and some members thus voiced their concerns over this unpreparedness. Study meetings became essential to the completion of their proposal. The city created a new position of "environmental coordinator" whose role was contracted to the Kiko Network. The first task of the Kiko Network was to organize and carry out a set of introductory study meetings with the Citizen Environmental Discussion Group while the group went to visit and observe the local environment. Taura facilitated the study meetings in plain language with concrete examples so that the members could easily grasp the essence of a highly technical expertise. These introductory meetings were prerequisite to writing their ordinance proposal.

It took six months for 15 meetings to explore the potential contents and finally complete their ordinance proposal in April 2001. Once submitted to the mayor, the proposal was expected to become the basis for the city administration to draft the actual ordinance. However, the Examination Committee was very reluctant to give official approval to the idea of inserting "partnership" as a key feature in the ordinance. At the sixteenth meeting with the Examination Committee members, some committee members argued that they should water down or postpone dealing with the idea. Under these circumstances, Taura played a crucial role in the start-up of collaboration between the two parties in the ordinance-drafting process rather than leaving it to the city administration. He bluntly pointed out the lack of understanding of the benefits of citizen participation within the city administration, while acknowledging the technical difficulties of administrative and legal requirements at the same time.[60] Both parties agreed that the Citizen Environmental Discussion Group would continue to involve and pursue consensus-building in this process. He facilitated a series of joint study meetings and exchange of opinions, which were designed to develop a shared understanding between the parties. He assisted them in adjusting the preferences of the lay group into a consistent legal framework for administrative and financial practice. It took five more months for 20 meetings to finalize the ordinance draft in October 2001. One of the principles stated in the ordinance draft was "the importance of citizen participation," and this principle provided the draft with detailed applications in the stages of policy-making and implementation.[61]

It is clear that the ongoing process of capacity-building, through which Citizen Environmental Discussion Group members enhanced their ability to understand both expert and local knowledge, was too short and too late for them to play an intermediate key role among stakeholders in the process of the ordinance-drafting. But the Kiko Network acted as an expert citizen in the collaborative process between local concerns and expert knowledge. The Citizen Environmental Discussion Group members were thus direct beneficiaries of the Kiko Network's coordination and facilitation.

But how were public preferences heard and represented in the process of local bylaw making, as the Citizen Environmental Discussion Group did not necessarily represent the diversity of Jōyō citizens? The discussion group became aware of this problem as the collaborative process between the discussion group and the city administration continued. The discussion group persuaded the Environmental Planning Department by saying, "As we initiated and drew up the draft ordinance, we'll talk to local residents."[62] In October 2002 the discussion group accordingly organized nine Neighborhood Chat Meetings (*idobata kaigi*), which were held at six community centers across the city to compile local concerns about proposing the city's environmental plan. Observation provided some very interesting insights as described by a member of the discussion group, Noboru Ashiwara, about the situation of Neighborhood Chat Meetings. He found the discussion (at the Neighborhood Chat Meetings), chaired by discussion group members, to be very useful for exchanging good opinions with participants, because the meetings would have ended up with citizens' one-sided accusations against the municipal authority if the discussion had directly taken place between the city and citizens.[63] In this respect, it appeared that the Citizen Environmental Discussion Group would undergo an embryonic stage before becoming expert citizens in the local policy networks. In October 2003 the Jōyō Environmental Partnership Conference (a non-profit organization) was established through the discussion group's initiative to collaborate with environmental experts, city departments, and local residents for conservation activities, policy-making, implementation, and evaluation.

Discussion

In the issue area of Japanese environmental policy, corporatist policy style has been consistently observed in the exclusive form of business-state relationships at the national level. A few nationally organized environmental groups have participated in national advisory councils but have rarely helped to draft national legislation. The ministerial state tends to invite environmental groups to participate in its advisory councils only if they take a pro-government stance or not engage in contentious politics. The industrial coalition of big business—powerful economic ministries—often rejects or emasculates progressive policy proposals in the legislative area of environmental policy. As seen in this chapter, most environmental groups in Japan have, until recently, been locally based, in terms of their goals and networking. Unlike those in the US, Japan's environmental groups at the local level do not have much in the way of backing from large, professionalized national environmental organizations (umbrella organizations), which citizens' movements largely failed to form. The necessity of expert citizens for public involvement thus does exist at the local level for successful environmental policy. The cases examined in this chapter indicate that specific events trigger the emergence of expert citizens. However, specific local factors need to be present before the localized expert citizens emerge. The findings of this study suggest a potential mechanism that could lead to expert citizen clusters and indicate the potential factors that constitute necessary or supportive prerequisites.

In the US, environmental scientists can be found in different capacities: scientists hired by national environmental non-governmental organizations to produce knowledge, federal government scientists, and a more autonomous and less economically interested body of scientists (who freely review data, government policy, and citizens' positions and engage in national policy networks). By emphasizing legalistic regulations in the US, as compared to administrative ones in Japan, scientists have more opportunities to present their independent views in the judicial system, even in order to establish legal standards for scientific thinking. In Japan, however, scientists are less likely to play a strategically independent role in national environmental policy networks. The basic problem is the alleged co-option of scientists and academics to the objectives of administrative regulations driven by the bureaucracy. According to this co-option account, scientists are expected to serve as "academic flunkies" (*goyō gakusha*) at regulatory advisory councils; some express dissenting opinions but these scientists are highly unlikely to be reappointed for additional terms. At the local level, Japan's environmental monitoring, environmental forecasting, and environmental assessment are often outsourced by local authorities to commercial consultant firms that tend to serve in favor of government projects to secure future contracts. As seen in this study, the primary focus of citizen-expert relationships in the issue area of Japan's environmental policy revolves around public involvement in the government administration at the local level. Expert citizens are thus expected to act as mediators in this context.

The findings from the field research undertaken in this study can be summarized in a few points, which can contribute to the new debate on citizen-expert relationships in environmental policy.

1   The case studies identify an avenue available to people who wish to become expert citizens: through organized and networked groups. Although many individuals do become interested in environmental issues and, on their own, learn and seek participatory avenues, the case studies show that the emergence of expert citizens requires organizations and networks through which individual citizens engage in public affairs. It is a collective citizen activity that is adept at accumulating a variety of resources and using them to gain expertise more effectively. It is citizen networking that allows individual citizens to know whom to contact, learn where to get information, and to connect with various community needs, priorities, and values. Individual citizens learn through citizens' organizations about environmental risk reduction, in terms of both scientific facts and local knowledge. Individual citizens who join those groups and networks tend to be driven by activism in the first place as they are eager to learn from experts, in order to find expert knowledge linking environmental risks with their community problems. In the case of Shiki city, about 70 environmental groups more favorable to the emergence of expert citizens already existed in the early 1990s. This precondition eventually brought all the environmental groups together to develop networks among themselves. These like-minded people had a shared sense of solidarity which subsequently emerged among those who had studied together for a common cause. In contrast, citizens' group activities in

Jōyō grew much slower and later than those in Shiki. Around 20 environmental groups in Jōyō were yet to develop their capacity to play an intermediate key role among stakeholders in the early 2000s.

2. Collaboration between community and experts provides socially mobilized citizens with an opportunity to learn more about a scientific understanding of environmental problems and trends as well as place-based local knowledge and experiences. In Japan in the late 1960s and early 1970s, the contentions of citizens' movements existed in more simple and often dichotomous interactions of polluters versus victims with established power relations. In the 1990s, Japan's urban movements in the area of environmental protection had been transforming into a far more complex process in which co-dependent interactions with traditional power holders were emerging. The line between victims and victimizers was not that clear, so to speak, although that transformation may be conventionally characterized as a process of the co-option of pre-existing local power-holders. By the mid-1980s, Shiki's conservationists began to lead environmental groups and they were willing to collaborate with the city administration, business, and academics. The opportunity structure that their networks of collaboration with experts created over time rewarded their learning of expert knowledge. It is safe to say that the collaboration enhanced and improved their understanding of, and ability to respond to, the process of decision-making in complex social-environmental systems. There was an emerging discourse among stakeholders that provided flexible adaptation to the city's environmental planning. This sort of collaborative governance is more likely to encompass complexity and cross-scale linkages of environmental issues, and the process of policy learning among participants. In the case of Jōyō, socially mobilized citizens were also direct beneficiaries of their collaboration with the Kiko Network, the city administration, academics, and local residents for the process of policy learning.

3. The heart of an intermediary role that expert citizens are to play at the local level lies in their capacity to facilitate the process of social learning by bridging gaps between stakeholders, leading to the integration of local and expert knowledge. Socially mobilized citizens occupy a strategic position to understand that expert knowledge continues to advance our understanding of the environment yet to recognize that there is a limited understanding or a degree of uncertainty in the complexity of environmental science, which requires local knowledge and experience to develop a more detailed understanding of environmental impacts at the local level. That strategic position does not automatically allow socially mobilized citizens to develop their skills to facilitate social learning processes among stakeholders. In the cases of Shiki and Jōyō, those skills were very limited and yet to develop further. The experience of environmental planning in both cities indicates some developing processes that will be useful for social learning to bridge the gaps between local and expert knowledge. Working together on joint problem-solving can be an important source for mutual learning among

stakeholders. The integration of local and expert knowledge is more likely to be effective when they engage in active communication through the sharing/exchange of knowledge and expertise and develop a sense of trust to realize mutual benefits. In a democratic sense, the ideal integration of local and general scientific knowledge is based on the use of participatory methods and a fundamental contribution to environmental justice, in order to foster the legitimacy of decision-making. The normative significance of expert citizens' role is to assist disadvantaged laypeople to be both knowledgeable and resourceful to communicate with power holders to integrate local and expert knowledge. EcoCity Shiki somewhat helped local residents develop their environmental literacy through group learning, and also allowed for them to produce clear democratic benefits through the deliberative process by which local residents who bear the consequences of policy-making should be able to be part of decisions.

4   Emerging expert citizens have the potential to act as a mediating force to set in motion a dialectic of expert knowledge and local knowledge while bridging the divide between experts and lay people. They offer platforms to open up spaces for dialogue, and thus integrate and harmonize the gaps, among actors involved in decision-making. The experiences of Shiki and Jōyō suggest that the processes of problem handling are more experimental and learning oriented. The way of expert-lay reflexive interplay may be practically more effective in dealing with the policy requirements emerging from the complexity, uncertainty, and ambiguity present in environmental science. The use of reflexive interplay implies that personal reflexivity (internal conversation) exists only to be relational to others. In other words, reflexive interplay refers to the relationships of actors who have their own reflexivity. As seen in the collaborative process between the citizen group and the city administration in Shiki, expert knowledge was not given but rather communicated and used, and likewise local knowledge might not necessarily lead to more environmentally sound or sustainable decisions thus seeking to reveal how it would improve environmental planning. This is regarded as a rather citizen-expert interactive co-production. EcoCity Shiki members, while trying to represent local residents' interests rather than remaining neutral, helped to open up a public space for a dialogue-oriented exchange of arguments and problem-solving. City department officials in Shiki initially wished to retain autonomy over technical issues and expected citizen participation to remain in the realm of implementation rather than planning and policy-making. In other words, expert knowledge and local knowledge are to be compatible in the sense that experts make decisions and local residents apply them to locally specific conditions. Contrary to their expectation, however, EcoCity Shiki acted as a contributor to all aspects of environmental planning decisions as its members successfully persuaded the city administration to bring forward publicly justifiable reasons for the procedural and substantive dimensions of legitimacy in decision-making. On-going reflexive dialogues, which are concerned with

5　Although the existing structure of social mobilization in both Shiki and Jōyō sets limits on the emerging process of expert citizens, personal ability can make a difference. Demographics and socioeconomic factors certainly create opportunity structures which constrain or enable the actors in political processes. But it is actors that perceive the political opportunities and assemble the knowledge, resources, and norms to achieve desired objectives. On the basis of community-outsider ECO Communication Center's and Kiko Network's experience of successful operation elsewhere, their individual coordinators used expertise and resources in Shiki and Jōyō, respectively. The facilitator from ECO Communication Center viewed Shiki's environmental projects, led by the Ministry of Education and the municipal government, as an opportunity to bring together a number of disconnected socially mobilized groups into expert citizens' training sessions. A series of participatory workshops on environmental issues, which were held by the city, provided a perfect networking venue among those groups. This led to the formation of EcoCity Shiki. A shared sense of solidarity or cohesion subsequently emerged among those who had studied together for three years. In contrast, faced with a smaller scale of socially mobilized groups' collaborative activities with the city administration in Jōyō, the coordinator of the Kiko Network acted to stimulate the creation of expert citizens while himself mediating between the actors involved in Jōyō's environmental ordinance and planning.

6　Expert citizens are expected to provide less-resourceful/less-informed citizens with technical and public relations support but to be mediators rather than advocates. Are expert citizens purely neutral actors who seek to mediate between the actors involved in decision-making? Are they sympathetic to a particular group/organization? Or do they politically lean more to the group/organization? EcoCity Shiki and Citizen Environmental Discussion Group (potential expert citizens) considered local experience and knowledge as resources to participate on an equal footing with power holders. They are expected to provide the less-informed individual and unorganized citizens with the resources and other technical support. EcoCity Shiki did not behave as a neutral mediator and clearly attempted to represent public preference. EcoCity Shiki had a closer and more direct access to environmental groups and socially mobilized citizens than to the city administration. EcoCity Shiki members were not disinterested actors but acted strategically to seek a solution among the actors involved in decision-making. They tried to establish a collaborative space through open workshops/seminars, expert consultations, and executive briefing in a multi-faceted process. However, the key issue of whether expert citizens need to remain neutral to effectively refashion expert knowledge into a more citizen-expert interactive governance requires further examination. The concept of expert citizens remains unsettled.

It is important to note that there are some clear limitations to be taken into account in the generalization of the analysis of two successful cases to other cases in Japan. Opportunity structures that influenced the emergence of expert citizens were unusual in the sense that other localities might not have such structures. At first, the opportunity structure for direct forms of public participation, which appears to be either empowered or constrained by demographics, plays a key role in promoting the necessity of expert citizens at the local level. Although a lack of case studies makes my observation only suggestive rather than definitive, there seems to be a threshold population size, probably exceeded only in the multi-million population cities, at which the greater number of organizations and the more complex decision-making processes come to outweigh the political efficacy of direct forms of public participation. Equally important, no reports on the smaller size categories of fewer than 30,000 are found in those case studies. Within this limit, the smallness of Shiki and Jōyō seems to have nurtured the rise of expert citizens by virtue of their accessibility and intimacy. Second, in the case of Shiki City, there had been no major issues involved in the relationships between the local administration and residents, which might otherwise force socially mobilized residents to engage in sustained contentious interaction with city departments. These stable relationships seem to have created political opportunities for residents to cooperate with city departments. The complexity of governance can be analyzed at three levels: politics, polity, and policy. In Shiki city, community planning became rather apolitical over time while the focus was on polity structuring and decision-making arrangements. This political climate seems to favor the emergence of EcoCity Shiki. However, despite the potential structural constraints, I must emphasize again that the success of Shiki and Jōyō derives largely from the innovative creation of new concerns, new interests and new ways of action by creative actors.

Conclusion

As the use of scientific knowledge and expert advice produces more uncertainty, stakeholders have little difficulty in accepting a need for a problem-solving mediator who is capable of striking a balance between expert knowledge and social concerns. The opportunities of expert citizens associated with this development seen in different countries represent considerable variation in institutional tradition, developmental paths, and social norms. Japan's traditionally strong yet divided bureaucracy has had little success in efficiently delegating governmental responsibilities to citizen-initiated organizations at the national level. In Japan, public involvement at the local level has consequently been viewed as a primary domain for political efficacy. In this context, opportunities for expert citizens have emerged to meet needs at the local level. This study has shown that access to citizens' organizations, through which they learn about both expert and local knowledge, is of crucial importance. Work by members of organized groups is a key pathway to becoming expert citizens. The case studies indicate that the ways of expert citizens' facilitation could increase the credibility and legitimacy of expert knowledge while helping to provide public participation with an "equal footing" with experts/policy-makers. No regularized solution can be found with respect to the balance between expert inquiries and local concerns. Finding a decision-making balance between experts/policy-makers and laypeople can be facilitated by emerging expert citizens through a more reflexive, ongoing interplay between expert knowledge and local understandings.

The primary rationale for the necessity of expert citizens is to enhance public engagement in the professionalized processes of policy-making. Expert citizens could facilitate the interactions of experts and laypeople to extend the principles of democracy to science-driven policy-making. They occupy an important position to help laypeople redress inequitable distributions of environmental burdens. One of the expected roles, played by expert citizens, is to increase public participation by bringing together experts and laypeople into the "scientization" and "expertization" of decision-making and incorporate laypeople in environmental risk management. The cases observed in this chapter represent only a small part of the variety of ways in which expert citizens have a potential to play an intermediary role between laypeople and experts. There is a great deal of research yet to be done. As the Japanese government emphasizes the need for greater public involvement in environmental decision-making, so do laypeople feel for the need of expert citizens. Even if local governments or individual citizens call for help from a third party, there is a clear shortage of the talent necessary for citizens to individually or collectively play such an intermediary role. Citizens' organizations now need to strengthen their organizational foundations and accumulate expertise and know-how for future use.

Expert citizen is a rather elusive term, carrying institutional dimensions (principles and rules for collective action), normative demands (democratic legitimacy), and epistemological implications (theory of knowledge). In the presence of inherent uncertainties in expert/scientific knowledge, expert citizens are expected to emerge as mediators to stop the declining public trust in science-driven policy. The effectiveness of expert citizens assumes that improved on-going dialogues between experts and laypeople will reverse the declining trend of public trust. A greater role of expert citizens is to reorient expert knowledge towards accountability and responsiveness to laypeople. It is likely that no universal/fixed solution can be found to prevent conflict between expert knowledge and local knowledge and strike a balance between scientific integrity and social concerns. Expert citizens are better positioned to facilitate the on-going dialogue of expert-lay reflexive interplay and find solutions through the very process of learning and knowing.

Notes

1 Robert Putnam, "Bowling alone: America's declining social capital," *Journal of Democracy*, Vol. 6, No. 1 (1995), pp. 65–78.
2 Japan, Association for Promoting Fair Elections, *Tōitsu chihō senkyo ni okeru tōhyoritsu no suii* [Trends of voter turnouts in the unified local elections], May 2003, available from: www.akaruisenkyo.or.jp/tohyo/top.html [accessed December 14, 2014].

3 Henrik P. Bang, "Between everyday makers and expert citizens," in John Fenwick and Janice McMillan, eds., *Public Management in the Postmodern Era: Challenges and Prospects* (Cheltenham, UK: Edward Elgar Publishing, 2010), pp. 163–92.
4 Paul Hirst, *Associative Democracy* (Cambridge, UK: Polity Press, 1996); Lance W. Bennett and Robert M. Entman, eds., *Mediated Politics* (Cambridge, UK: Cambridge University Press, 2001).
5 Henrik P. Bang, "Everyday makers and expert citizens: building political not social capital," unpublished, ANU, School of Social Science January, 2004, p. 7, available from https://digitalcollections.anu.edu.au/bitstream/1885/42117/2/Henrik.pdf [accessed December 14, 2014].
6 Oscar van Heffen, Walter J.M. Kickert, and Jacques J.A. Thomassen, eds., *Governance in Modern Society: Effects, Change and Formation of Government* (Dordrecht: Kluwer Academic Publishers, 2000); Will Hutton and Anthony Giddens, eds., *On the Edge: Living with Global Capitalism* (London: Vintage, 2001).
7 William Scott and Chris Oulton, "Environmental education: arguing the case for multiple approaches," *Educational Studies*, Vol. 25, No. 1 (1999), pp. 119–25; Fiona Clark and Deborah Illman, "Dimension of civic science: introductory essay," *Science Communication*, Vol. 23, No. 1 (2001), pp. 5–27; European Commission, *Sustainable Production and Consumption in the European Union* (Luxembourg: Office for Official Publications of the European Union, 2004).
8 Steven Yearly, "Making systematic sense of public discontents with expert knowledge: two analytical approaches and a case study," *Public Understanding of Science*, Vol. 9, No. 2 (2000), pp. 105–22.
9 Ulrich Beck, *Risk Society: Towards a New Modernity*, trans. Mark Ritter (London: Sage, 1992 [1986]).
10 Alan Irwin and Brian Wynne, *Misunderstanding Science? The Public Reconstruction of Science and Technology* (Cambridge, UK: Cambridge University Press, 1996); Harry Collins and Robert Evans, "The third wave of science studies: studies of expertise and experience," *Social Studies of Science*, Vol. 32, No. 2 (2002), pp. 235–96; Brian Wynne, "Seasick on the third wave? Subverting the hegemony of propositionalism," *Social Studies of Science*, Vol. 33, No. 3 (2003), pp. 401–17; Sheila Jasanoff, "Transparency in public science: purposes, reasons, limits," *Law and Contemporary Problem*, Vol. 69, No. 21 (2006), pp. 21–45.
11 Robert W. Collin and Robin Morris Collin, "The role of communities in environmental decisions: communities speaking for themselves," *Journal of Environmental Law and Litigation*, Vol. 13, No. 37 (1998), pp. 37–89.
12 Sarah Whatmore, et al., *Understanding Environmental Knowledge Controversies: The Case of Flood Risk Management*, Full research report ESRC end of award report, RES-227-25-0018 (Swindon, UK: ESRC, 2010).
13 James Wilsdon, Brian Wynne, and Jack Stilgoe, *The Public Value of Science: or How to Ensure That Science Really Matters* (London: Demos, 2005); Jack Stilgoe, Alan Irwin, and Kevin Jones, *The Received Wisdom: Opening up Expert Advice* (London: Demos, 2006).
14 Michel Callon, "The role of lay people in the production and dissemination of scientific knowledge," *Science, Technology and Society*, Vol. 4, No. 1 (1999), pp. 81–94; Robert W. Kates, Nancy M. Dickson, and William C. Clark, "Sustainability science," Discussion Paper 2000-33, Belfer Center for Science and International Affairs, Kennedy School of Government, Harvard University, 2000.
15 See, for example, Selvia Tesh, "Citizen experts in environmental risk," *Policy Science*, Vol. 32, No. 1 (1999), pp. 39–58.
16 Sally Eden, "Public participation in environmental policy: considering scientific, counter-scientific and non-scientific contributions," *Public Understanding of Science*, Vol. 5, No. 3 (1996), pp. 183–204.
17 Bang, "Everyday makers and expert citizens," p. 5.

18 Organisation for Economic Co-operation and Development (OECD), *Engaging Citizens in Policy-Making: Information, Consultation and Public Participation*, PUMA Policy Brief No. 10 (Paris: OECD, 2001); European Institute for Public Participation (EIPP), *Public Participation in Europe: An International Perspective* (Bremen: EIPP, 2009).
19 EIPP, *Public Participation in Europe*, pp. 11–15.
20 Robert D. Putnam, *Making Democracy Work: Civic Traditions in Modern Italy* (Princeton, NJ: Princeton University Press, 1993).
21 Daniel Lee Kleinman, ed., *Science, Technology, and Democracy* (New York: State University of New York Press, 2000); Judith Petts, "Barriers to participation and deliberation in risk decisions: evidence from waste management," *Journal of Risk Research*, Vol. 7, No. 2 (2004), pp. 115–33.
22 Dorothy Nelkin, *Selling Science: How the Press Covers Science and Technology* (New York: W.H. Freeman & Co., 1995); Jane Gregory and Steve Miller, *Science in Public: Communication, Culture, and Credibility* (New York: Basic Books, 1998); Martin W. Bauer and Massimiano Bucchi, eds., *Journalism, Science, and Society: Science Communication between News and Public Relations* (London: Routledge, 2007); Richard Holliman, Elizabeth Whitelegg, Eileen Scanlon, Sam Smidt, and Jeff Thomas, eds., *Investigating Science Communication in the Information Age: Implications for Public Engagement and Popular Media* (Oxford: Oxford University Press, 2008).
23 Hélène Joffe, "Risk: from perception to social representation," *British Journal of Social Psychology*, Vol. 42, No. 1 (2003), pp. 55–73; Léonie J. Rennie and Susan M. Stocklmayer, "The communication of science and technology: past, present and future agendas," *International Journal of Science Education*, Vol. 25, No. 6 (2003), pp. 759–73.
24 Maria Powell and Daniel Lee Kleinman, "Building citizen capacities for participation in nanotechnology decision-making: the democratic virtues of the consensus conference model," *Public Understanding of Science*, Vol. 17, No. 3 (2008), pp. 329–48.
25 Harriet Bulkeley, "Common knowledge? Public understanding of climate change in Newcastle, Australia," *Public Understanding of Science*, Vol. 9 (2000), pp. 313–33; Kleinman, *Science, Technology, and Democracy*.
26 Irwin and Wynne, *Misunderstanding Science*; Yearly, "Making systematic sense of public discontents with expert knowledge"; Theresa Garvin, "Analytical paradigms: the epistemological distances between scientists, policy makers, and the public," *Risk Analysis*, Vol. 21, No. 3 (2001), pp. 443–55.
27 Miranda A. Schreurs, *Environmental Politics in Japan, Germany, and the United States* (New York: Cambridge University Press, 2002).
28 Sheila Jasanoff, *Risk Management and Political Culture* (New York: Russell Sage Foundation, 1986); Tesh, "Citizen experts in environmental risk."
29 EIPP, *Public Participation in Europe*, p. 13.
30 The figures in this paragraph are taken from a survey conducted during February–March 2013 by the Ministry of the Environment. The questionnaires were sent to all local governments (1789). The response rate was 66.7 percent (35 prefectures and 1,159 municipalities). See the Ministry of the Environment, "Kankyō kihon keikaku ni kakawaru chihō kōkyō dantai ankeito chōsa" [Survey on basic environmental plans by local governments], September 2013.
31 In 1993, the ICLEI (International Council for Local Environmental Initiatives) launched the notion of Local Agenda 21, a participatory, multi-sectoral process, in which local participants voluntarily create long-term, strategic action plans and implement them to achieve sustainability by integrating environmental, social and economic priorities.
32 Global Environmental Forum (GEF), *Rōkaruajenda 21 sakutei gaido* [Guidelines for formulating Local Agenda 21] (Tokyo: GEF, 1995).

33 Yasuo Takao, "Making climate change policy work at the local level: capacity-building for decentralized policy making in Japan," *Pacific Affairs*, Vol. 85, No. 4 (2012), pp. 777–8.
34 Makoto Kayashima, "Hinoshi ni okeru kankyō kihon keikaku sakutei" [Formulation of Hino city's basic environmental plan], *Tokyo no Jichi* [Autonomy Tokyo], Vol. 18, No. 33 (1999), pp. 18–25; Kenji Kawasaki, "Aratana dankai o mukaeta shimin sanka" [An emerging new phase for citizen participation], *Chihō Zaimu* [Local Finance], No. 568 (2001), pp. 276–7.
35 Kenji Kawasaki, "Shimin to gyōsei no pātonāshippu ni yoru jichitai kankyō manējimento" [Local environmental management by a partnership between citizens and administration], *Chiiki Kaihatsu* [Regional Development], No. 426 (2000), pp. 56–61; Hideyuki Takahashi, "Jichitai kankyō kihon keikaku no genjō to kadai" [The state and problems of local basic environmental plans]. *Kikan Gyōsei Kanri Kenkyū* [Administrative Management Quarterly], Vol. 89 (2000), pp. 19–34.
36 Research Institute for Humanities and Nature (RIHN), 2012. *ILEK project outline*, online, available from: http://en.ilekcrp.org/summary/ [accessed February 23, 2015].
37 Research Institute for Humanities and Nature (RIHN), 2012. *ILEK project outline*.
38 Interviews by author with Kenrō Taura, Head of the Secretariat, Kiko Network, May 13, 2010 and December 5, 2013.
39 Kazuho Seko, *Kyōdō kōdinētā* [Collaboration coordinator] (Tokyo: Gyōsei, 2007).
40 Ryo Mori, *Fashiritetā nyūmon: kankyō kyōiku kara kankyō machizukuri e* [Introduction to facilitators: from environmental education to environmental community building] (Tokyo: Tsuge Shobō, 2002).
41 Interview by author with Ryo Mori, ECO Communication Center, December 9, 2013.
42 Japan, Ministry of Internal Affairs and Communications (MIAC), *Todō-fuken chichō-son tōkeihyō* [Statistical tables of prefectures and municipalities] (Tokyo: Statistical Bureau, 2011).
43 Interview by author with Masanori Moori, EcoCity Shiki, December 10, 2013.
44 *Asahi Shinbun*, "Shasetsu" [Editorial], March 14, 1999.
45 Interview by author with Makoto Amada, Representative Director of EcoCity Shiki, December 10, 2013.
46 EcoCity Shiki, *Shimin ga tsukuru Shiki-shi no kankyō puran* [Shiki city's environmental plan to be made by citizens] (Shiki: EcoCity Shiki, 1998).
47 Interview by author with Masanori Moori, EcoCity Shiki, December 10, 2013.
48 EcoCity Shiki, *Shimin ga tsukuru Shiki-shi no kankyō puran*, p. 14.
49 *Asahi Shinbun*, "Ashimoto no kankyō puran kansei" [Completion of the groundwork for an environmental plan], June 26, 1998.
50 *Asahi Shinbun*, "Ashimoto no kankyō puran kansei."
51 Yūji Nishikawa, "Sanka-gata chiiki kankyō keikaku no kadai" [Issues over participatory local environmental plans], *Mizushigen Kankyō Kenkyū* [Water Resources and Environment], Vol. 13 (2000), p. 87.
52 Masanori Moori, "Mizuka no bunka ni manabu" [Learning from Mizuka culture], in *Mizuka no bunkashi* [Report on Mizuka culture], ed., Ecosystem Conservation Society (Shiki: EcoCity Shiki, 2011), pp. 234–9.
53 Interview by author with Masanori Moori, EcoCity Shiki, December 10, 2013.
54 Moori, "Mizuka no bunka ni manabu," pp. 234–5.
55 Mori, *Fashiritetā nyūmon*, pp. 29–30.
56 Information in this section is based on Jōyō City, *Kankyō hōkokusho* [Report on the environment], 2014, available from: www.city.joyo.kyoto.jp/government/environment/e_report/24 [accessed January 17, 2014].
57 Hideyuki Takahashi, *Shimin shutai no kankyō seisaku* [Environmental policy by citizens] (Tokyo: Kōjinsha, 2000), p. 91.
58 Department of the Environment (DOE), Matsusaka City, "Senshinchi shisatsu" [Minutes of meeting with Jōyō City's citizen environmental discussion group and

Jōyō City departments concerned], October 9, 2003, available from: www.city.matsusaka.mie.jp/www/contents/1000006926000/index_k.html [accessed December 14, 2013].
59 Cited in Shun'ichi Hiraoka, "Shimin sankagata kankyō seisakukeisei ni okeru kōdinetā toshite no kankyō NPO" [Study of environmental NPOs as a coordinator in the formation of environmental policy through citizen participation], *The Nonprofit Review*, Vol. 17, No. 1 (2007), p. 19.
60 Environmental Planning Department (EPD), Jōyō City, Meeting minutes, the sixteenth meeting of the citizen environmental discussion group, April 26, 2001.
61 Hiraoka, "Shimin sankagata kankyō seisakukeisei ni okeru kōdinetā toshite no kankyō NPO," pp. 16–17.
62 Department of the Environment (DOE), Matsusaka City, "Senshinchi shisatsu."
63 Department of the Environment (DOE), Matsusaka City, "Senshinchi shisatsu."

References

Asahi Shinbun (1998). "Ashimoto no kankyō puran kansei" [Completion of the groundwork for an environmental plan]. June 26, 1998.
Asahi Shinbun (1999). "Shasetsu" [Editorial]. March 14, 1999.
Bang, Henrik P. (2004). "Everyday makers and expert citizens: building political not social capital." Unpublished, ANU, School of Social Science. Available from https://digitalcollections.anu.edu.au/bitstream/1885/42117/2/Henrik.pdf [accessed December 14, 2014].
Bang, Henrik P. (2010). "Between everyday makers and expert citizens." In John Fenwick and Janice McMillan, eds., *Public Management in the Postmodern Era: Challenges and Prospects*. Cheltenham, UK: Edward Elgar Publishing, pp. 163–92.
Bauer, Martin W. and Massimiano Bucchi, eds. (2007). *Journalism, Science, and Society: Science Communication between News and Public Relations*. London: Routledge.
Beck, Ulrich (1992 [1986]). *Risk Society: Towards a New Modernity*, trans. Mark Ritter. London: Sage.
Bennett, Lance W. and Robert M. Entman, eds. (2001). *Mediated Politics*. Cambridge, UK: Cambridge University Press.
Bulkeley, Harriet (2000). "Common knowledge? Public understanding of climate change in Newcastle, Australia." *Public Understanding of Science*, Vol. 9, pp. 313–33.
Callon, Michel (1999). "The role of lay people in the production and dissemination of scientific knowledge." *Science, Technology and Society*, Vol. 4, No. 1, pp. 81–94.
City of Jōyō (2014). *Kankyō hōkokusho* [Report on the environment]. Available from: www.city.joyo.kyoto.jp/government/environment/e_report/24 [accessed January 17, 2014].
City of Jōyō, Environmental Planning Department (EPD) (2001). Meeting minutes, the sixteenth meeting of the citizen environmental discussion group, April 26, 2001.
City of Matsusaka, Department of the Environment (DOE) (2003). "Senshinchi shisatsu" [Minutes of meeting with Jōyō City's citizen environmental discussion group and Jōyō City departments concerned]. October 9, 2003. Available from: www.city.matsusaka.mie.jp/www/contents/1000006926000/index_k.html [accessed December 14, 2013].
Clark, Fiona and Deborah Illman (2001). "Dimension of civic science: introductory essay." *Science Communication*, Vol. 23, No. 1, pp. 5–27.
Collin, Robert W. and Robin Morris Collin (1998). "The role of communities in environmental decisions: communities speaking for themselves." *Journal of Environmental Law and Litigation*, Vol. 13, No. 37, pp. 37–89.

Collins, Harry and Robert Evans (2002). "The third wave of science studies: studies of expertise and experience." *Social Studies of Science*, Vol. 32, No. 2, pp. 235–96.
EcoCity Shiki (1998). *Shimin ga tsukuru Shiki-shi no kankyō puran* [Shiki city's environmental plan to be made by citizens]. Shiki: EcoCity Shiki.
Eden, Sally (1996). "Public participation in environmental policy: considering scientific, counter-scientific and non-scientific contributions." *Public Understanding of Science*, Vol. 5, No. 3, pp. 183–204.
European Commission (2004). *Sustainable Production and Consumption in the European Union*. Luxembourg: Office for Official Publications of the European Union.
European Institute for Public Participation (EIPP) (2009). *Public Participation in Europe: An International Perspective*. Bremen: EIPP.
Garvin, Theresa (2001). "Analytical paradigms: the epistemological distances between scientists, policy makers, and the public." *Risk Analysis*, Vol. 21, No. 3, pp. 443–55.
Global Environmental Forum (GEF) (1995). *Rōkaruajenda 21 sakutei gaido* [Guidelines for formulating Local Agenda 21]. Tokyo: GEF.
Gregory, Jane and Steve Miller (1998). *Science in Public: Communication, Culture, and Credibility*. New York: Basic Books.
Hiraoka, Shun'ichi (2007). "Shimin sankagata kankyō seisakukeisei ni okeru kōdinetā toshite no kankyō NPO" [Study of environmental NPOs as a coordinator in the formation of environmental policy through citizen participation]. *The Nonprofit Review*, Vol. 17, No. 1, pp. 13–23.
Hirst, Paul (1996). *Associative Democracy*. Cambridge, UK: Polity Press.
Holliman, Richard, Elizabeth Whitelegg, Eileen Scanlon, Sam Smidt, and Jeff Thomas, eds. (2008). *Investigating Science Communication in the Information Age: Implications for Public Engagement and Popular Media*. Oxford: Oxford University Press.
Hutton, Will and Anthony Giddens, eds. (2001). *On the Edge: Living with Global Capitalism*. London: Vintage.
Irwin, Alan and Brian Wynne (1996). *Misunderstanding Science? The Public Reconstruction of Science and Technology*. Cambridge, UK: Cambridge University Press.
Japan, Association for Promoting Fair Elections (2003). *Tōitsu chihō senkyo ni okeru tōhyoritsu no suii* [Trends of voter turnouts in the unified local elections]. May 2003. Available from: www.akaruisenkyo.or.jp/tohyo/top.html [accessed December 14, 2014].
Japan, Ministry of Internal Affairs and Communications (MIAC) (2011). *Todō-fuken chichō-son tōkeihyō* [Statistical tables of prefectures and municipalities]. Tokyo: Statistical Bureau.
Japan, Ministry of the Environment (MOE) (2013). "Kankyō kihon keikaku ni kakawaru chihō kōkyō dantai ankeito chōsa" [Survey on basic environmental plans by local governments]. September 2013.
Jasanoff, Sheila (1986). *Risk Management and Political Culture*. New York: Russell Sage Foundation.
Jasanoff, Sheila (2006). "Transparency in public science: purposes, reasons, limits." *Law and Contemporary Problem*, Vol. 69, No. 21, pp. 21–45.
Joffe, Hélène (2003). "Risk: from perception to social representation." *British Journal of Social Psychology*, Vol. 42, No. 1, pp. 55–73.
Kates, Robert W., Nancy M. Dickson, and William C. Clark (2000). "Sustainability science." Discussion Paper 2000-33, Belfer Center for Science and International Affairs, Kennedy School of Government, Harvard University.
Kawasaki, Kenji (2000). "Shimin to gyōsei no pātonāshippu ni yoru jichitai kankyō

manējimento" [Local environmental management by a partnership between citizens and administration]. *Chiiki Kaihatsu* [Regional Development], No. 426 (2000), pp. 56–61.

Kawasaki, Kenji (2001). "Aratana dankai o mukaeta shimin sanka." [An emerging new phase for citizen participation]. *Chihō Zaimu* [Local Finance], No. 568, pp. 267–81.

Kayashima, Makoto (1999). "Hinoshi ni okeru kankyō kihon keikaku sakutei" [Formulation of Hino city's basic environmental plan]. *Tokyo no Jichi* [Autonomy Tokyo], Vol. 18, No. 33, pp. 18–25.

Kleinman, Daniel Lee, ed. (2000). *Science, Technology, and Democracy*. New York: State University of New York Press.

Moori, Masanori (2011). "Mizuka no bunka ni manabu" [Learning from Mizuka culture]. In Ecosystem Conservation Society, ed., *Mizuka no bunkashi* [Report on Mizuka culture]. Shiki: EcoCity Shiki, pp. 234–9.

Mori, Ryō (2002). *Fashiritetā nyūmon: kankyō kyōiku kara kankyō machizukuri e* [Introduction to facilitators: from environmental education to environmental community building]. Tokyo: Tsuge Shobō.

Nelkin, Dorothy (1995). *Selling Science: How the Press Covers Science and Technology*. New York: W.H. Freeman & Co..

Nishikawa, Yūji (2000). "Sanka-gata chiiki kankyō keikaku no kadai" [Issues over participatory local environmental plans]. *Mizushigen Kankyō Kenkyū* [Water Resources and Environment], Vol. 13, pp. 85–92.

Organisation for Economic Co-operation and Development (OECD) (2001). *Engaging Citizens in Policy-Making: Information, Consultation and Public Participation*. PUMA Policy Brief No. 10. Paris: OECD.

Petts, Judith (2004). "Barriers to participation and deliberation in risk decisions: evidence from waste management." *Journal of Risk Research*, Vol. 7, No. 2, pp. 115–33.

Powell, Maria and Daniel Lee Kleinman (2008). "Building citizen capacities for participation in nanotechnology decision-making: the democratic virtues of the consensus conference model." *Public Understanding of Science*, Vol. 17, No. 3, pp. 329–48.

Putnam, Robert D. (1993). *Making Democracy Work: Civic Traditions in Modern Italy*. Princeton, NJ: Princeton University Press.

Putnam, Robert (1995). "Bowling alone: America's declining social capital." *Journal of Democracy*, Vol. 6, No. 1, pp. 65–78.

Rennie, Léonie J. and Susan M. Stocklmayer (2003). "The communication of science and technology: past, present and future agendas." *International Journal of Science Education*, Vol. 25, No. 6, pp. 759–73.

Research Institute for Humanities and Nature (RIHN) (2012). *ILEK project outline*. Online. Available from: http://en.ilekcrp.org/summary/ [accessed February 23, 2015].

Schreurs, Miranda A. (2002). *Environmental Politics in Japan, Germany, and the United States*. New York: Cambridge University Press.

Scott, William and Chris Oulton (1999). "Environmental education: arguing the case for multiple approaches." *Educational Studies*, Vol. 25, No. 1, pp. 119–25.

Seko, Kazuho (2007). *Kyōdō kōdinētā* [Collaboration coordinator]. Tokyo: Gyōsei.

Stilgoe, Jack, Alan Irwin, and Kevin Jones (2006). *The Received Wisdom: Opening up Expert Advice*. London: Demos.

Takahashi, Hideyuki (2000). "Jichitai kankyō kihon keikaku no genjō to kadai" [The state and problems of local basic environmental plans]. *Kikan Gyōsei Kanri Kenkyū* [Administrative Management Quarterly], Vol. 89, pp. 19–34.

Takahashi, Hideyuki (2000). *Shimin shutai no kankyō seisaku* [Environmental policy by citizens]. Tokyo: Kōjinsha.

Takao, Yasuo (2012). "Making climate change policy work at the local level: capacity-building for decentralized policy making in Japan." *Pacific Affairs*, Vol. 85, No. 4, pp. 767–88.

Tesh, Selvia (1999). "Citizen experts in environmental risk." *Policy Science*, Vol. 32, No. 1, pp. 39–58.

van Heffen, Oscar, Walter J.M. Kickert, and Jacques J.A. Thomassen, eds. (2000). *Governance in Modern Society: Effects, Change and Formation of Government*. Dordrecht: Kluwer Academic Publishers.

Whatmore, Sarah, *et al.* (2010). *Understanding Environmental Knowledge Controversies: The Case of Flood Risk Management*. Full research report ESRC end of award report, RES-227-25-0018. Swindon, UK: Economic and Social Research Council.

Wilsdon, James, Brian Wynne, and Jack Stilgoe (2005). *The Public Value of Science: or How to Ensure That Science Really Matters*. London: Demos.

Wynne, Brian (2003). "Seasick on the third wave? Subverting the hegemony of Propositionalism." *Social Studies of Science*, Vol. 33, No. 3, pp. 401–17.

Yearly, Steven (2000). "Making systematic sense of public discontents with expert knowledge: two analytical approaches and a case study." *Public Understanding of Science*, Vol. 9, No. 2, pp. 105–22.

Conclusion

This book presents a first attempt to better understand the potential role played by sub-national governments in overcoming the policy coordination difficulty that cross-scale and multi-level approaches to environmental governance may create due to the emerging plurality of actors and organizational complexity. It proposes an alternative framework of decentralized environmental governance, where sub-national governments could act as intermediate agents to reconnect local action with national policy and turn global strategies into local action for problem-solving. It sets out to see if such a framework could be identified to support the future shape of Japan's environmental policy and governance. The findings demonstrate that Japanese local governments' intermediary involvement in cross-scale/multi-level interactions is successfully supporting the bridging of gaps among local actions, national mandates, and global strategies to build a decentralized space for policy coordination, and meet the needs of environmental risk reduction. The scope of this research is country-specific and limited but it suggests that a decentralized framework, if properly implemented, has the potential to lead to greater successes in policy integration. Further research is needed to test empirically the application of decentralized environmental governance in which sub-national governments take up a key role, and to establish whether it leads to greater policy coordination success.

Japanese local governments share a structural factor that places them in a strategic position to saddle the division between the national government and the community and that between the domestic and the foreign. However, it is left to individual local governments' capabilities and motivations to decide whether they identify and capitalize on a structural opportunity to act as intermediate agents. In many countries, sub-national governments do not have the fiscal capacity to include the needed funding requirements in their environmental programs. They also often lack sufficient jurisdiction over decision-making and the implementation of environmental policies. More importantly, it must be remembered that the range of experiences associated with the decentralized role of sub-national governments seen in different countries represents considerable variation in cultural tradition, developmental paths, and social norms. Both fiscal capacity and administrative ability are significant indicators of local governments' active engagement in cross-scale/multi-level interactions but many wealthy and competent local authorities eschew any active engagement. The central issue boils down to local authorities' willingness and capability to contribute to policy coordination to cater for locally specific needs, national mandates, and the global agenda in an integrated way. The findings show that different motivations (strong political leadership, historical experience, normative commitment, policy learning, and others) make a difference for active engagement, rather than having a uniform impact generated by local structural factors, the national political system, and international obligations. To put it another way, human agents need to collectively interpret and adapt to constraints and opportunities. I expect that the results of this study will give new impetus to future research in the comparative perspective.

To provide a blueprint for solving the policy coordination difficulty with the emerging plurality of actors and organizational complexity, two basic categories of reform options are available: the creation of a more authoritative and better-resourced international environmental organization or efforts by decentralized governance to better incorporate lower levels of government and social groups into the formal processes of environmental management. In my view, the establishment of a strong international organization is not necessarily incompatible with the other reform options in the sense that decentralized functions and policy networking are still necessary for more effective international environmental organization. To improve the performance of centralized governance efforts, an international organization still needs to redistribute the functions and responsibilities of environmental governance to other agents and networks, in order to meet the needs of policy diversity, flexibility, and innovation. In principle, environmental governance should be based on a decentralized division of labor among internationally recognized agents or networks, with greater attention directed towards policy coordination and coherence to bridge the policy gaps in the existing environmental governance. This policy coordination needs to derive from an on-going dialogue of reflexive interplay, and find solutions through the very process of learning and knowing, between the various actors involved in governance. Information flow in both directions between the stakeholders involved in policy coordination is essential to address the real gaps in the existing governing system.

Political opportunity structures

Environmental issues in Japan have been closely associated with the resource-poor nation's concerns with energy security. The national government has taken policy priority measures to ensure energy supplies and increase production, and the corporate bias has largely insulated the national government from popular pressures. In this context, spanning problems have become marked in environmental issues, as these issues are tangled with other policy areas, such as energy security. Nuclear energy is a case in point. The dominant industrial coalition members initially saw nuclear energy as instrumental in managing energy demand/supply for production. By the late 1980s, public opinion began to take this issue area as a matter of environmental policy regarding public safety and environmental risk. Yet Japan's nuclear energy remains a strong top-down national undertaking to lay the foundations for its prosperity and security and it establishes a division of labor among levels of government with a state-centric gate-keeping capacity. Central-local government relations are institutionalized to clarify local governments' roles in achieving national goals. Local governments are legally and formally instructed to primarily play an implementation role in achieving national energy targets. The policy priority of local governments, with community welfare at the top of the list, tends to be co-opted by national regulations into the pro-nuclear camp. Chapter 2 on Japan's nuclear energy indicates that coalition behavior was framed by the low degree of "openness" in the political opportunity structure, i.e., high territorial centralization and one-party dominance. Unitarism and local dependency regarding nuclear energy issues represented a minor opening for the anti-nuclear coalition, with limited opportunities to take a community-wide initiative for anti-nuclear advocacy and thus not easily expanding anti-nuclear coalition-building into the national level. The presence of strong state control largely constrained the choice of local governments in initiating specific balancing acts between national mandates and local concerns over nuclear energy development.

In general, however, the national government heavily depends on local governments for the successful implementation of policy measures regarding environmental issues and problems. Unlike nuclear safety, a large proportion of environmental policy measures in Japan are not driven by a strong top-down national undertaking, since national policy often enables the local level of participation under a delegation of decision-making power to local governments. Even if there is no clear delegation, the absence of national regulation, or the national government's inaction, represent an opening for proactive environmental policy at the local level but it is not open wide enough to progressively expand an environmental risk reduction coalition to the national level. A nationally led framework embedded within Japan's unitary system structurally remains intact. In the 1960s, Japanese local governments were known as the leading innovators in Japan's environmental policy. By the mid-1970s, the national government incorporated most local policy innovations into its nationally-led platform. Over the past three decades, some Japanese local governments have become involved in international environmental cooperation and go beyond what is mandated under national policy. They have deliberately decided to engage due to a lack of support from the national government or in the absence of national regulation. They often bypass the established national-local relations, but neither completely supersedes nor directly challenges the level of territorial centralization. In other words, there is little potential for the political opportunity structures that frame the "competition" between various advocacy coalitions at the national level. This type of competition can be seen in the context of the United States (US) political system on whose characteristics the advocacy coalition framework (ACF) draws heavily. But Japanese local governments, which are not only equipped with policy expertise but are also socially competent, have a good potential to act as intermediate agents in reconnecting local action with national policy and turning global strategies into local action. Within Japan's consensual quasi-corporatist regime, local governments may develop their capabilities to bridge the gap between state and society and the divide between domestic and foreign affairs in a less contentious way. The case of Kitakyushu city shows that the municipal government has successfully avoided engaging in sustained contentious or competitive interactions with power-holders at the national level and developed its long-term collaborative alliances with national authorities to advance its policy goals with local communities and businesses.

Advocacy coalitions

In general, the structural nature of Japan's state institutions is less likely to provide the political opportunity structures that induce the formation of coalition-building to create a dynamic process of high competition between coalitions of actors. The dominant governing coalition tends to control a given policy subsystem and produce coalition stability over a long period of time. The policy area of nuclear energy in Japan probably approximates to a unitary subsystem that is shaped by one dominant, united coalition dealing with minor oppositions. However, as environmental problem-solving involves multiple agencies and diverse stakeholders, Japan's territorial centralization no longer seems to be a major impediment for the formation of pluralistic competition among various coalitions within a policy subsystem. The policy area of climate change in Japan has indeed displayed the pluralistic elements (i.e., bureaucratic pluralism) of the ACF. The greater the degree of bureaucratic compartmentalization, the greater the political pressure different domestic groups exert on policy-making. Coalition-building is carried out between each national department and its supporting private institutions, especially business associations. In the process of the negotiations at the Kyoto climate conference, the politics of coalition bargaining was handled within the sectionalism-driven national bureaucracy (i.e., among the industrial coalition of the Ministry of International Trade and Industry's [MITI] Agency of Natural Resources and Energy and the Keidanren, the environmental coalition of Environment Agency [EA] technocrats and the National Institute for Environmental Studies, and the coalition of Ministry of Foreign Affairs' [MOFA] diplomatic interests), yet it was unable to respond to foreign pressures in a concerted way.

Despite experiencing two oil crises, in the policy area of industrial pollution, the formation of industrial pollution policy was essentially a domestic-level process occurring within the Japanese state. In other policy areas, whether nuclear energy (dominant coalition) or climate change (competitive coalitions), policy formation was observed not only as a domestic-level process, but also as the result of events, external to the policy subsystem, at the international level. Japan's nuclear energy policy became linked with US foreign policy to contain the Soviet Union in the context of the emerging Cold War. At the Kyoto climate conference, Japan's delegation was quite sensitive to the wishes of the US due to its close relations with the US. To ensure US participation in the protocol, the Prime Minister's Office intervened as a policy broker in the domestic political game. Foreign pressures influence domestic opportunity structures (that affect the resources and constraints of the subsystem actors) or affect the variations of how domestic political systems meet social demands. Foreign pressures can alter the nature and patterns of institutional access at the domestic level with actors who seek their policy beliefs and mobilize their skills and resources in forming coalitions with allies. The findings show that policy formation, especially in the context of cross-scale/multi-level environmental affairs, is understood better in terms of coalition-building taking place along the space in which domestic and foreign issues converge.

At the Kyoto Climate conference, most Japanese local governments simply monitored the negotiations, without getting directly involved in coalition-building, and ascertain Japan's climate change pledge, which might affect local governments in terms of achieving the national mandate. While Japanese negotiators, who were constrained simultaneously by domestic demand and international pressure at the Kyoto Climate conference (two-level game), acted as the only legitimate representatives of domestic interests to maintain the separation of domestic and foreign affairs (domestic-foreign gate-keeping), some Japanese local governments began to act along the domestic-foreign frontier in the absence of national regulation. The responsibility of local governments to formulate and implement their climate change action plans was clearly specified in the revised national Climate Change Law. Yet this law neither clearly granted a legal/formal authority nor provided the decentralized financial power for local governments to reduce greenhouse gas (GHG) emissions at the local level. Given Japan's internationally pledged target, some pioneering municipalities, such as Kawasaki, Kitakyushu, Kobe, and Yokohama, set up their own ambitious mitigation targets and linked local communities with the national mandates, although the national government failed to allocate a share of the international pledge to individual prefectures. This is even more impressive as municipal officials in Kitakyushu and Yokohama came to see themselves as direct participants in global sustainability strategies. These municipalities contributed to the policy-making process of international environmental cooperation without the supervision of the national government. They delivered a range of formalized forms of problem-solving cooperation with local entities in the developing world in a global North–South context. They facilitated two-way problem-solving responses to both globalizing and localizing needs. This environmental collaboration with developing countries was the result of their intermediary role in bringing together local entities on both sides of the transnational relationships to meet local specific needs and to adapt to the global agenda on environment and development. These local governments largely stayed out of the process of competition between coalitions of actors, especially in regard to bureaucratic politics at the national level. They apolitically connected local concerns and interests with the established national mandates and sought to turn global expectations into action to meet locally specific needs.

Finally, it is important to note that the dominant governing coalition was normally required to have some cross-coalition interactions with minor coalitions or potential pro-environment forces, in order to retain existing power relationships within a policy subsystem or prevent the opposition forces from adopting confrontational strategies (which the dominant industrial coalition experienced in the policy area of severe industrial pollution from the late 1960s to the early 1970s) outside of established policy channels. At the strategic level of learning to understand political feasibility, the dominant governing coalition that instituted a given policy program sought to remain in power within that jurisdiction. To this end, the various forms of the responses—such as location subsidies, compensation, environmental assessment, consultation, state agencies' reorganization, and others—to the opposition forces were used to neutralize opposition voices. In this context, local governments held an intermediary position between the dominant governing coalition and local voices to reduce the potential for political conflicts between them. Aside from statutory regulations and national administrative guidance restricting the room to maneuver available to local governments, the intermediary position allowed local governments to still hold significant leeway to intervene between them. As environmental issues and problems are often deeply divided over fundamental policy beliefs and values, local governments often chose one coalition/political force (i.e., local voices) over others. While helping less resourceful local actors develop their capacity to deal with power-holders, local governments tended to act as policy advocates, rather than policy brokers, to find feasible policy solutions. In this sense, Japanese local governments did not always support coalition stability or the status quo of the policy environment, bur rather they were often policy revisionists and thus pushed their innovative ideas for the proposed solution.

Cross-scale policy coordination

Environmental problems stretch across scales of geographic space. Geographical proximity is the natural and conventional criteria for the explanation of environmental protection. In Japan, the industrial coalition saw the costs of environmental risk reduction as primarily concentrated on a limited relationship between polluters and victims in the affected industrial areas. In Japan from the early 1950s to the mid-1980s, actors in the process of political coalition-building treated environmental protection as a local or national public good whose benefits extended to all members of a community situated within the nation or all the citizens of the nation. These benefits of environmental protection corresponded to national borders rendering the nature of local and national public goods territorial. As stakeholders in environmental protection had different priorities and preferences, the question of how to share the burden of financing them became highly politicized. Local governments played a strategic role in bringing social cohesion to both the division between economy and environment and that between the business sector and social groups at the local level. In the mid-1970s, the focus of environmental protection shifted from identifiable sources of industrial pollution to diffuse, no-point sources of non-industrial pollution. Environmental citizens' movements began to experience that environmental risk did not necessarily stem from a single identifiable source, such as electronic power manufacturers and oil refineries. Environmental protection required the inclusion of diffuse pollutant sources, such as cars and household appliances. It was becoming increasingly clear that the sources and causes of pollution were far more diffuse and interrelated than those experienced in early post-WWII Japan. Environmental problems that had once been local or national were now stretching beyond national boundaries.

A case in point is the inter-municipal cooperation between Dalian (China) and Kitakyushu (Japan) over pollution control. In the 1980s, the City of Kitakyushu was a polluted steel town but is now renowned for having successfully overcome some of Japan's worst environmental problems. As the city accumulated environmental management expertise, a neighboring city across the Yellow Sea, Dalian, was about to experience every imaginable environmental problem, much like those experienced in Kitakyushu. The trans-boundary spillover effects of Dalian's pollution (e.g., acid rain) became a serious concern for Kitakyushu. In the 1990s, Kitakyushu residents and local business clearly recognized that environmental degradation was spreading beyond national borders and could have a regional/global range. At the national level, policy-makers had to face two primary sources of constraints on environmental policy-making: domestic constituencies' demands and international pressures for the cost-sharing of environmental cooperation (global public goods). Environmental politics became a locus where national policy-makers had to choose how to reconcile both international and domestic concerns. The interplay between the two concerns can be viewed as mutually constitutive and thus less cohesive in managing the state of environmental problems. This decision-making environment provided an opportunity for the mayoral leadership in Kitakyushu to show how to realistically reduce environmental risks by reconnecting local action with national mandates and by using local expertise to promote international environmental business and turn the strategies of decentralized international cooperation into local action.

The above practices of Japanese local governments reveal the underlying dynamics and tendencies that have been shaping the sub-national level of participation in the resolution of transnational issues. Cross-border contacts on a daily basis turn local authorities on the border towards cross-border cooperation to promote their interests and solve the cross-border problems. Geographical proximity is indeed one of the most important factors driving local governments' activities across geographical borders but other factors allow the activities to transcend the constraints of geographical fragmentation. The most influential additional factor is probably the dual dynamics of internationalization and globalization. Internationalization can be seen as a sphere where external events influence domestic decision-making ("second image reversed") while globalization can be narrowly defined as a process of policy convergence, especially in the policy area of environmental standards. As discussed previously, while globalization cannot be accounted for by a set of driving forces in a deterministic way, I have directed attention to agent-specific and ideational factors as well as structural and economic factors. These dual dynamics facilitate the development of sub-national participation through greater spatial interaction.

Japanese cities and their counterparts in Southeast Asia are geographically far apart but internationalization and globalization made the physical distance less relevant to their partner selection for international environmental cooperation. Since the early 1990s, in response to the criticism of foreign aid tied to Japanese exports, the Japanese government has refocused its foreign aid towards environmental and "softer" types of aid such as poverty alleviation and social infrastructure. Both the structural change in aid policy and the global recognition of local governments' role in international cooperation (e.g., the 1992 Earth Summit and the 2005 United Nations [UN] Summit) provide favorable conditions for local authorities' involvement in dialogues to tackle the North–South divide and South–South cooperation. As international environmental cooperation has become part of global strategies for environmental risk reduction, the linkages between trans-local relations have revealed different geographical orientations, with a special focus on North–South issues. In the past, Kitakyushu has partly been driven by its immediate concerns about the trans-boundary spillover effects across the geographically adjacent areas, such as Dalian city in China. As environmental problems become global in scale, Kitakyushu's environmental business is now expected to form the basis of dialogue for mutual benefits and learning between Northern and Southern partners. The operation of the Kitakyushu Asian Center for Low Carbon Society has a good potential for developing a compatible way of balancing the normative commitment to North–South solutions and commercial self-interest. In the case of Yokohama, norms seem to outweigh both geographical proximity and immediate utility; its reputation as an international city provided a foundation for shaping a collective self-understanding of normative commitment to international contribution. The city took part in the creation of a multi-actor cooperation network, the Regional Network of Local Authorities for the Management of Human Settlements (CITYNET), among local authorities and communities in the Asia Pacific region and beyond. Yokohama's desire to enhance its role in the region helped to provide a mechanism to put local-to-local dialogue into trans-local practice.

Geographical proximity, which drives local governments' activities across geographical borders, can be observed in the physical space. The physical proximity of local communities to ecological effects may provide a potential for sub-national participation in decentralized environmental cooperation. The experience of environmental incidents may thus create or increase the need of sub-national participation and thus open opportunities for environmental reformism. Yet, as the case of Yokohama implies, policy-making is embedded in both the physical space (e.g., geographical proximity for cross-border problems) and the non-physical space (e.g., shared experience and ideas without geographical constraints). In the case of Shiga, the process of policy idea production occurred simultaneously in the physical space (i.e., that of local environmental protection) and in the non-physical space (i.e., that of international environmental cooperation). The worsening eutrophication of Lake Biwa, which had become a serious health hazard, triggered serious concerns for existing policy priorities in Shiga prefecture. These concerns allowed the prefectural government to reorient its policy towards quality of life and to avoid the scrutiny of voters regarding the costs of the policy shift. Environmental impacts were manifested locally and adaptive capacity was determined by local conditions. Environmental protection for Lake Biwa was a local public good whose benefits extended to all the members of a community situated within the prefecture. On the other hand, the primary motive of Shiga prefecture to reach out transnationally was policy learning without geographical constraints in the non-physical space. Shiga's motive behind its collaboration with the United Nations Environment Programme (UNEP) was to foster policy learning and find solutions in the absence of national support. Acting out of its own interest or utility, Shiga had begun to recognize that sub-national action would not suffice in producing the desired solution without international cooperation and policy learning. In this sense, Shiga's engagement in international environmental cooperation occurred, especially in the non-physical space, and formed cross-scale linkages in managing the environment.

Multi-level policy coordination

The case studies reveal both vertical and horizontal dimensions: the former referring to the linkages between vertical territorial levels of government and the latter referring to the horizontally formed networks across both sectors and jurisdictions. This book seeks to provide a better understanding of the relationships and the dynamics underlying transitions between the two types of multi-level governance in Japan's unitary system. One of the most important findings is that the case studies provide examples of particular attempts at strengthening the capacity of the local governments engaged in policy coordination between vertical territorial tiers of government and horizontally formed networks of governance. In particular, these studies locate and illustrate the processes of transitions between the different types for solving community issues and problems. The dual responses of local governments' participation in environmental governance to both globalizing and localizing trends facilitates the transitional process in which local governments are placed on the spot to connect the vertical and horizontal approaches and prevent any conflict between the two approaches to improve the provision of local, national, and global public goods.

In essence, Japan institutionally represents state-centric governance, which is based on a nationally-led framework embedded within institutional boundaries to extend decision-making authority above and below the national state while the national government remains a central actor. There are two models of the links between vertical territorial levels of government: a top-down model (or a hierarchically ordered system of direct/indirect coercion) and a bottom-up model (a decentralized form of decision-making). In the traditional state-centric framework, national policy either regulates or enables a sub-national level of participation in decision-making. In the top-down model, as national governments extend incentive schemes as well as national mandates towards local governments, sub-national actors have primarily an implementation role to play if national environmental targets are to be met. National governments may delegate decision-making authorities to lower levels of government, but establish a division of labor among levels of government with a state-centric gate-keeping capacity (its capacity to influence policy decisions) to meet the needs of aggregate progress at the national scale. The key issue of state-centric policy coordination lies in the capacity of the national government to effectively monitor progress at the sub-national level for an understanding of national scale progress. National inaction may create a harmful barrier to effective decision-making for the improvement of public policy. Without guidance at the national level, local policy innovations and regulations may emerge, as there is a policy vacuum where policy issues are not well addressed by the national government. The case in point is that Japanese local governments initially led the adoption of policy innovations against industrial pollution and the policy laggard, the national government, followed suit. If local action one-sidedly enhances policy diffusion to higher levels of government, this can be seen as a bottom-up model.

The institutional approach to policy coordination on climate change that is commonly used in most countries is a top-down model where national governments require sub-national authorities to work within nationally defined frameworks as well as assist sub-national authorities to develop their capacity to take action on their own. But national governments do not necessarily have such a strong commitment to climate action. In the absence of strong policy initiatives at the national level, as seen in the case of Tokyo's cap-and-trade, some sub-national authorities are capable enough to act independently to address climate change by lesson-drawing and policy learning. If local policy ideas one-sidedly promote policy transfer to the national government, this can be seen as a bottom-up model (a decentralized form of learning or copying). The case study of Tokyo's cap-and-trade, however, has found that a third model, that of interactive/mutual learning processes among levels of government, is revealed in the process of adopting policy ideas. The examination of organizational learning through interaction, even between hierarchized tiers of government, can tap into the abundant information about policy diffusion. In general, climate mitigation measures are less likely to be directly transferable to a different level of government while there is a growing need for coordinated decision-making processes between different levels of government. Learning agents are faced with a different structural context at each level of government. They interpret that structural context and make a conscious effort to have an improved understanding of what factors constrain a direct policy transfer. In the case study of Tokyo's cap-and-trade, the learning of mandatory reporting in national energy policy triggered the introduction of mandatory reporting in a different policy domain at the local level, that is, local environmental policy, to meet local conditions. The national government eventually made policy development a better fit in the national structural context of the same environmental policy domain and then introduced a national mandatory reporting scheme in a less stringent way to reduce GHG emissions.

Japan's unitary system does not formally recognize the legal right of sub-national authorities to represent themselves at the international level. This arrangement arises out of the traditional state-centric framework. Local governments' participation in global environmental governance is either constrained or promoted by the national government to clarify local governments' roles in achieving national goals within the context of international obligations. In this process, the local level of participation beyond national borders tends to be legitimized by national benefits rather than local needs. One would expect that Japan is more approximate to the vertical-top-down model with the gate-keeping capacity of the national government. But the patterns of Japanese local governments' participation in international environmental cooperation are extremely complex and require a close examination. As the detailed implementation of global strategies is specified, the necessity of sub-national participation in international cooperation becomes more salient. There are locally specific aspects of diplomatic representation that may not be suited to the national government. There will be various issues and problems that are not addressed in the state-centric diplomatic representation. Once attention is directed towards a decentralized form of decision-making by local governments, the static notions of governance cannot easily account for the dynamics of the real-life experiences in Japan. This is primarily due to the connections between *hierarchized* tiers (vertical dimension) and *de-hierarchized* new spheres (horizontal dimension) of authority. What is equally important is that, although sub-national participation can be conceived as horizontally ordered in new-shared spheres of authority, Japanese local governments do not normally challenge the hierarchized tiers of territorial jurisdictions in an explicit way while bypassing the state-centric gate-keeping. This is mainly because the multi-task jurisdictions of local governments (not only over environmental issues) continually have to deal with the hierarchical territorial tiers of authority on a daily basis while simultaneously moving across different spheres of authority. In particular, the financial needs of such sub-national participation in de-hierarchized new spheres bring the local governments back to deal with the hierarchical territorial tiers to access national financial resources.

In Japan's unitary system, as the case studies in this book suggest, local governments, while mobilized across institutional boundaries of polity, independently participate in environmental governance at the international level, either due to a lack of support from the national government or in the absence of national regulation. Without any familiar ground of institutionalized rules or the right to legitimately represent themselves at the international level, local governments find a way through non-institutionalized or informal channels to move across levels of government and deal directly with a transnational network of local governments and non-state actors, and supranational actors (i.e., horizontally formed networks) in a rather ad hoc fashion. Informal extra-national channels, such as the establishment of independent overseas offices for lobbying and representing their interests, are sought to push for the increased involvement of sub-national actors in decision-making at the international level, while engaging in direct exchanges with host nations and international organizations.

The story of Shiga's lake environmental management is a case where a local government transnationally reaches out for policy learning while experiencing the institutional capacity limitations of the national government to address the problem. The prefectural government pursued its own agenda independent of national policy, which facilitated its policy learning beyond national borders and recognized the greater governance gap that the inability of the national bureaucracy created to sense the need for a sub-national level of participation in international environmental governance. The prefectural government accordingly looked for overseas partners as a compensation mechanism. It called for help from UNEP to see how its counterparts in other countries were coping with lake environmental management (i.e., horizontally formed networks). Shiga was able to get involved only because the prefectural government successfully tapped into the legitimating power that derived from its local constituencies. The prefectural government then played an intermediary role in turning transnationally shared knowledge and expertise into local solutions. In advanced democracies, sub-national authorities represent their constituencies; therefore, sub-national activities need to be in the interests of the sub-national territories. By mobilizing transnationally, sub-national authorities might simply promote their narrowly defined sub-national interests as if they were just lobbying for particular interests. In the case of Shiga, however, the prefectural government and its local constituencies ended up sharing broad public interests (i.e., lake environmental knowledge as a global public good) in sub-national participation at the international level of environmental cooperation. The legitimacy of Shiga's participation in international environmental cooperation initially derived from the community values reflected in citizen-led issue framing. The experience of the international conference, which was then facilitated by electoral slack, raised public awareness and promoted the production and diffusion of information regarding the need to link the framed sub-national issue to international environmental cooperation. This was instrumental in placing the establishment of the International Lake Environment Committee (ILEC) on the policy agenda.

Perhaps, the most important role played by the prefectural government was its policy coordination between vertical territorial tiers of government and horizontally formed networks of governance. Since there were no domestic statutory provisions to authorize local governments to engage in international environmental governance functions, the ILEC was initially created as a private organization, which would be neither regulated nor protected by the national government. Later the prefectural government re-established it as a legally recognized foundational organization for public benefits. This arrangement provided Shiga with improved access to national funds, although the ILEC came under the supervisory jurisdiction of both the EA and the MOFA. Fund-raising was critically important for maintaining Shiga's involvement in international environmental cooperation. Many projects were heavily dependent on funding from the national government. To maintain its organizational autonomy, the ILEC acted as an independent provider of objective expertise on lake-basin management, while seeking external funds. Shiga's international environmental cooperation involved, to a degree, reciprocal relationships with the national government, although it was neither formally independent nor functionally interdependent on equal terms.

The real-life experience of Kitakyushu was driven by dynamic connections between hierarchized tiers (vertical dimensions) and de-hierarchized new spheres (horizontal dimensions) of authority in a depoliticized fashion. The municipal government, which was part of the state apparatus, was entitled to have close access to national ministries and then national aid, distributed by these ministries, provided the tools Kitakyushu's policy initiatives for the international environmental cooperation needed to become financially secure. The territorial state of Japan had difficulty in providing an integrated set of solutions for the spillover effects of environmental problems experienced through the unbundling of the functions of environmental protection to different governance levels and spheres. However, Kitakyushu experienced new spheres where its activities were neither confined to a fixed scale of geographic space nor to a rigid hierarchy of authority. Kitakyushu's environmental collaboration with developing countries was the result of an adaptive process between state and non-state actors in which the municipal government functioned as a pivot for connecting the horizontally formed transnational networks with the vertical territorial levels of government. The trans-local process facilitated the two-way responses of Kitakyushu's activities to both globalizing (aggregate effort of all countries to reduce GHG emissions) and localizing (locally specific environmental solutions) needs. Kitakyushu was an intersecting actor in multiple spheres of authority spanning many jurisdictions for coordinated action.

The case of Kitakyushu approximates neither the exclusively state-centric nor the exclusively autonomist in its institutional approach to international environmental cooperation. The city has been capable of effectively engaging in international environmental cooperation by using a number of avenues for the cross-fertilization of both institutional frameworks, so to speak. From a state-centric view, Kitakyushu's participation at the international level has largely been an active part of national policy. Kitakyushu has developed its cooperative relationship with the national government to provide its environmental management experience at the local level, which has been formerly unattended by national ministries. The city has been quite successful in receiving national funds, that is, grants and subsidies, to build its environmental business capacity and carry out various public work projects, including creating a hub of human resource development in Asia. Yet the city's activities have not been simply complementary to already existing national policies by engaging in assistance activities that were nationally defined, but rather has taken its own initiatives in response to locally specific issues and problems. The national government has often recognized the benefits and importance of Kitakyushu's policy innovations, such as the "Dalian Environmental Model Zone," and adopted them as part of national policy implementation. Over the years, the city has developed the capacity to act as an independent provider of expertise and human capital on environmental management for the successful implementation of national policy.

Normative responses to governance practice

Yokohama's participation in international environmental cooperation has also been an active part of national policy, while being involved beyond what was mandated under national policy. Yokohama's cooperation with several international organizations was an integral part of national mandates for Japan's international contribution (*kokusai kōken*). But Yokohama's international contribution to involve itself beyond the reach of the national government, such as coordination for South–South cooperation at the municipal level, was motivated largely by norms. A collective self-understanding of normative commitment to international contributions seemed to outweigh immediate utility for local communities. There are two fundamental priorities or commitments that induce local governments to get involved beyond national mandates in environmental governance: material motivations (the extent to which local authorities are committed to maximizing their local economic or material utility) and normative motivations (how committed local authorities are to obeying the norms and values of environmental governance for its own sake). In practice, as the case studies show, while holding a mix of these motivations, the local governments show significant differences in the weighting of material and normative motivations. Yokohama's historical legacy and international orientation, while supported by a strong fiscal capacity, led the city to respond to needs for international development assistance and environmental cooperation. Yet it is important to note that these patterns of local governments' involvement are not mutually exclusive over time. The case in point is Yokohama's new strategy to promote international cooperation for the benefit of local business.

The case of Yokohama demonstrates that environmental problem-solving cannot be simply assumed to be utility-driven. Unlike the functionalists' assumption that governance will shape its form in response to collective utility needs, Yokohama's story reveals the dynamic process of international cooperation in which normatively driven agents purposively steer the course of events. Neoliberal institutionalists' claim that the form of governance is fixed by predetermined material interests also overlooks the activities of individual agents involved in cross-scale/multi-level interactions for environmental problem-solving. Developmental and environmental issues are closely associated with a dimension of cultural tradition and social norms, which affect locals with a locally specific profile. Local norms established at one time may be stable; however, over time, multi-level/cross-scale consultations and negotiations among agents may lead to local adaptation to foreign norms. In this respect, Yokohama adapted its historical tradition and its reputation as an international city to international environmental norms to be congruent with the collective expectation of local communities.

In terms of normative responses to governance practice, there is another important issue that the case studies address: the divide between the social values of the community and the economic efficiency of the corporate sector and that between those values and expert knowledge of the national bureaucracy. Participation is the essence of multi-level and cross-scale approaches that open up opportunities for all of the stakeholders' interests to contribute their inputs in an inclusive way, while not responding to any particular interests but still making a better decision or providing a public good for all. This most difficult task could be carried out by holding each other accountable for their actions in a democratic way. In the issue area of environmental problems, since no single territorial level alone can tackle the challenges of environmental risk reductions, solutions must be sought flexibly by linking the cross-scale of the environmental problem with the jurisdictional and practical reach of governmental and non-governmental actors. These simultaneous interactions between governmental and non-governmental actors at the cross-scale and multi-level could result in organizational complexity or impose constraints on actual accountability. A possible source of cohesion for accountability coordination lies in the peculiar role of local governments. Local authorities are more likely to assert values based on social needs or collectivist values as a counter to both values based on profit maximization or the interests of the business sector and values based on fragmented or individualistic modes of private consumption. As described in this book, local governments also do not simply ignore hierarchical constraints to attain their desired goals but negotiate with national authorities to steer policy-making. Without directly challenging the governmental tiers, local governments may be capable of deliberately crossing the domestic-foreign divide and entering cross-border cooperation agreements to meet their social needs. While they may mobilize their own locally specific resources beyond national boundaries to understand themselves as part of global strategies, they are normally willing to keep redefining their relations with governmental tiers through coordination and negotiation. It may be an overestimation to designate local governments as the only possible venue of accountability coordination, but it would equally be a mistake to underestimate the potential for local governments' strategic position to bring all the stakeholders together.

Kitakyushu continuously sought to make the competing goals of economic efficiency and social values/environmental protection compatible. The important point of this balancing act by the municipal government is that when motivated by self-interest to supply a public good, an agent needs to act within the framework of norms to achieve environmental protection. The municipal government skillfully coordinated its collaborative achievements to restore the environment and its preventive environmental efforts between citizens' groups and the business sector. The municipal government made great efforts to deliberately utilize its environmental assets and local experience to bring economic benefits to the city, while promoting the norms of environmental protection for their own sake. The city successfully avoided a hard political choice between development and environment by simultaneously seeking both goals in a rather conciliatory way. Kitakyushu was also quite successful in overcoming the divide between national bureaucratic expertise and local social needs. The ex-bureaucrat mayor was able to acquire a high degree of bargaining leverage with national ministries and thus derived significant financial resources from Kitakyushu's cooperative relationship with the national government. In the cooperative pattern of central-local relations, national ministries were responsive to Kitakyushu's demands for the successful implementation of nationally-supported policy and tolerated a measure of local flexibility in promoting international environmental business to meet local social needs. As the general public supported the mayor's initiatives, the depoliticization of municipal decision-making was epitomized in the course of events regarding the activities of environmental business development.

Policy learning and diffusion

Local needs and adaptive capacity continue to ensure difference and diversity among the more self-motivated local governments, in contrast with weaker municipalities that remain over-dependent on national supervision. The patterns of environmental policy-making at the local level appear to reflect four major analytically distinct mechanisms: tutelage (by the national government), mimicry (emulating neighbors), learning (revising after drawing lessons), and pioneering (innovation). The majority of Japanese local governments who engaged in international environmental cooperation simply worked with state agencies to support national programs to train specialists from and dispatch local experts to developing countries.

Tutelage, exercised via conditions attached to national subsidies or top-down administrative guidance, is most likely to be important in explaining the similarities among local authorities' environmental policy. Mimicry also favors the diffusion of similar patterns of environmental policy and international cooperation; it explains how and why some cities copy neighboring localities' practices in order to catch up, rather than making their own policy choices. These two other mechanisms are found to be at work in the case studies. Learning is based on lessons drawn from experience, which gives guidance about the likely consequences of policy options. Pioneering, especially found in the case of Kitakyushu, is the initiative in which local actors use new information to update their prior beliefs and adopt new policy ideas. While both tutelage and mimicry tend to have a uniform impact on policy-making and implementation activities among "bandwagoning" local actors, learning and pioneering can reveal different motivations within local decision-making, as illustrated in the case studies.

The view of learning is conceptualized to improve policy-making. There are various forms of policy learning: (1) the broad level of learning about policy elites' beliefs, key policy objectives, or general policy direction, (2) the operational level of learning about regulatory/promotional instruments or implementation designs, and (3) the strategic level of learning to understand political feasibility and its policy process. Lesson-drawing as well as mimicry appear to take place among most Japanese local governments, with obligatory forms of "indirect coercion" (e.g., administrative guidance). The broad level of learning about general policy direction is less likely to be found in such a non-voluntary act, since policy objectives or general policy directions are given or defined by the national authority. For these weaker local governments, policy learning is likely to occur at the technical level of policy instruments and implementation designs. In contrast, pioneering local governments have been actively involved in voluntary acts of policy learning. The case studies demonstrate that such voluntary acts experience the interconnected lesson-drawing of hierarchized and dehierarchized dimensions of governance where local governments are capable of moving across levels and spheres of authority. These pioneering local governments are largely able to advance policy ideas by learning how to enhance political feasibility from lesson-drawing and can even alter a general policy direction, independent of national policy.

Policy learning and innovation are not inevitable processes deriving from greater fiscal capacity or other enabling factors. It is true that earlier studies indicate a positive and significant correlation between fiscal capacity and international cooperation at the aggregate level. Yet, some actors are more willing to adopt policy ideas than others; not all policy-makers are equally sensitive to the same information. This may result from various factors. Kitakyushu has one of the lowest levels of fiscal capacity among designated cities, yet it has engaged in more innovative international cooperation than any other locality. The city, which suffered from severe pollution and overcame it, has demonstrated an ability to use local experience and expertise to promote international environmental business. The potential economic benefits helped to legitimize Kitakyushu's involvement in decentralized international cooperation. Shiga is a landlocked, rural prefecture. The limits of indigenous institutional capacity to cope with lake-environment degradation are seen as a key factor driving Shiga to reach out transnationally for policy learning and solutions. Its partnership with UNEP unexpectedly led to Shiga's promotion of environmental management for developing countries. In both cases, political leadership—mayoral leadership in Kitakyushu and gubernatorial leadership in Shiga—has been a crucial ingredient in motivating local governments to get involved in decentralized international cooperation. Such political leadership was a necessary condition, in the sense that without the chief executives' commitment, the initiatives for international cooperation would never have appeared on the policy agenda.

Tokyo's policy learning is not easily adopted elsewhere due to the interaction of structure and agency peculiar to the capital megacity. The Tokyo Metropolitan Government (TMG) stands out in its fiscal capacity, with per capita local tax revenue amounting to roughly twice the level of the prefectural average. The TMG has a great deal of freedom in budgetary choice, which allows it to offer a more comprehensive incentive program for mitigation measures. The characteristics of the mega capital also increase the political feasibility of cap-and-trade proposals. No steel and petroleum facilities, which fall under the category of the targeted facilities under the cap, happen to be located in Tokyo. The TMG is thus able to limit instances of direct confrontation with the most powerful lobbying groups. There is evidence of both endogenous and exogenous sources of learning in Tokyo's climate change policy. All in all, domestic processes in conjunction with policy ideas from overseas are reflected in its policy package.

The key finding is that the opportunity for transferring overseas ideas into Tokyo arises from its adaptive capacity, which is determined by local conditions. The TMG obviously borrowed the idea of the European Union Emissions Trading Scheme (EU-ETS) but it had to adapt the policy instruments to the specific urban scale. The process of adopting the TMG's mandatory reporting scheme is a redesign of the national policy instrument and constitutes evidence of instrumental learning in the hierarchies of the state. A key departure from prior policy ideas towards Tokyo's cap-and-trade was the change in the shared policy beliefs of the environmental coalition from voluntary reduction to mandatory reduction, which policy network members had learned from the policy experience of a voluntary emissions reduction plan with mandatory reporting (the broader level of learning about core policy ideas).

Finally, a strategic position enables local governments to take up a key role in the decentralized functions of environmental policy coordination. Yet the necessary precondition for local governments to efficiently and effectively participate in decentralized policy coordination lies in their level of governing capacities. Key indicators for policy efficiency in climate policy are chief executives' leadership, administrative ability, and fiscal capacity. But, as the case studies show, a handful of Japanese local governments are both willing and capable enough to contribute to decentralized policy coordination without national supervision. There are governing capacity gaps between pioneering local governments and other local governments. The national government needs to structurally enable local levels of participation in multi-level/cross-scale governance. Decentralized environmental cooperation requires an adequate delegation of power to lower levels of government. In this regard, the significance of "expert citizens" needs to be added to the limited capacities of local governments. The primary rationale for the necessity of expert citizens is to enhance public engagement in the professionalized processes of policy-making. Expert citizens could facilitate interactions between experts and laypeople to extend the principles of democracy to science-driven policy-making. They occupy an important position to help laypeople redress inequitable distributions of environmental burdens. In the past, Japanese local governments have made increasing use of private consultants who provide more technical and complex planning services. Yet the case studies of Shiki and Jōyō suggest that the limited capacities of local governments to help less-resourceful laypeople to participate in decision-making also require expert citizens to facilitate public participation. A greater role of expert citizens is to reorient expert knowledge towards accountability and responsiveness to laypeople. Expert citizens are better positioned to facilitate an on-going dialogue of expert-lay reflexive interplay and find a solution through the very process of learning and knowing. As the Japanese government emphasizes the need for greater public involvement in environmental decision-making, so do laypeople feel the need for expert citizens. Even if local governments or individual citizens call for help from the third party, there is a clear shortage of talent necessary for citizens to individually or collectively play such an intermediary role. Citizens' organizations are thus required to strengthen their organizational foundations and accumulate expertise and know-how for future use.

Appendix I

Appendix I Two-tier system of sub-national government in Japan (as of January 2014)

Prefectural	Total 47
Prefectures [*to-dō-fu-ken*]	47

Municipal	Total 1,742
Designated cities [*seirei shitei toshi*]	20
Core cities [*chūkaku-shi*]	45
Cities [*shi*]	725
Special wards (Tokyo) [*tokubetsu-ku*]	23
Towns [*chō*]	746
Villages [*son*]	183

Source: figures adopted from database provided by Local Authorities Systems Development Center (LASDC).

Note
A designated city must have a population greater than 500,000 and has been designated as such by a Cabinet order under Article 252, Section 19 of the Local Autonomy Law. A core city has a population greater than 300,000 and an area greater than 100 square kilometers and has been created as such by the first clause of Article 252, Section 22 of the Local Autonomy Law.

Appendix II

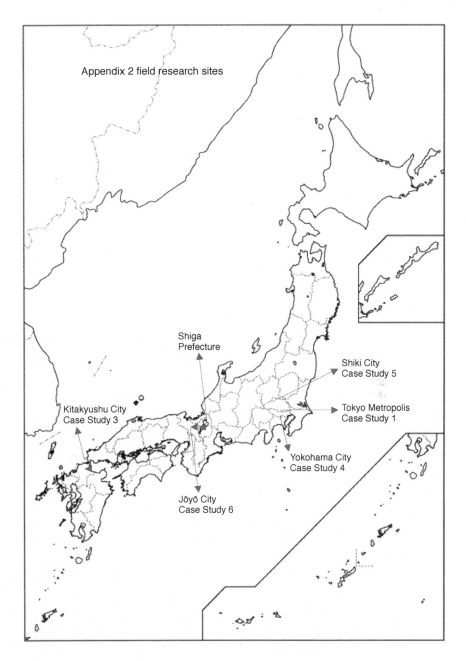

Appendix 2 Field research sites.

Appendix III
Major environmental legislation and local government's role in Japan

Basic Law for Environmental Pollution of 1967

This law defined the responsibilities of the national government, local governments, corporate firms and individual citizens for the prevention and control of pollution. It was to provide a framework for setting national environmental quality standards, specific implementation and planning measures at different levels of government. In the course of the drafting process, however, strong regulatory provisions were weakened by inserting a compromise clause to "harmonize" environmental protection "with sound economic development." In 1970 the electoral threat to the ruling national party at local elections forced its leadership to radically revise the 1967 comprehensive countermeasures against pollution. All regulatory power over business operators was delegated to municipal governments. This regulatory mechanism did not, however, specify any nationally-defined mandatory emissions standards but left regulation and enforcement to sub-national authorities.

Air Pollution Control Law of 1968 and Water Pollution Control Law of 1970

Within the statutory framework of these laws, a wide range of countermeasures was prescribed, including reporting on construction or installation of emission sources, setting permissible pollutant discharge standards from the emission source, regular guidance and on-site inspections of factories and businesses, and enforcing the law. Local governments are responsible for taking these measures. There are many cases in which, reflecting location-specific conditions in individual localities, discharge standards imposed by local ordinances are much stricter than those prescribed in the national laws.

Basic Environmental Law of 1993

This law completely revised the 1967 Basic Law for Environmental Pollution, in response to global strategies, especially Agenda 21's challenge. At the domestic level, from 1967 to 1993, there was a marked shift in the focus of environmental policy from industrial pollution to environmental conservation while Japan experienced many legislative failures in coping with industrial and non-industrial pollution. Article 34 acknowledges the importance of the roles played by local governments in promoting international cooperation with regard to global environmental conservation.

Environmental Impact Assessment Law of 1997

The national law is applied only to large-scale projects, and consultation at an early stage of projects does not fall within the scope of the national law. Small-scale projects and early stage consultation are left to local environmental impact assessment systems, which are established by local ordinances and guidelines. Long before the enactment of the national law, some local governments had already implemented relatively comprehensive assessments, responding to public pressure to take preventive measures rather than ex-post countermeasures against industrial pollution.

Climate Change Law of 1998

This law requires prefectural and municipal governments to prepare plans for taking specific mitigation measures. It gives statutory recognition to the advantages of decentralization, emphasizing that the nature of environmental problems is often location-specific and can be managed at different geographical areas. As Japan ratified the Kyoto Protocol in 2002, the national law was amended to increase local government's role in emissions reduction. Local governments were now instructed to create stakeholders' consultation committees and appoint expert advisors for making "voluntary" efforts to mitigate through local initiatives.

Appendix IV
International recognition of local authorities as key players in international agenda

1. European Charter of Local Self-Government of 1985: The "existence of local authorities with real responsibilities can provide an administration which is both effective and close to the citizen" and the "safeguarding and reinforcement of local self-government in the different European countries is an important contribution to the construction of a Europe based on the principles of democracy and the decentralisation of power."
2. Agenda 21 – Rio Earth Summit of 1992:

   Local authorities construct, operate and maintain economic, social and environmental infrastructure, oversee planning processes, establish local environmental policies and regulations, and assist in implementing national and sub-national policies. As the level of governance closest to the people, they play a vital role in educating, mobilizing and responding to the public to promote sustainable development.

3. UN-HABITAT agenda of 1996:

   We recognize local authorities as our closest partners, and as essential, in the implementation of the Habitat Agenda, we must, within the legal framework of each country, promote decentralization through democratic local authorities and work to strengthen their financial and institutional capacities in accordance with the conditions of countries, while ensuring transparency, accountability and responsiveness to the needs of people, which are key requirements for Government at all levels.

4. UN-HABITAT report of 2001: The report defines decentralized international cooperation as a locus "whereby cities (and indeed other institutions) work together on defining their problems and devising appropriate solutions on the basis of shared experience among peer groups."
5. Para. 174 of UN General Assembly, World Summit outcome of 2005: "We underline the important role of local authorities in contributing to the achievement of the internationally agreed development goals, including the Millennium Development Goals."

6 UN Secretary-General Kofi Annan's remarks to the UCLG World Mayors' Delegation of 2005:

> Global and local matters are more intertwined than ever before ... ultimately it is in the streets of your cities and towns that the value of what's decided here [at the United Nations] will be tested. You are essential partners. While our Goals are global, they can most effectively be achieved through action at local level.

7 Article 307 of the Lisbon Treaty of 2007:

> The Committee of the Regions shall be consulted by the European Parliament, the Council or by the Commission where the Treaties so provides and in all other cases, in particular those which concern cross-border cooperation, in which one of these two institutions considers it appropriate.... Where the Economic and Social Committee is consulted pursuant to Article 304, the Committee of the Regions shall be informed by the European Parliament, the Council or the Commission of the request for an opinion. Where it considers that specific regional interests are involved, the Committee of the Regions may issue an opinion on the matter.

Index

Page numbers in *italics* denote tables, those in **bold** denote figures.

Abe, Shinzo 74–6, 82, 92, 96–8
Acid Deposition Monitoring Network in East Asia (EANET) 57
Act on Promotion of Global Warming Countermeasures (1998 Climate Change Law) 53, 141n53, 176
Action Program to Arrest Global Warming (1990) 52
Aichi prefecture 159; Designated Special Major Port 261; Nagoya City 134, 145n119, 149, 158, 189, 242–3, 261, 263; Port of Atsuta 261; UN Centre for Regional Development (UNCRD) 189
Air Pollution Control Law (1968) 190
Akashi, Yasushi *see* Yokohama
Akita prefecture 159
Alger, Chadwick 54–5, 66n81, 66n82, 66n83
All-Japan Local Government Workers' Union 90
Allied Occupation 78, 82–3, 246–7
Argentina 189
Ariyoshi, Chūichi *see* Yokohama
Asano, Sōichirō *see* Yokohama
Ashio Copper Mine 2
Ashiwara, Noboru *see* Jōyō
Association of Southeast Asian Nations (ASEAN) 221
Asukata, Ichio *see* Yokohama
Atomic Energy Basic Law (1955) 79
Atomic Energy Law (US 1946) 78
Atomic Power Indemnification Law (1961) 84
Australia 28n15, 33n97, 34, 39, 132, 158, 165–6, 203n7, 207, 294n25, 296; Greenhouse Gas Reduction Scheme 165–6

ba (shared or interaction field) 2–3, 10, 27n2
Bang, Henrik 272, 274, 293n3, 293n5, 296
Bangladesh 255; Dhaka City 255
Basel Convention on the Control of Transboundary Movements of Hazardous Wastes (1989) 63n27
Basic Environmental Law (1993) 4, 56, 67n90, 70, 94, 111, 116, 189, 277
Basic Law for Environmental Pollution Control (1967) 44
Basic Law for Establishing the Recycling-based Society (2000) 4
Beck, Ulrich 273, 293n9, 296; *Risk Society* 273, 293n9
Belgium 11, *132*, 183
Brazil 198
Britain 24, 31n52, 35, 48, 50, 65n62, 66n69, 72, 75, *132*, 151, 275, 158, 176; Calder Hall reactor 24, 79–80, 84; Champions of Participation 275; DEMOS 276; Engage for Change 275; Involve 276; UK Local Government Alliance for International Development 144n106
Broadbent, Jeffrey 28n4, 32n84, 34, 62n8, 62n16, 63n28, 63n32, 63n33, 64n34, 64n45, 64n49, 69, 76, 101n7, 106
Brundtland (World Commission on Environment and Development) Report 15, 49

Cabinet Office: Committee on Economic Cooperation 130, 144n102
Cambodia 221; Paris Peace Agreement 221; Phnom Penh *see* Kitakyushu; Water Supply Authority (PPWSA) 221

Index 325

Canada 65n62, *132*, 158, *181*, 188, 203n16, 209; Canada Centre for Inland Water 188
Carter, Jimmy *see* nuclear energy policy
Chiba prefecture 125, 159, 163, 164; Ichikawa City 127, 278; Kashiwa City 119; Shiroi Town 125
China 48, 57, 58, 59, 75, 184–5, 204n23, 207, 211, 213–9, 221, 235n20, 235n22, 238n79, 239, 241, 306–7; Coastal Open Cities 215; Dalian *see* Kitakyushu; Hong Kong 245; National Environmental Protection Agency 214; Qingdao 219; Shanghai 245; Suzhou 219; Tianjin 219
Chōshū (present Yamaguchi prefecture) 245
civic science *see* expert citizens
civil society groups 5, 8, 9, 26, 271–2
climate change: aggregate efforts 163; Brundtland Report *see* Brundtland Report; cap-and-trade *see* Tokyo; carbon taxes 50; *chikyū kankyō* (global environment) 115, 140n29, 151, 203n13, 205n41, 204n42, 204n47, 206n61, 206n66, 208; *chikyū ondanka* (global warming) 66n74, 66n76, 66n78, 72, 115, 139n27, 140n30, 140n31, 141n53, 141n54, 143n83, 143n90, 143n93, 146, 147, 148, 151, 173n31, 173n32, 174n50, 175, 176, 178; Cities for Climate Protection 25, 33n97, 34, 136, 183, 203n7, 207; climate adaptation 2, 4, 30n35, 34, 51, 54, 110–12, 118–21, 124–5, 136–7, 167–8, 251–2, 254, 255, 279; Climate Leadership Group (C40) 165; climate mitigation 2, 25, 29n25, 35, 51, 54, 110, 113, 118–20, 123–5, 138n8, 140n30, 146, 147, 152–71, 173n31, 174n46, 174n52, 174n63, 178, 183, 204n27, 207, 224, 251, 252, 254, 255, 279, 304, 309, 316; coalition of diplomatic interests 53, 303; Conference of the Parties (COP7) – Marrakesh Climate 159; COP-3 (United Nations [UN] Framework Convention on Climate Change Conference) 2, 4, 52–4, 61, 63n27, 66n71, 66n77, 70, 191, 304; environmental coalition 41, 44–8, 51–3, 161, 170, 302, 303–5, 317; European Union Emissions Trading System (EU-ETS) 157, *171*; Experimental Emissions Trading Scheme 164; GHG Accounting and Reporting system (national system) 157–8, 168, *171*; industrial coalition 3, 23, 45, 48, 51, 52–3, 60–1, 161–2, 286, 301, 303, 305; International Carbon Action Partnership (ICAP) 165; Joint Crediting Mechanism (JCM) 224, 238n70, 238n71, 238n72, 238n73, 238n74, 238n75, 240; Kyoto City Global Warming Countermeasures Ordinance *see* Kyoto; Kyoto Protocol 4, 52–4, 61, 63n27, 66n71, 70–1, 191; National Institute for Environmental Studies 52, 318; National Level Cap-and-Trade Program (NLCTP) 164; North–South divide 49, 59, 198, 219–22, 307; Regional Level Cap-and Trade Program (RLCTP) 164; Toronto Conference 49; Voluntary Emissions Trading Scheme (JVETS) 164
Cold War 78, 79, 102n20, 144n101, 212, 246, 303
Constitution (Japan): Article 93 121
Container and Packaging Recycling Law (1995) 4
Convention concerning the Protection of the World Cultural and Natural Heritage (1972) 63n27, 191
Convention on Biological Diversity (1992) 197
Convention on Wetlands of International Importance (1971) 57, 191, 197
Convention to Combat Desertification (1994) 197
"core cities" 56, 133, 141n53

Davies, Jonathan 154, 172n17, 176
Democratic Party of Japan (DPJ) 75, 95
Democratic Socialist Party (DSP) 90
"designated cities" 56, 117, 119, 120–3, 133–4, 141n53, 145n112, 145n122, 158, 163, 169, 210, 215, 229, 243, 316
Deng, Xiaoping *see* Kitakyushu
Denmark 198
Deutsch, Karl 153, 171n1, 176
"developmental state" 23
Doi, Takako 90
Dolowitz, David 30n49, 31n50, 34, 35, 154, 172n4, 172n13, 172n16, 176
Dōmei (private sector labor confederation) 89
Dublin Principles 197
Dulles, John Foster *see* nuclear energy policy

Economic Planning Agency 248
Egypt 80
Eisenhower, Dwight D *see* nuclear energy policy
Energy Conservation Law (1979) 47
Energy and Environment Council 75, 95–6, 101n6, 105n88, 106, 107
energy policy: energy conservation 23, 47–8, 52, 64n47, 156, 162, *171*; energy demand/supply 48, 51, 88, 156, 301; energy efficiency standardization 47
Environment Agency (EA) 47, 51, 141n47, 147, 303; International Division 191, 193; Ueda, Minoru 193
environmental governance: adaptive governance 16, 18, 30n35, 35, 278; autonomous governance 183–6; citizen–expert interactive governance 27; "clustering" 184, 185, 203n16, 203n18, 209, 218; community awareness 60, 220, 223, 224, 228, 276, 311; "community participation model" (*kokumin-sanka gata*) 129; constitutive localization 267n57; cross-border effects 1, 220, 306, 307; cross-scale coordination 1, **6**, 8–15, 300, 305–8, 313, 314, 317; cross-sectoral 19, 155, 180–202; cultural match 267n58; decentralized coordination **5**, 7, 110, 300, 317; decentralized international cooperation 28n7, 39, 54–60, 110, 128–30, 132, 135–7, 180–202, 210–34, 242–64, 305–8, 310, 316; environmental equity 116, 127, 137, 281; environmental impact assessment (EIA) 3, 113, 118, 120–1, 142n61, 142n62, 142n64, 143n92, 148, 150, 151; environmental management systems (EMS) 125; environmental performance disclosure 3, 113, 121–2; fairness of government outputs 113, *114*, 126–7, 137; "free riding" 18, 112, 167, 272, 273; geographical proximity 58, 154, 219–20, 305, 306–8; global public goods 233, 306, 308; globalization 58–9, 61n2, 63n26, 69, 138n6, 153, 172n12, 177, 307; governmental performance 113, *114*, 123–7; governmental procedures 113, *114*, 117–23, 137; horizontal policy integration 12, 184, 186, 196; incentive mechanisms 3, 100, 113; information disclosure 3, 117–18, 121–2, 142n66, 142n67, 148, 158, 218; international environmental management standards (ISO14000) 49; international environmental management standards certificate (ISO 14001) 125, 143n84; International Organization for Standardization (ISO) 49, 65n54; internationalization 58–9, 130, 145n115, 151, 259, 306, 307; Japan Industrial Standards (JIS) 49; *kōchōkai* (public hearings) 91, 95, 104n71, 120; multi-level governance *see* multi-level governance; normative/ethical dimensions 12–15; officials' attentiveness 113, *114*, 121–3; officials' efficiency 113, *114*, 123–6; performance disclosure 3, 113, 121–2; political involvement 113, 115–17, 127, 277; pro-development policies 41, 45; *shimin sanka* (citizen participation) 116, 140n30, 140n37, 142n76, 143n93, 146, 147, 148, 277, 295n34, 295n51, 296n61, 297, 298; *shingikai* (advisory councils) 116, 277, 286, 287; state-centric coordination 11, 27, 74, 99, 309; sustainability *see* sustainability; transnational environmental governance 180, 181–3, 183–6, 203n11; transnational policy communities 155–6; transnational sectoral network 180–202; "transnationalization of policy" 155, 172n15, 172n18, 173n24, 178; transnationalism 24–5, 181–3, 210–34; vertical policy integration 184–5, 196
Environmental Impact Assessment Law (1997) 120
environmental politics: advocacy coalition framework (ACF) 18–26, 31n53, 31n54, 31n59, 31n61, 31n62, 32n69, 32n70, 32n72, 32n73, 32n74, 32n76, 33n85, 33n88, 33n93, 33n101, 33n102, 33n103, 37, 38, 39, 45, 74, 232, 302–5; bureaucratic compartmentalization 22, 303; bureaucratic politics 22, 65n59, 203, 304; bureaucracy-dominant models 85, 103n49; "devil shift" 26; domestic-foreign divide 7, 14, 24, 40, 42, 54, 192, 200, 303, 314; electoral politics 32n71, 32n77, 32n78, 32n79, 32n82, 35, 45, 60–1, 92–3, 95, 97–8, 104n75, 105n94, 106, 107, 108, 109, 155, 260, 271–2; epistemic communities *see* epistemic communities; industrial advocacy coalition 23, 45, 161, 303; international pressures/structures 7, 23, 77–81, 303–4; interpersonal trust 113, *114*, 115, 117, 139n26; leverage 7–8, 231, 314;

material groups 26, 77, 85, 86; mercantilist interests 129; non-state actors 1, 10, 12, 18, 25, 33n92, 33n96, 38, 40, 42, 182, 232, 310, 312; "policy brokers"/"policy coordinators" 25–6; policy subsystem 18–26, 31n61, 40, 44–5, 47–8, 74–101, 101n1, 105n87, 107, 109, 260, 303–5; political efficacy 113, *114*, 115–6; political fragmentation 22; political leadership 12, 110, 113, *114*, 123–4, 127, 135, 137, 155, 160–3, 187, 188, 201, 230, 233, 251, 258, 261, 301, 316; political mobilization 11, 18–26, 56, 89, 92, 180, 184–5, 191–2, 194, 200; political opportunity structures (POS) 18–26, 31n60, 31n63, 31n64, 31n65, 31n66, 31n67, 76, 100; politicization of science 19, 155; proportional representation (PR) 32n78; "a race to the bottom" 112, 167–8; residents' movements (*jūmin undō*); "second image" 42; "second image reversed" 24, 33n90, 35, 42, 58, 63n21, 69, 306; single-member districts (SMD) 32n78, 92; single-non-transferable-vote, multi-member system (MMD-SNTV) 22; "stable system parameters" 20, 31n61, 32n74, 81; structure-agency 20, 154, 171; territorial centralization 99, 100, 302, 303; "transgovernmental actors" 24, 182; transnational advocacy coalition/networks *see* transnational advocacy coalition/networks; "turf wars" 7, 76; "two-level-games" theory 24, 33n91, 37, 44, 63n22, 72

"Environmental Pollution Diet" (1970) 3, 45

epistemic communities 33n98, 35, 155, 172n19, 182, 203n9, 207

European Commission 186, 239n7, 297

European Union (EU): Committee of the Regions 55, 186; Members of the European Parliament 55

Evens, Mark 154, 172n7, 172n17, 173n23, 176

"expert citizens" 271–99; "bilateral knowledge translators" 278; citizen alienation 272, 275; "citizen experts" 274; civic science 271–99; "co-production" 273, 289; "counter-experts" 274; democratization of science 274–6; elite policy networks 154, 274; expert knowledge 13, 17–18, 19, 26, 27, 31n57, 39, 271, 273–4, 276, 277–8, 280, 285, 283, 287–92, 294n26, 299, 314, 317; "expertization" 278, 292; facilitator 254, 272, 276, 279, 281, 290, 295n40, 298; Formation of Integrated Local Environmental Knowledge (ILEK) project 278; functionalists 12, 274, 313; *goyō gakusha* (academic flunkies) 287; intermediary role 18, 271–99; knowledge-based adaptive governance 278; *kyōdō kōdinētā* (collaboration coordinators) 279, 295n39, 298; Mori, Ryo *see* Shiki; neutral third party 276, 283; participatory learning process 279, 281; place-based knowledge 273, 283, 288; public participation in science 27, 271, 273, 274–6, 292, 293n7, 293n8, 293n10, 293n11, 293n13, 293n14, 293n15, 293n16, 294n21, 294n24, 294n26, 293n 296, 297, 298; reflexive interplay 289, 292, 301, 317; scientific reasoning 18, 273, 274, 275; "scientization" 278, 292; Seko, Kazuho 279, 295n39, 298; socially shared understandings 275; structuralists 274

Factory Law (1911) 2
federal systems 11, 20, 168, 183
Federation of National Electric Power Workers Unions 89–90
Food and Agriculture Organization (FAO) *see* Yokohama
Fordism 250
France 65n62, 75, 81, *132*, 158, 205n50, 208, 275
Fukuoka prefecture 236n25; Fukuoka City 169, 189; Kitakyushu City *see* Kitakyushu City; UN Human Settlements Programme (HABITAT) Regional Office 189
Fukushima prefecture 86, 93, 103n55, 106, 159; Hokkaidō 127; Fukushima Daiichi 75, 76, 84, 86, 95, 99, 105n82, 105n91, 105n92, 107; Fukushima Daini 89; nuclear disaster 40, 74–7, 95–101

gate-keeping capacity 11, 27, 46, 54, 74, 184, 262, 302, 309
Geospatial Information Authority of Japan 196
Germany/West Germany 28n5, 28n8, 38, 39, 41, 48, 50, 62n17, 62n18, 73, 109; Lake Constance 188
Ghana 144n99, 198

Global Environmental Facility (GEF) 195; Global International Waters Assessment (GEF-funded GIWA) 196
gubernatorial leadership 123, 127, 160–3, 187, 188, 199, 201, 316

Harbor Law (1950) 246
Hashimoto, Ryūtarō 52
Hatoyama, Yukio 164
Hayashi, Fumiko *see* Yokohama
Hikone City *see* Shiga
Hino City *see* Tokyo
Hiranuma, Ryōzō *see* Yokohama
Hiroshima City 119
Hokkaidō 58, 87, 120; Northern Forum 58; Sapporo City 158, 159
Hooghe, Liesbet 10, 29n19, 29n24, 35, 36, 63n23, 69, 138n9, 147, 204n21, 204n24, 207
Hosoda, Kihachirō *see* Shiki
Hyogo prefecture 57, 120, 158; Kobe City 126, 304

Inaba, Minoru *see* Shiga
India 80
Indonesia: Bajak river basin *see* Kitakyushu; bank *sampah* 224; Developmental Planning Agency (BAPPEKO) *see* Kitakyushu; Jakarta *see* Yokohama; Pusdakota *see* Kitakyushu; Semarang *see* Kitakyushu; Surabaya *see* Kitakyushu
industrial pollution: anti-industrial pollution movements 2–3, 41–2, 44–8; conservative industrial coalition 23, 45, 47, 48, 51, 260; compensation scheme 42; emission regulations 42, 48, 54, 126, 152–71; minority anti-industrial pollution coalition 45–6; "point source polluters" 3, 122, 167; Pollution Countermeasure Agreements (PCAs) 42, 46, 62n13, 122; pollution-intensive sector 48, 65n53; Total Pollutant Load Control System (TPLCS) 42, 62n14
International Atomic Energy Agency (IAEA) 80, 103n34, 106
International Bank for Reconstruction and Development (IBRD) 192
International Council for Local Environmental Initiatives (ICLEI) 25, 56, 67n87, 67n91, 60, 111, 138n4, 147, 183, 294n31
international environmental cooperation 54–60, 128–36

International Environmental Management of Enclosed Coastal Seas (EMES) Center 57
International Monetary Fund (IMF) 13
International Tropical Timber Organization (ITTO) *see* Yokohama
International Union of Local Authorities Asia-Pacific (IULA-ASPAC) 254
Iran 80
Ishihara, Shintarō *see* Tokyo
Ishii, Hideo *see* Kitakyushu
Israel 158
itai-itai disease (cadmium poisoning) 2, 45
Italy 62n7, 72, *132*, 139n23, 150, 275, 294n20, 298

Japan Communist Party (JCP) 89, 98
Japan Fund for Global Environment 223
Japan International Cooperation Agency (JICA) 130, **131**, 132–4, 136, 144n100, 144n103, 145n110, 147, 190, 195, 198, 215, 220, 223, 225, 254–6, 262
Japan Livestock Technology Association 195
Japan Socialist Party (JSP) 89–90, 92–3, 105n79, 108, 260
Jenkins-Smith, Hank 20, 31n54, 31n59, 32n69, 32n70, 32n72, 33n88, 33n103, 33n104, 38, 102n14, 102n16, 105n87, 107, 109, 177
Jie, Zhenhua *see* Kitakyushu
Joetsu City 118
Johannesburg Summit (2002) 217; Johannesburg Declaration on Sustainable Development 227
Jōyō City: Ashiwara, Noboru 286; Basic Environmental Ordinance (2002) 283; Basic Environmental Plan (2003) 283; Department of Environmental Planning 284, 286, 296, 296n60; "environmental coordinator" 278, 281, 283, 284–6, 290, 296n59, 297; gravel pit 284; *idobata kaigi* (Neighborhood Chat Meetings) 286; Jōyō Environmental Partnership Conference (2003) 286; *kankyō shimin kondankai* (Citizen Environmental Discussion Group) 283–6; *kentō iinkai* (Examination Committee) 283, 284, 285; Kiko Network 278–9, 283–6, 288, 290, 295n38; Kizu River 284; Okamura, Noriko 284; Outsource 284, 287; Taura, Kenrō *see* Taura, Kenrō; Townspeople Conference against Gravel Digging (1967) 284

Kan, Naoto 95
Kanagawa prefecture 118, 120, 163, 164; Kawasaki City 119, 120, 121, 126, 189, 245, 304; Yokohama City *see* Yokohama City; Zushi City 120–1
Kasumigaura City 118
Keidanren (Japanese association of business organizations) 48, 49, 50, 52, 65n64, 80, 83, 84, 86, 96, *97*, 303
Kennan, George 247
Keohane, Robert 29n29, 36, 182, 203n5, 208
Kihara, Mitsuhiro *see* Kitakyushu
Kiko Network (formerly Kiko Forum) *see aslo* Jōyō City; "Strategic Forums for Low; "Carbon Regional Development" 278
Kishi, Nobusuke 102n20
Kitakyushu City: acid rain 214–15, 216, 236n23, 236n24, 240, 306; Action Plan of the Kitakyushu Eco-Model City (2009) *211*, 219, 237n48, 239; Aqua Tech Co., Ltd. 216; "Asia's International Resource-Recycling and Environmental Industry Base City" 219; Bajak river basin 220; Bay of Dokai *211*, 213; cleaner production technology (CPT) 213, 216; Dalian 4, 56–7, 58–9, *211*, 213–17, 219, 230, 234, 306, 307, 312; "Dalian Environmental Model Zone" *211*, 215–16, 230, 234, 312; "dead sea" 213; Deng, Xiaoping 214; Developmental Planning Agency (BAPPEKO - Surabaya) 225; Earth Summit 2002 Sustainable Development Award 217; Eco-Town Center 218; Environmental Cooperation Center 214–17, 235n14, 236n28, 236n38; Environmental Cooperation Network of Asian Cities 58; "environmental industry" 217–9; Environmental Pollution Control Bureau 213; Global 500 Award (1990) *211*, 214; "Green Sister City" 224, 237n61; Hai Phong 221–2; Hibiki landfill 217–8; Hibikinada Development Plan *211*, 218; International Conference on Acid Rain in East Asia 214; international environmental businesses 216, 217–25; Ishii, Hideo 220–1; Jie, Zhenhua 215; Kihara, Mitsuhiro 220; Kitakyushu Asian Center for Low Carbon Society *211*, 219, 220, 222, 224, 225, 237n59, 237n60, 240, 307; Kitakyushu Citizens' Association of Global Warming 228; Kitakyushu Council for the Promotion of Environmental Industry 218; Kitakyushu Eco-Town Project *211*, 218–19, 236n41, 237n46, 240, 241; Kitakyushu for Asia Women Forum (KWAN) 228; Kitakyushu Initiative Network 57, 67n98, 71, *211*, 219; Kitakyushu International Techno-cooperation Association (KITA) 67n94, 145n120, 149, 234, 235n14, 236n25, 236n27, 236n28, 236n30, 236n31, 236n32, 237n62, 240; "Kitakyushu Method" 213, 215, 233, 237n60; Kitakyushu Urban Center of the Institute for Global Environmental Strategies (IGES) 219, 237n51, 240; Kokura 211, 212; Kubota, Kazuya 221; low-carbon technology transfer 222, 229; merger of Yawata and Fuji 213; Mizoguchi, Hiroshi 217, 236n35, 238n79, 238n80, 238n82, 241; Mizuno, Isao 215; Moji 212, 213, 214; Multi-stakeholders Forum 227; Nakabaru Women's Association 212, 226; New Japan Chemical Environmental Consultancy Co., Ltd. 216; Nihon Denso Power Plant 212, 226; Nippon Steel 211, 213, 218; Nippon Steel Chemical 226; Nishi-Nippon PET-Bottle Recycling Co. Ltd. 218; Office for International Environmental Strategies 224; Phnom Penh 221, 255; pollution prevention ordinance (1971) *211*, 213; Pusdakota 223; Regional Centre of Expertise (RCE) 228, 238n84, 240; RISE Kitakyushu 228; Semarang 220; socio-technical export 222–5, 229; Song, Jian 215; Sueyoshi, Kōichi *221*, 217, 218, 230–1, 236n37, 236n39, 236n40, 241; Surabaya 223–5, 237n61, 238n62, 238n63, 238n64, 238n65, 238n66, 238n67, 238n68, 238n72, 240, 241; Takakura Home Method (THM) 223; Tobata 212–13, 226–7; UN Local Government Honors (1992) *211*, 214; Upward Biological Contact Filtration (U-BCF) 221; "venous" industry 217; Wakamatsu 212; "Water Business" 222; Water and Sewer Bureau 220–1, 225; waterworks technology 221, 237n53, 237n58, 241; "World Capital of Sustainable Development" (2004) 227–8, 238n79, 238n80, 238n82,

330 Index

Kitakyushu City *continued*
238n83; Xi, Jinping 219; Yada, Toshifumi 217; Yawata Iron and Steel Works (today's Nippon Steel Corporation) 211, 235n2; "zero emissions environmental industries" 217; Zhu, Rongji 215
Kitschelt, Herbert 19, 31n60, 31n63, 31n64, 36, 104n72, 107
Koizumi, Jun'ichiro 92–3
Komeito 97
Korean War 78, 83, 212, 246, 247; special procurement boom 247
Krauss, Ellis 28n3, 32n81, 36, 37, 62, 71, 92, 104n74, 104n76, 107, 138n2, 150, 265n24, 269
Kubota, Kazuya *see* Kitakyushu
Kusatsu City *see* Shiga
Kushiro International Wetland Centre 57; Ramsar Convention on Wetlands of International Importance 57, 197
Kyoto prerfecture: Jōyō City *see* Jōyō City; Kyoto City Global Warming Countermeasures Ordinance 119; Miyako Agenda 21 Forum 120

Liberal Democratic Party (LDP) 22, 23, 32n82, 36, 45, 47, 48, 75, 76, 84–93, 95–8, 99, 100, 104n74, 104n75, 104n76, 107, 109
Local Autonomy Law 27n1, 118, 189, 277
local government: adaptive capacity 27, 61, 110, 128, 130, 134, 152, 170, 180, 201, 263, 308, 315, 317; administrative ability 27, 124–5, 128, 137, 263, 300, 317; administrative evaluation/review 125; advisory environmental councils 116, 277; Agenda 21 4, 55–6, 66n84, 67n87, 67n91, 70, 72, 111, 113, 118–19, 120, 127, 138n3, 138n4, 141n46, 141n47, 141n48, 141n49, 141n50, 141n51, 147, 148, 149, 151, 197, 277–8, 294n31, 294n32, 297; "bandwagoning" 135, 264, 315; Basic Environmental Bylaws 116, 277; Basic Environmental Plans 116, 127, 140n34, 140n35, 140n38, 148, 150, 277–8, 294n30, 295n35, 297; city-to-city international cooperation programmes 55, 57, 67n100, 128, 143n96, 151, 213–17, 255, 262; delegated authority 8, 9; fairness of government outputs 113, *114*, 126–7, 137; financial capacity index 145n114; fiscal capacity 128; fiscal elasticity 125–6; Global Warming Countermeasures Promotion Office 122; institutional authority 8; international inter-city network programs 133–4, 144n108; *jinji-idō* (organization-wide job rotation practice) 123; *kankyō-shoku* (environmental specialists) 123; Local Agenda 55–6, 67n87, 67n91, 70, 111, 113, 118–19, 120, 127, 138n4, 141n46, 141n47, 141n48, 141n49, 141n50, 141n51, 147, 148, 149, 277–8, 281, 294n31, 294n32, 297; Local Allocation Tax 125, 129, 130, 152, 242–3, 243; Local Authority's Standards in the Environment (LAS-E); local capacity building 26, 59, 60, 110–27; local human capital 165, 213, 230, 250, 260–1, 312; local official development assistance (ODA) 57, 128, **131**, 131–2, 190–1, 215–7; Miyako Agenda 21 Forum *see* Kyoto; moral authority 8, 227; *ōru yotōka* (all parties ruling together without political opposition) 121; political legitimacy 8, 193, 251; *sōgō keikaku* (long-term comprehensive plans) 118; trans-local cooperation 128, 213, 215, 216, 219, 222, 223, 234, 307, 312; World Charter for Local Self-government 55
local knowledge 2, 13, 15, 17–18, 59, 156, 181, 188, 196, 200, 271–92, 267n57, 267
local norms 13, 17, 29n31, 34, 242–64, 313
Local Tax Law 125

MacArthur, Douglas 246
Management and Coordination Agency 89, 104n65, 107
Marks, Gary 10, 29n19, 29n20, 29n21, 29n24, 29n28, 35, 36, 37, 43, 63n23, 63n24, 71, 138n9, 147, 204n21, 204n22, 204n24, 204n25, 204n26, 204n31, 207, 208
Marsh, David 31n50, 31n55, 35, 154, 172n4, 172n8, 172n13, 176, 177
Matsuzawa, Shigefumi *see* Tokyo
Meiji emperor 245
Meiji government 245
Meiji Restoration *243*, 245
Mexico 41, 144n104, 151
Mie prefecture 121
Millennium Development Goals 55, 129, 144n97, 231
Minamata disease (mercury poisoning) 2, 3, 45

Ministry of Construction (MOC) 189–90, 195, 217, 230–1; Land and Water Bureau 190; River Bureau 190
Ministry of Economy, Trade and Industry (METI – formerly MITI) 65n61, 65n62, 70, 94, 95–6, *97*, 101n4, 107, 141n56, 147, 156, 164, 173n26, 177, 238n71, 240, 252, 255; Advisory Committee for Natural Resources and Energy 96; Next Generation Energy Infrastructure and Social System Demonstration Area 252
Ministry of Education, Culture, Sports, Science, and Technology (MEXT) 94, *97*
Ministry of the Environment (MOE) 64n46, 66n72, 66n75, 67n90, 70, *97*, 140n35, 140n45, 141n48, 141n50, 141n52, 141n53, 141n54, 141n57, 142n62, 142n64, 142n71, 143n83, 143n90, 147–8, 164, 173n34, 173n36, 173n37, 173n38, 173n39, 175n71, 175n73, 177, 231, 240, 297
Ministry of Finance (MOF) 143n88, 148
Ministry of Foreign Affairs (MOFA) 51, 52, 53, 57, 59, 65n58, 70, 130, 145n112, 190–1, 205n51, 208, 303, 311; Grassroots Grant Aid Program 59; United Nations Policy Division 193
Ministry of Health and Welfare (MHW) 44
Ministry of Home Affairs (MOHA) 46, 130, 131, 145n112, 190, 191, 251; Council of Local Authorities for International Relations (CLAIR) 67n92, 69, 132, **131**, 131, 133, 136, 145n109, 145n116, 146, 190, 254, 255, 262; Economic Affairs Bureau and Economic Cooperation Bureau 260; *kokusaika suishin taisakuhi* (promotion expenditure for internationalization) 130
Ministry of Internal Affairs and Communications (MIAC – formerly MHA) 130, 142n66, 142n68, 142n69, 142n70, 143n81, 143n86, 143n87, 143n89, 148, 269, 295n42, 297
Ministry of International Trade and Industry (MITI) 46, 48, 51, 52, 76, 84–6, 87, 91, 93, 94, *97*, 101, 103n49, 104n71, 107, 212, 213, 218, 219, 234n2, 235n3, 235n4, 235n5, 235n12, 240, 248–9, 303; Agency of Natural Resources and Energy 51, *97*, 156, 303
Ministry of Land, Infrastructure and Transport 252
Mizoguchi, Hiroshi *see* Kitakyushu
Mizuno, Isao *see* Kitakyushu

Moori, Masanori *see* Shiki
Mori, Ryo *see* Shiki: ECO Communication Center
multi-level governance: *de-hierarchized* spheres 10–12, 16, 232, 310, 312: *hierarchized* tiers 10–12, 16, 202, 232, 309, 310, 312; mutual accountability 9; organizational complexity 9, 14, 300, 30; stakeholders 1, 8–12; territorial jurisdiction 10, 12; Type I governance 10–11; Type II governance 10–11
multilateral environmental agreements (MEAs) 7, 43, 63n27, 183–4, 191, 205n53, 208; "clustering" *see* environmental governance

Nagano prefecture 119, 124, 158; Tanaka, Yasuo 124
Nagasaki 211
Nakasone, Yasuhiro 49, 78–9, 82, 85, 90
National Action Plan for Agenda 21 (1993) 4
Netherlands 144n98, 146
New Zealand 132, 158, *181*, 188; Lake Taupo 188
NHK (Japanese Broadcasting Corporation) 96, 140n39, 194
Niigata Minamata disease (Methylmercury) 45
NIMBY (not-in-my-backyard) 47, 88, 99, 101n11, 107
Nippon Telegraph and Telephone (NTT) 115, 140n32, 149, 225; NTT Data Institute of Management Consultant 225
Nishikawa, Yūji *see* Shiki
Noda, Yoshihiko 95
non-industrial pollution 3, 46–7, 115, 306
Non-profit Organization Law (1998) 117
Nozaki, Kin'ichirō *see* Shiga
nuclear energy policy: anti-nuclear energy activism/coalition 76, 88–90, 98, 99; "Atoms for Peace" 78, 83, 102n29, 107; Basic Energy Plan 75, 96; boiling water reactor (BWR) 83–4; Calder Hall type reactors *see* Britain; Carter, Jimmy 80; Central Intelligence Agency (CIA) 79; Chernobyl Nuclear Power Plant 90; confidentiality clauses 80; Cost Review Committee of the Energy and Environment Council 101n6, 106–7; Daigo Fukuryū Maru 79, 89; Defense Department (US) 79; "dual structure" 85; dual-use 8; Dulles, John Foster 78; "dynamic system events" 77;

nuclear energy policy *continued*
  Eisenhower, Dwight D. 78, 102n29, 107; Electric Power Development Co., Ltd (EPDC) 84, 248; Electric Utility Coordination Council (EUCC) 87, 91, 93; electric Power Development Tax 87; energy security 48, 82, 95, 30; Export-Import Bank (US) 78; external subsystem vents 77, 94, 100, 303; fast breeder reactor (FBR) 81–2; First Atomic Power Industry Group 83; Fukushima Daiichi *see* Fukushima; Fukushima Dainis *see* Fukushima; General Electric (GE) 78, 83–4; Green Energy Law Network (GEN) 94; International Bank for Reconstruction and Development 78, 192; Japan Atomic Energy Commission (JAEC) 79, *97*, 104n60, 104n67, 105n77, 106, 107; Japan Atomic Energy Enterprise Co. 83; Japan Atomic Energy Research Institute (JAERI) 83–4, *97*; Japan Atomic Industry Forum (JAIF) 83, *97*; Japan Atomic Power Company (JAPCO) 84, *97*; Japan Nuclear Fuel Limited 85–6; JCO Co. Ltd (Japanese nuclear fuel cycle company) 93; location subsidies 86–7, 91, 305; Mitsubishi Atomic Power Industries 83; Monju 82, 93; Mutsu 89; Nagashima incident 88; National Parliamentarians' Association for Promoting Renewable Energy 94; Nippon Television Network Service 79; Nuclear and Industry Safety Agency (NISA) 94, 96, *97*, 102–3n34, 105n80, 106; nuclear fuel cycle 78, 82, 86, 91, 93, 100; Nuclear Regulatory Authority (NRA) 75, 96, *97*; "outside forces" 76, 101n12, 106; overlapping policy subsystems 48, 74, 101n1, 101n2, 105n87, 109; Pentagon 80; political realignment 21, 23, 77; *Power Reactor & Nuclear Fuels Corporation 87*; pro-nuclear energy coalition 22, 24, 48, 74, 80, 82–6, 87, 88, 90, 91, 93, 96, 98–101, 302; Reagan, Ronald 80; Rokkasho 82; "ruling triad" 76; Science and Technology Agency (STA) 79, 83, 85, 87, 91, 93, 94, *97*; Sendai 1 reactor 75; Shikoku Electric Power Co. 90; Shōriki, Matsutarō 10, 33n89, 34, 79–80, 102n19, 102n23, 102n 26, 102n27, 102n28; Strauss, Lewis 80; Sumitomo Atomic Energy Industries 83; "techno-nationalism" 82; Tokyo Atomic Industry Research Institute 83; top-down national undertaking 74–101, 302; Truman, Harry S. 78; US Information Service (USIS) 79; US–Japan nuclear cooperation agreement (1955 and 1968) 79–80; utility companies 77, 82–6, 87, 91, 95, 101; Westinghouse 78, 83; Windscale reactor 80; Yokomichi, Takahiro 87; zaibatsu 83; *see also* Yokohama

Nye, Joseph 24, 33n95, 36, 182, 203n5, 208

Occupation Supreme Commander of the Allied Powers (SCAP) 246
official development assistance (ODA) 50, 57, 59, 65n59, 128–32, **131**, 135, 144n101, 144n102, 144n107, 190, 198, *211*, 215, 216, 217, 221, 231, 234, 240, 255; bilateral ODA 130, 131–2, *132*; "contracting-out method" 130; Development Assistance Committee (DAC) 131–2, *132*, 144n106, 144n107, 264n1, 268; grassroots ODA 59, 217, 231, 255; ODA Charter (1992) 50, 129, 135, 190, 231
oil crisis 3, 47, 86
Okamura, Noriko *see* Jōyō
Organisation for Economic Co-operation and Development (OECD) 1, 13, 40, 48, 49, 50, 52, 62n3, 64n48, 65n60, 65n63, 69, 70, 72, 111, 132, 138n7, 144n99, 148, 158, 175n67, 175n72, 176, 177, 192, 217, 236n36, 241, 242, 275, 276, 294n18, 298; OECD Development Co-operation Directorate 264n1
Osaka prefecture 118, 119, 158, 159, 164, 189; Toyonaka City 3, 116, 118, 127, 278

Pekkanen, Robert 32n82, 36, 92, 102n13, 104n74, 104n76, 106, 107
Perry, Matthew *see* Yokohama
policy convergence/interaction 40, 43, 44, 175, 176
policy learning/transfer 10, 15–18, 30n44, 30n45, 30n48, 31n52, 31n53, 31n54, 31n59, 32n69, 32n70, 33n88, 33n103, 33n104, 37, 38, 86, 91, 95, 102n16, 109, 129, 135, 151–71, 172n4, 172n5, 172n6, 172n7, 172n8, 172n9, 172n10, 172n11, 172n12, 172n12, 172n13, 172n14, 172n15, 172n16, 172n17, 172n18, 172n19, 172n20, 172n21,

172n22, 172n23, 173n29, 176, 177, 178, *181*, 181, 186, 189, 190, 191, 197, 199, 201, 202, 210, 222–3, 227, 233–4, 257, 260, 262, 263–4, 288, 301, 305, 308, 309, 311, 315–7; Bayesian learning 16, 30n45, 37, 177; bounded rationality 16, 17, 177; cognitive/ conscious factors 17, 153, 160, 170; collective/mutual learning 17; "consensual knowledge" 154, 160; cross-national policy diffusion 171n3, 172n6, 175; cross-scale and multi-level learning 154; decentralized form of learning 166, 309; deficit model 18; diffusion mechanism 46, 153, 171, 233, 315; free-riding problem 18; "front-runners" 159, 167; geographical proximity 58, 154, 219, 220, 305–7; ideational-based policy diffusion 154; interactive/mutual learning 17, 60, 156, 165, 166, 220, 233, 262, 288, 309; "lesson drawing" 16, 17, 18, 30n43, 31n55, 38, 135, 155–7, 162, 166, 171, 173n33, 177, 213, 222, 224, 263, 309, 315, 316; mimicry 135, 263, 264, 315; operation level of learning 17, 86, 91, 155, 157, 315; "perceptual transfer" 154; policy convergence 24, 40, 43, 44, 58, 61n1, 62n3, 69, 153, 158, 172n6, 173n25, 175, 176, 233, 306; policy elites' beliefs 17, 95–8, 159–60, 315; policy innovation 40, 41, 47, 57, 111, 125, 152, 153, 154, 155, 166, 167, 172n9, 172n10, 172n11, 172n12, 172n14, 172n20, 172n21, 175, 176, 177, 179, 181, 183, 188, 200, 226, 230, 231, 232, 233, 247, 248, 302, 309, 312, 316; regulatory/promotional instruments 17, 83, 86, 315; social learning 17, 30n40, 31n52, 35, 60, 288; "soft" and "hard" transfer 154, 165; tutelage 74, 118, 135, 263, 264, 315; *yokonarabi* (copycatting behaviour) 123
politicization of science and technology 19, 155
public goods 7, 9, 43, 44, 49, 65n57, 72, 196, 197, 200, 229, 233, 305, 306, 308
public opinion 23, 42, 44, 45, 74, 75, 77, 82, 89, 90, 93–5, 96, 99, 104n65, 105n82, 105n83, 105n87, 105n91, 105n92, 107, 115, 120, 139n27, 147, 188, 259, 277, 301
Putnam, Robert 33n91, 37, 63n22, 69, 72, 139n23, 150, 271, 292n1, 294n20, 298

Reagan, Ronald *see* nuclear energy policy
Reed, Steven 28n3, 38, 62n6, 62n9, 72, 98, 102n13, 104n75, 105n94, 106, 108, 109, 137n1, 138n2, 150
Rio Earth Summit (1992) 4, 49, 55, 111, 115, 129, 143n97, 214, 217, 231, 307
Risse-Kappen, Thomas 24–5, 33n92, 33n96, 38, 182, 203n6, 208
Russo-Japanese War (1904–1905) 211

Sabatier, Paul 20, 31n53, 31n54, 31n59, 31n62, 32n69, 32n70, 32n72, 32n76, 33n88, 33n101, 33n102, 33n103, 33n104, 38, 39, 101n1, 101n2, 102n14, 102n15, 102n16, 102n32, 102n33, 103n36, 103n38, 103n39, 103n50, 103n54, 105n81, 105n84, 105n87, 109, 15, 177
Saigō, Michikazu *see* Yokohama
Saitama prefecture 117, 121, 158, 159, 163, 164, 280; Kawagoe City 119; Shiki City *see* Shiki City; Tokorozawa City 282
Sakimura, Hisao *see* Shiga
Samuels, Richard 76, 101n8, 103n35, 103n45, 103n48, 103n51, 109, 137n1, 150
San Francisco Peace Treaty (1952) 246
Satsuma (present Kagoshima prefecture) 245
Science Council of Japan 83
sectoral networks 4, 56, 57, 179–202
Seko, Kazuho *see* "expert citizens"; Training and Resource Center 279
Seoul Metropolitan government *see* Yokohama
Shiga prefecture: *akashio* (freshwater red tide) *181*, 187; "BIWASO" (Lake Biwa Comprehensive Development Project) 190; Canada Centre for Inland Water *see* Canada; "causal story" 187; cultural tradition 282, 300, 313; degradation visibility 187; Environmental Bureau 181, 188, 189, 191–2, 201; eutrophication 57, *181*, 181, 187, 188, 199, 308; "framing" 187, 188, 192, 201, 202, 206n57, 311; gubernatorial leadership *see* gubernatorial leadership; Hikone City 118, 127; Inaba, Minoru 195; Integrated Lake Basin Management (ILBM) 198; International Lake Environment Committee Foundation (ILEC) 57, 67n96, 70, 180–202, *181*, 203n13, 205n38, 206n70, 206n76,

334 *Index*

Shiga prefecture *continued*
206n77, 206n78, 207, 208, 209, 261, 262, 311; International Lake Environment Conference (1984) *181*, 182, 193; international non-governmental standing committee 180, 182; Kusatsu City 119, 202n1, 206n70, 206n73, 206n76, 207, 208, 209; Lake Basin Management Initiative (LBMI) 195, 197; Lake Biwa 57, 67n97, 71, 180–202, 203n2, 203n4, 203n13, 205n35, 205n41, 205n42, 205n47, 206n61, 206n66, 207, 208, 308; Lake Constance *see* West Germany/Germany; Lake Taupo *see* New Zealand; lake environment policy network 181, 188; lake-environment risk reduction 57, 180, 187; *nin'i dantai* (unregistered private organization) 195; Nozaki, Kin'ichirō 187; Ordinance Governing the Conservation of Natural Scenery (1984) *181*, 188; Ordinance Relating to the Prevention of Eutrophication in Lake Biwa (1979) *181*, 187; public transnational networks 25, 136, 182–3; Sakimura, Hisao 192; *sekken undo* (soap campaign) 197; Takemura, Masayoshi *181*, 187, 205n36, 209; "Three-Drop" citizens' movement 187; Tolba, Mostafa 192–3; traceability of responsibility 187; "transgovernmental actors" 24, 182; Women's Organization Liaison Committee 187; World Lake Conference (WLC) 195, 197; "World Lakes Database" 196; World Lake Vision (WLV) 196–7, 206n73, 206n74, 206n76, 206n79, 209; *zaidan hōjin* (legally recognized foundational organization) 195

Shiki City: Basic Environmental Plan (1999) 280; Citizen's Environmental Conference (1998) 282; conservationists 280, 288; Council for the Promotion of Clean River 280; dioxin pollution 282; EcoCity Shiki 280–3, 289–91, 295n43, 295n45, 295n46, 295n47, 295n48, 295n52, 295n53, 297, 298; ECO Communication Center 279, 281, 284, 290, 295n41; Ecosystem Conservation Society (Shiki Branch) 280; Environmental Promotion Department 282; Field Club 280; heritage investigations 283; Hosoda, Kihachirō 280; Local Agenda Shiki Workshop 281; local historical legacies 282; *mizuka* (remnants of locally specific flood control facilities) 283, 295n52, 295n54, 298; Model City for the Promotion of Environmental Education 279; Moori, Masanori 280, 282, 295n43, 295n47, 295n52, 295n53, 295n54, 298; Mori, Ryo 279, 295n40, 295n41, 295n55, 298; Nishikawa, Yūji 282, 295n51, 298; Promotion Committee for Environmental Education 281; Shiki Citizen's Conference 280; Shiki Citizen's Environmental Plan (1998) 280, 281, 282; Shiki City Livelihood Club 280; "Shiki Ecomuseum" 283; Shimin Kankyō Daigaku (citizens' environmental university for facilitators' training) 279, 280, 281; Two Trees Club 280; workshop-driven planning process 281

Shizuoka prefecture 46, 119, 158, 169, 249; Mishima-Numazu 249; Nirayama Town 118

Shōriki, Matsutarō *see* nuclear energy policy

Social Demoratic Party (SDP – formerly JSP) 93, 98

"soft politics" 7

Sōhyō (General Council of Trade Unions of Japan) 89

solid waste management (SWM) 223, 224, 225, 255

Song, Jian *see* Kitakyushu

Southeast Asia 49, 58, 59, 139n21, 146, 173n23, 176, 221, 254, 307

Soviet Union 78, 80, 211, 303

spillover effect 5, 56, 95, 215, 220, 232, 306, 307, 312

Sri Lanka: Colombo 255

state-centric governance 1, 10, 54, 88, 184, 185, 308

Stone, Diane 154, 172n7, 172n15, 172n18, 172n19, 178

Strauss, Lewis *see* nuclear energy policy

Sueyoshi, Kōichi *see* Kitakyushu

sustainability 15, 28n14, 34, 67n87, 67n91, 70, 111, 129, 139n23, 150, 210, 228, 250, 277, 293n14, 294n31, 297, 304; "strong sustainability" 15; "weak sustainability" 15

Switzerland 11, 75

Takahide, Hidenobu *see* Yokohama
Takemura, Masayoshi *see* Shiga
Tamura, Akira *see* Yokohama

Index   335

Tanaka, Kakuei 87
Tanaka, Yasuo *see* Nagano prefecture
Tarura, Kenrō 2, 140n31, 151, 284, 285, 295n38
Thailand 198; Bangkok 32n84, 67n86, 69, 255
The Philippines 255, 256; Iloilo City 256, 267n54, 267n55, 268; Makati City 255
Tiebout, Charles 138n12, 150, 265n20, 270
Tokugawa Shogunate *see* Yokohama
Tokyo 2016 Olympic Game bid 124, 161, 174n51, 178; Asian Network of Major Cities (ANMC-21) 57; Association of Building Engineering and Equipment 161; Bureau of the Environment (BOE) 156–7, 159–65, 169–70; cap-and-trade 27, 50, 65n65, 117–20, 124, 134, 137, 152–71, 173n35, 174n62, 179, 309, 316, 317; "Carbon-minus Olympics" 124, 161; CBO Environmental Conservation Ordinance 162; Chiyoda Ward 119; Enterprise Planning System for Mitigation Measures 156, 173n31, 178; Environmental Collateralized Bond Obligation (CBO) Program 162; "Global Warming Countermeasures Fund" 161; Hino City 3, 116, 127, 140n38, 148, 278, 295n34, 298; Ishihara, Shintarō 124, 159–60; Kōtō Ward 47; mandatory emissions trading scheme 117–18, 152, 163–4, *171*, 317; Matsuzawa, Shigefumi 164; Metropolitan Assembly 160, 162, 173n41, 178; particulate-matter removal devices (DPF) 160; Special Wards 127, 143n76, 146; stakeholder meetings 119, 141n58, 151, 162, 174n53, 179; Suginami Ward 47; Tokyo Chamber of Commerce 120, 162; Tokyo Gas 161, 247, 252; Tokyo Metropolitan Environmental Council 161, 174n47, 178; Tokyo Metropolitan government (TMG) 46, 140n42, 141n55, 141n58, 142n67, 143n91, 143n92, 151, 152–79, 316, 317; "Tokyo's Climate Change Strategy" 159, 174n54, 178; Toyota Motor 161
Tokyo Electronic Power Company (TEPCO) 46, 76, 86, 103n56, 106, 248, 249, 252
Tolba, Mostafa *see* Shiga
transnational advocacy coalition/networks 24–5, 33n85, 33n86, 33n92, 33n93, 33n96, 33n99, 38, 39, 109, 203n6, 203n10

Truman, Harry S. *see* nuclear energy policy

U Thant *see* Yokohama
Ueda, Minoru *see* Environment Agency
unitary system 11, 20, 21, 136, 168, 183, 302, 308, 310
United Cities and Local Governments (UCLG) 59, 67n89, 73
United Kingdom (UK) *see* Britian
United Nations Center for Human Settlements (UN-Habitat) 55, 58, 128, 143n96, 151, 189
United Nations Centre for Regional Development (UNCRD) 189, 216; *see also* Aichi prefecture
United Nations Development Programme (UNDP) 58, 144n98, 151
United Nations Economic and Social Commission for Asia and the Pacific (UNESCAP) 57, 58, 189, 253
United Nations Educational, Scientific and Cultural Organization (UNESCO) 198
United Nations Environmental Programme (UNEP) 4, 12, 57, 180–202, 262, 308, 311, 316; Global Environmental Monitoring System (GEMS) 196; Regional Resource Centre of Asia and the Pacific 57
United Nations (UN) General Assembly 49, 67n88, 73, 78, 259
United Nations (UN) Human Settlements Programme (HABITAT II) of 1996 55
United Nations (UN) initiative of the Decade of Education for Sustainable Development (UNDESD) of 2005–2014 228
United Nations (UN) Stockholm Conference on the Human Environment of 1972 62n19, 196, 214, 235n18, 235n19, 239
United Nations University (UNU) 192, 228, 254, 259–60; United Nations University Institute for the Advanced Study of Sustainability (UNU-IAS) 228, 254, 259, 260
United States: California 165; Chicago 166, *181*, 188; Emissions Reduction Market System (ERMS) 166; National Resources Defense Council (NRDC) 271, 276; Regional Clean Air Initiatives Market (RECLAIM) 166; Regional Greenhouse Gas Initiative (RGGI) 165; US Congress 212; Vietnam War 212

United States–Japan: US–Japan Peace and Amity Treaty (1854) 244; US–Japan Security Treaty (1951) 102n20; US–Japan *Treaty* of Amity and Commerce (1858) *243*, 244

Vietnam 212, 221, 222, 237n56, 237n57, 237n58, 241, 255; Da Nang City 255; Hai Phong City *see* Kitakyushu; Hanoi City 222, 255

Wakayama prefecture 119
Watanabe, Katsusaburō *see* Yokohama
Water Pollution Control Act (1970) 190
Whatmore, Sarah 293n12, 299
World Bank 13, 59, 78, 195; Japan Trust Funds 195
World Food Program (WFP) *see* Yokohama
World Health Organization (WHO) 196
World Lake Vision (WLV) 196, 197, 206n73, 206n74, 206n76, 206n79, 209
World War II 44, 45, 81, 129, 211, 214, *243*, 246, 261, 272
World Water Forum 197
World Water Vision 197

Xi, Jinping *see* Kitakyushu

Yada, Toshifumi *see* Kitakyushu
Yellow Sea 56, 58, 216, 306
Yokkaichi asthma (Sulfur dioxide) 45
Yokohama City: Akashi, Yasushi 259; Ariyoshi, Chūichi 246; Asano, Sōichirō 245; Asukata, Ichio 46, *243*, 247–9, 251, 260–1, 265n19, 267; Awareness in Environmental Education (AWAREE) project 255; Basic Agreement on Town Development 252; "black ships" (American warships) 244; Brand Research Institute 242; building energy management system (BEMS) 252; *chokusetsu minshushugi* (direct democracy) 247; CITYNET Yokohama Project Office (CYO) 256; "cluster" approach 255; Commodore Matthew Perry 244; Community Based Adaptation and Resilience Against Disasters (CBARAD) project 256, 267n54, 267n55, 268; community energy management system (CEMS) 252; comprehensive assessment system for built environment (CASBEE) 252, 266n36, 269; Daikoku-chō 247; Department of Public Health 248, 265n21, 268; *ējanaika* ("who cares?") 245; Electric Power Development Co., Ltd (EPDC) *see* nuclear energy policy; Environmental Health and Preservation Committee 248; First and Second Regional Congress of Local Authorities for the Development of Human Settlements in Asia and the Pacific 253; Food and Agriculture Organization (FAO) 254; Great Kantō Earthquake *243*, 245, 249, 265n14, 269; Great Yokohama Air Raid *243*, 246, 249–50, 265n15, 268; Hayashi, Fumiko 257, 266n38, 267n56–267n59, 269; Hiranuma, Ryōzō 247; historical legacy 242, *243*, 257, 261, 313; home energy management system (HEMS) 252; Honcho area 44; Human Resources Division 258; *ichiman ni'n shūkai* (Ten Thousand Citizens' Meeting) 248; International Bureau 257; "international cultural center" 249; International Policy Office 255; "international trading city" 246; International Tropical Timber Organization (ITTO) 253–4; Investigatory Committee for the Redevelopment Planning of Yokohama City Center and Waterfront Area 250; Ishikawajima-Harima Heavy Industries 247; Isogo Medical Association 46; Isogo Ward 46, 248; Jakarta 255; *jōi* (the principle of excluding foreigners) 244; *kaikoku* (open-door policy) 242, 244, 264n7, 269; *kannai* (inside the barrier) 244, 250, 251; Keihin Industrial Zone *243*, 245, 247; *kokusai kōken* (contribution to the international community) 242, 254, 257, 313; *kokusai toshi* (international city) 259; *kyoryūchi* (designated foreigners' residence area) 244; Memorandum of Cooperation (MOC) 255; Minato Mirai 21 (MM21) 249–53, 254, 261, 266n28; Minato Mirai 21 Corporation 250, 265n25, 270; Mitsubishi 245, 250; Mitsubishi Dockyards 250; Mitsubishi Heavy Industries 250; Mitsui 245; Motomachi 244; Naka Ward 248; National Railways freight station 250; Negishi Bay 247; Nippon Yusen (NYK Line) 247; Nissan 252; Ōsanbashi Pier 247; PACIFICO Yokohama 259; Panasonic 252; Perry, Matthew 244; Petition for the Problem

Processing of the Requisitioned Land in Post-Peace Treaty 247; Regional Network of Local Authorities for the Management of Human Settlements (CITYNET) 4, 58, 59, 67n99, 67n101, 189, 205n43, *243*, 253–6, 257, 259, 262, 266n29, 266n39, 266n40, 266n44, 266n45, 266n47, 266n48, 266n50, 267n51, 267n52, 267n53, 267n54, 267n55, 268, 307; requisitioned land area and buildings 246; Saigō, Michikazu 251; *sakoku* (isolationist policy) 244; Seoul Metropolitan government 254; "smart city" 252, 266n37; "smart grid" 252; South–South cooperation 4, 58, 59, 189, 253–6, 257, 262, 307, 313; "sustainable building" 252, 266n36, 269; Takahide, Hidenobu 252–3, 267n59; Takashima rail yard 250; Tamura, Akira 250–1; *teito no genkan* (the gate way to the nation's capital) 246; Tokugawa Shogunate 244; Tokyo Electronic Power Company (TEPCO) *see* TEPCO; Tokyo Gas 247, 252; Toshiba 247, 252; Tsurumi River Networking 256; U Thant 259; Urban Development Bureau 251, 252; US Navy facilities 246; Watanabe, Katsusaburō 245–6; water and sanitation (WATSAN) 255; World Food Program (WFP) 254; Yamashita-cho (district) 244; "Yokohama City Center Plan Concept Proposal" 250; Yokohama General Plan (2006) 258, 267n60, 268; Yokohama Reconstruction Council 247; Yokohama Smart City Project (YSCP) 252; Yokohama Station 250; "*Yokohama's* City Planning – *Yokohama's Future* Made by Its *Citizens*" 248; *zaibatsu* (family-owned business combines) 245; *see also* nuclear energy policy

Yokohama International Port City Construction Law (1951) 246

Yokomichi, Takahiro *see* nuclear energy policy

Yoshida, Shigeru 78

Zhu, Rongji *see* Kitakyushu

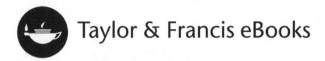

Helping you to choose the right eBooks for your Library

Add Routledge titles to your library's digital collection today. Taylor and Francis ebooks contains over 50,000 titles in the Humanities, Social Sciences, Behavioural Sciences, Built Environment and Law.

Choose from a range of subject packages or create your own!

Benefits for you
- Free MARC records
- COUNTER-compliant usage statistics
- Flexible purchase and pricing options
- All titles DRM-free.

Benefits for your user
- Off-site, anytime access via Athens or referring URL
- Print or copy pages or chapters
- Full content search
- Bookmark, highlight and annotate text
- Access to thousands of pages of quality research at the click of a button.

REQUEST YOUR FREE INSTITUTIONAL TRIAL TODAY

Free Trials Available
We offer free trials to qualifying academic, corporate and government customers.

eCollections – Choose from over 30 subject eCollections, including:

Archaeology	Language Learning
Architecture	Law
Asian Studies	Literature
Business & Management	Media & Communication
Classical Studies	Middle East Studies
Construction	Music
Creative & Media Arts	Philosophy
Criminology & Criminal Justice	Planning
Economics	Politics
Education	Psychology & Mental Health
Energy	Religion
Engineering	Security
English Language & Linguistics	Social Work
Environment & Sustainability	Sociology
Geography	Sport
Health Studies	Theatre & Performance
History	Tourism, Hospitality & Events

For more information, pricing enquiries or to order a free trial, please contact your local sales team:
www.tandfebooks.com/page/sales

 | The home of Routledge books

www.tandfebooks.com